NEGOTIATION
Readings, Exercises, and Cases

The Irwin Series in Management and The Behavioral Sciences
L. L. Cummings and E. Kirby Warren *Consulting Editors*
John F. Mee, Advisory Editor

Roy J. Lewicki
The Ohio State University

Joseph A. Litterer
University of Massachusetts

NEGOTIATION:
Readings, Exercises, and Cases

Homewood, Illinois   60430

ISBN 0-256-02634-3

Library of Congress Catalog Card No. 84–81264

Printed in the United States of America

12 13 14 V 6 5 4 3 2

PREFACE

Managers negotiate every day. During an average day, a manager may negotiate with

His boss over a budget request.

His subordinates over a work deadline.

A supplier about delivery of required raw materials.

A banker over the interest rate on a loan.

A government official regarding compliance with a federal pollution regulation.

A real estate agent on the price of a new home.

His spouse over who will walk the dog.

His children over who will walk the dog (still an issue after losing the previous negotiation).

In short, negotiation is a common, everyday activity that most people use to influence others and to achieve personal objectives. In fact, it is not only common, but also essential to living an effective and satisfying life. We all need things: resources, information, cooperation, support from others. At the same time that we have these needs, others from whom we expect these things have needs of their own. Negotiation is basic to satisfying our needs through others, while at the same time taking the other party's needs into account. It is a fundamental skill, not only for successful management, but for successful living.

Until recently, negotiation has not received full examination as a common, everyday process of interpersonal influence. Rather, scholars of negotiation have generally restricted examination of the process to basic theory development and laboratory research in social psychology, and to comprehending negotiations in the specific areas of international diplomacy and labor-management relations. There has been little or no effort to draw from and translate these isolated literatures into a broad view of influence in conflict settings, or to illustrate the broad variety of contexts that can be successfully understood and acted upon using influence and negotiation concepts. We believe that this book represents a new and unique effort to make that translation and application.

The *Readings* section of this book represents years of reviewing, clipping, and saving articles from contemporary periodicals and journals on the broad topics of negotiation, persuasion, power, and conflict management. Some articles are by well-known authors (both scholarly and managerial) in the field of negotiations, while others are by observant journalists or social commentators. Some articles attempt to define central problems and processes in negotiation, while others illustrate these points through descriptive writing and news reporting. The readings are organized into 13 sections; these sections parallel chapter headings in a companion text, *Negotiation*, also written by us and published by Richard D. Irwin, Inc. Each section begins with an overview prepared by one of us, highlighting the key points of each article. We hope you find the articles stimulating, and that reading them enhances your own understanding of the commonplace nature of negotiation, and yet the fascinating complexity of the process.

The second section of this book provides a variety of experientially based role plays, simulations, questionnaires, and cases. These materials have been included because it is our view—and our experience—that negotiation is a behavioral skill which can be best learned through actual practice and behavioral experimentation combined with training in effective diagnosis, conceptualization, and planning of negotiation situations. Some activities in this section are designed to explore the basic interpersonal processes of cooperation and competition; others are intended to expose you to more sophisticated negotiations, and still others focus on related concerns such as power, differences in personal orientation and style, or coalition behavior. Finally, we have included several cases on actual negotiations in this text in order to highlight key aspects of the negotiation process. The intent of these cases is to provide opportunities for you to determine what *you* would do at key points in a negotiation and/or how individuals have handled (and perhaps mishandled) key strategic and tactical decisions. The opportunity to examine a complete negotiation—from inception to conclusion—is provided by these cases, and creates another effective way to understand negotiation processes.

Students using these materials will discover that the materials in each activity are sometimes incomplete. Frequently, role positions or specific information will be omitted. Some of this information is located in the rear of this volume; other information will be found in the *Instructor's Manual*, available from Richard D. Irwin, Inc., to any instructor who adopts this book for an academic course or executive program.

In conclusion, the authors would like to thank

The many authors and publishers who have allowed their work to be reproduced in this volume.

The many teachers and trainers who have inspired or developed the role plays and questionnaires herein, particularly Bert Brown, Norman Berkowitz, Jim Ware, Ken Thomas, David Jamieson, Lee Bolman, and Terry Deal.

Our spouses, Debbie and Marie, who have frequently wined and dined us in less creative moments and put up with our idiosyncracies during our more creative ones.

Finally, our children, Karen, Susan, David, Aaron, and David, who have taught us most of what we *really* know about negotiation.

Roy J. Lewicki
Joseph A. Litterer

CONTENTS

Introduction

We negotiate every day. Each day, we may be involved in one or more of the following scenes:

Arriving simultaneously with three other cars at a four-way stop sign and deciding who should go first.

Deciding how to share a scarce resource—for example, a computer terminal or a library book.

Working out an arrangement with others to get tasks and chores done—for example, cleaning an apartment, shopping for food, or walking the dog.

Influencing a person to change his/her mind or point of view—for example, altering the due date of an assignment or project or obtaining a pay increase.

The list is endless. Regrettably, however, many of these situations are not recognized as negotiations. As a result, we don't handle them as effectively as we might. The purpose of this book is to help the reader recognize a wide variety of negotiation situations and to learn how to manage them more effectively.

Many people are surprised to find that there are situations in which they could or do negotiate every day. All too commonly, when we think of negotiating, we think of large, complex, formal negotiations between unions and management, between nations on a treaty, between businesses in a merger or a major acquisition. Even when we do see ourselves in "negotiation," we probably associate negotiating with infrequent behavior, such as buying an automobile or buying a house. In fact, we are faced with many situations where we do or could negotiate; for example, setting a salary for a new job, deciding when vacations will take place, coordinating reports with other departments. The list is endless. However, many of these are not recognized as negotiation situations and, as a result, are often poorly handled.

WHEN IS NEGOTIATION NEEDED?

A negotiation situation is one in which two or more parties have to make a decision about their interdependent goals or objectives; in which the parties are committed to peaceful means for resolving their dispute; and in which there is no clear or established method or procedure for making the decision. Like most definitions, this one means most to those who already understand what is being defined. Let's take an example. Two people want to take a vacation the first two weeks in June; however, both cannot be away at the same time. In some organizations, it is understood that the most senior person will get first choice. Such an understanding may be formal—that is, company rules or union contract—or it may be the tradition of the organization. In any event, there is a rule that can be referred to and used. An alternative way of getting the decision made is to refer the matter to a superior. When there are no rules and the superior is not available or will not make the decision, what are the parties to do? They could flip a coin. Some would feel that this is too important to be left to chance. At that point, the parties are left with no other option than to negotiate; that is, to persuade one another why one party's needs or priorities for this time period are most important or to compromise on the use of this time block.

FEAR OF NEGOTIATING

Even after recognizing the need to negotiate solutions to problems, many people still back off. They find the prospect of negotiating uncomfortable, even distasteful.

One reason is that negotiations involve, or appear to involve, a conflict. For a variety of reasons, most people do not want to get into a fight with their boss, spouse, friends, or associates. While this is an understandable and realistic concern, we have to recognize several things:

1. Conflict is unavoidable given our interdependent world—each of us has priorities and preferences different from those with whom we are interdependent.
2. If we fear conflict, we are likely to take a position that will guarantee we will lose what we want.

3. Negotiation does not have to be a bloody conflict to be successful. In fact, if it is bloody, it is not successful.

A second reason seems to be that many of us have the idea that, to be
successful at negotiation, we need to be very glib, very persuasive, even
capable of verbally manipulating others. People get what they want in
negotiations, it is thought, through being fast talkers, misleading, or devious
in what they say. Many people see these as skills and abilities they do not
possess or as reflecting personality characteristics they do not want to
possess or be seen as possessing.

If these perceptions are really true, it means we have to deal with three
main issues regarding negotiations. First, what is negotiation and what does
it involve? Second, what are the skills people need to carry out negotiations?
Third, what are the feelings, values, and beliefs people have about proper
conduct in negotiation, and how do the actions of others in negotiation clash
or appear to clash with them?

While these fears exist and have some basis, they are often greatly exaggerated. Like so many things, developing basic skills is far less difficult than
it appears. For one thing, while skills in persuasion, communication, and the
like are important, there are other, more important factors in negotiating
which we can all understand and use to increase the likelihood of success.
For another, while some people exploit negotiating situations in unethical
ways, this does not mean that unethical ways are needed to succeed. In fact,
this is not the way to succeed in the long term.

PURPOSE AND SCOPE OF THIS BOOK

Negotiating is a complex human activity. It involves a dynamic interpersonal
event. It involves skills, both behavioral and analytical. It involves the
values and moral systems that people hold. It is also a skill that can be
learned and can be done well, to support and exemplify a person's value
system.

In this book, we have compiled material written by a large number of
authors on a wide range of topics. It either describes various aspects of
negotiation or analyzes different aspects of the process. The material is
organized into 13 sections. The first section introduces negotiation and
further explores the issues and topics just discussed. Section Two describes
negotiation as a process to manage interdependence. The third section
reviews some of the factors that go into successful competition and also some
of the traps we can encounter. The next three sections show that successful
negotiation rests as much, perhaps more, on the planning that precedes actual
face-to-face dialogue than it does on the interpersonal processes that occur
once actual negotiation begins. Sections Seven through Eleven focus on
some of the key elements in the actual give and take of negotiation: communication, persuasion, power, and personality. In Section Twelve, the conflic-

tual nature of negotiation is addressed and ways of resolving conflict are examined. Last, in Section Thirteen, the values and moral systems of negotiators are examined and their connection to the process of negotiation is explored.

INTRODUCTION TO SECTION ONE: OVERVIEW

One view of negotiation, more commonly held than might be suspected, is that negotiation involves getting what you want from another person using any means available. Like most stereotypes, this view contains a vague resemblance to truth; but it is substantially off target—a bit like confusing lighting a match with arson. Successful negotiation does not imply taking care of oneself at the other party's expense but rather working to take care of the needs of both parties. We may think that successful negotiators are glib, articulate, forceful, perhaps even domineering. Some are, but other success-ful negotiators speak the way anyone else does, are quiet and listen patiently to the other side, and then explain their point of view without theatrics or bombast. Further, they often concede the other side has a valid point and even change their positions and preferred solutions. Rather than being aggressive and combative, successful negotiators are often understanding and conciliatory. This suggests that, to understand negotiation and to be successful at it, we need to have a somewhat different perspective and vision of what negotiation involves.

Andrew Tobias in the first article, "Winning through Negotiation," delves into the theories and art of negotiation expounded by Herbert Cohen. Cohen, in "You Can Negotiate Anything," points out that much of our difficulty in understanding and being successful in negotiation rests upon our misunderstanding of three basic elements in any negotiation: information, time, and power. The misunderstanding is that the other side seems to have more of all three than we do. Success, Cohen points out, rests upon successfully analyzing these elements and using that analysis to arrange our own strategy to achieve the results we want. A successful outcome is not always winning at any cost or even "winning." That approach assumes that there has to be a loser and ignores the possibility that to get what we want does not necessarily mean the other side has to lose. A strategy of winning at all costs may work if we do not have to deal with the same parties again; but, if we do (and that is usually the case in most negotiations), success at *any* cost may make all future success impossible. Cohen introduces a theme that we will follow throughout this book: Successful negotiation does not mean winning by defeating the other party, but winning by getting what both parties want.

This definition might suggest that negotiators need to trust each other to completely lay out their priorities and jointly arrive at a reasonable solution. Unfortunately, things are not that simple. For example, while people might be willing to pay $8,000 for a new car, they would be happier if they could get it for $7,000. In contrast, while the seller, if necessary, sells the car for $7,000, he would be much happier receiving $8,000. Furthermore, both parties probably have a hunch that this condition exists. It is to be expected that each will tend to hold back some information about what they are maximally willing to do and, perhaps, stress or promote information that will shape the other's understanding more to their favor. At the same time, both want to get as much information as possible about what the other party will really settle for. Hence, in any negotiation, there is a tendency to conceal and mislead about one's own information and also to probe for information about the other party. While all this is occurring, both parties are faced with the fact that they have to reach an agreement on a price that both will find acceptable. Hence, negotiation always involves a tense, stressful relationship where parties are working together, yet simultaneously working for themselves; where they will and are expected to manipulate information and impressions, yet cannot be deliberately dishonest or deceptive; where they have to trust, yet be alert to the fact that the other party is pursuing his own self-interest.

This stressful situation can spawn a number of problems. In his article, "The Virtues, Dangers, and Limits of Negotiation," Max Ways shows how a successful negotiaton can become an end in itself rather than a means to an end. When this happens, the parties involved may accept a bad agreement in order to *appear* to have a successfully completed negotiation and to avoid facing the fact that an acceptable agreement was not possible.

The stressfulness inherent in any negotiation can be magnified when negotiations drag on over a long period of time or seem to be getting nowhere. The heightened tension and stress can feed into other patterns of behavior that can work to the disadvantage of one, or perhaps both, parties. Ways identifies these problematic dynamics in negotiations and shows how they can impede the progress toward successful resolution.

In the third article, "The Significance of Human Conflict," Kenneth Benne discusses the nature of interpersonal conflict. Benne points out that most people view conflict as destructive and dysfunctional; this assumption has lead people to approach conflict with a negative frame of mind, and to evade it, deny it, or seek a win-lose approach to "solve it." In fact, conflict has many positive functions in our society. Benne discusses some of these positive aspects, and sets forth propositions for creatively and rationally resolving disputes.

ANDREW TOBIAS

Reading 1-1
Winning through Negotiation

Herbert Cohen, 47, teaches the art of negotiation. One day he conducts his seminar at the FBI ($1,650), then makes much the same speech to the Food Marketing Institute ($2,000) and then—all in the same day—fields questions for five and a half hours, from midnight to 5:30, on network radio. The day before, he was in Sault Sainte Marie; the day before that, in Toronto. In the next two weeks, he will be in Chicago (home base), Washington, Hyannis, Chicago again, Sands Point, Ottawa, Rochester, Manhattan, White Plains and Peoria. Typical weeks. After that, he will be at the State Department, counseling on Iran and Afghanistan, and will even get a handshake and a word of thanks from the President of the United States.

Figuring an average of $2,500 in fees per day (expenses are billed separately), and his working 250 days a year (his datebook is full through 1981), one estimates that Herb Cohen—former wise-ass kid from the streets of Brooklyn, former claims adjuster for Allstate Insurance (while he attended law school at night)—must now gross about $625,000 a year. And, says his wife, fees are going up. He charges the Justice Department ''only'' $6,000 for a two-and-a-half-day seminar on negotiation and leadership, because he likes the work; the National Dairy people, on the other hand, were milked to the tune of $4,000 for a single day's program. Whatever drives him, he is like an author on an eternal book tour or a politician whose campaign never ends. ''It's not the money,'' he is fond of saying (meaning money as a way to buy things); ''it's the *money*'' (meaning money as a way to keep score). It may also have something to do with Cohen's ego, which is not small, and his upbringing—he is the son of hard-working immigrant parents.

Cohen looks and talks exactly like Walter Matthau (except when he does a sort of Buddy Hackett); he greets every audience with the news that we are *all* negotiators, from the time we first cry for our mother's attention; and will leave us, his voice resonating with solemnity, recalling "two men who lived 2,000 years ago, two of the greatest negotiators in the history of the world— of course, I am talking to you about Jesus Christ and Socrates."

In between, whether it be a dessert-and-coffee engagement or a two-day management seminar, Cohen is a Catskills comedian whom we half expect, after every sketch, to bow, thank the crowd and disappear behind a curtain. Instead, his voice and diction turn suddenly oratorical—"And so I say to you"—as he reiterates the point of his story. You must be an entertainer first, Cohen says, and a teacher only second, if you want people to learn.

It is an open question whether or not attendees actually do learn to negotiate more effectively and, if so, whether or not they will ever have a chance to try out what they've learned. But they never fall asleep in class.

A senior vice-president of Chase Manhattan Bank wrote to Cohen: "Without a doubt, your sessions on 'negotiation' were the absolute high spot of the two-week [Chase Advanced Management Course]. . . . In fact, I've already put to use one of your tactics. . . . I felt we were being 'diddled' by a key New York City official in our negotiation. We broke off any further talks. This triggered certain responses which brought matters back into better focus and cleared the air for further negotiations." In other words, they creamed New York.

Another fellow claims to have saved $3,500 on the purchase of his home, thanks to Cohen's lecture.

The mayor of Tulsa wrote: "Your presentation [to a conference of mayors in 1978] had a greater impact on me than anything I have had since becoming mayor." The FBI loves him. The mayor of New Orleans calls whenever he gets into a jam. Mexicans listen to him eagerly through translation. Private individuals pay $225 to attend the one-day public seminars he sometimes gives.

Having watched the Herb Cohen show three or four times, twice live, once on tape and piecemeal in hotel suites, I give it to you here—not complete, to be sure; but not for $4,000, or even $225, either.

Cohen, dressed like a banker—Walter Matthau as community leader— begins a bit stiffly from the lectern.

"Persistence is to power," he says, "what carbon is to steel. If a rat gnaws long enough at a dike, it could sink an entire nation. This is how the Camp David peace accords were put together. Jimmy Carter, in my opinion, is a highly moral individual. High moral convictions. However"—and suddenly Cohen is banker no longer—"he is also one of the most boring people in the history of this country. So he got Begin and Sadat to go to Camp David. Camp David is a very boring place itself. It's not what you'd call a swinging modern-day Sodom and Gomorrah. He got 13 people up there with two bicycles and three films, so by the fifth day, they had seen all those films and had to helicopter in a fourth. He'd come around every day and say, 'Hi,

I'm Jimmy Carter. Let's talk for another five boring hours.' And if you were Sadat and Begin, obviously, you would have signed anything to get out of there, and that's what they did.

"I think, to some extent, the same thing was true in the Middle East. Carter would leave—he was supposed to leave—no, he's gonna stay a little while longer. In fact, I think he'd still be there, but to his credit, the persistence paid off. I think he achieved a great deal."

And when did "concession behavior," as Cohen calls it, occur? When it *always* occurs—at the deadline. Cohen learned this lesson and the importance of time and deadlines many years ago—before he went to work for Allstate, before he was promoted to handle the training of all claims adjusters, before he left 10 years ago to set up his Power Negotiations Institute.

COHEN'S FIRST NEGOTIATION

"Twenty years ago, I was employed by an outfit that was operating internationally. I was not, but the organization was." Cohen jumps off the dais and begins working the crowd. "I had one of those top management jobs where they would say, 'Hey, Cohen—two with cream, two with sugar.' You know—one of those key spots. And people would come back from overseas . . . you'd meet them for breakfast—'Where you been?' And they'd say, 'Aw, just got back from Singapore; pieced together this $9,000,000 deal.' Somebody else—'Where you been?' 'Abu Dhabi. Where *you* been?' What could I say? 'Well, I went to the zoo . . . the aquarium. . . .' I used to go in to my boss every Friday and ask for a shot at the big time. I bothered this person so much that eventually he sent me to Tokyo to deal with the Japanese. This was my moment.

"I'm on a plane on my way to Tokyo. It's a 14-day negotiation. I've taken along all these books on the Japanese mentality, their psychology. I'm really gonna do well. Plane lands in Tokyo, I'm the first guy down the ramp. I'm raring to go. Three little Japanese guys [at one time, Cohen weighed in excess of 200 pounds; now 155] are waiting for me at the foot of the ramp and they're bowing. I liked that quite a bit. Then they helped me through customs, they put me in this large limousine, sitting there in the rear all by myself, and they're sitting on those fold-up seats. I say, 'Why don't you guys join me?' They say, 'Oh, no—you're an important person. You need your rest.' We're driving along and one of them turns around and says, 'By the way, do you know the language?' I say, 'You mean Japanese?' They say, "Right. That's what we speak. This is Japan.' I say no. They say, 'Are you concerned about getting back to your plane on time?' Up to that moment, I have not been concerned. They say, 'Would you like this limousine to pick you up?' I say, 'Oh, yeah,' and hand them my ticket.

"Now, I don't realize it at the time, but what's happened? *They know my deadline, but I don't know theirs.*

"So we start negotiating, or I think we do. The first seven days, they send me to Kyoto to visit the shrine, they enroll me in an English-language course in Zen, they . . . I'm begging these guys to negotiate. They say, 'Plenty of time.'

"We finally start the 12th day. We end early, play golf. The 13th day, we resume. End early for the farewell dinner. The morning of the 14th day, we resume in earnest and just as we are about to get to the crux of things, the limousine pulls up to take me to the airport. We all pile in and just as we arrive at the airport, we consummate the deal.

"By the way—how well do you think I did?'

Cohen advises people to conceal their own deadlines as far as possible. Act as if you have all the time in the world, even though you haven't. (And if you can, take more than you might have planned, because that extra time will pay off. Try to keep your deadline flexible.) Meanwhile, you should know that your negotiating partner, cool though he is playing it, unconcerned though he seems, is also sweating a deadline. It may not seem that way, but it's almost always true.

THE PRISONER AND THE CIGARETTE

"Power is nothing more than the capacity to get things done. It's not moral, not immoral—it's neutral. What people tend to do is to confuse the power over with the power to. Power itself is neutral.''

Where some of the recent crop of power books seem largely based on stepping on other people—rationalizations for being selfish or unprincipled—one has the feeling, at least, that Cohen's pitch comes from a somewhat less cynical mold. Pushy he may be, but likely to be pushy on the right side of the issues.

"Power is based on perception. If you think you got it—you got it. And if you don't think you got it—you *don't* got it. Let me illustrate that point.

"A prisoner in solitary confinement is walking around, holding up his pants; he's lost a little weight. He craves a cigarette. Notices the guard is smoking his brand. He walks over to the steel door and he knocks and the guard ambles up, opens the door—'Whaddya want?' 'I'd like a cigarette.' *Bam,* the guard slams the door. He perceives the prisoner is powerless. But the prisoner thinks he has power. 'Hi, there,' he says through the bars. 'Let me tell you what's going on. If I don't get a cigarette in the next 30 seconds—see this head? [Cohen points with feeling to his head]—I'm gonna bang it up against that concrete wall, and I'll be all bloodied, and when they find me, I intend to swear you did it. Now, they're never gonna believe me—but think of all the hearings you'll be attending, think of all the reports in triplicate you'll be filling out, think of . . . [and now Cohen's voice is plaintive, indeed] as opposed to giving me one crummy cigarette and I promise not to bother you again.' Can the guy get the cigarette? Yeah. The guard is doing a little cost-benefit analysis. Why can he get the cigarette? One, because the prisoner thinks he's got power. Two, because the prisoner perceives he's got options. Three, because the prisoner is willing to take risks.

"Every one of you in this room [a gathering of small businessmen hosted as a customer-relations exercise by Citibank] always has more power than you think you have. You gotta start off believing it," says Cohen.

KILL ME, KILL ME

Cohen's advice is similar when it comes to fighting very big guys: Ask your adversary to step outside—so he will not lose face if he lets you go; then tell him, with maniacal conviction, that if he so much as lays a hand on you, he'll have to kill you. Anything less than that, tell him, and no matter what it takes, you will kill *him*. Maybe not then and there, but sooner or later.

As Cohen explains it, no one really wants to *kill* a guy—so your disputant may well just tell you to get lost, even though he could easily beat your brains out. Why should he kill you? Or *not* kill you and worry for the rest of his life that you might just be crazy enough to stick him with a knife some night or dynamite his house?

Impeccable logic. It is possible, however, that the man you are advising to kill you will be in less than a rational frame of mind himself—or not speak English—and break you into small pieces? It is vital when negotiating, Cohen says, to take risks.

DELAWARE IS CLOSED

"People in this society are enormously affected by signs," says Cohen. "If I were to tell you to do something, you would evaluate my request based on your needs; and if the two of them meshed, you might comply. But if a *sign* directed you to do it, the chances of your complying would be much higher. Do you buy that?

"Holiday Inn. The check-out time is one P.M. What percentage of the people do you think check out by the Holiday Inn check-out time? What do you think? *Ninety-five to 99 percent,* depending on where it is in North America. Don't you think that's a remarkably high figure? Fifty-five percent of the people vote, but 95 percent check out by the check-out time."

Or, asks Cohen, do you remember the time *Candid Camera's* Allen Funt put a sign up on a major highway leading into Delaware—DELAWARE CLOSED? "You'd see guys drive up in their cars and they'd pull over and they'd get out and here's Funt and they'd go, 'Hey, what's going on in Delaware?' And he'd say, 'You read the sign.' The guy says. 'Yeah, yeah, but I've got a family—when do you think it will be open again?' And so I say to you, legitimacy is very potent."

Legitimacy. Cohen has some suggestions on using it to your advantage. E.g., don't have the price you want to charge merely in mind, have it typed up formally on an authoritative-looking price list. Better yet, keep that price list *under glass* on your desk. How can you change it if it's under glass? You, on the other hand, should not be cowed by such things. Cohen isn't.

HIS TAX AUDIT

"Four years ago," says Cohen, "the IRS called me in to audit my tax return. There was one area of questioning about a building that I had elected to depreciate over a number of years. Now, the IRS claimed that number should have been 30. I took the position during the audit that it should have been 20. We're discussing this, the auditor and myself, we're having nice discussions. Suddenly, the auditor reaches in the right-hand corner of a desk drawer, whips out a large book and as I am speaking, he is turning pages. He comes to one page, looks up—'The book says 30 years.' I get up, walk around the table, look at the book. I say, 'Does the book mention my name?' He says, 'Of course not.' I say, 'I don't think it's my book.' I say, 'Otherwise, it would have my name and my building.' I start taking down other books. The guy says, 'What are you doing?' I say, 'I'm looking for my book.' He says, 'You can't look at the books.' I say, 'Why not?' He says, 'I dunno, no one ever did that.'

"Now, what was that book he had? That book was not written in stone. That book was thought up by two bureaucrats somewhere to the best of their ability to implement some regulations. The book itself was the product of negotiation—and anything that's the product of negotiation is negotiable." Or, if you make people crazy enough and are willing to take enough time— if, that is, you have no sense of decency, dignity or decorum—there's no telling what concessions you might get. Witness:

THE NIBBLE

"Why was it so hard for the United States to extract itself from the war in Vietnam? Because we had invested 50,000 lives in it. It's known as the nibble. Let me describe it to you.

"You go into an exclusive clothier in the downtown area where you reside. You want to get a fine suit. You start trying on suits. Each suit you ask the salesman, he says, 'Terrific.' You spend three and a half hours trying on 39 suits. Each one you ask the salesman, he says, 'Terrific.' The salesman is fed up with you. He's about to blow his cool, when suddenly you say, 'I'll take the one right there for $270.' 'You will?' The salesman breathes a sigh of relief and starts writing up the order. He takes you to a little room in the rear where they do the alterations—you've been in that room, you know that room—the one with the three-way mirror and they stand you on this little box and there you are, looking at yourself. The salesman is writing up the sales slip, calculating his commission. Beside you as you stand on the box is this little guy with pins in his mouth, a tape measure around his neck. He's taking these pins and shoving them in your cuff, he's poking you up the rear and he's always saying to you, 'This is a beautiful suit—it hangs very well on you.' Whenever you go, the guy's got the same accent. Maybe it's not an accent. Could be the pins. Anyway, you get the picture. You're standing there on the box, the salesman's writing up the slip, counting his commission, man on the floor shoving in the pins, making the chalk marks—when suddenly you turn to the salesman and say, 'What kind of tie will you throw in?'

"The salesman stops writing. He looks at the guy on the floor; the guy on the floor looks up. He doesn't know whether to shove another pin, make another chalk mark—he lets go of your crotch. Ladies and gentlemen, that's what we call the nibble.

"Now, I ask you—what is going through the mind of the salesman after the first wave of heat has disappeared. He's thinking: Three and a half hours of my time, 39 suits I put on the guy's back, $30 on a $270 sale—as opposed to taking four bucks out of my pocket. I'm going to give this guy a tie and hope that I never see him again.

"Will you get that tie? Yes."

Was it worth the effort and demeaning yourself? No. Would Cohen have gone through all that himself? Presumably not. But by using simple stories from everyday experience, he communicates better—even to bankers and auditors—than he would if he told the story of the two accountants negotiating the treatment of foreign-currency losses in a not yet consolidated subsidiary. Still, one suspects Cohen isn't the easiest guy in the world to deal with—and that he cannot always resist the temptation to chisel and buck or two even on the little things. "It's not the money"—he has plenty of that—"it's the *money.*"

POOR HERTZ

"Have I ever shown you my legitimacy card?" Cohen asks over six-dollar cups of lobster bisque in his hotel suite. (Six dollars well spent, I might add.)

Most people know that Hertz and Avis give a variety of corporate discounts—usually 20 percent—when you rent one of their cars or if you use their credit cards. It seems, according to Cohen, that Hertz gives IBM *37 percent.*

"I find this out and I think it's inappropriate for me not to get the same discount."

At most airports, Cohen says, you need only say you're with IBM and the attendants don't even check. Off goes the 37 percent. But at La Guardia, they're really sticky. "They say, 'Who are you with?' I say, 'IBM.' They say, 'Yeah? Let me see your card.'"

Whereupon Cohen pulls out of his wallet one of those preprinted cards that says IBM in the upper-left-hand corner and has Cohen's name typed in the middle. He was a speaker at one of its conferences, where everybody gets a card under plastic to wear on his lapel, and Cohen kept the card.

Not only does he get 37 percent off, he says, they throw in free collision coverage. Works with Avis, too.

The only problem—evaluate it as you will—is that you have to lie to get the discount.

THE NEW HOUSE

Nowadays, it's not enough to issue orders and expect the job to get done. You've got to negotiate for the commitment of your organization—get it behind you. Otherwise, it can kill you just by doing exactly what you say—"malicious obedience."

What does it mean to have your organization behind you?

"Six and a half years ago, I lived in a community in Illinois called Libertyville. A rustic community, acres of land—thought I was very happy there until my wife explained to me that we weren't that happy. She said that area was not quite right for us, we ought to move.

"Since I'm away from home a great deal, it fell upon her shoulders to move us. And, you know, when you've been out of the real-estate market for seven years and then come back, you're in for a shock.

"She's looking two weeks, four weeks—and, to be honest with you, it does not bother me that she's looking—but I call home every night. Wherever I am, I call home every night. I am not a creative telephone conversationalist, by the way. I have a standard opening every night—'Hi, how's everything?' And I even have a preferred answer, which is, 'Fine.' I always move on to my second question, which is, 'What's new?' My preferred answer is, 'Nothing.'

"Monday night, Tuesday night, Wednesday night, I got good answers. Thursday night: 'Hi, how's everything?' 'Fine.' 'What's new?' What could be new? I just talked to her last night. 'I bought a house.' I said, 'No, you phrased that incorrectly—semantically, you're wrong. You mean to say you saw a house you liked and you offered money on it.' 'Yes, except they accepted the money and we got it.' '*A whole house? How could you buy a whole house?*' She said it was really easy."

It turned out, shortening the story, that Cohen's wife had made the deal subject to her husband's approval. That cheered him up somewhat.

"OK, I get home late Friday night, I'm up early Saturday morning—the wife and I are going to his home, and I, alleged technical titular leader, am ready to reject the whole deal. We are driving along and I say to my associate, 'By the way. Does anybody know about this home you almost bought?' She says, 'Oh, yeah.' I said, 'Who could know? It just happened.' 'A lot of people know.' 'Who?' 'Well, all our neighbors, all our friends know—in fact, they're throwing us a gala farewell party.' I said, 'Who else

COHEN'S CRASH COURSE IN NEGOTIATING

**Got a meeting in an hour? Here's a handful of nuggets
to make you shine.**

• Always remember, says Herb Cohen, that people are different. They have different needs and they understand things differently. ''In the Midwest, you tell people a nine-o'clock meeting—what time would you have to arrive at such a meeting before you would be considered late? You know what people tell me? Eight forty-five. It's Vince Lombardi time or something. In California, they say 9:15. In New York, guys say, 'According to Jimmy Walker, as long as you get there before it's all over, you're not late.''"

• Make things personal. ''Commitments are never kept with institutions. They're too big, too impersonal. What's the difference if Chase loses $100,000? What you want to do, see—you're with Chase, but you negotiate on behalf of yourself. A guy waffles on his commitment and you say, 'Look, you told me you were going to do this, and I told my boss—you're not going to let me down, are you?' The guy says, 'Hey, you're not taking this personally, are you?' [Plaintive, not hostile] 'Yeah.''"

• If you box people into taking a stand publicly, they will tend to resist change. Do your negotiating before the public meeting, if you can.

• Similarly, boxing someone in with an ultimatum is one of the worst mistakes you can make—unless you are prepared to back up that ultimatum. If the other party *believes* you are prepared to back it up, you probably won't have to.

• It's much easier to say no over the phone. So if you want something, you'll do better getting it face to face.

• The caller is always at an advantage—he's prepared, knows just what he wants to say. If you are the callee, bury the caller with gratitude for calling—but ask if you can call him back. That gives you time to prepare. Or, if that's awkward, hang up on yourself. Let him talk a little, start to answer—and in the middle of your sentence, hit the button. Must have been the lousy switchboard. Gather your thoughts while you wait for him to call back.

• If one of you is going to write a memo confirming your understanding, you be the one to do it. That way, you get the initiative, you set the priorities, you control the situation. The guy gets the memo and has five problems with it. ''You mean you want me to do this all over again?'' You are incredulous, hurt, perhaps a trifle annoyed. The guy has to fight for each one of his five points and feels lucky to get three. (If he'd written it, the five problems would have been in his favor, not yours, and you would have been stuck with two of them—down two rather than up two.)

• Likewise, note taking. Asks Cohen: Who's in a better position to interpret the chicken scratchings than the chicken?

• Don't be afraid to ask for help, to say you don't understand. People respond to that; it helps make the negotiations more ''collaborative'' and less ''competitive'' (making it more likely that you will both emerge more satisfied); and

> sometimes, in reiterating and explaining his list of outrageous demands, your counterpart—perhaps embarrassed by their outrageousness or taking pity on you—will let one or two drop without your even having to argue.
> • Consider timing. When is the best time for a hooker to negotiate—before or after performing her services? Anticipation is always (or almost always, anyway) greater than reality.
>
> *Andrew Tobias*

knows?' 'Well, our families know—your family, my family. In fact, my mother has already ordered us custom-made drapes for the living room—I called in the measurements.' I said, 'Who else could know?' She said, 'Well, our children know; they told their friends, they told their teachers; they selected bedrooms they like. . . .'

"In other words, what is happening is that the organization is moving away from the leader. It is the zigzag theory of organizational behavior. In this case, the alleged technical titular leader was in the zig, while the organization was in the zag.

"What do you think the alleged, technical, titular, lonely leader did in order to keep the title of alleged, technical, titular leader? He ratified the decision his organization had already made. It seems my wife knows more about negotiations than I do. When the body moves, the head is inclined to follow.

"And so I say to you: See people in context, get the commitment of others in the organization. Find out who's important to you and influence the people who are important to that person and you'll influence him."

THE REFRIGERATOR

"If you want to deal effectively with people, if you want to convince them, if you want to negotiate, if you want to persuade, then you've got to approach people based on their needs. And that's all negotiation is. It is meeting the needs of people.

"You want to negotiate with Sears about the cost of a refrigerator. So you go into Sears and say, 'Hey, I'll tell you what—I'll take 20 bucks off your price, but I'll pay cash.' Does that work at Sears? No. Sears is not any retail establishment—it wants you to think it is, but in reality, it is a financial institution. It wants to grab off 18 percent of your money on its revolving charge account. Sears doesn't *want* you to pay cash. Does the cash ploy work with somebody else, though—the guy on the corner with a cash-flow problem? Sure it does. And so I say to you: Every approach should meet the needs of the people."

(In fact, Cohen maintains you *can* negotiate with Sears and similar "one-price" stores. Most people don't think so, so they don't try. But the salesmen are authorized to come down on prices, to arrange trade-ins, to deal on "floor models," and more.)

Cohen speaks of refrigerators but actually has his mind on larger things, such as labor negotiations, or Salt II.

"Find out what the other side's needs are. How do you do this? You don't start out when the negotiation begins; people won't tell you anything then. You've got to see all your encounters with people not as an event but as a process. You see, we think literally in terms of When does it start? It starts April sixth at two P.M. But negotiations, like mental illness, are a process. When somebody has been declared mentally ill at two P.M. on April sixth, when does he actually become mentally ill? Does anyone think he was fine at 1:59 and at 2 P.M. he went bananas? Use your lead time to gather information.

"Also to give information. Why do I say you should give information? Three reasons. One, it is more blessed to give than to receive. Two, you've got to give a little to get a little. Three, when you give information to people, it influences the expectation level of the other side. It takes people a while to get used to a new idea. Throw something out to somebody over here—well in advance—and he will say, 'I don't buy that. No, sir.' You mention the same thing over here—a little closer to the event—but when you bring it up, you change the name of it. Do this a few times and what happens? 'Oh. That's been around for a while.'

"It takes a while for people to get used to any new idea. Allow for acceptance time to occur."

THE CLOCK

"A husband and wife are looking through an architectural magazine and they see a magnificent clock. They agree that if they can get it for $500, they'll be happy. They spend months looking for this clock—flea markets, antique shops, weekend trips—and finally they see the clock of their dreams. As they near it, they see one potential problem, a sign that says $750. One of them is appointed negotiator in an attempt to secure the clock. That individual walks up to the person selling the clock and says, "Sir, I notice you have a little clock for sale. I notice a little dust around that sign on the top. Now, I am going to make you one offer and one offer only and I know it's gonna thrill you very big—are you ready for it?—here it is: $250.'

'And the seller says: 'You got it. Sold.'

"Now, how do you feel when that happens to you? Why do some of you smile when you hear this? You smile because you've *been* there, that's why—and I've been there, too. What's your first reaction? Is it that you got a great price? No. Your reaction is: 'I could have done better. I was stupid. I should have started lower.' Your second reaction? 'What's wrong with the clock?'

"If the seller had been a decent compassionate human being, he would have allowed you to fight for every dollar and finally settled with you for $497. You would have been happier.

"I'm saying to you that human beings have needs beyond just dollars. And they are different."

Creative negotiators, Cohen believes, can often turn the process into a "win-win" situation, where *both* sides' needs can be met. In essence, he says, successful negotiation lies in finding out what the other side *really* wants and showing it a way to get it while you get what you want. He recalls a corporate acquisition he once was involved in for which the seller asked $26,000,000
—and refused to budge. The buyer offered $15,000,000, $18,000,000, $20,000,000, $21,000,000, $21,500,000—the seller refused to budge. Only after some days, by chance over dinner, did it develop that the seller's brother had sold *his* company for $26,000,000. Suddenly, Cohen's group realized that its man had needs other than money. It wound up working out terms that fell within its budget but allowed the seller to feel he had done better than his brother.

The incident of the clock also illustrates another of Cohen's basic tenets: Start low. Or, if you're selling, start high. Any three-year-old knows to do that, of course, but Cohen says—no, *even lower* (or higher) than that. That gives you more room to maneuver, tests the waters and lowers the opposition's expectations. Of course, if you had been planning to offer so little (or ask so much) as to be downright insulting, this advice could serve to shatter any chance of making a deal.

Well, don't start *that* low, says Cohen.

THE SERAPE

"Ever see people who come back from Southern climates, who take winter vacations and wind up at Northern airports—ever see what they're wearing? A week away from New York and they're wearing muumuus. I myself own two Mexican serapes. To tell you the truth, I never thought of myself as being with a serape. I don't like them.

"Five years ago, my wife and I go to Mexico City and we're walking through the streets and suddenly she says, 'Ah, yonder I see lights.' She speaks that way, you know. I say, 'Hey, I'm not going over there, that's the commercial area. I did not come here to wallow in commercialism. You go; I'll meet you back at the hotel.' I go off on my own, and as I'm moving with the ebb and flow, I notice this person approaching me wearing serapes. He's calling out, 'Twelve hundred pesos.' I'm trying to figure out who he can be talking to. It couldn't be me—how did he know I was a tourist? I look straight ahead and keep walking. The guy walks right up to me—I'm not even looking at him—and says, 'A thousand pesos.' I'm still moving. 'Eight hundred pesos.' I stop. I say, 'My friend, I certainly respect your initiative and your diligence; however, I do not need a serape, I do not like a serape, I do not desire a serape—would you kindly sell elsewhere?' I walk away; the guy's still following me. 'Six hundred pesos.' I'm running down the damn street, I'm hot, I'm sweating, and he's chasing me. He says, 'Four hundred pesos.' I'm irritated. 'Damn it, I just told you I don't want a serape—now beat it.' 'Two hundred pesos.' I say, 'What did you say?' 'Two hundred pesos.' I say, 'Let me see the serape.' Why am I asking to see the serape? Do I need a serape? Do I want a serape? Do I like a serape? No. See how a man changes his mind? I didn't think I wanted a serape, but maybe I do.

"You see, the guy started at 1,200 pesos, he's now down to 200—I don't know what the hell I'm doin', but—I mean, I haven't even started negotiating and already I got the guy down 1,000 pesos. Now, I find out from this guy that the cheapest anyone ever bought a serape in the history of Mexico City was a fellow from Winnipeg whose mother and father were born in Guadalajara. He paid 175 pesos. I get mine for 170, thereby giving me the serape record for Mexico City. I am now walking down the street wearing my serape. It is hot, I am perspiring—but wearing my serape."

He rushes back to his hotel to show his wife. "How much did you pay?" she asks him.

"The guy wanted 1,200 pesos, but the internationally renowned negotiator picked it up for 170." She opens the closet to show him the identical serape, for which she paid 150 pesos.

"Why did I buy that serape? Did I need a serape? Did I like a serape? I didn't think so, but on the streets of Mexico City I encountered not a peddler but an international psychological negotiating marketeer. By some sort of process, he met needs I didn't even know I had."

It is Cohen's contention that we all have a serape or two in the closet.

PRESERVING YOUR OPTIONS

A man went out to Cohen's new house (you know, the one his wife bought) to install a couple of locks. The bill came—$142. He had been there 45 minutes, Cohen says—$142. "So I call up the guy and he says, 'Look, pal, that's the price.' 'Maybe we can talk about it.' 'No—that's it.' I said, 'Well, do I have any options in this situation?' He says, 'What do you mean, options? If you don't like it, I'll take out the locks.' I said, 'Good. That's a very good idea.' He says, 'What do you mean—you'll have holes in the door.' I say, 'No problem; take them out.' He says, 'How about $95—would that sound better?' I said, 'Yeah.'"

And there, in the relatively trivial difference between the $142 that many of us would resignedly have paid and the $95 that let us assume for the sake of argument *was* a more equitable price, lies the kernel of Herb Cohen's philosophy. He is not talking about "looking out for number one" or "winning through intimidation" or "screwing the Government because it is screwing us."

"I want people to have power," he says. "To have options and know they have options. When people are powerless, it's bad for everybody. Either they become hostile and try to tear down the system or they become apathetic and throw in the towel. We don't want either one."

MAX WAYS

Reading 1–2
The Virtues, Dangers, and Limits of Negotiation

Once upon a time a hunter named Noneck had in his cave more rabbit meat than he needed; however, he had lost his hunting club. His neighbor, Twelvetoes, happend to have two clubs but no meat. Twelvetoes could have bopped the unarmed Noneck and taken his food. Or both could have ignored the opportunity for an exchange. Instead, they squatted by the fire (for in those days the three-martini lunch was unknown) and haggled until they agreed on exactly how many rabbits were worth one club. That's how negotiation began.

Down the centuries the practice gradually spread. In recent years it has surged and now seems to crop up everywhere. Sports news used to concentrate on athletic contests, but reporters have become so fascinated by stars' salary negotiations that it's sometimes hard to find out who won yesterday's games. Negotiation has entered areas formerly determined by authority or by the norms of society. Parents speak of negotiating curfews with their children. Troubled spouses say they are renegotiating the terms of their marriages. In criminal courts most defendants are never tried; after negotiations they plead guilty to lesser charges.

Business has long been the main matrix of negotiation. Financial pages now are full of merger talks begun, aborted, or concluded. Corporations are negotiating huge settlements of lawsuits brought by other corporations, by governments, or by interest groups.

In politics "the will of the people" has been fragmented into a thousand splinters; politicians, trying to compromise among these contending wills are enmeshed in negotiations with one another. States, cities, and universities negotiate for federal grants. Cities negotiate with unions and ethnic communities. President Carter's first two years had few highlights, and two of them, the Panama Canal treaty and Camp David, were connected with negotiations. Ahead of the president lie major stresses produced by negotiations: the Israel-Egypt tension continues, a SALT agreement will set off intense debate, and the [1979] Teamsters contract will test, and perhaps bust, the wage-price guidelines.

All these kinds of negotiations, disparate in substance, have some common patterns and roots. Though almost everybody has negotiated (for a car or a house, at least), the nature of the process is not well understood. Popular opinion tends to oscillate between two misleading attitudes. One bias puts too much faith in negotiation, believing it to be applicable to all situations; this view is sometimes expressed as "any compromise is better than conflict." The opposite bias regards the process as ethically tainted because it often involves dissembling or moral compromises.

Until a few decades ago, there was little effort to theorize about negotiation as a general process. Since then a respectable, though still sparse, body of analytical writing has appeared. From this literature a definition has been adapted: *Negotiation is a process in which two or more parties, who have both common interests and conflicting interests, put forth and discuss explicit proposals concerning specific terms of a possible agreement.*

Explanation of some terms in the definition may throw light on such questions as why negotiation is increasing, how the process operates, what its ethical implications are, and what hazards and limits restrict its usefulness.

Parties may be individuals or groups (e.g., nations, corporations, unions, associations) that are autonomous enough to make and keep contracts. They are, in a word, "free." Individuals and groups who can meet these requirements are far more numerous now than in former centuries. The proliferation of potential parties is the most obvious cause of the rise of negotiations.

Within societies that are tightly controlled from the top (e.g., the Soviet Union), negotiation among ordinary people occurs—and probably is increasing. But the process is far less important there than within the advanced democracies, where power, in the sense of freedom to act, is much more widely dispersed among the population.

The core of the definition lies in the interplay of two phrases, "common interests" and "conflicting interests." Unless *both* are present, in either an overt or a latent way, negotiation makes no sense. Negotiated accords are usually specific and not intended to abolish all conflict between the parties. A SALT agreement, for example, would not end the antagonism between the United States and the U.S.S.R. They do, however, have a common interest in reducing the costs and risks of an arms race.

In the United States, competition has sharpened and widened during the 20th century. As individuals and groups pursue their interests more intently, conflicts inevitably multiply. In the same period, interdependence among peoples and groups has also increased. Indeed, the most usual way of pursuing self-interest in this society is to enter into relationships based on common interest.

Each party, acting in self-interest, tries to increase the value placed on his goods or services by others who act in their self-interest. This is what people do in jobs and what companies do in searching for customers. The society that results is not, as is often said, an "atomized" chaos of self-seeking units. It is an intricate web of relationships that are both competitive and cooperative. The simultaneous rise of self-interest and mutual interest increases the aggregate of contracts, some of which are negotiated.

Obviously, not all or even most agreements are made that way. The words "put forth and discuss specific proposals" are inserted in the definition to distinguish negotiation from the ways in which most agreements are reached. Except for some big-ticket items, retail trade in the United States is conducted on a take-it-or-leave-it basis by sellers who seldom negotiate with individual customers. Transactions in capital markets, too, are organized in stock and bond exchanges where a continuing auction eliminates negotiation. At the present volume of economic transactions, there would be no time left for producing goods and services if Americans haggled over each trade in the pattern that survives in the Arab *souk*.

The process of negotiation does not always develop quickly when parties with common interests find themselves in conflict. The first American strike occurred in the late 18th century, and many other "turnouts" followed during the first half of the 19th century. But these disputes were neither preceded by nor settled by negotiation. An employer would establish by unilateral action a scale of wages. Journeymen would draw up a higher scale, sometimes inserting it in a bible on which each swore he would not work for less. The scale was presented to the employer, and if he did not agree the workers "turned out" and stayed out until one side or the other caved in. No counterproposals, no discussion, no negotiation.

Horace Greeley, who was simultaneously a union sympathizer and an employer, found a better way. In 1850 he told a workers' mass meeting in Tammany Hall, "I do not agree that the journeymen should dictate a scale, but they should get the employers to agree to some scale." A few years later Greeley proposed that workers come to negotiations with statistics and arguments supporting the fairness of their cause. He set the United States on the course known to the 20th century as "collective bargaining."

When individuals bargain as consumers or to fix the terms of their employment, they usually act for themselves. Today many agreements are negotiated by agents. Much bitterness and grief have been generated when agents are deemed to have conceded too much or—less often—too little. A dramatic and costly example of faulty communications between agents and principals occurred in last winter's coal strike, prolonged at great cost to the U.S. economy when the union's rank and file rejected a draft agreement approved by the leadership. The union negotiators had obtained a hefty wage increase—larger, perhaps, than the miners expected—but had given up certain medical benefits that had a high value to the miners.

In numberless instances negotiators have been accused of selling out to the other side. Even without venality, negotiations sometimes take on a life of their own; agreement—any agreement—becomes the overriding goal. Fred Charles Iklé, a distinguished analyst of modern diplomacy, points out in his book *How Nations Negotiate* that diplomats "are generally praised for the good agreements they concluded, not for the bad ones they avoided, since historians find it hard to reconstruct what the terms and consequences of such unborn accords might have been." Iklé quotes Sir Samuel Hoare, who was a member of the British Cabinet during the successful—though disastrous—negotiations with Hitler in 1938: "The longer it went on and the more serious the issue became, the more anxious I grew to see it succeed. This is almost always the course of negotiations. As they proceed, the parties concerned in them become increasingly obsessed with the need to prevent their final failure."

At a level deeper than the relation of bargaining agents to their principals, the bargaining process is surrounded by ethical ambiguities. The process does not necessarily involve dishonesty, but it is seldom open and candid. Even in commonplace negotiations (e.g., purchasing a car) buyers do not candidly disclose their eagerness to sellers; nor are they under any moral obligation to do so. Patterns of commercial bargaining, anciently established, allow—and sometimes require—negotiators to practice what in other contexts would amount to immoral deceit.

One negotiator may react to another's proposal by feigning more indignation than he feels. He may bluff. He may assert with every appearance of sincerity that he is unchangeably committed to a price beyond which he will not budge—and then budge.

When negotiators, departing from conventional bargaining practices, are too quick to concede a point, they may give an impression of weakness. That happened in the negotiation of the armistice ending the Korean War. The Communists, predictably, proposed a truce line far to the south of the battle line between the opposing armies. The United Nations negotiators, as they had been instructed to do, proposed a line to the north of the battlefront. But then, trying to be reasonable, they immediately retreated. In the words of Admiral C. Turner Joy, who led the UN negotiating team, the northern line "was a bargaining position, and even while proposing it we made plain our interest in a solution on the line of ground contact." The UN negotiators did not owe the other side this degree of candor. It could be argued that they owed their principals a vigorous defense of the northern line even though they expected to fall back to "the line of ground contact" eventually.

Admiral Joy later acknowledged that the American desire to be reasonable gave the Communists a tactical edge. "Because of our American tendency to feel that a deadlocked issue should be solved by mutual concessions," he wrote, "the Communists are on favorable ground in applying their delaying tactics. By proposing that 2 plus 2 equal 6, and by then delaying an agreement interminably, the Communists hope to lead us to agree that 2 plus 2 equal 5.''

Yet negotiation is not a process where anything goes. Some negotiators get a reputation for trickery that destroys their effectiveness. Others negotiate successfully for years and enjoy among their opponents and their principals a reputation for probity and fairness. They know how to draw delicate lines between what is ethically permissible in negotiations and what is not.

A negotiator has no right to lie about what purports to be an objective fact. For example, if an employer in negotiation decides to produce figures showing that his business is in bad shape, he must not present false figures. But he does not owe the union candid exposure of his own subjective view of what the figures imply for the future of the business; he may be less depressed by his accounts than he seems to be. The union representatives will routinely test his attitude by continuing to insist on their demands and by pretending to be less depressed by the employer's figures than, in fact, they are. Through such well-worn and twisting—though not necessarily immoral—paths, negotiators frequently reach a ''striking point'' where each is convinced the other will make no further concessions.

In these maneuvers, the parties are not really ''deceived.'' Each recognizes that the other is playing a role, and that the negotiating context does not require his partner-opponent to make a premature disclosure of how much he is prepared to give. The outcome of negotiations depends largely on what is in the minds and hearts of the negotiators and what each thinks is in the other's mind and heart. Each tries to change the other's perception and values, partly by persuasion and partly by assertions, which may not be candid, about what is in his own mind and heart. During negotiations one side may—and often does—change its values and goals because of what it has come to believe about the other's values and goals.

This subjective aspect of negotiation is one reason it does not readily lend itself to analysis by the logical techniques developed in the theory of games. Those techniques work best in situations of ''pure conflict'' and in zero-sum games where one party's gain is exactly equal to the other party's loss. Most negotiations result in exchanges where both sides are supposed to gain. Game theory can rise to brilliant heights of intellectual complexity, but its psychological assumptions are too simple to be applied to negotiation, where ''winning'' is never the sole motive of the parties.

In determining the outcome of a negotiation, the skills of the negotiators often will be less important than the objective circumstances surrounding the bargaining. The most adroit and strong-willed negotiator can seldom make headway if the facts are heavily and plainly against him. It is always unfair to blame negotiators for a disadvantageous agreement without taking into account the objective situation of their principals.

Of course, it is broadly true that a strong party confronting a weak one is in a position to make advantageous deals. But this generalization can mislead because it is subject to so many qualifications and exceptions. In the first place, ''strong'' should not be equated with size or wealth or power. If a very large company wants to acquire a small company by merger, both may know that the big company needs the little one and the little one does not need the big one; the price that the larger will have to pay for the shares of the smaller may reflect the inequality of desire rather than the inequality of size.

Weakness itself can be a source of bargaining strength. A bank may call a large debtor and express an incipient anxiety about the safety of the loan. The debtor may laughingly reply, ''So you're waking up. My condition is so much worse than you suspect that your only chance of repayment depends on a lower interest rate and a postponement of payments on the principal.'' If the loan is big enough, the very weakness of the debtor's objective position may undercut the bargaining strength of the creditor. Unions with empty treasuries, incompetent leaders, and dissentient memberships have been known to negotiate quite advantageous contracts with managements who feared a stronger, tougher union waiting in the wings.

One of the most amazing examples of the bargaining strength conferred by weakness was the relationship between the United States and the government of South Vietnam. The Saigon government for years was dependent for its very survival on military and economic help from the United States. Again and again the United States tried to negotiate agreements committing Saigon to undertake military, economic, and political reforms. In vain, Saigon always pleaded that it was too weak to make the changes suggested. The frustrating failure to reform the Saigon government has often been blamed on the American negotiators, but in truth Saigon's weakness was the objective foundation of its intransigence.

The definition of negotiation concludes with the words ''specific terms of a possible agreement.'' The word *specific* should be stressed. Negotiated accords work best when their substance is quite limited and clearly defined. The 1928 Kellogg-Briand Pact, signed by 64 nations, which renounced ''war as an instrument of national policy'' was trash; its agreement was too broad, too vague, and too ambitious.

The usefulness of negotiation has logical limits. No single negotiation can be expected to produce a grand and constructive advance in human relations. Negotiated accords are strongly influenced by precedent and by the values of the society. They are evolutionary steps allowing a society that uses them to be both stable in its main institutions and flexible in detail.

When words like *fair* and *just* occur in negotiation, as they often do, something outside the negotiation process itself is being appealed to—norms of justice that have been accepted by the overarching framework of the society. Negotiations should not be used to create norms of justice. Definition of a fundamental social institution, such as marriage, should not be determined by private agreement between the parties. Some parts of the U.S. Constitution were explicitly negotiated by founders who represented conflicting regional interests. But the essence of the Constitution was not negotiated; it flowed from a broad consensus of political experience, tradition, and emergent values.

Just as the Constitution sets limits on what the government may do, so government may forbid certain kinds of private contracts; for example, price-fixing conspiracies among sellers. Belief that consumers are victimized by certain contracts between labor unions and employers has raised the question of whether restraints should be applied to this important kind of private contract. In debating such issues, attention should always be paid to the long-range danger that limiting freedom of private contract will throw upon government kinds of responsibilities it is ill-equipped to handle.

Even within its proper limits, negotiation often falls short of the ideal of benefiting both parties. Sometimes one wins and the other loses. A really bad bargain is when both lose. Many negotiations go on for weeks or months, only to be broken off. Such waste of time and effort is a risk inherent in the process.

Despite its limitations, abuses, and hazards, negotiation has become an indispensable process in free societies. More effectively than any alternative anybody has thought of so far, it enables us to realize common interests while we compromise conflicting interests. Since these are among the basic objectives of rational people, negotiation has to be counted among the greatest of human inventions.

Reading 1-3
The Significance of
Human Conflict

Were I to ask you to associate freely to the word *conflict,* I predict I would receive three kinds of responses. One set of terms would have grisly and negative connotations—*war, death, destruction, disorder, aggressiveness, violence, rape.* A second set of terms would have positive connotations—*adventure, opportunity, drama, fun, excitement, development.* A third set of terms would be relatively neutral, affectively speaking—*tension, competition, scarcity, mediation, bargaining, reconciliation.*

Some of us would produce terms belonging to two or to all three sets. If I am right in my predictions, the results indicate a basic ambivalence in us, individually and collectively, toward *conflict.* And these mixed attitudes are justified in empirical reality. Conflicts can and do bring disorder, destruction, and death to human affairs. But conflicts also can and do bring opportunity, drama, development, and growth to human individuals and societies. In fact, I am prepared to defend the thesis that all individual growth and social progress involve the facing and rationally creative resolution of conflicts.

CONFLICT CAN LEAD TO GROWTH

I will make one other prediction about my fantasied data collection. Since we are for the most part middle-class Americans here, I predict that a large majority of our free associations to "conflict" would be negative, implying that conflict is a bad thing in human life. It is. But if it is also potentially a good think—the motor of individual growth and social progress—will not an attempt to deny, suppress, or eliminate conflict, if successful, also deny, suppress, or eliminate growth and progress? As a matter of fact, if conflict cannot be eliminated from human relationships, as I fully believe that it cannot, an attempt to deny, suppress, or eliminate it will therefore lead to destructive modes of expressing and handling it, and so justify and reinforce the fears that led to its denial and suppression in the first place. The schoolteacher who suppresses open expression of hostility between factions in her class reaps a harvest of unctuous tattling and informing upon one another "for the good of the group" or the persons informed upon. The conflict is still present but in a form more ugly and less rationally manageable than before. Thus the painful self-fulfilling prophesy of the unmitigated evil of conflict reenacts itself.

How can the cycle be broken? Here is where the neutral vocabulary for characterizing conflict—the third set of responses—finds its usefulness. Scientific study demands a neutral vocabulary for objectifying data collection about and interpretation of human events, however fraught with painful or joyous connotations the terms for these events in commonsense language may be. If we are to understand conflict we must, for the time of diagnosis at least, get outside our fears or our exultation in order to estimate the nature of the conflict, its potentialities in terms of growth or destruction for those involved, and the best deployment of our resources for helping to actualize more of the former potentialities than of the latter. The neutral language and concepts of social and behavioral science are important tools in such dispassionate diagnosis.

Unfortunately, social and behavioral scientists have also tended until recently to avoid the serious study of conflict. Lewis Coser in his *The Functions of Social Conflict* makes this point in a telling way:

> Even a cursory examination of the contemporary work of American sociologists clearly indicates that conflict has been very much neglected indeed as a field of investigation. . . .
>
> In contrast [to early American sociologists], the majority of sociologists who dominate contemporary sociology, far from seeing themselves as reformers and addressing themselves to an audience of reformers, either have oriented themselves toward purely academic and professional audiences, or have attempted to find a hearing among decision-makers in public or private bureaucracies. . . .
>
> They center attention predominantly upon problems of adjustment rather than upon conflict; upon social statistics rather than upon dynamics. Of key problematic importance to them has been the maintenance of existing structures and the ways and means of insuring their smooth functioning.

Recently a new interest in the scientific study of human conflict has developed. This is illustrated by the publication of *The Journal of Conflict Resolution,* devoted exclusively to attempts to generalize beyond the specific areas in which conflict has been studied empirically—race relations, labor-management relations, and international relations particularly—toward more inclusive theories of conflict and strategies of conflict resolution. At the Human Relations Center in Boston University, a cross-disciplinary group has been studying conflict and conflict resolution over several years. Our conviction is that psychological, group, social, and cultural factors in conflict must be seen and studied together if adequate growth-releasing strategies of resolution are to be devised and developed.

I cannot summarize here all of the propositions about conflict that today find some support in the literatures of various social and behavioral sciences. I will state a few propositions that may be useful in our thinking about valid and invalid strategies for handling the ambivalences inherent in the concept and the actuality of human conflict.

Conflict always occurs within a context of interdependence. It is a relationship between parts of a system of interrelated parts. If the "parties" in conflict were not interdependent in the sense that the actions of one "party" have consequences for the opposed "party" and vice versa, conflict could not occur. This helps in part to explain the fear of conflict—at the least it disrupts the order and the productive output of the system in which it occurs; at the most it may lead to the dismemberment and destruction of the system. This proposition also offers hope for constructive resolution: If the system of interdependence has value for all parts of the system and if perception of the common values of maintaining the system can be kept alive in all parties to the conflict, this provides a force toward creating some mutually satisfactory and acceptable resolution of the conflict, which, in effect, means the improvement of the system. (The "system" as used here may be a person, an interperson, a group, an organization, a community, a nation, or an internation.)

One type of conflict grows out of similarities in the needs and values of parts of a system in the presence of scarce and undistributable goods required to satisfy these needs and realize these values. Johnny and Jimmy, siblings, both want the same toy to play with—there is only one toy. Johnny and Jimmy are in conflict. It is not differences in needs and valuations which induces the conflict; it is rather the similarity of needs and valuations in the presence of scarce goods. Enlarging the supply of scarce goods may resolve the conflict. Changing the image of the good desired to joint utilization of the toy rather than sole possession may also resolve the conflict. If the toy is a fire truck and Johnny and Jimmy can find more value in playing a game utilizing the fire truck along with other available resources than in either child's possessing the fire truck exclusively, the conflict may be lifted onto a higher level of cooperation. The main point is that similarities in need and value systems need not lead to cooperation but may rather lead to conflict. Creating distributable and nonscarce values in the conflict situation may be a growth-releasing way of resolution if emphasis can come to be placed upon joint utilization and manipulation of distributable goods rather than on exclusive possession of scarce values.

Another type of conflict grows out of differences in needs and valuations as among parts of a system. The needs and values of one part of a group, for example, may favor one direction of movement for the group; the needs and values of another part of the group may favor another direction of movement. Or the differences may lie not in direction but rather in methods of moving toward the agreed-upon goal. Resolution may lie in breaking up the group, in compromise, in bargaining, or in some creative synthesis of a new direction or method of movement, developed out of the very clash of differing needs and valuations. Out of the last kind of experience may grow appreciation of persons with differing values and needs in an association as sources of fruitful conflict and creativity. The sights of all parties must be lifted toward utilization of differences in a common quest and away from defensiveness toward loss of *my* present distinctiveness, in order to accomplish creative resolution.

TRUST AND RATIONALITY

The "ideal" resolution of the two types of conflict just noted involves two requirements. First, each party to the conflict must accept the right of the other party to his claim upon the situation along with his own—must, in effect, trust him. Second, all parties must be capable of locating realistically and rationally the sources of the conflict. When conflicts are not faced and recognized, when full-bodied communication about the nature and genesis of the conflict is not released and maintained, the parties tend to develop unrealistic versions of each other and of the conflict situation. Projection by one party of his or its undesirable motivations upon the opponents occurs and vice versa. If one party feels at some level he is selfish and cannot admit this to himself, he comes to find "pure" selfishness as characteristic of his opponents. The motives of the opposition are impugned on both sides; the drama of conflict becomes a melodramatic and externalized struggle of good and evil. Noncommunication with the enemy comes to be seen as a virtue. Also, realistic acceptance by a member of "my" party of the enemy's right to oppose us comes to be seen as disloyalty and treason in the member. Or if the source of the conflict realistically involves a revered or powerful person or faction in opposition, displacement of negative affect toward a less powerful and less revered "opponent" takes place, and responsibility for the conflict is heaped upon a more or less helpless scapegoat.

In other words, under conditions of denial and noncommunication, "unrealistic" versions of the conflict tend to obscure the "realistic" sources of the conflict. Both *trust and rationality,* essential elements in creative resolution of conflict, tend to be lost and excluded from the situation. Preventing the emergence of nonrealistic conflicts and converting a nonrealistically perceived conflict situation into a realistically perceived one become major concerns of those who would encourage the creative utilization of conflict in human affairs.

EVADING OR DENYING CONFLICT

What forms do strategies for denying and/or eliminating conflict from human situations take? Most of these have already been suggested. Perhaps renaming them here will be helpful:

Segregation of conflicting elements in a situation.   Segregation seldom works well because of the actual interdependence within the system which it thwarts.

Melodramatic externalization of the conflict.   The conflict is all out there between the evil "Them" or "Its" and the holy "I's." The conflict is actually within Me and within You as well as between Me and You. Externalization thus beclouds reality.

Making a virtue of submission to established power relations. To maintain an existing order against all internal attack is to assume that whatever is, is right; and since in human affairs this is never true, reality is falsified again.

Myth that "we are all alike essentially."   This is false as well as suicidal—I am I and Thou are Thou. But even if it were accepted as true, it would not eliminate conflicts which grow out of similar needs and values in the presence of scarce and undistributable goods.

Undermining "partial" identifications in the name of devotion to the whole.   I am responsible not alone to maintain the whole of whatever systems I belong to but also to change them in areas where I believe they need changing. My "partial" identifications within the whole are my leverage for changing the whole over time. To deprive me of these levers is to crush me into passivity.

Legalistic punishment of aggressive acts without consideration of the merits of the context in which aggression and counteraggression occur.   We frequently assess the merits of the parties to a conflict by trying to answer the question "Who started it?" rather than "What are the rights in the situation?" This is to substitute chronology for ethics and theology.

FACING AND RESOLVING CONFLICT

And what of the conditions and strategies for facing and creatively and rationally resolving conflicts in human affairs?

Facing and accepting the complexity of the motivations of myself and of my own party and of those in opposition within the conflict situation.   To oversimplify a complex situation is to falsify it, however flattering to the ego, and out of falsification further falsifications grow.

Humanizing and rehumanizing my party and the opposition party in the conflict situation.   This is related to the previous point, but humanization involves more than a fair assessment of faults and virtues. It involves acceptance of the dignity and potentiality for growth and learning of self and of others. It is to see the drama of human conflict as essentially tragic rather than melodramatic.

Internalization of the conflict.   Objectivity toward a conflict situation can be achieved only if the claims of my opponents upon the situation can be internalized and entertained along with my own. What is at stake in the conflict is felt as well as cognized.

Envisioning values inherent in the situation as changed.   Conflicts generated in situations as they now are cannot be resolved without altering the situation, including the parties within it. Rejuggling the situation as now perceived and enacted can lead only to compromise resolutions. Creative resolutions require changes all around.

Acceptance of conflict as inherent in human life.   This does not mean passive drift in the presence of conflict or joyous exultation in the destruction of values, which is always a potential in conflict situations. It does mean an attitude of not being so threatened by conflict as to resort consistently to strategies of evasion or denial.

Maintaining and building in each person and other human systems a methodological character attuned to division, and enacting growth-releasing resolutions of conflicts whenever they may appear.   To rely on commonly acceptable methodologies to carry us through situations where our own values are under challenge and review is not to forsake old values. It is rather to accept the premise of continuing creation of new values through conflicts jointly, imaginatively, and rationally faced and resolved. It is to remember John Dewey's wisdom—"He who would think of ends seriously must think of means reverently."

SECTION TWO

Interdependence

As a people, we treasure independence and autonomy, and believe we have a great deal of it. Politically, we do. But socially? Economically? That is another matter. We may feel we are free to do many things until a truck hits a power line and shuts off our electricity, or the rubbish collectors go on strike, or relatives or friends get sick, or OPEC quadruples crude oil prices, or we move to a new community. These sudden breaks in routine events sharply bring home how interdependent we are with others; people (perhaps some we have never seen) and events we have no control over can drastically upset our lives. The number of people we are involved with and the number of ways we are involved is far greater than most of us appreciate.

Even without the major disturbances mentioned above, we are continually adjusting to other people in big and little ways. We almost unconsciously work out who will get on the elevator first; interrupt someone eating to pass us the salt; with a little more effort, we successfully adjust our vacations to fit in with others; or trim a shrub on the border of our property to the mutual satisfaction of us and our neighbor. The very ordinariness of this process is very important, for it shows that many interdependence situations that could lead to conflict do not; instead, with relatively little effort, they almost routinely conclude with success. However, the ease, the ordinariness of this success means we are unlikely to carefully examine what took place in handling this interdependence successfully; so we are not aware of what is involved when the process is not going well. The articles in this section examine various aspects of events and behavior that occur in ordinary, everyday situations and bring out basic processes and structures that need to be used to understand bargaining situations. How can we explain that many of these events go smoothly and others have difficulty?

Bertram Raven and Jeffrey Rubin, in "The Interdependence of Persons," analyze the structure of dependency relationships and explore the many means one can use to gain information and exchange offers and rewards to reach an agreement or to coordinate efforts. They bring out two powerful points. First, once we recognize that we are in an interdependent situation, where we have to consider another person's actions (and particularly their responses to our actions), we should pursue a search for a solution that gives us the maximum joint return rather than seeking maximum individual return. The second point, as already noted, is that we influence others in a variety of ways, sometimes through written and spoken words, sometimes through actions.

However, we do not deal with others only as individuals. Many of our actions toward others results from the fact that we, and often they, are members of groups. Groups have a powerful effect on individual behavior. People take great risks for groups in hazardous situations (i.e., loyalty to a group in combat) or because of pressures from groups. How we treat another person may be more determined by the group of which she or he is a member than by what we know about the person as an individual.

Jerry Harvey, in "Some Dynamics of Intergroup Competition," explores these phenomena and goes on to examine what happens when groups are in conflict. He points out that what happens within the group is almost directly the opposite of what happens between the groups. During conflict with another group, people within a group pull together, see each other in more favorable ways, and are more tolerant of each other and their actions. The members of the competing group are looked upon less favorably; they are stereotyped in unfavorable ways, and their individual and collective actions are judged more harshly.

Harvey points out that these shifts in perception occur because people are in groups and the groups are in competition. The same people would be seen differently if they were not in a group or if the groups were not in competition. Hence, if we are going to work to reduce conflict between groups, we can begin by recognizing that how we see the other party and how they see us is shaped by the competitive situation.

BERTRAM H. RAVEN and
JEFFREY Z. RUBIN

Reading 2–1
The Interdependence
of Persons

INTERDEPENDENCE DURING AN UNEVENTFUL DAY

In the course of a single, not especially eventful day in the lives of most of us, we are expected and required to make an extraordinary number of judgments that pertain to the complex ways in which we are interdependent with others. Here, for example, is a sequence of events that happened one day in the life of a professor of social psychology.

Beginning in the late morning, at the conclusion of my weekly graduate seminar in social psychology, the students and I are discussing plans for our next meeting. We agree to spend our next session critiquing a body of social psychological research and decide that, in order to have a really fruitful discussion, each person will read the same set of experimental papers. I have most of the articles the students are to read, but many of them are too long to duplicate. As a consequence, the students must decide on some sharing arrangement. Phone numbers are exchanged, and an elaborate plan is established for coordinating the reading. Since there are five students in the seminar and five articles to be reviewed, each student will read a different article on the first day and then, round-robin fashion, pass the article along to someone else. In this way, each student will be able to study each of the papers by the following meeting.

After the seminar, I join several other faculty members and students for lunch at a local restaurant. Midway through our meal, we overhear four businessmen at the next table each insisting that today *he* must pay the check. Soon, however, it becomes clear that none of them *really* wants to pick up the tab; the bill is lying in the middle of the table, and any one of them could easily pick it up if he really wanted to. Why, then, this elaborate ritual? And what strategy is each using to make his offer seem honest—while not getting stuck with the bill?

Later in the day I have a brief meeting with the department chairman. After our other business has been completed, I decide to broach the subject of my salary for next year. With as much delicacy as I can muster, I inquire about the possibility of a raise. His response is surprisingly disarming. He points out, first of all, that he considers me worthy of a raise, and that he will do his very best to help me. But, he cautions, I must remember that his hands are tied. The university administration has allotted him only a fixed amount of money for departmental salaries, which he must distribute as he sees fit. Thus, if I get the raise that I deserve, someone else will not. I experience pangs of guilt at the thought that one or more of my equally competent and deserving colleagues may suffer because of my avarice. After a moment or two, I suggest that we solve the problem by encouraging the administration to allocate a larger sum of money to our department, thereby allowing all who deserve raises to receive them. The chairman assures me that he will try his hardest.

That evening, my wife and I set about the task of preparing dinner. Following our usual division of labor, I fix the salad while she prepares the meat and salad dressing. After dinner, I wash the dishes and empty the garbage, while she waters the plants. Since it is Friday, and thus the end of a workweek, we decide to go out for the evening. But where? During the course of our conversation, the following dialogue takes place:

Me: Why don't we go to a movie?
My wife: That's fine with me. Or we could go to a play.
Me: It sounds like you'd rather see a play.
My wife: That would be nice—but a movie is fine also. I'm easy.
Me: Me too.
  (Silence)
Me: So how are we going to decide?
My wife: What movie did you want to see?
Me: *Cries and Whispers.*
My wife: It may be difficult to get seats.
Me: That's true. What play did you want to see?
My wife: *Don Juan in Hell.*
Me: It'll probably be just as difficult to get seats for that as for the movie.
  (Silence)
Me: So how are we going to decide?
My wife: What would you like to do?
Me: I'd like to go to a movie—but only if you'd like to also.
My wife: *Cries and Whispers* is fine.
Me: Okay. But do you *really* want to go—or are you just saying that because you know I want to go and are being nice?
My wife: *Cries and Whispers* is fine. (Pause) Look, why don't you stop fooling around and decide. I made the decision last time.

Me (thinking to myself): She says she's willing to go to the movie, but I suspect she really wants to see the play. She's saying the movie is okay because she knows my preference and wants to please me. But her impatience with my ambivalence suggests that she isn't as "easy" about what we're going to do as she's letting on. I think I'll give her a pleasant surprise.

Me: Okay. Let's go to the play. We'll see the movie another time.

And so it goes—one example of interdependence following another. But now, let us examine this scenario of events, the details of which vary from person to person, and from day to day. In what ways are the events recounted here similar? In what ways do they differ? And, most important, what are the consequences of these similarities and differences for the ways in which people behave with one another?

THE PROBLEM OF COORDINATION

The individual actors in our drama of an uneventful day were busily, and characteristically, engaged in a process that we shall call *coordination:* they were each trying to phase their preferences, intentions, and/or expectations with those of others. It is by means of coordination that people transform their interdependent relationships into behavioral reality. Coordination, in other words, is interdependence made visible.

People are often fully aware of the coordination process in which they engage. For example, I knew perfectly well that my wife preferred a play to a movie and plant-watering to dishwashing. At other times, however, people are only dimly aware of their interdependence or have no awareness at all. Thus, while speaking to another person, we may adjust the tone of our voice and our articulation so that we will be understood by, but not annoy, him. If he is socially sensitive, he will adjust his own speech in turn. And all this may take place without either person being consciously aware of it.

In order to study the coordination process that emerges when neither person is aware of his interdependence with another, three psychologists conducted a rather interesting experimental study of a "minimal social situation". . . . Two subjects were placed in separate rooms, but neither was told of the other's existence. Each subject was presented with two buttons; although he was not informed of the purpose of the buttons, he was told that he could press them in any manner or order that he wanted. He was further informed that he would receive points on a counter in front of him, but that he might also receive a shock through an electrode that was attached to him. He was instructed to try to get as many points as possible and to avoid shocks. Unknown to the subjects, one of Subject A's buttons was wired to give a point to Subject B and the other was wired to shock Subject B. B's buttons were similarly wired to Subject A. Note that neither subject could reward or shock himself, but only the other.

You might think that in a situation such as this, complete and utter chaos would result. To the contrary, the experimenters found that the number of shocks received by both subjects steadily decreased, while the number of points obtained increased. Thus, despite the subjects' ignorance of their interdependent relationship (not to mention their ignorance of one another's existence), they still learned to help, rather than hurt, each other. But how could this happen? It appears that, over time, each subject learns to adopt the identical, simple strategic rule—"win-stay, lose-change." That is, each person tends to repeat (stay with) his last response after receiving a positive outcome (a point), but he tends to change it after getting a negative one (a shock). For example, if Subject A receives a point and B receives a shock, then we might expect A (who "won") to repeat his last response and B (who "lost") to change. Now both A and B would get a shock. If they both changed their response, then they would both get points. And, since they have both "won" now, both might be expected to repeat their last response—and continue to win.

In many relationships people are unaware of their interdependence. The central implication of the "minimal social situation" research is that in any relationship where people are uncertain about which of several courses of action to pursue, they may adopt the strategic "win-stay, lose-change" rule. But note the inherent conservatism of this rule: If things are going well, it says, continue doing whatever you have been doing ("you must be doing something right"), but if things are not going well, change ("you have little to lose—and possibly much to gain"). By adhering to this rule, we learn to persist in behavior for which we are rewarded (by ourselves, but even more so by others) and to change behavior for which we are punished (or at least not rewarded).

Now that we have seen how coordination may occur even when people are ignorant of one another's existence, let us look at the more frequent case in which people do know about their interdependence. In analyzing this situation and the various strategies that result, it may be useful to distinguish among three types of coordination problems: those in which people's interests are either *convergent* (common), *divergent* (different), or both *convergent and divergent*.

Convergent Interest Coordination

Try to solve the following problem: . . . You and a total stranger, whom you have never met and with whom you cannot communicate, are seated in separate rooms. On a table in front of each of you is a pencil and a piece of paper. Your task is to write down a sum of money. If you and the stranger both name the same amount, you can each have as much as you have named. But, if you and the other person write down a different amount, neither of you will win anything.

Guessing What the Other Person Will Do.   Okay; what amount did you indicate? $1? $5? $1 million? Next, ask yourself how you went about trying to solve this problem. Perhaps you said something like this to yourself: "Since I know nothing at all about this other person, why not assume that he is just like me? I will figure out the amount of money *I* want to write down, and then assume that he will do exactly the same thing.'' Or perhaps you reasoned as follows: I cannot really assume that the other person is just like me [I'm probably a bit smarter], but I'll try to guess what he [an average person] might put down and then give the same answer myself.'' Or perhaps, if you were especially clever, you thought to yourself: ''In order to decide what amount to put down, I will first have to figure out how much the other person thinks *I'm* going to write down—which will be the amount *he* will then specify to match my choice—which will be the amount *I* will put down to match his guess about my choice.'' And so on, perhaps endlessly, this cycle of interpersonal perspectives might continue, each person making his choice dependent upon his guess about the other's guess about his guess about the other's guess . . .

Picking a Prominent Solution. Obviously, in attempting to solve a problem like this, each person must try his best to coordinate his preferences, intentions, and expectations with those of the other. In this particular problem, each person knows only that the other person is in exactly the same interdependent relationship as he—and that the other is aware that he knows this. Given this limited information about one another, perhaps the wisest course for each to take would be to seek out a ''solution'' that is somehow prominent. . . . Thus, $1 is a more prominent solution than $0.73. Heads is more prominent than tails in the flip of a coin, and so forth. Of course, if you knew anything at all about the other person, this would greatly increase your chances of finding a prominent solution. If, for example, you thought he was a student, you might guess that he would write down a relatively small amount of money—$1, $10, or $100 perhaps, but certainly not $1,000. On the other hand, if you were a millionaire playing with Howard Hughes in a game conducted by Aristotle Onassis, $1,000 or even $1 million might emerge as a more prominent solution.

Using Additional Information about the Other Person. What we have done so far is to take the ''minimal social situation'' and modify it by letting each of our two people know that there is another with whom he is interdependent in a particular kind of way. Let us now further enrich and complicate this situation by systematically introducing new information about the other person. The following example is based upon a study conducted by Arlene F. Frank and Jeffrey Z. Rubin. . . . Suppose that you and the stranger are once again seated in separate rooms without any means of communication. On the table in front of each of you is a pencil and a piece of paper, on which six circles have been drawn in a horizontal row. The circles are of equal size and are spaced evenly apart. Your task is to put a check mark in *one* of the six circles. If both of you check the same circle, you will each win some identical (but hypothetical) sum of money. But if you and the other person check different circles, neither of you will win anything. Let us suppose that you are a native-born American who reads from left to right; therefore (others things being equal) you have a natural preference for the extreme left circle.

If I were to tell you that the stranger was also an American, you might readily assume that he had the same left preference and thus check off the extreme left circle. But suppose I informed you that the stranger came from a Middle Eastern country (where words are written from right to left). Then you could assume that he would have a preference for the extreme right circle and simply pick that one. Fine! But wait a minute. Does *he* know that *you* are an American? If so, he might expect you to choose *left,* and so he would do likewise—despite his own inclinations—in order to coordinate with you. Then you would both lose, although each had been trying to accede to the other's inclinations.

To go one step further, suppose that before making your choice, I told you your partner's preference and told him yours (and informed you of this). Now your partner knows that you prefer the extreme left circle, but he does *not* know that you are aware of his preference for the extreme right. What would you do? Probably you would stick with your initial preference. After all, if he knows your preference (and you are aware of this), but he does not know that you are aware of his preference, it will probably be incumbent upon *him* to change his preference to match yours. However, if each of you knows not only the other's preference, but also that the other person is aware that you know, you would both be in a quandary again about what to choose.

Knowing the Other too Well May Hinder Coordination.   In sum, perfect knowledge about the other (and his knowledge about you) may not facilitate a coordinated solution; to the contrary, it may hinder progress. Recall the example of my wife and I trying to decide how to spend Friday evening. She wanted to see a play, while I wanted to see a movie, and we were each aware of the other's preference. Given this state of knowledge, as well as our shared desire to spend the evening together, it was difficult to make a decision. If only my wife had not known that I wanted to see a movie, yet had known that I was aware of her desire to see a play (or vice versa), we might have easily settled on a course of action and been relatively satisfied. The one who was ignorant of the other's choice would "stay," while the one who knew would "change." However, we each knew the other's choice and were aware that we both wanted to do whatever the other preferred. It was extremely important for us to please each other. Therefore, how could I know that when my wife said that seeing a movie was fine with her, she really meant it? Perhaps she only said it in order to please me. If only I had been ignorant of her desire to please me, I could have accepted her offer to go to the movie at face value and been pleased with our solution. And if only I had not been so intent on trying to please her, I might not have invested so much energy in trying to determine what she "really" wanted to do. But such is life!

People are forever trying to "get inside one another's heads"—to take the other person's perspective in order to coordinate behavior. A humorous aspect of such role-taking is presented in the Jewish folklore of Eastern Europe as, for example, in the tragicomic stories of the ghetto community of Chelm. One of the "wise men of Chelm," while visiting the big city, wrote home to his wife:

Please send me your slippers. I say send me your slippers because I really want my slippers. But if I had written "Please send me my slippers" then you would have read "my slippers" and you would have sent me your slippers. But I do not want your slippers, I want my slippers. And that is why I write and ask you to please send me your slippers.

Divergent Interest Coordination

The Aalsmeer Flower Auction.   For study of coordination of divergent interests in a natural setting, one would be hard-pressed to find a more colorful example than a Dutch flower auction. In the small town of Aalsmeer, the preparation begins at night, as barges arrayed with the most amazing concentration of color and fragrance float down the canals into the village. Early the next morning, the buyers assemble in a large sales room, each with an assigned and numbered seat that is equipped with a signal button. The flowers are wheeled in before the buyers in huge lots. As each lot number and a description of the flowers is announced, the auctioneer sets in motion a large clocklike meter, which starts ticking down the price of the flowers: "100 guilders, 95, 90, 85." Suddenly the meter stops, and the result flashes on a board: Buyer number 16 has pressed his button to stop the clock at 85 guilders, and so the lot is now his. The next lot is then brought forth, and the auction continues. The whole proceeding takes place rather quickly so that a large number of flowers can be shipped off early in the morning for sale to the public.

Imagine that you are a merchant bidding for flowers at the Aalsmeer auction. A cart full of especially attractive flowers has just been wheeled in. You would like to buy this lot, since you know that the sale of these flowers will bring you a handsome profit, and you suspect that the other bidders feel very much as you do. The meter begins ticking down the price of the flowers. How long should you wait before stopping the clock? The longer you wait, while the meter lowers the purchase price of the lot, the greater will be your potential profit when the flowers are sold at retail later in the day. However, the longer you wait, the greater will be the chance that another bidder will stop the meter and buy the flowers instead. What you need to do, therefore, is to try to stop the meter just a few guilders ahead of anyone else. However, other buyers may be watching you, trying to figure out when you will make your bid, so that they can bid just a moment earlier. You may decide to stage something of an act—pretending to have no real interest in a given lot of flowers—until you are ready to make your move. But perhaps other buyers seem disinterested also—and perhaps they are also play-acting for your benefit.

Of course, the buyers at the Aalsmeer flower auction may not always engage in this sort of strategic reasoning and behavior. They probably meet each other on a daily or weekly basis, know each other quite well, and know what each is likely to bid; therefore, they may not try to disguise their intentions by bluffing. Moreover, since the buyers are aware that many lots of flowers are to be auctioned off, they may believe that even if they don't get a particularly desirable lot, they can probably get another one that is almost as good at a reasonably good price; therefore, they may not bother to try to figure out what the other buyers are going to bid. Trying to outfox others at an auction may be more likely to occur when the bidders know little or nothing about one another and when they are vying for a single, highly coveted item such as a rare stamp, an unusual antique, or any unique acquisition.

Comparing Convergent and Divergent Interest Coordination.   Let us now examine some of the points of similarity and difference between problems of convergent and divergent interest coordination. Both require the use of complex chains of interpersonal reasoning that are fundamentally alike. In trying to decide how to act, one must first try to take into account the other's expected behavior, his expectations of your behavior, and so forth. Then each must correctly coordinate his own behavior with his guess about the other's. Convergent and divergent problems differ, however, in the purposes for which these guesses are made. In the former, interpersonal information is used in order to reach a solution that is mutually beneficial; if you make a mistake, *everybody* loses. In the latter, information is used for the purpose of obtaining a competitive advantage; if you make a mistake, *you* lose!

To successfully outwit the other bidders at an auction, one must first figure out what the highest other bid is likely to be and then bid just more than that oneself. If your judgment is incorrect, you stand to lose in one of two ways: either you fail to get the object you seek (if you bid too little) or you end up paying more for it than you really had to (if you bid too much).

As the Democratic primaries were drawing to a close in the late spring of 1972, four Democratic senators—McGovern, Muskie, Humphrey, and Jackson—were still in contention. Senator McGovern was building up a commanding lead, and it appeared increasingly probable that he would have the support of a majority of the delegates by convention time. Among his rivals, there appear to have been two prominent goals: to win the nomination or, failing that, to obtain a position of prestige and influence within the party. Think about the dilemma facing Senator Muskie during the late California primary: At what strategic point should he concede and throw his support to McGovern? To do so too early would mean giving up any chance of winning the nomination as well as any possible bargaining power with McGovern. To do so too late would mean that all or most of the other candidates would have already done so; McGovern's candidacy would be assured and Muskie's endorsement would have little value and gain him little bargaining power.

Finally, recall the example of the four businessmen "fighting" over the luncheon check. In trying to decide how many times to offer to pick up the tab, so that he does it one time less than the next guy, each man must first make a shrewd guess about the probable behavior of the other three. Up to this point, it can be seen that the problem is somewhat similar to that which confronts the participants in a convergent coordination task: each wants to have an accurate understanding of the other. However, each person's guess about the other's probable behavior is then used not for mutual, but for individual, advantage. Each businessman, in effect, said to himself: "In order to solve this problem, I must estimate how many times each of my colleagues (none of whom really wants to pay the bill) will offer to pay. Then I will try to coordinate my actions with theirs so that I avoid two possible mistakes: the Scylla of offering to pick up the tab *too often,* in which case I'll get stuck, and the Charybdis of *not offering often enough*—in which case I may be seen as cheap by the others. So I should offer to pay exactly one time less than the man whom I believe will make the greatest number of offers."

In some instances it is neither knowledge alone nor ignorance alone, but the coupling of one person's knowledge with the other person's ignorance that makes convergent interest coordination problems relatively easy to solve. My ignorance of your preference, coupled with your knowledge of my preference (and your awareness of my ignorance) can result in a mutually beneficial, coordinated solution: I stick with my preference, while you change you choice accordingly. He who is ignorant "stays," while he who knows "changes." Does this "ignorance-stay, knowledge-change" rule apply to divergent coordination? The answer is no, for the following reason: If our interests are divergent, and I am ignorant of your preference while you know mine, you would surely win and I would surely lose. You would be able to exploit your knowledge and my ignorance to your competitive advantage. Similarly, in order to be able to outwit you, I would have to begin with some knowledge (or at least a good guess) about your preference.

Of course, one person could *pretend* to be ignorant of the other's preference, in order to gain a strategic advantage in the relationship. Suppose you and another driver are approaching an unmarked intersection at right angles, each apparently wanting to cross first. How might you manage to prevail in this conflict of interest? One possibility would be for you to adopt a strategy of staring straight ahead into space, thereby communicating your total unawareness of his desire to cross the intersection first—and even your ignorance of his very existence. Assuming that he has good eyesight and can see that you "don't see him" (which is untrue, of course, but hopefully he doesn't know that), your "unawareness," coupled with his knowledge of this, compels him to cede the right of way. What you have done, in Thomas Schelling's . . . language, has been to "bind" (irrevocably commit) yourself to a course of action, thereby shifting the locus of control over a possible collision from your shoulders to his. Note, however, that if the other driver even suspects that you are only pretending, he is far less likely to yield.

Mixed-Motive Relationships: Coordinating Convergent and Divergent Interests

Although many relationships exist in which the parties' interests are either purely convergent or divergent, the most common interdependent situations are those that contain both convergent and divergent interests. These situations are called "mixed-motive" since the parties are motivated both to cooperate and to compete.

Many relationships that appear, at first glance, to be examples of pure divergent interests are, in fact, mixed-motive relationships—they contain convergent interests as well. The two drivers racing to be the first to cross the intersection appear to be in a purely competitive relationship. Yet, although they want to beat each other, they also share a common interest in getting across the intersection safely and thus avoiding a collision. Similarly, in the event described earlier, my colleagues and I appeared to have purely divergent interests with respect to our salaries (the larger my raise, the smaller theirs would be, the chairman argued). Our interests would also be convergent to the extent that we might collectively urge the administration to increase the departmental budget, or to the extent that we might use one professor's raise to try to extract raises for the others.

Minimizing Divergence through Redefinition.   Under some circumstances, a relationship that is characterized by divergent interests can be redefined as a convergent one. Consider, the behavior of two boys in a badminton game, as observed so sensitively by the psychologist, Max Wertheimer. The 12-year-old boy (we'll call him Johnny) was obviously much more skilled than the 10-year-old (Billy), and was defeating him in game after game. Billy finally threw down his racket and said that he would not play anymore. Johnny was puzzled and a bit angry. He had enjoyed the game and especially the winning. Billy had enjoyed playing at first, but he did not like being beaten over and over again. Johnny tried to persuade Billy to continue the game, for without Billy he could not play and, thus, could not win. Suddenly he thought of a solution: "I have an idea—let us now play this way: Let's see how long we can keep the bird going between us, and count how many times it goes back and forth without falling. What score could we make? Do you think we could make it 10 or 20?" Billy agreed readily, and so they played the game that way. Billy enjoyed it more, of course, and so did Johnny—for apparently he realized that beating the younger boy at a game at which Billy was unskilled was not really such a rewarding experience. In fact, what had happened was that both boys had redefined a divergent interest situation as a convergent one. . . .

In many respects our interaction with others day in and day out can be viewed as a game in which we have both convergent and divergent interests. . . . Social exchange theory is a way of analyzing interpersonal attraction and rejection. Let us see how this theory applies to mixed-motive relationships.

Social Exchange Theory

The social exchange approach in social psychology originated in economic analysis and game theory. . . . Although it has been presented in various forms . . . , our approach is the one proposed by John Thibaut and Harold Kelley. . . . Thibaut and Kelley began by examining the limited social interaction of two people and later extended their analysis to more complex interaction in larger groups. The social exchange relationship is often represented in matrix form, as in Exhibit 1, which depicts the exchange relationship between a husband and a wife on a Sunday afternoon. Each has five possible activities in which he or she may engage. Clearly, they have both divergent and convergent interests. The satisfaction or dissatisfaction that each receives is a function of the combination of what they both do. (The wife's costs and rewards are above the diagonals, and the husband's are below.) Note that the wife would most enjoy going with her husband to the museum ($+10$). The husband would not like to go to the museum at all (-5), but, if he does go, he would rather go with his wife than alone (the other cells in that row show -8). What does the husband want to do? He really wants to play squash ($+10$); furthermore, he wants to play no matter what his wife does (the other cells in that row also show $+10$). Although the wife's first choice is to go to the museum with her husband, she would rather

EXHIBIT 1
Social Exchange Relationship

		Wife's Possible Activities				
		Go to Museum	Read Sunday Newspaper	Go Bicycling	Visit Aunt Suzie	Write Article
Husband's Possible Activities	Go to Museum	+10 / −5	−2 / −8	+4 / −8	+4 / −8	+5 / −8
	Read Sunday Newspaper	−5 / +4	+6 / +3	−3 / +4	+4 / +4	+7 / +4
	Go Bicycling	−5 / +7	−5 / +7	+8 / +5	+4 / +3	+5 / +7
	Visit Aunt Suzie	−5 / −5	−5 / −5	−5 / −5	+9 / −2	+5 / −5
	Play Squash	−5 / +10	+1 / +10	−5 / +10	+4 / +10	+5 / +10

A social exchange analysis of a husband's and wife's activities on a Sunday afternoon. In each box, the value above the diagonal represents the wife's costs or rewards, and the value below the diagonal represents the husband's. The wife prefers most of all to go to the museum with her husband, while he prefers most of all to play squash—regardless of what she does.

do anything with him than by herself. But playing squash is not available as an alternative to her (since she doesn't even belong to the squash club), so, in all likelihood, the husband will spend the afternoon playing squash and the wife will do some more work on an article she is writing—the most attractive activity in that row ($+5$).

Social exchange theory provides a useful conceptual scheme for analyzing a variety of social interaction phenomena. A matrix analysis is, of course, not without its limitations. For example, it is often difficult to determine the values that should be assigned to the cells; moreover, only a few activities can be included in a simple matrix. Obviously, we did not deal with the possibility of the husband nagging his wife or of being inconsiderate to her at a later time if she refused to let him play squash. Nevertheless, analyzing social interaction in terms of mutual rewards and costs has proved to be very useful. . . .

The Prisoner's Dilemma Game: A Paradigm for Mixed-Motive Problem-Solving

Let us now apply the exchange analysis of costs and rewards to a research problem that has captured the imagination of large numbers of social psychologists—the Prisoner's Dilemma. Imagine that you and an incommunicado stranger are seated in separate rooms. In front of each of you are two buttons, one black and the other red. Your task is simply to push *one* of these buttons. Depending upon the choices made by both you and the other person, you will each win or lose an amount of money, as follows: If you both push black, you will each win $1, if you both push red, you will each lose $1, and if one pushes red while the other pushes black, the one who pressed the red button will win $2 while the one who pressed the black button will lose $2. The amounts of money you and the other person can win or lose, depending upon your combined choices, are summarized in Exhibit 2.

When confronted with this problem, many people are inclined to choose

EXHIBIT 2
Black–Red Problem

		The Other Person Chooses	
		Black	*Red*
You Choose	**Black**	+$1.00 / +$1.00	+$2.00 / −$2.00
	Red	−$2.00 / +$2.00	−$1.00 / −$1.00

The number in the lower left-hand corner of each box is the amount of money you can win or lose by choosing black or red. The number in the upper right-hand corner of each box is the amount of money your partner can win or lose by choosing black or red.

red, perhaps reasoning as follows: "Since I don't know anything about the other person, I don't know whether he would be more likely to choose red or black. What I should do, therefore, is to figure out what choice to make if he pushes black and what to do if he chooses red. Let's see. If he pushes his black button, I can make more by choosing red ($2) than by choosing black (only $1); therefore, I should push my red button. If, on the other hand, he pushes his red button, I'm going to lose regardless of what I choose—but I will lose less by choosing red (−$1) than by choosing black (−$2); therefore, I should push my red button in this case as well. In other words, regardless of what the other person does, I should choose red because I stand both to make the most (if he presses black) and lose the least (if he presses red)."

Sound logic, indeed! The only problem is that the other person may have reasoned in exactly the same way—in which case, you will each choose red and lose $1, whereas you could have each chosen black and won $1!

This particular situation is called the "Prisoner's Dilemma" game, because of the example originally used by R. Duncan Luce and Howard Raiffa . . . to illustrate this type of coordination problem. In their example, which is not too far afield from some real-life situations, two burglary suspects are apprehended together by the police. Since the evidence is not sufficient to convict either one, the police interrogators devise a clever stratagem. One of the suspects is isolated in a room and told: "Look. We know we don't have the evidence to convict you, but we are questioning your partner. We will make it worth his while to squeal on you, and we believe he will. If so, you will get four years for burglary and he'll get off scot-free. But you can make it a bit easier on yourself by telling on your partner; you will then get a reduced sentence for turning state's evidence—only 18 months. If your partner doesn't tell on you, we will still get you on a vagrancy charge, which will keep you in jail for six months. And even then, it would be worth your while to squeal on him, for then we would let you free." The prisoner correctly guesses that his partner has been told the same thing. The payoff matrix is presented in Exhibit 3.

Of course, the possibility that you both end up in the reduced sentence cell of the matrix in the Prisoner's Dilemma, as well as in the—$1 cell of the black-red game, is due in part to your inability to communicate and work out a convergent arrangement. Communication is obviously important. (In the badminton game, if Billy and Johnny had become so angry that they could not speak to one another, Johnny could never have conveyed his plan for a convergent relationship.) It should be stressed, though, that communication is meaningless without mutual trust. If the two prisoners had met and were suspicious of each other, then a mutual agreement to remain silent still might not be honored when they were separated again. Each might suspect that the other was using him to get off free. When there is communication without trust, we try all sorts of stratagems to mislead the other person.

Consider, for example, the old parable about the two competing mer-

EXHIBIT 3
Prisoner's Dilemma

		Choices of Prisoner 2	
		Remain Silent	*Squeal on Partner*
Choices of Prisoner 1	*Remain Silent*	Jailed for Vagrancy −6 / Jailed for vagrancy −6	Set free 0 / Full sentence for burglary −48
	Sequal on Partner	Full sentence for burglary −48 / Set free 0	Reduced sentence for burglary −10 / Reduced sentence for burglary −18

Here are the jail sentences for each of two burglars, depending upon whether each remains silent or testifies against his partner.

chants (call them A and B) who meet at the train station one day. A turns to B and inquires where he is going, to which B replies "To Minsk." After some thought, A retorts: "You say you are going to Minsk in order to make me think that you are going to Pinsk, but I know you are *really* going to Minsk. Do you think you can fool me?" Notice that A has a choice in this situation. He has the option of trusting B and simply accepting his reply ("to Minsk") at face value. But, instead of this, he appears to proceed from the assumption that B is untrustworthy and out to fool him. Paradoxically, through this double-think process, A ends up by accepting B's statement as fact after all. Question: By what path of reasoning could B best outwit A?

A participant in a mixed-motive relationship has a choice not unlike that confronting A. He can view the relationship as one of convergent interests, in which case he should behave cooperatively (while expecting the other person to do the same). Or he can view the relationship as one of divergent interests, in which case he should attempt to outwit and exploit the other person. Whether he decides to view the relationship as one of convergence or divergence depends upon both how much he *trusts* the other person to behave cooperatively and how much he *can be trusted* to behave cooperatively himself. Two hostile nations that can decide either to limit their arms production to an agreed upon level or to compete with each other for military superiority are in very much this sort of situation.

Factors That Affect Cooperation and Competition in the Prisoner's Dilemma

Mixed-motive games, particularly the Prisoner's Dilemma, have given rise to hundreds of experiments in the past decade—largely, we suspect, because of the intrinsic interest, importance, and prevalence of relationships that contain a mixture of cooperative and competitive motives. . . . Let us now look at a few of the factors that affect the degree of cooperation.

1. Number of Interactions. As you might expect, when pairs of strangers are asked to play the black-red version of the Prisoner's Dilemma game just once, they tend to act less cooperatively than when they play the game repeatedly. Why? Because when playing just once, each person knows that he cannot be held accountable for his future behavior and is therefore more willing to attempt to exploit the other (by choosing red). Both players thus tend to choose red, and both lose.

When the Prisoner's Dilemma game is played over a series of turns, and both players are told the other's choice at the end of each turn, there is more likely to be cooperation, although it may eventually deteriorate. In general, social psychologists have observed a pattern of choice behavior in games with multiple turns like the hypothetical one depicted in Exhibit 4.

EXHIBIT 4
Hypothetical Choices in the Prisoner's Dilemma Game (black-red version)

Turn	Person A		Person B	
	Choice	Outcome	Choice	Outcome
1	Black	+1	Black	+1
2	Black	+1	Black	+1
3	Black	+1	Black	+1
4	Red	+2	Black	−2
5	Red	−1	Red	−1
6	Red	−1	Red	−1
7	Red	−1	Red	−1
8	Black	−2	Red	+2
9	Red	+2	Black	−2
10	Red	−1	Red	−1

The two players typically begin the game cooperatively (black-black). Eventually one person (A) defects, and then both compete and miscoordinate to their mutual disadvantage.

Assuming that neither Person A nor Person B begins with prior information about the other or how to act toward him, our two players might start by choosing black on their first turn. In this way, each shows that he is willing to trust the other and to be trustworthy himself; the result is a set of outcomes ($+1$, $+1$) that is mutually and equally beneficial. Once A and B have established this kind of cooperative relationship, they typically maintain it for quite some time. After a while, however, one person, A (turn 4 in our diagram), may decide to defect. The reasons for this defection are not completely clear. Perhaps A decided that B was an ''idiot'' who could be exploited readily and indefinitely; perhaps A simply became more greedy, rivalrous, or even just plain bored with so much cooperation. In any event, he defects, while poor B (totally unaware of A's decision) once again gives a trusting and cooperative response. As a result, A succeeds in exploiting B. On the following turn (5), things typically deteriorate further. A, in effect, says to himself: ''It worked once. Why shouldn't it work again? And anyway, if B gets angry, he will surely choose red to protect himself. So I should chose red in either case.'' B, on the other hand, probably thinks: ''That dirty, rotten S.O.B.! I can't afford to trust him anymore. I've got to choose red to protect myself against further exploitation.'' So both choose red, and both lose. For the next several turns, this mutually competitive pattern will probably continue, A hoping that B will slip back into a trusting black choice, and B remaining totally committed to defending himself against A's aggression. After a while, however, as the pair continues this costly, destructive course, losing money on every turn, one person (typically the one who defected in the first place) tries to return the relationship to its earlier, more prosperous state. Perhaps A thinks to himself: ''Wow, did I make a mess of things! If it weren't for me and my errant ways, we'd still be riding the high road to mutual fortune. I've got to show B that I want to change. I will choose black.'' B, however, knows nothing of A's plan to reform, and so he continues to choose what he feels he must in order to protect himself—namely, red. The result (turn 8) is that A loses, while B inadvertently exploits A and wins. Now A may say to himself: ''Things are hopeless. It's just not going to work. I've made an irreconcilable enemy of B. He's going to continue to defend himself. Therefore, I've got to defend myself as well. I'll choose red.'' B, meanwhile, is thinking: Wow! A has finally seen the light. I'll choose black and everything will be okay again.'' So A chooses red, while B chooses black (turn 9), and the pair miscoordinates once again. And so, in this Kafkaesque way, A and B may continue—one person making a cooperative overture while the other behaves competitively (or defensively). Eventually what often happens is that the pair slips back into a pattern of mutually competitive, costly behavior (turn 10), locks into this pattern, and remains there.

Gloomy? Indeed it is! However, some pairs eventually manage to find a way out of this impasse. This happens when one person chooses black not once but at least *twice consecutively,* thereby indicating his willingness to trust the other and conveying his conviction that cooperation represents the only reasonable course of action. Such persistent attempts at cooperation by one person, especially after the pair has pursued a mutually destructive course of action, typically enable the pair to restore a cooperative relationship. And once restored, cooperation tends to continue.

2. *Initial Orientation to the Situation.* By varying the introduction to the Prisoner's Dilemma game, experimenters have elicited vastly different behaviors on the part of the two participants. When the players are told that they are in a competitive game and that their goal is to try to get a higher score than their partner (and that he will be doing the same thing), the participants almost invariably end up in the red-red square. However, when the situation is presented as a cooperative game, in which each player is supposed to try to help the other beat the bank and to get the banker to pay out as much as possible, the players generally finish in the black-black square. And finally, when the game is presented as an individualistic endeavor, in which each player is supposed to try to get the highest score for himself (without regard for the other's winnings or losses), there is greater variability in behavior. However, the players typically end up in the red-red cell (with both of them losing) more often than in the black-black cell. . . .

3. *Personality Predispositions.* Individual differences in personality are especially inclined to affect behavior in the Prisoner's Dilemma game when the players begin with an individualistic orientation. A person who is inherently suspicious of others, distrusting, or malicious is especially apt to make a red response. He expects his partner to be untrustworthy, and so he chooses competitively, causing his partner to do likewise; therefore, his own expectations are confirmed as a self-fulfilling prophecy. If both partners are open and trusting, however, a black-black response is much more probable. . . .

4. *Communication.* As we have mentioned, communication may help to reduce competition, so that the players can redefine the situation as a cooperative one. An explicit cooperative communication (for example, "I would like you to choose black. I intend to choose black. But if you continue to choose red, then I shall choose red also") will probably elicit a cooperative response. . . . But once distrust and hostility have been initiated, they are extremely difficult to change. . . .

5. *Partner's Strategy.* When the Prisoner's Dilemma game is played for a series of turns (as depicted in Exhibit 4), each choice becomes a form of communication. A black response is perceived as an intention to be cooperative; a red response is viewed as an intention to be competitive. A series of black responses may elicit cooperative responses in return, so that the more favorable black-black cell pattern is established. However, there is one danger. Sometimes a succession of cooperative responses is perceived as a sign of ignorance or naïveté, and so it invites exploitation. There is evidence that a more realistic strategy for eliciting cooperation from one's partner requires some form of matching—after one's partner chooses black once or twice, one should begin to reciprocate by choosing the same color as he did on the preceding turn. If your partner chooses red, retaliate with red on the next trial to show that you mean business. Turning the other cheek is often not the best strategy. . . .

6. Cultural Factors and Cooperation.   Cultural norms can influence a person's cooperative or competitive orientation in a manner that is very similar to one's personality predisposition. As the cultural anthropologist Margaret Mead demonstrated many years ago, . . . some cultures encourage a cooperative, trusting orientation toward people, while others foster competition, distrust, and hostility.

JERRY HARVEY

Reading 2-2
Some Dynamics of
Intergroup Competition

Jim Smith, age 16, stands before the judge in juvenile court. He is charged with assaulting another juvenile, Johnny Rocco, with a blackjack. Luckily, a policeman broke it up before either boy was seriously injured. The judge questions Jimmy:

> "Jimmy, have you ever had trouble with Johnny Rocco before?"
> "No sir. I have never seen him before last night."
> "Has he ever bothered any of your family or friends?"
> "No, not that I know of. He just happened to be walking down the street."
> "Did he call you a name or something?"
> "No, he didn't do anything like that."
> "Were you trying to steal something from him?"
> "Nope. All I did was clobber him."
> "Why did you do it?" the judge asks.
> "Well, he's a member of the Robins gang. We guys in the Dragons hate their
> guts."

No doubt the judge, as do other people, finds Jimmy's behavior extremely puzzling. But in a broad sense, it reflects a causation force in behavior which judges, psychiatrists, psychologists, managers, and laymen frequently overlook in dealing with others. This is the effect of group membership upon individual behavior. For, in a broad sense, Jimmy is a representative of a group, the Dragons, which is in a state of hostile relations with another group, the Robins. Viewed in this context, Jimmy's hostility and aggression

Jerry Harvey, "Some Dynamics of Intergroup Competition." Used with permission of author. From a theory session presented at Institute IX, the National Council of Juvenile Court Judges Institute and Conference Programs, Monticello, Illinois. The format of part of the paper follows an outline which has appeared in a number of NTL Laboratory Proceedings. The author wishes to acknowledge help from the various people who contributed to its development.

represent not a problem of personality deviation, but rather the effect of loyalty to a group, as that group exists in a competitive relationship with another group. Thus, we frequently make the error of assuming that individual personality dynamics are always the primary causal force in shaping behavior, including hostility toward another, love toward another, dislike toward another, or devotion toward another; while in reality much of this behavior can better be understood by recognizing the effect of group membership as it works to shape and modify the basic personality tendencies. Stated differently, Jimmy's behavior makes relatively little sense if we look solely at the personality level, but it does make sense if we look at the concept of group loyalty, with its concomitant demands and pressures, as they act on Jimmy at a given time.

Look at the culture around you. You see that we each belong to groups and that these groups are divided in many ways. On a broad cultural level, these divisions are frequently competitive rather than cooperative: Russia versus the United States, labor versus management, Democrats versus Republicans, Catholics versus Protestants, Negroes versus whites, students versus administrators, one delinquent gang versus another—and delinquents versus law-abiding society as a whole. Each of these schisms, vividly described in our daily newspapers, has a number of elements in common.

1. They involve individuals who are members of definable groups, which in turn exist in various levels of competition and conflict with other groups.
2. They involve individuals who are either selected by formal procedures as representatives of the groups or individuals who, because of their membership in and loyalty to the group, act as informal representatives. Thus, negotiators meet on labor-management relations; congressmen, on political issues; ambassadors, on international relations; and, less formally, an American tourist represents his country abroad. Central to the dynamics of group membership and intergroup competition is the concept of representational behavior, where representatives serve to carry their group's ideals, values, and beliefs forward in dealings with others. Such representational behavior is a normal behavior process. In Jimmy's case the behavior was not, by an criterion, constructive to society as a whole; but in many cases the same dynamics operate but are channeled into more constructive ends.

The purpose of the intergroup exercise as a component part in a training laboratory is to look at problems that group membership and intergroup competition pose for the individual and the groups involved.[1] Specifically, we hope to examine the ways in which representative behavior is influenced

---

[1] Copies of the exercise, including directions, sample instruments, and so on, may be obtained by writing the author.

by group pressures, to look at problems of judging and arbitration, to look at the manner in which intergroup conflict can be resolved and dealt with constructively, and to provide a general framework for examining problems which face individual group members as they relate with one another and as they serve as representatives of their in-group in relating with members of other groups. It should be made clear that the effort is to focus on *normal* behavior of individuals and groups rather than on individual and group psychopathology, as we frequently do when studying competition, conflict, and aggression in human behavior.

What generally happens when groups meet in a competitive relationship as in this exercise?

WITHIN THE GROUPS

Group members pull in close. They begin to see the members of the other groups as "enemies." Loyalty to the in-group increases, and allegiances and friendships with out-group members are strained or broken.

Group members begin to see only the best in their own group and the worst in the other group. Competition, conflict (or friendly relations, for that matter) create psychological filters which screen each group member's perceptions of what the other group members say or do. One good example of "filtering" is the quantitative data showing the judgments by each group of the quality of the other group's solutions. Each group sees its solution as superior to that of the other group, and the feelings become more and more clear-cut in favor of the in-group's solutions to the problem as the competition becomes more intense.

Groups begin to demand more conformity from their members. Thus, any group member who preaches moderation or tact or "softness" in dealing with the other group is likely to be confronted with extreme pressure to change his viewpoint to coincide with that of the larger group. This behavior can be clearly observed on the political level, where greater uniformity and solidarity are demanded on the part of the individual members of the Democratic and Republican parties, respectively, immediately before a presidential election. Likewise, greater group pressure will be put on Jimmy, the closer his gang comes to a "rumble" with the Dragons.

The style of the leadership changes. More autocracy is accepted by group members. Militancy on the part of the leader becomes more acceptable. Thus, the president generally is given much greater freedom to act unilaterally under conditions of national crisis than under conditions of peacetime.

The group atmosphere changes from one of relaxed, unhurried consideration of problems to one of work, and from one in which personal problems of members are given consideration to one in which they are discounted.

The group structure changes. Subgroups may form which cause internal discord, but such discord is visible only to the in-group. For instance,

Democrats and Republicans may disagree violently over foreign policy, but when our country is attacked by an outside enemy bipartisanship prevails.

BETWEEN THE GROUPS

Inaccurate and uncomplimentary stereotypes form. Judgments are made about individuals belonging to the other group on the basis of group membership, not on the basis of accurate knowledge and information.

Interaction and communication decreases among group members. Group members don't wish to interact with one another and when they do, they tend to distort the meaning of one another's behavior. Herein lies a paradox. At the time when valid, accurate communication between groups is of utmost importance if misperceptions are to be eliminated and problems are to be solved, our tendency is either to "break off" communication or to distort it so that it creates additional problems, rather than to communicate in a more constructive manner. For example, research in similar situations[2] indicates that group members don't listen to their adversaries when they communicate. They tend to hear only that which supports their own position. Specifically, the research indicates that when groups have similarities in their solutions to common problems, they tend not to see the similarities; rather, they see only the differences. Thus, if group members are given a surprise test on the solutions they have produced in the intergroup exercise, they tend to know much more about their group's solution than they know about the solution of the other group. They tend to see the differences in their solutions but to be unable to see the extent to which their solutions are similar. As a consequence, they lose an important avenue for cooperation and for resolving tension and differences.

THE FORMAL REPRESENTATIVES OF THE GROUPS

The representatives feel more tension from being responsible for the group's success or failure.

Representatives frequently suffer a conflict between their own beliefs and the mandate given to them by their group. Thus, a representative in many cases is not free to negotiate as his conscience or his insight into the problem would lead him to do. Rather, he must be responsible to his group, and this responsibility frequently results in inflexibility and rigidity.

The reason underlying the representative's anxiety and his "rigidity" is clear. Research findings indicate that if a representative does not follow the mandate given him by his group he is desposed as representative and, in varying degrees, is ostracized by the group. Stated differently, the representative who capitulates to the other group, regardless of the reason, is

---

[2] R. R. Blake and Jane S. Mouton, "The Intergroup Dynamics of Win-Lose Conflict and Problem-Solving Collaboration in Union-Management Relations," in *Intergroup Relations and Leadership*, ed. M. Sherif (New York: John Wiley & Sons, 1962).

frequently termed a *traitor*. Herein lies one of the fundamental problems of representative behavior. The representative may see the validity of the other group's position, but because of the pressure put on him by members of his own group he is not free to negotiate according to the objective merits of the situation.

TO THE JUDGES

Judges who belong to one of the two groups in competition generally find it difficult to divorce themselves from the group and, therefore, find it difficult to be neutral and unbiased. Thus, each judge in the exercise tends to vote for his own group, not because of conscious group loyalty but because he actually feels and believes that his group has produced a better solution. At times, however, the judges experience an initial period of deep conflict between loyalty to their own group and the role of judicial neutrality; and in this case the decision is more difficult to make. However, over time, they tend to develop logical and rational thought processes to support their voting for their own group's position. Again, it should be stressed that the process that they undergo is certainly not one of dishonesty or conscious bias, but rather a normal process involving the complex dynamics of group loyalty and group membership.

The culture apparently recognizes the judges' conscious and unconscious plight and the problems it poses. For example, in recognition of this dilemma, judges or referees for athletic contests, such as football games, are chosen so that they don't also represent the institutions involved in the contest. And on a more formal level, safeguards are frequently taken to insure that judges in our formal legal system are not beholden to those about whom they sometimes have to render judgment.

The neutral judge in the intergroup exercises generally casts the deciding vote, and the vote in most cases is three to two, with each of the other two judges voting for the position expounded by his own group.

The participants in the winning groups tend to see the judges as being fair, unbiased, honest, intelligent and capable of dealing rationally and objectively with the material about which they judge. They are satisfied with and are willing to implement the judges' decision.

Participants of the losing group tend to see the judge as being unfair, biased, inadequate, lacking in intelligence, and unable to judge the issues on the basis of merit. As a consequence, they are dissatisfied with the decision and are unwilling to implement it. (In the language of the judiciary, they generally wish to appeal.)

TO THE GROUP THAT WINS

It retains and builds cohesion.

Members release tension and lose their fighting spirit. They become complacent and unable to deal innovatively with similar kinds of problems.

Thus, in another paradox, the fruits of victory frequently may sow the seeds of future defeat.

TO THE LOSER

The group frequently splinters, seeks the reason for its defeat, and then reorganizes.

Members frequently demonstrate scapegoating behavior and, as a consequence, the representative or judge is frequently blamed for the defeat. They learn a lot about themselves and their group and tend to improve the operation of their group.

HOW CAN INTERGROUP FRICTION BE REDUCED?

And related to this, how can the individual representative, both formal and informal, be freed to react to the objective, intrinsic needs of a situation, rather than on the basis of group loyalty and group pressures? In other words, how can we get productive effects from group membership and inevitable intergroup competition without suffering the destructive side effects?

> *By understanding the effects of group membership and intergroup competition on individual and group behavior.*   Participating in training exercises on intergroup competition is one way of obtaining such understanding.
>
> *By finding goals which require intergroup cooperation if the goals are to be attained.*   These goals, termed *superordinate* goals, must be of such a nature that the accomplishment of them will be beneficial to both groups. Stated differently, this means to direct group membership and intergroup competition into constructive channels. Thus, two delinquent gangs might compete under supervision in building park facilities for a neighborhood. Here, the dynamics of group life could be maintained but put to constructive use.
>
> *By developing flexible solutions to group and intergroup problems.*   Thus, to the degree that groups are not inflexibly committed to solutions, it is possible to develop new solutions which are satisfactory to members of both groups; and to that extent it is possible to provide the individual representative with the freedom to act according to the objective merits of the situation.

Many delinquent acts in society can be attributed not to psychopathology or personality deviation but to the normal process of individual behavior in a group context. Said another way, the same dynamics which may lead a judge to represent his political party in a constructive political process or to represent his society as a symbol of law and order when dealing with the lawless, may lead a delinquent to commit an act destructive to the society which the judge protects and may lead his parents to protest the judge's role in protecting that society.

Following from this is a second notion—that it is frequently easier to induce change in whole groups than to change individual group members. Thus, although psychiatric care and individual therapy is appropriate as a treatment procedure for many kinds of delinquents, some variety of group change process may be a more appropriate procedure for many other cases.

SECTION THREE

Planning and Preparation

PLANNING

Successful professional negotiators agree on one thing: the key to success in negotiation is preparation and planning. Persuasive presentation, skillful communication, nimble shifting of position, and a host of other skills used during actual negotiations are important, but they cannot recoup the disadvantage created by poor planning, nor can they help negotiators who lock themselves into untenable positions before or during the early stages of negotiation. Further, while interpersonal skills during negotiation can reap the most from a strategy, a well-laid plan has its own strength; and even modest skills can see it through to an acceptable conclusion. Preparation and planning is divided into several parts. The first section deals with preparation for planning; the next two sections discuss the strategy and tactics of competitive and integrative bargaining situations, and the last with a more extensive examination of the fundamental characteristics of strategy.

PLANNING AND PREPARATION

There are at least two levels or stages of preparation for negotiation. One involves getting ready for a specific negotiation, when we want to learn more about the other party, the situation we face, and so on. The other involves making ourselves ready to negotiate at any time. In football, players prepare for Saturday's game, but they have also been preparing themselves all year, in fact for many years, to play football. Given that we are all going to face negotiation situations regularly, we need to know how to adequately prepare.

Competition is a part of life, welcomed by some, regretted by others, but, nonetheless, present. Nowhere is this more unavoidably so than in negotiation. Some bargaining, as when two parties have different and mutually exclusive objectives, such as haggling over the price of something, is obviously competitive. Even in integrative bargaining, when the parties are working toward joint or congruent goals, there may still be substantial conflict about how much each will contribute or how much each will benefit. Hence, conflict, while varying in intensity, is inherent in any negotiation situation and needs to be recognized and handled.

Jack Vance, in his article "Winning: A Leading Consultant Tells How," looks at some of the things that successful competitors do. He finds that successful competitors continually prepare themselves to compete, seek out situations where they can compete, and assess their opponent's strengths, weaknesses, needs, and resources before they begin. They prepare for the really demanding parts of a competition; they work at winning and not at impressing observers. They also develop an outlook or attitude about competing that focuses their attention, encouraging flexibility and a certain level of modesty, to keep them open to change and to learning.

This theme of how we approach encounters with other people is explored further by Jeffrey Rubin in his article, "Psychological Traps." A psychological trap is an outlook or mental set that we get into which works to our disadvantage and which we find difficult to get out of. A common trap in negotiation occurs when people set goals to put the other party down or to "win" by achieving some arbitrary standard. Some auto salespersons boast that they always sell a "loaded" car; that is, one with stereo, better-grade upholstery, and so on. What they do not talk about are the number of people who do not buy at all because they left when they felt they were being pushed into something they did not want. It is all too easy in negotiation to want to get more than the other person and, in the process, actually get less than might have been attained. There are other traps, such as wanting to complete a negotiation (at any cost) once it has been started. Determination in seeing something through is a good virtue, but there are times when we start things and soon have information that tells us we are into an unwise effort. Then, getting out as quickly as possible makes good sense. However, appearing to "give up," even then, is something many people find difficult. It is hard to get out of a trap even when one is aware of it. Regrettably, we often are unaware of the traps we set up for ourselves. Rubin identifies common traps and suggests some ways to prepare to avoid them.

Finally, Jeb and Earl Brooks define the role of top management in negotiations. They argue that senior management frequently wastes considerable time and effort in negotiations, in two ways: (1) by becoming personally involved in day-to-day deliberations rather than retaining the "big picture," and (2) by not allowing people with the technical skill and expertise to play a greater role. Brooks and Brooks provide a detailed outline of the flow of negotiations and the key role of top management in each stage. They also supply a helpful checklist for gathering and analyzing information that will help the chief executive plan for both the technical and strategic aspects of the negotiation process.

JACK O. VANCE

Reading 3–1
Winning:
A Leading Consultant Tells How

Competition is as old as recorded history: The warriors of ancient times competed in tournaments; Plato had a shoe factory that had some rough going; and the Aztecs enjoyed vying with one another in organized team sports. Although the physical stakes are less dire today, competition remains fundamental to the whole of Western culture, forming the foundation of our free enterprise system and permeating our lives.

Yet, what is it that makes for a strong competitor—a winner? People who don't compete well and/or try to avoid competition cannot seem to pin down the elusive elements that make for success. Many of us, in fact, are prone to wonder: Is it luck, ability, or a certain intuitive sense that, when all else is equal, gives winners a slight edge?

I believe that there is actually an ''art'' to effective competition; that consistent winners have certain common characteristics and perceptions which, while practiced unconsciously by some, are studied, learned, and even rehearsed as techniques by others.

These techniques, as I see them, form both a *methodology* that provides a strong external approach to every competitive situation as well as a unique *mental attitude* that provides inner strength. Together, these make contenders out of ordinary mortals.

THE METHODOLOGY OF SUCCESSFUL COMPETITORS

In many years of observing the winning process, I have come to believe there is a distinctive methodology to successful individual competition. What may appear to be opportunism and chance is usually, upon closer analysis, a

Reprinted courtesy of the Association of MBA Executives, Inc., New York, N.Y.

carefully constructed approach. I have observed six techniques that are characteristic of winners.

1. Most Winners Seek Competition. Undoubtedly there is a correlation between long years of successfully competing and "winning ways." In other words, *winners often practice winning.* The person who consistently seeks competition gains poise and polish under stress that the infrequent competitor will not achieve. The industrial tool salesman with 20 years of experience as a competitor has a distinct poise and confidence that enhances his or her knowledge of customer needs. This knowledge helps the salesman win orders.

2. Successful Competitors Assess the Competition in Advance. A winner may appear to be casual, but the seemingly calm exterior is built upon the confidence of having sized up the opponent. Competitors have different methods of studying the forces they will face. Whatever their approach, however, it is likely to include adequate time for research and/or scouting (i.e., watching the competitor in action somewhere), and it will probably culminate in a formal plan—often documented on paper. Weekend tennis winners, for example, claim to learn a great deal by simply jotting down their opponents' strengths and weaknesses, as well as the game plan they intend to employ to prevail over these. There is nothing "offhand" or "spur of the moment" about the preparation of the successful competitor. The essence of this step is emphasized by the massive resources corporations dedicate to marketing research. The information this research generates is ammunition for product managers and salesmen.

3. Successful Competitors Practice. This is a corollary to the second point, as research and planning bring into focus that which must be practiced. Specific technique practice for each contest may appear to be an elementary concept, but religious adherence to this step is nevertheless a key distinguishing characteristic between consistent and sporadic winners. Practice and training involve two elements: Self-discipline—a guaranteed strengthening factor, no matter when or how it is applied in the process—and time scheduling, or the knack of meeting all other commitments and still achieving the desired level of preparation. Many would say that this is an art in itself. Few would deny its inestimable value.

4. Successful Competitors Train Themselves to Prepare for Critical Periods Requiring Peak Performance. In sports this involves a plan for pacing, and in business it means holding resources in reserve for as long as possible. Here again we see the benefit of a game plan and an understanding of the competitor's strengths and weaknesses, since these will help identify where one's energies and abilities are most sorely needed. Obviously, no one can play any game at peak output at all times. The big winner usually has a knowledge of the most likely critical points and has a plan for redoubling efforts at those periods. Some of the most successful consumer goods advertising campaigns target their emphasis at the critical period in the buying decision.

5. Successful Competitors Are Consistent. This style may not be spectacular or what is known as playing to the grandstands''; it rather seems to be a series of applied techniques that consistently net better-than-average results. This performance style may appear fairly mundane but it can create a "folklore" type of reputation that has a precontest impact upon opponents. It is this practice that comes into play as some corporations continue to hold their market share without major challenge for years, or when all the world (including the opponent) marvels at a famous tennis star's backhand. The one danger of such a solid reputation is that you may become overly confident of your own invincibility. Always remember the quickest way for a competitor to gain fame is by destroying yours. As you climb to the top of the competitive ladder you become a clear target. At the same time the idea of grandstanding your downfall becomes more tempting for your opponents. Fight the temptation to relax in glory or to grandstand. Stick to your proven skills. They will net you a victory when all is said and done.

6. Strong Competitors Are Resilient through Flexibility. Haven't all great golf and tennis pros come back with miraculous performances on the brink of defeat? When this occurs we are aware primarily of the competitor's great self-control and iron-willed determination. We may not be as aware, however, that applications of strength are usually combined with an intelligent overview of the situation and the flexibility to change a game or strategic plan when spontaneous events so dictate. This is the most difficult technique to develop as it is not an instinctive competitive reaction; it seems to create a conflict of purpose in terms of the previously recommended adherence to the researched game plan. But the two are not, in fact, mutually exclusive. When the plan isn't working, a competitor must have "on the spot" creativity and flexibility to come up with a new *approach;* poor competitors often maintain the same *modus operandi* no matter how many losses or defeats it keeps producing. Often a change of program will confuse the opponent just enough to allow you to "spring back."

MENTAL ATTITUDE OF SUCCESSFUL COMPETITORS

Winning competitors have mental attitudes that support their techniques, and training in the techniques can help you strengthen your attitude. There are several mental attitudes characteristic of successful competitors.

1. The Superior Performer Is Free of All "Pregame" Anxieties. The ability to "clear your mental decks for action is much easier said than done. What about all this planning we have talked about? How can we plan, yet not let destructive elements of concern creep into our consciousness? The answer is practice, experience, and discipline: Keep trying until you find something that works. The most successful technique I know involves rehearsing the game plan in great detail. This singleness of purpose can either completely occupy you or tire you of the situation so much that you will temporarily forget the whole thing. The business equivalent of this is the new product campaign that is prepared and rehearsed for each new market area.

2. The Successful Competitor Maintains an Attitude of Deep Concentration during the Competitive Process.   It is easy to say that all outside distractions should be eliminated. The problem is doing it. The executive typically has myriad domestic and community involvements that sap his or her concentration on the competitive challenge. The athlete in any spectator situation must deal with increased tension created by audience presence. In either case, most competitors will tell you it is better to concentrate your mental energies on what you are doing, rather than trying to shut out the superfluous. Like the swimmer who concentrates on the word "pull," the effect can be almost hypnotic.

3. The Ability to Compete more Effectively than Others Usually Incorporates a High Level of Mental Alertness.   The competitive process demands that you study the reactions of your opponent. This should complement your concentration on yourself. First concentrate on what you are doing, and then concentrate on the impact this makes on your opponent, adjusting your strategy accordingly. This requires practice and intelligence. The popular caricature of the hulking athlete with the vacuous mind is a fallacy. I believe that there is a high degree of correlation between coordination and a person who "thinks right." The only problem some competitors face is training themselves to fully use their mental prowess. Practically any winner will tell you that competition is a mental challenge as well as a physical one. In business we often see the flexible plan win because it has incorporated check points for change if necessary.

4. A Self-Supportive Attitude of Confidence Is a Must for Anyone Involved in Competitive Activities.   Self-doubts can destroy effectiveness in a flash. This is as true in the boardroom as it is on the playing field, as meaningful on the podium as on the market floor. All the previous words about methods and mental approach will not work without self-confidence. In fact, the very ability to apply any of the methods and attitudes listed above depend on your own basic belief that you will succeed. This fundamental need to believe in yourself extends beyond the competitive arena and relates to leadership ability in general and even to basic satisfaction in life. Again, any successful competitor will tell you that anyone who does not believe he or she will win, won't.

5. To Be a Competitive Success You Must Be a Continual Student, and This Requires a Certain Level of Modesty.   Once you are convinced that there is no further room for improvement, you have begun your own demise. We have all seen how success can destroy modesty and self-appraisal. Obviously, one of the major rewards of winning is the pleasure of regarding yourself on the summit. But you will need special self-discipline techniques to get off the pedestal or you won't stay there long. I have seen business executives and athletes who, moments after winning, began to critically analyze what they did wrong. They remained winners. If you have ever sat in on a Monday postgame film session and listened to the coaching staff's critique, you would know that the study of each success component is a fine technique for the restoration of modesty.

COMPETITION IS PART OF LIFE

Competition is a rigorous process requiring a methodology and controlled mental attitude for success. Achieving this is clearly an act of determination. And yet, we know that only half the participants in sports can be successful. On the business front there are more subtle shades of success, but competition remains a frustrating process for many of its participants.

Occasionally we hear of ideas for eliminating some elements of competition, such as controlled economies, and removing the grading system from our schools. To my knowledge these have not succeeded in eliminating stress, nor have they improved performance. If the zest for winning continues to be a strong human motivation, as it has been up to now, competition is likely to remain a basic fact of life. And, as long as it is, those who strive to become better at it will reap the rewards.

JEFFREY Z. RUBIN

Reading 3–2
Psychological Traps

*Even when it no longer makes sense, we may step up our efforts to save a
relationship or a career that is yielding diminishing returns. Not knowing
when to cut our losses, we continue to pour money into an aging automobile, a
risky investment, or a doubtful poker hand. Caught in traps of our own
devising, we can only climb out by understanding how they work.*

You place a phone call and are put on hold. You wait. And then you wait
some more. Should you hang up? Perhaps. After all, why waste another
second of your valuable time? On the other hand, if you hang up you'll only
have to call again to accomplish whatever business put you on the phone in
the first place. Anyway, you've already spent all this time on hold, so why
give up now? So you wait some more. At some point you finally resign
yourself to the likelihood that you've been left on hold forever. Even as you
hang up, though, your ear remains glued to the receiver, hoping to the bitter
end that all the time spent waiting was not in vain.

Almost all of us have spent too much time caught in little traps like that.
Even when it no longer makes sense, we continue to spend money on a
failing automobile or washing machine, on an aging and decrepit house, a
risky stock investment, or a doubtful poker hand. We simply do not know
when to cut our losses and get out. And the same goes for more serious
situations. Some of us remain longer than we should in a marriage or love
relationship, a job or career, a therapy that is yielding diminishing returns.
On a grander scale, entrapment is part of the dynamic in political controversies—Abscam, Watergate, the war in Vietnam.

A common set of psychological issues and motivations underlies all such
situations, a process of entrapment that shares many of the characteristics of

Reprinted from *Psychology Today* Magazine. Copyright © 1981 Ziff-Davis Publishing
Company.

animal traps and con games and has been studied in a variety of laboratory and natural settings. As researchers, we are attempting to describe the properties of psychological traps: what they have in common, where they lurk, whom they tend to snare, and how they can be avoided.

When I was growing up in New York City there was a cunning little device that we called the Chinese Finger Trap—a woven straw cylinder about three or four inches long, with an opening at each end just large enough for a child's finger to be inserted. Once you put a finger into each end, the trap was sprung. The harder you tugged in opposite directions in an effort to get free, the more the woven cylinder stretched and pulled tight around each finger. Only by pushing inward, by moving *counter* to the direction in which escape appeared to lie, could you get free. So it is with entrapping situations. The tighter one pulls, the greater the conflict between the lure of the goal and the increasing cost of remaining in pursuit of it. And the tighter one pulls, the greater the trap's bite. Only by letting go at some point can the trap be escaped. Or, as the Chinese philosopher Lao-tzu put it: "Those who would conquer must yield; and those who conquer do so because they yield."

To understand psychological entrapment, we must first understand the simplest traps of all—physical traps for animals. Sometime rather early in the evolution of our species, human beings came to understand that the active pursuit of quarry by hunting was often impractical or undesirable. Thus, trapping was invented. A trap allows hunters to outwit their quarry, to offset any advantage that the quarry may have by virtue of its greater power, speed, or the limited destructive capacity of the hunters' weapons. An animal trap accomplishes these ends in a strikingly simple and clever way: it brings the quarry to the hunter rather than the other way around. Instead of continuing to hunt for quarry, often in vain and at considerable cost, trappers get the quarry to catch itself. Once set, the animal trap takes on a life of its own, a surrogate hunter waiting with infinite patience for the quarry to make an unwise choice. The consequence of having this surrogate is that hunters' limited resources can now be devoted to other pursuits, including the construction of additional traps.

Ingenious devices, these animal traps, devilishly clever and efficient— and utterly sinister in their effect on the victims who fall prey to them. What properties, then, make them work?

First of all, an effective trap must be able to lure or distract the quarry into behaving in ways that risk its self-preservation. Often this important first step is accomplished with some form of bait that is so tantalizingly attractive, so well suited to the quarry's particular needs, that the animal is induced to pursue it, oblivious to the trap's jaw.

Second, an effective animal trap permits traffic in one direction only. It is far easier for a lobster to push its way through the cone-shaped net into the lobster trap than, once in, to claw its way out. The bait that motivated the quarry to enter the trap in the first place obscures the irreversibility of that move. Doors that yield easily, inviting the quarry's entry, slam shut with a vengeance.

Third, an effective trap is often engineered so that the quarry's very efforts to escape entrap it all the more. The bear's considerable strength, applied in an effort to pull its paw from a trap, only sinks the trap's teeth deeper into its flesh. A fish's tendency to swim away from anything that constrains its free movement only deepens the bite of the hook. An effective trap thus invites the quarry to become the source of its own entrapment or possible destruction.

Finally, an effective animal trap must be suited to the particular attributes of the quarry it is designed to capture. One cannot catch a guppy with a lobster trap or a mosquito with a butterfly net. Consider the awful and awesomely effective 19th-century American wolf trap. The simplicity and frightening elegance of this trap is that it depends on the wolf's appetite for the taste of blood. A bloodied knife blade was left to freeze in the winter ice. While licking the knife, the wolf would cut its tongue and begin to bleed. It would then start to lick at the knife all the more, which in turn led to a greater flow of blood—and the wolf's ultimate undoing. The animal's blood attracted other wolves, who then attacked the victim, and, eventually, one another. Thus a whole pack of wolves could be destroyed with just one trap.

Confidence games are psychological traps for capturing people and are remarkably similar to self-entrapment. Like animal traps, they rely for their effectiveness on the trapper's (con artist's) ability to lure the quarry (mark) into a course of action that becomes entrapping. The lure is typically based on the mark's cupidity; the fat, wriggling worm is the tempting possibility of getting something for nothing, a big killing that appears to happen at the expense of someone else.

The effective con also depends on the mark's willingness to cheat another person in order to reap large and easy profits. As a result, the mark's progressive pursuit of the lure tends to obscure the fact that the path taken is not easily reversible. With the con artist's kind assistance, the mark is increasingly rendered a coconspirator in a crime against another, a bit like Macbeth: "I am in blood/stepp'd so far that, should I wade no more,/ Returning were as tedious as go o'er."

In addition, the mark's very efforts to escape—by making a quick, glorious, and final big killing before quitting once and for all—only lead to deeper entrapment. The more money the mark is persuaded to put up in this effort, the more carefully he or she is apt to guard the investment—and to justify it through the commitment of additional resources.

Finally, just as an animal trap is tailored to its quarry, so must a con be geared to the brand of avarice and dishonesty of the mark. "Different traps for different saps" is the rule.

There are two kinds of cons: so-called short cons, such as Three-Card Monte or the Shell Game, in which the mark is fleeced for a few dollars on the spot; and big cons, in which the mark is directed to a "big store"—a place where the con is played out. Big cons reached their heyday around the turn of the 19th century in this country and lined the pockets of skilled con artists with hundreds of thousands of dollars. Big cons include the Rag, the Pay-Off, and the Wire, the last of these made famous by Paul Newman and Robert Redford in *The Sting*. In that con, a mark was persuaded that horserace results had been delayed long enough for him to place a bet *after* the race had been run, thereby betting on a sure thing. The con took place in a large ground-floor room, rented for the week as the big store. All the roles in the drama, save that of the mark, were played by confederates, creating an elaborate and complex ruse.

The steps or stages involved in most big cons are remarkably consistent:

1. "Putting the mark up"—finding the right person to fleece.
2. "Playing the con"—befriending the mark and gaining the mark's confidence.
3. "Roping the mark"—steering the victim to the "inside man," the person who is in charge of running the big store.
4. "Telling the tale"—giving the inside man an opportunity to show the mark how a large sum of money can be made dishonestly.
5. "Giving the convincer"—allowing the mark to make a substantial profit in a test run of the swindle.
6. "Giving the breakdown"—setting the mark up to invest a large sum of money for the final killing.
7. "Putting the mark on the send"—sending the mark home for that amount of money.
8. "The sting"—fleecing the mark in the big store.
9. "Blowing the mark off"—getting the mark out of the way as quickly and quietly as possible.

In psychological entrapment, one person may simultaneously play the role of roper, inside man, and mark. In so doing, we manage to ensnare ourselves. As with physical and psychological devices for capturing others, these traps only work when people are, first and foremost, interested in—and distracted by—the lure of some goal. Final victory in Vietnam, a happy marriage, a big killing at the gambling table, or simply the return of the person who pushed the hold button: all may be viewed as worthy goals—or as bait that conceals a dangerous hook. In entrapping situations, marks initially look in one direction only—forward—as they pursue the mirage of a goal that lies just beyond their grasp.

In their single-minded rush toward the objective, marks neglect the possibility that they are being sucked into a funnel from which escape may prove remarkably difficult. The first stage of entrapment—eager, forward-looking pursuit of one's goal—is thus followed by attention to the costs that have been unwittingly incurred along the way. The compulsive gambler's drive for a killing is inevitably followed by attention to the mounting costs of the pursuit, costs that in turn need to be justified by greater commitment. Similarly, when our personal or professional lives are disappointing—and our efforts to achieve a turnaround do not pay off quickly enough—we may decide to justify the high cost by renewing our commitment and remaining on the treadmill.

But notice that the more resources committed to attaining the goal, the greater the trap's bite. Each additional step toward a rewarding but unattained goal creates new and greater costs, requiring greater justification of the course of action than ever before. With each additional year that a person remains in a dissatisfying job, hoping it will take a turn for the better, he or she feels more compelled to rationalize the time invested by remaining in the job even longer.

In certain entrapping situations, those in which several people are competing with one another, reward pursuit and cost justification are followed by a third stage, in which people try to make sure that their competitors end up losing at least as much—if not more—than they. Like two children in a breath-holding contest or two nations in an arms race, many entrapping situations evolve to the point where each side's focus is no longer on winning or even on minimizing losses, but on getting even with the adversary who engineered the mess.

In the last major stage of entrapment, marks must finally let go, either because their resources are gone, because they are rescued by another person, or because they recognize the desperation of the pursuit. Just as the Chinese Finger Trap can be escaped only by pushing inward, entrapment can be avoided only by letting go.

One devilishly simple and effective example of entrapment is a game known as the Dollar Auction, invented about 10 years ago by Martin Shubik, an economist at Yale. As his proving ground, Shubik allegedly used the Yale University cocktail party circuit. Anyone can make some money—but perhaps lose some friends—by trying it out at a party.

Take a dollar bill from your pocket and announce that you will auction it off to the highest bidder. People will be invited to call out bids in multiples of five cents until no further bidding occurs, at which point the highest bidder will pay the amount bid and win the dollar. The only feature that distinguishes this auction from traditional auctions, you point out, is the rule that the *second-highest* bidder will also be asked to pay the amount bid, although he or she will obviously not win the dollar. For example, Susan has bid 30 cents and Bill has bid 25 cents; if the bidding stops at this point, you will pay Susan 70 cents ($1 minus the amount she bid) and Bill, the second-highest bidder, will have to pay you 25 cents. The auction ends when one minute has elapsed without any additional bidding.

If my own experience is any indication, the game is likely to follow a general pattern. One person bids a nickel, another bids a dime, someone else jumps the bidding to a quarter or so, and the bidding proceeds at a fast and furious pace until about 50 or 60 cents is reached. At around that point, the number of people calling out bids begins to decrease, and soon there are only three or four people still taking part. The bidding continues, at a somewhat slower pace, until the two highest bids are at about $1 and 95 cents. There is a break in the action at this point, as the two remaining bidders seem to consider what has happened and whether they should continue. Suddenly the person who bid 95 cents calls out $1.05, and the bidding resumes. Soon the two remaining bidders have escalated matters so far that both bids are over $4. Then one of the guests suddenly escalates the bidding by offering $5, the other (who has already bid $4.25 or so) refuses to go any higher, and the game ends. You proceed to collect $4.25 from the loser and $4 from the "winner."

Several researchers have had people play the Dollar Auction game under controlled laboratory conditions and have found that the participants typically end up bidding far in excess of the $1 prize at stake, sometimes paying as much as $5 or $6 for a dollar bill. The interesting question is, of course, why. What motivates people to bid initially and to persist in a self-defeating course of action?

Thanks primarily to the extensive research of Allan Teger, a social psychologist at Boston University, the question has been answered. Teger found that when Dollar Auction participants were asked to give reasons for their bidding, their responses fell into one of two major motivational categories: economic and interpersonal. Economic motives include a desire to win the dollar, a desire to regain losses, and a desire to avoid losing more money. Interpersonal motives include a desire to save face, a desire to prove one is the best player, and a desire to punish the other person.

Economic motives appear to predominate in the early stages of the Dollar Auction. People begin bidding with the hope of winning the dollar bill easily and inexpensively. Their bids increase a little bit at a time, in the expectation that their latest bid will prove to be the winning one. If the other participants reason the same way, however, the bidding escalates. At some subsequent point in the Dollar Auction, the bidders begin to realize that they have been drawn into an increasingly treacherous situation. Acknowledging that they have already invested a portion of their own resources in the auction, they begin to pay particular attention to the amount they stand to lose if they come in second. As the bidding approaches $1—or when the amount invested equals the objective worth of the prize—the tension rises. At this stage, Teger has found, the participants experience intense inner conflict, as measured by physiological measures of anxiety and nervousness; about half of them then quit the game.

People who remain in the auction past the $1 bid, however, typically stick with it to the bitter end—until they have exhausted their resources or their adversary has quit. Interpersonal motives come to the fore when the bid exceeds the objective value of the prize. Even though both players know they are sure to lose, each may go out of his or her way to punish the other, making sure that the other person loses even more, and each may become increasingly concerned about looking foolish by yielding to the adversary's aggression. Teger found that this mutual concern occasionally leads bidders to a cooperative solution to the problem of how to quit without losing face: a bid of $1 by one player, if followed by a quick final raise to $2 by the second, allows the first person to quit in the knowledge that both have lost equally.

If entrapping situations are as ubiquitous and powerful as I have suggested, how do people ever avoid getting into them? What, if anything, can people do to keep from getting in deeper? Over the past six years or so, I have been working with a research group at Tufts University to find some answers to these questions. We have conducted most of our research in the laboratory, using the Dollar Auction and several other procedures. We have begun to study entrapment in naturalistic settings, by holding contests in which residents of the Boston area, chosen at random, are invited to solve a series of increasingly difficult problems that require more and more of their time.

In one experimental model, people were invited to pay for the ticks of a numerical counter in the hope that they would obtain a jackpot—either by reaching a number that had been randomly generated by computer or by outlasting an adversary. A second laboratory paradigm challenged people to solve a jigsaw puzzle correctly within a limited period; if they succeeded, they received a cash jackpot, but if they failed, they had to pay for the number of pieces they had requested. Finally, in a third type of experiment, undergraduates were instructed to wait for an experimenter or another participant to arrive at the laboratory so that they could receive a research credit; naturally, the experimenter was always late, and the subjects had to continually decide how much longer they would wait.

In one such experiment, Tufts undergraduates were seated in individual rooms, given $2.50 in cash for agreeing to come to our laboratory, and invited to win an additional $10 jackpot by solving a crossword puzzle. The puzzle consisted of 10 words of varying difficulty, eight or more of which had to be correctly solved in order to win the jackpot. Each student was given three ''free'' minutes to work on the puzzle; after that, 25 cents was deducted from the initial $2.50 stake for each additional minute. People could quit the experiment at any point and leave with their initial stake—minus 25 cents for each minute they remained in the study past the first three. If they remained in the study after 13 minutes had passed, they had to begin paying out of their own pockets, since their initial stake was exhausted at that point. The study was stopped after 15 minutes.

Almost everyone found the puzzle too difficult to solve without the aid of a crossword puzzle dictionary, which they were told was available on request. Participants were also told that because there were two people working on the puzzle and only one dictionary, it would be available on a first-come, first-served basis. (No such dictionary was actually available.) When students requested the dictionary, they had to turn their puzzles face down, so they were not able to wait for the dictionary and work on the puzzle at the same time. Surprisingly, nearly 20 percent of the students stayed in the experiment the full 15 minutes.

We investigated several important influences on the entrapment process here. First, we created either a competitive or noncompetitive relationship between the participants by telling the students either that the $10 jackpot would be awarded to the first person who solved the puzzle or that it would go to anyone who was able to do so. We found that students who believed they were in a competition became more entrapped—they played the game far longer and spent more of their money—than those not in competition.

We also studied the nature of the investment process by giving participants different instructions about quitting the experiment. Some were told that they could quit at any time. Others were advised that the experimenter would ask them every three minutes if they wished to continue. We expected that the experimenter's intervention would serve as an indirect reminder of the cost of continued participation and that those students who were spoken to would become less entrapped than the others. That is exactly what happened. Students who were not asked if they wished to continue remained in the experiment far longer and, as a group, lost more than twice as much money.

In all of our experiments, as in the one described above, we encourage subjects to move toward some rewarding goal, while we increase the time or money they must invest in it and give them the option to quit at any time. Both our research and Teger's reveal certain repeating themes in the behavior of the participants, which I can summarize in the form of some advice on how to avoid entrapment:

- *Set limits on your involvement and commitment in advance.*   We find that people who are not asked to indicate the limits of their participation become more entrapped than those who do indicate a limit, especially publicly. Depending on the entrapping situation you are in, you may wish to set a limit based on your past experience (for example, the average time you've spent waiting on hold); your available resources (the amount of time or money you have left to spend); the importance of reaching your goal on this occasion (you may be able to call later to make a plane reservation); and the possibility of reaching your goal in some other way (using a travel agent to make the reservation).
- *Once you set a limit, stick to it.*   We all play little games with ourselves—we flip a coin to make a decision and then when we don't like the result, decide to make the contest two out of three flips. We set limits that are subsequently modified, shaded, and shifted as we get close to the finish. Each new investment, like the addition of an AM/FM radio to a new car that has already been decked out with extras, tends to be evaluated not in relation to zero (the total cost of the

investment) but in relation to that inconsequential, minuscule increment above and beyond the amount we've already agreed to spend. If you're the sort of person who has trouble adhering to limits, get some help. Find a friend, tell him or her the limit you wish to set, and have your friend rope you in when you get to the end of your self-appointed tether. Uylsses used that method to resist the deadly temptation of the Sirens' wail.

• *Avoid looking to other people to see what you should do.*   It's one thing to use a friend to rope you in, and it's another matter entirely to deal with your uncertainty about what to do by sheepishly following others. Given the uncertainty in entrapping situations, it is tempting to look to others for clues about the appropriateness of one's own behavior. Our research indicates that the presence and continued involvement of another person in an entrapping situation increases one's own entrapment, and that this occurs even when the behavior of each person has no effect on the other's fate. Proprietors of Las Vegas gambling casinos know what they're doing when they use shills to ''prime the pump'' and get the gambler's competitive juices flowing. Similarly, one is far more likely to continue waiting for a bus that has not yet arrived—and even wait for an outrageous, irrationally long time—if other people are also waiting.

• *Beware of your need to impress others.*   Other people are not only a source of information about what to do in entrapping situations; they are also a critically important source of praise or disapproval for our behavior. We all want to be liked, loved, and respected by people whose opinions matter to us. This motive is perfectly healthy and often appropriate, but not in entrapping situations. Our research shows that people become more entrapped when they believe their effectiveness is being judged and scrutinized by others. This is particularly powerful when the perceived evaluation occurs early in the game, and diminishes in importance if evaluative observers are introduced later on. We also find that people who are especially anxious about their appearance in the eyes of others and who feel that they have something to prove by toughing things out get more entrapped than their less anxious counterparts.

• *Remind yourself of the costs involved.*   Our research indicates that people are less likely to become entrapped when they are made aware early on of the costs associated with continued participation. Even the availability of a chart that depicts investment costs is sufficient to reduce entrapment. The net effect of such information about costs is to offset the distracting, shimmering lure of the goal ahead—especially if the cost information is introduced right away. If you don't start paying attention to the costs of your involvement until fairly late in the game, you may feel compelled to justify those costs by investing even more of your resources.

• *Remain vigilant.*   Entrapping situations seem to sneak up on us. People who understand and avoid one brand of trap often manage to get caught in others with surprising frequency and ease. Just because you knew when to bail out of that lousy stock investment doesn't mean that you will have the good sense to give up on an unsatisfactory relationship or a profession in which you feel you have too much invested to quit. Obviously, people who are told about entrapment and its dangers are less likely to become entrapped. Our studies also show that being forewarned about one kind of trap, moreover, can put people on guard against other kinds of traps.

Although very little is known at this point about the kinds of people who tend to get entrapped, we have recently begun to study this issue and can therefore engage in a bit of informed speculation. First, people who go for bait are also likely to end up hooked. Those who are exceptionally ambiguous or greedy or unusually self-confident and self-assured about their ability to reach a goal must tread warily. There may be icebergs lurking in those calm and glassy seas ahead. Second, the sort of person who believes that he should—indeed must—profit according to his efforts may also be ripe for the plucking. Those who tend to trust excessively in a just world, who think that people get what they deserve and deserve what they get, may end up caught in a version of the Chinese Finger Trap. They use their belief in justice to rationalize continued investments—and so tighten the noose all the more. Finally, the man or woman who tends to get swept up in macho ideology, who feels that nothing else applies, is also especially vulnerable to entrapment. Such people may be willing to invest more and more in order to avoid some small embarrassment—only to suffer greater humiliation in the final reckoning.

Despite cautionary advice, we all still manage to get ourselves entrapped. When the inevitable happens, when you find yourself asking "What have I done?" remember there are times when the wisest course may be to quit, not fight. There may just not be a way of salvaging the time, effort, money, even the human lives that have gone into a particular sinking ship. Know when to give it up, when to push rather than pull those fingers, when to yield and wait for victory another day. For there is almost always another day, despite our proclivity for ignoring that fact.

JEB BROOKS and
EARL BROOKS

Reading 3–3

The Role of Top Management
in Negotiations

The president of a medium sized manufacturing firm believes in giving individual managers free rein in handling intercompany negotiations. "They're the best judge of their operating needs and strengths," he explains. "Give them the responsibility and they'll produce." Accordingly, when a contract with a major customer comes up, the sales manager is given full authority to conduct the negotiations. Although highly motivated, the manager lacks the knowledge to speak for, much less integrate, the different needs and priorities of other parts of the company that are also affected by the negotiated terms of the agreement. Because he knows his own department best, he ends up maximizing its interests and commits the firm to a five-year contract that severely strains both production and finance. Company profits fall.

The president of a retail company is proud of the reputation she earned as a negotiator during the building years of her business. Whenever her firm is engaged in negotiations, she monitors them closely and often intercedes in the talks at the first sign of difficulty. Her authority, she feels, can help expedite decisions and cut through all that unnecessary muddle. However, as her company has grown in size and complexity over the years, she has become less knowledgeable about the specifics of her products. Executive responsibilities limit the depth of her preparation. The quick settlements that she achieves are often lopsided—in favor of the other party.

Neither of these approaches to managing negotiations is unusual in American business today. Both, unfortunately, are ineffective. Top management par-

Jeb Brooks works with Boston Financial, a real estate equity syndication firm. Earl Brooks is a professor of administration, Graduate School of Business and Public Administration, Cornell University.
Reprinted from *MSU Business Topics*, Michigan State University, Summer 1979.

ticipation is critical to successful negotiating, yet too few presidents understand the role they must play. On the one hand, the high stakes involved in intercompany negotiations demand the concentrated involvement of top management; on the other, it is a complex and time-consuming activity which requires judicious delegation of responsibility and authority.

What little has been written about negotiations is concerned with tactics and the actual process between parties. Scant attention has been directed toward understanding the chief executive officer's point of view. This article speaks to this gap. We begin with a brief overview of the role, then focus in depth on a practical analytic framework for the chief executive to use in planning objectives, guiding preparation, monitoring progress, and assessing results. While the degree of the CEO's direct involvement depends on the type and magnitude of the particular negotiating situation, he or she must provide direction for all negotiations. The costs of ignoring this role can be high.

Robert L. Katz has pointed out that in successively higher levels of management, two abilities become increasingly important: (1) coordinating all the activities and interests of the organization toward a common goal (conceptual skill), and (2) understanding and motivating individuals across departments (intergroup skill).[1] Nowhere is competence in these two skills more important than in managing the negotiating process.

The flowchart set out in Exhibit 1 traces both the conceptual and intergroup responsibilities of the CEO from the preplanning stage to the final point of assessment and evaluation. The specific actions called for fluctuate between (1) the CEO being directly involved with the negotiating team and the other party, and (2) the CEO taking a back seat, delegating responsibilities, and playing supportive and coordinating roles.

The flowchart includes set points at which the chief executive officer can check that the long-term welfare of the total organization is being considered. However, as perhaps the only person in the company who holds and can speak for this perspective, the CEO is responsible for maintaining this overview role throughout the negotiating process.

PREPLANNING

Top management should decide, often after considering staff recommendations, what operational objectives may best be realized through negotiations. For example, the policy decision by the president of a sporting goods company to concentrate on the development of highest profit areas led to a task committee's recommendations to sell off the fledgling camping equipment operation and to acquire a sailboat manufacturer to round off the small boat line. Both proposals called for intercompany negotiations.

---

[1] Robert L. Katz, "Skills of an Effective Administrator," *Harvard Business Review* 74 (September-October 1974): 90–102.

Exhibit 1
Flow Chart—The Role of Top Management in Negotiations

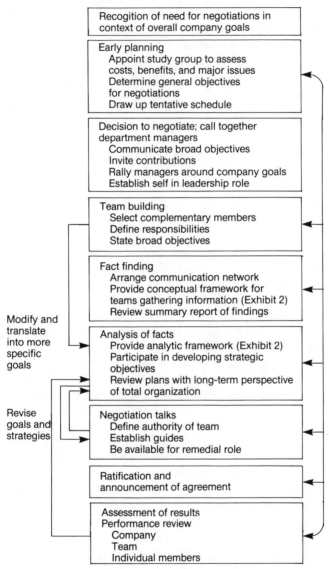

At this point the negotiating process starts. The chief executive's first step involves directing the task committee or a separate study group to prepare a preliminary report on the costs and benefits of negotiations, the issues likely to be involved, and the companies that might be approached. This information enables the chief executive to undertake the second step: to draw up a tentative schedule regarding planning, preparation, and the duration of the negotiating talks.

Too often negotiating teams face a single-choice situation because management did not plan enough lead time. The more alternatives open to a company, the greater is its power in negotiations. Whenever possible, the chief executive must allow sufficient time to explore, develop, and use options. Time is needed not only for in-depth preparation and analysis of issues but also to enable public and private sources of information to be tapped early. It is far easier to learn the other party's pricing and decision-making processes six months before the negotiations than it is on the eve of the session.

This initial information gathering should be expanded prior to actual negotiations.

RALLYING THE COMPANY BEHIND A COMMON GOAL

As mentioned above, the chief executive officer is responsible for viewing the company as a whole and recognizing interrelationships; that is, how various functions depend on one another and how a change in one part has consequences for all others. The CEO must also think in terms of relative emphases and priorities and must strike a balance among conflicting needs and values of departments. (In fact, negotiations occur continuously *within* every organization—from vice presidents vying for capital budget funds to a salesperson arguing with a credit manager over what terms to offer a customer. However, intracompany negotiations are not within our scope and will be discussed only as they relate to negotiations with outside companies.) In the face of change—such as accompanies intercompany negotiations— intracompany competition is heightened. Top management must pay special attention to this conflict and try to direct it into a constructive mode.

Soon after deciding to proceed with negotiations, the chief executive should meet with concerned department managers to discuss their needs, views, and preferences. The CEO must not commit himself or herself to specific plans, but rather should agree to explore options. This early participation can foster a cooperative sense among department managers so they all feel their specific values have validity; it can help ensure that each department knows there have to be trade-offs and compromises in negotiations but that decisions to advance the overall welfare of the organization will benefit everyone. The CEO must clearly convey the message that he or she will assume responsibility for making those tough decisions.

These preliminary meetings serve a purpose beyond motivating and gaining the commitment of personnel holding different views. They pave the way for subsequent fact-finding efforts. In effect, the chief executive has given authority to the negotiating team in the eyes of individual department managers. Opening these channels of communication is essential for the planning and preparation that must go into the negotiations.

BUILDING THE TEAM

In large companies, the chief executive generally lacks: (1) detailed current knowledge about products, technologies, and customer needs, (2) the necessary patience or time to prepare in depth for and engage in the actual negotiations, and (3) the specific skills required at the bargaining table. For these reasons the CEO must concentrate on broad strategic issues and rely on a team of skilled negotiators. This team will work with members of the organization to develop background information, goals, strategies, and tactics, and then conduct the negotiations.

Most negotiating teams include a leader who organizes and speaks for the group, supporting specialists to provide technical assistance, experts to bolster credibility, and a note-taker to record what is said—and not said—during the negotiating sessions. Management must judge the situation the company faces and select team members accordingly. (If dealing with a monopolistic seller, management might select a persuasive negotiator with an encyclopedic capacity for facts and figures. If the firm itself is the sole seller, a negotiator of high status and low tolerance might be most effective.)

While there is a tendency for chief executives to pick members in their own image—hard-nosed bargainers to mirror their own tough-mindedness, or technical people if they themselves are engineers—research indicates that an effective negotiator has a combination of traits: competitiveness and cooperation; skepticism in perception and positiveness in presentation; ability to speak and listen well; and good business sense and a practical understanding of human nature. Because such individuals are rare, management often builds a team with members who complement one another. A large retail company has had outstanding success pairing a "dumb questioner" with a sharp cost accountant at the negotiating table. Respectful but persistent, the questioner needs to understand thoroughly most assumptions the opposing party considers as given. Needless to say, he and the accountant work well together.

Management also must know when to bring in outside consultants for the team. During the 1950s, a drug company began negotiations with government officials to build a plant in Latin America. Their central approach was to stress the financial advantages of their proposed project. Fortunately, management included on the team a consultant familiar with Latin American operations who pointed out that decision makers in this particular country placed far greater weight on political than on economic considerations. The company revised its approach and now enjoys successful operations throughout Latin America.

PREPARATION OF THE TEAM

Many companies prepare for negotiations in a loose, haphazard manner. This is surprising because rarely can the investment of time and effort return as great a profit as in negotiations.

Both experience and research findings indicate that a negotiator's commitments to (1) gather information, (2) set high goals, and (3) take risks produce higher settlements. The chief executive should clearly demand these commitments of negotiators, then follow through in providing the time, resources, and atmosphere for their development.

Gathering Information. Commonly, negotiators underestimate their own power and overestimate that of the other party. Knowledge is power in negotiations. The more a company knows about its own position, that of the other party, and the marketplace, the better is its bargaining position. The chief executive can facilitate information gathering in two ways. First, the CEO must help set up a communication network. The initial meeting with department managers, which we mentioned earlier, helps serve this purpose. It is important that the negotiating team follow through by expanding upon and using these channels of communication. Second, the chief executive officer can install a framework to guide the team in its overall preparation. Such a framework is shown in Exhibit 2. The approach must be flexible. In certain situations, some stages will become more or less important; others may have to be added.

- The Company.   Study its situation and concerns, including the needs, strengths, and limitations of each department and how each will be affected by various negotiated conditions. Brainstorm for alternative solutions.
- The Other Party.   Study its situation and concerns. Project possible strategies, questions, and alternative proposals it may raise during the talks.
- External Trends and Developments.   Place the negotiations within economic, government, and social contexts. An upcoming labor contract, for example, will be influenced by other settlements in the industry.
- Opportunities for Mutual Gain.   Negotiating is not all conflict and competition; two parties get together because of complementary needs. The outcome, therefore, should benefit both parties; even if they never conduct business together again, they still must carry out the terms of the agreement. Look for issues that lend themselves to cooperative problem solving.

Top management is rarely directly involved in this technical, fact-finding stage. However, once information has been collected, management is responsible for helping place it within the context of long-term company goals. This placement leads, in turn, to the development of strategic objectives and the setting of specific goals.

Setting Goals and High Targets. Effective leaders are those who lift the aspirations of their followers from lower to higher goals. This observation by Abraham Maslow applies to the leadership role of management in negotiations. Research indicates that a negotiator's commitment to high targets is a

EXHIBIT 2
Checklist for Gathering and Analyzing Information

Your Company	*Other Party*

Your Company

Assess product and service need
   Break down into components
      Characteristics of product and
      service
      Time requirement
   Determine relative flexibility and
   alternatives for meeting need

Project worth of their product and
   service to you

Assess department capabilities
   Needs
   Strengths
   Limitations

Determine major issues

External factors
   Trends
   Condition of market
   Economic, government, and social
      contexts

Other Party

Assess their product and service need
   Break down into components
   Determine their flexibility and
      options

Project worth of your product and
   service to them

Evaluate company
   Organizational structure
      Decision-making process
      Authority of their negotiators
   General business and financial
      conditions
   History
      Performance record
      Description of prior negotiations

Project their major issues

Project negotiating position
   Strengths and limitations
      Time
      Knowledge
      Resources
   Brainstorm to determine their likely
      demands, strategies, tactics,
      questions and answers

The Negotiations

Determine
   Relative position and power
   Opportunities for cooperative problem solving
   Trouble areas

Set goals—Refine broad objectives into specific goals
   Categorize as essential, desirable, tradeable
   For each issue prepare:
      High target
      An acceptable minimum
      Starting price
      Reason for that starting price

Develop primary strategy and alternatives

Develop tactics

Prepare support data for
   Internal company use
   Presentation to other party

Suggest agenda for negotiation talks

Conduct dry runs

Prepare questions to test assumptions and estimates

key factor in results. The crucial word is *commitment.* High targets should not be unilaterally set by the chief executive officer because this may cause resentment in the team and the attitude that "they're the CEO's goals—not ours." But neither should the target-setting be left entirely to the discretion of subordinates—it is too important a task.

We suggest that the chief executive state broad objectives, then guide the team in breaking down and translating them into operational issues and goals. Such a process can be used in simple but effective ways. The president of a small consumer products company, for example, often instructs his negotiating team to aim for the "best possible terms." "I know that may sound imprecise," he says, "but I rarely have precise figures available. We get our people together, sit down and figure out just what 'best possible terms' means. First we try to define them objectively, then we discuss how to achieve them. People come out of these discussions really motivated. We do well in negotiations."

A Framework for Analyzing Issues.   In larger organizations in which such active participation is impractical, the chief executive officer can provide the team with a framework to guide the analysis and development of goals.

Few negotiable issues can be ranked neatly in order of priority. Often, however, they lend themselves to general categorization. The team can put each issue into one of the following categories:

1. Essential.
2. Desirable.
3. Tradeable.

For each quantifiable issue, the team can plan:

1. A high target price or demand.
2. A minimum offer that the company would accept.
3. A starting price.
4. A cogent reason for that price.

The importance of this comprehensive analysis cannot be over-emphasized; company negotiators must have a facility with the issues that allows them to understand and deal with the varied combinations the other party may present. In addition, the analysis of issues will help the team prepare its own alternative strategies and package proposals.

The chief executive must instruct the team to preserve flexibility. The negotiating process is dialectical: What one party does depends on the moves and countermoves of the other. An unexpected concession by one side may allow the other to change a nonnegotiable demand. Options must remain open. Although issues and priorities may change, they must alway be understood.

Taking Risks.   Few business opportunities can be known with certainty; instead, they present themselves in terms of relative tendencies and probabilities. This is especially true with negotiations. (If terms were known in advance, there would be nothing to negotiate.) Reducing uncertainty can reduce risk. The knowledge gained from the planning and preparation processes discussed here should lessen uncertainty for the negotiating team.

There are two additional actions the chief executive can take to encourage risk-taking by the team. First, state that he or she understands and accepts the risks of planned strategies and objectives. Commitment to high goals also increases the likelihood of stalemate. Every part of the organization, including the board of directors, if appropriate, must be prepared for the implications of deadlock. Second, the CEO can give team members a general assurance that they are regarded as competent professionals who will not be second-guessed at every turn.

The Role of Top Management with Respect to Tactics.   The CEO helps develop strategic objectives and priorities but leaves tactics, for the most part, to the discretion of the negotiating team.[2] Certain tactics, however, such as the use of publicity or the take-it-or-leave-it gambit, should not be used without management's approval. Also, the chief executive officer is responsible for the ethical and legal standards of those representing the company and must never condone lying, deliberate misrepresentation, or illegal acts. A policy based on presentable facts will best serve the interests of the company.

Management should assure itself that tactics used by the team are in the company's long-run interests. Squeeze tactics used in a one-shot deal with a real estate agent, for example, would be inappropriate for negotiating the latest contract with the union. However, in some situations this distinction is not so clear.

In investment projects in Third World countries, the balance of power often shifts over the course of the project.[3] When terms are negotiated at the entry stage, the investing company has the relative power. But as the host country begins to gain knowledge (perhaps as expectations prove unrealistic or new investors accept less attractive terms), the power balance changes. At this point, the host government may insist on renegotiating the terms of the original agreement, disrupting company operations.

Top management, with the aid of its broad perspective, might foresee this danger and consider providing officials of the host country with more information in an effort to make their expectations more realistic and to reduce the area of future dispute. Although such action initially would result in less favorable investment terms, the long-term prospects of the project would be enhanced.

Final Preparation.   As seen in Exhibit 2, the dry run and drawing up the agenda for negotiations are the final steps in the preparation. Management should direct team members to hold practice sessions to pool and assess all

---

[2] Tactics, generally speaking, are airy plots designed to distract the other party from real bottom line issues. The leading book on tactics is Chester L. Karrass, *Give and Take* (New York: Crowell, 1974).

[3] Ashok Kapoor, *Planning for International Business Negotiations* (Cambridge, Mass.: Ballinger, 1975).

they have learned and to anticipate how the negotiations are likely to unfold. Drawing up the agenda—that is, outlining what issues need resolving and the order and timing of those decisions—presents an opportunity to gain control of the talks. It is clearly advantageous for the team to suggest an agenda.

Finally, the CEO should caution the team not to assume too much. Research is an invaluable aid in preparing for negotiations, but misjudgments can be costly. Early in the session, the team should plan to ask questions to test its assumptions and estimates.

THE NEGOTIATING TALKS

If the planning and preparation have been done well, the actual negotiations should go smoothly. The chief executive officer rarely will be directly involved in the talks and, in fact, must refrain from trespassing. Interference can cause serious damage to the credibility and sense of authority of the team in the eyes of the other party.

This is not to suggest that top management should never sit at the bargaining table. Its presence may be necessary in certain situations, such as (1) initial meetings, to display interest and commitment, (2) to speed decisions or break deadlocks, and (3) to arrive at an agreement in principle (the legendary Onassis handshake), with details to be worked out by respective staff.

Related to this topic is the decision the CEO must make about how much authority to delegate to the team. Restraint is essential. Full authority is often a great handicap—history is filled with blunders made at summit meetings—whereas limited authority gives the negotiator additional time to think and plan countermoves while checking upstairs for approval. Also, with limited authority, negotiators can give budget limitations, company policy, and an adamant boss as reasons for not making a concession. (During the acquisition heyday of the 1960s, a major conglomerate often used a representative of relatively low status to make the initial approach to the president of the target company. In the event the feeler was refused outright, this tactic left room for a high-level executive to follow up with a sweetened offer.)

Generally, a negotiator who has easy access to decision makers and who can obtain quick and decisive responses will not lose credibility or power.

Occasionally, a representative of the other party may go over the head of the team and attempt to deal directly with top management. This can set an unfortunate precedent. A few years ago the president of a large trucking firm permitted the traffic vice president of an automotive company to circumvent his negotiating team and deal directly with him. Not only was the morale of the president's team damaged, but also this action established a pattern in future negotiations for leapfrogging at the first sign of difficulty.

Once the negotiations begin, the CEO should be available to play a mediative role. The other party may spring a surprise, such as a sudden change in demands, authority, deadlines, or negotiations. The team should be instructed never to respond to such situations until it is prepared. In the event additional information needs to be gathered and new goals and strategies developed, the role of top management with respect to the team proceeds as in the earlier preparation.

The CEO has other responsibilities. He or she should arrange to be informed of significant progress in the talks and, to the extent other departments of the organization are affected by different negotiated packages, should make certain that they are kept informed of developments. However, as mentioned above, the CEO must resist monitoring progress too closely. By their nature, bargaining sessions are confidential, and the frequent reporting of tentative agreements or lack of progress can cause leaks harmful to the delicate negotiating process.

In addition, the chief executive is responsible for all decisions to introduce extra resources, to make changes in the negotiating team, or to discontinue the talks.

RATIFICATION

When the parties are moving toward agreement, provision usually is made for periodic noting of progress. In the Paris fashion industry, for example, there is a wire around the negotiating room on which daily summaries of tentative agreements are posted. Successful negotiators can sense a willingness to settle. Often, at this stage, a private meeting of one member of each party is held to reach an understanding, the details of which are filled in by representations of the two teams, subject to further refinement by legal and other staff groups. These drafts are then submitted to the top management of each side for approval. If ratification is not forthcoming from one party and additional concessions are requested, the other CEO should consider carefully the ramifications of granting additional demands.

Generally, top management should not be afraid to ratify a contract that is in substantial agreement with the company's goals. If an important issue remains unresolved, a statement to this effect should be included in the final agreement. The act of ratification may serve as impetus to work out the additional compromise.

Often, ratification is simply a formality. If the chief executive officer has received periodic reports over the course of the negotiations, there should be no surprises in the final agreement. Once a careful study has been made to assure that the contract is a complete and accurate representation of the terms agreed upon during the session, the executive may commit the company to implementing the agreement.

ASSESSMENT AND PERFORMANCE REVIEW

The CEO is responsible for appraising the results of the negotiations in light of performance objectives. The framework presented in Exhibit 2 provides essential points of reference. Within each area—from planning and preparation to the actual sessions—the CEO should evaluate successes and errors and look for ways to improve negotiating performance in the future.

This evaluation should include an assessment of the team and its individual members. Although negotiating tactics may be a technical skill not everyone can master, managing the negotiation process, including understanding how negotiations can be used to meet needs and create opportunities, is an ability that managers need to learn and develop. The CEO should make certain that negotiating skills are included in the management development program of the company.

CONCLUSION

In summary, the role of the chief executive officer in negotiations is a complex one that demands many executive skills. The CEO's responsibilities include providing the necessary overview and conceptual framework, organizing staff and team, helping plan and make decisions regarding priorities and objectives, and motivating negotiators to achieve them.

There are no simple solutions in negotiations; there are only intelligent choices. It is the responsibility of the CEO to provide the framework and direction to help accomplish the company's objectives.

SECTION FOUR

Competitive Bargaining: Strategy and Tactics

Earlier in this volume, we referred to different types of bargaining situations as different "structures" of bargaining. In this section and the next, we will look at the various structures of bargaining and how they pose different conditions and problems for negotiators.

In distributive (competitive) bargaining, two parties have different but interdependent goals. When two parties are in a situation where they have incompatible goals, the condition is described as a fixed sum, variable share payoff structure, and, sometimes, a win/lose situation. In labor negotiations, labor and management are looking at the profits being made by the company (the sum) and negotiating as to what share the workers will get as a salary increase and how much the firm will keep as profit. There is a clear conflict of interest, and each party is motivated to obtain the largest share. The more one party knows about the other's strategy, the better able they are to plan their negotiations and know what can probably be obtained. Hence, much effort before and during negotiation is directed to getting as much information as possible about the other party.

Of course, the same process holds true for the other side; and, hence, it is to each side's advantage to keep their own information as private as possible while trying to learn about the other side. Therefore, in distributive bargaining, we face a situation where both parties are attempting to obtain as much information about the other as possible and, at the same time, give out as little information as they can.

In integrative (collaborative) bargaining, the total size of the resources at stake is not fixed. Therefore, if the amount of what is to be divided can be increased, both parties can get more, even though the proportions stay the same. Hence, in labor-management discussions, if workers agree to give up rigid assignment of jobs and management agrees to put more resources into product improvement and they also agree to a profit-sharing plan, there may be both a larger dollar amount of profits and more take-home pay in the future. For this reason, distributive bargaining is sometimes referred to as a "fixed-pie" situation and integrative bargaining as a "variable-pie" situation.

One of the most dramatically competitive, zero-sum negotiating situations arises when hostages have been taken and police or other authorities move in and try to arrange for their release. In exchange for the hostages, the kidnappers usually want something: money, release of prisoners, transportation to another place, or publicity of their cause. The authorities insist, at first, that they are not going to give anything. Jed Horne, in his article "Cop to the Rescue," describes how a special police unit handles negotiations with hostage-holders. He describes how they work to establish and keep open a dialogue with the hostage-holder, how they try to determine what actually is on his or her mind, and how they work to reach an agreement. Above all, Horne brings out the extensive preparation needed to deal with this type of negotiation.

The importance of getting information about the other party has been mentioned several times already. One of the key ways negotiators obtain information is by asking questions. While we all use questions, few of us are aware of the many different types of questions that can be asked. Gerard Nierenberg, in his paper, "The Use of Questions in Negotiating," identifies 16 different types of questions. He points out that some of them are very useful and others often lead to trouble during negotiations. (For example, he points out that when people ask questions they think "clever" negotiators would ask, they are likely to ask questions that will cause problems.) In addition to getting information, questions can serve other functions, ranging from calling attention to some issue to drawing things to a conclusion. He also discusses the reverse side of using questions in negotiation—how to respond when asked a question so as to neither give away valuable information nor to be unnecessarily vague or evasive.

Nierenberg is discussing the conscious or deliberate purposes to which we put questions. As Jacques Lalanne points out in "Attack by Question," we are at times using questions to conceal another message and may be unaware of what we are doing. Therefore, we may unintentionally lead a discussion in a direction that we neither want nor intend.

JED HORNE

Reading 4-1
Cop to the Rescue

Midnight in April. Terry Hammonds is jumpier than he is crazy. But he's got a gun. His girlfriend Otelia Faison bolts from her fifth-story Bronx tenement the second he pulls it out. A lover's quarrel. By the time police arrive, Hammonds has himself barricaded inside the apartment and is riding herd on four hostages: Otelia's cousin James Faison, two of Faison's five kids, and one of their friends, Loriann Good, aged 11. Hammonds hears the cops inching up the hallway and immediately grabs Loriann, shoving his gun against her temple.

The cops radio for New York City's hostage negotiating team. Within minutes, two police negotiators have taken positions by the door, backed up by the unit's commander, Captain Frank Bolz. He is wearing his customary baseball cap. The negotiators have one option: keep talking. Talk about anything, and get Hammonds to talk back. If talk doesn't work, they will have to try something else. Something more dangerous. Storming the apartment, for example. Behind the trio of negotiators lurks a two-man assault team armed with Ithaca deerslayer shotguns. On rooftops surrounding the Faison apartment, sharpshooters equipped with night-vision devices try to keep Hammonds in sight. At the impromptu command post downstairs, support police personnel have begun to interview friends and neighbors, radioing for out-of-state records that could shed light on the gunman's motives or personality. (Hammonds, it turns out, has a record of 15 arrests.)

Slowly, as the negotiators talk, Hammonds begins to soften. Would he like a cigarette? The cops throw in a pack. Within an hour the gunman has agreed to release the two Fiason kids. But now he retreats into the darkened interior of the apartment to contemplate the fate of his remaining two hostages.

From *Quest*, July/August 1981.

Suddenly, Captain Bolz hears footsteps moving toward the door in front of which the hostage negotiators stand positioned.

He calls out, "Halt!"

No response.

"Stand aside," Bolz orders his men. "He may be charging us." The well-disciplined men of the assault team level their shotguns, trigger fingers tensed, ready to offer instantaneous assistance if it's needed.

"Hold your fire!" cries Bolz. It's Loriann Good, who races through the doorway and into his arms. "Why didn't you *tell* us it was you?" Bolz asks the terrified girl. She looks up at him and shakes her head quizzically. For all the wealth of data volunteered downstairs by friends and neighbors—even Loriann's own mother—no one thought to tell the police that Loriann is hearing-impaired.

Grace under pressure. Cool under fire. Such qualities haven't always been police department strong suits. But thanks largely to the pioneering work of Captain Frank Bolz, police all over the world have come to appreciate the benefits of tactical restraint, negotiation, and patience in certain explosive situations. The biggest obstacle to the quiet revolution wrought by Bolz has been an attitude still prevalent both with the public and with law enforcers. Bolz calls it the John Wayne syndrome: "Police have always been viewed as the good daddies of society. People expect them to *perform*, to fix any situation. Inaction has been deemed inappropriate. So the police are frequently goaded into taking actions that are violent, risking injury to the victims, the criminal—and to the police themselves."

After Loriann Good's dash to freedom, Terry Hammonds finally was talked into surrendering. It took more than four hours and, at the last minute, police had to jump Hammonds when he panicked and lost confidence in the negotiated promises not to open fire. But no one was killed. No one was hurt. With equal success, Bolz's hostage team has talked a younger father off a Harlem rooftop; he threatened to jump with an infant son in his arms. A disgruntled laborer who threatened to blow up the World Trade Center with a suitcase full of dynamite was persuaded to give up by Bolz's team. And then there was the paranoid Panamanian sailor Luis Robinson, who hijacked a Vermont Transit bus and ordered it driven to Kennedy Airport. There he demanded a plane to Havana and $6 million in exchange for the release of the terrified bus passengers—two of whom he had already murdered during the first chaotic moments of the hijacking Bolz's crew negotiated for hours, playing for time, and finally persuaded Robinson to surrender.

In its nine-year existence, Bolz's negotiating team has handled more than 200 incidents. Except for one distraught male who committed suicide in a Broadway dress shop—he was on the verge of surrender, thought Bolz—the team has not lost a single hostage, hostage-taker, or cop. At least, not after the negotiating team established contact with the hostage-holder.

Negotiation is no panacea," says Bolz in his office. "It's another tool at the commander's disposal, in addition to sharpshooters, tear gas, assault teams. What we suggest is that police response *begin* with negotiation. It's nonviolent and there's less chance of hostages being hurt, less chance of cops being hurt. The perpetrator's well-being is also important to us. Often he's only going through a transitional situation; given help and an opportunity to readjust, he can return to a normal productive life. He can take care of his family and himself. Blow these people away and you wind up with more people in the welfare rolls. That's the cold, statistical point of view. But you also have to remember: you cannot bring back life. That's the idea that runs through our whole program.''

Bolz's office is a cluttered cell tucked away on the 11th floor of the fortresslike New York Police Department headquarters, just north of the Brooklyn Bridge. An overburdened coat tree in the corner is crowned with the baseball cap Bolz habitually wears while negotiating. An ancient, hand-cranked siren lies on the floor in front of some file cabinets. (Bolz and his wife are zealous weekend antique hunters.) A budless, dust-laden geranium endures a kind of endless autumn on the office windowsill. Wedged in beside it are a portable television set (with an American flag attached to the aerial) and a police band radio that fritzes and crackles with news of the latest stickup. Periodically, Boltz's voice cuts dead, mid-sentence, and he sits frozen, his head cocked toward the radio like a robin listening for the sound of another worm gnawing into the Big Apple's pulpy flesh.

When he has to leave the office—on his lunch break—Bolz drives the few blocks to his favorite hangout so as not to lose precious minutes retrieving his car in the event of a hostage emergency. The gray Dodge sedan is a veritable rolling arsenal of equipment, some of it esoteric, some downright quirky. Its trunk is packed to the brim. There is Bolz's bullet-proof vest, a gas mask, several cans of Mace, pairs of goggles, a bullhorn, and various coils of rope, including a 200-foot length for rappelling down buildings. There is also a carbine and a shotgun, adhesive tape, a wedge for holding doors open, a generator for powering a telephone hookup, a pair of binoculars, assorted hand tools, including gear for picking a lock, a straight-edge razor, a dental mirror (for peering around corners), two children's toy periscopes (same purpose), and, for listening through walls, a stethoscope—Bolz's latest addition to his continually evolving kit. The trunk also holds envelopes of instant soup, lest the night grow long and the stomach empty. Dictionaries in several languages and copies of the Bible and the Koran offer other means of communicating with hostage-takers. Snuggled next to the tire jack lies a loose-leaf binder with documents that gain Bolz access to restricted areas at New York City airports. The list goes on and on. There are also two tape decks: one for recording the negotiation so it can be studied later (the entire situation is also videotaped, when possible); the other for playing music that Bolz has found an excellent mood manipulator. More than one hostage-holder has surrendered to the soaring strains of Wagner's *Ride of the Valkyries.*

The overwhelming majority of hostage incidents arise from domestic squabbles, burglaries, and holdups, and most—as many as 2,000 a year in New York City—are effectively defused by regular police response. The situation has to have ripened for an hour or so, to a standoff, before Bolz brings in his team. This happens roughly 25 to 30 times a year, which would be an average of more than twice a month if so many incidents weren't clustered in March—or April, if spring has been slow to arrive. "People are coming out of the doldrums of winter, getting over cabin fever," is Bolz's explanation for the seasonal epidemic. "A lot of people want to put themselves into a catharsis." Not incidentally, springtime is also the suicide season, and Bolz sees a connection. "Many hostage incidents are subconscious attempts at suicide. The hostage-takers haven't got the guts to shoot themselves, so they get into a situation where a cop will do it for them."

In its broadest terms, Bolz describes the technique of hostage negotiation as a matter of managing and manipulating anxiety, the ultimate goal being to reduce it. "Basically, the man holding the hostages is going through a crisis. Crisis creates anxiety. Whether he's a bank robber who grabs some hostages as he comes into confrontation with the police, or an emotionally disturbed person who has taken the hostages as a means of getting attention, he's completely up in the air. What we try to do is to bring the hostage-holders down. First of all, we try to communicate that they're not going to be hurt. Hostage-holders are afraid that they're going to be killed. Don't forget that. It's the main thing that keeps them from surrendering. They see guys out there with shotguns. Their perception is that they've played the game and lost by the rules. 'The cop is the good guy. I'm the bad guy. Now I get shot.'"

Bolz moved into the hangar at Floyd Bennett Field, an antiquated city airport, from which the emergency service was operating—and which is still used for emergency service and negotiating-team training. Through simulations and role-playing, officers were taught to depersonalize situations, to withdraw their own egos from the negotiation process, to make it possible for concessions to be made to a hostage-taker without a cop fearing a loss of his own status. Officers were instructed in the interpretation—and communication—of body language nuances, as well as verbal strategies that might reinforce or stabilize a gunman's mood.

Bolz's original team was 25 strong, a group of officers ranging in age from 27 to 50, all of them members of the elite detective division. A few were women—who have seen some action and proved invaluable. Only a female negotiator could have provided the sisterly sympathy that finally induced a young parochial schoolgirl to release a nun she had taken hostage. But in general, from Bolz's experience, women are simply too disturbing to both sexes for use in hostage work. Men have difficulty giving up to a "mere woman," notes Bolz, and when a woman has seized hostages, he encounters an even greater obstacle: "I don't care how good or bad our negotiator looks," says the captain, "the female perpetrator will perceive her as looking prettier—and jealousy will start to build."

What makes a good negotiator? Dr. Schlossberg, now retired from the police department and in private practice, stresses Bolz's glibness. "He's an easy talker, very open, very much on the surface. There's little that he holds back." Bolz himself looks for a negotiator's ability to draw out the other person. "He has to be a good listener," he emphasizes, "but enough of a talker so that he can stimulate the perpetrator to talk. Kind of like a talk-show host."

Certain restraints on the dialogue, however, must be upheld. The hostage-taker can be reassured that he will not suffer bodily harm upon surrender, but no effort should be made to cajole him into thinking that he will walk away free. Seductive lies may coax one gunman into surrendering, but ultimately a reputation for dishonesty undermines the credibility of the entire hostage unit.

There are a few other nonnegotiable absolutes. In no circumstances will Bolz provide a hostage-taker with firearms. Nor will he ever yield to the temptation to substitute police officers for the panicky and terrified hostages. Similarly, wives, relatives, friends, and priests are not encouraged as stand-in negotiators. In Bolz's view, they only tend to inflame a situation that is already charged with too much emotion. As Schlossberg has observed, "If the perpetrator thought his mother loved him, or if he believed in the teachings of the church, he wouldn't be doing what he's doing."

Both Bolz and Schlossberg use a Freudian term to zero in on another key element in hostage situations: transference. It is a volatile component because its influence can go either way. On the one hand, transference bonds hostages and their captor in a curious alliance that first permits but then greatly complicates the negotiation process. In its extreme form, the subservient loyalty of hostages to the man or woman threatening their lives is called the Stockholm syndrome—so named after a Swedish bank robbery and siege during which hostages actually stood guard against the police who were attempting their rescue while their captor caught up on some sleep.

In one critical sense, transference works to the distinct advantage of the hostages. "If a person intends to kill, there's nothing you can do about it," Bolz explains. "But if a person takes a hostage, it's not very likely that he intends to kill that person. A hostage has value only for the audience he can create." This was the fundamental insight that allowed for the development of negotiating strategy in the first place. Time is on the side of the cops. The longer a hostage is held, the less likely it is that his captor will turn and kill him.

A dramatically different kind of transference can also develop between the hostage-taker and the cop attempting to reason with him. "The negotiator almost begins to act as the perpetrator's advocate," Bolz explains. "Whatever the perpetrator is doing, the negotiator is right behind him in terms of anxiety. He fluctuates with him. We encourage this kind of transference." The process, says Bolz, helps to attune and sensitize the negotiator to shifts and nuances in the hostageholder's mood—but it requires careful monitoring. It's one reason the hostage unit always works in teams of two. The backup negotiator is available to lean over the primary negotiator's shoulder, acting as a kind of therapist, regrounding the frontline man in the reality outside the perpetrator's troubled imagination. There's another reason for the backup negotiator: stress. One negotiator suffered a heart attack right on the scene. Another collapsed immediately after a hostage incident was successfully resolved.

GERARD I. NIERENBERG

Reading 4–2
The Use of Questions
in Negotiating

Asking questions is an effective way to uncover your opposer's thoughts and to assist him in the formation of his ideas. Questions permit you to channel the stream of conversation in any direction you may choose—you can make the conversational stream return to you. Questions are not only a window on the opposer's mind; they are implements for perception. As the playwright Eugene Ionesco comments, "It is not the answer that enlightens, but the question." Asking a question is like sharpening a pencil: Each apt question helps to whittle down the problem.

HOW TO FORMULATE QUESTIONS

Subconsciously your opposer realizes the tremendous force that is potentially contained in questions. Therefore, if the questioning process is not handled in an understanding way, it can cause great anxiety in the person being questioned. This anxiety is a sign that one feels that one's self-esteem, self-regard, or person is endangered. If your opposer shows signs of anxiety during the questioning process, you should do something about it—you should act immediately to remove the source of discomfort. You can progress into another area or eliminate the uncertainty of the question by making your purpose clear. As Dr. George Gallup points out, "When you start asking questions, the other person immediately wonders, 'Why does he want to know?'" One way to help eliminate this doubt is by laying a foundation for the question in advance. This will help put the other's mind at ease, because you have told him what you are going to try to achieve. You have given him

Reprinted from Gerard I. Nierenberg, *Creative Business Negotiating*. Used with permission of the author.

some insight into what you are doing and why you are doing it; that is, not "Where did you get that tie?" but "I would like to buy a tie like yours. Where did you get it?"

Creating anxiety can also be avoided by giving attention to transitions. When it is necessary for you to change subjects, know in what direction you want to proceed, making sure the shift is smooth and logical. Finally, be sensitive to the knowledge that the questioning process causes reactions in the other person's mind and be aware of his reactions. Comprehend what you are trying to evoke in the other person's mind. Don't ask questions haphazardly without regard to possible consequences. Remember the story of the young lawyer who had a witness on the stand.

"Did you see the alleged fight start?"

"No."

"You did not arrive on the scene until the altercation was over?"

"That is correct."

Rather than be satisfied with his cross-examination and stop it there, the lawyer continued. "Then how do you know that the defendant bit off part of the plaintiff's ear?"

"I saw him spit it out."

Some people have divided questions into categories: what questions to ask, how to phrase them, and when to ask them. They have said, for example, that if a question was put one way you might get a worthwhile contribution; put another way, however, the question might infuriate or confuse the opposer or cause him to pull away. Let us consider these arbitrary categories briefly. They permit some useful insights, in spite of the fact that they do not actually help us to formulate a particular question for a specific requirement.

What

Questions should not offend. They are not disciplinary measures, nor should they show signs of leadership. Questions should be relevant to help form new meanings and insights and help provide new "experiences." When an employee comes in late and you say, "Do you know what time it is?" you do not really want to know what the time is, you want to discipline him, you want to show who is boss. An entirely different way to handle the situation is to start by asking, "Do you have any problem that is causing you to be late, and can I help with it?" Perhaps difficulty at home has caused his tardiness.

How

Questions should be nonforcing; they should not put a person in a spot. St. John reminds us, "It is the modest, not the presumptuous inquirer, who makes a real and safe progress." As I have mentioned before, if you lay a foundation as to why you want the information, you will help to eliminate anxiety. If you are dealing with a question concerning the future, it is important that you recognize what you are looking for: Are you asking in terms of *evidence* or in terms of *estimates*? The one asks for facts, the other for opinion. Finally, phrase your questions so that the answer that you want is easier; for example, if you are selling soda, ask, "Do you want the large glass?" rather than "Do you want the small or large glass?"

When

If you want to gain control of a conversation or overcome an interruption, a question can be used. First, incorporate the interruption into your next question. Let us say a telephone call from the buyer's wife interrupts a 15-minute sales talk just before the close. You cannot start the sales presentation all over again. You might say, "Look, the big decisions we reserve for our wives, but we still have to make the little business decisions, don't we? We still have to decide whether to buy 300 tractors this year. As I was saying, with 300 tractors. . . ."

Second, if you incorporate the last statement of a group with your question, this can lead the group thinking back to where you want it applied. You will find it a very useful questioning process. For example, you have called a conference for the purpose of getting some information on a *production* problem. For an hour after the conference has started they are still discussing the *supply* problem. Try, at the appropriate time saying where you honestly can, "Jim, can you apply the same insight you have shown for the supply problem to the production problem?" You have them back on your track.

As useful as a classification approach to questions seems to be, it fails to show how to formulate questions for your conversations. Let us consider a different method. What purposes does a question serve in the communication process? This avenue can provide useful insights and can be helpful in enabling you to compose questions.

Questions appear to be able to be divided into five basic functions:

Five Functions of Questions
1. Cause attention. Provide preparatory conditions for the operation of the other's thinking. Example: "How are you?"
2. Get information. Provide questioner with information. "How much is it?"
3. Give information. Provide the other with information. "Did you know you could handle this?"
4. Start thinking. Cause the other's thinking to operate. "What would your suggestion be on this?"
5. Bring to conclusion. Bring the other's thinking to a conclusion. "Isn't it time to act?"

There are advantages to this form of approach in considering the questioning process. Understanding that a question can serve one or more of these functions allows you to prepare a series of functional questions which can be used during the course of a negotiation. Having a reserve of functional questions ready at any time will permit you to direct the stream of conversation in any manner you want. You can make up several questions that will help guide your overall strategy. At the same time, under each individual tactic, have several questions ready for moment-to-moment guidance. Even where the opposer is doing most of the talking, you can safely permit this because with the use of a question you can always obtain conversational control. Let us consider each separate function of questions:

Function I. To Cause Attention

When the commuter that you meet asks you the question "Beautiful morning, isn't it?" this is more or less devised to break your preoccupation. Many of the ritual questions (i.e., "How are you?") that are asked are under this function. Here are some specific examples: "Wouldn't it be wonderful . . . ?" "Would you mind . . . ?" "Could you help me . . . ?" "By the way, how often have I . . . ?" "How many times have I . . . ?" "May I . . . ?" "Could you tell me . . . ?" "If you would be kind enough . . . ?" You can see that in this function of questions there is little that would cause any anxiety.

Function II. To Get Information

These are questions designed to obtain information. Some words that lead off this type of question are as follows: *who, what, when, where, should, shall, could, is, do, for instance, will.* Anxiety can be caused if the reason for wanting the information cannot be ascertained.

Function III. To Give Information

We know very well that many times questions contain and give a great deal of information in spite of the fact that they might seem to be grammatically structured to get information. For example, take the desperation questions "Why was I born?" and "What is there to live for?" These contain a great deal of information which anyone listening to them can readily understand. Questions can accuse. There is the story of an automobile that ran down a hill and hit the side of a house. The mother inside immediately looked for her young son. She shouted the question, "George, where are you?" A timid voice replied, "Mother, I didn't do anything." Other questions serving this function might be used to bring hidden objections out into the open: "All right, why don't you want to go?" Some other illustrations are: "Do you like being pushed?" "Was it also . . . ?" "Can *any* of *your* problems be solved?" "Oh, really?" Sometimes you want to sustain the interest of the other person and say: "Have you ever . . . ?" Or perhaps you want to put the listener on the defensive: "Isn't it so . . . ?" Some words that are used in these forms of questions are: *because, if you, did you, would you.*

    The questioning process itself is a way of supplying information. Questions have a kind of educational force that carries through. They carry information along with them. People who are asked the same question twice may answer differently a second time because their attitude has been changed by having been asked the question the first time. Questions asked in a certain series have a tendency to carry information—for example, "Is there justice in the United States?" "Is there justice for all?" "Is there justice for the blacks?" Follow-up questions tend to give more and more information.

Anxiety is caused by Function III when the replier feels that the information given is threatening.

Function IV. To Start Thinking

These are such questions as: "Have you ever . . . ?" "Are you now . . . ?" "How much would you guess that it sells for?" "Aren't we lucky to . . . ?" "To what extent . . . ?" "If I were to . . . ?" "Is there . . . ?" Some of the words used in these questions are: *how, why, did, would, describe.* Anxiety can be a by-product of the thinking if the replier feels endangered.

Function V. To Bring to a Conclusion

This function can cause anxiety when you want to lead the listener where you want him to go and where he might not want to go. This may happen when you start out with questions such as: "Isn't it true?" "Which do you prefer?" "Is this the only way?" "Where would you rather eat, here or there?" "Was it also because . . . ?"

THREE OR MORE FUNCTIONS IN A QUESTION

A question can also contain three functions. Sometimes such questions can be misleading or dangerous; they become rather confusing since they are loaded with so many functions. For example, "Do you think that the sale of old police horses to meat packers should go through or not?" In this case a "No" answer and a "Yes" answer can mean the same thing. "No" might mean that the sale should not go through. "Yes" might mean that the sale should not go through. A typical three-function question would be gaining attention, giving information, and asking for a conclusion. The telephone receptionist's question was an example of this. Many salesmen's closing questions are three-function types: "Would you mind looking this over to see if the information is correct, then would you sign here?" It contains I, IV, and V functions.

OLD QUESTION CLASSIFICATIONS AS COMPARED TO NEW USE OF QUESTION FUNCTION

Let us compare some of the question classifications and see how they reveal the functions they contain. The following are a list of question classifications: The first group are questions that have been classified as manageable; the second, classified as difficult. You will notice that the first group have I,

II, and IV functions, while the second group tend to have III and V functions. This does not imply that you should not use questions with III or V functions, but merely that it is more difficult to give the listener information and make him come to a conclusion by the questioning process than it is to get information, start thinking, and gain attention.

QUESTION CLASSIFICATIONS THAT ARE MANAGEABLE

Functions

IV   Open-end questions cannot be answered with a simple "Yes" or "No." They usually begin with *who, what, when, where, why,* or *how*—for example, "Why did you do it?"

II–IV   *Open questions* invite the other person to express his thinking freely. It gives him latitude in answering. "Will you tell me, Tom, how this looks to you?"

II–IV   *Leading questions* gives the direction of the reply. "Then couldn't you send a letter to Tom?"

IV–II   *Cool questions* have little emotion involved. "Now, what would you say that the next step in the solution of this arithmetic problem is?"

IV   *Planned questions* are part of an overall logical sequence thought out in advance. "And after you take care of the first part what would your suggestion be on this?"

I–II   *Treat questions* let the respondent know that he can help when he expresses his view. "Could you help me, Joe, with one of your excellent suggestions?"

IV–II   *Window questions* help you look into the other person's mind. "Why do you feel that way about her?"

IV–II   *Directive questions* focus on a particular, understood point. "How excessive do you think the cost might be?"

Functions

IV   *Gauging questions* give feedback about the state of the other person. "How do you feel about that?" "How does that strike you?"

QUESTION CLASSIFICATIONS THAT CAN CAUSE DIFFICULTY

Functions

III–V   *Close-out questions* force the other person into your preconceived point of view. "If you were convinced that the action was destructive for you, you wouldn't take it, would you?"

III–V   *Loaded questions* put the other person on the spot, whatever his answer may be. "Do you mean to tell me that your

	solution is the only solution to this problem, and the right one?"
III–V	*Heated questions* reflect a good deal of feeling toward the respondent. "Having already spent a great deal of time discussing your problem, don't you think we should move on?"
I–V	*Impulse questions* just occur to questioner. "By the way, what is your impression of how your boss would handle this situation?"
IV–V	*Trick questions* would appear to require a frank answer, but are actually going to put the respondent on the spot. "What are you going to do about your marital problem—get a divorce, separation, or annulment?
III–V	*Reflective or mirror questions* simply reflect another point of view, or your own. "Here's how I see it, don't you agree with me?"
V–III	"You think this plan would not work because it is too costly?"

GRAMMATICAL QUESTIONS AND THE FUNCTIONS

There are four ways of grammatically structuring a question, and some of these structures lend themselves more easily to one function of a question than another. First, by placing the subject after the auxiliary verb we can make a Function IV type question: "Are you going?" Or a Function II question: "Did you study last night?" The second way of making a question is by using an interrogative pronoun or adverb: *who, which, where, how.* These usually are a Function II or IV question: "Who studied last night?" The third type of question is formed by adding an interrogative statement to a declarative statement: "You did study, didn't you?" These can be used for a Function V question. The fourth way of making a question is by putting a question mark at the end of a declarative statement: "You've been studying?" This can be used for Function V questions.

Any of these four ways can be used for the Function I questions and the Function III questions. Further, when we consider speech emphasis and content, we can see how almost any one of these grammatical structures can be used for any of the five functions of questions.

PROCESS OF QUESTION CONSTRUCTION

Understanding the function of a question is still only one aspect of a process. The framing of a question requires other abilities. It involves your intuitive feelings for the situation and your ability to devise a question that takes into account a number of conscious and unconscious clues that the situation bears at the moment.

Many examples of forms of question have been provided. Still it must be borne in mind that the form of any spoken question can be varied by accent, innuendo, emphasis, and the other speaking devices that we use to carry on and emphasize aspects of conversation. The full context of a written message can also be varied in similar manners.

The simple use of the question "How are you?" can be changed from one function to another by emphasis:

"How are you?" No emphasis on any particular word. Causes attention. (I)
"How *are* you?" Gets information. (II)
"How are *you*?" Gives information. (III)
"*How* are you?" Starts thinking. (IV)
"*But* how are you?" Brings to a conclusion. (V)

Then there are situations in which a question can serve all five functions as example. Have you ever been in a restaurant when the waiter would like you to sign the check? He comes over and asks, "Another drink?" He is doing this basically to gain your attention (I), and also at the same time he wants information (II) to another function. He may want you to leave (III). This question could start you thinking (IV), and finally it could have you come to a conclusion (V). Therefore when you question, remember, in the context of the situation and of the moment it is capable of being interpreted as serving any function by the listener. The responsibility is on the speaker. If the conversation misfires he must be prepared with understanding and alternatives.

HOW FUNCTIONAL QUESTIONS OPERATE

It would appear that we cause much less anxiety by the functions I, causing attention, II, getting information, and IV, starting the other person to thinking, rather than III, giving information, and V, bringing the other person to a conclusion. Let us see how this operates in day-to-day situations. Let us say that it is possible to ask another person his opinion without putting him on the spot or forcing him to respond, as: "Would you like to add anything further?" (a I- and II-function question) rather than "What is your opinion?" (a V question). Another example: As a door-to-door salesman, you ask, "Would you like to buy the Encyclopaedia Britannica?" That is a V question. The answer may be "No," and the door slams in your face. Instead, you might start off "Do you have any children in school?" to gain the attention of the person and get information (I and II functions).

The telephone company spent millions of dollars sending representatives around to suggest different methods of answering the switchboard. Some receptionists, they found, answered the phone with "Who's calling?" That tends to be antagonistic to some people. They feel that the person will only be in to certain people (III function). The suggestion was made that the receptionist ask instead, "May I ask who's calling?" This gains attention (I), and more or less gives the other person a choice in answering. A still better way of answering the phone might be "May I tell Mr. Smith who's calling?" This is a multiple-function question, containing a I, a III, and a V function. It gains attention, provides you with information that Mr. Smith is there, and allows the caller to come to a conclusion. You have the right to say "Yes" or "No."

Let us compare other types of questions as illustrations. "You're not working now, are you?" has a III and a V function. Another way of handling it would be "Are you looking for a job right now or waiting for a while?" This contains two IV functions. Another illustration, "Do you quarrel to settle your domestic conflicts?" is a III and a V function. Another way of handling this might be "When conflicts arise, how do you try to settle them?" which is a III and a IV function.

In an interviewing situation, there are questions that you as an interviewer should ask. Your purpose is to gain attention, certainly to get information, and start thinking. Therefore questions designed around these three functions are quite useful, and if you find that functions III and V are coming through, then you should reexamine the type of questions you are asking. Let us assume that we were using the type of question we should not ask, as "I assume you wouldn't smoke pot?" That is a question that contains a V function and a III function. It might better be asked, "Mr. Smith, would you care to discuss your opinions on marijuana?" This contains a IV and a II function. Another way is "Can you tell me anything I've missed that you might like to bring out?" That is a IV and a II function. The open questions, which are II and V functions, also fall into this category. In interviewing, the II and IV functions are all-important.

THE IMPORTANCE OF FUNCTIONAL QUESTIONS IN PREPARING FOR NEGOTIATIONS

To reemphasize, in the course of a negotiation set up an overall group of functional questions, questions that cover the entire negotiation from start to finish, each one performing its various functions at the particular time. Also have small clusters of functional questions that can serve the immediate purposes and move the negotiation tactically over your entire strategic plan. You can then let your opposer do almost all the talking. You can control the direction of the negotiation by thoughtfully interjecting a question now and again.

HOW TO ANSWER (OR NOT) WHEN QUESTIONED

Professor Chandler Washburne in an excellent article in the General Semantics magazine *ETC.*, March 1969, on the vital subject of how to answer when questioned, ends his discussion with "The future of this much-needed science is in your hands.'' I would like to propose a similar statement to you and show you some of the various applications that might be considered. These are not offered as suggestions to follow but merely as examples of alternatives that you may have been subjected to or used on others. The field may be divided as follows: (1) leave the other person with the assumption that he has been answered, (2) answer incompletely, (3) answer inaccurately, (4) leave the other person without the desire to pursue the questioning process further.

1. Leaving the Other Person with the Assumption That He Has Been Answered

In the questioning process we deal with two sets of assumptions—those of the questioner and those of the person questioned. In answering we should try to handle the questioner's assumptions and attempt to leave out our own. An army captain once made the wrong assumption when faced with a question. He had been in charge of his company's officers' club funds, which he had slowly misappropriated over a long period of time. While in the PX one day he was accosted by two military policemen. One put his hand on the captain's shoulder and said, ''Captain, would you come outside with us?'' The officer replied, ''Could you excuse me for one moment?'' He went into the men's room at the rear of the PX and shot himself. The MP's were astonished. They had come in to tell the captain his jeep was parked by a fire hydrant. He would be alive today, but possibly behind bars, if he had made an effort to consider the question on the basis of the other person's assumptions rather than his own. He might have answered the MP's question with a challenging ''Why?'' and acted accordingly.

2. Answering Incompletely

An incomplete answer is one in which we cover a much more limited area than the questioner intends. Let us say you have just had dinner at the home of a newly married friend and his wife has cooked the meal. The next day the husband asks you, ''Well, how did you like my wife's dinner?'' Your answer might be, ''She certainly sets a beautiful table. The silver was especially fine. Was it a wedding present?''

Use restricted meanings to the questions asked. Sometimes in a negotiation if details are presented and both sides are concerned that they could never agree on the specifics, they will ask questions which are subject to restricted answers rather than obtain an absolute rejection which they do not want. When, for example, the question was asked of the manufacturer, ''Could you handle this order?'' the manufacturer, considering a restricted meaning, said, ''Certainly we can handle an order of this sort.'' Neither side was asking or receiving an answer to the question of when delivery could commence.

As previously stated, you should ask questions considering the level that you wish to receive answers on. If you ask a high-level question you will probably get a high-order, abstract answer. A lower-level question will elicit more precise, detailed information. In answering questions, however, this process can be reversed. When you are asked a high-order question, you can give a low-order answer by prefacing your answer with "Well, to be more fundamental . . ." When the question is asked, "How do you think the disarmament talks are going?" the answer might be "As skilled diplomats, our representatives are in direct and constant communication with the representatives of the other side." A low-order question can be given a high-level answer, as when asked, "Why didn't the president of Columbia take more immediate action against the S.D.S. students when they started their disruptive activity?" The answer might be "Rugged individualism is dead in the United States." There was a man fishing in a bayou in Louisiana. Two men came up to him and asked if there were any snakes in the water. The fisherman assured them there was none. After the men had taken a swim, one asked the fisherman, "How come there aren't any snakes?" "The alligators ate them all," he answered.

Another method of answering incompletely is to sidestep the question. Let us say that you are a salesman and are in the middle of your presentation. At this point the customer asks, "How much does it cost?" Your object is not to answer at this time; you wish to complete your presentation before revealing the price. You might reply, "The dollar value is what I'm sure you're interested in. Therefore, let me round out the details and present the various costs so that I may more fully be able to answer your question." You might also say, "When I've finished my presentation of the entire article, I'm looking forward to asking your opinion of the price." Sometimes use of the restricted meaning can be of assistance; tell him the price of the part that is being demonstrated at the time, then go on with the presentation.

3. Answering Inaccurately

Use an analogy beginning "As I understand your question . . ." and then set forth your own version of the question; or begin with "A similar situation . . ." and state a situation that you are prepared to compare it to; or set forth a typical analogy to which you would like to relate the question. You can also change the question by substituting a different question. Suggest that you are going to answer and deftly change the subject: "I thought you might say that, and you deserve an answer. But before I reply, let me ask this question." "Yes, I agree with the intent of the question, but let me rephrase it slightly." If the questioner is still unsatisfied and says, "I don't think the answer is pertinent," your answer might be "Perhaps you're right. How would you phrase it?" or "How would you have stated it?" or "Would you prefer that I put it this way?" or "How would you like me to say it?"

4. Leaving the Other Person without the Desire to Pursue the Questioning Process Further

State many answers without committing yourself to any one. For example: "Why can't we improve railroad service?" Answer: "When we consider shifting population, the change in the economic conditions of people in various sections of the area, the failure of the state to supply necessary funds, the federal government's preoccupation with supersonic jets, labor's inclination to give as little for the dollar as possible . . .''

State that the answer to the question is that the question cannot be answered: ''That's one of those unanswerable questions.'' ''The future holds the key to that problem.'' ''It would serve no purpose in this instance to speculate on the future.''

Give a ''nothing'' answer: ''That *was* a dinner.'' ''*What* a dress.''

Use disarming praise: If the mother of a girl asks a reluctant bachelor, ''What are your views on marriage?'' he could answer, ''If I could only be sure that all mothers looked as charming as you. Tell me, how do you manage to do it?''

If the question cannot be refuted logically, use a remark designed to stigmatize the opposer's point of view as being below notice: ''Isn't it the duty of government to assist its needy citizens?'' Answer: ''Do-gooders are taking away people's initiative.''

Use humor in answering questions: ''Who were the first people to discriminate against you?'' (This was asked of a Jewish comedian.) Answer: ''My parents.''

Counterattack on a point quite irrelevant to the point at issue: ''Isn't it the duty of government to assist its needy citizens?'' Answer: ''Some people want to destroy free enterprise.''

Don't answer. The method used can take many forms: You are distracted; you cause a distraction; you intentionally continue creating a distraction by choosing another question or appointing someone else to answer the question.

Consider what occurs when a person asks a question. He has problems too—and look at the interrogator's problems! He lacks the depth and the knowledge of the circumstances that the other party may have to answer the question and he may even lack knowledge of the vocabulary used to describe the circumstances that are involved. He may not really have decided on what he wants to know, and he is not at ease in asking his question. The inquirer may also feel that he cannot reveal the true question because of its sensitive nature. He may also have prejudices against various groups or occupations and consequently may avoid giving a true picture of his own feelings. And finally, the inquirer may lack the confidence in the respondent's ability to deal with the question. These elements must be considered as natural barriers in the questioning process.

JACQUES LALANNE

Reading 4–3
Attack by Question

Questions have their place. Anyone who has seen a skillful lawyer break down a carefully constructed lie knows the value of effective questions, or cross-questions, as weapons.

But in everyday conversation, questions are usually a poor substitute for more direct communication. Questions are incomplete, indirect, veiled, impersonal and consequently ineffective messages that often breed defensive reactions and resistance. They are rarely simple requests for information, but an indirect means of attaining an end, a way of manipulating the person being questioned.

> Where did you go?
> Out.
> What did you do?
> Nothing.

This classic parent/child exchange illustrates in 10 words how ineffective questions may be. The parent isn't really asking for information, but making a charge. What come across is: "You know you're not supposed to cross the street," or, "I told you not to go anywhere after eight o'clock," or, "You got your dress dirty again."

The child's answers, brief as they are, are just as devious. He's learned the hard way that a straightforward answer is likely to lead to trouble. So he uses evasion—"Out," or a half truth—"Nothing."

"WHEN DID YOU GET HOME?"

It's no surprise that questions make most of us feel uneasy. They remind us of times we'd rather forget. As children, before we learned the small skills of excuse and evasion, questions were often a prelude to accusations, advice, blame, orders, etc. At home we'd be asked what we did, or what we didn't do, and one seemed as bad as the other. At school, most questions seemed designed to ferret out what we didn't know rather than what we did.

When we become adults, the questions keep coming. As spouses, salespeople, bosses, even friends, we all use questions to manipulate in some way, convince of some truth, or convict of some error.

"Have you spoken to him about it?" often means, "You should speak to him, and soon." "When did you get home last night?" usually means, "You should have called me as you promised."

A person asking questions may feel in control of a conversation, but that type of conversation isn't very nourishing for the questioner, either, because he's not really involved. Instead of examining our own feelings, as questioners we focus attention on the other person. We replace what is going on inside us with what is happening outside; facts take on more importance than feelings.

For example, instead of saying, "I'm disappointed," we often ask, "When did you decide?" Joy and gratitude remain veiled behind "How did you prepare all that?" and instead of showing that we are worried, we ask, "Where were you, for heaven's sake?"

"I WAS AFRAID . . ."

It's easy to fall into the question-answer conversational trap, and we'd be better off consciously avoiding it. When we feel a question coming on, we could start listening to ourselves, identify our real feelings and express them, rather than hiding them in a question.

Instead of asking coolly, "Are you going out tomorrow afternoon?," we can become involved by revealing, "I'd appreciate it if you took me downtown tomorrow." The question, "What were you doing there so late?," does not express our real feelings as much as, "I was afraid you'd been in an accident."

Personal disclosures of this kind involve risk. By showing our real feelings, we chance direct refusal or rejection. But we also create a warm climate for direct, fruitful contact with the other person—something the tepid questioning approach rarely accomplishes.

When a questioner has us in his clutches, we can break the spell by paying careful attention to the speaker's tone of voice, gestures, and other hints to see what the real message is, and then respond to that deeper meaning. Feedback establishes communication and lets it circulate.

It could work like this. "Where were you so late last night?" might be answered, "You seem quite worried about it," a response which opens the door for a discussion of what is really bothering the questioner. In answer to "Are you going out Friday night?," words such as "Maybe we can make plans for that night" get at the real message in considerably less time.

BEYOND THE QUESTION MARK

Here are some everyday questions that work better as honest statements:

What time is it?
I'm tired. I'd like to go home now.

Is it far?
I don't feel up to a long trip this weekend.

Do you love me?
I wish you'd spend more time with me. You work every day and read in the evenings.

How much did you pay?
I hope we have some money left for the rest of the week.

Is it good?
I need to know if you like my soup, if I made it the way you prefer.

SECTION FIVE

Integrative Bargaining: Strategy and Tactics

As noted above, integrative, or cooperative, bargaining occurs when both parties in a negotiation are working together toward common or convergent goals. For integrative bargaining to occur, the parties first must agree on the overall goal that they jointly share; the discovery rests on the accurate exchange of information, just the opposite of what is needed in distributive bargaining. Because this need to share, rather than to conceal, information is different from what we normally expect in negotiation; people often find it difficult to accept and do what is necessary for success in integrative bargaining. Simison, in his article "UAW Struggles with a New Idea: Cooperation," describes the political and perceptual difficulties experienced by the United Auto Workers union, a traditionally competitive group, in working toward a more collaborative position with the automobile manufacturers.

In part, integrative bargaining is a search for synergy, a way of pulling together into a new whole those things which were formerly separate. It involves, as Jones and Pfeiffer point out in "Synergy and Consensus-Seeking," learning to attend to things which are opposites or paradoxical and looking for what they have in common or that support each other rather than, as we more commonly do, attending to differences. The effort involves finding what is or can be shared and avoiding things that differentiate or divide. Hence, discussion works toward decision making by consensus rather than toward a vote. "Horse trading, which gives people what they want, is avoided in preference for package agreements, in which all can share, rather than compromise, in which all parties get less.

For successful integrative bargaining to happen, different strategies and tactics are needed. A brief synopsis of some key differences between competitive and cooperative bargaining are given by Glass and Foote in "Winning by Negotiation."

Finally, David Ewing in "How to Negotiate with Employee Objectors," offers an integrative bargaining approach to working with dissident and dissatisfied employees. Rather than ignoring these "employee objectors," as many employers are prone to do, Ewing suggests an approach that actively listens to their concerns and works toward finding a mutually acceptable solution that incorporates the employee's perspective. Using negotiating tactics in this way, and in this context, is integrative bargaining at its best.

ROBERT L. SIMISON

Reading 5–1

UAW Struggles with a New Idea: Cooperation

Detroit—For months, the big auto companies had been raising a public clamor for lower labor costs. Meanwhile, local union leaders were nervously facing reelection contests. It clearly was no time for the United Auto Workers union to appear indecisive.

Without waiting for a formal bid for new talks, therefore, the union declared last month that it will not renegotiate terms at General Motors Corp. or Ford Motor Co. At least, not right now. While this apparently hasn't discouraged Ford or GM, it did permit local union politicians to show their continued willingness to stand up to the companies, often a key to retaining office in the unions.

This accommodation to internal politics illustrates one of the most taxing dilemmas the UAW has had to face. Deeply worried by the U.S. auto industry's dismal situation, top union leaders have concluded they must adopt a new, cooperative stance to help the industry recover. The UAW, however, is an institution built on confrontation, not cooperation.

"We've been teaching our local leaders and our members all these years to be aggressive and militant toward the companies," says a high union official. "Now we have to turn around and undo all that."

It's a problem other unions face, too. In a number of industries, "strained economic circumstances are forcing the bargaining parties to reexamine the assumptions underlying the adversary principle, a foundation stone of American industrial relations," says Jack Barbash, a University of Wisconsin economics and industrial relations professor.

In the auto industry, both labor and management are rethinking their

117

traditional adversary relationship. "It's been us versus them for 40 years," says Lee A. Iacocca, chairman of Chrysler Corp. "As long as the golden goose kept getting bigger and bigger, it was okay to have a shootout every three years to see who got what piece. But now that it's getting smaller, we have to develop a new relationship based on cooperation."

But neither side is quite sure what that means. "We are in uncharted waters," Mr. Iacocca acknowledges. A union man ponders, "Where are we going to end up?"

The risk of failure is high. The UAW's latest package of concessions to help Chrysler, for example, stirred stiff resistance among some Chrysler workers, even though rejection might have bankrupted the company. "Many recent efforts have . . . foundered on the rocks of rank-and-file suspicion," Mr. Barbash comments. "Management, for its part, is reluctant to take a flexible view of management rights."

The U.S. auto industry is fundamentally restructuring itself to compete in a new, energy-conscious market that demands smaller, more fuel-efficient cars. This will pit Detroit more directly than ever against efficient foreign cars—made with lower labor costs.

Companies and the union have already joined this fight in a couple of ways. In public, they've formed a political alliance to press the government for limits on car imports. In the plants, labor and management are working together in joint committees to improve the cars' quality; superior quality has been a major contributor to imported cars' sales success.

The UAW has even been passing out bumper stickers that say, "UAW pride is quality, safety."

"Can you believe that?" a union man marvels. "Quality and safety used to be management's responsibility. We always had bumper stickers kicking management in the tail."

As an adversary, though, the UAW can do little to preserve its members' jobs, an issue of growing importance as the auto industry contracts, argues Douglas A. Fraser, UAW president. "We must have a more effective voice in the destiny of our members at all levels," he says.

Now, the UAW is trying to carve itself a role in management. Borrowing ideas from European and Japanese labor, the UAW has charted a course intended to involve workers in decision making, a clear break with American labor traditions. In doing so, they are imitating the Japanese, who credit much of their industrial success to labor-management cooperation. In the U.S. industry these loosely defined programs generally involve workers and supervisors in joint efforts to make jobs more interesting and more efficient and to boost productivity by ironing out production snags.

GM, Ford, and the UAW are all enthusiastic about initial success of these efforts. "We've found that people have a great deal more to contribute than their physical labor; they can contribute their ideas," says Peter J. Pestillo, Ford's vice president for labor relations. Adds Donald Ephlin, a UAW vice president, "The old adversary relationship was a win-lose situation. Employee involvement is a win-win situation."

In agreeing to $1.07 billion of wage and benefit reductions for Chrysler, the UAW has set a pattern of extracting a bigger management role in return. At Chrysler this includes a board seat for Mr. Fraser, access to sensitive financial data and some influence over plant closings and supervisory ratios. A parallel thrust is to make workers financial partners through employe stock purchase and profit-sharing plans.

This strategy is raising questions about the union's role. Both UAW and Chrysler officials attest to Mr. Fraser's absolute integrity in simultaneously sitting on the board and bargaining with the company. But some in the rank-and-file wonder how he does it, and few outsiders believe any other labor leader could credibly play both roles.

"It's very difficult to mix being a representative of the workforce with the responsibilities of being a corporate director," comments W. Michael Blumenthal, chairman of Burroughs Corp., who has written about the West German experience with labor directorships. "I'm sure any American labor leader who did this on a regular basis would risk being thrown out by his membership."

Similarly, the various "employee involvement" and "quality of work life" efforts have stirred controversy. The idea has been slow to catch on in the UAW, and both the union and the companies have found it necessary to declare that the programs aren't supposed to affect collective bargaining or grievance procedures. "We aren't abandoning the adversary role," the UAW's Mr. Ephlin maintains.

Moreover, UAW leaders run some risk of diluting the union's bargaining clout. "How do you conduct a slowdown or a walkout if you're all stockholders?" asks a union man.

And as an institution the UAW depends on a certain amount of "us versus them" rivalry. "It's easy for the top leadership to talk about becoming a mature, responsible union," says one union official. "But on the local level, you've got guys who have to run for office. They have to create an atmosphere of politics; that's the nature of our institution."

Flexible and pragmatic though the UAW may be, its new role clearly won't happen overnight. But as it does evolve, both the UAW and the auto industry are adhering to well-established public rituals for the workers' consumption.

For the companies' part, Roger B. Smith, GM chairman, warns that jobs are at stake. "We're going to have to come closer to working with the UAW every day now to get this industry's problems solved," he declares.

For the union's part, Mr. Fraser reassures the workers that GM's profits don't justify concessions just now. But he offers to listen to the industry and cooperate by getting an early start on new contract talks. "We always bargain based on economic realities," he says.

The workers themselves just may be receptive to the new direction, if not quite ready to settle for less. "Attitudes are changing," suggests a UAW man. "I think maybe the workers are getting tired of screaming at the foreman all the time."

J. E. JONES and
J. W. PFEIFFER

Reading 5-2

Synergy and Consensus-Seeking

There is a myth about group productivity that is sometimes humorously expressed as, "A camel is a horse put together by a committee." It is probably more accurate to say that a camel is a horse put together by a very bad committee. There is a tendency to think about the outcomes of group activity in terms of one's experience with an array of unproductive efforts rather than in terms of possibilities. Almost everyone has been a member of groups whose outcomes were less than dramatic.

Ordinarily, task groups are put to work without any effort being expended toward building the group as a functioning unit. The most common lack is processing how work gets done, discussing how members feel about what is happening, and exploring what they are willing to contribute. Individual members are presumed to know how to be effective group members, and democratic mechanics such as voting are presumed to result in collective judgments that are satisfactory because people are "involved."

One value that often gets introjected into persons who grow up in our culture is to win, to be number one, to beat out someone else, and this results in highly competitive behavior in group situations. There is a presupposition that competition gets better results. In ambiguous situations, individuals are likely to inject a competitive element because that posture in relation to other persons has been overlearned. This tendency is rationalized in statements such as, "It's a dog-eat-dog world," and "Free enterprise is the answer."

Closely related to the phenomenon of competition is the cognitive style that is sometimes referred to as "either-or" thinking. We tend to over-simplify situations by reducing them to dichotomies, to discrete, mutually exclusive categories, and to polar opposites. This way of looking at the world

Reprinted from John E. Jones and J. William Pfeiffer, eds., *The 1973 Annual Handbook for Group Facilitators* (San Diego, Calif.: University Associates, 1973). Used with permission.

gets translated into human relations in win-lose, zero-sum terms. "Either you're for me or you're against me." "Who's in charge?" "If he gets an A, that hurts my chances." "If I give it all away, I won't have anything left." "More of this means less of that." We often are impatient with paradoxes, such as "Giving is receiving," "Good and evil can coexist," and "Being unselfish is selfish."

Synergy means looking at what appears to be opposite or paradoxical in terms of its commonalities rather than its differences. It is looking for meaningful relationships between what are often thought of as dichotomous elements of a situation. It is an attempt to break out of the either-or mentality to look for bridging abstractions, to look for wholes rather than parts. One is thinking synergistically when such seeming opposites as work and play, sensuality and spirituality, now and not-now, aggression and kindness, etc. are seen as fused.

Applied to groups, the concepts of synergy means looking at outcomes in a nonzero-sum way. Collaboration in planning, problem-solving, etc., generates products that are often better than those of any individual member or subgroup; whereas competition often means creating not only winners but also powerful losers, who can make the price of winning high. Collaboration and competition are seen as meaningfully related processes, both of which can result in incremental outcomes owing to group interaction. Consensual validation of points of view held by individuals in interpersonal interchange can cause the outcome to exceed that of persons working parallel to each other. A synergistic outcome results from the "groupness" that is greater than the sum of the parts of the group.

Work groups can obtain synergistic results when the process of working heightens sharing and functional competition. The mechanics of democratic decision making get redefined to achieve consensus as the goal (members of the group reach *substantial* agreement, rather than unanimity) rather than splitting the group into a majority and one or more minorities around an issue. Conflict becomes viewed as an asset rather than something to be avoided. Winning becomes a group effort rather than an individual quest. Individuals who do not "go along" are seen as catalysts for improved production rather than as blockers. "Horsetrading" is viewed as failing to look at polarized points of view on a larger plane.

Consensus-seeking is harder work than formalistic modes of decision making, but the investment in energy expended to make the group function effectively without violating its members can have a dramatic payoff. A number of suggestions can be made about how consensus can be achieved.

1. Members should avoid arguing in order to win as individuals. What is "right" is the best collective judgment of the group as a whole.
2. Conflict on ideas, solutions, predictions, etc. should be viewed as helping rather than hindering the process of seeking consensus.

3. Problems are solved best when individual group members accept responsibility for both hearing and being heard, so that everyone is included in what is decided.
4. Tension-reducing behaviors can be useful so long as meaningful conflict is not "smoothed over" prematurely.
5. Each member has the responsibility to monitor the processes through which work gets done and to initiate discussions of process when it is becoming effective.
6. The best results flow from a fusion of information, logic and emotion. Value judgments about what is best include members' feelings about the data and the process of decision making.

A sculptor viewing a block of granite can see a figure surrounded by stone. In an analogous way, a decision that is best can be seen inside group effort, if we can find ways of chipping away the excess. Consensus-seeking offers promise of marshaling group resources to produce synergistic outcomes without denying the integrity of members.

ARIC PRESS with
CHARLES GLASS and
DONNA FOOTE

Reading 5–3
Winning by Negotiation

They were among the sacred texts of the Me Decade—books that told strivers to slip on their power shoes, square their assertive chins and intimidate their way to success. That ethos remains alive and well in America, but today hymnals to slash-and-parry narcissism are being replaced in bookstores by manuals on collaborative negotiation. The pacesetter is Herb Cohen's "You Can Negotiate Anything," a how-to-haggle blueprint that preaches the gospel of bargaining so that everyone wins—a message nearly lost in a book laced with enough manipulative ploys to make Niccolò Machiavelli nervous. Now from the Ivy League comes "Getting to Yes," a more coherent brief for "win-win" negotiations which, if it takes hold, may help convert the Age of Me to the Era of We.

The point of both books is to help the public understand bargaining as something more than starting at polar extremes and then splitting the difference. Their theories are not billed as just another tool for settling disputes; negotiation now is nothing short of a way of life, with benefits on the same grandiose scale. Cohen says negotiating skills can give a person control over his life. And Roger Fisher, a Harvard law professor and co-author of "Getting to Yes," maintains that his four points can lead to victory over insecurity. With such promises, they have found their slice of America's bottomless if-only market: if only I could lose 10 pounds, I'd find a perfect mate; if only I dressed better, I'd get a raise; if only I could write a self-help book, I'd get rich.

GROWTH INDUSTRY

Despite their obvious appeal to the magic-pill crowd, the books deserve to be treated seriously. "More and more occasions require negotiation," write Fisher and his co-author, William Ury. "Conflict is a growth industry." Generally, the response to confrontation—whether in a showroom or at a SALT talk—is to stiffen one's position or make an appeasing gesture in the interest of being nice. The former tactic, Cohen says, is bargaining "Soviet style,"—I must win, you must lose. The latter, Fisher says, is the "hostess phenomenon"—the only way to be a decent person is to give more. Both techniques are flawed. Instead, the experts say, negotiators must try to forge a settlement that satisfies both sides.

Which guidebook do you use to reach negotiators' nirvana? Fisher and Ury build from their experience with the Harvard Negotiation Project, an informal Cambridge group that explores bargaining issues. (Fisher was involved in negotiations to free the American hostages in Iran, and Ury has mediated a mining dispute in Kentucky.) Their strong suit is providing a comprehensive framework in which all problems can be approached. Cohen, who has advised the FBI, . . . Ronald Reagan and a host of private companies, is also interested in mutual-benefit results, although he admits that he's not above some Soviet-style shenanigans when the situation calls for them. Fisher and Ury, in short, are the guys you'd want on the other side of the table—they'd walk away rather than finagle. You'd want Cohen, if he must be there, on your side.

Sometimes Cohen's ploys seem a bit much—like hanging up the phone in mid-sentence so the other guy thinks you were cut off, thereby buying a few minutes to reorganize. But no technique has brought as much backlash as "the nibble." That maneuver consists of wearing down an opponent, appearing to agree, then asking for a final concession. Cohen uses the example of a customer leading a clothes salesman through 40 suits, then deciding on an expensive one. As the tailor is marking the trousers, the customer asks the weary salesman whether he's going to throw in a free tie. Simple negotiation or simply piggish? "I was showing why the 'nibble' works," pleads Cohen. "I was not advocating its use."

PERCEPTIONS

Fisher and Ury have no patience for such tactics. Instead, they focus on specific steps for successful negotiators to follow. First, separate the people from the problem. That means trying to develop a working relationship with an adversary by examining the other fellow's perceptions, clearly communicating your own, making allowances for emotional outbursts and giving the other side a stake in the outcome. (That last factor, by the way, is what makes the nibble work.) For all their emphasis on accommodation, however, the pair also acknowledge the value of aggressive behavior: "Do not let your desire to be conciliatory stop you from doing justice to your problem,'' they say.

With the negotiation concentrated on issues and not personalities, Fisher and Ury prescribe developing options that offer mutual gain. In other words, instead of carving the pie, expand it. The trick is to present choices. In Cohen's terms, if an employer can't meet a prospective employee's salary demand, he might find other means of compensation—a company car, a club membership or more life insurance.

The final stage comes when both sides have satisfied their common interests but some conflicts remain. This is the time, Fisher and Ury say, to settle by using objective criteria: ''Commit yourself to reaching a solution based on principle, not pressure.'' They cite an episode from a Law of the Sea conference when underdeveloped nations feared that large companies would pick off the best deep-sea mining sites for themselves. Instead, the nations agreed that each time private developers wanted to start a project, they had to present two sites to the United Nations mining group. The UN could then choose the one it wanted.

If some of these suggestions sound familiar, that's because the authors admit that what they have done is to collect bits of common wisdom and give them a structure. ''This is not an answer to every problem,'' says Fisher, ''but it gives you a coherent way of dealing with every problem.'' Mothers have known it for centuries: when two kids have to share a piece of cake, one of them gets to cut it—and the other gets first choice.

DAVID W. EWING

Reading 5–4

How to Negotiate with Employee Objectors

Two of your employees have told you that a certain company practice is unsafe. You know that a lot of thought went into establishing that practice, and you believe their suggestion to improve the situation is ridiculous. Your instinct is to ignore their complaint, laugh at their suggestion, or get rid of them. But you don't want any bad publicity or lawsuits on your hands, and you know you're playing with fire. So what do you do?

First of all, listen. Those so-called dissidents may be valuable and dedicated employees with very real concerns. Second, try to learn what motivates them to speak out, and let them know what your concerns are. Talking things over honestly and openly—but with certain goals in mind—can often point the way to a solution that everyone feels good about.

Few executives need to be told about the current proliferation of employees who criticize or resist management decisions. In one sense, the problem is an old one. Many types of recalcitrants have been with us for a long time— chronic complainers, malcontents, incompetents, and misfits. Perhaps they always will be. But other types of employee critics are relatively new to the business scene.

These are employees who, perceiving what appears to be wrongdoing, speak up against it; or who, believing a company action to be unwise or irresponsible, object to it; or who, convinced that a company practice or procedure is hazardous, resist it. Variously referred to as whistleblowers, dissenters, or dissidents, more often than not they are able and well-intentioned people. Not surprisingly, they stir the concern of many executives and fellow employees. To separate them from the traditional recalcitrants, I refer to them as *employee objectors*.

The increasing number of employee objectors is one reason for concern. While no quantitative studies of the trend have been made, increases in the frequency of lawsuits, complaints handled by employee assistance departments, executives' personal experiences, and other information suggest that employee objectors are at least 10 times more numerous today than they were, say, 10 or 15 years ago.

What is more, objectors may be costly to an organization. One well-known Eastern company has spent many millions of dollars defending itself against the legal attacks of a single determined objector, and its struggles may be far from over. An organization in Texas that tangled with an objector has received the not too kindly attention of dozens of newspapers, an eminent scientific publication, and scores of speakers at professional meetings. One chief executive of a giant corporation has had to make a long and painful court appearance in his company's defense to testify against a whistleblower. A struggle with dissidents in the construction of the San Francisco Bay Area's rapid transit (BART) system is the subject of a book written by a team of scholars.[1]

One could go on and on with such examples. Yet until only about a decade ago, around the time that the famous case of Pentagon whistleblower A. Ernest Fitzgerald caught national attention, such examples were almost unknown. However, the trend is not unexpected. Some time ago, Peter McColough, chairman of Xerox, predicted that the 1980s would be the decade of employee rights. And Peter E. Drucker made similar predictions. As both men saw, the sources of the trend had been in the making for some time.

A few companies, including Bank of America, Donnelly Mirrors, IBM, Northwestern National Bank, Pitney-Bowes, Polaroid, and Puget Sound Plywood Company, have been testing organizational procedures for responding to objectors.[2] In government, the Nuclear Regulatory Commission established in 1981 a carefully devised system for meeting "professional criticism" from its employees. But, of course, systems alone are not enough. Indeed, they are not the most important thing. The most useful, valuable, and economical management response to employee objectors is the one that only superiors and supervisors can make: prompt and effective person-to-person handling of the problem when it arises.

How should managers deal with able, well-intentioned employees who begin to "make waves" about perceived wrongdoings? In principle, the

---

[1] Robert M. Anderson, Robert Perrucci, Dan E. Schendel, and Leon E. Trachtman, *Divided Loyalties* (West Lafayette, Ind.: Purdue University, 1980).

[2] See David W. Ewing, "Due Process: Will Business Default?" *Harvard Business Review*, November-December 1982, p. 114.

wheel of this answer need not be reinvented, for it lies in techniques developed over the years by many negotiators and mediators. Some of the approaches have been written up in manuals on negotiation and conflict resolution. Of the many offerings, my own preference is the four-step sequence proposed by Roger Fisher and William Ury in their book, *Getting to Yes,* which considers negotiation in a wide range of government, business, and domestic settings (but not employee dissidence).[3] Here I will use that book's sequence, simplified and adapted to the employee objector problems. For the sake of simplicity, I illustrate its various steps with the three "mini-cases" shown in the ruled inserts.

DRAW OUT THE OBJECTOR'S PERSONAL CONCERNS

While you may see the facts, arguments, and positions advanced by an employee objector as inaccurate or misconceived, you would be wise to treat the person's fears and worries as important facts. This is the first principle of conflict resolution in the Fisher-Ury scheme and probably accounts for more successes with employee objectors than any other step. Get the objector's personal reactions into the open. Consider them respectfully, even if you find the person's arguments foolish and irritating. Especially if the objector is wrought up, it is wise in the beginning to keep the focus *off* substantive ideas and positions taken.

Quick Descent to Disaster

Unfortunately, managers and supervisors repeatedly forget this simple first step when they confront a worried subordinate. Turning the case of the concerned airline pilot (boxed text) into a hypothetical situation, here is the way the crucial opening discussion may go:

> **Manager:** What's going on here, Mr. Pilot? It was bad enough when you complained about the "automatic hold" equipment to the vice president, but now you've gone and written the National Transportation Safety Board.
>
> **Pilot:** But if a pilot accidentally presses the wheel control column, the "automatic hold" can disengage.
>
> **Manager:** You had training in how to use this equipment, and your instructors showed you how to avoid that problem. The other pilots aren't complaining. I read your letters and I've listened to my engineers, and I'm convinced the equipment is safe. Are you disputing my judgment?
>
> **Pilot:** I've flown the plane myself and—
>
> **Manager:** I know, you told us all about that, and you told the Safety Board, too. Are you saying we don't know our job?
>
> **Pilot:** No, sir, I'm saying no such thing, only—

---

[3] Roger Fisher and William Ury, *Getting to Yes* (Boston: Houghton Mifflin, 1981).

PROTESTING AIRLINE PILOT

The senior pilot of an airline believed that a piece of equipment used in certain planes, an automatic control device ("automatic hold") to maintain a set altitude level, could become disengaged under certain circumstances without a warning to the pilot on the annunciator panels. After a plane crash that he thought might have been caused by such a failure, he wrote a letter to three top executives of the airline detailing why the automatic control device was defective.

When the operations vice president replied without promising action to investigate or correct the problem, the pilot sent a similar letter to the Air Line Pilots Association and the National Transportation Safety Board, which was conducting hearings on the crash. The board called him to testify, which he did. After the board decided that pilot error, not equipment failure, was the cause of the crash, the pilot continued to note possible failures in the equipment when he was flying. After writing a 12-page petition to the board, with a copy to the operations vice president, he was demoted to co-pilot. He protested this demotion and was grounded. Victorious in a grievance proceeding, he resumed flying. Later he took the airline to court.

Manager: Now listen, we're paying you to fly these planes in the best way you know how, and we're doing everything we can to make them as safe as possible. What kind of fools do you take us for? Do you think we're going to sit by while you go around writing letters to everybody saying the equipment is unsafe? We won't have it. We'll speak with one voice on this issue. As of now, Mr. Pilot, you're grounded. Good day.

Openers like this one are likely to take you right into a thunderhead. Taking the objector's self-esteem on such a bumpy ride, dropping it in one air pocket after another, is a risky thing to do with motivated professional and technical people. The bitter-sweet maxim attributed to a government autocrat—"First we drive them crazy, then we tell people not to listen to them because they're crazy"—is dangerous advice for today's manager.

In addition, objectors are not likely to be as impressed as you are with your understanding of the situation, nor are they likely to appreciate the value of your sources of information—your discussions with other managers, perhaps, or your knowledge of confidential company information, or possibly your familiarity with a new company plan that alters the situation.

Better Approach

Far better to avoid any evaluations or judgments and make some such opening statement as this: "Mr. Pilot, you complained about the 'automatic hold' in a letter to the vice president, and you sent a copy of it to the National

Transportation Safety Board. Naturally we're concerned.'' Then encourage him to tell his side of the story. Listen as attentively as you can, avoid using words that prejudge his behavior, and ask open-ended questions that invite him to lay out in detail his fears and criticisms. Questions that begin with ''what'' or ''how'' and requests that begin with ''tell me'' or ''would you describe'' work best. Nod your head. From time to time restate the objector's views in your words. ''So what you're afraid of is that accidentally a pilot might push the wheel,'' you might say, or ''In other words, you felt that the vice president wasn't paying any attention to your first letter. . . .''

The beauty of this approach, as Fisher and Ury point out, is that it keeps the objector's personality from becoming entangled with the issues. The accident that the pilot fears may be unreal, but his fears *are* real. Demolishing the factual basis of the fears does not necessarily demolish the fears.

Just as you encourage the pilot to express his fears and concerns, so should you tell him your own. You're afraid of the bad publicity. You're afraid the criticism will lead to a chain reaction, igniting needless complaints from other employees. You're concerned your leadership will be questioned. And so on. This discussion should take place frankly and honestly, without either side blaming the other.

Though dissidents may be too emotional to talk this way at first, after a while they should react positively to your good example. The pilot confides, ''Well, to tell the truth, Mr. Manager, there's this guy Hottemper in operations control. And you know, I went to him about this way back in March—a couple of us were worried about it then—and you know what he tells me? 'You goddamn pilots think you know everything, just because you get paid so much.' And before he got through, he was saying something about my ancestry, too.''

Strive to avoid giving any impression that your response is a routine that you learned in some training program. Don't let your eyes suggest that you're listening just to make the person feel better. Interrupt occasionally to ask, ''Do I understand correctly that you're saying that the vice president never answers those letters himself anyway?'' or ''Excuse me, but you just said some operations controllers were spies for management. How do you mean that?'' Don't be concerned about how far off base you think the objector is. Put these questions or rephrasings in his or her own words.

And remember: listening sympathetically does not mean you agree with employee critics, only that you take them seriously. As A. W. Clausen, erstwhile head of Bank of America, said when I asked him how his organization handled ''frivolous'' employee complaints: ''*No* employee complaint is frivolous. To the employee, that complaint is serious.'' But Clausen by no means agreed with the *substance* of every complaint.

One well-known university administrator is unusually adept at defusing angry complainants and getting talks on a constructive basis. The reaction of one objector gives the secret: ''I hardly ever saw eye to eye with him, but he always made me feel important.''

Finally, Fisher and Ury offer this counsel: "In many negotiations, each side explains and condemns at great length the motivations and intentions of the other side. It is more persuasive, however, to describe a problem in terms of its impact on you than in terms of what they did or why: 'I feel let down' instead of 'You broke your word.' 'We feel discriminated against' rather than 'You're a racist.' . . . A statement about how you feel is difficult to challenge. You convey the same information without provoking a defensive reaction that will prevent them from taking it in."[4]

FIND OUT WHAT MOTIVATES THE OBJECTOR

Even after drawing out the objector's fears and concerns, continue to avoid a head-to-head hassle over the merits of his or her argument. Don't get led into a debate. Instead, try to understand the person's purposes and interests in challenging management. Ask yourself what this person is trying to achieve and what gain he or she seeks. This is much more likely to help you progress than focusing only on the position taken.

The difference between positions and interests was brought out forcefully to me one time when I was talking with a hospital employee. As an objector, she argued that the hospital should set up a staff group to monitor the enforcement of a bill of rights published for patients. This was totally impractical; in no way could the hospital afford an extra staff group, nor could such a group hope to inspire most medics and patients to cooperate. But the objector's interests—her desire for better understanding of and respect for patients' rights—deserved (and later got) sympathetic management attention.

How can you ascertain an objector's true interests? The person may not oblige by candidly reporting them to you. You may have to figure them out by inference and deduction, paraphrase them for the objector, and see if they are acceptable.

Using this time the mini-case of the chemist (see boxed material), ask yourself why this chemist and his wife have gone to all the work of writing a novel criticizing the way management treats scientists and engineers. Is their motive to put public pressure on companies like yours to recognize the rights of professional people to bargain with top management? And if so, what kinds of management unfairness are they most concerned about? Unequal pay? Unfair discharge? Arbitrary assignment and transfer? Is their motive to attract publicity and attention? Or perhaps to "get back" at the company for some wrong in the past? Perhaps as you're sitting there listening, it will become clear that one of these is their real interest.

If this approach does not yield a good answer, ask yourself (*a*) what the objector may think you want him or her to do, and (*b*) why the person chooses not to do it. For instance, suppose you believe Mr. Chemist realizes

---

[4] Ibid., p. 37.

NOVEL-WRITING CHEMIST

A chemist with 16 years of service and promotion in a chemical plant believed that scientists and engineers deserved more rights and the kind of protection of rights afforded production workers under the National Labor Relations Act. He and his wife collaborated on writing a novel, published by a local firm, that portrayed the disadvantaged situation of professionals. The novel did not name his employer or identify him with the employer company. Shortly after the novel came out, the chemist ran unsuccessfully in the state primary for the U.S. House of Representatives. During the campaign, he distributed several thousand copies of the book. Shortly after, he received a letter from his superior indicating that he was dismissed. When he went to the superior's office to protest, he got nowhere. After dismissal, he began a series of legal actions against the company.

---

how much you want him to get that antibusiness book off the market—to expunge it, if possible. If he sees that, why doesn't he oblige? Does he see this issue as one on which he has a right to speak out, just as a person has a constitutional right, say, to speak out against a governmental action?

"If I do what the company wants and take the book out of circulation," you may see Mr. Chemist thinking, "I sell out to management. Professionals like me will look weak, our superiors will scoff at us for doing nothing. But if I refuse to comply with management's obvious wishes, I uphold the rights of professional people to speak out, I will be praised by my colleagues, others will be encouraged to do what I have done, we'll get publicity and public support, we'll gain more respect and recognition by executives. . . ."

Perhaps you cannot forgive Mr. Chemist for writing a book that is contemptuous of management. But, you realize, he is doing something that to him seems completely logical. He practically *has* to keep promoting it and subsidizing more printings in order to justify himself.

Usually, an employee dissident, or a group of them, has more than one interest. The chemist, for instance, may be seeking not only a preferred status for professional employees as a class but also security and advancement for himself. He may also be after increased status and recognition from his colleagues, or perhaps from professional associations. Possibly, intending to run for Congress again, he sees the book as a medium for keeping himself in the voters' eyes.

Instead of just letting these thoughts pass idly through your mind, Fisher and Ury recommend that you write them down when you have a moment to yourself. In so doing, you will remember them better and perhaps hit on some good ideas for dealing with them. If possible, rank them in order of their probable significance to the employee.

Encouragement by Example

To encourage the objector to talk about his purposes and desires, be candid about your own. "You see, Mr. Chemist, what management is worried about is that a union will come in and organize the technical people. We don't want to get involved in the kind of bitter rivalry that Detroit suffers from." Or if managment's right to manage is a salient concern: "Frankly, Mr. Chemist, some of the executives around here think that if this goes on they won't be able to manage any more—keep high standards, get rid of non-producers, that sort of thing. Now personally, I'm not concerned so much about what your book has done as about what it might start some of the others to writing."

Be as specific as you can in outlining your interests. Details make your view more convincing. "Just last month, for instance, we asked your colleague Nohelp to assist us in interviewing candidates for the agricultural chemicals department, and he refused. He said that was below his level, an administrator's job, not a professional's." Or: "Maybe you'll recall, Mr. Chemist, that we all got together at the beginning of the year and budgeted $200,000 for modifications of the equipment in Y-Lab. Well, they used up that amount in three months and went right on spending as if the budget didn't mean a thing, never bothering to tell us. Can you blame management for getting uptight? Everybody can't go flying off in his own direction."

When the objector begins to discuss his interests, show that you have listened and understood. "What I hear you saying, Mr. Chemist, is that you want credit for what you're doing, and you don't think the company has been fair with you. Am I right? Is there more to it than that?"

The object, as in the first step, is to get the focus off positions, away from a pointless debate over who's right. Once interests become the subject of attention, you and the objector won't get trapped in recriminatory argument, with you asserting, "Mr. Chemist, you can't treat us like that; don't forget who's in charge," and him accusing, "The company wants to treat me like a blue-collar worker and I'm not going to let them!"

THINK UP MUTUALLY BENEFICIAL OPTIONS

Having gotten the discussion away from "I'm right and reasonable and you're wrong and ridiculous" to "Now you know what I'm really interested in, and I think I know what you're really interested in," you can begin the payoff stage: devising options and alternatives that will leave you both better off. What might be an exercise in futility if you were trying to reconcile conflicting positions can become a productive negotiation because each side understands the other's motives and desires.

DISSIDENT ENGINEERS

Holger Hjortsvang, Max Blankenzee, and Robert Bruder, three engineers working on the construction of the San Francisco Bay Area Rapid Transit system, became concerned about faults in the design of the control equipment. They reported their worries to their supervisors but got little response. Convinced that going to top management would be an equal waste of time, they wrote an unsigned memorandum spelling out their concerns and left copies of it on the desks of many engineers, middle managers, and senior managers. Then they met confidentially with a member of the board, laying out all their concerns to him and explaining their fears that to continue to object openly, as they had at first, would lead to their being branded as troublemakers and being penalized.

After the director gave the facts to an outside consulting engineer, the consultant produced a highly critical report of BART's technical planning. A newspaper learned about the report and ran a story on it. Incensed, BART's top management learned the identities of the three engineers and fired them. The action precipitated spates of hostile newspaper articles, resolutions of support for the engineers from professional societies, criticism from legislators, and a legal action by the engineers (settled before the case came to trial).

For an example, let us take the story about dissident engineers working on San Francisco's BART system (see boxed text). Your interests as a manager would be speedy and efficient construction of a safe transit system with favorable publicity in the media. You don't want leaks to the press about problems. You don't want anonymous memoranda about perceived mistakes circulating among engineers. On the other hand, Hjortsvang, Bruder, and Blankenzee, the employee objectors, would be fearful of being made the scapegoats for operating failures, worried about management's perceived obsession with speed at the expense of safety, and interested in gaining credit for contributing to a successful, innovative venture. For the sake of their job prospects and reputations with their peers, they want the BART project to succeed in engineering terms (whatever the cost).

With such divergent interests, what kinds of solutions might you propose? Perhaps the engineers would agree to put aside their objections for 10 months and go all-out on the present program if management would agree to hire an impartial outside consulting team to evaluate progress at the end of the period and, if necessary, recommend major changes in approach. If the engineers pooh-pooh budget restrictions that management regards as very important, they might agree to respect a new budget for a period of six months, at the end of which time meetings will be called to consider changes in the amounts budgeted.

If management wants harmony and unison in the ranks but the engineers feel more comfortable in an atmosphere that permits disagreement and encourages individual opinion, management's interest in the organization's image might be preserved by a code of strict confidentiality, while the engineers' interest might be served by regularly scheduled rap sessions. If the engineers are more interested in job security than management is, both sides' interests might be served by management's agreement to a policy of no layoffs except for reasons approved by an impartial panel of arbiters.

Throughout this stage, avoid trying to influence the three objectors by warnings; instead, emphasize the beneficial consequences of adopting your proposal. For instance, a 10-month moratorium on resistance followed by a critical review would give management an opportunity to prove its belief in the current program without delaying too long the engineers' desire to see a thorough critique carried out—and the critique should serve the interests of both sides. Again, your layoff proposal is not going to hurt capable people like Hjortsvang, Bruder, or Blankenzee; it will, however, enable BART to deal with incompetents and misfits who are a pain to everybody.

Try to keep in mind the politics of the other side's agreement with your proposed solution. In advance of the meeting, jot down on the back of an envelope how your proposal for a moratorium may be seen by the engineers' peers. Will it be criticized as a sell out? Would it be more agreeable if the technical review panel were named in advance? Suppose one of the three dissidents decided to seek a job elsewhere in the months ahead. How might your proposal affect the track record he can claim for his work at BART?

Keep referring to the goals that both you and the objectors are interested in. "We want these trains to work. . . . We don't want to disappoint the public. . . . We want the best technical thinking we can get. . . . We don't want any last-minute surprises. . . . If the budget isn't right, we need to know enough in advance so we can get it revised. . . . We don't want to scare away good people. . . ."

The late Eli Goldston, chief executive of Eastern Gas & Fuel Associates, told of his troubles with efforts to reduce lung disease in coal mines owned by the company. After equipping miners with face masks, management found workers often didn't wear the devices. Although efforts were made to increase use of the masks, many miners obstinately laid them aside, claiming that they interfered with visibility or "didn't work right." After some talks, Goldston and others realized that the balky miners indeed had a strong interest in protecting their lungs—only they didn't want to admit it because they wanted to smoke while working. So the company set up work breaks during which smokers were allowed to light up away from the areas of heavy air pollution. At all other times, they would wear the masks.

PROPOSE OBJECTIVE TESTS TO DETERMINE OUTCOMES

In seeking a resolution of a conflict with employee objectors, don't let the outcome depend on willpower or staying power. And don't settle for a solution that is a compromise between your interests and the employees' interests and in effect satisfies no one. If experience teaches anything, such compromises are not a solid answer. If you and the objectors cannot agree on a solution that meets both of your needs, as described in the third step, try to devise objective tests or criteria, agreeable to both sides, that can be used to decide on an outcome.

For example, in your negotiations with the BART engineers, a stumbling block might be differences of opinion over what constitutes reasonable and adequate safety from collisions due to faulty switching. You might take this tack:

"We're both interested in safety, right? But management also is interested in keeping operations going at a profit and in minimizing downtime, and in the long run that's in your interest too. So what would be a fair way to decide on the proper safety level? If an arbiter from the Institute of Electrical Engineers won't do, what about one from the CalTech faculty? Or what about a list of nominations from you engineers and a list of nominations from management, so we can draw up a panel of arbiters using both lists?"

Remember that, as management's representative, you generally have an important advantage in these discussions. For instance, as a top executive of BART, you're known to the business and government communities, whereas the engineers have no public identities. The visibility and authority of your office enable you to communicate to many more people—and faster—than the engineers can. As a manager of the chemical company, you have instant access to support and resources that are beyond the reach of the chemist. As an executive of the airline company, you have similar advantages.

"Look," you can say to Mr. Chemist, "you don't think your campaigning is prejudicial to the company, but I think it is. Now, isn't there some way we can find out what other people think? What about an independent outside survey? Depending on the outcome of that, we'll decide on a rule for clearing future publications and speeches." Or, to Mr. Pilot, "All right, now, we both want safe planes but we disagree on this altimeter equipment. How about agreeing that nothing more will be said about it until we can get a good outside opinion? What about asking the National Transportation Safety Board to recommend an expert to look into it and render an opinion?" So long as your proposal is reasonable, your advantage as a member of management makes it difficult for the objector to reject your suggestion.

Values and Variations

In essence, this was the successful approach worked out by one chief executive of an industrial manufacturer when confronted with complaints from foundry workers who thought the air was unfit for breathing. He suggested they get the air quality measurements of a well-known rival foundry and use them as a benchmark. They agreed, and the dispute was resolved. In another situation, the head of Sentry Insurance Company was challenged by several employees who felt that the company's tests for job applicants were an invasion of privacy. He suggested that the next employee opinion survey include a question on what other employees thought. In the first case, after the results were in, management decided it had better make some improvements in a few areas; in the second, the dissidents learned that few others agreed with them, so they dropped their complaint.

An interesting wrinkle in this approach is to ask the other side to put in writing the most reasonable proposal he or she can make; you do the same for your side. Then give the two ''most reasonable'' proposals to an arbitrator to choose between. The idea is that such a procedure puts pressure on both sides to make their proposals as fair as possible. In professional baseball and in states where the procedure is compulsory in certain types of public sector disputes, this approach reportedly has produced more settlements than have conventional types of arbitration.

If you and the subordinate agree on a criterion or procedure for resolving the dispute, ask the subordinate to summarize the discussion and agreed-on solution and send you a memorandum. Write a memo on the talk for your own records too, and if there is much divergence between the two, get in touch again with the dissident.

PARTING OBSERVATIONS

In most organizations in most states, managers are not legally compelled to negotiate with employee objectors who are not union members. Managers can thumb the objectors out of the company, if they want to. As a practical matter, however, it is becoming less desirable to do so. Especially with employees who have served the company for a while and whose capabilities are proved, it pays to seek a mutually advantageous solution.

Still, even the most adept managers do not always find employee objectors responsive to negotiation. What should be done then? If the objector seems to be more interested in being a gadfly or rabble-rouser than in being cooperative and helpful, then, if you have done your best to negotiate and assuming you comply with any company policies on the subject, it may be time to fire the person.

If anyone questions you, offer your notes on the discussions. If one or two others joined you at some stage, they can attest to your efforts. If company policy or government regulations require you to submit to a hearing procedure, your duly noted discussions should serve as documentation for your decision. To broaden your understanding of procedures at this stage, consult one of the good books available.[5]

The guiding principle is simple: aim to keep the conflict from becoming

[5] See, for example, Robert Coulson, *The Termination Handbook* (New York: Free Press 1981); *Employee Termination Handbook* (New York: Executive Enterprises Publications, 1981).

an "I win, you lose" affair and instead approach it as a "we both can win" situation. Don't make the mistake of the superior who, feeling that his or her managerial prerogatives are threatened, refuses to negotiate with the objector because of "principle." The approach you take can be judged by the three criteria proposed by Fisher and Ury: "It should produce a wise agreement if agreement is possible. It should be efficient. And it should improve or at least not damage the relationship between the parties."

SECTION SIX

Essence of Strategy

In the preceding sections, we have been looking at how one might proceed in handling negotiations to get the best outcome through preparation and planning. This implies that negotiation is inherently systematic, rational, and predictable. Preparation and planning do pay off, but not in such a deterministic fashion. We have pointed out that there is no proper way of determining the best settlement in negotiation. The settlement is always arbitrary. We have also explained how negotiations are never cool, harmonious, or generous and mutually supportive. There is always a tension, a troublesome trade-off between individual and joint interests. These conditions may be accentuated and multiplied when one or, perhaps, both parties structures the relationship as competitive, as an effort to win at the other party's expense. Doing this, of course, engenders defensiveness, distrust, and a counteroffensiveness, resulting, usually, in a less satisfactory outcome for both parties. Our key message has been that these conditions can be attenuated and made subordinate by structuring the relationship as cooperative, where parties work together on joint or mutually supportive goals, work to trust each other, and to find ways to collaborate.

In the earlier discussions, we may have been misleading by suggesting that in integrative bargaining there is cooperation while in distributive bargaining cooperation does not exist. The fact is that, even in distributive bargaining, there must always be a certain minimal level of cooperation. Suppose that you are selling a used car and drive a hard bargain, getting as much as the buyer can possibly pay, and withholding many of the special features that had earlier been part of the car; for example, an extra set of stereo speakers, snow tires, and so on. You may have "won" in the sense of getting as much as possible from the situation; and the other party may have "lost" as much as possible because they did not get any concessions from you in what was a heated, highly competitive negotiation. Yet, you will have nothing if the other party does not cooperate and go through with the deal. In most states, for a limited amount of time after a deal has been reached, people can walk away from an agreement to purchase a house, a car, and most major appliances. In less legal types of arrangements, like an adjustment made between two managers about the transfer of materials between their departments, both parties have to continue to see it to their advantage for the agreement to work.

These aspects of negotiation are difficult to fully understand; and, hence, strategy in negotiation takes a while to comprehend. In this section, having had one look at strategy, we step back and look at some of its more underlying characteristics. We begin with a cameo picture of the U.S.–Iranian negotiations over the release of American hostages held by the Iranians (Powell, Salamon, and House, "Crisis Diplomacy"). At first reading, it describes much confusion; "minor miracles" described as pulling a rabbit from a hat, many strong and varying emotions, many people serving, or claiming to serve as communication links, pleadings, coercion, actions, and changes of position that were puzzling and never understood—a virtual cauldron of confusion, conflicting communication, contradictions, which, nonetheless, eventually lead to concession and agreement. In "The Non-Logical Strategy," Henderson reminds us that confusion and nonlogical behavior may be the elements of the soundest negotiating strategy. The appearance of being nonlogical may be the most logical way to get the best of the arbitrary decision that must be made. He describes how the other party actually has a range of positions that will be accepted and that appearing to be nonrational may be the way to get the best position for us which the other party will accept. His argument is that we win in setting a strategy by first understanding the other party well and then by winning the mind of the other party.

The idea that there is no completely safe, tension-free, unambiguous strategy in negotiation is explored further by Johnston in "Negotiation Strategies: Different Strokes for Different Folks." He examines three common strategies: competitive, collaborative (what we have called cooperative), and subordinative; that is, where one party consistently gives in to avoid conflict and stress. All three have advantages, and all three have disadvantages. Put a little differently, Johnston argues that none of these strategies is adequate by itself. The successful negotiator needs to be able to pursue all three as needed. In short, the most sensible strategy is to be flexible.

The important message of these beginning sections is that what happens before beginning negotiation in preparing, planning, and setting strategy is important, perhaps the most important part of negotiation. Preparing and setting strategy are complex processes requiring a different perspective on ourselves, the other party, and what is going on between parties than we typically hold in everyday events. Such a shift does not occur quickly or easily. As Jack O. Vance in Section Three, points out, competing—and we can also say negotiating— takes study and practice.

EILEEN ALT POWELL,
JULIE SALAMON, and
KAREN ELLIOTT HOUSE

Reading 6–1
Crisis Diplomacy:
How U.S. Negotiators Saved
Hostage Deal at the Eleventh Hour

The financial deal freeing the American hostages in Iran almost collapsed in the final hours of negotiations last Tuesday.

The crisis struck about 9 A.M. local time Tuesday in Algiers, where a U.S. negotiating team was going over final details of the multibillion-dollar exchange of frozen Iranian assets for the 52 hostages.

The negotiators, only hours before, had cleared what they believed would be the last hurdle by deciding to withdraw from the agreement an appendix that the Iranians publicly charged had misstated their assets.

But then, without warning, another snag developed: The Iranians privately notified the Algerian intermediaries that they wouldn't sign the section of the agreement to which the appendix had been attached. The section outlined the technical responsibilities of the Algerian central bank, which was to manage Iranian funds in escrow.

The negotiators representing the Carter administration reacted with despair, fearing that this new problem just couldn't be solved in the few hours of authority left to them before President Reagan was to take office.

"It was the lowest of the low points," recalls Robert Mundheim, a former Treasury Department general counsel who was in Algiers as a consultant for the department. "Everyone was sure it was over. It could have been a misunderstanding or deliberate on Iran's part. I don't know the answer to this day."

The negotiators immediately phoned the Oval Office at the White House, where President Carter, Vice President Walter Mondale and several top aides were spending the night. It was 4 A.M. in Washington, and Chief of Staff Hamilton Jordan was asleep on the couch.

"We have another problem," Warren Christopher, the chief U.S. negotiator, told Mr. Carter.

"At that late hour to find we had a new problem was about more than could be borne," recalls Lloyd Cutler, counsel to the President, who joined Mr. Carter on an extension.

TRUSTING ALGERIA

The new Iranian objection triggered frantic discussions among the U.S. negotiating team, officials of the Algerian central bank and banking officials in Washington. Finally, the Americans decided to "trust the Bank of Algeria," as one U.S. negotiator put it, and dropped the offending technical section as well as the appendix.

Thus, the last impasse ended, and at 11:18 A.M. Algerian time (6:18 A.M. in Washington), U.S. officials initialed the final deposit and escrow accords. The signing in the first-floor meeting room of the Algerian foreign ministry cleared the path for one of the biggest, most complex, most emotion-fraught movements of money in history. Some $7.98 billion of Iranian assets was unfrozen by the United States and moved to England. Shortly before 12:30 P.M. EST the 52 American hostages were flown out of Tehran toward Algiers and freedom after 444 days in captivity.

While the agreement brought an end to the long negotiations to free the 52 captive Americans, it also marked the beginning of what is becoming an intense debate over the terms of the deal. The Reagan State Department said yesterday it would carry out U.S. obligations assumed by the Carter administration, but a spokesman added that a careful review would still be needed. . . .

Some individuals and corporations with claims against Iran that are to be settled out of a separate, yet-to-be-established $1 billion escrow account are calling the accord unconstitutional. They are moving in U.S. courts to try to block transfer of the estimated $4 billion in Iranian assets remaining in the U.S.

RABBIT FROM A HAT

In addition, some attorneys, such as Gail Borden in Washington, also believe the financial settlement is "ambiguously written in places and unfair, because it appears to favor banks over other American companies." Mr. Borden adds, however, that "perhaps it had to be what it is in order to get the hostages out."

The people closest to the financial agreement, which was the key to the lock, believe that completing the arrangement at all was a minor miracle. "We pulled a rabbit out of the hat," says Robert Carswell, who served as the Treasury's point man in the negotiations. "Nothing like it had been done before. We put it together from the bottom."

The agreement was negotiated, Mr. Carswell and others note, with diplomatic, banking and legal officials on three continents. Documents had to be drafted in three languages: English, Farsi for the Iranians, and French for the Algerians. And the U.S. negotiators were under pressure to produce an agreement before President Carter's administration ended at noon Tuesday.

As that deadline approachd, officials at the State and Treasury departments in Washington and the Federal Reserve Bank in New York went 72 hours or more without sleep. Bankers gathered in the 32nd-floor law offices of Shearman & Sterling in mid-town Manhattan and slept intermittently on couches or the floor. Many of the bankers wore blue blazers with brass buttons that reminded one banking source of "the opening day at the yacht club." Officials in law firms in London and at the Bank of England monitored telex machines for their marching orders.

In the Oval Office of the White House President Carter surrounded himself with aides to await word on the final agreement. When the last documents were signed, Mr. Carter invited television crews in to film the moment for eventual inclusion in his presidential library. "Right on," he said of the deal.

The "guiding principle" in the negotiations according to former Secretary of State Edmund Muskie, was "to return matters, insofar as possible, to where they stood before the hostages were seized."

The Iranian assets were frozen in U.S. banks and their European branches by President Carter on November 14, 1979—10 days after Iranian militants overran the U.S. embassy in Tehran and imprisoned the diplomatic staff and other Americans who were there. In subsequent weeks, Mr. Carter moved to squeeze Iran further by blocking exports and imports. U.S. banks, which weren't any longer able to collect loan payments from Iran, declared more than $5 billion in loans in default. Those banks that also had Iranian deposits in their overseas branches, such as Citicorp and Chase Manhattan, moved to "offset" more than $1.8 billion of the deposits against the loans, as authorized in Treasury regulations carrying out the freeze.

A private U.S. lawyer who has been closely involved with the negotiations says U.S. banks first made overtures to Iran early last March. "They wanted to see if it was possible to work out an agreement to reconstitute or restructure the loans," he says. "The idea was to settle their disagreements, understanding that it would have to be put eventually in the context of an overall diplomatic settlement."

Discussions by West German and British lawyers for both sides led to a proposal by the banks in September. It was rejected in Tehran, "largely for want of a sponsor," the lawyer says.

One New York banker says that these talks began and continued "with so many frustrations you didn't know whether to laugh or cry." The biggest obstacle, he says, stemmed from the factionalism in Iran. "We'd offer a proposal. They'd respond. We'd try to handle their objections in the next proposal. Then we'd get a response that didn't seem to have anything to do with what came before it," he recalls.

Participants disagree on when negotiations involving U.S. government officials really began moving forward. Mr. Muskie, for instance, believes that "the line was a pretty straight one" after September 12, when Ayatollah Khomeini outlined four conditions for release of the hostages. The conditions included the unfreezing of Iranian assets and cancellation of all claims against the Islamic nation.

Others believe the key was the November 2 action by the Iranian parliament formally adopting the conditions. This decision signaled what one State Department official terms "a crucial victory" for the faction in Iran that wanted the hostage problem solved. In any case, the United States dispatched Deputy Secretary of State Warren Christopher to Algiers on November 10 to respond to the four conditions, and talks mediated by the Algerians began.

In December, Iran rejected another proposal by the banks. This one was crafted by European lawyers to try to get Iran to agree to bring its loans up to date and to set up an escrow account to cover future payments of principal and interest. Then, on December 21, Iran unveiled its demand that the United States provide $24 billion in guarantees that Tehran would eventually recover its frozen assets and the late shah's wealth.

For U.S. negotiators that was a turning point. "For the first time Iran was saying it didn't want everything back when the hostages were turned over but was prepared to wait for some of its money," says a State Department official who took part in the negotiations. From that point on, American negotiators say, the two countries began to focus on how much money Iran would get back at the time of the hostages' release.

About a week into 1981, the European attorneys flew to New York to assist attorneys for a consortium of 12 U.S. banks. Bankers say they met more than a half dozen times, mostly in the offices of Shearman & Sterling, Citicorp's lead law firm.

One participant in the New York talks says the meetings produced a series of "feelers" that were sent to Treasury officials in Washington, who in turn relayed them to lawyers in Algiers, London and West Germany. Those in New York "really never knew where the proposals were ending up," this participant says, but most of the Iranian-American contact appeared to take place in London and Germany.

On January 12, Iran rejected a formal proposal that would have required Iran to get its loans current and set up an escrow account to cover principal and interest payments for two additional years. A revised version sent less than 48 hours later evoked the response from Iran that, bank officials agree, allowed for the eventual agreement. For it was on January 15 that Tehran officials notified U.S negotiators through the Algerian intermediaries that the Islamic nation wanted to pay off all its debts.

Americans may never know why Iran changed signals. One Iranian expert speculates that there may have been internal political reasons, the greatest of which may have been a desire by the leadership ''to tell the people that they had broken all ties with the United States.'' Officials in Kuwait note that Iran was down to less than $4 billion in reserves because of the Iran-Iraq conflict and needed its cash. And a Washington attorney suggests that ''every crisis has a life, and it was probably concluded in Iran that it was time to end this one.''

Spurred by Iran's overture and a call from the Treasury's Mr. Carswell, the bankers met all day in Washington last Friday, January 16. The basic structure of the final agreement was hammered out that night in the State Department, one banker says. Over the weekend, ''refinements'' were hashed out by telephone between lawyers in New York and at the Treasury Department in Washington. The agreement became the basis for the transfer of funds that followed the Tuesday morning signing ceremony in Algiers.

Of the $7.98 billion unfrozen and transferred to the Bank of England for holding, some $3.67 billion was set aside to repay the syndicated bank loans, which were loans made by groups of U.S. and foreign banks to Iran. American banks managed about half the 17 or 18 syndicates, taking responsibility for the 100 or more bank participants, banking sources say. The dispersal of the bank syndicate money will send about $1.4 billion to U.S. banks and $2.3 billion to foreign banks.

In addition, $1.4 billion has been put into escrow at the Bank of England to cover about $700 million of nonsyndicated bank loans and $800 million that U.S. banks believe they were overcharged on interest they paid at a rate near 17 percent on the deposits.

Other documents commit the United States to stopping litigation against Iran in the United States and freeing an additional $4 billion in assets, out of which a $1 billion escrow account will be set up to cover the claims of individuals and nonbank corporations. The U.S. government has yet to release documents on the bank deal, leading William Rand, an attorney at the New York firm of Coudert Brothers, to ask, ''Why aren't we being told why the banks got the deal they did?'' Mr. Rand's firm represents General Telephone & Electronics, which had a $109 million lawsuit pending against Iran.

The agreement with the banks was crucial to the transfer of the assets, says a Treasury official, who adds that it was the Iranians who decided that the outstanding loans should be paid in full. The bank agreement also had to be completed before the final documents could be signed. The last two documents were the ones in Algiers that authorized the Bank of England to act as the depository institution for the transfer and that instructed Algeria on the escrow accounts.

But early Tuesday morning a last-minute hitch arose when Iran objected to an appendix to the Algerian escrow agreement. Iran's alternative to the appendix was a telex message from Tehran to London telling U.S. banks to move specified Iranian deposits in Europe.

Mr. Carswell says that the telex line was opened at 2:30 A.M. EST, although transmission didn't begin until 3 A.M. "But the test number at the top of the cable was wrong. There was a typo. We had to get it corrected." The first transmission also was garbled, he says. For example, it listed Iranian deposits in First National Bank of Chicago accounts at zero rather than $70 million.

Attorneys for bankers who saw copies of the telex in New York were upset. Robert Douglas, chief counsel for the Chase Manhattan Bank, says that "everyone was exhausted. The tension . . . was unbearable." The question of the hour, he added, was, "Were they trying to wreck the deal?"

The Iranians sent the telex again, and the second transmission was accepted when "Mr. Carter decided it was good enough," Mr. Carswell said. As a result, the United States at 3:46 A.M. told the bankers to move the Iranian money to the Federal Reserve in New York for transfer to special holding accounts in the Bank of England.

A few hours later, the whole deal again threatened to unravel when the Iranians said they wouldn't sign the section of the agreement to which the appendix had been attached.

This second crisis was resolved in a series of telephone conferences that Carter administration documents indicate lasted "over an hour." The resolution came when New York Fed President Anthony Solomon authorized the signing of the escrow agreement. In so doing, the United States agreed to a more-general definition of duties for the Algerian handling of the escrow account while abandoning the more-specific second chapter.

The steps to move the funds from U.S. control to Iranian control then began.

At 6:41 A.M. EST, Harold Gooding of Brooklyn, a 34-year-old supervisor in the New York Fed's cable division, began feeding a message into a blue-gray telex machine instructing the Bank of England to move the U.S. funds from the special Federal Reserve holding accounts to the escrow account in the name of the central bank of Algeria. The message cleared two minutes later, Fed spokesmen confirm.

The Bank of England then certified, via an open telephone line from London to the British central bank's deputy governor in Algiers, that the Algerian escrow account had been opened and filled with $7.98 billion. With this completed at 8:04 A.M., the Algerian central bank at 8:06 A.m. certified to Iran that the money was available for the swap with the hostages.

With everything set for the hostages' release, President Carter waited. Gary Sick, a National Security Council aide, was in the White House Situation Room with a telephone to each ear—one to hear word from

Algerian intermediaries that the hostages' aircraft had left Tehran and the other to tell Mr. Carter the 52 Americans were free.

Every few minutes he called Mr. Carter—in the family quarters, in the limousine enroute to the Capital for Mr. Reagan's inauguration, and finally in the room at the Capitol just before Mr. Reagan took the oath of office. Mr. Sick never got to deliver the news Mr. Carter wanted to hear.

Mr. Carter left office shortly after noon on Tuesday. The first plane bearing hostages left Tehran at 12:33 P.M. EST. ''The worst part of all this,'' says Mr. Sick, ''was the petty cruelties.''

BRUCE D. HENDERSON

Reading 6–2

The Non-Logical Strategy

The goal of strategy in business, diplomacy and war is to produce a stable relationship favorable to you with the consent of your competitors. By definition, such restraint by a competitor is cooperation. Such cooperation from a competitor must seem to be profitable to him. *Any competition which does not eventually eliminate a competitor requires his cooperation in a stabilization of the situation.* The agreement is usually a tacit nonaggression. The alternative is death for all but one competitor.

In business, as in war and social affairs, those who compete also have common interests. Only a little reflection on conflict situations will dramatize how often the rewards of victory can be increased for both parties if fighting is minimized. Conflict arises because of the difficulty in getting both parties to accept the final decision in advance.

This is why it is necessary to appear irrational to competitors. For the same reason you must seem unreasonable and arbitrary in negotiations with customers and suppliers. A stable competitive situation requires mutual self-restraint. But mutual self-restraint means mutual agreement. Such agreement cannot be arrived at by logic. It must be achieved by an emotional balance of forces.

Competition and cooperation go hand in hand in all real life situations. Otherwise all conflict could only end in complete extermination of the competitor. There is a point in all conflict where both parties gain more or lose less from peace than they can hope to gain from any foreseeable victory. Beyond that point, cooperation is more profitable than conflict. But how will the benefits be shared?

In a negotiated conflict situation, the participant who is coldly logical is at a great disadvantage. Logically, he can afford to compromise until there is no

Bruce D. Henderson, "The Non-Logical Strategy," The Boston Consulting Group, Inc. 1973.

advantage left in cooperation. The negotiator/competitor whose behavior is irrational or arbitrary has a great advantage if he can depend upon his opponent being logical and unemotional.

The arbitrary or irrational participant can demand far more than a reasonable share and yet his logical opponent could still gain by compromise rather than breaking off the negotiation.

Likewise, all cooperation has an important element of conflict. If the benefits cannot be obtained without cooperation, then how much can be demanded from the other party without destroying the cooperation?

When there is anything short of a death struggle, the result is a form of tacit cooperation. Whenever it is of any mutual advantage to cooperate or stop short of unlimited competition, there is always the question of who will benefit the most. This sharing of the benefits of cooperation is always arbitrary.

- "Nearest to whose aims is the peace treaty signed?"
- "Closest to whose terms is the labor contract settled?"
- "Nearest to whose desires is the merger consummated?"
- "Nearest to whose interests is the patent-license granted?"
- "On whose conditions are commercial practices developed?"

The decision on what is an acceptable compromise is essentially emotional and arbitrary. Logic, reason and intellect only set the limits within which the decision must be made. If both parties are too arbitrary, the result is either intensified competition or the breakdown of mutually advantageous cooperation. If one party is clearly less arbitrary in his demands, he will benefit correspondingly less from the cooperation.

Cooperation does not mean collaboration. Cooperation in this sense means pursuing your own interests to the exclusion of everything else. Unavoidably, however, there are many areas in which a tacit agreement to cooperate is mutually advantageous in spite of the conflict. The critical question is: "Cooperate on whose terms?"

A steel company and an electric equipment company enter into a joint research effort. As the result of this effort, a vastly superior electric steel is developed. The electric equipment made from this steel is not only better but it is less expensive. By the nature of the research agreement, only the steel company can make the product and only the electric company can buy it. How should the cost advantages between the two research partners be shared? They must cooperate to have any profit. They are in competition for that profit.

In the classic labor negotiation situation, both sides stand to lose substantially by any work stoppage. Yet there is a very important difference in benefits depending upon whose terms an agreement is reached.

Both of these situations can be translated into mixed cooperative-competitive strategies. In a price war, all participants lose substantially by a continuation of below cost sales. Everyone would gain by a return to normal conditions. Yet the differences in market share afterwards can be substantial depending upon who takes the initiative in raising prices and how closely the competitors follow.

It is a common matter in business to have customer-supplier relationships which are mutually advantageous yet in which it is necessary to set a price level periodically. This level can often vary over a considerable range without eliminating all the advantages to either party. The question is: "How much should each party benefit at the expense of the other?"

Absence of monopoly in business requires voluntary restraint of competition. At some point there must be a tacit agreement not to compete. Unless this restraint of trade were acceptable to all competitors, the resulting aggression would inevitably eliminate the less efficient competitors, leaving only one. Antitrust laws are an attempt to formally limit competition. All antimonopoly and fair trade laws are restraint of competition.

Utter destruction of a competitor is almost never profitable unless the competitor is unwilling to accept peace, no matter how advantageous it might be to him. In our daily social contacts, in our international affairs and in our business affairs, we have far more ability to damage those around us than we ever dare use. They also have the same power to damage us. The implied agreement to restrain our potential aggression is all that stands between us and eventual elimination of one by the other. Both war and diplomacy are mechanisms for establishing or maintaining the self-imposed restraint on all competitors. The conflict continues, but within the implied area of cooperative agreement.

The prevalence of the parallel self-restraint is not as well recognized in business as it is in national affairs. Yet it requires little experience in business to realize that the attitudes and beliefs of your competitors with respect to you can be vital to your success regardless of how vigorous the competition between you may be.

The heart of business strategy, the essence of diplomacy and the key to military strategy is the creation of attitudes upon the part of competitors which will cause them either to restrain themselves or to act in a fashion which is more advantageous to you than to them.

There are several ways that this balance is struck.

The most easily recognized way of enforcing cooperation is by exhibiting obvious willingness to use irresistible or overwhelming force. This requires little strategic skill. Even here, though, there is the problem of convincing competitors that force will be used without incurring the cost or inconvenience of actually doing so. The classic name for this situation is Pax Romana. The Roman peace was based upon the demonstrated willingness to use force. Most police effectiveness as well as underworld peace is based upon the well developed general conviction that force will be used without hesitation.

Maintaining competition under antitrust laws depends upon restraint of aggressive competition. The paradox is that this restraint is illegal. But the lack of it inevitably leads to monopoly if competition is preserved.

The most common situation occurs when the available force is not over-whelming but is clearly able to inflict major punishment. If both parties can inflict such punishment on the other, we have the classic case. In case of open conflict, both parties lose. In case of cooperation, both parties are better off but not necessarily equally—particularly if one is trying to change the status quo.

When both parties can severely punish the other, their equilibrium de-pends upon three things:

- Their respective willingness to accept the risk of punishment.
- Their belief about each other's willingness to accept the risk of punishment.
- Their degree of rationality in behavior.

Certain observations about these factors are strategically very important.

- Lack of willingness to accept the risk of punishment is almost certain to produce either the punishment or progressively more onerous conditions for cooperation—provided the competitor recog-nizes the attitude.
- Beliefs about a competitor's future behavior or response are all that determine competitive self-restraint. It is not actual capability; it is the anticipated use of capability that counts.
- The less rational or predictable the behavior appears to be, the greater is the advantage in establishing a favorable competitive balance. This is limited only by the possibility of forcing a competitor into an untenable position where he has nothing to lose, or by the possibility of creating an emotional antagonism or hostility of equal unreasonableness and irrationality.

Many illustrations of these factors in operation are easy to recall from diplomatic and military history.

In business these competitive détentes are less visible. They occur in many ways: in pricing, in hiring of key people, in the observance of trade practices. Behavior patterns are codified into fair trade practices or ethics. Such behavior may fly in the face of both sound economics and national policy with respect to competition. It is still rational behavior. It is the choice between self-restraint and commercial death.

For some competitors, such predictable behavior may be very much in opposition to their best interests. In this case, the competition has won a strategic victory by establishing a particular set of assumptions on which it can base its decisions.

The goal of most business strategy is to cause competitors to forego opportunities or withhold effort while you exploit them. There are many ways this can be done.

It is possible to obtain a product lead or market hold which puts a competitor at an irreparable disadvantage. It is important for him to recognize this, otherwise his efforts to compete can still be very costly to you, as well as to him.

Often such a commercial advantage is not insuperable, but it may still be possible to cause a competitor to believe that it is and thereby either delay or avoid a major challenge.

The purest kind of strategic victory occurs when your competitive advantage is minimal or nil, but your competition can be induced to believe that your behavior will be so irrational that both of you will be involved in unacceptable costs or risks. If you can convince your competitor that you are reckless or irrational, you can always win at Russian roulette without actually playing.

More business victories are won in the minds of competitors than in the laboratory, the factory or the marketplace. The competitor's conviction that you are emotional, dogmatic or otherwise nonlogical in your business strategy can be a great asset. This conviction on his part can produce an acceptance of your actions without retaliation, which would otherwise be unthinkable. More important, the anticipation of nonlogical or unrestrained reactions on your part can inhibit his competitive aggression.

In business the most visible area of competition or cooperation is price policy. In this area the government is a silent partner whose opinions can be decisive. Several things must be said about this:

- Tacit or implied cooperation is implicit in any situation in which competitors do not actively seek to destroy each other. Either course is apt to be regarded as illegal.
- No matter how vigorous the competition, the goal is optimizing the results. Consequently, a forecast and anticipation of competitive behavior is mandatory. Failure to act against specific competition is failure to compete. If you are not predatory, you are acting in restraint of trade.
- Near term cooperation on price is self-defeating. It merely shifts the competition and costs to nonprice items. It also invites the non-cooperating competitor (usually the smaller one) to revert to price competition when nonprice services cost more than they are worth to the user.

In the absence of full collusion, not only on prices but production, it can be assumed that prices are the least rewarding area for competitive cooperation. Certainly this is true over the long term for the low-cost competitor. This is why the antitrust laws regarding collusion are superfluous unless the collusion includes restraint of capacity and production.

The real rewards for induced cooperation by competitors lie in inhibiting otherwise logical behavior. Convince the competitor that an invasion of a new market will be unprofitable. Convince him that introduction of a new product will be too expensive. *Most important and above all, convince him that the addition of new capacity will not increase his market share.*

In the final analysis, true competition means improving your performance at the expense of competitors. Skillful use of nonlogical persuasion can often produce the benefits of victory on your terms without the cost of a direct confrontation and the mutual attrition of an actual struggle. Such persuasion is almost always by actions, not words; by implication, not regulation.

For example, there was a company which took over industry price leadership, and made publicly known that it intended to meet competitors' price cuts with individual customers by extending equivalent prices to all customers. As long as its competitors believed this, they had little to gain and much to lose by a special price to a special customer. The price leader was being very nonrational. He was promising voluntarily to take large cuts in margin just to retaliate against a single price cut with a solitary customer. In fact prices have been stabilized for considerable periods by such tactics.

As another example, *A,* an automotive parts producer, was threatened with price competition in the "after market." He managed to make it clear that any price competition would produce retaliation. When a competitor, *B,* did in fact cut the price on replacement parts, *A* retaliated by cutting his own price to one of the big three auto makers by an even larger amount, even though he had been selling very little to them for original equipment. The original price cutter, *B,* was faced with a major loss either in price or volume on his major customer. *A,* who cut the price in retaliation, had no volume to begin with in the market area in which he cut prices. The interchange and action was based upon mutual expectations about essentially arbitrary nonlogical reactions.

There is a definite limit to the range within which competitors can expect to achieve an equilibrium or to negotiate a shift in equilibrium even by implication. Arbitrary, uncooperative or aggressive attitudes will produce equally emotional reactions. These emotional reactions are in turn the basis for nonlogical and arbitrary responses. So nonlogical behavior is self-limiting.

This is why the art of diplomacy can be described as the ability to be unreasonable without arousing resentment. It is worth remembering that the objective of diplomacy is to induce cooperation on terms that are relatively more favorable to you than to your protagonist without actual force being used.

The long-term and the short-term consequences of a hardnosed attitude can be quite different. Short-term gains can be cancelled eventually by the cumulative long-term effects. For instance, Hitler conquered an empire without fighting. His annexation of Poland was not essentially different from those aggressive acts which preceded it, yet that act started World War II. It is interesting to observe that the British and French declaration of war was no more a logical decision than previous refusal to take that same step. The cumulative result of Hitler's actions resulted in a deep emotional commitment of the British which kept them fighting against apparently hopeless odds in a nonlogical dedication.

For businessmen the philosophy of arbitrary behavior has certain corollaries which are fundamental in nature.

- You must know as accurately as possible just what your competition has at stake in his contact with you.
- Logic sets the limits. But logic is a competitive handicap within those limits.
- The less the competition knows about you, the less advantage he has.
- It is absolutely essential to know the character, attitudes, motives and habitual behavior of a competitor if you wish to have a negotiating advantage.
- The more unreasonable and unpredictable you *seem to be,* the more leverage you have.

There are two essential conclusions. The first is that an intimate knowledge of the competition is a prerequisite to a superior strategy. The second is that your victories must first be won in the minds of the competition before they can be converted into competitive net gains.

Victories achieved by use of superior force are not victories at all. They are failures to achieve the potential results without the waste inherent in a test of strength.

The true strategist knows his competition in depth. He is meticulous in his logic. He seems to be impulsive, arbitrary and irrational. He avoids arousing the emotions of competition. The true strategist lives at peace with stronger competitors who use self-imposed restraint which is highly advantageous to the superior strategist.

ROBERT W. JOHNSTON

Reading 6–3
Negotiation Strategies:
Different Strokes for Different Folks

Negotiation is a lifelong process. As infants we learn that we can barter gurgles, giggles, and wailing for attention and affection. From that point on—day after day, year after year—we engage in innumerable negotiations: We bargain with teachers for better grades, with clients for their business, and with supervisors to give us more money. Human resources managers, in particular, must negotiate on behalf of their employer every day—with individual employees, with supervisors and managers, with unions, and so on.

Some negotiations are clearly defined—for example, bargaining with a union. Others are more amorphous and often pass unnoticed as negotiations per se. Consider this interchange, for example: "Golly, boss, I really goofed up that time." "Oh, no, John, you performed as well as could be expected under the circumstances." The result is that John gets his ego stroked, and the boss feels parental and supportive.

The purpose of this article is to examine the factors involved in choosing among three common strategies of negotiation—competitive, collaborative, and subordinative. Emphasis throughout will be placed on the application of these strategies within your work environment.

CHARACTERISTICS OF COMMON
NEGOTIATING STRATEGIES

In the business/professional community all three strategies are seen. For example, a purchasing agent's interaction with a used equipment dealer in an effort to arrive at the highest possible trade-in value for a used machine is an example of competitive bargaining. Each party is intent upon a win-lose outcome. In contrast, interactions among fellow members of a research team may be largely collaborative or integrative; their goal is to achieve a winning situation for all parties. The "yes man" who, as an interim negotiating strategy, consciously agrees with the boss is operating in the subordinative mode of behavior. Though he may appear to be losing at the time, the "yes man" may be ensuring a future victory or setting up a situation in which he can apply the collaborative or competitive mode.

The distinguishing characteristics of these three negotiation strategies differ markedly from one another and may vary in form and emphasis from situation to situation. Exhibit 1 lists the characteristics of each of the three strategies. Exhibit 2 gives a synopsis of these three modes, including their dynamics, characteristics, and predicted results.

DETERMINING WHICH STRATEGY TO USE

How does one determine which strategy—competitive, collaborative, or subordinative—to adopt for such business situations as negotiating next year's objectives with one's supervisor, negotiating for new personnel, settling a grievance, or negotiating a contract? Deciding on the appropriate strategy enables one to select the appropriate behavior. The key lies in the relationship between the parties' goals.

The pivotal discriminating question is: If I reach my goals, will the other party, in some degree, be unable to reach his or her goal? If the answer to this is "yes" and to the extent to which it is true, the parties have entered into a competitive negotiation. On the other hand, the extent to which your own goal achievement involves or leads to the other party's goal achievement is the extent to which the situation is collaborative and integrative. But if you consciously subordinate your own goals to avoid conflict, then you have assumed a subordinative role.

PROBLEMS CREATED BY EACH STRATEGY

The preceding discussion suggests a major source of problems in both social and business situations. The competitive and collaborative negotiating games are generally played simultaneously, and sometimes these games involve subordinating on small points to gain a position of strength on larger goals or principles. For example, a company negotiator facing the union must, on the one hand, try to keep the settlement as close as possible to the low range of concessions set by industry patterns—knowing full well that the union representative is in an adversary position and has opposite intentions. At the same time, the company negotiator must be able to work with the union representative to find solutions to the problems of seniority, job jurisdiction, retraining programs, and so forth—demands created by the union's need to

EXHIBIT 1
Characteristics of Negotiation Strategies

	Competitive	Collaborative Negotiations	Subordinative Negotiations
1.	Behavior is purposeful in pursuing own goals at the expense of the other party.	Behavior is purposeful in pursuing goals held in common with others.	One party consciously subordinates own goals to avoid conflict with other party.
2.	Strategy involves secrecy and keeping one's cards close to the vest. It is characterized by high trust in one's self and low trust in the other party.	Strategy calls for trust and openness in expressing one's thoughts and feelings, actively listening to others, and actively exploring alternatives together.	Strategy means that one party is totally open to the extreme of exposing his or her vulnerabilities and weaknesses to the other.
3.	Parties have accurate personal understanding of own needs, but publicly disguise or misrepresent them. Neither party lets the other know what it really wants most, so that the other won't know how much it is really willing to give up to attain the goal.	Parties have accurate personal understanding of own needs, and represent them accurately to the other party. Each party has empathy and cares about the needs of the other party.	One party is so concerned with the other's needs that his or her needs are buried or repressed.
4.	Parties use unpredictable, mixed strategies and the element of surprise to outfox the other party.	Parties' actions are predictable. While flexible behavior is appropriate, it is not designed to take the other party by surprise.	One party's actions are totally predictable; his or her position is always one that caters to the other party.
5.	Parties use threats and bluffs and put each other on the defensive. Each always tries to keep the upper hand.	Parties share information and are honest with each other. They treat each other with mutual understanding and integrity.	One party gives up own position to mollify the other.

6. Search behavior is devoted to finding ways of appearing committed to a position; logical and irrational arguments alike may serve this purpose. Each party engages in destructive manipulation of the other's position.	6. Search behavior is devoted to finding mutually satisfying solutions to problems; utilizing logical, creative and innovative processes; and developing constructive relationships with each other.	6. Search behavior is devoted to finding ways to accommodate to position of other party.
7. Success is often enhanced (when teams or organizations are involved on each side) by creating a bad image or stereotype of the other, by ignoring the other's logic, and by increasing the level of hostility. These tend to strengthen in-group loyalty and convince competitors that one means business.	7. Success demands that bad stereotypes be dropped, that ideas be given consideration on their merit (regardless of sources), and that hostility not be induced deliberately. In fact, healthy, positive feelings about others are both a cause and an effect of other aspects of collaborative negotiations.	7. Success is determined by minimizing or avoiding all conflict and soothing any hostility. Own feelings are ignored in the interest of harmony.
8. Unhealthy extreme is reached when one party assumes that everything that prevents the other from attaining its goal facilitates movement toward one's own goal; thus each party feels that an integral part of its goal is to stop the other from attaining its goal.	8. Unhealthy extreme is reached when one party assumes that whatever is good for others and the group is necessarily good for one's own self, when one cannot distinguish one's identity from that of the group or the other party, or when one party will not take responsibility for itself.	8. Unhealthy extreme is characterized by complete acquiescence to the other's goal at the expense of personal or organizational goals. Concern with harmony results in total avoidance of conflict; the subordinate party becomes a doormat for the other party.
9. Key attitude/behavior is "I win, you lose."	9. Key attitude/behavior is "What is the best way to meet the goals of both parties?"	9. Key attitude/behavior is "You win, I lose."
10. If impasse occurs, a mediator or arbitrator may be required.	10. If difficulties arise, a facilitator skilled in group dynamics may be used.	10. If behavior becomes chronic, assertiveness training or a psychotherapist may be used.

EXHIBIT 2*
Three Modes of Negotiating Behavior and Their Predicted Results

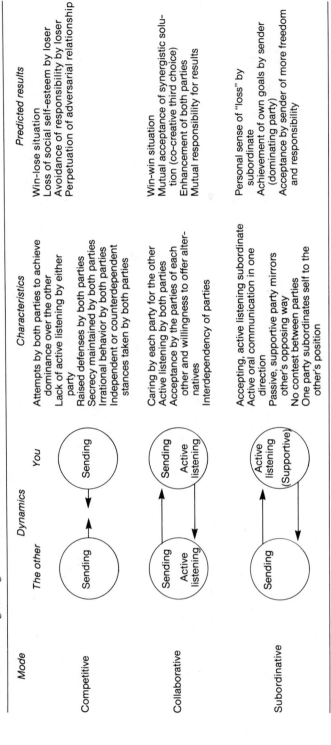

Mode	Dynamics		Characteristics	Predicted results
	The other	*You*		
Competitive	Sending	Sending	Attempts by both parties to achieve dominance over the other Lack of active listening by either party Raised defenses by both parties Secrecy maintained by both parties Irrational behavior by both parties Independent or counterdependent stances taken by both parties	Win-lose situation Loss of social self-esteem by loser Avoidance of responsibility by loser Perpetuation of adversarial relationship
Collaborative	Sending Active listening	Sending Active listening	Caring by each party for the other Active listening by both parties Acceptance by the parties of each other and willingness to offer alternatives Interdependency of parties	Win-win situation Mutual acceptance of synergistic solution (co-creative third choice) Enhancement of both parties Mutual responsibility for results
Subordinative	Sending	Active listening (Supportive)	Accepting, active listening subordinate Active oral communication in one direction Passive, supportive party mirrors other's opposing way No contest between parties One party subordinates self to the other's position	Personal sense of "loss" by subordinate Achievement of own goals by sender (dominating party) Acceptance by sender of more freedom and responsibility

* Prepared in collaboration with David C. Wigglesworth.

provide job security. Such demands often conflict with, but may sometimes coincide with, the corporation's need for operational flexibility. To cast the issue of economic settlement entirely into a collaborative model would be to risk granting a larger-than-necessary package. And to cast such issues as seniority provisions wholly into a competitive model would be to ignore whatever possibilities there are to meet union needs without management's making a corresponding sacrifice, and vice versa.

The question often becomes, then: What are the drawbacks of engaging in competitive, collaborative, or subordinative negotiating "games"? Let's look at each of the strategies in turn and discover the problems associated with each.

Drawbacks of the Competitive Game

Playing the competitive game creates a "win-lose" complex with the following consequences—each of which makes problem solving between the competitors more difficult:

1. *"We-they" and "superiority-inferiority" complexes.* Individuals, factions, or groups under competitive negotiating pressure invariably rate themselves "above average" in both cohesion and ability, while rating their competitors inferior.

2. *Distortions in judgment.* Under competitive pressure, individuals or groups invariably evaluate their own contributions as best and, as a result, they frequently fall into the trap of downgrading others' efforts. Consequently, the others feel put down, angry, and hostile; warfare—visible and/or invisible—often ensues.

3. *Distortions in perception.* Experiments demonstrate that under competitive pressures and the emotions that accompany them, people perceive, or claim to perceive, that they understand the other's proposal when, in fact, they do not. Consequently, areas that they share in common are likely to go unrecognized, obscured by emotional barriers and preoccupations with offensive and defensive maneuvering and the heat of battle.

Drawbacks of the Collaborative Strategy

The collaborative negotiating strategy, with its inherent goal of "win-win," can also be disastrous if it is followed too closely and too completely. Some of the consequences of this strategy can be:

1. *Exploitation of the opponent's strengths and weaknesses.* The amount of openness required can lead to a revelation of strengths and weaknesses that can be too easily exploited if either party reverts to a competitive negotiating mode.

2. *Manipulations tied to predictable patterns of behavior.* The amount of predictability required in collaborative negotiating can, if used too often and freely, result in one competitive party's using a

pattern of behavior that can be manipulated by the other to his or her advantage, resulting in a loss of bargaining strength.

3. *Overbearing attitude of negotiators.*   Very often, collaborating negotiators develop a "We can solve it" attitude and viewpoint detrimental to those whom they represent. As a result, they work out an agreement or position totally unacceptable to their clients, and new negotiations that frequently involve different, more intransigent bargainers, must be undertaken.

Drawbacks of Subordinative Strategy

The dangers involved when either or both of the negotiators use the subordinative mode to too great an extent would appear obvious. Several of these are:

1. *Regular capitulation to the other party.*   A pattern of "giving in easily" is established that may be difficult or impossible to reverse when vital issues that the subordinating party wants to influence are under negotiation.

2. *Suppression of the subordinating party's own interests.*   The subordinator begins to work harder at appeasing the other side than in seeing that his own or his client's interests are expressed and pursued.

3. *A false sense of well-being.*   The phony harmony produced in negotiation creates a false sense of well-being that does not carry over into the "real world" and can even cause hard feelings and resentment among those who are not involved in the negotiations.

A General Problem: The Mixed Character of the "Game" Itself

The preceding suggests an important source of our problems: We really have to play the competitive, collaborative, and subordinative negotiating games simultaneously. For example, if you are a company negotiator facing the union, you must, on the one hand, try to keep the settlement near the lower end of the range set by industry patterns—knowing full well that your union counterpart is an adversary with opposite intentions. Yet, on the other hand, you have to be able to jointly explore solutions to problems concerning such issues as seniority, job jurisdiction, retraining programs, and so forth— problems created by your opponent's need to gain job security for union members and your need to achieve production flexibility for the company. To cast the economic conflict wholly into a competitive model would be to ignore whatever possibilities there are to meet union members' needs without a corresponding sacrifice on your part, and vice versa.

However, I think the more common problem with those of us in business and industry today is cynicism: We characteristically approach situations as if they were competitive even when they are not. Why are we so competitive in situations where collaborative negotiations would clearly produce the more effective and satisfying results? Some would say that the answer lies in human nature—that we can blame our genes for our competitiveness. Others say that it is our cultural heritage that taught us to be competitive. Be that as it may, management team-building experience, as well as our general knowledge of organizational life, tends to bear this out.

SHIFTING FROM COMPETITION TO COLLABORATION

Note the key role of values and attitudinal change as a factor that permits collaborative behavior to be substituted for competitive behavior. The important thing is that the parties begin to get to know each other and develop some trust in each other. Then they can begin to reexamine the situation to find its collaborative aspects. This, of course, is just what can happen in our management team-building efforts and within work teams in the factory and office.

In examining problems for which you have usually used the competitive negotiations approach, you can make three possible diagnoses:

Diagnosis 1. No real conflict exists even though such conflict has been assumed. That is, if you reexamine the logical aspects of the situation, you discover that no real conflict of goals or of opportunities for rewards (raises, promotions, and so forth) exists. In such a situation, you may find new collaborative and integrative possibilities for day-to-day negotiations with your supervisor, peers, and subordinates.

Diagnosis 2. There is no real goal conflict (a fact that you and the other parties involved already recognize), but different basic attitudes and antagonistic interpersonal relations between you and others are preventing negotiations from moving toward a common goal or goals. Here, it is best to work directly on improving interpersonal relationships—thereby creating mutual trust and concern for better teamwork and improved results.

Steps you can take toward that end include the following:

• As a starter, accept the other party's position in good faith.
• If antagonistic groups are involved, such as union and management committees or an operating department and the controller's department, break the groups down into smaller units and assign members to these joint subunits to enable the individuals to interact on a more direct, face-to-face basis.
• Increase the amount of time spent in fact-finding meetings.
• Use active listening techniques, and explore alternative solutions to problems instead of trying to argue that differences are more apparent than real.

Diagnosis 3. You may discover that apparent goal conflict is significant and real. If the reward structure in your situation is determined exclusively by others, you may have no choice but to play a competitive game in which the parties are competing for a larger slice of the same pie.

However, if you are a manager who establishes the nature and rules of the game, including the reward system, you can choose whether you use competitive, collaborative, or subordinative negotiation behavior. As you consider the relative advantages of the three types of negotiating strategies and as you use them, you might look for some developments in your area of influence that indicate a shift from a competitive stance to a collaborative negotiating mode. Such indications include:

    a. Better coordination of efforts.
    b. Better division of labor and equitable distribution of work.
    c. Internal or external motivation from individuals to achieve goals.
    d. Increased amount of communication, particularly active listening to achieve understanding.
    e. Mutual comprehension and common appraisals of communications.
    f. Increased attentiveness to other members of the organization.
    g. An orientation toward goals and a willingness to implement suggestions.
    h. Increased productivity per unit of time.
    i. Higher quality of product and more informed discussion about the job.
    j. Friendliness during discussions.

APPLYING STRATEGIES ON THE JOB

The situation in a work environment is frequently based on a reward structure that encourages some elements of all three types of behavior. A prime example of such a mixture involves the competition for promotion to higher levels of management. Obviously, only one person will "win" such a competition. Interactions among the competitors may take on very hostile, uncooperative overtones. However, other aspects of the reward structure, such as bonuses for meeting commitments, may demand that the competitors collaborate to meet company or departmental goals.

There are also situations in which subordinative behavior would be most advantageous—for instance, when one party is dealing from such a tremendous position of power that the other must "give in" to avoid losing completely.

Through practice and experience you can learn the value of each strategy and the advantages to be derived from learning to employ each of the three negotiating modes—competitive, collaborative, and subordinative—in accordance with your goals and the goals of those with whom you work.

SECTION SEVEN

Communication

At the heart of the negotiation process is communication. Without communication, negotiation would be no more than a series of bids or offers exchanged between parties. There would be no additional information provided to support a bid or offer, nor would there be information provided as to why that bid or offer was unacceptable. Without more information there would be no reason, other than the passage of time, for parties to make concessions. In short, there would be no negotiation.

The readings in this section provide several interesting viewpoints on communication during bargaining. In the first article, "Bargaining and Communication," Fred Ikle addresses concerns about both the economic and communication aspects of bargaining. He highlights the fundamental tension created by a negotiator's common interests versus his competing interests, and the need for communication as a process to resolve the tension. These competing pressures among negotiators lead to critical negotiating dilemmas and dynamics. One dilemma centers on the nature of truthful communication in negotiation. On the one hand, the parties need to accurately communicate with each other in order to explore their true preferences and priorities. At the same time, they need to recognize that there are incentives for not being completely truthful with their opponent—for example, for not disclosing their true "bottom line." Bluffing, deception, and concealment of minimally acceptable preferences can be advantageous to negotiators in obtaining more desirable outcomes. Bargainers thus have to choose between the advantages of being deceptive in communication, at the risk of not being believed, or the advantages of being completely truthful, at the risk of putting themselves at a disadvantage.

A second common communication problem is that negotiation frequently involves misunderstandings and miscommunications. Ikle argues that many people attribute breakdowns in negotiation to miscommunication—and that if the parties somehow communicated more accurately or more fully, negotiating problems would be more easily resolved. While this argument may be frequently true, better communication is not necessarily the best solution to all negotiating problems. Enhanced communication *can* reduce the possibility of misunderstanding and improve the relationship between parties over the long term, but stalled negotiations frequently also require more structural approaches to bring the parties closer together.

As a third point, Ikle discusses the function of ambiguous communications. Just as it has been assumed that negotiation would be improved if the parties eliminated misunderstanding and miscommunication, so has it also been commonly assumed that communication in negotiation should be as clear and accurate as possible. Ikle points out the circumstance under which ambiguous communication, both in verbal expression and the specificity versus vagueness of agreements reached, actually may be functional.

Finally, Ikle examines the role of rhetoric and propaganda in negotiation. Negotiators, particularly when they are accountable to larger organizations, governments or institutions, often need to employ rhetoric and propaganda in the negotiation process. The function of this propaganda is only partially directed toward influencing the actual outcome. Its more immediate purpose is to persuade or influence constituencies, bureaucracies, or outside observers that the negotiator is taking a "hard-line" position. As Ikle states, the more rhetorical and propagandistic the communication is, the more polarizing it is likely to be, and the less likely it is to be able to be helpful within the negotiation in terms of achieving jointly acceptable outcomes.

A second approach to communication in negotiation is provided by Frank Acuff and Maurice Villere in "Games Negotiators Play." Ikle approaches negotiation as an economic game with specific economic payoffs; in contrast, Acuff and Villere view some negotiation games as destructive communication rituals. This view draws on the theory of transactional analysis, an approach to understanding individual psychological behavior in social interaction. Transactional analysis creates a framework for examining interactive communication patterns between individuals, and for determining whether those interactive patterns are productive or destructive to each party's aims. Acuff and Villere identify a number of destructive games in the communication-negotiation process. Each of these games has a fairly common format and scenario, and leads to an unproductive outcome. Using transactional analysis, negotiators can learn to assess how destructive communication games occur, and how these processes can be counteracted to turn negotiations toward more productive ends.

A number of Acuff's and Villere's examples highlight the fact that miscommunication frequently occurs because the parties frequently attract complex statements, or because the message they send are vague and ambiguous. The remaining two articles in this section specifically focus on this ambiguity, the degree to which negotiators often talk "in code," and the degree to which communication is, therefore, open to misinterpretation. "The Negotiator's Art," by Joel Forkosch identifies some of the negotiator's commonly used codes, and the meanings of these coded statements. These statements sometimes have the positive effect of ambiguity that Ikle identified, but also can lead to confusion and misinterpretation as well.

The article "Meta-Talk: The Art of Deciphering Everyday Conversations," by Gerard Nierenberg and Henry Calero pushes the examination of coded messages further by showing that the way we use words, particularly everyday expressions and phrases, has a distinct psychological impact on the listener. If negotiators can effectively understand how to use these expressions, with their desired impact, then they can more effectively prepare the receiver for the message to be sent. These authors' insights into the nature of communication are useful and demonstrate how attention to communication detail can strongly shape the basic message that negotiators want to send.

To successfully use communications in negotiation, we need to know what contributes to clarity and understanding, and also to know when we want, or do not want, to achieve clarity and understanding.

FRED CHARLES IKLE

Reading 7-1

Bargaining and Communication

All bargaining requires communication. In fact, almost all the action in bargaining consists of communication if the term *communication* is defined broadly enough to include everything that a party does to make its opponent aware of its wishes, intentions, and interpretations of the adversary relationship. In everyday interpersonal bargaining, opponents communicate with words, signals, or gestures. In international negotiations, the parties may also communicate through their many postures, economic measures, and policy changes. Even such moves as personnel changes can be used to communicate in a bargaining situation: for instance; the placement of a "dove" by a "hawk" in a government position can convey a threat.

THE ESSENCE OF BARGAINING

Bargaining can be defined as a process of interaction between two or more parties for the purpose of reaching an agreement on an exchange, or an agreement to satisfy a common interest where conflicting interests are present. The agreement may be explicit (for instance, expressed in a contract) or tacit (i.e., an unspoken mutual understanding). Agreement, by definition, is the coincidence of offer and acceptance, both of which are acts of communication. Three conditions are necessary for bargaining to occur:

1. The parties must have some common interests, which means that they jointly prefer certain outcomes over other possible outcomes (e.g., the joint preference that war not break out, or that a sale take place).
2. The parties must have conflicting interests, which means that

Reprinted from *Handbook of Communication,* Ithiel de Sola Pool and Wilbur Schramm et al., eds. Copyright 1973 by Houghton-Mifflin Publishing Company.

some of the jointly preferred outcomes are better for one party whereas others are better for the other party (e.g., divergent preferences regarding the conditions under which a conflict is settled short of war, or regarding the price of a sale).

3. The parties must be able to communicate somehow.

It is useful to distinguish between *negotiation* as a form of bargaining where explicit proposals are being put forward, and *tacit bargaining* where the parties do not explicitly propose terms or explicitly consent to a settlement. Note, however, that in negotiation the explicit exchanges are only part of the bargaining process. In international negotiation, especially, the most important moves are often tacit, while the verbal exchange is secondary.

Bargaining can also be examined in terms of economic variables alone. Indeed, for many real-life bargaining situations, the essentials are explainable with the concepts and language of economics (Cross, 1969). Yet, the role of communications in bargaining tends to be oversimplified in such approaches, and other social and psychological aspects, of course, fall outside an economic analysis.

The basic moves in bargaining and negotiation are commitments and threats. A *commitment* can be defined as an action whereby one party changes his *own* incentives in order to alter the opponent's expectations about his future conduct. That is, one party seeks to convince his opponent that he will carry out some prediction (such as holding firm or implementing a threat) by making it more difficult for himself not to do so—in other words, by committing himself.

A *threat* can be defined as a special kind of conditional prediction that a party addresses to his opponent. To threaten is to let one's opponent know that, should he fail to comply with your position, you will make a special effort to inflict a certain damage on him (Ikle, 1964, 1968).

Since the nuclear era, the concept of the threat has been extensively analyzed in writings on military strategy and disarmament. Nuclear deterrence, of course, is based on a threat. A key question about threats is their credibility: Will they be carried out if the opponent fails to comply, or will the first party be "caught bluffing"? To make threats more credible, they are usually buttressed by commitments.

THE FUNCTION OF LYING AND TRUTHFULNESS

As seen by the opponents in a bargaining situation, communication ordinarily serves to convey some truthful information as well as to give false information (or at least to conceal the truth). If one or both parties conveyed either only false or only truthful information, bargaining would tend to atrophy. Thus, if a party became known to give information that is almost invariably false, its threats and commitments would lose credibility, while its offers to agree would lose all value. If, on the other hand, a party consistently conveyed truthful information, its explicit commitments and threats would become highly rigid. With complete truthfulness, every explicit threat would be carried out whenever the opponent failed to comply, and every explicit commitment would be upheld. For instance, if a completely truthful seller argued that he would not accept a lower price, he would in fact be predicting with certainty that a sale at a lower price will never take place.

If the definition of truthfulness is extended to mean that the parties not only abstain from knowingly making false statements but also fully reveal their intended moves and their own (cardinal) preferences, the process of bargaining atrophies to a "game with complete information" (in the mathematical game-theory sense of the term). The outcome is then given by the parties' payoff structure. Stated in this form, the fact that bargaining is incompatible with completely truthful communication sounds like a truism. However, in many proposed "rules" for negotiators, the requirement for and complexity of *partial* truthfulness is lost sight of.

To exploit the common interests in a bargaining situation, the parties can often benefit from mutual frankness. Of course, the more they are like partners engaged in common enterprises—rather than like hostile antagonists—the better can they jointly search for common interests. This search takes the form of discovering, or inventing, outcomes that leave both parties better off—a process that will be facilitated if the parties reveal their true preferences. Thus, bargaining can become partly common problem solving (Walton & McKersie, 1965, pp. 356–357; Shure & Meeker, 1969).

MISUNDERSTANDINGS AND LONG-TERM CONDITIONS

The possibility for exploring common interests is related to the notion that conflict frequently stems from misunderstandings. The valid core of this notion must be separated from unwarranted extensions. Of course, the proposition that conflict would be eliminated if people (or nations) understood each other better can become tautologically true, depending on the definition of "understanding." But the view that people and nations would overcome their conflicts if only they could better communicate their objectives and intentions to each other is based on too rosy a picture of the world. Indeed, one can easily find illustrations where a full communication of antagonistic objectives would only have deepened existing conflicts. Also, evidence from experiments in interpersonal bargaining indicate that the opponents would have been unable to converge on certain mutually advantageous outcomes had they had more complete information about each other's payoffs (Shure & Meeker, 1969).

One of the interesting features of the "prisoner's dilemma" game is the very fact that the parties' knowledge of the opponent's payoff matrix does not help in resolving the conflict. Indeed, one can invent "prisoner's dilemma" games where misinformation between the parties would help both sides to achieve a better outcome. If communication between the parties cannot be blocked or used for misinformation, the mutually deleterious outcomes of a "prisoner's dilemma" will be avoided only if the parties remain concerned about a long-term "super game," that is to say, if they expect and plan for recurrent conflicts of the "prisoner's dilemma" type.

The valid core of the notion that conflict can be reduced through better communication has several elements:

First, there is the before-mentioned possibility that through frank discussion the parties can discover new outcomes that are to their mutual advantage.

Second, if the actual differences between parties have been exaggerated, better communication will help to reduce antagonistic feelings.

Third, clear communication of a commitment or threat can help to deter the opponent from an initiative that would exacerbate the conflict. That is to say, if a party really means to carry out its threat or to stick with a commitment, and if the opponent will yield if he learns of this determination, communicating firmness obviously helps to prevent a clash. Since World War II, this thought has found wide expression in the literature on international relations and nuclear deterrence. For instance, it has often been argued that the Communist attack on South Korea would not have taken place had the United States made it clear that it would come to South Korea's help.

Fourth, communication in bargaining serves what might be called a "systemic" purpose; that is, the purpose of altering the long-term relationship with the opponent rather than the outcome of a particular negotiation. Indeed, the full implications of threats and commitments cannot be ascertained realistically without reference to long-term expectations among the parties. In simulation experiments in bargaining, where subjects (say, college students) take the role of parties, it is most difficult, if not impossible, to introduce realistically these long-term expectations and the processes by which they change. This is one reason why the results of simulation studies of threats are difficult to apply to real-life situations.

Another reason for the limited applicability of game experiments is the richness and importance of the context of bargaining situations, which modifies the nature and functioning of threats and commitments. As one reviewer of the extensive literature on such games observed:

> Game experiments on "threat" have shown most clearly the futility of posing psychological hypotheses containing terms like "threat" in a way that suggests the existence of a "theory of behavior under threat." Hypotheses so formulated cannot be tested, because the "threat conditions" set up by different investigators may have little in common except a designation as such (*Journal of Conflict Resolution*, 1970, p. 65).

Even if the researcher is prepared to disregard the long-term context (or "super game") in his gaming experiments, he will find it difficult to operationalize the concept of threat. Several otherwise interesting experiments have been criticized on this score (Kelley, 1965).

Since full communication of a threat or commitment is required to make it

effective, the opponent, whose bargaining position is supposed to be soft-
ened by such moves, may have an interest in not receiving this communication. The efficacy of this "burning of communications bridges" has been
observed in the way children bargain with parents, in day-to-day bargaining
among adults, and even in labor-management negotiations (Schelling, 1960,
pp. 17–18, 146–150; Walton & McKersie, 1965, pp. 113–115). It has much
less application in international negotiations for the simple reason that
modern governments cannot convincingly pretend that they do not hear
messages that the opponent broadcasts to them. (Sometimes governments
refuse to accept a diplomatic note that a messenger from a foreign embassy
attempts to deliver. This occasional practice has symbolic meaning only: it
conveys strong disapproval or disdain regarding the content of the note, or
underlines the lack of diplomatic relations with the sender country; but it
cannot mean that the message has not been heard.)

AMBIGUITY VERSUS SPECIFICITY

Ambiguity has several important effects in negotiation. On the one hand,
ambiguous agreements can lead to a reopening of the conflict later on. On the
other hand, an attempt to introduce specificity might prolong negotiation or
even prevent agreement altogether. Hence, parties often tolerate ambiguous
agreement deliberately, thereby postponing the residual points of disagreement—perhaps in the hope that these would never lead to conflict. Ambiguity in an agreement can also be unintended, resulting from inadequate
communication between the parties regarding each other's understanding of
the terms on which they converge.

In international negotiation, particularly in East-West conferences, a great
deal of time is sometimes spent in disputes about how specific an agreement
should be made. These disputes are essentially a symptom of disagreement
about the substance of the settlement, not about its form. If there were
agreement on the substance of the settlement, there should, on the one hand,
be no objection to spelling it out in detail and, on the other, little interest in
recording the details. If a party objects to giving an agreement greater
specificity, this is usually a concealed way of communicating that there is
continuing disagreement. Sometimes, disputes about how specific an agreement should be can stem from different preferences as to how much latitude
future mediators should have (Ikle, 1964, pp. 8–15).

Ambiguity in conveying commitments or threats serves to soften these
moves. Thus, an ambiguous threat is unspecific concerning either the occasion when the threatened action would occur or the content of that action.
From the point of view of the threatening party, an ambiguous threat has the
disadvantage of being less credible, but the advantage of allowing more
freedom to react mildly without proving oneself a bluffer. Moreover, the
opponent might give in (or stay deterred) regardless, since he, too, faces
uncertainty.

PROPAGANDA AND RHETORICAL DEBATE

If the bargaining parties are not private individuals, but organizations or institutions (such as governments or labor unions), the communication flow affects third parties as well as the internal bureaucracy of each party. Consequently, much of what is said in negotiations may be addressed to (1) outsiders, in the hope that they in turn would influence the opponent (for instance, through propaganda to affect "world opinion"); or (2) one's own internal bureaucracy. Representatives of labor unions have to make statements for the benefit of rank-and-file membership; government delegates at international conferences may have to address themselves to interagency conflicts back home or to domestic public opinion. Indeed, such internal audiences are often the only justification for the negotiator's rhetoric.

The exchange of words across the conference table thus is only partly relevant to the outcome and, even when relevant to the outcome, is often effective indirectly through third parties. This limited relevance can be analyzed in more detail:

1. Weak rhetoric at the conference table may lead to weak delegation reports to the home government. The delegate at the conference site, as a result of his ineffectiveness in debating tactics, may get the impression that his government's position is difficult to defend and that the opponent is unlikely to budge. Hence, he will report to his government that the opponent's position is firm and advise making a concession. (This hypothesis might be tested by correlating weak defenses at the conference table with the recommendations that the delegation sends back home afterwards.) The same applies to the conference talk between delegates of nongovernmental organizations, such as labor unions and business corporations.

2. Weak rhetoric at the conference makes it easier for "soft" allies to maneuver a party into concessions. If the opposing ideas are strong adversaries, the rhetorical aspects of the debate will have little direct effect on their positions, since the relationship between such opponents cannot be affected much by words alone. However, *within* a team of close allies (such as the United States and the United Kingdom in the nuclear test ban negotiations), where words *are* used to settle differences, the "rhetorical loss" of a point with the common opponent might lead to the "forensic loss" of the same point in the private debate with an ally who prefers to soften the common allied position. Thus, while the rhetoric in long-winded negotiations may have little effect on "world opinion" because the news media will have long ceased to pay attention to it, debating defeats might, nonetheless, be exploited by allies (the ever-present witnesses at the green table) in the private forum where the interallied policy is hammered out.

3. In a protracted conference where little real bargaining occurs, the formal debates may nonetheless generate major themes that become

part of the agenda or the negotiating position for subsequent bargaining. This may be a deliberate tactic of one or the other party, or it may be inadvertent. In the 1957 London Disarmament Conference, principal aspects of the nuclear test ban—such as the moratorium and the isolation from other arms controls—were already raised to such a status during the prolonged debates that it would have been hard to reject them out of hand when the real negotiations started a year later (Zoppo, 1961).

4. Sometimes negotiators at the conference table—like human beings in other situations—talk without really knowing what they wish to accomplish with their words. That is, communication during bargaining situations may serve no bargaining purpose at all—or, at the most, may serve merely to fill the time until new conditions lead to a change in the position of one or the other side.

One of the advantages of mediation is that it tends to do away with the largely dysfunctional rhetoric so common in direct negotiations. Part of the function of a mediator is to facilitate, as well as to filter, communication between opponents. Proposals and counterproposals conveyed through a mediator are more tentative, since the mediator can be more easily disavowed than an official delegate. Also, a mediator, not being part of the bureaucracies of either side, does not have to insert statements addressed to these home constituencies.

SUMMARY

The many functions of communication in bargaining situations can be grouped as follows:

1. Communication, especially of the explicit, verbal types, serves to convey or to accept offers. When an offer is made very precisely and explicitly, or when an acceptance is final, the statements of the negotiator become, in part, "performative sentences" (in J. L. Austin's meaning of this term). That is, the very saying of the sentence is also the act described in this sentence: e.g., "my government offers, . . ." "I accept" (Austin, 1965).

2. Communication, explicit as well as tacit, is used to change the opponent's expectations as to the probable outcome from the time bargaining begins until agreement is reached or contact is broken off.

    a. Expectations are changed through the terms of offers and counteroffers (they convey the range of the outcome), as well as through commitments (they indicate the probability that a position will be maintained) and through threats (they alter the expected loss in the event no agreement is reached).

    b. In addition, the way in which offers are conveyed and the language used to describe the issues can highlight one particular outcome within a range. The communications signal a "focal point" toward which the opponent's (and perhaps one's own) expectations regarding the outcome are being guided (Schelling, 1960, pp. 111–113).

3. Communications between the opponents can also accomplish changes in the way in which they *evaluate* alternative outcomes. In interpersonal bargaining, this may take the form of direct persuasion. In international negotiations, direct persuasion between opposing governments occurs rarely. Nonetheless, in prolonged international negotiations, a similar, although somewhat more indirect, process can be of prime importance. The ways in which the parties evaluate their own payoffs and those of their opponent can be changed gradually, not because diplomats are such persuasive people, but because these evaluations are highly complex, often result from intricate intragovernmental compromises, and involve a great deal of uncertainty. Hence, the gain and loss calculations regarding specific outcomes tend to be uncertain and can be modified by the casualness or reluctance with which a concession is given, the way in which a certain outcome is labeled, the boundaries that are drawn around the bargaining issues, and other ways of defining or describing the situation (Ikle, 1964, Chap. 10).

    This change in the evaluation of a specific outcome should not be confused with a change in expectations as to the characteristics of possible outcomes. (The former, for instance, would be the view that a certain territorial settlement means a loss or a gain. The latter would be the expectation that agreement can be reached that the 18th or 19th parallel will become the new boundary.) Incidentally, diplomatic histories tend to neglect the fact that such a change in evaluations often results from the communications flow in prolonged negotiations.

4. Finally, communication between negotiators serves to reveal new outcomes. The parties, by exchanging information about their preferences and about various constraints and opportunities regarding the issues under negotiation, might help each other to discover or to invent outcomes that would leave both sides better off than with the outcomes initially sought.

References

Austin, J. L.   1965.   *How to Do Things with Words.* New York: Oxford University Press.

Cross, John G.   1969.   *The Economics of Bargaining.* New York: Basic Books.

Ikle, Fred C.   1964.   *How Nations Negotiate.* New York: Harper & Row.
———— .   1968.   "Negotiation." *International Encyclopedia of the Social Sciences,* ed. David L. Sills. Vol. 11. New York: Macmillan, pp. 117–20.
Journal of Conflict Resolution.   1970. "Editorial Comments." *Journal of Conflict Resolution* 14:65.
Kelley, Harold H.   1965.   "Experimental Studies of Threats in Interpersonal Negotiations." *Journal of Conflict Resolution* 9:79–105.
Schelling, Thomas C.   1960.   *The Strategy of Conflict.* Cambridge, Mass.: Harvard University Press.
Shure, Gerald H., & Robert J. Meeker.   1969.   "Bargaining Processes in Experimental Territorial Conflict Situations." *Peace Research Society (International) Papers,* ed. Walter Isard and Julian Wolpert. Vol. II. Philadelphia: Peace Research Society, pp. 109–22.
Walton, Richard E., & Robert B. McKersie.   1965.   *A Behavioral Theory of Labor Negotiations.* New York: McGraw-Hill.
Zoppo, Ciro E.   1961.   *The Issues of Nuclear Test Cessation at the London Disarmament Conference of 1957: A Study in East-West Negotiation.* RM-2821-ARPA. Santa Monica, Calif.: RAND Corporation (September).

Additional Readings

Borah, Lee A., Jr. "The Effects of Threat in Bargaining: Critical and Experimental Analysis." *Journal of Abnormal and Social Psychology* 66 (1963):37–44.
Hermann, Margaret, and Nathan Kogan. "Negotiation in Leader and Delegate Groups." *Journal of Conflict Resolution* 12 (1968):332–344.
Rapoport, Anatol, and A. M. Chammah. *Prisoner's Dilemma: A Study in Conflict and Cooperation.* Ann Arbor: University of Michigan Press, 1965.
Shubick, Martin. "Some Reflections on the Design of Game Theoretic Models for the Study of Negotiation and Threats." *Journal of Conflict Resolution* 7 (1963):1–12.
———— . *Games of Status.* Santa Monica, Calif.: The RAND Corporation, August 1968.

FRANK L. ACUFF and
MAURICE VILLERE

Reading 7–2
Games Negotiators Play

The process and outcome of negotiations can have an enormous impact not only upon the parties involved, but on third parties and the public interest itself. For example, a recent transit strike in a large metropolitan area completely shut down mass transit operations in the city for over three months. This strike affected not only the salaries of the union employees and the profits of management, but the industries and individuals dependent on mass transit—primarily retail establishments and the poor.

Much of the delay in settling disputes is attributable to the negotiating practices of the parties involved. Some practices are efficient and effective in meeting the goals of all concerned. Other practices lead to long and tedious dickering which brings severe hardship to many who should not be involved and many who cannot bear such a hardship.

Many of the examples to be discussed in this article are drawn from labor negotiations for illustration purposes, but have an applicability to many other personnel or business transactions. Whether an attempt by junior to get dad's car keys or a diplomatic strategy to obtain pivotal concessions of international impact, the negotiating process is a pervasive one to all of us. Moreover, productive negotiations will become even more imperative as industries and institutions become larger and more complex.

One poor negotiating practice which is present in all types of negotiations (regardless of the nature of the business or the parties involved), and which is a major deterrent to effective and efficient settlements, is game playing.

"Game" is defined here in the terms of transactional analysis (TA).

F. Acuff and M. Villere, "Games Negotiators Play," *Business Horizons,* February 1976. Copyright, 1976, by the Foundation for the School of Business at Indiana University. Reprinted by permission.

TRANSACTIONAL ANALYSIS PRINCIPLES

Transactional analysis (TA) divides the individual's personality into three ego states. An ego state is defined as a consistent pattern of thinking and feeling attached to a pattern of behaving. The three states are defined as follows:

Parent—that part of the personality dealing mainly with values, opinions and how-to prescriptions. It may be expressed two ways. First is the critical parent state, which only accepts the individual if he follows instructions very closely. This state is the prime dispenser of negative strokes. Second is the nurturing parent, the supportive type of authority which accepts the individual unconditionally.

Adult—the rational part of the personality. Rather than being concerned with outdated parental dictums, the adult part of us acts as a computer by digesting current factual data for problem-solving purposes. The adult often plays the role of executive of the personality, utilizing parent and child data for decision making and permitting the activation of the other ego states where appropriate.

Child—the emotional part of the personality. It may be expressed through: (*a*) free child, the source of straightforward feelings, creativity and spontaneity; or (*b*) adapted child, which expresses itself as rebelliousness or over submissiveness—the "yes man" in all of us.

Parent Cues (*Verbal*)	*Adult Cues* (*Verbal*)	*Child Cues* (*Verbal*)
Shoulds	Who?	I need
Oughts	What?	I feel
Do's	Now?	Wow
Don'ts	Why?	Gee
Be like me.	Let's consider this.	I want it my way.

According to TA, a game is an implicit interactional strategy where the outcome is negative. By implicit, we mean that in a game a person appears to be doing something agreeable and profitable on the surface while the actual motive is negative and is disguised ulteriorly.[1] The negative payoff is usually in the form of a subtle or not so subtle put-down or negative stroke addressed toward an opposing party. In the terminology of TA, games arise out of "not OK" positions. In the negotiating setting, the position is often I'm OK but my opponent is a not OK enemy to be dealt with. For those not familiar with TA terms, see the accompanying box of definitions.

A: Excuse me, Fred, what time do you have?
B: About 10:15.
A: Didn't we agree to meet at 10:00 on the nose?

---

[1] Eric Berne, *Games People Play* (New York: Grove Press, 1964).

B: Right, I'm sorry. One of the team got a phone call at the last minute.

A: Let's stick to our word, then, Fred, and not keep the members of my committee away from all their other obligations. I should certainly hope these negotiations are as high a priority for you as they are for us.

A classic example of a game in TA terminology is NIGYSOB, or Now I've Got You, You Son of a Bitch. In negotiating, this game may come about, for instance, when one party uses a trivial error (tardiness) of the opponent's as a basis for belittling the opponent's overall considerateness and sincerity. A thus has an excuse to show displeasure against B and is actually delighted to have a vehicle from which to vent pent-up feelings.

The joy A gains from such self-righteous anger may easily overshadow the original provocation. The problem with game playing is that, in the end, nobody wins. One may get the temporary feeling that he is one up on someone else (that he has really put someone else down; for example, by making him feel foolish), but in the long run nothing is accomplished. Certainly, the demeanor of mutuality and cooperation, the basis for effective negotiating, is severely jeopardized. In fact, often an atmosphere of hostility replaces the previously cooperative one. Now rather than attempting to pull in harness toward just terms, hurt parties will become primarily concerned with protecting their egos and getting even. As a consequence, games prevent honest and open relationships, promote distrust, destroy rapport and, in the final analysis, inhibit the attainment of objectives.

NEGOTIATING GAMES

In order to deal effectively with game players, one must first be aware that a game is in progress. A prime way to achieve this awareness is to become familiar with typically played negotiating games. The following 10 games appear to be typical in a multitude of negotiating settings. Though obviously not complete, these games should introduce the reader to games generally played during negotiating sessions.

Expertise

The apparent purpose of this game is to establish that one has a knowledge of the facts affecting the negotiations. Expertise is usually played early in the negotiations, thus trying to achieve a position of credibility by giving the impression one's homework has been done.

A: We have been able to determine the economic factors affecting this negotiation through the prodigious efforts of our resident economist, Dr. Adam Smith, and the cooperation granted us by the U.S. Bureau of Labor Statistics.

B: We likewise have gathered the data necessary to assess the economic needs and strains in force upon the parties through the use of a fourth generation computer and the most advanced systems analysis and programming available in data processing.

A: Advanced data processing techniques are fine, but unless these are based on useful information, the output will be of little use to us. "Garbage in, garbage out," as they say.

B: We agree. That is why that instead of depending on a single individual who is interpreting governmental statistics perhaps irrelevant to our situation, we would enlist the help of DP techniques that would make a great deal of information immediately relevant.

This game appears to be played only on the adult-adult level, since the tool of this game is purportedly "the facts," or an easy access to them. Actually, however, A's ego state is closer to that of the critical parent whose purpose is to demean B's competence through A's "superior" grasp of the subject matter.

Snow Job

This game is similar to Expertise in that purported facts and figures are its main tool and its use may be that of trying to establish credibility. Snow Job is played by A and B trying to overwhelm the other with facts and figures, a game often played throughout the negotiations process.

A: It is clear that by your proposal the 30 percent increase affects the lower 72 percent of the workers with gains of less than 9 percent increase, and the top 10 percent wage earners with gains of $0.67 per hour, a proportion our membership can hardly tolerate, particularly when the whole package represent 7 percent less than the average real wages now paid by (X competitor), and 15 percent less than (Y competitor) pays its middle 18 percent of the wage earners.

B: I really didn't understand all that. Could you please summarize the details?

A: I don't think that's necessary. It's obvious that any one of those facts will tell you we must have a 57 percent increase.

So What?

This game is played by the parties immediately after a concession has been won at the bargaining table. Regardless of the priority given the item prior to concession, the post concession posture is that the item really wasn't important in the first place.

The winning position is to de-emphasize the conceded item so that the party gaining the concession can maintain leverage for gaining other concessions. In other words, "What you gave us was small potatoes, now let's get on to the biggies." The party granting the concession will attempt, of course, to escalate the importance of the concession. The transaction might look like this.

A: The parties then agree that one company-paid holiday per year will be added.

B: Right. Now, let's get on to some of the demands central to these negotiations.

A: What could be more central than this one holiday? You've been stressing this issue since the last negotiations. We've spent several hours this week negotiating an item which will have a major cost and scheduling impact on our operations. This concession should wash out some of the remaining negotiable items.

B: Hardly. This is something we really shouldn't have had to bargain over in the first place.

Wheat and Chaff

This game has perhaps the longest life span of any negotiating game. It is established early and nurtured throughout negotiations. Wheat and Chaff is played by putting in chaff (minutae or not really priority items) in order to obtain the wheat (priority items). The idea is to pad the demands with items you can give away. Ideally, this course of action leads to the position, "We've given so much (chaff disguised as wheat) but gotten so little (wheat)," or "We're doing all the giving." B naturally responds that what they have received are really items of low priority (chaff). While B stresses the lack of *quality* (wheat) in the concessions A has made, A will continue to emphasize the *quantity* of items conceded.

Wheat and Chaff may be played for political reasons, espousing the multitude of items the rank and file wishes voiced during negotiations. Wheat and Chaff, therefore, may serve the purpose of at least introducing these items if not resolving them. In this way those represented will know that their representatives have "fought the good fight."

Wooden Leg

The thesis of this game is "What would you expect of a man with a wooden leg?" A argues that he is suffering from a limitation that makes him unresponsible for his action. Examples in everyday life are a headache and drunkenness in order to avoid doing a full day of productive work. This game is played from A's child ego state, and is complemented by B's parent.

A: We haven't been able to show the real impact of your counterproposal because we are lacking representation from each of the subdepartments affected.

B: That would bring your committee size to 27. Our sessions would be unmanageable.

A: True, but we're at a severe disadvantage without having full representation from all groups.

A wooden leg often used by both company and union negotiators are the respective constituents whom they represent—management and the rank and file. A, for example, contends that B's proposal is on its face acceptable, but the unruly mob back at the union hall or the management team just won't buy it at this time.

A popular wooden leg of union negotiating teams is a purported lack of financial resources and staffing with which to prepare for negotiations. Being careful not to infringe upon the Expertise game, the union will stress that it has not been blessed with the wealth of resources possessed by management's negotiating team.

Between a Rock and a Hard Place

In this game, A argues, "I hear you, I know what you need, and I'd like to give it to you, but I can't win for losing." Like Wooden Leg, a purported helplessness abounds. Separation appears to be momentarily established between A and his constituents. Ostensibly a strong attempt is made by A to establish an empathy and identification, and even temporary coalition with B. Actually, however, A is creating a noncompromising posture by claiming to be caught in a dilemma.

Sandbagger

In this game, A attempts to negotiate from a position of strength by establishing his own weaknesses. A creates, or feigns the degree of his wounds and weaknesses in order to exaggerate the relative strength of the opponent. By emphasizing his own weakness, A hopes to gain relative strength by preying upon B's sympathy or uncautiousness.

A, for example, may claim that negotiating is a new experience, and ask for B's patience and understanding. Or, A may state that even though he lacks the eloquence which comes from B's formal education and training, A will nevertheless attempt to struggle on. A will argue that such an imbalance is but yet another example of the uphill battle which "simple earnest men" must fight.

A: Tell me, none of us have had much of a chance to look into the world of high finance. I notice in the newspaper that your stock rose 93 points last year. What does that mean?

B: The points are equivalent to dollars.

A: It is good that the points increased?

B: Certainly our shares are now worth more. Investors have increased confidence in our business.

A: Interesting. What would cause all these points, as you call them, to increase so much?

B: Largely because of our record year of profits.

A: You don't say! It doesn't really matter, I was just curious.

A's own weaknesses are created or magnified in both Sandbagger and Wooden Leg. In the former, A is more likely to be cognizant of the degree of his exaggeration, whereas in the latter, the actual or imagined weakness is more likely an unconscious crutch. In Sandbagger, the con man in all of us is at work.

Boredom

The game is best played during a time when the opponent is making his most salient and forceful points. Body language is often an important supporting device, courteously notifying the opponent that his points fail to impress. A often plays boredom during points which B is reiterating. By such reiteration, B risks terminating the game if actual ennui sets in.

If It Weren't for You

This game shields A from acknowledging his own inadequacies. A union-initiated game might look like this:

> **A:** If it weren't for your narrowminded views on each of the issues, our rank and file wouldn't be so discontented.
> **B:** Your excessive demands have made the rank and file unduly optimistic.
> **A:** Our demands are in fact great because of the substandard base on which the rank and file has been living.

Presumably, all would be well with the rank and file if only B would bow to demands. If, in fact, B presented A with no differences on the various bargaining issues, there would be nothing left to bargain about. A's constituents might question the effectiveness, and even the necessity, of their leadership—there are no battles to be won if there are no battles. B has thus performed a service for A by providing opposition.

"Yes, But"

In the "Yes, But" game one individual appears to be seeking advice from another. In fact, his true purpose is to give negative strokes by discounting all the advice given. Every time a solution is suggested for solving his problem, he derides it with a "yes, but . . ."

> **A:** We very much feel the need to negotiate next week, but our schedule looks awfully tight for our regular morning sessions. Any suggestions as to when to get together?
> **B:** Well, instead of our usual morning meetings, let's try afternoons.
> **A:** Yes, we would, but it looks like full agendas for every afternoon next week except Friday.
> **B:** Okay, let's shoot for Friday afternoon. We can at least discuss remaining items on through—
> **A:** Yes, but do you really think we could accomplish anything in just one afternoon?
> **B:** Well, we've met at night in the past. Perhaps the afternoon meeting combined with one or two evening meetings.
> **A:** Yes, but we've often questioned the real utility of bargaining when tired. Why don't we shoot for week after next?

COUNTERACTING GAMES

A number of general strategies can be used to counteract or avoid game playing.

Be Aware

Sometimes it is difficult to know if you are in a game because of the subtle nature of games. However, if you feel discounted or believe you are not getting anywhere in the negotiating, you are probably in a game.

Cultivate Openness

You and the other party are in the negotiating process together. If you both do not pull together in a straightforward manner, you will be pulling apart. As a result, costly negotiating time will be prolonged and, in the end, key issues and facts may be left out of the final contract—issues and facts which might mean the difference between a fair and livable settlement and an ineffective and unpopular one.

Give an Unexpected Response

Games are between at least two people and require cooperation to be successfully completed. Completion of a game is not possible if the second party does not give the proper response that will lead to the negative stroke. The critical parent, the main stroke dispenser, is trying to put down an adapted child. Similarly, the adapted child is setting himself up to be put down by a critical parent or be rescued by a nurturing parent.

By responding from an ego state other than that of the adapted child, critical parent or nurturing parent, one will be much more successful in getting out of the game.

Stop Exaggerating

Games involve one-upmanship. *I am better or stronger than you* is their implied meaning. Games can be terminated or avoided by getting down to the facts and by resisting the temptation to impress or depress the other party. Egotists and masochists are often on the receiving end of most negative strokes. If a negotiator comes to the bargaining table to prove something about himself, his organization, or the other parties involved rather than for the purpose of equitably settling a dispute, that's game playing.

Positive Strokes

The payoff of any game is a negative stroke or a put-down. When disputes become defensively charged or frustrating, it is easy to push the blame off on someone else in the form of a negative stroke. Attacking the other party closes, rather than opens, further communications. The following are examples of converting negative game strokes into positive, cooperative statements:

> *Negative Game Stroke.*   "That statement doesn't make any sense."
> *Positive Version.*   "Could you explain fully what you mean?"
> *Negative Game Stroke.*   "Do you really think you can get away with that?"
> *Positive Version.*   "We are more optimistic in meeting other demands than we are with this one."

Avoid Victim/Persecutor Roles

The persecutor dishes out the negative strokes and the victim collects them. Do not put yourself in the role of the victim by coming to the bargaining table unprepared with poorly researched information. By the same token, it is profitable to avoid the role of persecutor. You may have to negotiate tomorrow with the party you put down today. Supplant a spirit of persecution or hostility with one of cooperation. Cooperation has a way of being contagious. It is also the spirit which leads to effective and efficient results.

Game Inducing Stimulus	*Game Perpetuating Response*	*Unexpected Game Disrupting Response*
"This whole interchange is irrational." (Critical Parent)	"What's the use of arguing with you. You're going to get your way anyway." (Adapted Child)	"Any suggestions for getting us back on the track?" (Adult)
"I know you're not prepared only because you've had a lot of other problems at the office. No problem." (Nurturing Parent)	"I've got so many other things on my mind that I'm no good to anybody today." (Adapted Child)	"Based on the information I brought with me, let's see in what areas we can move forward." (Adult)
"Your demands are unrealistic!" (Critical Parent)	"You're the one who's unrealistic." (Critical Parent)	"Why?" (Adult)

JOEL A. FORKOSCH

Reading 7-3
The Negotiator's Art

Despite the impact that collective bargaining has on our daily lives, the general public—and even the majority of businessmen—are only dimly aware of the negotiation process.

Newspaper and other media reports of positions taken, statements made and concessions granted across the bargaining table are generally disseminated and accepted at face value. Rarely do such reports seek to distinguish between proposals asserted primarily as the basis for further negotiations and those that actually reflect a party's real position.

The proliferation of news media has also in recent years added a third party to the bargaining table, the public. Negotiators frequently say things for the sole purpose of creating a favorable public reaction, thereby hoping to exert pressure on the other side.

Collective bargaining as it has developed in the United States since the 1930s is premised on the existence of a "settlement range" within which both labor and management feel that it is in their interests to reach agreement rather than resort to economic pressure in the form of slowdowns, strikes, lockouts or boycotts.

The prime requisites for a good labor negotiator are:

- To be able accurately to identify this settlement range.
- To have the skill to negotiate a settlement that gives the other side just enough to make it willing to agree, but no more.

This "negotiating sense" is to a large degree a product of the negotiator's understanding of the language of collective bargaining and of his appreciation of the other side's real, as opposed to its announced, demands. The

J. Forkosch, "The Negotiator's Art," *The New York Times,* April 22, 1973. Copyright © 1973 by The New York Times Company. Reprinted by permission.

failure to develop these skills often means a strike that could have been avoided or a settlement much more expensive than could have been obtained.

Phrases that occur over and over in the language of collective bargaining include:

No Contract, No Work. To certain unions this unequivocably means that if a new contract is not reached before the expiration of the old contract they will strike. But many negotiators use the phrase loosely and wind up choking on it.

This is especially true if the old contract expires in midwinter. Even if the employes have voted strike authorization to the negotiating committee, two days on a picket line in freezing weather often proves the most effective tactic management possesses.

We Cannot Agree to More Than a One-Year Contract. This is generally used by unions, which favor short-term agreements as a hedge against a rising cost of living.

Management, on the other hand, prefers longer contracts so that it can calculate its labor costs for several years.

Management will often ignore a union demand for a one-year contract and gear its offers to a longer period. Unions, just as often, negotiate terms for a second and third year without explicitly backing off their initial demand for a one-year agreement.

Frequently, the new contract is for two or three years with a provision for reopening wage negotiations in the second or third year or for tying second- or third-year wage increases to rises in the cost of living.

This Proposal Is Acceptable in Principle. This is an answer often used by management to respond to a union proposal for a new economic benefit, such as a dental or optical plan.

This usually implies that management couldn't care less how the union divides the economic pie that it is being offered, but that the increased cost of the new benefit must come out of that pie, thus reducing other increases.

Just as often, though, management rejects such proposals for fear of opening the door to new cost items in the agreement.

Our Members Demand Establishment of a Company-Funded Day-Care Center So That Our Members' Wives Can Work. This or any other similar, seemingly revolutionary, concept broached as part of a union's initial package of demands is probably a trade-off item that the union will give up in return for something else, such as money.

This demand may have been something bandied about at a meeting held by the union's negotiating committee with the rank and file. The committee incorporated it into its demands to placate the employes and to serve as the basis for the refrain throughout negotiations that the company doesn't pay a living wage.

This Item Is Critical to Our Members. This can and often is applied to almost any type of union demand. It often signifies that union politics require that management offer something in a specific area to preserve the credibility of the negotiating committee in the eyes of the rank and file.

This frequently occurs where a dissident element has arisen within the union that is seeking to oust the present leadership. The union will often accept just a small part of the proposal in the contract or possibly just a promise by management to study the matter.

Sometimes, though, this may auger things to come in future negotiations and the present proposal is presented in earnest to set the stage.

This Proposal Requires Extensive Consideration; We Will Study It and Discuss It Later.   This should be contrasted to "absolutely unacceptable."

Frequently, proposals made during the course of negotiations, especially those presented in written form, necessitate careful and detailed analysis to discover any hidden meanings or pitfalls. In this context the phrase can be entirely neutral.

Yet just as often a party's initial response to even a complex proposal signifies that it may or may not be acceptable in principle.

This Is Our Final Offer.   As with "no contract, no work," this phrase is often used too loosely.

When employed by negotiators with a long history of bargaining together, it may have significance and mean what it says. Too frequently, however, it is used whenever a negotiator runs out of things to say and feels compelled to take a firm stance.

This can be disastrous because he frequently will back off (or be ordered to do so by his superiors) and thus lose his credibility with the other side.

This Is Our Rock Bottom Limit; We Can't Budge Another Inch; You Can't Squeeze Blood from a Stone.   These and similar variations are connected to "this is our final offer" and used interchangeably.

In negotiations between parties with a relatively long and stable relationship, a pattern may develop between the negotiators so that each knows the litany by heart and understands which, if any, of these phrases is intended to be meaningful. Otherwise, the phrases themselves have no intrinsic meaning and both the negotiator and the public must infer a meaning from the surrounding circumstances.

Your Entire Course of Bargaining to Date Reflects a Complete and Utter Lack of Good Faith.   Since a refusal to bargain in good faith is a violation of the National Labor Relations Act, there may be occasions when this or similar phrases presage the start of legal proceedings.

More often, however, its use elicits similar vituperations from the other side and the negotiating session erupts into name calling. Just as often, though, the phrase has no significance.

We Are at an Impasse.   This is another term indicative of an inability of the parties to agree.

Since the word "impasse" may have legal consequences, the good negotiator must be aware whether it is being used in the legal or colloquial sense. It often precedes the arrival of a neutral mediator to encourage and help the parties to reach agreement.

It may also precede the breaking off of negotiations before the exertion of economic pressure or in expectation that the economic position of the other side is so weak that it will be compelled to request a resumption of negotiations and thereby lose face.

Any Agreement We Reach Is Subject to Approval by the Membership. This is a standard union refrain. The management counterpart is that the company negotiator is unable to accept a proposal without clearance from higher up.

Often rank and file approval is a foregone conclusion, especially when the contract is heartily endorsed by the union leadership. On occasion, however, the union anticipates membership rejection and then returns to the bargaining table for something additional for the membership.

In reaction, management often holds something back for just such a situation. Every so often, though—and with greater frequency in recent years—rank and file rejection of an agreement comes as a surprise to both the union leadership and management. This creates extremely difficult problems and in some cases may unravel everything to which the parties previously agreed.

This brief glossary may suggest that collective bargaining is nothing more than gamesmanship played for extremely high stakes, devoid of meaningful exchanges on substantive issues. This may be true where one side or the other, or indeed both, are represented by unskilled negotiators.

In the vast majority of situations, however, it is the skill of the negotiators, employed against the backdrop of the parties' economic positions and their recognition that each needs the other, that results in the creation of viable compromises concerning seemingly intractable problems.

GERARD I. NIERENBERG and
HENRY H. CALERO

Reading 7–4
Meta-Talk: The Art of Deciphering Everyday Conversation

"In daily life, our conversation says both much more and much less than is intended," write Gerard I. Nierenberg and Henry H. Calero. *"For these meanings behind our ordinary talk, we have coined the word 'meta-talk.'"* Their book Meta-Talk, *analyzes a lot of language that is all too familiar in the offices of top executives and the corridors of middle management.*

FALSE HUMILITY

Recently an expert was asked to testify regarding the possibility of anticipating earthquakes along the San Andreas fault in California. He started his testimony with the expression "In my humble opinion . . . ," which drove the person asking the question into a rage. He shouted, "We are not interested in your false humility, we are seriously concerned about future earthquakes and determining where and when they may occur. Please tell us what you believe to be the best approach to the problem."

The expert, visibly shaken, squirmed in his seat, adjusted his pants, sat up straight, and replied sternly, "At present, no one can accurately predict where or when an earthquake will occur on the surface of this planet."

Variants on "In my humble opinion" are: "I do the best I can" and "Far be it from me to say." All are clichés of false humility.

False humility is also present in the use of the expressions "As you are aware" and "As you well know." These phrases seem to suggest that the

Reprinted from *MBA Magazine*, January 1974. Used with permission of the author.

speaker is not taking any chances of insulting the listener's intelligence by saying something he is already aware of. This is often not the case. For example, a scientist while telling his colleagues about his newest discovery may say, "As you are aware," knowing full well they are *not* aware. Rather than softening the blow, he draws sharp attention to their ignorance and sets himself apart from them.

SOFTENERS

Most of us at some time have prefaced our words with an expression intended to influence the listener in a positive manner. We call them "softeners." In such situations we might say, "It goes without saying . . ." (attempting to get agreement before stating something); "What I'm about to tell you . . ." (usually a disclosure that must be handled very carefully and involves the listener); "I venture to say," "Don't take me seriously," "off the top of my head" or "at first blush" are sometimes used to mean the same thing.

"Would you be kind enough to . . ." is a softener that attempts to influence another with praise or flattery. "I'm sure someone as intelligent as you . . ." strokes a person's ego, as does "You're very perceptive about . . ." "What is your expert opinion of my . . ." asks for concurrence, not censure, as the individual who tells that speaker he disagrees will soon learn. No one uses such expressions looking for negative responses. The meta-talk means: "I've scratched your back and you should scratch mine."

"You are right but . . ." attempts to avoid conflict by feigned agreement. Acceptance statements often are followed by the incongruous qualifiers—"but," "yet," "however," and "still." They communicate that the person doesn't think you are right, but would like to soften the blow. A husband arguing with his wife about his conduct at a social gathering says, "You are right, I shouldn't have done that, but . . ." then he explains the logic and reason behind his behavior. Instead of contrition, justification is the theme. Seldom do we encounter someone who says, "You are right," and lets it go at that. Even less seldom do we find a person who follows "You are right" with "What should I have done?"

FOREBODERS

Often we put listeners in a negative, anxious frame of mind with the use of "foreboders," as when we say, "Nothing is wrong" ("There *is* something wrong. However, I don't want to talk about it").

Similar foreboders that have a negative effect on the listener are: "It really doesn't matter" (it sure does); "Don't worry about me" (please do); and a statement Oliver Hardy used to make to Stan Laurel, "I have nothing more to say," before lashing out at him verbally and physically.

INTERESTERS

Some statements and questions attempt to arouse the interest of the listener.

"And do you know what he said?" is a strong plea for interest and is used to get undivided attention. Used once or twice it is very effective, but eventually it no longer creates interest but rather boredom or even distaste. We begin to anticipate the question, no longer listening but waiting for its repetition. This phrase often becomes a verbal tic, revealing the speaker's feeling of insecurity.

"Guess what happened?" When this question is used the listener is being told to ask, "What?" so that in complicity with the speaker he will share an unimportant bit of information. The question does not give the listener a choice—it demands his attention and reveals that the speaker is uncertain that he has anything relevant or interesting to say.

"What do you think of . . . ?" This query calls for interest and agreement. But the question is often used to insist on agreement with the speaker's opinions. For the meta-talk expert, then, "What do you think of . . . ?" is followed by insights into the foibles and prejudices of the person who uses it.

"I could say something about that." This statement can cause both interest and conflict. In a discussion between two persons, a long-suffering soul who resists disclosing his true feelings may utter this expression only after a long sigh to demonstrate his patience. Yet the person who dislikes conflict attempts not to fuel arguments by using such trite phrases, remaining silent instead. On the other hand, the I-don't-want-to-cause-trouble-but-will-anyway type tends to use this expression. He draws attention to a conflicting statement or issue by seeming to avoid a confrontation. "I could say something about that" may provoke the response, "Well, why don't you?" Then the fight is on.

DOWNERS

Downers are used intentionally to put the listener in a defensive state of mind.

"How about . . ." is used in numerous negotiating situations to arouse tension in an otherwise cooperative environment. Most of us have the emotional stability to handle one, two, or even three "How abouts." However, when the phrase is repeated again and again, the cumulative effect serves to make us defensive, angry, and sometimes irrational. "How about" serves to stimulate our opposition to the person uttering it.

"Don't be ridiculous!" heads the list of commands beginning with "Don't." The person saying it is authoritarian, incapable of seeing any colors except black and white. Very few listeners would resent a command that makes sense ("Don't walk on the grass"; "Don't smoke in bed.") But, "Don't be ridiculous!"? Is one supposed to abjectly renounce all his characteristic ways to please the person making the demand? Not likely. "Don't be ridiculous!'' usually prompts the question, ''What do you mean by ridiculous?'' This continues the downward spiral of the conversation that will probably end in angry words or blows. A popular variation is ''Don't be unreasonable.''

''Needless to say'' is a phrase often used to impose an opinion. ''Needless to say, we would all like to be handsome and rich.'' Or would we? Sometimes we project our own feelings and needs on others by using this phrase. Because we feel very strongly about something we want others to share our feelings and we take the liberty of assuming they do. A similar device appeals for consensus by threatening ostracism from the group: ''I think we all agree that . . .'' These phrases and statements may unconsciously express contempt for the listener.

Self-doubt is revealed in the many expressions that plead with the listener to accept without question the veracity of everything that the speaker has to say. ''Believe me,'' ''I'm not kidding,'' ''I have to tell you,'' ''I wouldn't lie to you'' have little value except as communication stoppers. Probably everything that follows is going to be a lie or a half-truth.

Hostility in communication often indicates weakness. ''Mind your own business,'' ''Stay out of this,'' ''The matter is closed,'' ''I don't want to hear any more,'' and other abrupt attempts to terminate a conversation can frequently be traced to the fact that the speaker feels he has lost an argument. He tries to regain control of the situation by displaying his power to choose what will or will not be discussed.

Denial is a device often used by people to pretend that things are better than they actually are. An example is the man who asks, ''You don't think something's happened, do you?'' when he means, ''I think something's happened!''

Uncertainty about our ability to do a job well may produce meta-talk that indicates we cannot do it at all. An individual who has been asked to undertake a difficult assignment may reply, ''I'll do my best'' or ''I'll try.'' The boss may wonder about such statements. Does ''I'll do my best'' mean ''My best is none too good,'' ''I can't do it,'' ''I'm not sure I can do it,'' or what? The same is true of ''I'll try.'' Either statement can prompt the anxious question: ''Don't you think you can do it?'' That is because the statements are rationalizations that prepare for failure. The lower the aspirations of an individual, the more probably it will be that he will anticipate failure. Those who are more highly motivated ''try'' less and ''do'' more.

Others prepare for failure by using ''if-then'' statements: ''If you will grant X, Y, and Z, then I'll be able to . . .'' This can be a perfectly legitimate statement if X, Y, and Z are realistic requests. Often they are not. They merely serve to interrupt communications and try to place blame for the failure on the other person. The meta-talk here is, ''Play the game my way or I won't play well and it will be your fault.''

Concealed aggression is a common element in many adult conversations. Polite prefaces are often used to soften penetrating questions or abrupt statements: "Do you mind if I ask you . . ." or "Have you ever considered doing . . ." These and similar phrases if used sparingly can grease the wheels of communication but if overused they tend to build up resentment by pressing a point of view too hard.

META-TALK IN BUSINESS

The hot air of talk is as important to a salesman as a cool breeze is to the yachtsman: neither can make his landing without some wind. Some salesmen, however, have learned to minimize the use of small talk and have become outstanding listeners. They realize that many prospective purchasers can talk themselves into buying.

Questions are vital, of course, to the buy-seller relationship. However, people have become very sophisticated and a deal can be destroyed if questions are too frequently answered with questions. "How much will it cost me?" brings the reply, "How much do you think it should cost you?" This device to avoid saying "I don't know" can quickly degenerate into a downward spiral of increasingly hostile questions and evasive answers.

When a buyer or seller says he will "try" to do something, he is often signaling that you should be prepared for his future inability to produce. If you are confronted with a promise to "try" to get certain terms on a deal, be ready to hear sometime later, "Well, I tried" (and failed). Frequent cost overruns on defense contracts would indicate that this and similar clichés ("I'll see what I can do," "We will make every effort") are used far too often in government contract dealings. On the individual level as well as the corporate, "trying" is the meta-talk of one preparing to be an underachiever.

"Trying" puts a distance between the subject and the desired object because the infinitive "to do" is much weaker than the active use of the verb, "I will do it." Similarly the person who relates well to others in a buyer-seller situation will avoid other indications of distance.

Not all such distance-putting verbal devices are the result of injured pride. Many of us try to soften criticism by putting a string of words between "I" or "we" and the complaint: "I don't know how to say this . . ." "I am doing this for your own good . . ."; "We've done business for a long time . . ."; "I wish I didn't have to say this, but . . ." All of these clichés leave an impression that there is something not quite right about offering criticism. Yet it is often necessary to straighten out a relationship that has taken a wrong turn. Many successful executives are very aggressive and seldom waste time in softening criticism. So long as the criticism is valid and is kept impersonal this may be a good way for them to handle the problem. A frank revelation of feelings can actually improve a relationship by removing the "polite" distance between two people.

Meta-talk abounds in relationships between superiors and subordinates, particularly those characterized by a lack of openness. An aware employee would recognize at once that if his boss says, "I want there to be complete frankness between us at all times," he may really be saying, "Don't tell me anything I don't want to hear." No superior can obtain frankness or any other quality from an employee merely by requesting it. He may get a semblance of frankness or honesty in this way. To achieve an open relationship, however, trust must first be established. Similarly, statements such as "This is the way I'd like to see it done" can really mean, "You are incapable of thinking for yourself. *I'm* the only one who thinks around here." The boss who signals this through his meta-talk is not getting as much as he should from his employee. No intelligent person enjoys a relationship that limits his creative ability to come up with alternatives to problems, and "This is the *only* way" certainly does that.

If employees confident of their abilities resent such signals from their superiors, less confident subordinates employ meta-talk to beg for reassurance while denying any weakness in their performance. "On the whole . . ." and "Under the circumstances . . ." often introduce these self-serving statements: "On the whole I'm satisfied with the job I did"; "Under the circumstances, I don't see how I could have done anything differently." The meta-talk of these statements is, "I don't have any specific strong points to bring out, so I'll generalize."

An employer may say, "On the whole, your idea sounds all right." If he follows up with, "Let me sleep on it," chances are he doesn't think it is important enough to keep him awake. The employee who eagerly awaits the next day to get the verdict is in for a jolting disappointment.

Quite naturally, money and its allocation produce a great deal of meta-talk in superior-subordinate relationships. Oddly some employees can be quite forthright and aggressive about getting every penny of a proposed departmental budget, let us say, and yet be very reluctant to discuss their personal financial needs for fear of being rebuffed. Asking for raises and forestalling such requests provide cartoonists with limitless material. They also can be time-consuming in offices where there is no open communication between employee and boss. One seemingly open conversation with a superior might go like this: "Dave, this company is confronted by a strong competitive market dominated by buyers. In order to survive, we must minimize all costs in order to compete." The subordinate has no difficulty translating this. It means, "Don't expect any increase in pay" or "You're not going to get the increase I promised you last year." For some timid souls the meta-talk is enough, but a more desperate one might venture: "I was wondering how you felt about considering giving me a raise?" Note the distance put between "I" and "raise." It almost becomes an abstract speculation. Therefore, if it is answered with a terse "lousy!" the employee can gracefully but quickly take cover.

A stronger person might preface his request with what he hopes are rhetorical questions: "Do you like my performance?" or, "Have you found any significant weaknesses in my department?" If the answers are favorable, he can then proceed with, "In view of that fact . . ." or, "Considering that . . ." both are meta-talk for "I am too good to refuse." The superior may simply acknowledge that fact or say, "I'll tell you what . . ." meaning "You're not going to get a pay increase that easily." A negotiating situation at least has been set up.

Some employees say only what they know will please the boss. Often they preface their remarks with, "Tell me if I'm wrong." This is a perfectly safe thing to say since any boss who can be taken in by this ruse is also probably not going to be critical of his own ideas. This situation is destructive. Words are used as weapons, not as instruments for transmitting and sharing ideas.

There are certain "buzz" words that have become clichés. These are used to obtain feedback and may have a limited positive use. However, when used to excess, such expressions as "Right?" "Is that clear?" "Okay?" "Check?" "Do you follow?" are verbal tics that unconsciously express a doubt that the listener is capable of clearly understanding anything. They also become unreliable guides since they practically demand an affirmative answer. The speaker assumes he will get one and rushes on, ignoring verbal and nonverbal feedback. There is a hidden assumption that for every problem there is but one correct and one incorrect solution. Most of life's problems do not lend themselves to such a simplistic approach. No successful businessman can afford to come up with "the" solution. Generally, there are many alternatives, one of which seems especially appropriate in a given time and place. It often takes time and a supportive relationship to come up with an appropriate answer. Clichés only hamper the process.

Some executives try to conceal their sense of self-importance with statements of self-importance with statements that minimize their ability or power: "May I make a modest suggestion?" or "If I may venture an idea . . ." Probably no one is fooled by such preliminary statements, but subordinates are alerted that a "great thought of Western man" is about to make its appearance and they had better like it.

A well-intentioned friend, determined to "help" an out-of-work executive, begins to offer "off the top of his head" (meaning, "I'm a genius, I can turn out ideas like popcorn") solutions to his employment problem. Suddenly, the executive interrupts with "Now wait a minute!" What does the meta-talk mean? The friend has made the hidden assumption that the executive is over the hill and incapable of making a decision for himself. He must be "told" what to do. The "Wait a minute" is a protest from the victim who is being talked to, not communicated with. The conversation has added to his problems and increased his self-doubts.

In a supportive relationship, this would not happen. The priorities would be reversed: instead of the friend offering solutions to assumed problems, the problems would be thoroughly analyzed and, more important, the executive's aims and aspirations for the future would shape proposed solutions to the problems. The term *Job's comforters* means those who discourage or depress while seeming to give consolation. These abound in both business and social situations. Don't be one. Communicate.

Persuasion

In the previous section, we stated that communication is the heart of negotiation, and that breakdowns in communication are frequently (but not always) a cause of negotiation ineffectiveness. Linked closely to communication is the process of persuasion. How arguments are constructed, and how they are joined together in a persuasive message, is another important element in understanding the dynamics of successful negotiation.

Many of the important elements of the persuasion process have been covered in the earlier discussion of distributive and integrative bargaining processes. We noted previously that information, per se, may be the strongest possible persuasive force in negotiation; each of these strategic approaches uses information for different motivational ends. However, there are a variety of other factors to be considered in constructing a persuasive message, and in understanding how receivers are persuaded by various verbal and nonverbal elements. The articles in this section focus specifically on the more subtle, nonverbal, and tactical approaches to persuasion that can be used in negotiation, and examine the impact of these particular approaches.

In the first article, "The Tactics and Ethics of Persuasion," Philip Zimbardo reviews a variety of tactics that can be used to change another party's attitudes. This article was prepared to help social activists learn how to be more persuasive in promoting attitude change on important social issues—that is, antiwar issues, environmental issues, social issues. Zimbardo suggests that one's tactics can be organized into three major categories:

preparing the initial contact, gaining access to the person to be persuaded, and maintaining and directing the relationship. While many of his examples are drawn from simple persuasion situations in which college students or other social activists seek to change individual attitudes regarding major social issues, the basic elements and process relate to most negotiation situations. The article also examines the ways that police use persuasion strategies to extract confessions or compliance from people who are arrested, and explores some of the more "Machiavellian strategies" for obtaining compliance or change in another's point of view. Zimbardo believes that using some of these strategies may raise ethical "concerns" for the persuader, and addresses this question in discussing the tactics.

Donald Moine, in "To Trust, Perchance to Buy," also reviews a variety of very subtle and seductive tactics derived from his study of successful salespeople. Moine argues that a successful sales presentation is much like a form of indirect hypnosis, and that it is most useful to analyze the strategies of very effective salespeople by comparing them to the techniques of master hypnotists. There are three critical elements which both professionals have in common. First, both groups establish a mood of trust and rapport with their target person. They do this by a form of mirrorlike matching of communication gestures ("getting in sinc"), in which the persuader attempts to model, as closely as possible, the words, phrases, expressions, manner of speaking, etc. of the target person. A second critical element is the "soft sell" approach; the persuader hopes that the bond of trust and rapport which has been created can be supplemented by suggestions and indirect commands intended to get the target person to comply. "Leading arguments" are used, by which the persuader helps the target person to formulate a pattern of arguments that leads directly to the conclusion desired by the persuader. Finally, successful persuaders use anecdotes, parables, and stories, usually to handle possible resistance to complying with the persuader and to "close the sale." Metaphors and parables are used as clinching arguments, as the way to make the final point, to draw imagery that helps the target person go along while feeling good about his/her actions. Moine suggests that we can be very persuasive if we pay attention to many of the more subtle details of the persuasion process. However, such techniques require extensive training and practice in order to be used effectively.

The techniques described by Moine work as a form of flattery, by enhancing the target person's ego, sense of self-worth, and hence his/her negotiating position. These tactics are clearly designed to seduce the target person into compliance, rather than to use hard argumentation and competitive force, and can be very effective under the right conditions. One might question whether everyone is susceptible to these tactics. The article "How People Respond to Flattery," by Andrew Colman suggests that everyone is not. Colman's research indicates that strategies such as flattery can only really work when the target person does in fact see himself or herself in a positive light. Individuals who have high self-esteem and are flattered tend to view the persuader in a much more positive light than when the persuader makes neutral comments. In contrast, individuals with low self-esteem feel more negatively toward the persuader when they are flattered than when they receive neutral comments. The results suggest that flattery works only when it confirms the individuals own self-image; positive comments toward the target person, in an attempt to "soften him up for persuasion," may only work when the target person sees himself in a positive light.

The last article in this section is an excerpt of a sociological classic by Erving Goffman. Goffman's "On Cooling the Mark Out: Some Aspects of Adaptation to Failure" explains con games, and the behavior of both the con artists and the "mark" (i.e., recipient of the con). Goffman illustrates how the con game is in fact a common social phenomena in which one individual is deceived by another. Goffman's particular emphasis is on the mark, and the need for the con to help the mark "cool out" to prevent him/her from retaliating against the con artist. Hence, cooling the mark out is a process of keeping the target of a persuasion attempt from resorting to retribution or escalation, particularly if the persuasion attempt has been unusually successful and the persuader has gained significant tactical advantage. Goffman reviews the ways that the mark can be helped to regain status or to save face without retaliating, while at the same time recognizing that he or she has been significantly taken advantage of. In negotiating context, such processes are extremely important when one party has gained a great deal from the other, and when their relationship will continue. Given that they have a long-term relationship and may encounter one another in the future, the mark must be cooled out in order to minimize the risk of retaliation or revenge in future interactions.

PHILIP G. ZIMBARDO

Reading 8–1
The Tactics and Ethics
of Persuasion

The police interrogator is recognized by society as an agent of change whose job it is to persuade witnesses and suspects to give evidence, admissions, and confessions of guilt. When he is successful, the individual may lose his freedom or life, but society is presumed to be the beneficiary of this loss. The salesman's effective persuasion may or may not benefit either the "target" of his sales attempt or the society, but it certainly brings personal gain to the salesman and those he represents. What is similar about both is that they are "formal" persuasive communicators insofar as their goal to effect a specified change is explicitly formulated and their tactics often are laid down in training manuals used in their initiation. Examination of their tactics reveals a further basis of similarity—a willingness to employ virtually any means to achieve their goals. Indeed, for one, it has been necessary to establish Supreme Court rulings to limit the use of third-degree physical brutality and excessive psychological coercion; for the other, the Better Business Bureaus and Ralph Nader are needed to limit the excessive exploitation of the consumer.

Every social interaction, however, carries the burden of being a potential attitude change encounter. The ethical issues raised by deceptive business practices or police coercion are often ignored in other equally compelling influence situations. Parents, educators, priests, and psychotherapists, for example, represent some of the most powerful "behavioral engineers" in this society. It is rare that the appropriateness of evaluating what they do in ethical terms is even considered. This is largely because they are not perceived as formal agents of attitude and behavior change. They function

Reprinted from *Attitudes, Conflicts and Social Change,* Bert King and Elliot McGinnes (eds.), 1972, pp. 81–99. Used with permission of Academic Press and the author.

with the benefits of socially sanctioned labels which conceal persuasive intent: parents "socialize," teachers "educate," priests "save souls," and therapists "cure the mentally ill."

There are two other characteristics of the influence situations in which they operate which minimize any issue of unethical, deceptive, or coercive persuasion. First, there is an illusion that the goal of the situation is defined in terms of the best interests of the target person: the child, student, sinner, sick patient. Second, an attribution error process typically occurs by which we judge that the individual could have resisted the pressures brought to bear upon him. One would want to believe that people change only when they want to or when they are subjected to overwhelming *physical* forces. The extent to which behavior is controlled by external social and psychological forces is denied in favor of the presumed strength of individual will power to resist. Given these three characteristics, then, the most persuasive communicators are not acknowledged as such, or are not recognized as exerting a potentially negative effect on the individuals with whom they interact.

Upon closer analysis, however, these underpinnings of this naive view of such attitude-change agents lose some of their foundation. For example, all of them can be viewed as "salesmen" for the established *status quo* with the best interest of society placed before the best interest of the individual. "Socialization" to be a Hitler *Jungn,* "socialization" to repress impulses, to be a good child, to do what one is told, to be seen and not heard, to be patriotic, to be polite, not to question elders, and so forth are goals of the adults in the society, which may be at odds with the child's personal growth. "Education" can mean to bias, to present prejudiced opinion as scientific or accepted fact, to perpetuate preferred ways of thinking. For example, the Russians teach the doctrine of Lysenko, some U.S. schools reject Darwinism, teachers can be models of racial prejudice, and the like. To save sinners may involve making people feel guilt, shame, anxiety—deny the pleasure of physical contact; accept the poverty and *status quo* of this world for a pie in the sky when you die. To cure the mentally ill sometimes involves communicating what the person must do in order that society not label him a "deviant" and cast him out into a madhouse. Psychotherapy can be seen as conformity training in which there is a unilateral influence attempt to make the patient's "abnormal" behavior "normal" (like everyone else's) again.

Such a predisposition to make the attribution error of overestimating internal relative to external causality is seen repeatedly in those phenomena which most intrigue and fascinate us. Hypnosis, voodoo deaths, brainwashing, placebo effects, Asch's conformity, and Milgram's obedience findings all share this property. Dramatic changes in behavior occurs in others, which we believe we personally could resist. The strength of the situational forces are not appreciated, while our own ability not to be tender minded, or weak willed, or suggestible, or controlled by words is magnified.

Research from many disparate areas clearly reveals how easy it is to bring behavior under situational control. Hovland (1954) has noted that it is almost impossible *not* to get positive attitude change in a laboratory study of attitude change. Orne (1962) despairs at being able to find a task so repulsive and demeaning that "experimental subjects" will *not* perform it readily upon request. Milgram (1963) shows that the majority of his subjects engage in extremely aggressive behavior in a situation which psychiatrists had believed would only have a weak effect in inducing blind obedience. We comply, conform, become committed, are persuaded daily in the endless procession of influence situations that we enter, yet each of us continues to maintain an illusion of personal invulnerability. It is only when the situational forces become so obviously unfair—so physically suppressive or psychologically repressive—that we question the ethics of the change situation.

In this sense, then, one may talk about the politics of persuasion since an influence attempt backed by society is persuasion sanctioned by established policy. If a *communicator* advocates change which is not acceptable to the power structure controlling the resources of the society, then pressure is applied to change the communicator. Attempts are made to bring him back in line or, failing this, to reject him through relabeling as a "revolutionary," "radical," or "traitor."

Society in the United States is now in a state of confusion because agents of change whose persuasive influence once was sanctioned by society are no longer granted dispensation to use the approved labels "educator," "pediatrician," and so forth, or to be immune from persuasion attempts themselves. It then becomes obvious to former "targets" that there was previously an implicit contract of complicity and that there still is with other agents. When people become aware of this duplicity and cognizant of the hidden situational forces, they lose trust in parents, educators, politicians, and all those who now reveal themselves as undercover agents of change. They become cynical toward a system which professes to function for the people when, in fact, it functions for the communicator and his powerful backers, the "Society." Finally, when the illusion of individual assertiveness, resistance, and willpower disintegrates under the realization of the overwhelming forces operating to keep even their "personal" communicators in line, then feelings of hopelessness come to the surface.

If a society, through its political power base, wanted to make war and not peace, and most of its traditional communicators have supported this view (or did not openly oppose it), how could the society ever be changed? The two alternatives are revolution, which destroys the established base of power, or persuasion, which redirects available knowledge and tactics and utilizes former "targets" as new agents of communication.

The remainder of this paper presents one attempt to apply the research findings of social psychology and the salesman's intuition to just this problem. Can "students" and young people effectively persuade adults, who collectively have the power to change the system, to use their voting power in an effort to promote peace?

Tactics and strategies designed to achieve this goal will be formulated explicitly, and then, for purposes of comparison, the tactics of the police interrogator will be outlined. The ethical issues involved in attempting "to turn a society around" by working through its system will not be discussed, but the question of using "Machiavellian" techniques on an individual in order to do so will be raised.

PERSUADING FOR NEW POLITICS

Preparing for the Initial Contact

A. Be Informed. Get as much accurate, up-to-date, reliable evidence as you can. Commit important facts, arguments, statistics, and quotations to memory so they are "natural" when you need them. You should see yourself as more expert on the particular issue of concern than the people you will try to persuade. Your perceived competence is a very important source trait. However, *do not use information as a put-down.* Do not overkill. Hold your storehouse in reserve and select only the facts you need.

B. Learn as Much as You Can about Those You Will Engage. Be familiar with their neighborhood, local issues, basic values, language style (use of diction, clichés, homilies), source of local pride and discontent, the nature of usual influence media, attitudes on the issue in question, and the like. You can obtain this information from local businessmen (barbers, cab drivers, grocery store employees, bartenders,and others), salesmen, letters to the newspaper, and distinguishing characteristics of the neighborhood or the individual home. You can also encourage people to state their opinions on preliminary telephone surveys. When you are in this learning phase, do not try to exert influence.

C. Actively Role-Play with a Friend the Anticipated Situation. Imagine and then work through as realistically as possible the persuasion situation in which you will operate. If available, tape-record or videotape such dress rehearsals and then critically analyze your performance. Switch roles and try to be the target person in the situation where he is experiencing the pressure to comply to a request for some commitment.

D. Do a Critical Self-Appraisal. Analyze your own personal strengths and weaknesses, your appearance, and discuss any source of fear, anxiety, anticipated embarrassment, and so forth with one or more persons with whom you feel comfortable before you actually start out.

E. Be Confident. Expect that you will be effective more often than not. You must expect some setbacks, but you must be dedicated to winning, to making the "sale." If you do not handle the situation carefully, you may produce the undesirable effect of increasing the person's resistance to any further influence attempts by others, or you may generate a backlash effect yourself. If you blow it once or twice, or if you get doors slammed in your face before you even start talking (this will surely happen in some neighborhoods), keep trying. If you lose your confidence, however, or you get negative results in a variety of neighborhoods with a variety of techniques, then perhaps you are not suited for face-to-face confrontations and your talents could be put to better use elsewhere.

F. Be Sensitive to the Varied Reasons underlying the Attitude(s) in Question.   Attitudes are formed and maintained because of needs for information, for social acceptance by other people, or for ego protection from unacceptable impulses and ideas. Deeply held attitudes probably have all three of these motivational bases. Information *per se* is probably the least effective way of *changing* attitudes and behavior. Its effectiveness is maximum at the attitude-formation stage when the person has not yet taken a stand and put his ego on the dotted line. Your general approach must acknowledge that the individual is more than a rational, information processor—sometimes he is irrational, inconsistent, unresponsive to social rewards, or primarily concerned about how he appears to himself and to others.

G. Even as a Stranger You Can Exert Considerable Influence.   You can be an effective agent for change by serving as a model for some behavior by publicly engaging in it, selectively reinforcing some opinions rather than others, and providing a new source of social contact, recognition, and reward for many people.

Gaining Access to and Establishing the Contact

A. Before you can persuade, you must get the person to acknowledge your presence, to attend to you and to follow your presentation. People are wary of an assault on their privacy and "life space" by an unknown person on their doorstep. You might want to consider an initial phone call or letter to contacts to be made at home.

B. If you are making a home contact, be aware of the particular situation you have encountered. Be sure that the person is willing to give you the required time. You might be interrupting dinner, a phone call, a family quarrel, a visit with guests, or some bad news. You do not want the dominant motivation of the homeowner to be to get rid of you as soon as possible.

C. Although strangers can influence everyday behavior, persuasion is enhanced when the target perceives some basic similarity with the source. This "strategy of identification" (practiced by all good entertainers and politicians) involves finding something in common between you. Physical similarity is the most obvious: age, sex, race, ethnic features, dress (distribution of hair). In addition, similarity is inferred from voice dialect, regionalisms, and appropriate slang, jargon, or group-membership-identifying phrases (for example, "such a lot of *chutzpah* he's got, that vice president," or "People like us who work for a living have callouses on their hands; a politician like X who talks about working for the people, probably has them only on his mouth.") Canvassing should be arranged to optimize this perceived similarity by selecting neighborhoods and locations which are approximately matched to the available canvassers. The canvasser should try to uncover as many points of similarity as possible because similarity breeds familiarity, which breeds liking and enhances credibility and greater acceptance of the message.

D. Students are not seen as credible sources on most issues that concern them directly, and to be effective, it is important that they increase their source credibility. This may be accomplished in a number of ways:

1. Impress the audience with your expertise, concern, and dedication, being forceful but not overbearing.
2. Make some points which are against your own best interest: indicate the sacrifices you have made and would be willing to make.
3. Have a respected person introduce you, make the contact for you.
4. Begin by agreeing with what the audience wants to hear, or with whatever they say first.
5. Minimize your manipulative intent until you ask for the commitment.

E. Avoid group situations where the majority are known or expected to be against you, since they will provide support for each other and their cohesion might make salient the group norm that you appear to be attacking (which they never cherished so much before your attack).

Maintaining, Intensifying, Directing the Interpersonal Relationship

Once you have managed to get the person to receive you, then you must hold this attention, while trying to get your message (and yourself) accepted.

A. You have the power to reinforce many behaviors of the target person, a power you should use judiciously but with conscious awareness of what and how you are reinforcing.

1. Listen attentively to what the other person has to say about anything of personal interest. This not only "opens up" the person for a dialogue, and helps in establishing what are the primary values, beliefs, and organization of his (or her) thinking, but establishes you as someone open to what others have to say. (The opportunity to tell a college student where to get off is very rewarding for many people.)
2. Maintain eye contact with the person and as close physical proximity as seems acceptable to the person.
3. Individuate the person, by using names (with Mr. or Mrs. or titles where there is an age or status discrepancy). Make the person feel you are reacting to his uniqueness and individuality—*which you should be*—and are not reacting in a programmed way to your stereotyped conception of a housewife, blue-collar worker, etc. Similarly, help the other person to individuate you, to break through the categorization and pigeonholing process which makes you just an anonymous canvasser. At some point, describe something personal or unique about your feelings, background,

interests, and so forth (which you expect will be acceptable). However, once accomplished, then do not allow yourelf to be the exception to the stereotype—say, "most other students are like me in how we feel about X."

4. Reinforce specific behaviors explicitly and immediately, by nodding, saying "good," "that's an interesting point," and the like. Reinforce more general classes of behavior by smiling, and by making it obvious you enjoy the interaction and by being impressed with the person's openness, sensitivity, intelligence, or articulateness. As a student with a lot of "book learning" you can still learn a lot from people who have gone to the "school of hard knocks," who have "real-life learning" and "street savvy" to offer you. Let them know that this is how you feel when talking to someone who has not had the benefit of your degree of education.

5. The person must perceive that you personally care about and are enthusiastic about the item(s) under discussion; moreover he/she must perceive that *you* as a person really care about the complaint act—at a personal level and not merely as part of your role.

6. Your reinforcement rate should increase over the course of the interaction, so that ideally, at the end of the time, the person is sorry to see you leave.

B. Be aware of sources of resentment against you for what you represent by your physical appearance, group membership (as a student), and the like; work first to differentiate those biased and often unfounded feelings and reactions from those reactions you want to elicit by your influence attempt.

Working class people in particular will resent you for having an easy life. They have worked with their hands, strained their backs, calloused their knees, scrubbing, lifting, sweating, struggling, ekeing out a measly subsistence, while you (as they see it) sit on your butt and have every need catered to. You can blunt this resentment in at least two ways: (1) by showing respect, even awe, for how hard they work, acknowledging that you found it really tough that summer you worked as a hod-carrier, and so forth; (2) by offhandedly noting what a sweat you had studying for that last calculus exam, that while other students may have a lot of money, *you* don't and you don't know whether you can afford to make it through college, and the like— whatever you can honestly say to undercut the perception that you are privileged and spoiled.

In contrast, middle-class office workers are likely to resent you for a different set of reasons: that (according to the stereotype) you do not show respect for your elders, that you are an uncouth, dirty, disruptive, pot-smoking libertine, and so forth. A neat appearance and considerate, respectful manner will do much to combat this stereotype.

C. Plan the organization of your approach well enough so that it seems natural and unplanned, and be flexible enough to modify it as necessary.

1. Do not surround your best arguments with tangential side arguments or a lot of details. Arguments that come in the middle of a presentation are remembered least well. Put your stronger arguments first if you want to motivate or interest uninvolved people.
2. Draw your conclusions explicitly. Implicit conclusion drawing should be left for only very intelligent audiences.
3. Repeat the main points in your argument, and the major points of agreement between you and the target person.

D. Tailor your approach to the target person.

1. Do not put him on the defensive, or even encourage or force a public defense of (and thus commitment to) any position against you. Opposing beliefs are seen as providing the opportunity for open discussion, and as a starting point to find areas of common agreement. If the person is for you, then get a public commitment early, and try to make that commitment more stable and more extreme than it was originally.
2. If possible, have the person restate your ideas and conclusions for himself, in his own words (encourage active participation).
3. If the person appears to be very authoritarian in manner and thinking, then he will probably be more impressed by status sources, decisiveness, and one-sided generalizations than by informational appeals, expert testimony, unbiased presentation of both sides of the issue, and so forth. Make any approach responsive to the dominant personality and social characteristics of the person to whom you are talking.
4. Work in pairs. Although a more personal relationship can be established in a two-person interaction, there is much to be gained from teamwork. Working in pairs provides each student with social support, lowers apprehension about initiating each new contact, and allows one of you to be "off the firing line" appraising the situation, to come in when help is needed, to refocus the direction, or respond to some specific trait detected in the target person. There are several ways in which teams can be composed to produce interesting effects. There is a general principle covering them all; namely, *the two members of the team should differ in some obvious characteristic, such as temperament, age, or sex.* There are two reasons behind this principle: first, it maximizes the chances that either one or the other member will be similar to the target person and therefore can gain a persuasive advantage at the appropriate moment; second, it pro-

motes that subtle idea that even when people differ in outward characteristics, they can still agree on the important issue of peace—therefore, the target person, who may differ from both persuaders, can be encouraged to agree also. The obverse of this "team difference" principle is also important: *it is very inefficient for similar canvassers to accompany each other.*

Getting the Commitment and Terminating the Contract

Do not insist that the person accept and believe what you have said before he makes a behavioral commitment. Get the behavioral commitment anyway, and attitude change will follow. The ideal conclusion of the contact will also leave the person feeling that the time spent was worthwhile and his self-esteem will be greater than it was before you arrived.

A. Do not overstay your welcome or be forced to stay longer than is worthwhile according to your time schedule. Timing is essential both in knowing when to ask for the commitment and in knowing when to quit with an intractable person. For a person who needs more time to think, encourage him if you get a promise to allow you to come back.

B. Provide several levels of possible behavioral alternatives for the person: pushing the most extreme is likely to get a greater level of compliance even if the extreme is rejected.

C. Be clear as to what actions are requested or what has been agreed upon or concluded.

D. Use a "bandwagon" effect, if called for, to indicate prestigious others who have joined in the action.

E. When you believe the target person is about to make the commitment (or after a verbal agreement is made), stress the fact that the decision is his own; it involves free choice, no pressure. This maximizes the dissonance experienced by the decision made and forces the individual to make his behavior internally consistent by generating his own intrinsic justification for his behavior. Each person is his own best persuader. After the final commitment, honestly and openly thank the person and reinforce his behavior.

F. Broaden the contact in two ways. First, get the name of one or more neighbors who would agree with that person's position—you will talk to them too and use the person's name if that is O.K. with him. Second, honestly react to something about his person which is irrelevant to the main social/political issue at hand—the house, decor, hair, clothes, and avocation mentioned, or a favor which you can do related to something mentioned.

G. Extend your influence if you can get the target person also to be an agent of influence. Try to enlist his aid in getting at least one other person to agree to do what he has just done. He should be motivated to proselytize at this time, especially if he is an outgoing person good at persuading others. If he convinces others, that will reduce his own doubts about whether he has done the right thing.

MACHIAVELLIAN STRATEGIES

Just how far should you go to make the "sale," to get the commitment? The answer to such a question depends ultimately on a complex interplay of ethical, ideological, and pragmatic issues. Each individual must establish his own set of weighting coefficients to determine how much pressure he is willing to exert. Assuming that your approach will achieve your purpose, it is "right," "proper," "decent," "humane," "moral" for you to deceive someone, to hit him below his unconscious, to arouse strong negative feelings of guilt, anxiety, shame, or even positive feelings of false pride? Behaving unethically for whatever reason pollutes the psychological environment by replacing trust, understanding, and mutual respect with deceit, lies, and cynicism.

Police interrogation manuals state: "When you break a man by torture, he will always hate you. If you break him by your intelligence he will always fear and respect you" (Kidd, 1940, p. 49). This generalization may hold only when he does not realize that you, in fact, have broken him by intention. When deception techniques are employed by a sophisticated, trained practitioner, the "victim"—be he a criminal subject, collegiate experimental subject, or "mark" in a pool hall hustle—does not realize he has been conned. But *you* always know what your intention was and that you "broke a man" thus. What effect does such knowledge have upon you? Do you respect yourself more because of it? Do you begin to depersonalize other human beings as they become notches on your gun handle, "hits/misses," "easy cases/tough customers"? Thus, you must reflect upon the psychological effects of behaving unethically, both upon the target person and upon yourself. If you are so ideologically committed to your cause or goal that any ends justify the means, then ethical issues will get a zero weighting coefficient. But that alone should give you pause.

a. Will it be possible to restore ethical precepts after your ends have been achieved?

b. If you have been converted to such an extreme view, can others be similarly moved without recourse to deception?

c. Have you not been duped into the extreme position you now hold?

d. Are you being honest with yourself in recognizing that you are about to be dishonest with others, and are not covering up the fact with rationalizations about "the other side did it first" (if that's true then the poor victim gets it from both ends).

Finally, if you cast ethics to the wind, yet proceed firmly convinced that Goodness, Justice, and Truth are what you stand for, then ask one more practical question: "Is it likely to work?" How much effort, training, staging, and time will it take to carry off the caper? Are you the type of person who can be effective at this game? What happens if the person discovers the gimmick? Will each "miss" turn into a "boomerang" or a backlash that will actively work against your cause? Will you then get only the immediate, small behavioral compliance, but blow the hoped-for bigger subsequent commitment and attitude change? Have you "ruined" the person for further persuasion attempts (or experiments) by your colleagues?

Having posed and answered such questions to your own satisfaction, and if you still want to go for broke, then the time has come to go Machiavellian. Once such a decision has been made, your only concern is to find the weak points of the target person, and learn what conditions to manipulate and how best to exploit the unsuspecting victim.

Before describing several concrete examples of how Machiavellian tactics can be utilized in even such an incongruous situation as a "peace campaign," let us see how they are already effectively being used.

The Police Interrogator Misrepresents a Little Bit

Confessions are often obtained by either minimizing the seriousness of the offense and allowing the suspect a "face-saving" out, or by the opposite through misrepresenting and exaggerating the seriousness of the crime.

The first approach can be accomplished through "extenuation"—in which the investigator reports that he does not take too seriously a view of the subject's indiscretion, since he has seen thousands of others in the same situation. Or he may "shift the blame" to circumstances, the environment, or a subject's weaknesses, any of which might lead anyone to do what the suspect did. A more morally acceptable motive may be suggested for the crime, such as self-defense, an accident, a mistake, heat of passion, and so forth. In order to "open up" a suspect, it is recommended that good "bait" is to blame anyone who might be associated with the crime other than the suspect; for example, an accomplice, a fence, a company, loan sharks, or even the victim.

Some provocative examples of the way in which experts use this approach in order to misrepresent the nature of the crime to the suspect in order to get him to talk about it are:

1. A 50-year old man accused of having taken "indecent liberties" with a 10-year-old girl was told:
   "This girl is well developed for her age. She probably learned a lot about sex from the boys in the neighborhood and from the movies and TV; and knowing what she did about it, she may have deliberately tried to excite you to see what you would do" (Inbau & Reid, 1962, p. 45).
2. Or, in forcible rape cases, "where circumstances permit, the suggestion might be offered that the rape victim acted like she might be a prostitute . . . that the police knew she had been engaged

in acts of prostitution on other occasions" (Inbau & Reid, 1962, p. 46).
3. "During the interrogation of a married rape suspect, blame may be cast upon the subject's wife for not providing him with the necessary sexual gratification. "When a fellow like you doesn't get it at home, he seeks it elsewhere'" (Inbau & Reid, 1962, p. 51).

Once the suspect is in a state of emotional confusion, then "he is unable to think logically and clearly, since his sense of values has been disturbed and his imagination is distorting his perspective. It is possible for the investigator to obtain admissions or even a confession from the suspect by further misrepresenting the picture" (O'Hara, 1956, p. 105).

This misrepresentation can take the form of a "knowledge bluff"— revealing a few known items and pretending to know more, or lying to the suspect that his fingerprints, blood, etc. were found at the scene of the crime (even show him falsified samples and records). In some cases of murder, it might be stated that the victim is not dead or, as happened in Minneapolis, a youthful offender, John Biron, might be told that he will be tried as a juvenile when it was known that he is legally an adult (see *Time Magazine*, December 3, 1965, p. 52; April 29, 1966, p. 65).

Since modern interrogation involves establishing "rapport" or a meaningful interpersonal relationship between the suspect and the interrogator, it must involve a distortion of the social-psychological situation. Even before the questioning begins, the interrogator is urged to role-play the position of the subject in order to be able to respond to him—"man to man, not as policeman to prisoner" (Inbau & Reid, 1962, p. 19).

Under this category would fall all the appeals which depend upon the interrogator being friendly, kind, sympathetic, understanding, "a Dutch uncle," or an older brother. He is the one who provides social approval and recognition, who accords the suspect status, and is aware of and able to manipulate the suspect because of his social values, feelings of pride, and class or group membership.

The police manuals recognize that "It is a basic human trait to seek and enjoy the approval of other persons." Therefore, it is wise to flatter some subjects, for example, by complimenting an accused driver of a getaway car for his maneuvering and "cornering," or by comparing a juvenile with his movie idol, or a member of a racial group with a respectable, outstanding member of that group. This approach apparently works best with "the uneducated and underprivileged," since they "are more vulnerable to flattery than the educated person or the person in favorable financial circumstances."

A slightly different approach is needed for the white-collar first offender, which includes clerks, managers, cashiers, office workers, professionals, and teachers—in short, most of the audience of this book. Since these people traditionally subscribe to orthodox ethical principles and conventional moral standards, the calm, dignified approach of the physician is respected and effective. One police manual author states rather boldly: "The character of a person in this category is weak and must be exploited fully" (O'Hara, 1956).

To create rapport, the interrogator could pat the suspect on the shoulder, grip his hand, or offer to do a favor for him—get water, talk to his wife, employer, etc. O'Hara says (1956): "Gestures of this type produce a very desirable effect. They import an attitude of understanding and sympathy better than words."

For suspects who have pride in their family, if an attempt to get their parents to cooperate fails, their attention is called to a (faked) circular being prepared for broadcast and distribution throughout the country. It not only describes the fugitive, but lists all of his known relatives' names and addresses as possible leads for approaching him. Cooperation quite often is obtained in this way.

The reader may recall that in the famous case of George Whitmore, Jr. (who confessed to the slaying of two society girls in New York in 1963), he gave a 61-page typed confession after 20 hours of interrogation. He virtually sentenced himself to death or life imprisonment with this confession—which later was proved false and coerced when the true murderer was subsequently exposed.

MAKING MACHIAVELLI WORK FOR PEACE

The following hypothetical examples do not have the time-tested validity of those reported in the police interrogator's literature; rather, they merely illustrate how such tactics can be adapted to suit virtually any cause. The content of our cause will be related to "canvassing for peace," but one could imagine an adversary who could use them to canvass for war.

A. Mutt and Jeff. The so-called Mutt and Jeff technique of police interrogation involves a sneaky one-two punch in grilling suspects. A rough analog of this tactic in political persuasion can be devised. One persuader is militant in style and extreme in his position; the second persuader is moderate and reasonable as if to save the listener from the excess of the first, but in fact exacts a considerable concession by virtue of his soothing performance.

A very skilled and aggressive antiwar debater, who is dying to be turned loose but who may sometimes turn people off, can be paired with a sympathetic gentlemanly type who can gently chide him in the presence of the listener with remarks such as, "My friend may be overdoing it a little because he feels so strongly about the war, but what I would say on this point is that the war is much too expensive. I think that this is a position with which most hard-headed Americans can agree." Thus, the "moderate" brings the listener over to his side by using the "militant" as a foil.

This technique at best must be used very delicately and sparingly. It is double-edged. Too much "Mutt" militance on the doorstep will drive the listener up the wall, and both may get thrown out before Jeff can intervene. Furthermore, it takes a couple of good ham actors to carry it off, and too much "con" in the canvassing operation would be unfortunate, especially if neighbors compare notes.

B. The Stigmatized Persuader.   Recent research has found that a person with a visible stigma (such as blind or crippled) elicits a mixed reaction. There is sympathy and a tendency to want to help in some way, but also considerable tension from guilt, revulsion, and resentment (the disabled person has intruded himself upon the complacent life space of the individual). These basic motives to help and to ignore can both be elicited by having a person with a real or faked stigma appear on the doorstep (for example, a pretty girl with a scar, a boy on crutches, a team of whom one member is apparently blind). After the general introduction, the person with the stigma clearly states the level of commitment desired and then suggests that if the person does not want to act on it now, they could perhaps spend some time together talking it over. Embarrassed sympathy will make it difficult to terminate the interaction brusquely, but if an easy way out is provided by the canvasser, it will be the preferred way of resolving the conflict. They may sign now to avoid facing the stigmatized of the world any more than is necessary.

C. The "Overheard" Communication.   It is a well-known result of studies of persuasive communication that a message accidentally overheard can be more effective than when the speaker is aware of the listener's presence. In the "accidental" case, the listener has no reason to be suspicious that the speaker is trying to manipulate him.

The following setup tries to utilize this advantage of overhearing. Since it is an artifice, it is not recommended for widespread use.

In a possible one-person version, a coed enters a busy laundromat with a basket of laundry, puts the clothes in the machine, and asks another customer for change of a quarter to make a phone call to her mother. While pretending to call Mom she describes the chores she is doing and checks on the groceries she is to buy at the supermarket. "A daughter like that, I should only have," is the kind of thought running through the heads of the women there. "Good Daughter" then proceeds to talk to her mother briefly about the war and agree with her mother that it is awfully important to end this terrible war very soon and that she is happy that the mother has written to her congressman, and hopes she will also vote for Candidate X. She talks loudly enough to let the target audience hear, but goes about her business when she is finished, unless someone in the audience initiates a conversation.

Variations on this idea can be adapted for use in bus stations, drugstores, barber shops, and other such places, although this technique suffers from the general difficulty that the same person cannot wash the same bundle repeatedly, call the same Mom over and over, or get more than a few hair cuts a day without seeming very peculiar indeed.

The two-person version is more practical. This can be enacted when riding back and forth on crowded subways or buses, never traveling the same line at the same hour of a weekday. A student and an older person (his uncle or Dad, presumably) make the ideal team. The two get into a spirited argument about today's mood of campus protest. Even though they argue, it is obvious that they have a great deal of affection for each other, and the student (or son) slips in references to good behaviors ("When I was fixing our sink last night with that rusty drainpipe, I was thinking down the drain, down the drain, boy, all the money we're spending in Vietnam is just going right down the drain, totally wasted"). Their voices are raised just enough so that people can hear, but not enough to be obnoxious. The Dad complains that students aren't working hard like he did in his day (avoid references to riots, drugs, and the like—the most intense antistudent issues). The son agrees that this may be true, but the reason is that they are disillusioned because America is fighting an expensive, faraway war when there are all these problems that need working on at home. The Dad tentatively offers a few lukewarm arguments in favor of present war policy, but soon changes his mind when the student confidently (but not arrogantly) cites facts and arguments for quick withdrawal. The Dad agrees to write against the war to his congressman, but counterattacks with gusto on the issue of student laziness. The son now concedes this point (it would not leave a good taste with the listeners if the cocky son triumphed completely over the wishy-washy Dad). The son resolves to get back to his campus and get all his buddies more involved in their own education and in constructive action. He complements his Dad on his understanding and on all he has done all these years for his son. They now chat amiably about other things.

POSTSCRIPT

The fundamental thesis of this paper is reflected in Bandura's (1969) perceptive concern for the potential misuse of the therapist's influence in his one-way power relation with those labeled "patients."

> As behavioral science makes further progress toward the development of efficacious principles of change, man's capacity to create the type of social environment he wants will be substantially increased. The decision process by which cultural priorities are established must, therefore, be made more explicit to ensure that "social engineering" is utilized to produce living conditions that enrich life and behavioral freedom rather than aversive human effects. [p. 112].

References

Bandura, A. *Principles of Behavior Modification.* New York: Holt, 1969.
Hovland, C. I. "Reconciling Conflicts Results Derived from Experimental and Survey Studies of Attitude Change," *American Psychologist* 14, 1954, pp. 8–17.

Inbau, F. E., & Reid, J. E. *Criminal Interrogation and Confessions*. Baltimore: Williams & Wilkins, 1962.

Kidd, W. R. "Police Interrogation," *The Police Journal*. New York, 1940.

Milgram, S. "Behavioral Study of Obedience," *Journal of Abnormal and Social Psychology* 67, 1963, pp. 371–378.

Mulbar, H. *Interrogation*. Springfield, Ill. Charles C. Thomas, 1951.

O'Hara, C. E. *Fundamentals of Criminal Investigation*. Springfield, Illinois: Thomas, 1956.

Orne, M. "On the Social Psychology of the Psychological Experiment: With Special Reference to Demand Characteristics of Their Implications", *American Psychologist*, 17, 1962, pp. 776–785.

Time Magazine, December 3, 1965, p. 52.

Time Magazine, April 29, 1966, p. 65.

DONALD J. MOINE

Reading 8–2
To Trust, Perchance to Buy

The real estate agent, who normally speaks quickly and loudly, is responding in a slow, soft, rhythmic voice to her slow-speaking, quiet customer. The agent opened the sales interview with a series of bland and flatly accurate remarks about the cool weather and the lack of rain. Now she is explaining her hesitation in showing her customer a particular house: "I know you want to see that house, but I don't know whether I should show it to you. It is expensive, and"—an imperceptible pause—*"just looking at it will make you want to buy it."* A bit later she repeats something that, she says, a previous customer told her about a house he'd bought: "The house has been worth every penny. My wife and I enjoy it so much"—another pause—*"we can't understand why we took so long to buy it."*

The agent, an extremely successful saleswoman, is instinctively using weapons from the arsenal of the skilled clinical hypnotist, whose initial aim is to create in a subject a state of intensified attention and receptiveness, leading to increased suggestibility. All successful persuaders produce such an effect, probably without understanding the exact nature of the techniques that accomplish it. Our real estate woman is lulling her customer into a mood of trust and rapport by taking on his verbal and emotional coloring, and her techniques are almost identical to those that therapists like Herbert Spiegel use with patients who come to them to be hypnotized out of, say, their fear of cats.

The conclusion that a successful sales presentation is an intuitive form of indirect hypnosis is the most provocative finding of a psycholinguistic anlaysis that I performed in 1981. My initial study focused on eight life insurance salesmen, four of whom were identified as "top producers" by the presidents of their companies, and four as only average. The two groups were closely matched on such characteristics as age and experience. Taking the role of the customer, I spoke with the eight men, recorded their comments, and analyzed those comments for the 30 techniques of persuasion that Richard Bandler and John Grinder had identified in the work of the master hypnotist Milton Erickson. I next examined the work of 14 top sellers of real estate, luxury automobiles, stocks, commodities, and trust deeds. Since 1981, I have tested my findings with more than 50 other people, who sell, among other products, jets, computers, and oil and gas leases. My basic finding was confirmed: Superior sellers use the techniques of the clinical hypnotist; mediocre ones do not.

GETTING IN SYNC

The best salespeople first establish a mood of trust and rapport by means of "hypnotic pacing"—statements and gestures that play back a customer's observations, experience, or behavior. Pacing is a kind of mirrorlike matching, a way of suggesting: "I am like you. We are in sync. You can trust me."

The simplest form of pacing is "descriptive pacing," in which the seller formulates accurate, if banal, descriptions of the customer's experience. "It's been awfully hot these last few days, hasn't it?" "You said you were going to graduate in June." These statements serve the purpose of establishing agreement and developing an unconscious affinity between seller and customer. In clinical hypnosis, the hypnotist might make comparable pacing statements: "You are here today to see me for hypnosis." "You told me over the phone about a problem that concerns you." Sales agents with only average success tend to jump immediately into their memorized sales pitches or to hit the customer with a barrage of questions. Neglecting to pace the customer, the mediocre sales agent creates no common ground on which to build trust.

A second type of hypnotic pacing statement is the "objection pacing" comment. A customer objects or resists, and the sales agent agrees, matching his or her remarks to the remarks of the customer. A superior insurance agent might agree that "insurance is not the best investment out there," just as a clinical hypnotist might tell a difficult subject, "You are resisting going into trance. That's good. I encourage that." The customer, pushing against a wall, finds that the wall has disappeared. The agent, having confirmed the customer's objection, then leads the customer to a position that negates or undermines the objection. The insurance salesman who agreed that "insurance is not the best investment out there" went on to tell his customer, "but it does have a few uses." He then described all the benefits of life insurance. Mediocre salespeople generally respond to resistance head-on, with arguments that presumably answer the customer's objection. This response often leads the customer to dig in his heels all the harder.

The most powerful forms of pacing have more to do with how something is said than with what is said. The good salesman or -woman has a chame-leonlike ability to pace the language and thought of any customer. With hypnotic effect, the agent matches the voice tone, rhythm, volume, and speech rate of the customer. He matches the customer's posture, body language, and mood. He adopts the characteristic verbal language of the customer ("sounds good," "rings a bell," "get a grip on"). If the customer is slightly depressed, the agent shares that feeling and acknowledges that he has been feeling "a little down" lately. In essence, the top sales producer becomes a sophisticated biofeedback mechanism, sharing and reflecting the customer's reality—even to the point of breathing in and out with the customer.

I have found only one area in which the top salespeople do not regularly pace their customers' behavior and attitudes—the area of beliefs and values. For example, if a customer shows up on a car lot and explains that she is a Republican, a moderately successful salesman is likely to say that he is, too, even if he isn't. The best sales people, even if they are Republicans, are unlikely to say so, perhaps because they understand that "talk is cheap" and recognize intuitively that there are deeper, more binding ways of "getting in sync" with the customer.

THE SOFT SELL

Only after they have created a bond of trust and rapport do the top salespeo-ple begin to add the suggestions and indirect commands that they hope will lead the customer to buy. One such soft-sell technique is using their patently true pacing statements as bridges to introduce influencing statements that lead to a desired response or action. For example: "You are looking at this car and you can remember the joy of owning a new reliable car," or "You are 27 years old, and we figure that your need for life insurance is $50,000." These pacing-and-leading statements resemble the way a hypnotist leads a client into hypnosis: "You are sitting in this chair, and you are listening to my voice"—the unarguable pacing statements—"and your eyelids are get-ting heavy, and they are beginning to close. . . ."

There does not have to be any logical connection between the pacing statement and the leading statement. They can be totally unrelated, yet when they are connected linguistically, they form a "sales logic" that can be powerfully effective, even with such presumably analytic and thoughtful customers as doctors and college professors.

The power of these leading statements comes from the fact that they capitalize on the affirmative mental state built by the undeniably true pacing statements, with which the customer is now familiar. Customers who have agreed with salespeople expect, unconsciously, further agreement, just as customers who have disagreed expect further disagreement. The "tradi-tional" truth of these pacing statements rubs off on the leading statements, and, without knowing it, the customer begins to take more and more of what the sales agent says as both factual and personally significant. Using hypnotic language, the agent activates the customer's desire for the product.

Average sellers combine pacing and leading statements less frequently and with less skill than do their superior colleagues. They also speak in shorter, choppier sentences, and thus fail to create the emotional web of statements in which the truthful and the possible seem to merge.

One of the most subtle soft-sell techniques is to embed a command into a seemingly innocuous statement. "A smart investor knows how to *make a quick decision, Robert.*" I'm going to show you a product that will help you, *Jim, save money.*"

Salespeople insure that their embedded commands come across by changing the tone, rhythm, and volume of their speech. Typically, as they pronounce the commmands, they intuitively slow their speech, look the customer directly in the eyes, and say each word forcefully. A clinical hypnotist does the same thing deliberately. "If you will *listen to the sound of my voice,* you will be able to relax."

The placement of an individual's name in a sentence seems like a trivial matter, yet the position of a name can make a significant difference in how strongly the sentence influences the listener. Placed before or after the command portion of a sentence, it gives the command an extra power.

By changing their speech rate, volume, and tone, the best sales agents are able to give certain phrases the effect of commands. "If you can *imagine yourself owning this beautiful car,* and *imagine how happy it will make you,* you will want to, *Mr. Benson, buy this car.*" The two phrases beginning with 'imagine' become commands for the customer to do just that. Owning the car is linked to the leading statement of how happy it will make the customer. Finally, the statement carries the embedded command: *"Mr. Benson, buy this car."*

THE POWER OF PARABLES

A final soft-sell technique of the best salespeople is the ability to tell anecdotes, parables, and stories, and to frame their comments in metaphors. For thousands of years, human beings have, been influencing, guiding, and inspiring one another with stories and metaphors, so it should be no surprise that salespeople routinely use them to influence customers. What is surprising is the frequency and skill with which they do so.

Some sales agents I have studied do almost nothing but tell stories. They tell them to get the customer's attention, to build trust and rapport, and even to deliver product information. A piece of information that in itself might be boring takes on a human dimension and stays in the customer's memory when placed in the context of a story. "I sold a receiver like this a week ago to a surfer from Torrance and what he liked best about it was its FM sensitivity of 1.7 microvolts."

Metaphors and stories are used to handle customers' resistance and to "close" on them without endangering rapport. A top insurance agent was attempting to close a deal for a policy with a young man who was considering signing with a smaller company. As part of his clinching argument, the salesman wove the following metaphor into his pitch: "It's like taking your family on a long voyage across the Atlantic Ocean, and you want to get from here to England, and you have the choice of either going on this tugboat or on the Queen Mary. Which one would you *feel safe* on?" Had the salesman tried to make his point with a litany of facts and figures, he might never have focused his customer's attention; the discussion could have descended into a dispute about numbers. Instead, his story spoke directly to the customer's concern about his family's safety and implied that it was now in the customer's power to decide between two choices that were clearly unequal.

Note, too, that the salesman used conjunctions to link the metaphor in one unbroken chain and give it a hypnotic cadence. Mediocre salespeople who know such a story would probably tell it as several separate sentences. In addition, they probably would give no special emphasis to the phrase "feel safe" even if they had heard better sales people do so. The skill in telling it is more important than the material itself.

The same can be said about all the skills that constitute the intuitively hypnotic arsenal of the best sales agents. But obviously, these skills are not exclusive to sellers. They are common to others—politicians, lawyers, even preachers. No less than salespeople, these persuaders try to influence their audiences. No less than salespeople, they attempt to implant in their audiences a resolve to do something. And, like salespeople, all of them use, to some extent, variations of the techniques of Mesmer, Cagliostro, and Rasputin.

ANDREW COLMAN

Reading 8-3
How People Respond to Flattery

"Every woman is infallibly to be gained by every sort of flattery, and every man by one sort or another." Lord Chesterfield expressed this dogmatic opinion in a letter to his son in 1752, and his sentiments have been shared by numerous subsequent writers. In *How to Win Friends and Influence People*, Dale Carnegie recommended the unstinting use of flattery as part of his formula for "how to make people like you instantly." He believed this policy would invariably yield positive results. Recent experiments I have undertaken with my colleagues at the University of Leicester in England, however, have revealed that things are not so simple, and that there are circumstances in which flattery is likely to cause a decrease in liking for the flatterer.

The background to our experiments was provided in the 1960s by the work of Edward Jones, now professor of psychology at Princeton. Jones and his colleagues were curious about all the various methods, collectively called "ingratiation tactics," that people sometimes adopt to make themselves appear more attractive to others. They carried out a series of experiments in which people were given a chance to get acquainted with strangers. They devised various ingenious methods to get their subjects to behave ingratiatingly, usually creating situations in which the subjects had something to gain by making themselves attractive to the strangers.

The subjects persuaded to behave ingratiatingly usually did so in a way clearly distinguishable from that of the subjects who were given no particular incentive to ingratiate themselves. They used four main tactics: they usually tried to present themselves to the strangers in a manner that both emphasized what they thought were their more attractive qualities and played down their weak points; they generally pretended to share the strangers' attitudes and

First published in *New Society*, London, England, 1980. Reprinted with permission of the publisher and the author.

opinions on important issues; they often offered unsolicited favors to the strangers; and finally, they very often resorted to flattery.

One unexpected finding about vanity and self-deception emerged from these experiments. When the ingratiation tactics succeeded, even the most candid subjects were later unwilling to admit to Jones and his colleagues that they had taken any active steps to enhance their attractiveness. They seemed to have convinced themselves that the strangers had liked them for no other reason than their inherent likableness.

These early experiments investigated the *active* features of ingratiation. My colleagues and I, on the other hand, have been investigating the *responsive* aspects of ingratiation—that is, the way in which a particular kind of ingratiation; namely, flattery, influences the recipient's liking for the flatterer.

There are two main theories about the effect of flattery: the "self-enhancement" theory and the "cognitive consistency" theory. Although they are both quite simple and almost commonsense, the two theories lead to conflicting predictions about what will happen in certain circumstances.

The self-enhancement theory is based on elements of Carl Rogers' theory of personality and on the concept of "need satisfaction." The fundamental assumption is that people have a powerful need to evaluate themselves favorably. Flattery helps to satisfy this need. It is always reassuring, according to this theory, to be told that one is likable; it satisfies a basic human need and evokes reciprocal liking for the flatterer.

The cognitive-consistency theory is based on a different kind of human need—the need to organize one's thoughts, feelings, and behavior in a meaningful and harmonious way. People therefore usually like those who share their attitudes and opinions on matters of importance to them. Since a person's attitudes toward himself or herself clearly fall into this category, cognitive-consistency theory predicts that flattery will cause the flatterer to be liked only when the flattery supports the recipient's self-image. One of R. D. Laing's poetic "knots" makes this point:

I am good
You love me
therefore you are good.
I am bad
You love me
therefore you are bad.

It is interesting to see what happens when a person who has very low self-esteem is flattered, or when a compliment is delivered on some personal quality that the recipient believes he or she is lacking. According to cognitive-consistency theory, this type of flattery is liable to backfire. Self-enhancement theory, on the other hand, predicts that this kind of flattery will be most effective in eliciting liking for the flatterer, because the recipient's need for reassurance is strongest where he or she lacks self-esteem.

To test these two theories against each other, we recently carried out an experiment on 30 subjects who had been specially selected by means of a standard questionnaire for their very high or very low self-esteem. Each subject was interviewed separately for 10 to 15 minutes in a laboratory fitted with a one-way screen. The interview covered biographical details, relations with other people, problems with work, incidents the subject was proud or embarrassed to recall, and so on. Subjects were told they were being observed through the one-way screen by a psychologist who would later provide an expert character analysis.

Each subject, in fact, received one of two standard evaluations. One was very flattering: "He creates a very favorable impression. He's the kind of person I enjoy talking to. . . . He shows healthy psychological adjustment." The other standard evaluation was neutral: "He creates a fair impression. . . . There's nothing really outstanding to say." After receiving the flattering or the neutral evaluation each subject was asked to give impressions of the evaluator.

The results provided clear support for the cognitive-consistency theory. The high self-esteem subjects generally ended up with a much more favorable impression of the evaluator when he flattered them than when he offered neutral comments. Subjects who had a low opinion of themselves preferred the neutral evaluator to the flatterer—that is, the flattery backfired when it was used on these subjects. The results suggest that flattery succeeds in eliciting liking from the recipient only when it confirms the latter's self-image. People who have low opinions of themselves are not merely impervious to flattery—they react against it by disapproving of the flatterer.

We also carried out a subtler experiment with 48 subjects to discover some of the limits of cognitive-consistency theory. In this experiment, instead of selecting subjects for high and low overall self-esteem, we capitalized on the fact that nearly everyone has qualities that they like and qualities they dislike. For example, a woman may possess high aesthetic self-esteem (she may think she is beautiful), but low intellectual self-esteem (she may think she is not intelligent). In this case, a compliment on her good looks would be an example of what we call "valid flattery," and a compliment on her brightness would be "phony flattery." The nature of the flattery—whether valid or phony—is therefore defined from the viewpoint of the recipient rather than that of the flatterer.

According to the cognitive-consistency theory, only valid flattery will elicit liking for the flatterer, because it satisfies the need for consistency. The self-enhancement prediction is precisely the reverse: phony flattery will elicit more liking than valid flattery, because the recipient's need for reassurance is greatest in those areas where he or she has low self-esteem.

We expected the outcome would depend upon the status differences between the flatterer and the recipient. When a low-status person delivers phony flattery to someone of relatively higher status, common sense suggests that the recipient will reject the flattery in order to maintain cognitive consistency. ("He says I sing beautifully, but he doesn't know what he's talking about.") Compliments from a flatterer of relatively higher status, on the other hand, are likely to seem more authoritative and to carry more weight even if they are phony. ("He says I sing beautifully, of all things. Well, what about that!")

In this experiment, therefore, we introduced the evaluator to each under-graduate subject either as a relatively high-status person (a graduate student) or as a relatively low-status person (a high school dropout). In addition, the flattery was individually tailored to each subject's self-image, which had been carefully assessed by a previous paper-and-pencil test. We expected that both valid and phony flattery would result in increased liking for the high-status flatterer, but that only valid flattery would succeed with the low-status flatterer.

The results partly confirmed our predictions. Status alone had no effect on liking: when they refrained from flattery, the high-status and low-status evaluators were equally liked by the subjects. When they indulged in flattery, however, the high-status flatterers became much more attractive to the subjects and the low-status flatterers became much less attractive. As ex-pected, it made little difference whether the high-status evaluators used valid or phony flattery. However, subjects disliked the low-status evaluators most when they indulged in phony flattery. Unexpectedly, even valid flattery tended to backfire when used by the low-status evaluators.

These results suggest that all kinds of flattery are liable to fail when used by someone of lower status than the recipient, and that phony flattery is liable to fail dismally in such cases. When used by a high-status person, however, flattery seems to evoke liking, whether valid or not. The explanation for the different effects of status probably lies in the apparent insincerity of flattery delivered by a low-status person. Praise from a lowly quarter may suggest not only that the flatterer's opinion is of little worth but that he or she is trying to gain some advantage, particularly if the flattery seems phony. Praise from someone whom we admire or respect is less easy to reject, and we are less likely to attribute manipulative intentions to such a flatterer.

The results of this experiment support both theories of the effect of flattery: people seem to need both self-enhancement and cognitive consis-tency, depending on the circumstances. Flattery that is inconsistent with a recipient's self-image may create positive and negative reactions simul-taneously: the flatterer may be liked at an emotional level, but regarded as a fool from a more rational point of view.

ERVING GOFFMAN

Reading 8-4
On Cooling the Mark Out:
Some Aspects of Adaptation to Failure

In cases of criminal fraud, victims find they must suddenly adapt themselves
to the loss of sources of security and status which they had taken for granted.
A consideration of this adaptation to loss can lead us to an understanding of
some relations in our society between involvements and the selves that are
involved.

In the argot of the criminal world, the term *mark* refers to any individual
who is a victim or prospective victim of certain forms of planned illegal
exploitation. The mark is the sucker—the person who is taken in. An
instance of the operation of any particular racket, taken through the full cycle
of its steps or phases, is sometimes called a play. The persons who operate
the racket and "take" the mark are occasionally called operators.

The confidence game—the con, as its practitioners call it—is a way of
obtaining money under false pretenses by the exercise of fraud and deceit.
The con differs from politer forms of financial deceit in important ways. The
con is practiced on private persons by talented actors who methodically and
regularly build up informal social relationships just for the purpose of
abusing them; white-collar crime is practiced on organizations by persons
who learn to abuse positions of trust which they once filled faithfully. The
one exploits poise; the other, position. Further, a con man is someone who
accepts a social role in the underworld community; he is part of a brotherhood whose members make no pretense to one another of being "legit." A
white-collar criminal, on the other hand, has no colleagues, although he may
have an associate with whom he plans his crime and a wife to whom he
confesses it.

From *Psychiatry* (1952) 25:451–463. Copyright © 1952 by the William Alanson White
Psychiatric Foundation, Inc. Reprinted by special permission of the William Alanson White
Psychiatric Foundation, Inc.

The con is said to be a good racket in the United States only because most Americans are willing, nay, eager, to make easy money, and will engage in action that is less than legal in order to do so. The typical play has typical phases. The potential sucker is first spotted, and one member of the working team (called the outside man, steerer, or roper) arranges to make social contact with him. The confidence of the mark is won, and he is given an opportunity to invest his money in a gambling venture which he understands to have been fixed in his favor. The venture, of course, is fixed, but not in his favor. The mark is permitted to win some money and then persuaded to invest more. There is an "accident" or "mistake," and the mark loses his total investment. The operators then depart in a ceremony that is called the blow-off or sting. They leave the mark but take his money. The mark is expected to go on his way, a little wiser and a lot poorer.

Sometimes, however, a mark is not quite prepared to accept his loss as a gain in experience and to say and do nothing about his venture. He may feel moved to complain to the police or the chase after the operators. In the terminology of the trade, the mark may squawk, beef, or come through. From the operators' point of view, this kind of behavior is bad for business. It gives the members of the mob a bad reputation with such police as have not yet been fixed and with marks who have not yet been taken. In order to avoid this adverse publicity, an additional phase is sometimes added at the end of the play. It is called cooling the mark out. After the blowoff has occurred, one of the operators stays with the mark and makes an effort to keep the anger of the mark within manageable and sensible proportions. The operator stays behind his teammates in the capacity of what might be called a cooler and exercises upon the mark the art of consolation. An attempt is made to define the situation for the mark in a way that makes it easy for him to accept the inevitable and quietly go home. The mark is given instruction in the philosophy of taking a loss.

When we call to mind the image of a mark who has just been separated from his money, we sometimes attempt to account for the greatness of his anger by the greatness of his financial loss. This is a narrow view. In many cases, especially in America, the mark's image of himself is built up on the belief that he is a pretty shrewd person when it comes to making deals and that he is not the sort of person who is taken in by anything. The mark's readiness to participate in a sure thing is based on more than avarice; it is based on a feeling that he will now be able to prove to himself that he is the sort of person who can "turn a fast buck." For many, this capacity for high finance comes near to being a sign of masculinity and a test of fulfilling the male role.

It is well known that persons protect themselves with all kinds of rationalizations when they have a buried image of themselves which the facts of their status do not support. A person may tell himself many things: that he has not been given a fair chance; that he is not really interested in becoming something else; that the time for showing his mettle has not yet come; that the usual means of realizing his desires are personally or morally distasteful, or require too much dull effort. By means of such defenses, a person saves himself from committing a cardinal social sin—the sin of defining oneself in terms of a status while lacking the qualifications which an incumbent of that status is supposed to possess.

A mark's participation in a play, and his investment in it, clearly commit him in his own eyes to the proposition that he is a smart man. The process by which he comes to believe that he cannot lose is also the process by which he drops the defenses and compensations that previously protected him from defeats. When the blowoff comes, the mark finds that he has no defense for not being a shrewd man. He has defined himself as a shrewd man and must face the fact that he is only another easy mark. He has defined himself as possessing a certain set of qualities and then proven to himself that he is miserably lacking in them. This is a process of self-destruction of the self. It is no wonder that the mark needs to be cooled out and that it is good business policy for one of the operators to stay with the mark in order to talk him into a point of view from which it is possible to accept a loss.

In essence, then, the cooler has the job of handling persons who have been caught out on a limb—persons whose expectations and self-conceptions have been built up and then shattered. The mark is a person who has compromised himself, in his own eyes if not in the eyes of others.

Although the term, *mark,* is commonly applied to a person who is given short-lived expectations by operators who have intentionally misrepresented the facts, a less restricted definition is desirable in analyzing the larger social scene. An expectation may finally prove false, even though it has been possible to sustain it for a long time and even though the operators acted in good faith. So, too, the disappointment of reasonable expectations, as well as misguided ones, creates a need for consolation. Persons who participate in what is recognized as a confidence game are found in only a few social settings, but persons who have to be cooled out are found in many. Cooling the mark out is one theme in a very basic social story.

* * * * *

In all personal-service organizations customers or clients sometimes make complaints. A customer may feel that he has been given service in a way that is unacceptable to him—a way that he interprets as an offense to the conception he has of who and what he is. The management therefore has the problem of cooling the mark out. Frequently this function is allotted to specialists within the organization. In restaurants of some size, for example, one of the crucial functions of the hostess is to pacify customers whose self-conceptions have been injured by waitresses or by the food. In large stores the complaint department and the floorwalker perform a similar function.

One may note that a service organization does not operate in an anonymous world, as does a con mob, and is therefore strongly obliged to make some effort to cool the mark out. An institution, after all, cannot take it on the lam; it must pacify its marks.

One may also note that coolers in service organizations tend to view their own activity in a light that softens the harsher details of the situation. The cooler protects himself from feelings of guilt by arguing that the customer is not really in need of the service he expected to receive, that bad service is not really deprivational, and that beefs and complaints are a sign of bile, not a sign of injury. In a similar way, the con man protects himself from remorseful images of bankrupt marks by arguing that the mark is a fool and not a full-fledged person, possessing an inclination towards illegal gain but not the decency to admit it or the capacity to succeed at it.

In organizations patterned after a bureaucratic model, it is customary for personnel to expect rewards of a specified kind upon fulfilling requirements of a specified nature. Personnel come to define their career line in terms of a sequence of legitimate expectations and to base their self-conceptions on the assumption that in due course they will be what the institution allows persons to become. Sometimes, however, a member of an organization may fulfill some of the requirements for a particular status, especially the requirements concerning technical proficiency and seniority, but not other requirements, especially the less codified ones having to do with the proper handling of social relationships at work. It must fall to someone to break the bad news to the victim; someone must tell him that he has been fired, or that he has failed his examinations, or that he has been by-passed in promotion. And after the blowoff, someone has to cool the mark out. The necessity of disappointing the expectations that a person has taken for granted may be infrequent in some organizations, but in others, such as training institutions, it occurs all the time. The process of personnel selection requires that many trainees be called but that few be chosen.

* * * * *

I have mentioned a few of the areas of social life where it becomes necessary, upon occasion, to cool a mark out. Attention may now be directed to some of the common ways in which individuals are cooled out in all of these areas of life.

For the mark, cooling represents a process of adjustment to an impossible situation—a situation arising from having defined himself in a way which the social facts come to contradict. The mark must therefore be supplied with a new set of apologies for himself, a new framework in which to see himself and judge himself. A process of redefining the self along defensible lines must be instigated and carried along; since the mark himself is frequently in too weakened a condition to do this, the cooler must initially do it for him.

One general way of handling the problem of cooling the mark out is to give the task to someone whose status relative to the mark will serve to ease the situation in some way. In formal organizations, frequently, someone who is two or three levels above the mark in line of command will do the hatchet work, on the assumption that words of consolation and redirection will have a greater power to convince if they come from high places. There also seems to be a feeling that persons of high status are better able to withstand the moral danger of having hate directed at them. Incidentally, persons protected by high office do not like to face this issue, and frequently attempt to define themselves as merely the agents of the deed and not the source of it. In some cases, on the other hand, the task of cooling the mark out is given to a friend and peer of the mark, on the assumption that such a person will know best how to hit upon a suitable rationalization for the mark and will know best how to control the mark should the need for this arise. In some cases, as in those pertaining to death, the role of cooler is given to doctors or priests. Doctors must frequently help a family, and the member who is leaving it, to manage the leave-taking with tact and a minimum of emotional fuss.[1] A priest must not so much save a soul as create one that is consistent with what is about to become of it.

A second general solution to the problem of cooling the mark out consists of offering him a status which differs from the one he has lost or failed to gain but which provides at least a something or a somebody for him to become. Usually the alternative presented to the mark is a compromise of some kind, providing him with some of the trappings of his lost status as well as with some of its spirit. A lover may be asked to become a friend; a student of medicine may be asked to switch to the study of dentistry[2] a boxer may become a trainer; a dying person may be asked to broaden and empty his worldly loves so as to embrace the All-Father that is about to receive him. Sometimes the mark is allowed to retain his status but is required to fulfill it in a different environment: the honest policeman is transferred to a lonely beat; the too zealous priest is encouraged to enter a monastery; an unsatisfactory plant manager is shipped off to another branch. Sometimes the mark is "kicked upstairs" and given a courtesty status such as "Vice President." In the game for social roles, transfer up, down, or away may all be consolation prizes.

A related way of handling the mark is to offer him another chance to qualify for the role at which he has failed. After his fall from grace, he is allowed to retrace his steps and try again. Officer selection programs in the army, for example, often provide for possibilities of this kind. In general, it seems that third and fourth chances are seldom given to marks, and that second chances, while often given, are seldom taken. Failure at a role

[1] This role of the doctor has been stressed by W. L. Warner in his lectures at the University of Chicago on symbolic roles in "Yankee City."

[2] In his seminars, Mr. Hughes has used the term *second-choice* professions to refer to cases of this kind.

removes a person from the company of those who have succeeded, but it does not bring him back—in spirit, anyway—to the society of those who have not tried or are in the process of trying. The person who has failed in a role is a constant source of embarrassment, for none of the standard patterns of treatment is quite applicable to him. Instead of taking a second chance, he usually goes away to another place where his past does not bring confusion to his present.

Another standard method of cooling the mark out—one which is frequently employed in conjunction with other methods—is to allow the mark to explode, to break down, to cause a scene, to give full vent to his reactions and feelings, to "blow his top." If this release of emotions does not find a target, then it at least serves a cathartic function. If it does find a target, as in "telling off the boss," it gives the mark a last-minute chance to redirect his defenses and prove to himself and others that he had not really cared about the status all along. When a blow-up of this kind occurs, friends of the mark or psychotherapists are frequently brought in. Friends are willing to take responsibility for the mark because their relationship to him is not limited to the role he has failed in. This, incidentally, provides one of the less obvious reasons why the cooler in a con mob must cultivate the friendship of the mark; friendship provides the cooler with an acceptable reason for staying around while the mark is cooled out. Psychotherapists, on the other hand, are willing to take responsibility for the mark because it is their business to offer a relationship to those who have failed in a relationship to others.

It has been suggested that a mark may be cooled out by allowing him, under suitable guidance, to give full vent to his initial shock. Thus the manager of a commercial organization may listen with patience and understanding to the complaints of a customer, knowing that the full expression of a complaint is likely to weaken it. This possibility lies behind the role of a whole series of buffers in our society—janitors, restaurant hostesses, grievance committees, floorwalkers, and so on—who listen in silence, with apparent sympathy, until the mark has simmered down. Similarly, in the case of criminal trials, the defending lawyer may find it profitable to allow the public to simmer down before he brings his client to court.

A related procedure for cooling the mark out is found in what is called stalling. The feelings of the mark are not brought to a head because he is given no target at which to direct them. The operator may manage to avoid the presence of the mark or may convince the mark that there is still a slight chance that the loss has not really occurred. When the mark is stalled, he is given a chance to become familiar with the new conception of self he will have to accept before he is absolutely sure that he will have to accept it.

As another cooling procedure, there is the possibility that the operator and the mark may enter into a tacit understanding according to which the mark agrees to act as if he were leaving of his own accord, and the operator agrees to preserve the illusion that this was the case. It is a form of bribery. In this way the mark may fail in his own eyes but prevent others from discovering the failure. The mark gives up his role but saves his face. This, after all, is one of the reasons why persons who are fleeced by con men are often willing to remain silent about their adventure. The same strategy is at work in the romantic custom of allowing a guilty officer to take his own life in a private way before it is taken from him publicly, and in the less romantic custom of allowing a person to resign for delicate reasons instead of firing him for indelicate ones.

Bribery is, of course, a form of exchange. In this case, the mark guarantees to leave quickly and quietly, and in exchange is allowed to leave under a cloud of his own choosing. A more important variation on the same theme is found in the practice of financial compensation. A man can say to himself and others that he is happy to retire from his job and say this with more conviction if he is able to point to a comfortable pension. In this sense, pensions are automatic devices for providing consolation. So, too, a person who has been injured because of another's criminal or marital neglect can compensate for the loss by means of a court settlement.

I have suggested some general ways in which the mark is cooled out. The question now arises: what happens if the mark refuses to be cooled out? What are the possible lines of action he can take if he refuses to be cooled? Attempts to answer these questions will show more clearly why, in general, the operator is so anxious to pacify the mark.

It has been suggested that a mark may be cooled by allowing him to blow his top. If the blow-up is too drastic, or prolonged, however, difficulties may arise. We say that the mark becomes "disturbed mentally" or "personally disorganized." Instead of merely telling his boss off, the mark may go so far as to commit criminal violence against him. Instead of merely blaming himself for failure, the mark may inflict great punishment upon himself by attempting suicide, or by acting so as to make it necessary for him to be cooled out in other areas of his social life.

Sustained personal disorganization is one way in which a mark can refuse to cool out. Another standard way is for the individual to raise a squawk; that is, to make a formal complaint to higher authorities obliged to take notice of such matters. The con mob worries lest the mark appeal to the police. The plant manager must make sure that the disgruntled department head does not carry a formal complaint to the general manager or, worse still, to the board of directors. The teacher worries lest the child's parent complain to the principal. Similarly, a woman who communicates her evaluation of self by accepting a proposal of marriage can sometimes protect her exposed position—should the necessity of doing so arise—by threatening her disaffected fiancé with a breach-of-promise suit. So, also, a woman who is de-courting her husband must fear lest he contest the divorce or sue her lover for alienation of affection. In much the same way, a customer who is angered by a salesperson can refuse to be mollified by the floorwalker and demand to see the manager. It is interesting to note that associations dedicated to the rights and the honor of minority groups may sometimes encourage a mark to register a formal squawk; politically it may be more advantageous to provide a test case than to allow the mark to be cooled out.

Another line of action which a mark who refuses to be cooled can pursue is that of turning "sour." The term derives from the argot of industry but the behavior it refers to occurs everywhere. The mark outwardly accepts his loss but withdraws all enthusiasm, goodwill, and vitality from whatever role he is allowed to maintain. He complies with the formal requirements of the role that is left him, but he withdraws his spirit and identification from it. When an employee turns sour, the interests of the organization suffer; every executive, therefore, has the problem of "sweetening" his workers. They must not come to feel that they are slowly being cooled out. This is one of the functions of granting periodic advancements in salary and status, of schemes such as profitsharing, or of giving the "employee" at home an anniversary present. A similar view can be taken of the problem that a government faces in times of crisis when it must maintain the enthusiastic support of the nation's disadvantaged minorities, for whole groupings of the population can feel they are being cooled out and react by turning sour.

Finally, there is the possibility that the mark may, in a manner of speaking, go into business for himself. He can try to gather about him the persons and facilities required to establish a status similar to the one he has lost, albeit in relation to a different set of persons. This way of refusing to be cooled is often rehearsed in phantasies of the "I'll show them" kind, but sometimes it is actually realized in practice. The rejected marriage partner may make a better remarriage. A social stratum that has lost its status may decide to create its own social system. A leader who fails in a political party may establish his own splinter group.

All these ways in which a mark can refuse to be cooled out have consequences for other persons. There is, of course, a kind of refusal that has little consequence for others. Marks of all kinds may develop explanations and excuses to account in a creditable way for their loss. It is, perhaps, in this region of phantasy that the defeated self makes its last stand.

The process of cooling is a difficult one, both for the operator who cools the mark out and for the person who receives this treatment. Safeguards and strategies are therefore employed to ensure that the process itself need not and does not occur. One deals here with strategies of prevention, not strategies of cure.

From the point of view of the operator, there are two chief ways of avoiding the difficulties of cooling the mark out. First, devices are commonly employed to weed out those applicants for a role, office, or relationship who might later prove to be unsuitable and require removal. The applicant is not given a chance to invest his self unwisely. A variation of this technique, that provides, in a way, a built-in mechanism for cooling the mark out, is found in the institution of probationary period and "temporary" staff. These definitions of the situation make it clear to the person that he must maintain his ego in readiness for the loss of his job, or, better still, that he ought not to think of himself as really having the job. If these safety measures fail, however, a second strategy is often employed. Operators of all kinds seem to be ready, to a surprising degree, to put up with or "carry" persons who have failed but who have not yet been treated as failures. This is especially true where the involvement of the mark is deep and where his conception of self had been publicly committed. Business offices, government agencies, spouses, and other kinds of operators are often careful to make a place for the mark, so that dissolution of the bond will not be necessary. Here, perhaps, is the most important source of private charity in our society.

A consideration of these preventive strategies brings to attention an interesting functional relationship among age-grading, recruitment, and the structure of the self. In our society, as in most others, the young in years are defined as not-yet-persons. To a certain degree, they are not subject to success and failure. A child can throw himself completely into a task, and fail at it, and by and large he will not be destroyed by his failure; it is only necessary to play at cooling him out. An adolescent can be bitterly disappointed in love, and yet he will not thereby become, at least for others, a broken person. A youth can spend a certain amount of time shopping around for a congenial job or a congenial training course, because he is still thought to be able to change his mind without changing his self. And, should he fail at something to which he has tried to commit himself, no permanent damage may be done to his self. If many are to be called and few chosen, then it is more convenient for everyone concerned to call individuals who are not fully persons and cannot be destroyed by failing to be chosen. As the individual grows older, he becomes defined as someone who must not be engaged in a role for which he is unsuited. He becomes defined as something that must not fail, while at the same time arrangements are made to decrease the chances of his failing. Of course, when the mark reaches old age, he must remove himself or be removed from each of his roles, one by one, and participate in the problem of later maturity.

The strategies that are employed by operators to avoid the necessity of cooling the mark out have a counterpart in the strategies that are employed by the mark himself for the same purpose.

There is the strategy of hedging, by which a person makes sure that he is not completely committed. There is the strategy of secrecy, by which a person conceals from others and even from himself the facts of his commitment; there is also the practice of keeping two irons in the fire and the more delicate practice of maintaining a joking or unserious relationship to one's involvement. All of these strategies give the mark an out; in case of failure he can act as if the self that has failed is not one that is important to him. Here we must also consider the function of being quick to take offense and of taking hints quickly, for in these ways the mark can actively cooperate in the task of saving his face. There is also the strategy of playing it safe, as in cases where a calling is chosen because tenure is assured in it, or where a plain woman is married for much the same reason.

It has been suggested that preventive strategies are employed by operator and mark in order to reduce the chance of failing or to minimize the consequences of failure. The less importance one finds it necessary to give to the problem of cooling, the more importance one may have given to the application of preventive strategies.

* * * * *

Social Context of Negotiation

A significant element in any complex negotiation is the presence or absence of other parties. Some negotiations are exclusively conducted by two parties: a buyer and a seller, a husband and wife, or boss and subordinate. However, many more negotiations involve other parties. The negotiators themselves may be representing larger groups of people, as when a union leader represents his rank and file, a diplomat represents his country, or a manager negotiates a contract for his company. There may also be other interested third parties who are not as directly affected by the negotiation but who can observe the process. When constituencies, third parties, or audiences become involved in the negotiation, their very presence changes the nature of the negotiating process. Experienced negotiators know how to assess the impact of this larger social context on the negotiation process, and to effectively employ it to either protect one's self, or to increase the pressure on the other person to change his/her point of view. The importance of playing this role effectively is emphasized in the first article. Thomas Colosi in "A Core Model of Negotiation" points out that while most of the popular writing on negotiation depicts it as a one-on-one process, much negotiation is in fact rich and complex social interaction. Bargaining teams seldom agree among themselves as to their position, no less agree with the position of their counterparts. Individuals play different roles, often protracting the dispute as opposed to resolving it. Finally, deliberations are likely to occur hierarchically in the power structure as well as across the table. Thus, Colosi's article accurately represents the rich complexity that is characteristic of much real-life organizational negotiation.

A second way that the broader social environment impacts negotiation is through the customs, cultural rules, and procedures followed in various social contexts. The easiest way to observe this is to understand the impact of national differences on individual approaches to negotiations, which Howard Van Zandt explores in his article, "Comparative International Negotiating Practices." The purpose of this article is to teach American businesspeople the distinctive characteristics of their counterparts in Japan, and how these characteristics must be understood in order to effectively negotiate with them. Van Zandt highlights 13 characteristics which distinguish Japanese from Westerners, and explores in detail the implications of these characteristics for planning, preparing, and actually negotiating agreements. It is clear from both Van Zandt's approach, and the examples that he cites, that failure to understand the impact of these cultural and nationalistic differences can cause considerable difficulty for Westerners who want to successfully negotiate with Japanese.

In the third article, "Saving Face," Bert Brown focuses on one characteristic that is presumed strong among the Japanese, but which in fact is strong in most negotiators: the need to save face. While face-saving is an important attribute in Oriental cultures, Brown shows that is highly valued among Western negotiators as well. When people are told that they look foolish and that they look weak, and when that information is presented to them by observers who had a chance to evaluate their behavior, negotiators will change their negotiating strategy and engage in much more costly strategies in order to "regain face" or to regain favor among the negative observers. This face-saving behavior often leads negotiators to take tough and unyielding stands, even when those stands are unproductive for the negotiation's long-term economic outcomes. Brown's research clearly shows that negotiators can be made to act highly "irrationally" if told that they look foolish, and that the need to maintain a positive social image may be much stronger than the need to attain strongly positive and tangible outcomes. Everyday, the national press gives us interesting examples of politicians and other public figures seen doing some very unusual things, apparently to redeem their public image. For most of these situations, the negotiator has found that his constituency does not support a public stand on posture that he had made, and the negotiator is trying to regain his or her social stature.

THOMAS COLOSI

Reading 9-1

A Core Model of Negotiation

THE CONVENTIONAL PERCEPTION OF BILATERAL NEGOTIATION

Negotiations are typically depicted as involving one group sitting across a bargaining table from a second. One side presents its demands or proposals to the other, and a discussion or debate follows. Counterproposals and compromises are offered. When the offers are eventually accepted on both sides, the dispute is settled and an agreement is signed.

Within this model, all the interesting and relevant action is presumed to occur back and forth between the two sides. The model assumes that each party is monolithic, even if represented by bargaining teams. The way in which the participants are billed—labor versus management, prisoners versus guards, environmentalists versus industry—reflects the same monolithic assumption; that is, that all team members share the same set of demands, agree on a strategy for handling the opposition, and have come to the table with equal enthusiasm for the negotiating process.

Unfortunately, the conventional model of negotiation obscures much of the richness and complexity of the bargaining process. In practice, bargaining teams are seldom monolithic. Team members often have conflicting goals and values; some sort of consensus must develop internally before agreement can be reached with the other side. While some students of negotiation have recognized the importance of this internal bargaining, conventional models do not explain their relationship to the functioning of the larger process. By contrast, the model developed in this article attempts to incorporate this dimension and thus to present a richer and more realistic view of negotiation.

Adapted from Thomas Colosi, "Negotiation in the Public and Private Sectors," *American Behavioral Scientist,* vol. 27, no 2, November/December 1983, pp. 229–237. Copyright © 1983 by Sage Publications, Inc. Reprinted by permission of Sage Publications Inc.

For the sake of simplicity, the model presented below assumes—at this point—just two bargaining teams. Later in the article it is expanded to incorporate multiparty situations; conceivably it might also be applied to cases involving just two individuals. In any event, the model is intended to describe the structure or core of negotiation, regardless of the particular issues at stake, the identity of the parties, or the sector (public or private) in which the dispute takes place.

STABILIZERS, NONSTABILIZERS, AND QUASI-MEDIATORS

Within each team, negotiators usually hold quite different attitudes. Some negotiators tend to settle at any cost. They may be called *stabilizers*. They seek agreement with the other side to avoid the disruptive consequences of nonsettlement, particularly such lengthy, expensive, or disruptive alternatives as litigation, strikes, demonstrations, riots, and wars. A second general type, the *nonstabilizers,* do not particularly like the negotiation process. Nonstabilizers tend to disagree with most of the proposals of their own team and all of the counterproposals of the other side. They would rather see disruption through raw contests of will and power than compromise on a given position. The terms *nonstabilizers* would accept are far more stringent than those to which the stabilizers would agree.

Finally, in the middle is a third type, the *quasi-mediator,* who plays several roles. He or she is usually the spokesperson charged with the success of the effort. To those sitting across the table, the quasi-mediator may simply look like another negotiator, but within a team he or she often acts as a kind of mediator between the stabilizers and the nonstabilizers. As will be shown later, the quasi-mediator can also be a mediator between the team and its own constituents or clients.

HORIZONTAL, INTERNAL, AND VERTICAL NEGOTIATIONS

Although most conventional models limit their analysis to the bargaining that goes on across the table, relatively little true negotiating goes on horizontally. Instead, speeches are made, symbols and platitudes are thrown out, and emotions are displayed. If the communication is healthy, the two teams use this time constructively to educate each other: They explain proposals and counterproposals, compare data, show videotapes, share printouts, and present experts. Except for this opportunity to educate and to learn, however, all of this may be less important than the real activity going on internally.

The standard model also misses another important dimension of negotiation: the interchanges that occur between a bargaining team and its vertical hierarchy. A team is rarely and independent of a larger constituency. It is at the bargaining table because it has been sent to accomplish something. In the context of private sector labor negotiation, for example, management's vertical hierarchy is the company's leadership; for the union's bargaining committee, it is the international union and, most times, ultimately the membership who must vote on a proposed contract. Almost always, important negotiations must take place between a team and its vertical hierarchy at one point or another in the bargaining.

Since negotiators are continually being reeducated through the horizontal negotiations occurring at or near the bargaining table, they are frequently far more advanced in their thinking than are their constituents back home. The resulting gap can be a dangerous trap for all concerned. Part of the art and skill of being a negotiator is recognizing how far from the constituents the bargaining team has moved. The negotiator must also know when and how to go back and educate his or her own constituents.

Sometimes the vertical hierarchy will tell a negotiator what should be achieved at the bargaining table, but after several sessions with the other side, the negotiator may come to believe that these goals cannot be reached. It is within this context that negotiation between the team and its own vertical hierarchy takes place. The quasi-mediator is often responsible for negotiating with the hierarchy of the team's parent organization. In labor-management negotiations, for instance, the spokesperson or quasi-mediator on the union team may wind up intellectually positioned between the local's viewpoint on an issue and management's last known position. In such a case, the union spokesperson not only tries to get management to go along with labor's point of view but may also have to try to get the rest of the union team to accept management's view on some points.

INTERNAL TEAM NEGOTIATIONS

Resolving differences between the stabilizers and nonstabilizers may be a prerequisite for effective negotiation with the other side, as well as one for reaching accommodation with the team's own vertical hierarchy if settlement is the objective. Unless some means exist for coordinating positions and goals over time, there will be serious problems. When a team is considering making an offer, for example, the stabilizers likely will want to present a generous package, while the nonstabilizers will not want to offer anything. The quasi-mediator must begin to explore with the stabilizers why the concessions might be excessive. At the same time, of course, the quasi-mediator must discuss with the nonstabilizers why the proposal may be good and why the team should not be so rigid. In the same way, when a team receives an offer from the other side, the quasi-mediator must show the nonstabilizers why the team should not hold out for more while checking the stabilizers' tendency to grab the offer too quickly. Much like a neutral mediator, the quasi-mediator may meet jointly and separately with the stabilizers and nonstabilizers. If the team is not well disciplined, these discussions unfortunately may take place at the table. Ideally, they should take place in a separate caucus, away from the other side.

RAISING AND MAINTAINING DOUBTS TO FOSTER SETTLEMENT

In a sense, this internal team negotiation process is a microcosm of the larger negotiations that occur across the table. Similar aspects of bargaining positions come into play; the same kinds of negotiation skills are required. As in across-the-table bargaining, the most important efforts are those directed at changing the minds of parties who do not want to settle.

It is reasonable to ask why the focus should be on those who oppose settlement: Perhaps those who are anxious to settle—to sell the farm— should be challenged with at least as much force. The answer lies in the true essence of negotiation. Negotiations are not squabbles or battles between two sides. The goal of the process is not for one team to extract huge concessions from the other. Instead, the essence of negotiation is to provide an opportunity for parties to exchange promises through which they will resolve their differences with one another. A settlement thus is no more—and no less— than an expression of an exchange of promises. Because the emphasis in negotiations is on the resolution of differences through the exchange of promises, the process is oriented in favor of settlement. Attention is naturally focused on parties who seem to stand in settlement's way.

Settlement is fostered through the raising and maintaining of doubts. In all negotiations, parties that want to reach some settlement (e.g., the stabilizers and quasi-mediators) work to raise or maintain doubts in the minds of others as to the viability of their particular positions, as well as doubts about the consequences of nonagreement. This effort is focused on nonstabilizers and the team across the table. The nonstabilizers are asked to consider the implications of nonsettlement, what it would mean to them personally, or to their organization, objectives, ideals, and reputations. Thus, the same techniques and strategies teams may use to raise and maintain doubts in the minds of parties across the table are also appropriate internally with the non-stabilizers. By the same token, of course, the nonstabilizers engage in a parallel effort to raise doubts in the minds of stabilizers and the quasi-mediator about the consequences of settlement.

Because a particular settlement may not be in the interests of the non-stabilizer, he or she frequently must be convinced to accept a settlement through some method other than fostering doubts. Negotiators have an additional tool when dealing with a nonstabilizing teammate: the discipline of the parent organization. This discipline, which might rely upon power, title, prestige, or majority rule, operates within the team. The decision-making process is normally carried over from the parent organization through the chief spokesperson or team leader, which reinforces the roles and relationships of the vertical hierarchy. For instance, an organization that makes most of its important decisions by a majority vote will probably be represented in negotiations by a team that also makes its decisions by majority vote.

According to most practitioners, negotiation is a consensual process. The negotiators come to agreement precisely because they find settlement preferable to nonagreement. But it is erroneous to conclude, as some have, that everyone wins or gains from a negotiated agreement. The notion of "win-win" outcomes is another reflection of the limits of the conventional model of negotiation. Both sides across a table may appear to win, but within each team—where so much more bargaining goes on—there are often non-stabilizers who may view themselves as definite losers in the process.

TARGETING UNDERLYING CONCERNS

The creation and maintenance of doubts about the consequences of nonagreement (or one decision versus another) is central to inducing skeptics to settle. This is true whether they are nonstabilizers within a team or nonstabilizers across the table. But where should this effort be directed?

Fisher and Ury (1981) observe that a negotiator can move the opposite side closer to settlement by convincing it to participate in joint problem solving. This may be accomplished by separating the opposing side's *position* from its underlying *interests*.

Although positions are usually explicit, the interests that underlie them often are left unstated. For example, a community coalition might oppose the establishment of a home for mentally retarded adults in its neighborhood. Yet what is its true interest? Frequently, the community feels that the retarded adults would make the neighborhood less safe. Preserving safe streets may be the real interest at stake. A sophisticated advocate of the home would try to raise doubts about whether the community's stated position will actually satisfy its interests: "Might not additional numbers of sincere, capable adults contribute to community safety? Look at their abilities as well as their problems." An educational process showing that the retarded adults would pose no danger to neighborhood residents—and in fact might improve their security—could foster doubts in the minds of the neighbors about their flat refusal to consider the proposal. Even if opponents are not convinced on this particular score, identifying safety as their prime interest allows the parties to explore mitigating measures.

Education can be the most effective way to raise doubts. It is used, therefore, in every phase of negotiation: across the table, within a team, and between a team and its constituents. The plan of attack is to move the opponent to a more agreeable position.

As Fisher and Ury observe, the effective negotiator aims for the underlying interests that form the foundation of the adversary's position. What happens, however, if a negotiator cannot identify the opponent's interests?

Where else can doubts be targeted to get others to adopt a more flexible stance? An answer requires a closer look at the different levels of concern that are often negotiated: issues, proposals, problem definitions, and assumptions.

ISSUES, PROPOSALS, PROBLEMS, AND ASSUMPTIONS

The negotiator's job is to raise and maintain doubts on all four levels of concern. Consider, for example, a proposal to site a hazardous waste management facility that requires the approval of a community board. If there is local opposition, it probably will be based on the assumption that such facilities are inherently dangerous. If that assumption cannot be questioned, no basis exists for negotiations between the community and the developer. As a consequence, the facility will be blocked.

Moreover, even if the project sponsors can convince the community that such facilities are not necessarily dangerous, they may encounter a different obstacle—that of problem definition. For example, the community might contend that its opposition is not to treatment facilities in general but to the proposed location of this particular plant. (It might be near a flood plain.) Casting the problem in these terms obviously would affect proposed solutions. The range of proposals could include the following: having no facility at all, putting the facility at another site, using control technologies to make the facility fit the site, or making the site more acceptable for the proposed use. The issues to be discussed in negotiation would be tied to such proposals. For example, discussion might focus on the need for such a facility, the reasons for (and against) this particular location, and the cost-effectiveness of various mitigating measures.

The task of the facility sponsor would be to raise doubts about the viability of any unacceptable proposals or issues. As assumptions and problem definitions are revealed—which is much more likely than the disclosure of an opponent's real interests—the sponsor would also question them. Since the issues and proposals are derived from the problems and assumptions, the sponsor would probably try to move the negotiations into discussions of the latter before considering specific issues and proposals. In short, the sponsor would focus on the underlying concerns.

EXPANDING THE CORE MODEL

Multilateral Negotiations

The core model that has been described above includes five axes of negotiation: one horizontal, two internal, and two with vertical hierarchies. This model was based on the simplifying assumption that only two teams are at the table. While there are many instances of two-party negotiation, in other cases—particularly those that arise in the public sector—many more parties may be involved. How must the core model be expanded to accommodate additional parties?

The most important difference between two-party and multiparty negotiation is that the latter opens up the possibility of coalition. For example, three parties—A, B, and C—may come to full agreement or no agreement, but they also may be able to forge alternative side deals. Any two parties may strike a deal that leaves the third out. Were A negotiating with just one other party, he could simply weigh any proposed settlement against the consequences of nonagreement. Here, however, he must also compare a possible settlement with both B and C with the advantages of different agreements with B alone or C alone. The addition of each new party at the bargaining table greatly increases the number of theoretical alliances. The introduction of additional parties, necessary as they might be, greatly complicates the negotiation process. Some coalitions may hold for the entire negotiation, but often alliances shift with various issues. Moreover, the lineup of coalitions may shift over time as events, personalities, and loyalties change. Consensus building is always a delicate balancing act.

Finally, the presence of so many parties at the table usually will mean that much more business must be transacted. The important education process usually requires much more time, as the negotiators at the table have the burden of carrying far more information back through their vertical hierarchy. Perhaps we should not be surprised that so many public disputes seem to take months—even years—to negotiate.

The Solitary Negotiator

When only two individuals are negotiating, each acting on his or her own behalf, the conventional model with its emphasis on two independent units bargaining across the table may afford understanding. Yet perhaps even here it is an oversimplification if we do not look at the negotiation that occurs within each of us. Individuals often have mixed feelings and competing priorities. People must admit (to themselves at least) that they sometimes vacillate between accepting a settlement and holding out for more.

Speculation as to whether stabilizing, nonstabilizing, and mediating impulses may exist in one mind is best left to psychiatrists, psychologists, behaviorists, neurologists, and theologians. It does seem true, however, that even in one-on-one bargaining, there can be distinct and contradictory attitudes toward a particular settlement. One strength of the model developed here is that it recognizes the stabilizing and nonstabilizing forces within each bargaining unit (be it a team or an individual), and attempts to understand the means by which they may be integrated.

Quasi-Mediators and Mediators

Outside mediators enter disputes for a very specific reason: to fill a trust vacuum that exists at an impasse among and within the parties. The quasi-mediator and mediator play separate, yet related, roles: Both use the creation and maintenance of doubts to move other negotiators closer to settlement. The quasi-mediator, like the other negotiators, has personal, organizational, and institutional stakes in the outcome of the negotiation process. The truly neutral mediator does not. The quasi-mediator also has some power to make decisions about substantive and procedural issues. Whatever power the mediator might enjoy is procedural.

Reference

Fisher, R., and W. Ury. *Getting to Yes*. Boston: Houghton Mifflin, 1981.

HOWARD F. VAN ZANDT

Reading 9–2
Comparative International Negotiating Practices

International negotiating practices are as varied as the races of mankind. Diplomats, international businessmen, academics, and others would be well advised, before making a trip to some foreign country, to learn as much as they can about the negotiating expectations, methods, techniques, strategems, tactics, customs, and so on, they will face. In this paper an effort will be made to draw attention to some of them.

I. IMPORTANCE OF PERSONAL RELATIONS

In the industrialized nations of the world, many decisions would appear to be made based upon the data that spills forth from computers and telex machines. Negotiations conducted at computer or telex terminals are as impersonal as it is possible to be. They are the epitome of "dry." On the opposite side are negotiations between personal friends, dealings that are face-to-face and often involve warm handshakes, embrace (abrazo), and pats on the back. These are what are termed *wet*.

American negotiating is basically "dry," whereas the methods followed in Latin countries, much of Asia and Islamic and black Africa are "wet." It should not be assumed that all advanced countries are dry and the others wet. Actually, the Japanese are, in some respects wet, and they find their neighbors in China to be dry!

In U.S. universities, particularly in schools of business, so much time is given to quantitative subjects that students sometimes receive their degrees and spill out into the business world without having been taught that success,

For the session on "The Art of International Business Negotiations" in the International Management Division, Academy of Management Conference—August 16, 1983. Used with permission of the author.

even in a dry society, is dependent to a considerable degree on establishing and maintaining good personal relationships. Fortunately, Americans are regarded by foreigners as being an especially friendly lot, and it is probable that this innate characteristic lubricates their negotiating machinery and facilitates their success despite any shortcomings in their education.

In many foreign countries, for instance, Japan, France, and Germany, friendships are not made as swiftly as in America. Once they are made, however, they are likely to be longer lasting and to weigh more importantly in negotiations than is the case in the United States. In France and Spain a salesman develops friendships with his customers by treating them fairly and responsibly. If the salesman moves to a competing company, he will likely take his customers with him. Even in the Soviet Union, despite its huge bureaucracy and central planning, much is accomplished through the simple device of getting on friendly terms with those who may be able to help and influence policy.

II. EMOTIONS AND NEGOTIATING

In some cultures argument should be avoided. Japan is a conspicuous example. In China, on the other hand, people are likely to express their feelings naturally. Latin Americans tactfully avoid arguing. Australians are often laconic and cynical, and freely make critical remarks about situations, conditions, and people, sometimes giving the impression that they are sarcastic.

Orientals make an especial effort to conceal their emotions. Americans are far more open and usually show their feelings. In some instances it is to their disadvantage, say, when exhibiting enthusiasm for a product being offered. Once they do this, sharp-eyed Orientals will raise their prices. Other Asians and North Africans also watch for reactions and set their prices accordingly.

It is wise to avoid displays of impatience when dealing with Orientals. As one Chinese told the writer: "Even a mild impatience will lower respect." It is also desirable to keep your temper. The Japanese have a proverb: "Tanki wa sonki," which translates, "If you lose your temper you will lose your case." When negotiating with Japanese, it is desirable to avoid letting them get your goat, and goading you into a display of temper. Goading can, of course, have a negative effect on both parties. In Thailand, for instance, although the natives have a reputation of being quiet and reserved with ready smiles, when irritated enough, they become uncontrollable!

Face is important in many foreign countries, including the Arab nations, China, Thailand, and so on. It is wise to avoid reprimanding Chinese and Thai in the presence of others. If criticism is in order, it is best to do it privately. In Nippon, on the other hand, employees are sometimes criticized by Japanese supervisors in public in order to serve as a warning to others! Non-Japanese, however, had best help them "keep face," by criticizing privately.

Japanese and Chinese, among others, often tell of their shortcomings while talking to foreigners from advanced countries. They engage in self-criticism in order to demonstrate their modesty. Westerners often misunderstand and agree with the criticisms and even add some of their own. This leads to resentments and should be avoided.

Americans would do well to be modest when dealing with Orientals. As a Chinese told the writer: "Just because an American has an expensive education, wears fine clothing, and drives a big automobile, does not mean that he is a superior human being. He should know that Chinese picture Americans as barbarians with hideously big noses, the repulsive body hair of animals, and the offensive body odor that comes from eating too much meat. They would be wise to avoid showing any trace of arrogance."

People should also remember, when negotiating, that many foreigners have much pride in their own culture. It is desirable not to act in a condescending fashion or "talk down" to them. When dealing with Arabs and Iranians, it is well to remember that their heritage is a rich one, and that during the Dark Ages in Europe, they carried the torch of civilization high.

III. BUYING AND SELLING

In many countries haggling is common, expected, and a part of the game. This is especially true in the Near and Middle East where the natives take pride in having sharp wits. In neighboring Soviet Union, long and tough bargaining may take place over all the details in a business proposal.

In Japan, hard bargaining is the rule in Osaka and the prefectures closest to China. In Tokyo and vicinity, the samurai legacy of looking down on crass merchants and their ploys still influences behavior. The typical Tokyo buyer is not a patsy, however, and like others of his fellow countrymen, demands thorough explanations before he will agree to a purchase. On major procurements, the Nippon custom is to require far more documentation than is the case in the West. It is helpful when making a presentation in Nippon to provide published evidence. Orientals generally do not consider that oral statements are as reliable as published ones. Natives of countries at the other end of Asia often make oral promises and declarations that they cannot back up, and which may clearly be in error. Japanese do not exaggerate or overstate the attractions of products they are trying to sell.

Germans have the reputation of being hard bargainers. When they buy something important, they expect it to be presented in an orderly fashion and extensively described.

When negotiating with Spaniards it is wise to be fully prepared as they demand that all details be at hand, including precise prices and exact delivery terms.

Australians and the British tend to resent foreign salesmen who openly exaggerate the attractions of what they are offering. Both Australians and the British characteristically understate, so when negotiating with them, this should be kept in mind.

Negotiations take far longer in the USSR, Japan, China, and many other countries than in the United States. In the Soviet Union, stalling is a deliberate tactic. Japanese, Koreans, and Chinese sometimes use silence as a negotiating tool. Whereas in most of the rest of the world conversations are like Ping-Pong, with one person saying something, and then another person replying; in Northeast Asia, even though a question has been asked, silence may ensue as the one questioned hopes to get the other side to make a concession in order to get the discussion moving again.

It should be kept in mind that in the Orient and many other parts of the world, when dealing with someone of the same or higher level, it is customary to say what the other person would like to hear rather than give the facts. The traditional avoidance of saying "no" among Japanese and Chinese even though "no" is intended, comes from this custom.

When doing business with Asians or Latin Americans it should be kept in mind that if the American or other foreign negotiator has authored a book or articles in respected journals, or lectured at a university, his credibility will be increased as there is respect for a person who is believed to be scholarly.

IV. FORMALITY VERSUS INFORMALITY

In the United States, it is considered helpful if negotiators come to know one another well enough to use first names. Often it takes only five minutes of conversation to switch from "Mr." to "Bill." This is not the case in most foreign countries. In Japan, for instance, men may work in the same office together for 30 years and never use the first name! Generally, in Japan and most other foreign countries, first names are only used among members of the same family and between school classmates. Americans should keep this in mind and refrain from using first names in countries where it would be inappropriate.

In Germany, Japan, and many other countries it is proper to address people using their titles.

When preparing for a trip, it should be noted that in the Far East and many other parts of the world, unless on holiday, it is proper to dress conservatively. The writer recalls an experience when he took some consulting clients from Los Angeles to a business meeting in Tokyo one Saturday morning. The Californians, since it was a weekend, wore casual sports garb. The Japanese immediately concluded that they were not serious but just in Nippon for a vacation!

In the Orient and the Arab world calling cards should be presented at the beginning of meetings rather than at the end. Orientals make more use of calling cards than is done elsewhere, one reason being that there are so many homonyms. Only when seeing the name printed on a calling card is it possible to know which Chinese characters are used. Unless the proper ones are known, it is impossible to address a letter, or for that matter, find a name in a telephone directory.

It is best to refrain from kidding and idle banter when dealing with most foreigners. What may seem clever and witty to an American may be incomprehensible to a foreigner.

It goes without saying that it is a firm rule to be courteous to the foreigners with whom you are doing business. In public opinion polls conducted in Japan, the English and French were regarded as the most polite. Americans and Australians were classed as the least! It is not considered polite, or effective, to try to conduct business over the telephone in the USSR, Japan, and many other countries. Also, in the USSR and Japan, it is better to do business face-to-face rather than by mail.

V. COUNTRIES WITH HIGH RATES OF ILLITERACY

In many of the developing countries, particularly in Africa, South Asia, and tropical Latin America, a substantial proportion of the population is illiterate. If people cannot read and write, it is obvious that printed explanations, letters, memoranda, cables, and computer printouts will not be effective. In such countries it will be best to use pictures, drawings, samples, models, and the like in making presentations. Natives of developing countries are for the most part not as concerned with time schedules as are those in industrialized nations. Good business and political personal relationships are vital to success.

BERT R. BROWN

Reading 9-3
Saving Face

Some time ago a newspaper article described the achievement pressures put on students at the Harvard Business School. One young man, explaining why he and his peers worked unusually hard, said: "Fear of embarrassment is the great social motivator. There are a hundred people who can annihilate you in those classes. You don't want to look like a yo-yo in front of a hundred guys."

On April 30, 1970, President Nixon defended his decision to send troops into Cambodia by saying: "If when the chips are down the world's most powerful nation . . . acts like a pitiful, helpless giant, the forces of total-itarianism and anarchy will threaten free nations. . . . I would rather be a one-term President . . [than] . . . see this nation accept the first defeat in its proud 190-year history."

Bibb Latané of Ohio State and John Darley of Princeton did an experiment to discover when people will help in a crisis [*P.T.*, December 1968]. They found that individuals were less likely to intervene to help a person in distress when other persons were nearby and that the likelihood of intervention decreased as the number of others present increased. The researchers noted that some of the subjects were concerned not to make fools of themselves by overreacting.

NEED

The student, the president and the bystander all illustrate, in diverse ways, a universal psychological mechanism: the need to save face. Ten years ago, Erving Goffman identified this pervasive need, suggesting that it motivates us (1) to appear capable and strong whenever possible, and (2) to avoid situations that would make us look foolish in front of others. "Face" is thus heavily dependent on one's supposed status, prestige, or recognition in the eyes of others. Goffman was first to observe that individuals will guard against loss of face even if it becomes very costly for them to do so.

With introspection, we can see the face-saving mechanism at work in our everyday lives, when we often go to elaborate, contorted extremes to offset embarrassment, avoid looking foolish, and protect our fragile self-esteem. And if we look around us, we see increasing evidence of the important role that this motive has had historically: for example, in the alignment of nations in the First and Second World Wars, in the Korean War and subsequent negotiations, in the Cuban missile crisis, in the Arab-Israeli conflict, and of course in our involvement in Indochina.

SMOKE

Because of the fundamental nature of face-saving, and because it can have so many serious real-world repercussions, I have become interested in learning more about this motive: when it is likely to occur, what situational factors are likely to provoke it. If we can answer these questions, I reasoned, we might be better able to deal constructively with the smokescreen that face-saving sets up between friends and governments alike.

The first step was to define the motive in specific, behavioral terms. *The need to maintain face is expressed in the sacrifice of tangible rewards to avoid looking foolish or incompetent in public.* This definition includes two essential points: the motive (1) is *costly;* the need to preserve or restore self-esteem outweighs opportunities for financial gain; and (2) requires the presence of an *audience,* real or imagined.

Two components of the need to maintain face are *face-saving* and *face-restoration.* The former is designed to prevent a loss of face before it actually occurs. We may construct extravagant facades to protect ourselves in situations that might be embarrassing; we withdraw from experiences that might prove humiliating. In this sense, face-saving is anticipatory. Face restoration, by contrast, occurs after one has suffered humiliation. In such cases the individual tries to counteract his loss of face, by either retaliation or reassertion. Armed with this definition, we have conducted a number of laboratory experiments to explore the situational factors that affect face-saving. We have primarily used two paradigms: a bargaining game that involves aggressive exchanges between players and an embarrassing performance situation.

We based the bargaining task on a two-person trucking game originally devised by Morton Deutsch and Robert Krauss. Each player operates a trucking company, Acme or Bolt, and he must move his truck over a road system to his destination. The faster he completes the trip, the more money he will earn. Of course there is a dilemma: one must choose between two routes to the finish—a short, direct route and a longer, more circuitous one.

A portion of the short route narrows to a one-lane pathway; if both trucks attempt passage at the same time they will collide, causing both players to lose time and money. One player, then, has to yield. The longer route has no common pathway but is twice as long; its use permits a player to avoid encounters with his opponent, but it automatically limits the amount he can earn. In order for each to win the maximum amount, therefore, the opposing players must cooperate.

To complicate the game further, each player also controls a tollgate at one end of the common pathway on the short route, through which his opponent's truck must pass. In each trial we required players either to charge one of several specified tolls or to grant free passage. If a truck refuses to pay a demanded toll, it must then back out of the common pathway and take the longer route.

FEEDBACK

In our first experiment, 60 male subjects played this game with a stooge (Bolt) who had sole use of the tollgate and who systematically exploited them during the first round of 10 trials. That is, the stooge charged high tolls, causing subjects to lose much of their initial stake. At the end of this round, subjects got written feedback from—we told them—an audience of peers who had been observing.

Half of the subjects received evaluations that derogated them for allowing themselves to be exploited: for example, "Bolt was out to beat Acme and he really made Acme look like a sucker," or, "Bolt played tricky. He ran rings around Acme and made him lose a lot. Acme looked pretty bad." The rest of the subjects read comments that commended them for playing fair: "Bolt was rough and tricky but Acme came out okay because he played it straight," or "Bolt was out to beat Acme and make him look like a sucker, but Acme played fair and looked good."

Now the subjects played another round of 10 trials, and this time they, not the stooge, had control of the tollgate. We gave them the following toll schedule:

Toll you may charge:						
00	10	15	20	30	40	50
Costs to self:						
00	00	00	10	25	40	60

In other words, subjects could retaliate against the stooge by charging high tolls, or increase their own earnings by charging lesser ones. The more severe the retaliation, the smaller one's own gains became.

REVENGE

The results were clear. Students who had received the sucker feedback from their audience were far more likely to retaliate against their opponents than subjects who had received favorable feedback. More importantly, the first group retaliated at high personal cost; they were willing to lose money in order to restore face with their opponents. The second group, who did not feel that they had played foolishy, went on to maximize their profits.

It is possible, of course, that these results can be explained by revenge—the desire to inflict harm on one's opponent—rather than by the face-saving motive. We do not think that simple revenge was the primary factor here, since the "not-foolish" group was far less retaliatory than the "foolish" group, though all had been objectively victimized in the same way. Our postexperimental questionnaire also showed that subjects who felt humiliated were more concerned with appearing strong to the stooge than were the other subjects. We concluded that young men will try to reassert capability and strength after being made to look foolish—even if it is costly.

The price one pays for such sweet retaliation, however, must not be known to one's enemy. If X is aware that Y must sacrifice money for the pleasure of defeating him, Y's ability to restore face is greatly reduced. A variation on the bargaining experiment showed that the costs one willingly incurs to save face (or restore it) are likely to be greater when one knows that those costs will not be publicized. We told half of our subjects that before the second 10 trials their costs for retaliation—the toll schedule—would be shown to their opponents, while the rest thought that these costs would remain private. The latter group retaliated more frequently, tending to lose more money than the former.

PACIFIER

We next turned to a different experimental paradigm: public embarrassment. We told subjects, 48 freshman males, that they were participating in a perception study. Their task was to form detailed impressions of an object during a three-minute "sensing period"—but using only one prescribed sense. Each student sat in a private cubicle, blindfolded ("so as not to confound visual perception with other forms of perception being studied," we told them).

In the "embarrassing" condition, we gave each of one group of subjects a four-inch rubber pacifier (sterilized, in a cellophane packet) and told him to "sense it orally": "suck, bite, and lick the object to form detailed impressions of it." Each remaining subject got a four-inch rubber soldier; we told him to "touch and feel the object with your hands to form detailed impressions."

It appears that there is almost nothing more embarrassing to a freshman male than sucking a baby pacifier, except perhaps having to describe the experience. After the "sensing" part of the experiment, we gave each subject the choice of discussing his impressions before a panel of evaluators (to increase a monetary reward) or of declining public exposure (thereby forfeiting the reward). Subjects who had had to suck the pacifiers sacrificed far more money, on the average, than those who had had the less embarrassing task. The pacifier group said that they simply didn't want to look foolish.

The evaluative role of the audience is important in face-saving, too. In a similar experiment, subjects had to perform the same embarrassing task. But half of them believed that the audience was convened specifically to evaluate them as they discussed the experience; the rest thought that the audience was only a casual gathering of visitors, convened merely by coincidence. Subjects declined public discussion much more often in the first case.

SING

Our most recent set of experiments has explored the influence of felt incompetence, audience acquaintanceship, and expected feedback on face-saving. We used a different sort of embarrassment in this series.

We asked our subjects—72 freshman males—to sing "Love Is a Many-Splendored Thing" privately, after which they received apparently objective computer evaluations of their vocal abilities: "competent" or "incompetent." We selected that song for its high embarrassment potential, having discovered that most college students are willing to blunder their way through folk songs and easy ballads without undue embarrassment.

After receiving their voice evaluations, subjects sang the same song to a panel of evaluators (ostensibly sitting behind a one-way mirror). We explained that the purpose of the study was to compare the computer evaluations with those made by the audience. Further, we would pay the freshmen according to the length of time they continued to sing—the longer they kept going, the more they would earn.

EXPECTATIONS

We hypothesized that singing time would be: (1) shorter (and monetary sacrifice greater) in the "incompetent" group than in the "competent" group; (2) shorter when subjects expected to get feedback on their performances than when feedback was not expected; (3) longer before an audience of strangers than before acquaintances or friends. The results supported the first and third predictions.

In further support of the face-saving concept, the most common reason the freshmen gave for declining to sing was the desire to avoid looking foolish or incompetent. "I seriously did not feel it worth my time to stand there and croak like a frog, which is what my voice is like," explained one student. "I don't need the money particularly, and my embarrassment overcame my dedication to science," another rationalized. "I stopped because I couldn't remember the rest of the song and I know I can't sing so I felt really stupid," said a third.

Contrary to several theories and common sense, close friends do not liberate individuals from face-saving. Quite the reverse. Our subjects were more likely to withdraw from public performance in front of their friends than in front of strangers, and similarly they sacrificed more money before strangers they expected to meet later than before strangers whom they would not meet. Knowledge about future dealings with one's audience, therefore, evokes the motive to save or restore face.

SEX

Thus far we had used males in most of our research, since we wanted first to get hold of the situational factors involved in face-saving. We suspected that there would be differences *between* the sexes in face-saving, and also *within* each sex group depending on the sex of the audience. After reviewing the research on sex differences in several related areas (embarrassment, blushing, empathy, and status-associated sex), we predicted that:

1. Women would be more prone to face-saving than men;
2. Among women, face-saving would increase in the presence of males, but among males face-saving would decrease in front of females;
3. Overall, a male audience would be more likely to induce face-saving than a female audience would.

We used the public-singing situation to test these predictions, asking males and females to sing "Love Is a Many-Splendored Thing" before male or female evaluators. The primary measure of face-saving was length of singing time in front of the audience (subjects were paid for each five seconds they sang). The results:

Average Singing Time (in seconds)

| | Sex of Subjects | | |
Sex of Audience	Male	Female	Overall
Male	77	65	71
Female	90	16	53
Overall	84	41	

This shows: (1) that females sang for significantly shorter periods of time than males, regardless of the sex of the audience, and (2) that face-saving was most pronounced among women who had to sing to a female audience. Recall that the less one sang, the greater the face-saving.

MIX

We next tried to understand the reason for the increased face-saving in the female-female condition. Answers to a postexperimental questionnaire showed that women expected a female audience to be more critical than a male audience. They also attributed greater singing ability to women, and this increased their embarrassment—which in turn made them stop singing sooner. Interestingly, this process was not at work among the males; the sex of the audience had no significant effect on their singing times.

This finding suggested that for women the expertise of the audience has an important effect on the need to save face. To test this, we did an experiment with women only, using the same singing paradigm. We informed subjects that the (female) audience consisted of either "excellent" or "poor" singers. The results were clear: women who had to perform in front of the excellent group sang, on the average, for 32 seconds; those who sang for the poor group carried on for an average of 119 seconds.

POINTS

Taken together, these two studies of sex differences tell us, not so much that men and women are unlike in their needs to maintain face, but that they differ in their responses to particular situations. All of us use face-saving to keep from looking foolish, but some circumstances make us feel more foolish than others.

From our research we draw six conclusions about the nature of face-saving:

1. Face-saving is heightened when one's audience gives him derogatory feedback rather than supportive feedback.
2. The costs one will incur to save (or restore) face are far greater when one is sure that only he will know those costs.
3. Face-saving, by withdrawal from the public eye, is a likely response to public embarrassment even if this involves high cost to oneself. We are not motivated solely by rational, economic interests.
4. Face-saving increases when one's audience has an evaluative role.
5. Face-saving is likely to occur if one feels personally incompetent, and if this incompetence threatens to become publicly visible.
6. Individuals are more likely to save face in front of friends or strangers they will meet later, than before acquaintances or strangers they will never meet.

PEACE

These findings point to a generalized strategy to cope with the need to save face in settling conflicts. For example, if derogatory feedback increases face-saving, mediators should encourage negotiators to be supportive of each other. Compromises can be rationalized by pointing out that disputants are being wise, not weak, in making them. In short, mediators should be interpersonally skillful as well as impartial, and should be attuned to the strength and subtlety of the motive to maintain face.

Perhaps if the universality of this motive is brought into the open and better understood, we can learn to control it, negotiate around it, and not let it get in the way of our best interests. Students could study out of the motivation to learn; governments could admit to mistakes, however tragic; and we would be less likely to let the Kitty Genoveses die because we are embarrassed to intervene.

SECTION TEN

Power

Within the context of negotiation, as well as other social influence situations, power is one of the most captivating attention-getting topics. Power and its effective use have fascinated students and practitioners of social influence for thousands of years. The writings of Machiavelli, almost 600 years old, continue to stand as an excellent treatise to practitioners on the effective use of power. More recently, political scientists, economists, psychologists, philosophers, politicians, statesmen, as well as people from all walks of life have had extensive things to say on power, its use and misuse.

One way to account for this fascination with power is to recognize that, on the one hand, people understand how necessary a thorough understanding of power is to effective action, and at the same time, they recognize how difficult it is to know how to acquire and how to use power effectively. There remains a certain mysticism about power, a certain elusiveness that makes it hard to clearly define it and explain its dynamics; yet there is a very strong need to do just this. A general definition of power is that it is the ability to influence people to do something they otherwise would not do—clearly something a negotiator would like to be able to do.

The articles in this section will offer a variety of perspectives on power and power use, and will enhance the negotiator's understanding of how power works. In the first article, "Power and Influence," David Bell struggles with the definitions of power, influence, and authority. Taking a political science and communication approach to the understanding of power and authority, he defines power as the potential to take action that can directly influence another, and the communication of this potential to the other. These communications are primarily in the form of threats and prom- ises, or the intentions of the power holder to reward or punish the target person for desired or undesired behavior. Thus, power (as defined by Bell) is the ability to manipulate positive or negative sanctions for compliance or noncompliance with the power holder's wishes. Such power may be used explicitly or tacitly as desired or needed. While there are a variety of other types of power and power use in negotiation, Bell's approach reflects a common and easily understood perspective on effective power use.

Walter Guzzardi, in the next article, "How the Union Got the Upper Hand on J. P. Stevens," describes an active struggle for power: the long and protracted conflict between J. P. Stevens, a major textile manufacturing company, and the Amalgamated Clothing and Textile Workers Union's (ACTWU) efforts to unionize the J. P. Stevens's mills. In 1963, J. P. Stevens made a commitment to actively oppose unionization of its plants. The parties squared off and prepared for battle. What ensued was a 15-year fight with the National Labor Relations Board, the courts, as well as frequent union strikes and boycotts, and negotiating power tactics by both sides. The article clearly points out how such power struggles can drain both sides of valuable resources, but that the fight goes on nevertheless in order to win the intangibles of psychological victory and future negotiating leverage.

Because power tactics can be so costly in both the short and long run, they need to be carefully examined and understood. In the article, "Power, Alinsky, and Other Thoughts," George Peabody does this with many of the tactics used by Stevens and ACTWU. Peabody advocates an approach to power based on the writing of Saul Alinsky, a well-known community organizer. Peabody lays out a very pragmatic approach to power based on individual self-interest. He also describes the mechanisms by which power is effectively employed in order to forward one's own interests. This strategy begins with building an organization to coalesce around power, using the organization to apply leverage to particular issues or problems, and con- sciously focusing on strategy and tactics for achieving these objectives. These three action strategies—collaboration, fight, and negotiation—are all designed to accomplish ones's self-interests in the context of a political environment. Peabody uses as his examples the environments in which Alinsky's approach and tactics have been most commonly effective: social change, political action, and community organizing for exercising political goals.

Laurel Leff, in "Community Spirit: Local Groups That Aid Poor Flourish by Using Confrontation Tactics," presents us with a case example of the Peabody-Alinsky approach to community organization and its impact. Leff describes the work of the United Neighborhood Organization Group in Los Angeles and its work to organize the Hispanic community for social im- provement and effective political action. For the negotiator who represents a constituency, who has to be concerned with audiences, these techniques offer rich food for thought.

The next article, "Various Dimensions of the Issue of Personal Power," by Shel Davis, shifts the emphasis from the organizational and community approach to power to the individual approach. Davis comments on several ways that individuals act to decrease their own power by the way that they choose to behave in society. These ways include: not assuming responsibility for their own behavior, not pursuing their dreams for a better society, and being taught to feel uncomfortable with effective power use and application. Similarly, Gerald Nachman in "Squeak Up: My Turn," offers a tongue-in-cheek exploration of many popular books and articles that appeared in the late 70s, advocating self-assertiveness and personal strategies for overcoming powerlessness. Nachman offers his humorous insights into everyday situations in which people could be powerful but choose not to be, and some biting social commentary on what happens when we really try to use power but don't do it very well.

The last article in this section, "Get Things Done through Coalitions," by Margo Vanover, offers a perspective on one of the most important ways organizations and individuals get power—through forming coalitions. Coalitions are affiliations of people with common social objectives, who choose to pool their collective strengths and self-interests in order to accomplish a common goal. Professional trade associations, political action committees, or even groups of individuals with a similar purpose or goal are good examples of coalitions in action. Vanover shows how to make coalitions work effectively in order to apply leverage successfully to those who have power as a means of attaining goals and objectives.

DAVID V. J. BELL

Reading 10-1
Power and Influence

Power, influence, and *authority*—in everyday speech, their meanings overlap; the terms are sometimes used interchangeably. But at other times they
conjure quite different images. There are at least some circumstances in
which we would not substitute one of these three terms for the other. To
describe a man as powerful is not the same as calling him *influential;* and
neither term captures the connotations of the adjective *authoritative.* We
would hardly find appropriate a book entitled *How to Win Friends and
Overpower People.* Nor would we speak of an armed robber "exerting his
authority" to obtain cash from a teller.

Presumably, therefore, power, influence, and authority are not perfectly
congruent synonyms. Yet even sophisticated students of politics have usually
failed to distinguish them. Hannah Arendt must be credited with a sharp
understanding of the costs of such linguistic insensitivity:

> It is, I think, a rather sad reflection on the present state of political science that
> our terminology does not distinguish among such key words as "power,"
> "strength," "force," "authority," and finally "violence" . . . To use
> them as synonyms not only indicates a certain deafness to linguistic meanings,
> which would be serious enough, but it has also resulted in a kind of blindness
> to the realities they correspond to.[1]

But with what methodology are we to arrive at the "correct" means for
distinguishing among these terms? Do we turn to etymology in the hope of
finding the key? Or do we instead decree, as it were, that the terms mean
exactly what we wish? Although I firmly believe that the failure to draw
important distinctions has led to analytic confusion and meaningless debate,
this position poses a logical and linguistic dilemma: to argue that the words

---

From *Power, Influence, and Authority: An Essay in Political Linguistics* by David V. J.
Bell. Copyright © 1975 by Oxford University Press, Inc. Reprinted by permission.
[1] Hannah Arendt, *On Violence* (New York: Harcourt Brace Jovanovich, 1970), p. 43.

must be distinguished because they intrinsically mean different things is to adopt an essentialist position that is indefensible; while to argue that the words can mean whatever we want them to mean is to adopt the equally indefensible posture of Humpty Dumpty, who insisted that he could "make" words mean whatever he wanted because he was their "master." (He admitted, however, to "paying" them extra "when he made them do a lot of work.")

My position is made more difficult by the fact that even while agreeing wholeheartedly with Hannah Arendt's plea for distinctions, I find myself unable to accept her own definitions of the terms. Obviously there is a great deal of "private vision" in the picture of politics each writer draws.

To identify differing patterns of social/political relationships without resorting to neologisms, an investigation of these concepts must proceed along a path that runs between inductive "discovery" of "intrinsic" meanings and the deductive pronouncement of arbitrary definitions. Throughout, I place considerable emphasis on the "commonsense" usages of the terms while recognizing that at times our everyday language is inconsistent and self-contradictory. The goal of this investigation is to find concepts that illuminate politics, or—more accurately—bring it into focus. We view the political world through a series of conceptual lenses which in turn allow us to see certain features. Clear conceptual vision predetermines the quality of analysis—both empirical and normative—that may follow.

Power, influence, and authority refer to certain forms of human relations; that is, these phenomena exist only in a plural setting where two or more people interact with each other.[2] That these phenomena are *relational* seems quite obvious, and yet it is often forgotten. Perhaps because our language is virtually choked with a plethora of nouns rather than verbs, we tend to assume that power especially is a concrete thing that an individual can somehow "possess" like a fast car or a lot of money. But this usage is quite misleading, for, in the words of Eric Hoffer, "Power does not come in cans." To talk about power as a possession is therefore elliptical. What is really meant by the assertion "A possesses power" is that A "possesses" the *potential* for exercising power effectively.[3] In this discussion we will care-

---

[2] Note that the term *relation* can imply a repetitive, almost institutional quality of interaction and not merely a single disconnected act. "Power *relations* are built of repetitive, durable patterns of action, but microsociological taxonomic schemes, when stretched beyond their useful limits, tend to dissolve relation into individual acts." E. V. Walter, "Power and Violence," *American Political Science Review* 58, no. 2 (June 1964), p. 352.

[3] "Unfortunately, power lacks a verb form, which in part accounts for the frequent tendency to see it as a mysterious property or agency resident in the person or group to whom it is attributed. The use of such terms as 'influence' and 'control,' which are both nouns and verbs, as virtual synonyms for power, represents an effort (not necessarily fully conscious) to avoid the suggestion that power is a property rather than a relation." Dennis H. Wrong, "Some Problems in Defining Social Power," in *Recent Sociology*, ed. Hans P. Dreitzel, No. 1 (London: Macmillan, 1969). Cf. also Wrong's use (following Gilbert Ryle) of the notion of "dispositional" as contrasted with "episodic" words to distinguish potential power from the exercise of power.

fully distinguish between "potential power" and power. The former, of course, implies the existence of certain power *resources* that may be used in the attempt to exercise power.

Similarly, authority is not something that can literally be held, although the symbols of authority are often quite tangible. Authority is a relationship between a superordinate and one or more subordinates which, when "activated" by communication, leads to compliance with "orders" or "commands" issued from above. Finally, someone who "has a lot of influence" is an individual who either has influenced many people in the past or is likely to be able to do so in the future. His analogue in the economy is the person who "has a lot of credit," which is not equivalent to "having a lot of money."

Following our axiom that "politics is talk," we wish to discover in general what kind of communication among actors can affect their action, and then proceed to a further subdivision of this kind of communication into three categories. Let us narrow our initial interest to communications expressed in words rather than other nonverbal signals such as gestures.

At first glance our task seems more akin to linguistics than political science, for we are concerned with identifying verbal communication that can be understood or comprehended. Suppose that the structure of a shared language is understood by two actors A and B. Obviously, the rules of grammar and syntax for their language limit the sentences A and B can construct and understand. But within these constraints, what types of sentences are likely to affect their action?

The problem is that almost anything said by A can under certain circumstances affect B's action, perhaps substantially. For example, B may be so upset over something that if A even says "Boo," B will burst into tears. Ordinarily "boo" seems quite innocuous. It is probably impossible to construct a theory that will allow us to predict in advance whether a given sentence or expression will affect a given actor in a particular way.

The English philosopher of language J. L. Austin has elaborated some concepts that illuminate this discussion. In attempting to investigate the "uses" of language, Austin distinguishes among (*a*) the mere act of speech as a proper use of words (locution); (*b*) the uttering of a sentence as an act-in-itself, for example, saying the marriage vows before a minister (illocution); and (*c*) the "successful" use of words to bring about an action on someone else's part, for example, issuing an order which is then obeyed (perlocution). But Austin further distinguishes words with a perlocutionary *object* from those which merely give rise to a perlocutionary *sequel*. In the first instance the effect is *intended,* whereas in the second instance it is not. And while one may fairly easily identify in advance statements that have (intended) perlocutionary objects it is virtually impossible to predict which statements will have (unintended) perlocutionary *sequels*. "For clearly *any,* or almost any, perlocutionary act is liable to be brought off, in sufficiently special circumstances, by the issuing, with or without calculation, of any utterance whatsoever. . . ."[4]

More progress can be made if we first pick out certain types of verbal communication that express identifiable relationships in the form of either threats or promises. While in everyday encounters a threat may be conveyed by a mere gesture or even a raised eyebrow, verbal threats display remarkable uniformity of logical structure. They take the form of hypothetical or contingent statements[5] expressed in the "first person":

$$\text{If you do } X, \text{ I will do } Y.$$

This simple paradigm can be "filled in" with appropriate symbols or words to represent any given "threat-communication." For example, "If you say that again, I'll break your neck." Here the form of the threat follows exactly the form of the paradigm. But the basic structure remains the same even if we change the "sign" of X from positive to negative: "If you do *not* give me your money, I'll blow your brains out." Of course a would-be holdup man might very well use a different construction from the paradigm. He might say "Your money or your life." Or he might simply brandish a gun and say, "Give me your money." But implicit within the context of this situation is a threat which, were it not for the ellipsis of action and gesture, would take the basic form of the paradigm.

Thus in a threat-communication, the performance of action Y by the "threatener" is made contingent on the performance (or nonperformance) of action X by the recipient of the threat. In other words, action Y is the penalty you must pay if you refuse to comply with my demand that you do X. But what is it about action Y that makes it a penalty for you? Clearly, action Y must involve some loss or pain or suffering on your part; you must stand to lose something by my performing action Y, or else my threat would be "empty." We can describe Y, therefore, as a *sanction* which I will apply if you fail to comply. And since we are here concerned with threats, action Y can be further described as a *negative* sanction. It would make little sense whatever if as a "penalty" for noncompliance I "threatened" you with a "sanction" that consisted in some action you found immensely enjoyable.

---

[4] Cf. also the following: "A judge should be able to decide, by hearing what was said, what locutionary and illocutionary acts were performed, but now what perlocutionary acts were achieved." I shall say more about Austin's analysis below. J. L. Austin, *How to Do Things with Words* (Cambridge, Mass.: Harvard University Press, 1962), pp. 109, 121.

[5] It is also possible, as John Searle, *Speech Acts* (Cambridge: Cambridge University Press, 1969), pp. 55–56, has pointed out, to make "categorical" threats and promises. These would be expressed in the simple declaration "I will do X." But categorical threats are usually made in some sort of context which implies a contingency. A "normal" person simply does not go around uttering (or muttering) threats "for no reason." This fact was tragically illustrated in the case of the resident of Hamilton, Ontario, who earned the nickname "Me Shoot" because he frequently uttered this categorical threat in the course of arguments. One day during a dispute about a fence he shot to death three neighbors.

Indeed, this is one reason why it is difficult to use threats effectively against a masochist. Presumably his desire for pain and punishment transmutes "negative sanctions" into a source of pleasure. In the end, however, the plight of the masochist is pathetic. Like Oscar on "Sesame Street," the masochist finds himself in an infinite regress of contradictory sentiments. He is only happy when he is sad, so being sad makes him happy. But this of course makes him sad which in turn makes him happy . . . , etc.

The agonizing ambivalence of the masochist under threat should not obscure the fact that the "nonsense" of a pleasurable threat is semantical nonsense only. The world is full of pleasurable threats, except that we call them by a different name—promises. From this perspective, a promise is simply a positive threat, or rather a first-person hypothetical in which the Y is a positive sanction.[6] "If you go to bed with me, I'll give you $50." Or, as the popular kiddies' song has it, "If you show me yours, I'll show you mine." Here again, X may be either negative or positive: "If you *don't* tell mother, I'll let you play with my truck." In short, threats and promises share an identical syntactical structure illustrated in the paradigm,

If you do X, I will do Y.

where X and Y may each be either positive or negative.

It is to communications which involve either threats or promises that I wish to attach the name *power*. Notice that this usage makes no presuppositions about the likely effectiveness of a power communication. I am decidedly not assuming that power will result in compliance, or conversely that compliance must occur before power can be said to exist. Rather the concept refers to a certain relationship, embodied in a communication, by which A presents B with an "offer" to which is attached a contingency in the form of a reward (promise) or a penalty (threat).

It may at first appear curious (and perhaps misleading) to classify threats and promises together under the category of power.[7] Behavioral psychol-

---

[6] Cf. Searle, *ibid.,* p. 58: "One crucial distinction between promises on the one hand and threats on the other is that a promise is a pledge to do something for you not to you; but a threat is a pledge to do something to you not for you." See also his list of nine "conditions" for promising.

[7] Other writers, most notably Talcott Parsons, have used the distinction between positive and negative sanctions itself as the basis for distinguishing influence from power. Thus, for Parsons, power involves "mobilizing the performance binding obligations [of others], with the conditional implication of the imposition of negative sanctions." Influence, by contrast, operates through the use of what Parsons calls positive "intentional" sanctions. The term *intentional* is introduced to distinguish "influence" from "money." The latter also operates through the use of positive sanctions, which are "situational." Thus the two types of positive sanctions permit Parsons to distinguish between "inducement" and "persuasion." Ultimately there are several similarities between Parsons' concept of influence and my own. I do feel, however, that the term *sanction* is inappropriate to his discussion of persuasion, and should be reserved for what he calls inducement. Furthermore, I would include "negative intentional" relations under influence, and "positive situational" relations under power. See Talcott Parsons, "On the Concept of Influence," *Public Opinion Quarterly* 27, no. 1 (Spring 1963), p. 44.

ogists have carried out numerous studies to show the differential effectiveness of what they call positive versus negative "reinforcements." A common finding is that positive reinforcement is less likely to inspire hostility or resentment and therefore functions more effectively, especially in learning situations. Regardless of specific findings, the point is that experimental psychology has uncovered important reasons for distinguishing between negative and positive types of reinforcement. I have no intention of trying to refute such findings, nor do I propose that we overlook the differences between threat-power and promise-power. The rationale for the decision to classify them both under the concept of power will become apparent when we investigate the meaning I have given to the notion of influence.

However much threats and promises differ with respect to the reactions they may engender, the degree to which they represent "coercion," etc., they nevertheless share a number of crucial characteristics. Structurally, as I have already shown, they are identical (i.e., both can be reduced to the paradigm, "If you do X, I will do Y"). But they are alike in another way as well. If we imagine an individual as occupying (at a given point in time) a certain "position" along various continua with respect to several different values—wealth, security, knowledge, personal health, etc.,—then power takes the form of a declared intent to "shift" the individual's value position either in the direction of *more* enjoyment of the value (promise) or of *less* (threat). The promise is "kept" only if compliance is forthcoming, whereas the threat is "carried through" if compliance is *not*. But the outcome is identical: the individual in either case is "better off" (i.e., more favorably positioned along the value continua) if he complies than if he does not. In the first instance, he actually moves "ahead" whereas in the second instance he avoids being moved "back." Furthermore, even a positive sanction can be manipulated negatively if our "supplier" threatens to "cut us off." Absence of reward is in many instances equivalent to punishment.

The notion I am struggling so awkwardly to express in academic prose was made unforgettably vivid in the novel/movie *The Godfather*, Michael is explaining to his girlfriend how his father, Don Corleone, managed to secure the release of the singer Johnnie Fontaine from an unfair but legally binding contract. Don Corleone went to the bandleader who held the contract and offered him $10,000 if he would release Fontaine. The bandleader refused.

> "The next day my father went back to see the bandleader. He went in with a certified check for $1,000 and came out with a signed release."
>
> "How did he do that?" asked Kay.
>
> "He made the bandleader an offer he couldn't refuse."
>
> "You mean more money?"
>
> "Not exactly. This time my father took Luco Brasi with him when he went to see the bandleader. Luco held a gun to the bandleader's head and my father told him 'Either your signature or your brains are going to be on this contract.' . . ."

In view of the popularity (or notoriety) of *The Godfather,* no future reference to "making an offer that can't be refused" will escape ambiguity: does it refer to an unusually large positive sanction or to a painfully compelling negative sanction?

To this point, we have merely succeeded in identifying power communications by referring to their structure and intent. In effect we have skated around such important issues (which will be taken up later) as how an individual gets into a position to issue a power communication, under what conditions such communications are "credible," and whether power will indeed result in compliance. Similarly, we have failed to examine the alternative responses to power communications.[8] Nor have we said anything to illuminate the phenomenon of power in large-scale, complex social units. Indeed, most of our remarks have assumed a "dyadic" (i.e., one-to-one) relationship between only two actors, *A* and *B.* But the analysis so far has at least set the stage for an elaboration of the concept of *influence,* which we define as a communication intended to affect the action of *B* in the absence of sanctions (i.e., threats or promises).

How then does influence work? Let us examine the syntactical structure of an influence communication, even though this exercise is only a partially satisfactory description of influence (which ultimately serves as a kind of residual category for nonpower, nonauthority relations). The problem we face is this: can a relationship between two actors avoid threats and promises and yet be "important"? To put it differently, can we construct a sentence that does not take the form of a threat or promise but is nevertheless capable of affecting someone else's action?

Surprisingly, the basic power paradigm requires very little modification to provide at least one "solution" to this problem, thereby "proving" the possibility of influence. To transform the threat/promise expressed in first-person contingent statements into a sanction-free influence statement, we need only introduce the second-person construction:

> If you do *X, you* will do (feel, experience, etc.) *Y*
> (second-person contingent statement).

The effect of this minute change is profound. Contrast the power communication, "If you marry that girl, I'll cut you out of my will" with the far subtler influence communication, "If you marry that girl, you'll be miserable for the rest of your life!" In place of a threat or promise, influence involves a kind of *prediction* in the form of advice, encouragement, warning, and so on. "Advice is cheap," cynics may counter. Yes, but advisers are often very highly paid. Figure that one out.

---

[8] In most instances, the uttering of a promise or threat occurs as a "move" in a social "interchange." It will usually be followed by at least one more move (i.e., response by B) and possibly further moves by both actors. For the concepts of interchange and move, see Erving Goffman, *Interaction Ritual* (New York: Anchor Books, 1967), p. 20.

The assertion that influence is sanction-free does not necessarily contradict the assumption that human behavior is shaped or generated by contingencies of reinforcement. The "prediction" that "you will be miserable" indeed forecasts a very undesirable contingency attendant to your marrying "that girl." The difference is that this contingency, unlike the act of cutting you out of "my will," is *not* being manipulated by "me." To forewarn of a "threatening situation" is not the same as to make a threat. We would not speak of the weatherman as a "powerful" person, and yet the information he provides often has a considerable "influence" on the plans of millions of people.

Viewed from this perspective, the "influence" of religious leaders can be assimilated to a new version of the influence paradigm. The priest serves in effect as an adviser, predicting a whole range of contingencies (including "fire and brimstone," "everlasting damnation," eternal salvation, etc.) which will be dispensed by God either in this life or the life to come. Thus the new influence paradigm is,

> If you do X, He (God) will do Y
> (third-person contingent statement).

By now it should be clear that while power rests on the ability to manipulate positive or negative sanctions, influence does not. In either the second-person or the third-person contingent statements which we have proposed as paradigms of influence, the influencer, rather than manipulating the contingencies of reinforcement, is attempting to manipulate *perceptions* of those contingencies. He says, in effect, "If you do X, Y will happen," where Y is beyond his control.

TACIT INFLUENCE AND TACIT POWER

Occasionally we find that people decode messages that have never been sent! Indeed, there is a whole range of tacit influence (and indeed tacit power) that falls into the category of "anticipated reactions."[9] An actor tacitly subjects himself to influence or power by *asking himself* questions about the likely outcome of his actions. When the self-questioning takes the form of an inverted first person hypothetical, we can speak of tacit power. Thus,

> If I do X, will you do Y?

But if the question takes the form of an inverted second- or third-person hypothetical, it represents an example of tacit influence. Erving Goffman splendidly illustrates the point:

---

[9] The "rule of anticipated reactions" was "discovered" by Carl J. Friedrich in 1937 (*Constitutional Government and Politics*. pp. 16–18). A discussion of the rule appears in his *Man and His Government* (New York: McGraw-Hill, 1963), ch. 11. Despite its obvious importance, very little has been done by others to develop the implications of the concept beyond merely citing the rule.

The socialized interactant comes to handle spoken interaction as he would any other kind, as something that must be pursued with ritual care. By automatically appealing to face, he knows how to conduct himself in regard to talk. By repeatedly and automatically asking himself the question, "if I do or do not act in this way, will I or *others* lose face?" he decides at each moment consciously or unconsciously, how to behave. [10]

---

[10] Goffman, *Interaction Ritual,* p. 36. (Emphasis added.) Note that even the pronouns used in interaction affect and reflect deference, social status, etc. See Roger Brown et al., "The Pronouns of Solidarity and Status" in *Psycholinguistics* (New York: Free Press, 1970).

WALTER GUZZARDI, JR.

Reading 10–2
How the Union Got the
Upper Hand on J. P. Stevens

Joseph Williams, a worker at a J. P. Stevens textile mill in Roanoke Rapids, North Carolina, was given this warning one day in April 1973: "Joseph, on Monday morning you called Jasper Daniels, a fixer, over to the frame where you were. You then stopped your work and handed him some literature and tried to talk him into signing up with the union. You must not neglect your work nor interfere with the work of other employees in this or any other way. If you do, we cannot keep you in our employment."

When Williams ignored the warning and continued to pass out leaflets, his supervisor sent him home. After a discussion with other superiors, Williams was reinstated. Then one night Williams was told to clean the spindles on his loom. While he admitted later that cleaning spindles was part of his job, he also claimed—and his supervisor denied—that his work load was being unfairly increased. Williams told the supervisor, "I'm not going to clean those spindles." He was fired.

The union complained to the National Labor Relations Board. After Stevens appealed the NLRB ruling, the Court of Appeals found that Williams had been illegally fired because of his union activities. The court required the company to let Williams return to his job, and to give him back pay with interest. Since Stevens had been previously enjoined to "cease and desist" from unfair labor practices, the court also cited the company for contempt.

Crystal Lee Jordan was a worker in a Stevens fabricating plant and an active union organizer. One day in May 1973, her supervisor protested when she started to copy from a plant bulletin board an anti-union letter written by the management, and used a pay phone during work time to call her union representative. (When she argued about the phone call, one supervisor said to another, "Let it go, Melvin, let it go.") After the union had advised Jordan of her rights, she insisted on copying the letter.

That night some supervisors called her into an office. First she refused to go; then she went; then she would not talk to them unless each identified himself and spelled his name. She clapped her hands over her ears, and became shrill and defiant. She was fired.

Ruled the Court of Appeals: "The possibility that the company had legitimate cause for the discharge does not end the inquiry, for a discharge partially motivated by anti-union discrimination is also illegal. Jordan's outburst was used as a pretext for the dismissal of an active union organizer." Contempt again.

Those incidents—snippets from records running to millions of pages—are full of the hated taste of defeat for J. P. Stevens, the nation's second-largest textile company. Fifteen years ago when the company's battle with labor began, contempt of court judgments such as those—and all the complicated, highly damaging consequences for Stevens that flow from them—seemed impossible. But now, in an incredible turn of events, court rulings in hundreds of such episodes have given the Amalgamated Clothing and Textile Workers Union tremendous leverage over the company.

In the corporate management, the only executive who refuses to acknowledge the realities of the present situation is the chief executive officer, James D. Finley, a 61-year-old Georgian of iron character and rigid bearing. "I wouldn't change anything if I could do it all over again," he says, and such is the man's quality that one has to believe him.

But in his resolve he stands alone, a man isolated in an isolated corporation. The deeply worried executives around him are eagerly looking for ways to repeal the old decision to fight to the death, and are anxious to find a compromise. For the company stands today beleaguered in the courts, besmirched in public, an embarrassment to the business community. Even Finley, after asserting stubbornly that "we don't have any problem, the union has a problem," contradicts himself a moment later. "The next move is up to them," he says. "The union holds all the cards."

Back in 1963, the old Textile Workers Union seemed hardly important enough to be in the game with J. P. Stevens. The union's former president, Sol Stetin, 68, whose unamplified voice can still fill a union hall, admits that "we saw our organization dwindling." A fading brotherhood with aging leadership, the TWU could only helplessly watch textile companies flee the union's New England turf to the congenial, nonunion South.

But that fading brotherhood suddenly changed its character two years ago when it joined hands with the Amalgamated Clothing Workers of America. The merged union, the ACTWU, is hardly the most potent force in trade unionism, but it has its strengths—located exactly where they count, in the capacity for skillful lawyering. The ACTWU's president, Murray H. Finley, 56—no kin to the boss of J. P. Stevens—is a lawyer, knowledgeable in both the courtrooms and the court of public opinion. And the ACTWU's general counsel, Arthur M. Goldberg, is a recognized authority on labor law. It would be hard to find an adversary better equipped for just the kind of battle that the union has waged against Stevens.

When it was looking around for a textile company to unionize in the South, the TWU made one of the most felicitous mistakes in labor's history. The TWU had lost a big battle with that old buccaneer, Roger Milliken, then head of Deering Milliken, who had closed a plant in South Carolina rather than negotiate. The union had also been busted after a long strike at Harriet & Henderson Mills, and been beaten off by Cannon Mills and Burlington Industries. So the union's eye fell on J. P. Stevens. It looked like a soft adversary. The company's chief executive, Robert T. Stevens, was a former secretary of the army best known for having been browbeaten on national television by Senator Joe McCarthy. "Very truthfully," Stetin admits today, "I never imagined that the company would carry on the way it has." Unexpectedly, the thought of union organizers at the company gates turned mild-mannered Robert Stevens into Fighting Bob, and management decided to do battle.

Looking back at that critical moment today, James Finley insists that "We've always done everything we could to abide by the law." Even if that is true—and the courts have held otherwise—Bob Stevens and Finley must have decided to carry on the battle at the law's outer limits, to push and probe out where the boundaries between legal and illegal behavior are vague. Labor laws are primarily remedial, and there is not usually a heavy penalty for a misstep—so the decision did not look nearly as risky as it turned out to be.

So in 1963 when union organizers arrived at Roanoke Rapids, where Stevens has a seven-plant manufacturing complex, they found that war had already been declared. "Our positive intention," announced a company notice to employees, "is to oppose this union and by every proper means to keep it from coming in here. It is our sincere belief that if this union gets in here, it would operate to your serious disadvantage." In a foreshadowing of what was to come, that notice, the company's first thrust, made trouble—it was later declared to be illegal. What was worse, that declaration and other mistakable signs led the supervisors on the plant floor to conclude that they were expected to get tough, which probably suited their inclinations anyway. Then, out of stupidity, obtuseness, perversity, or laxity—or a mingling of these failings—the company's executives took years to get those supervisors under control. So began all those little dramas, each in several acts, that look so tragic to Stevens today.

Supervisors accosted employees over the size of the union button that an employee was wearing (the supervisor said it was too big, and might get caught in plant machinery); over where employees could distribute leaflets and whether it was dangerous to distribute them in doorways and hallways; over which cafeteria a worker was supposed to use and whether the rules were really clear; over whether Avon ladies were allowed to make sales on company property; over exactly what were the duties of blow boys and tenders and doffers and carders and fixers, and when they could go to the toilet and when they could smoke and how long they ought to take about it. Did supervisors really say, "People get hurt when they fool around with unions" and "I guess you know about your brother Theodore" and "Go home and take that T-shirt off," and were those threats, and were they followed by firings?

All those dramas were recalled very differently by witnesses and participants. But by the judgments of law just about all of them that went to trial were held to be violations of the National Labor Relations Act. There were gross incidents: within two days after their names were posted as new union members, three employees were fired. And there were trivial ones: a supervisor asked two employees walking through a plant drumming up attendance at a speech by a union organizer, "Can I help you?' and was held to have made a "gratuitous, condescending, and unjustified remark." But they were all ruled coercive acts, and therefore illegal. Stevens was like a man flipping a coin for high stakes, hearing his opponent forever cry, "Heads," and with unbelieving eyes seeing the coin come up heads every time.

Before it entered the game, Stevens ought to have taken a closer look at the rules. The central institution in labor law litigation is the National Labor Relations Board: charges are filed with NLRB regional offices, cases are prosecuted by lawyers from the NLRB, decisions are handed down by administrative law judges from the NLRB, and the place of first appeal is the full board of the NLRB. Over the years, NLRB boards have been pretty much the same: larded with career bureaucrats, sympathetic to labor, and blind to the realities of business. Today's board seems typical: it is, in the words of Edward Miller, a former chairman of the NLRB, "an ivory-tower board." Only two out of its five members have had any extensive experience outside of government; John Fanning, the chairman, has served on the board for 20 years.

Decisions of the NLRB can be appealed to the federal circuit courts. But what becomes critical then are "findings of fact," meaning, in labor cases, determination about the credibility of witnesses, a matter of whom to believe in a dispute about who said what to whom and in what tone of voice. And there, circuit court judges are very reluctant to reverse the courts below: last year they upheld the NLRB 80 percent of the time. Time and again Stevens came to the courthouse to hear a judge intone, "The NLRB's findings of fact are of great weight in this court . . . the conclusions are upheld." Concludes James Finley: "The law is pro-union." But Stevens should have known about its chances in that legal environment before it began appealing every case to its bitter end.

What Stevens probably could not have anticipated was the ACTWU's acumen in capitalizing on all those proved, triply certified, bound-in-iron illegal acts. The union has used them to conceal from public awareness the most arresting, least noticed, most crucially important fact in the whole arresting history of the Stevens affair: time after time, at plant after plant, in southern town after southern town, the union lost election after election. From 1965 to 1975, 12 elections were held at Stevens facilities. The union lost all but one. But by persuading the courts that the company was guilty of those unfair practices, the union was able to have many election results set aside. From there, it went on to turn the defeats into victories of rather special kinds.

Nothing illustrates the union's feats of magic better than the experiences at Roanoke Rapids, (population: 14,000) one of those renewed southern towns where there seem to be more cars than inhabitants. There Stevens now employs about 2,800 of the company's 44,000 people. The TWU lost an election there years ago by a big margin. Then it brought massive cases against the company, consolidating allegations of more than 100 illegal practices. Stevens challenged the cases, but the union was upheld, and the election results were set aside.

Then the union showed how to build on the foundation of that courtroom triumph. By bringing a stream of new charges, the union managed to put off a rerun election at Roanoke Rapids for something over nine years. It finally made its move in 1974, when the stock market was scraping bottom, employees' profit-sharing plans were down in value, and union organizers had long been hard at work in Roanoke Rapids. So there, for the first and only time in the history of its efforts to organize Stevens, the union finally won an election—by 237 votes out of 3,205 cast.

Against a background of anger and distrust, employer and union negotiators then seated themselves around a table to begin collective bargaining. But Stevens was far too eager to keep the newly installed union from being able to claim that it had won any special benefits for its constituency. So one day the company's negotiators suddenly announced that the company was putting a wage increase into effect for all its other employees, and asked the union team, led by a forceful man named Scott Hoyman, whether it wanted the same increase at Roanoke Rapids. The scheme was intended to leave the union with the choice of either accepting the increase, thus in effect conceding that it couldn't win better pay for its membership, or turning down the increase and negotiating—leaving the Roanoke Rapids members making less than unorganized workers elsewhere in the company.

But what the company had really done, Scott Hoyman said in a charge to the NLRB, was fail to bargain in good faith, and his complaint was upheld by an administrative law judge. So the company stands today bound to appeal, hardly likely to win, and fearful that it will be heavily fined.

In smaller matters the union has sprung similar traps. Last year the North Carolina Department of Labor ordered Stevens to supply its employees with a new respirator to filter out cotton dust. Since bargaining was going on, the union was entitled to full information about anything changing the conditions of work. It asked for a lot of technical data about the respirator and cotton dust, but did not get everything it wanted. Stevens put the respirator into use

anyway. Then the ACTWU successfully charged the company with a violation because some data had been withheld. Union brochures still accuse
Stevens of running dirty plants where employees contract brown-lung disease.

There seems to be no end to the possibilities of entrapment. Since it lost
the second Roanoke Rapids election in part because of that drop in the value
of its profit-sharing plan, the company later put a floor under the plan. But
while Stevens was doing that, the union happened to have a preelection
campaign going on at plants in Wallace, North Carolina. The union argued
that improvements in employee benefits during a campaign constituted an
unfair attempt to influence the election's outcome—a complaint that has
been sustained in court. Thus when Stevens improves benefits—refuting
claims that it underpays and exploits its workers—it is held guilty of a
violation in another locale. The more the company struggles, the deeper into
the legal morass it sinks.

Given its losing ways, the fact that Stevens was always so bullheaded in
its insistence on appealing also put the company in a bind. Last year, after he
had heard yet another case involving a batch of unfair labor practices
committed by Stevens, Judge Wilfred Feinberg of the Second Circuit Court
in lower Manhattan lashed out as though he were putting away a mass
murderer. Feinberg summarily dismissed the disputes over the petty who-
said-what-to-whom incidents—heads they all were, he said. Then he noted
that the conduct of the corporation "raises grave doubts about the ability of
the courts to make the federal labor laws work . . . the company has
undermined respect for this court." In anger, but probably with pleasure too,
he cited Stevens for contempt of court.

From there, Feinberg gave a demonstration of how to put punitive wallop
into those remedial laws. He ruled that Stevens was to be fined $100,000 for
any single future violation, and $5,000 a day for "continuing violations."
That addendum is of horrendous importance, since years can often go by
while charges of labor law violations are being litigated. (The NLRB's
administrative law judges are themselves responsible for a lot of the delay.)
So each violation of which it is found guilty could cost Steven's, say, $6
million—$1.5 million a year for four years. Hundreds of violations have
been proved against the company, and the ACTWU can easily find more to
allege. If necessary, the union might not be above provoking a few, and
stuffing them into the legal pipeline. One begins to see the meaning of
Finley's remark that "the union has all the cards."

In a different locale, the ACTWU has used the invalidation of a lost
election to equally good purpose. Its election loss at Wallace was set aside
because of coercive acts proved against the company. Then the ACTWU
launched an intricate legal maneuver to make this one of its loss-into-win,
dross-into-gold conversions. NLRB procedures provide that before an election unions must get signed cards from at least 30 percent of the involved
employees indicating they want a union to represent them. The card signing

is carried on in public by union organizers. The results of election, conducted afterwards in secret, may differ from this preliminary balloting: employees signing cards know they can change their minds in private later.

As its postelection move at Wallace, the union set about proving that it had won a majority in the card count preceding the election. After a lengthy dispute over whether union organizers had used coercion to get cards signed, the union won: 135 out of 143 challenged cards were declared valid. Once that was settled, the union was able to press its assertion that a free election was impossible because of the company's illegal acts. On the basis of the card majority, the ACTWU urged the NLRB to recognize the union as bargaining representative for the Wallace employees. In a surprising decision, the administrative law judge assented. The Circuit Court of Appeals for the Fifth Circuit upheld a similar ruling at Statesboro, Georgia. Although slim, the possibility thus exists that the union, by going to the courts rather than the workers, may eventually come to represent Stevens employees everywhere.

When at Statesboro a rump union began to bargain with Stevens on behalf of employees who had never properly voted it into power, the company promptly fell into a still deeper pit. Contract negotiations dragged along. The union brought bad-faith bargaining charges. And then, incredibly, Stevens closed the Statesboro plant.

Stevens insists that the closing was for strictly economic reasons and had nothing to do with the union's presence at Statesboro. "Our market for all-wool carpeting had just about dried up," says Whitney Stevens, son of Bob and now president of the company. But even if one grants that, the question remains whether the decision to close was balanced against costs such as the further loss of the company's standing with the courts, the additional supply of ammunition for the union's propaganda guns, and the additional damage to the company's reputation.

In any case, a panel of judges from the Fifth Circuit was obviously skeptical. The panel gave the NLRB sweeping powers to review the company's records to make sure that the plant was not closed "with intent of frustrating this court," and it conferred on the board other powers of discovery that may make endless trouble for Stevens in the future. The panel then clamped on the same heavy fine for "continuing violations" in its circuit as Judge Feinberg had in New York.

Finally, the Fifth Circuit judges took the ultimate step. They indicated that future punishment could include *"the issuance of attachment against the company's officers."* So Whitney Stevens and the indomitable James Finley may set another precedent in this remarkable case: they may be the first corporate executives ever to go to jail for labor law violations. James Finley responds defiantly: "I do not want to go to jail. But I am not fearful of it. I would go to jail for what I think is right."

While all the legal battles were raging, company and union were choosing very different ways of fighting the other big campaign—the one for public support. James Finley, as a matter of startling fact, decided not to join that particular passage of arms at all. He ordered his executives "to run the business as though this isn't happening," and to refer all union matters to headquarters. But at headquarters, Finley refused all public comment, never saw the press, and never made public arguments on his company's behalf. Except for his appearance at shareholders' meetings—and he got pretty testy there sometimes, too—Finley stayed in the background. "I give them a chance once a year to work me over," he says, "and that's enough."

In contrast, the ACTWU's first move was to launch a nationwide boycott against Stevens. Financially, it hasn't damaged Stevens a bit (James Finley even insists that it has helped). The company makes so many different textiles and fabrics marketed under so many different brand names that its products are mostly beyond the reach of a boycott. Last year gross revenues, where a boycott's impact would be most likely to appear, were up over 1976. And the boycott actually hurts the union with many Stevens employees, who think it puts their jobs at risk.

But the true purpose of the boycott is to drum up wide public support for the union cause, and there it is successful. The NAACP, the National Council of Churches, and women's and students' groups have all endorsed it, helping to arouse press and congressional opinion against Stevens. It apparently matters not at all that these groups do not have a very clear fix on what the fight is all about. The National Council of Churches favors the boycott to abet "the current struggle of J. P. Stevens' workers for industrial justice," despite the fact that most of those workers have not voted on whether they want a union. One clergyman who supports the boycott, the Reverend Donald Shriver, president of Union Theological Seminary, on the occasion of the union merger implored God to "take up the affairs of this union into your great Kingdom." Shriver went on to thank the ACTWU "not only for the undershirts that men walking down the streets of America are wearing, but also for the hundreds of pieces of other clothing that have been wrapped around this body of mine." The Reverend's cry penetrated even to irreverent Harvard, where students hung sheets labeled "Boycott Stevens" out of their windows.

Even where the ACTWU has made mistakes in its public campaign, it has not paid in full measure for them. There has been little audible disapproval from the business community over the union's use of threats to force other companies to cut ties with Stevens. By bringing pressure on Manufacturers Hanover Trust, the union succeeded in displacing Finley from the bank's board. And by pressuring Avon Products, it pushed Chairman David Mitchell off the Stevens board.

To spread that kind of discomfiture may give ACTWU officials some pleasing publicity and a gratifying sense of power, but the moves make no sense. Retribution at the secondary level is inequitable and pointless. But in this case, fear of getting too close to Stevens has inhibited businessmen: Irving Shapiro of Du Pont and Reginald Jones of GE, the business community's leading spokesmen, have shied away from criticizing the union's action. It's the kind of display that doubles one's respect for Finley's courage.

Losses in the courts, threats of fine and imprisonment, isolation from other businessmen, public judgment that the company is a retrograde monster—the convergence of all these elements has compelled a change in Stevens's policy. Hard and stubborn as always, Finley grimly denies the shift, but evidence of it is all around him.

For one thing, the command of the company's legal battalions has been changed. James Grady, 53, who became the company's general counsel a year and a half ago, is assuming an active role in the struggle, assisted by Jerrold Mehlman, who was formerly a trial attorney for the NLRB. Stevens comes very late to the idea of hiring talent from the agency that has been giving it so much grief, but still, it's a start. And the company has hired a new outside counsel, J. Frank Ogletree of Greenville, South Carolina, a lawyer with a bent toward compromise and conciliation.

Compromises in several areas attest to the new policy. Recently, Stevens actually settled a dispute with the NLRB instead of fighting it to the end. The board, striving for public recognition as a slayer of dragons, asked for an unprecedented nationwide injunction, which would have extended the punitive terms of circuit court rulings to every Stevens facility in the country. With James Grady setting the legal policy, the company worked out a settlement, and the injunction was never issued. (In the way of government agencies, the NLRB claimed a total victory anyway.) At the bargaining table at Roanoke Rapids, Stevens has also shown a new pliancy. Originally it opposed arbitration procedures and checkoff of union dues. Now it accepts both principles.

Helpful as all this may be, it still does not get Stevens off the hook. Specifically, the ACTWU has responded to the concessions at Roanoke Rapids by increasing its demands. Originally, Scott Hoyman was outraged when Stevens wouldn't agree to a checkoff. Now, he sounds just as outraged because the company proposes to give employees the right to cancel the checkoff whenever they want to do so. But many collective-bargaining agreements contain just that kind of withdrawal privilege—including the contract that the ACTWU has in effect with Fieldcrest Mills.

That union recalcitrance at Roanoke Rapids raises the question whether, even as it presses bad-faith bargaining charges against the company, the ACTWU really wants a settlement there at all. Right now, the union can very conveniently claim that it would certainly be the victor in company-wide elections among Stevens employees, but that, unfortunately, the company's conduct has made fair elections impossible. A handshake at Roanoke Rapids might begin the process of what the NLRB calls "purging the atmosphere"—restoring conditions under which free elections can be held. Should that happen, the ACTWU would face the real issue: the test of its popularity with the majority of Stevens employees. It is not impossible—

indeed, at this moment it is likely—that the union might then suffer the defeat that would wipe out all its victories to date. The ACTWU may be thinking that it will do better by sticking close to the courtrooms.

On a larger stage, the labor movement is served best by keeping Stevens in the role of villain and lawbreaker. Organized labor badly wants a labor law reform bill, which it hopes might make possible a reversal of its declining national fortunes. Now before the Senate, the bill would increase labor's chances of winning elections, impose heavier penalties on employers for labor-law violations (although that hardly seems necessary in view of what the courts may do to Stevens), and under certain circumstances give an expanded NLRB the power to dictate the terms of collective-bargaining agreements. Unsurprisingly, the NLRB favors passage of the bill. Union lobbyists have been calling it "the J. P. Stevens bill," and quoting from the most extreme language of the courts as a compelling argument for the bill's passage. The ACTWU may have agreed with the AFL-CIO that it would be a shame to begin settlements with Stevens at this inconvenient moment.

Stevens is also useful to organized labor for the rousing cause that the company has supplied. Says Benjamin Aaron, professor of labor law at U.C.L.A.; "Where Stevens is concerned, all union disagreements disappear. The Teamsters, Meany, and the UAW can all come together on the Stevens issue, where there's great ideological harmony." Adds Michael Zimmer, law professor at Wayne State: "The Stevens case may even be serving to mask a great truth—that labor unions are obsolete."

To negotiate bargaining agreements for Stevens employees, therefore, may now be only incidental to organized labor's larger purposes. So it may be quite a while before the union allows the company's long nightmare to end.

GEORGE L. PEABODY

Reading 10–3
Power, Alinsky, and Other Thoughts

In the spring of 1969 black students at Cornell University legally armed themselves with shotguns and rifles. University policies changed.

In the fall of 1969 the United States threatened to cut off tourism to Mexico. Marijuana crops were destroyed.

These were two effective actions because they produced intended results. They demonstrate that power is simply the ability to act effectively.

I shall deal here with a working description of power and its solid basis— self-interest. Then I shall show how men organize for power. Finally, I shall provide guidelines for the strategic and tactical use of power.

PRACTICALLY SPEAKING

The measure of power is results, regardless of the force of the applied effort. In the above examples, force was only threatened, not applied, but the strength of the power is clear.

Consider other examples: A manager sends a directive and people jump. A lady raises an eyebrow and men flock. Minimal efforts but effective results. That is power. However, a boxer may smash only air with a wild punch. Half a million American soldiers fight for years in a country the size of Montana. Much effort; no results. That is impotence. Any social effort that fails to get results is not power. It is only effort. Power is as power does.

"Power is the ability to give rewards and punishments *as seen by* the persons receiving them."[1] While no shots were fired at Cornell and no U.S.

Reprinted from *Social Intervention: A Behavioral Science Approach*, H. A. Hornstein et al., (eds.). Copyright © 1971 by The Free Press, a Division of Macmillan Publishing Company.

[1] Richard Beckhard, *Organizational Development: Strategies and Models* (Reading, Mass.: Addison-Wesley Publishing 1969).

tourism was cut off from Mexico, both the university and the Mexican government *believed* they were confronted by overwhelming forces to which they had to accede.

If A is the agent(s) exerting power and P is the person(s) upon whom power is exerted, then P's perception of A's strength is more important than A's actual strength. Of course A's power is related to his objective strength, but the two are not identical as they are in physics. *Social* power is in the eyes of the beholder.

Early in the power game, Gideon routed a large army of Midianites (a host, to be exact) with three hundred noisy men. At night they gave the illusion of being a host themselves (Book of Judges, Chapter 7). Illusion has been the name of the game ever since, except that now we have technicians paid to project images into the minds of voters, consumers and enemies. If A is to have power, then his first task is to make P perceive him as one able to reward or punish.

Men organize for power. All individuals have power; everyone can do some things effectively by themselves, but in the power world individuals have the weight of social dust. Whatever the purposes (to govern, make money, pray, administer, have a party, make war, teach), the reason for the organizing effort is to act more effectively. In union is the strength to give substantial rewards and punishments.

Organization may mean a network of friends or a loosely structured movement or a disciplined outfit. The type of organization depends on the amount of power needed—the more muscle required, the more solid must be the organizational skeleton.

In the first Federalist Paper, Alexander Hamilton wrote, "The vigor of government is essential to the security of liberty." Calling for the acceptance of the new Constitution, he proposed to discuss "The utility of the Union to your political prosperity and the insufficiency of the present Confederation to preserve that Union." Hamilton was calling for "a more perfect union" in order to constitute power on a more solid basis. With organization, then, there is significant power to act.

SELF-INTEREST

Politicians assume that what makes a man move is his own self-interest. If P sees A as strong enough to reward or punish his self-interest, then A has power. Therefore, a keen understanding of self-interest is a practical necessity.

We live in a culture where self-interest is not openly valued. People with "higher" motivations feel uneasy about their own self-interests, or don't wish to recognize such "base" motivations in others. Quite simply, working with self-interest produces results, regardless of how noble or base the motives. Power is what works and that is our only concern for the moment.

A change agent who wishes to be effective cannot afford to be confused about his *own* self-interests. Most people feel naked if they reveal their true motivations. Understandably, they design wonderful morals and rationalizations to clothe this reality. As Mark Twain wrote, "Humanity lives a life of uninterrupted self-deception." But at the critical moments, when power confronts power, there is the deepest kind of personal confrontation. Your allies have to know exactly "where you are at." "Are you with us or not?" If they don't know and you can't tell them, they will be justifiably afraid to move with you. Adlai Stevenson once said "The important thing is not to believe your own propaganda." When recognizing one's own interests, it is vitally important to be unprincipled. And when Harry Truman said, "I can't be moral on my country's time," he was saying quite succinctly that national interests cannot be entrusted to a moralizing man.

Only the solidly supported people and institutions can afford to believe their own rhetoric (for example, the very rich, some monks and the fellows of academies and foundations). The protected state of their self-interests enables them to live in outer space. Mark Twain described an ethical man as a Christian who holds four aces. If you've got them you can afford to be "ethical"; the rest of us must live more functionally.

Nor can an effective change agent afford to be confused about the self-interests of *others*. We already know that illusion is the first rule of the game. It is essential to distinguish self-interest from propaganda, naked power from its disguises, four aces from bluffing, Gideon's army from the noise. Political survival depends on it. "What is prestige?" John Kennedy once asked. "Is it the shadow of power or the substance of power? We are going to work on the substance of power."[2]

There is no reason to believe the propaganda of the antipoverty program, for instance. Is anyone still naive enough to think that it was enacted in the spirit of the American myth of "maximum feasible participation" of its citizens, or because poverty is a tragic condition? The punitive welfare program already attests to the general public perception of the "lazy" poor. Antipoverty programs exist because ghetto residents see the affluence around them and are beginning to demand a share of it. The fact that the programs have been poorly funded and disastrously administered suggests that more powerful interests might be affected if the programs were to succeed.

President Kennedy knew that the fairness, if not the favoritism, of the reporters had helped to elect him, but he was not fooled. He also knew that most of the editors and publishers had been out to defeat him. "Always remember," he once told Sorensen, "that their interests and ours ultimately conflict."[3]

BUILDING AN ORGANIZATION—A CHANGE MODEL

Whatever your role—company manager, self-styled Castro, college dean, missionary or society hostess—if you need more power to act, your aim must

---

[2] Arthur Schlesinger, *A Thousand Days* (Boston: Houghton Mifflin, 1965).

[3] Theodore Sorensen, *Kennedy* (New York: Harper and Row, 1965).

be to build (or change) an appropriate organization to provide it for you. The change processes you must consider are defined by the change needs of any human system.

I will describe Saul Alinsky's[4] model for building a community organization, with a few alterations in his terminology. The model contains most of the change phases that are also described by Lippitt, Watson and Westley in *Planned Change*.[5] Moreover, the core of Alinsky's model (Entry, Data Collection, Goalsetting, and Organizing) corresponds exactly to the four model concerns in group development identified by Jack and Lorraine Gibb (Acceptance, Data flow, Goal Formation and Social Control).[6] These parallels are no coincidence; the study of power requires the keenest observation of social dynamics. Whether or not he read any of these behavioral scientists, Alinsky made similar observations years ago, and applied them to his own imaginative manner. Let us look at his model:

A CHANGE TEAM IS ORGANIZED

A few people coalesce over several similar self-interests. These interests are no vague, do-good concerns; the problem is clear to them, they own it and feel keenly about it. Alinsky stresses that no change can occur until people are hurting.

They analyze the self-interests of persons and groups in the social system to determine who can significantly reward or punish their efforts—a power analysis.

They decide that the anticipated results will be worth the organizing effort.

They Move into the Larger Organization or Community to Coalesce Power

Two tasks become apparent:

Entry.   "Entry" really means developing credibility, or getting a licence to operate. The power given with this trust is essential for further activity. Even elected leaders have limited credibility, and it is their task to obtain further authorization. It is a subtle testing process. Has A been checked out by the local leaders? Has he been introduced by the right people? What is *his* self-interest? Can he be depended upon to understand and work competently

---

[4] Saul Alinsky is a professional community organizer, and executive director of the Industrial Area Foundation in Chicago. He wrote *Reveille for Radicals* over 20 years ago, and *Rules for Radicals,* published by Random House in 1971. Much of this paper is based on the things this author has learned as he traveled and studied with Alinsky.

[5] Ronald Lippitt, J. Watson, and B. Westley, *The Dynamics of Planned Change* (New York: Harcourt Brace Jovanovich, 1958).

[6] Jack Gibb, "Some Dimensions of Group Experience" (Lecture delivered at the National Training Laboratories, Bethel, Maine, July 19, 1962).

for our interests? Has he proved himself at critical times? Can he be trusted to mean what he says?

John Kennedy made instant entry into Germany when he resolved these questions in a single dramatic sentence "Ich bin ein Berliner!" Usually, it takes more time for the people to understand and believe. You work and you wait, knowing that nothing can happen until you are authorized. The doors are opening when you begin to see signs of confidence and acceptance. Or else you don't. If public opinion crystallizes against you, the closed doors are locked. Lyndon Johnson lost his license because a "credibility gap" forced him to abdicate. His successor has had similar difficulties. A newspaper columnist put it this way: "It (Vietnam war) has robbed the average citizen of a precious heritage: his feeling of trust in his government. We are lied to by the Pentagon, the CIA, the Army and—most shameful—by the President."[7] The media are so instantaneous today that the effective lie is far more difficult to execute than it was in Lincoln's day, for example. Credibility and entry today require the most simple truth-telling, or else much more skillful mendacity than is being practiced.

Data Collection.   Two kinds of information are particularly needed: (1) What are the self-interests of the people? Go to them directly. No one knows their interests as well as they do.

(2) Who are the natural leaders in the system? These are the people to work with. "If you know who these are," says Alinsky, "you have the telephone number of the community." When I was working with an organizer among the "Untouchables," along the Malabar coast in southwest India, we would create situations requiring leadership; then we would see who moved. We would stop to care for a sick man, lying in the road, and call out for water, a place to shelter him or strong hands to move him. In the gathering crowd, a few townspeople responded. We ran a similar test the next week, and selected those who had responded both times.

A friend of mine opened a storefront pool room as a base for organizing people in a Connecticut town. For several weeks, he noticed that only a few young men were coming in to play pool and talk with him; after a while, others drifted in. When he asked them why they came, he was told that he had been checked out and approved by the earlier fellows. By accident, he had found his local leaders, and had also made entry.

Goal-Setting and Organizing

The power of self-interest is harnessed when it is translated into common goals. Alinsky's experience in community organization has shown that as people come together to unify their efforts for power, they tend to see that their self-interests are related to those of their colleagues. "I need your help with my housing problem and you need my help with your school problem, so let's make a deal. I'll support you if you support me." After this

---

[7] Harriet Van Horne, *New York Post,* October 10, 1969.

negotiation is completed, the dynamics for collaboration begin. People begin to learn that "my" work needs other people and communities—this is at the heart of organizing. There will be a variety of interests requiring several goals; together they make up the program (or platform).

Alinsky specifies three criteria for working goals:

1. They must be highly *specific:* people won't work for "justice" but they will work to prevent a highway from being built through their community.
2. They must be *realizable:* there should be reasonable hope of success, however small. A limited goal gives the opportunity for visible success, and success is needed by most people in order to feel their strength. The gained confidence will enable them to take more vigorous steps next time.
3. They must be *immediate:* people get excited when they feel they can do something effective immediately. Hope releases energy, and this is power if it is used right away.

Establish a Tight-Knit Organization That Can Stand up Under Pressure

A movement without any organization can lose its shape and become impotent under pressure from other power groups. Therefore, its structure and discipline should enable it to make its own independent decisions and to sustain efforts toward its goals. In Alinsky's model, this process culminates in an organizing convention, where representatives of the community groups meet to elect officers and establish a legal constitution and by-laws for the community organization.

One final note about organizations: One of the pervading myths about power is that 51 percent of the people are required to effect change. Nothing could be further from the truth. A survey of several organized groups (that is, Unions and Churches) revealed that 4 percent of the membership was giving the direction;[8] 96 percent of the people were politically passive, either neutral or apathetic. As long as the general mass of the people is not against a small organization, it appears that the organization has a license to operate in that community. According to Alinsky, when the mass is generally *in favor* of the organization, then a well-disciplined core of as little as one to 2 percent has that power. "History is made and saved by creative minorities" (Arnold Toynbee).

You may remember the Old Testament story in which the Lord told Abraham that he would not destroy Sodom if there were as many as 50 righteous men in the city. After further negotiations with Abraham, he reduced the number to 10. That is a very small minority. Since even 10 could

---

[8] Saul Alinsky, *Reveille for Radicals* (Chicago: University of Chicago Press, 1946), Chapter 10.

not be produced, the city was destroyed. In that case, the minority necessary for urban renewal was just too small.

THREE ACTION STRATEGIES: COLLABORATION—FIGHT—NEGOTIATION

Strategy is the policy selected for exerting power for one's interests. Tactics are the maneuvers made to effect the strategy.

Action begins when one man moves out to confront another. He can collaborate with him to build power, fight to take the other's power, or negotiate for a desirable exchange of power. When power groups do business, they have the same three choices. A city politician described these three power strategies as "Personal, Clout and Chits." How is the proper strategy selected? The test is: If one party satisfies his self-interest, will the other be able to satisfy his? Let us consider this further.

Personal

The currency is trust and the action is collaboration. If two men belong to the same political party, same athletic team, or same business, they both can win if their groups win. It may even be that one can win only if the other wins also. Their self-interests converge; collaboration is appropriate.

Putting together a program which reflects the various self-interests of a community is a highly collaborative process. As people learn that they can meet their own needs better by helping each other, they are ready to move together.

Clout

The currency is force and the action is coercion. If two parties are political opponents campaigning for the same office, or tenants and landlords concerned about rent levels or two business concerns producing the same product, both cannot win. Their interests conflict. To the degree that one wins, the other loses. Fighting is appropriate, provided at least one party estimates the cost of the fight to be worth it. Otherwise, negotiation is in order.

It is naive to assume, as many do, that power is used only in fight strategies. Power is used just as much, if less dramatically, in negotiation and collaboration. But it is equally naive to assume that fighting is avoidable or unproductive. When fight conditions exist, it is dangerous to collaborate and useless to negotiate.

Alinsky, who has helped thousands to collaborate, says that "Change means movement and movement means friction and friction means heat and heat means conflict. . . . You just can't get the rocket off the ground discreetly and quietly. . . . Disengagement from conflict is disengagement from the world, and that is death, not peace." Senator Fulbright has said the same thing, perhaps more elegantly: "It is our expectation that these proceedings may generate controversy. If they do, it will not be because we value controversy for its own sake, but rather because we accept it as a condition of intelligent decision making."⁹

Chits

The currency is obligation and the action is exchange. It is appropriate to consider negotiating when the parties have conflicting interests, but *both* respect the other's power enough to reject fight strategies as too costly. By entering into negotiations, both sides admit that they have power, and that they are willing to compromise their interests in an exchange of value for value. The important thing to remember is that the powerful and the powerless cannot negotiate. If both should come to the same bargaining table, the latter is simply a beggar.

Informal negotiating goes on every day. When I do you a favor, this gives me a chit of obligation which I can cash in for a favor from you. A press officer in New York City spends most of his time doing favors for the key people in his work. When a story breaks he will need help fast and won't have time to go about negotiating for it; he simply cashes in his chits.

FIGHT TACTICS

As we have seen, the appropriate strategy is determined by the relative self-interests and power of the groups involved. When the strategy has been selected, action is required to make that strategy effective. The action steps (or tactics) are always tailored to the immediate situation, but they should be carefully designed along certain guidelines.

The following guidelines are for designing fight tactics. They were developed by Saul Alinsky (a master tactician), during his experience in mass-based community organizations. Showing a keen perception of human behavior, these guides are also helpful in designing tactics for negotiation and collaboration, although these two strategies will not be stressed here.

"Start from Where You Are and Use What You've Got"¹⁰

Obviously one can't do anything else, but many people still find it difficult to take the world as it is and not as they would like it to be. When I was consulting with a national organization in East Africa, my clients were incapable of planning a vigorous strategy because they saw themselves as poor. They had only £50,000 sterling and saw nothing else that they had as usable resources. They would not start from where they were. Once they realized how rich they were in land and people, they made splendid plans.

When Gandhi was fighting the British for control of India, he was

---

⁹ J. William Fulbright, *The New York Times Magazine,* May 15, 1966.

¹⁰ Since these tactical guidelines are Alinsky's, they are reported as his quotations.

confronted by a well-disciplined imperial army.[11] What did Gandhi have?—millions of illiterate, demoralized, undernourished fellow countrymen. All over India they just sat around apathetically. There was no chance of mobilizing and training this rabble to do battle. Gandhi didn't try. What else did he have? At the time, the imperial power was knit together by the railway network, which provided necessary communications and transport. Gandhi designed a tactic to employ his fellow Indians, simply by asking them to do their natural sitting-around—on the railroad tracks. They ultimately disrupted communication and transport as effectively as any well-trained army. Gandhi had something else which he needed to make this tactic possible—a certain decency of the British in their unwillingness to shoot the rail-sitters. This was critical; without this "support" the tactic could have been a disaster.

Surely Gandhi, like Dr. Martin Luther King, is revered as much for his nonviolent philosophy as for the social leadership he provided. A tough-thinking political pragmatist, however, must necessarily consider the possibility that these nonviolent rationales are splendid clothing for the lack of naked power available to their authors. It will not come as a surprise to a fight tactician to hear that Gandhi changed his rationale when he was in different circumstances some years later. When independent India and independent Pakistan were confronting each other in Kashmir, Gandhi said he had been "an opponent of all warfare. But if there was no other way to secure justice from Pakistan . . . the Indian Union would have to go to war against it."[12]

"There Is a Positive and Negative to Every Situation"

Every cloud has a flip side and so does every silver lining. You may not immediately see them both but they are there. Keep turning a situation around and around until they both stand out. Then you can exploit the positive and be on guard for the negative.

The apathy of the Indians, and decency of the British toward them, must appear at first glance to be negatives for Gandhi. It's difficult to arouse an apathetic people, particularly if the colonial government is not all bad. Yet Gandhi discovered the positives in these factors and used them to his advantage.

Imagine the several steps required by a savings bank to open an account: an interview, a form to fill, a minimal $1.00 deposit, a stamped bank book and a signature. To stop a savings account requires similar steps in reverse order. This process is a positive for the bank since it provides firm and

---

[11] Alinsky discusses Gandhi's situation in detail in "Of Means and Ends," *Union Seminary Quarterly Review* 22 (January 1967).

[12] Arthur Koestler, "The Yogi and the Commissar," *New York Times Magazine*, October 5, 1969.

orderly control. Turn this around and the negative shows up: the complexity and expense of opening and closing a $1.00 account. That negative for the bank might be a positive for an organized group fighting the bank's policies. What if they opened 50 new $1.00 savings accounts on Monday, closed them on Tuesday and repeated this over and over? Just imagine it!

"Men Won't Move Except under the Thrust of Threat"

Particularly in fight situations, men will move when they believe that something worse will happen to them if they don't move. "Do it, or else." Design your fight tactics to be seen by the opposition as punishing to their self-interest. Then threaten to use them. It's a stickup, pure and simple, and it's popular in all circles.

In 1969 a Mississippi senator threatened to withhold his important support for President Nixon's missile program unless the integration processes in his home state were slowed down. Only the threat was made, but Nixon believed it enough to acquiesce. Only threats were made by the United States to Mexico and by the Cornell students to the university. They were believed; that was enough.

It is better to threaten than to fight because it is less costly, but bluffs work only so long. You *can* fool all the people much longer than is generally thought (illusions being so widespread and untested), but you can't do it all the time. You have power only so long as the opposition believes you can and will do what they say you'll do. Be ready, therefore, to back up your threats. If you are challenged and can't deliver, your opposition will correctly see you as an impotent empty threat. To reduce the possibility of being challenged, it is worthwhile to fight easy fights just to "prove" you can, and will, deliver. This makes threatening easier at a later time.

Alinsky says, "You've heard it said that it's better to light a candle than to curse the darkness, but *I'm* telling you its better to light a candle and apply it to the tenderest portion of your enemy's anatomy." And when your enemy will believe you, it is easier just to light the candle.

"Communicate within the Experience of Your Allies and outside the Experience of Your Opposition"

Clear communication is essential, of course, in uniting your allies in trust and common action. To be understood, you must talk and act in ways that are already familiar to them. That's why an organizer tries to discover the local leaders—they can communicate and interpret for him. Any teacher or speaker knows he must provide llustrations familiar to his listeners. The training director of a large company offered to double my fee if I would shave my beard before working with his department. He was right; a beard was outside the experience of his men and would prevent communication. When Gandhi asked his people to sit on the tracks, that was something they understood and trusted. It was within their experience.

With your opposition, however, design your tactics to be outside their experience. Surprise or shock them. Violate their expectations or do something they have never seen before—it will make them confused, frightened and irrational. They may even withdraw, but they definitely won't be able to cope with the problem. This is just what a fighter wants in his opponent.

General Sherman had tried for weeks to catch and destroy the Confederate army of General John B. Hood, "but he had not had much luck, and he complained bitterly, if illogically, that the real trouble was Hood's eccentricity: 'I cannot guess his movements as I could those of (General) Johnston, who was a sensible man and did only sensible things.'"[13] Apparently Hood could move outside of Sherman's experience. Sherman soon gave up the pursuit entirely and made plans for his march to the sea, "the strangest, most fateful campaign of the entire war, like nothing that happened before or afterward."[14] By moving outside the confederate experience, the march created panic.

My white-haired mother is a bishop's wife and a "Boston brahmin." In the deep South she is recognized as a "lady," though she is a Yankee to her breezy soul. In April 1964, she lunched with a black lady in a restaurant in St. Augustine, Florida. Their purpose was to help Martin Luther King give high visibility to the town's segregationist practices. Since St. Augustine depended largely on tourists, it could ill afford bad press, especially on the eve of its 300th anniversary. It was outside the experience of the local citizenry for a "lady" to eat publicly with a Negro, and it confused them into making the serious mistake of jailing her. Once in jail, she was news, and the very *type* of person St. Augustine was hoping to lure to its expensive hotels was now pictured across the nation receiving another kind of hospitality. Having a "lady" in jail was *entirely* outside their experience, and the local white leaders became frantic. Some of them told me, "For God's sake, get that lady out of jail and take her home!" With her purpose splendidly accomplished, she flew home to her delighted family.

Picketing and demonstrations used to be effective, but now they are a familiar sight and rarely excite the opposition. At a big-city antipoverty agency there are black police officers on regular duty, city commissioners assigned regular days for meeting with the demonstrators on their frequent visits, and a room kept ready for the purpose. It is all very relaxed. The familiar tactics don't work. New and unfamiliar tactics need to be designed.

Mass Jujitsu

"Design your tactics to use the strength of your opponents to advantage, and you can count on them as your greatest 'ally.' Work outside his experience. Confuse him. Goad him to react irrationally—then use what he does! *The real action is in the reaction.*"

---

[13] Bruce Catton, *This Hallowed Ground* (Garden City, N.Y.: Doubleday Publishing, 1956), 354.

[14] *Ibid.*, 356.

When Saul Alinsky rose to speak in a Texas city, he was confronted by a large delegation of the Klan which filled up the front rows in the auditorium. As he reported it, "There were so many sheets around, I thought there was a white sale." A tasteful powder-blue sheet indicated the Klan leader. As he spoke, Alinsky continued to wonder what his opponent's strength really was. Deciding that it was their racial bigotry (a negative for Alinsky), he designed a jujitsu tactic to turn the situation into a positive. Interrupting his speech, he said in effect, "You know, I took physical anthropology years ago. Among other things, we studied the facial characteristics of the different races. Now I've been looking carefully at the face of that man in the powder-blue sheet, and I could *swear* that he is a Negro." There was a shock among the Klansmen as Alinsky continued his speech, but they began to stare fixedly at the Klan leader. In their irrational, bigoted eyes, he was somehow already becoming a Negro. The strength of the opposition was now being used against itself. Suddenly the leader folded his tent, rose and left with a few Klansmen straggling after him.

In the spring of 1969, SDS students were leading a mass meeting in the Harvard Yard. They were trying to enlist the sympathies of the moderate students—the great majority of those present at the meeting. The university strength was represented by large numbers of police. SDS successfully goaded the police into such punitive action that the moderates were shocked. Their sympathies were immediately aroused against the university, and SDS had won the day. Without the help of their university "ally," they could not have done so well. The action was in the reaction.

"When You Act, Go 100 Percent"

No issue is absolutely clear, with 100 percent right on one side and 100 percent wrong on the other. There are so many positives and negatives, that it is usually around 52 to 48 percent. "The mark of a free man is that gnawing doubt about whether or not he is right" (Learned Hand). No one can be absolutely sure. But once you have decided to move into action, the task is no longer to decide but to mobilize your strength; now you are "completely sure" and you create the illusion among allies and opponents alike that you are 100 percent right. There can be no doubts showing.

There was nothing objective about the Declaration of Independence.[15] Honest thought was not intended. It was a manifesto whose tactical purpose was to arouse Americans to arms. The difficult decision to fight had already been made, and it was time for action. It declared that the purpose of the King of Great Britain was to establish "an absolute tyranny over these States," and submitted "Facts" to a "candid World." The "Facts" reported the King's activity in the colonies:

---

[15] Alinsky, "Of Means and Ends."

"quartering large Bodies of Armed Troups among us," not mentioning the fact that the troups sometimes provide helpful protection; "imposing taxes on us without our Consent," not mentioning that some of these taxes were channelled back for the support of the colonies.

The Declaration laid it on thick: "He has plundered our Seas, destroyed our Coasts, burnt our Towns and destroyed the lives of our People."

When it is time for action, let the trumpet blow a certain blast.

LAUREL LEFF

Reading 10-4
Community Spirit:
Local Groups That Aid Poor Flourish
by Using Confrontation Tactics

Notwithstanding the maxim about looking a gift horse in the mouth, the United Neighborhood Organization believes in doing exactly that—and, if need be, kicking it in the teeth.

When the UNO, a Los Angeles community group, received a $1,000 gift from a local savings and loan association, officials of the group took one look at the check and promptly returned it. "We asked for $3,000," explains Sister Maribeth Larkin, the UNO's chief organizer.

The S&L followed up with a new check for $3,000.

Such successes are commonplace for the UNO, which comprises 20 parishes (19 Roman Catholic and one Episcopal) and 93,000 families in the heavily Hispanic district of East Los Angeles. So far this year, the UNO has raised about $55,000 in business contributions, which will be added to some $100,000 in dues paid by church members. Since its founding in 1976, the UNOs annual budget of $150,000 has allowed it to pursue such activities as persuading the police to increase patrols, forcing city hall to improve public services, and pressuring insurance companies to lower auto insurance rates.

Sharing the UNO's successes is its parent, the Industrial Areas Foundation, a group founded by the late political activist Saul Alinsky. Indeed, it might be said that without the IAF, the UNO would have gone the way of the many community organizations for the poor that have either faded or failed since their heyday in the Great Society days of the 1960s.

TRANSFER OF POWER

The IAF's stated objective is to take some of the power held by politicians, bureaucrats and businessmen and return it to families and churches by organizing democratically run community groups. "We're only teaching poor people what the business community has been doing for a long time," says Edward Chambers, the IAF's 50-year-old executive director. "Top management hasn't got the corner on brains, although it does have the corner on money. But organized people with a little money can beat management money."

IAF-affiliated groups are always based on churches, which provide an established structure, a base for dues and an aura of respectability. Directing each local group is a cadre of experienced, highly trained professional organizers who teach members to concentrate on winnable issues. Tactics taught by organizers range from planning and participating in carefully orchestrated meetings with community officials to staging confrontations known as "actions." Such actions have included tying up banks (by having hundreds of people line up to change dollar bills into pennies) and threatening to dump live rats on the steps of city halls.

"They're frustrating, annoying, relentless and irritating to politicians," says New York's lieutenant governor, Mario Cuomo, who has dealt with an IAF group in the New York City borough of Queens. "But that's part of the secret to their success."

FOUNDING FATHER

Much of that success is attributed to Mr. Alinsky, who founded the IAF in 1969 as an institute to train organizers of community action groups. Then 60 years old, Mr. Alinsky had begun organizing major community projects in the years after World War II.

Known for his brilliant organizing tactics as well as his brash comments (he once called a Catholic cardinal "an unchristian, prehistoric mutton head"), Mr. Alinsky opened the IAF with grants from the Rockefeller Foundation and the Midas Institute, a private philanthropic organization. The purpose of the new group was to train organizers, and it adhered to that aim despite Mr. Alinsky's death in 1972. Mr. Chambers, one of Mr. Alinsky's principal organizers, assumed the leadership of the group when the founder died; and under his leadership, the IAF has evolved into a professional training facility and sponsoring unit for a network that today comprises community groups in 11 cities across the country and a statewide group in Wisconsin.

True, some IAF organizing attempts have failed, notably in Kansas City and Pittsburgh. Nevertheless, the group today has more work than it can handle, forcing it to decline a recent request for an IAF presence in Denver.

Currently, organizing efforts are starting in south-central Los Angeles and the Texas cities of El Paso and Fort Worth.

CONFEDERATIONS OF CHURCHES

The IAF operates out of a small office on New York's Long Island and is financed by money from each of its local groups (about $20,000 per group per year). The groups differ in their structure, but all began as confederations of churches. And while some church officials frown on the IAF, complaining that religion shouldn't be entwined with politics in any way, the IAF's Mr. Chambers sees the role of the religious institutions as vital.

"Churches are already organized—they're little pockets of power," Mr. Chambers explains. "Loyalty to the church is a tremendous plus. We can play on that and parlay it into loyalty to the community group." What's more, national church denominations also help IAF groups meet their annual budgets, which typically range from $150,000 to $300,000.

(Even though Mr. Alinsky was Jewish, synagogues have eschewed IAF involvement. The IAF says that Jews often have their own organizations and are suspicious of the church involvement in IAF groups.)

The IAF's church base helps to explain the particular success of Alinsky-style groups among heavily Roman Catholic Hispanic communities. IAF successes in Los Angeles and San Antonio, Texas, have belied conventional wisdom that Hispanics are unable to exert political clout. But IAF organizations have also been effective among blacks and whites and among various Protestant denominations. For example, the Queens Citizens Organization, an IAF group made up of 30 Catholic and Protestant parishes representing 250,000 people in the predominantly middle-class New York City borough of Queens, has been particularly effective in dealing with public officials and businessmen.

Founded in 1977, the QCO got off the ground with an Alinsky-style flourish. In what now is a celebrated incident, New York's Mayor Edward Koch, then newly elected, stormed out of a meeting with the fledgling QCO when the group refused to allow him five minutes for a speech instead of the two minutes that had been scheduled. The mayor's action received considerable criticism, and the QCO received abundant attention. With a certain coyness, the QCO now refers to Mayor Koch as one of "our founding fathers."

Recently, the QCO invited all its state legislators to a meeting to discuss the borough's growing arson problem. When only about half showed up, QCO officials vowed to tell the group's congregations which legislators weren't willing to meet with them. At the next meeting, a month later, all the legislators or their representatives attended. (The QCO and the legislators recently agreed on proposed bills to help reduce arson by such means as stiffer penalties for insurance fraud; the bills have been submitted to the state legislature, which hasn't yet acted on them.)

"Our congregations are a valuable communications network, and the politicians know that," says Gregory Pierce, a 33-year-old ex-seminarian and IAF organizer. Mr. Pierce says involvement in groups such as the QCO is also beneficial to churches. "QCO stabilizes the neighborhoods which support (churches) and provides their people with a vehicle to fight for their values," he explains.

Another reason for the IAF's success is that it resists dependence on a charismatic leader or a single issue, both of which could die or disappear. Rather, it is the group itself that is important; and the group is taught to function effectively without seeking outside help.

"Our iron rule is never do for others what they can do for themselves," says Mr. Pierce, who notes that the IAF's staff in one locale never numbers more than four so the main burden falls on the community members. "That's what differentiates us from social workers, politicians and 80 percent of all ministers," he says. "We're interested in people getting more control over their lives, not in substituting one power elite for another power elite."

As part of that localized control, IAF affiliates can hire and fire IAF-trained organizers. And the IAF itself usually recommends rotating organizers between different cities every couple of years. "After two or three years in one place, an organizer tends to try to keep power for himself," says Mr. Chambers, the IAF executive director.

(Local groups pay organizers between $20,000 and $40,000 a year, a much higher range than that recommended by founder Alinsky. "Saul always believed in hair-shirt salaries, but he was wrong about that," Mr. Chambers says. "I want political organizing to be a profession, with a professional salary.")

As part of its emphasis on winnable issues, IAF organizers train community groups to begin with small projects. For example, one of the IAF's newest groups, the East Brooklyn Churches in New York City, isn't launching its organizing drive with an assault on crime even though it is based in a crime-infested Brooklyn neighborhood; instead, it is negotiating with the Port Authority of New York and New Jersey to ensure that an industrial park planned for the area provides jobs for neighborhood residents.

More difficult to teach are the tactics of confrontation. Sister Maribeth Larkin of the UNO recalls she was so nervous during her first action that she became physically sick. But she went ahead with her presentation to the Los Angeles City Council, she says, and "my shyness dropped behind the role I was supposed to play." She adds: "You learn a lot about your potential."

As part of its confrontation tactics, the IAF deliberately creates a tense atmosphere during meetings; the object is to forestall stock speeches or soothing platitudes from those on the other side of the table. And local groups are taught to go right to the top if meetings with underlings prove unsatisfactory. A case in point, and a good example of an IAF group in action, involved the UNO; Safeway Stores Inc., the Oakland, Calif.-based supermarket chain; and the investment firm of Merrill Lynch, Pierce, Fenner & Smith Inc.

After going through Safeway's normal channels to complain about an unclean store in East Los Angeles and receiving no satisfaction, the UNO requested a meeting with Safeway's chairman and chief executive officer, Peter Magowan; Mr. Magowan declined to meet. The UNO then sent a telegram to Merrill Magowan, Peter Magowan's brother, who is a Safeway director and a Merrill Lynch vice president in San Francisco.

Merrill Magowan didn't respond to the telegram. On a Monday morning at 10 A.M. 300 UNO members and a horde of press people descended on the Merrill Lynch office in downtown Los Angeles. The UNO's president, a tiny woman named Gloria Chavez, knocked on the office door and told the manager the group had an appointment with the vice president. (It isn't clear whether the UNO didn't know—or didn't care—that Merrill Magowan was in San Francisco.) The manager became so upset when he saw the throngs of people in the lobby that he shoved Mrs. Chavez, who stumbled backward; the manager retreated into his office.

The UNO then sent a priest into the office demanding an apology for Mrs. Chavez and an answer to the telegram. Finally, the manager arranged for Merrill Magowan to telephone his brother, the Safeway chairman. Following that phone conversation, Safeway agreed to fly five UNO leaders to the company's Oakland headquarters. After the meeting, the store was cleaned up; furthermore, Safeway has since announced plans to build a new store in East Los Angeles.

"Everyone at that action really had a sense of power," Sister Maribeth recalls of the Safeway confrontation. "We proved we could move a financial institution as remote from our community as Merrill Lynch."

The UNO now is trying to make the entire Los Angeles business community less remote. It has met with top executives of 70 Los Angeles companies, using the meetings to explain how the UNO works and to request "investments" in the group. "We don't accept charity," Sister Maribeth says. "We're looking for an investment. We think our organization improves the quality of life in the community, which makes it a better place to do business as well as a better place to work."

SHEL DAVIS

Reading 10–5
Various Dimensions of the
Issue of Personal Power

As I observe managers in a variety of settings and think about what I would have wanted for them in their academic careers, the issues that come to mind deal with power. I am struck with the various ways in which people act that decrease their own power and hence their own effectiveness in organizations.

BY NOT ASSUMING RESPONSIBILITY FOR
THEIR OWN BEHAVIOR

While it is true that all of us live in a world in which external forces influence and limit our choices, it is also true that managers too frequently compound this problem by acting as if they have even less choice about what they can and cannot do than is actually the case. Even though other people, organizational rules and task variables constrain one's options, people hold back from exploring alternatives and refuse to make the choices that are possible. Too automatically the response is "the system would not allow that to happen here" or "the risk would be too great."

This tendency to blame the system for decisions and indecisions means that the manager does not assume responsibility for what happens to him. Instead he acts as if he had no option because "the boss made me." But frequently one of the reasons the boss has such great power is that the subordinate acquieses and allows this control to be exercised! After all, it does take "two to tango," and all too frequently subordinates do not recognize and acknowledge what they have done that gives the superior such great power.

Reprinted from *Exchange: The Organizational Behavior Teaching Journal.* Used with permission.

299

It is important that an individual understand the choices he does or does not make and the responsibility he does or does not assume. Only with such understanding is he able to make choices. While an intellectual understanding of this phenomenon is important, it is critical that students also gain insight into themselves about their feelings which lead to acceptance or avoidance of responsibility.

ENCOURAGE STUDENTS TO STOP REPRESSING THEIR MORE HEROIC IMPULSES

Another significant way I see managers losing influence is by not listening to their own heroic impulses. One of the most pervasive and profoundly tragic aspects of organizational life is that so many managers repress their dreams, beliefs, and personal values. These are dreams not just about what can be accomplished in a task sense but also dreams about building a more affirming human experience in their organization. There is too great a tendency to rationalize one's present world—to settle for what is required just to get along rather than to dream about what could be. This repression is perhaps the most significant way in which we give up power within the system.

I do not believe this is easy to teach. Most difficult of all, perhaps, is that it may require that the faculty member recognize and articulate his own heroic impulses which is too frequently repressed in academia.

DEVELOPING SKILLS IN INCREASING THE POWER OF OTHERS

Too often we think of power as a fixed amount, so that if one person increases his power in the group, it must be at the expense of others. But this is not the case. It is just as possible for several people in a group to be powerful and heroic and assume responsibility for their own behavior. Not only is it possible but, personally, I am not very willing or enthusiastic about being in a group where an aspect of membership—in fact the price to be paid—is to be less powerful. This applies not only to members but to the leader as well for members attempt to reduce the leader's influence under the guise that "your power diminishes mine." I only want to belong to groups and to organizations where everybody can be fully influencial and fully heroic. That requires people to have the skills to confront others who play these power-diminution games. It also requires skills in assisting others to be more fully themselves.

One of the crucial ways in which all people can increase their power is through "due process"—the process by which individuals are given the opportunity to state their views, express their feelings, agree or disagree with others. I would like to see people skilled in using their influence not to suppress or coerce others (the common way we think of being powerful) but to support the appropriate group decision-making process so that all members are fully involved. And once so involved, they then would be expected to, in fact required to, support the implementation of whatever is decided.

FEELING COMFORTABLE IN USING LEGITIMATE POWER

Although the common conception of the manager is that he feels comfortable with power, I have frequently found this not to be the case. Often there is hesitancy in using power when doing so may lead to disapproval from others. If "due process" has taken place and a commitment has been made by organizational members through that process, then the leader should be able to—in fact, must be able to—direct others to then carry out this commitment. I stress this because I have too frequently observed in academia that what first appears to be a firm commitment later turns out to be simply a momentary and highly conditional agreement. I believe this is not a healthy model. Following "due process," an organization must be able to have leadership that is willing to use the power legitimately vested in it to see that things get done.

*   *   *   *   *

Reading 10–6

Squeak Up!: My Turn

I wonder what happens when somebody who has read "Winning Through Intimidation" sits next to someone at a party who just finished "Power: How to Get It, How to Use It," and Mr. Power tells Mr. Intimidation to put out his cigar and make it snappy.

Assuming Mr. I doesn't say yes when he means no, it could end up with somebody in tears, or possibly dead, but I doubt it—not if I know my fellow mice.

No matter how many advice-to-the-hatelorn books they've read, people who hope to learn a little harmless fascism to use around the office are sure to slip when shove comes to push. If you try doing Charles Bronson numbers on everyone when, underneath, you're still Charles Nelson Reilly, you are bound to *(a)* look pretty silly and *(b)* mess things up even worse as a semipro bully.

All the self-assertiveness best sellers claim that once you stand up for your rights, maître d's will step aside with a flourish and say, "Yes, *sir,* Mr. Mitty, your table is ready!" and bosses will be so deeply moved by your sudden tablethumping skills they'll boost your salary that afternoon with a hearty, "By Jove, Milquetoast, I can see now you're a man on the move, whereas just two days ago I took you for a real schnook!"

In my own spotty experience of standing up for my rights, statistics show that about 83 percent of the time I'm wrong—a cruel blow to your up-and-coming Machiavelli. Whenever I call a waiter over to growl that the bill is $2.35 too high, he growls back that I forgot to add the onion soup. Exit scampering.

CRACKPOT RAVINGS

If, by some quirk, it turns out I'm right, I have to wait around for the manager to get back from lunch or fill out a 12-page complaint form. Standing up for your rights involves much standing up.

When you *can* force someone to bend to your demands, they make it doubly rough on you. To quote the *Mouse Manual:* "Leave bad enough alone," In the classic case of sending back an undercooked steak, the chef always sends it right back out with sixth-degree burns, just to let you know who's really in control. (Most of the people who've benefited from aggression books seem to be waiters, chefs, desk clerks, etc.)

If you ask a hotel clerk for a nicer room, say with a view, you'll get your lousy room with a view, all right, but it will also have cold and cold running water. As the *Mouse Manual* notes: "You can't win."

All serious attempts to get my way are treated like crackpot ravings. A Manhattan bakery that advertises "San Francisco sourdough French rolls" invites you to call the company president with any complaints. When I phoned him to say that his rolls would get him arrested in San Francisco for bread pollution, a secretary told me, "Gosh, nobody ever complained before."

SWAGGERING DEFEATS

In any given disaster, I'm always the "only one" to fuss. If I told the manager of the Leaning Tower of Pisa that his building appeared to be teetering, and I'd like to check out, he would just chuckle and say, "Funny—you're the first person to complain."

Conditions are never ideal for asserting myself. If my stereo breaks a week after it's been fixed, the man who did the job is in Lapland for a year. If I demand my way, I'm suddenly "causing a scene" and now everyone is mad at *me;* the mouse suddenly dwindles to pest.

Recently, I swaggered into Nathan's with free passes for two hotdogs and the henchperson said, "Ain't no good here, Next." After I'd illustrated with sound logic (more sound than logic) that it plainly states "Good at any Nathan's," the manager grudgingly agreed to fork over the wieners. I felt I'd won my first clear-cut intimidation victory, good for at least a Gold Cluster from awed bystanders, but I'd somehow lost again, shot down from behind by an ex-ally: "Boy," said my wife, "were *you* obnoxious."

Look who's talking—little Ms. Power-Grabber herself, a born self-asserter who simply assumes she's always right and if not—well, she deserves it anyway. No matter how often I watch her in action in the ring, and hold her coat, I can't seem to get that attitude to rub off. Advises the *Mouse Manual:* "Marry into power."

Whereas I was born looking over one shoulder, she's always on the lookout for holes in the defensive line. One summer, we went to Clint Eastwood's outdoor restaurant in Carmel, Calif., but it was 3 P.M.—Patio Closing Time—and we were told to eat our avocadoburgers inside.

They hadn't figured on Mugsy, who pointed out that her watch showed 2:59, that we'd come clear from Egypt and that if we were not seated outside she would "take it up with Mr. Eastwood, a family friend." Well, it was a fistful of intimidation that Dirty Harry would have loved. We got a pretty patio table, overlooking a two-inch high manager.

Now if I'd tried this gambit (as if I can think that fast on my feet; mice tend to think best in the tub a day later), I'd have been arrested for impersonating a lion.

Not that we macho mice don't have our own cute little power plays—none of which works, but they make us feel lots better, and that's what counts. I go for moral defeats. One of my favorite tactics is WALKING OUT IN A HUFF, a swell way to assert yourself without risking a scar. When things get hot, I can be counted on to clench my fists and snort, "OK: if they don't serve us in *five* more minutes, we leave." (If anybody ever noticed us leave, they'd be destroyed.)

THE POWER OF PUNITIVE THINKING

Another pet ploy is known as GLARING. I have perfected an arsenal of withering scowls and triple whammies that wear me out but that noisy people behind me at the movies just take to be my normal scrunched-up expression.

Then there is my famed HEAVY SIGH OF DISGUST. This must be done with great melodramatic exhaling, enough so that outsiders can tell you're burned up as hell but not so extreme that people think you're having an asthma attack.

My last-ditch technique is LEAVING A NASTY NOTE. I used to live in an apartment under a man who liked to see how loud he could yell at 2 A.M. It was a hobby and he got awfully good at it. I could have marched upstairs and simply beat him up but I preferred to write a violent note that read "QUIET!!", slip it under his door, push the bell and run like crazy.

I don't recall if it worked, for I was so flushed with joy at my own ingenuity that I didn't care. And I was so tired from sitting up all night thinking of what I *might* do to him that I fell fast asleep.

As the *Manual* firmly whispers, "Better a drowsing mouse than a dead rat."

MARGO VANOVER

Reading 10–7
Get Things Done through Coalitions

What do the American Paper Institute, National Coffee Association, Milk Industry Foundation, and American Council on Education have in common?

It may seem unlikely, but the answer is "an interest in sewer user charges."

These four associations and 11 others formed the Coalition for ICR Repeal to protect their members' interests in sewer user charges. Coalition members term industrial cost recovery (ICR) as "an unfair, unnecessary, and costly provision of the 1972 Federal Water Pollution Control Act."

This particular example of a coalition illustrates two very important points that you, a leader of your association, should be aware of. First of all, the coalition was successful. The industrial cost recovery provision was repealed on October 1, 1980, and coalition members frankly admit that they could never have done it alone. It took the efforts and—even more important—the clout of all 14 members to accomplish their goal.

The second point is this: Coalition members seemed like unlikely allies. Who would have thought they had anything in common?

"It's an interesting conglomeration of business groups with one similar interest," acknowledges Sheldon E. Steinbach, general counsel for the American Council on Education, Washington. "We all had one common problem—a proposed increase in sewer user charges.

"I remember the stunned look on the faces of the people at the first coalition meeting," he says with a chuckle. "They found out quickly that my association had the exact concern theirs did."

WHO ARE OUR ALLIES?

Right now, your association is probably a member of a coalition. But do you know what the coalition's purpose is? If you don't, ask your association's

Reprinted with permission from the December 1980 issue of *Leadership* magazine. Copyright 1980, by the American Society of Association Executives.

chief paid officer. He or she usually represents an association's interests in a coalition effort.

And while you are talking to your chief paid officer, ask what other associations comprise the coalition. You could be surprised. Like the Coalition for ICR Repeal, their names might not suggest a tie-in with your association's cause. In fact, they may be the names of associations that have been adversaries or competitors in the past.

It's not all that unusual, says Mr. Steinbach. "We look for common cause with other groups. We may be allies on one cause and enemies on another. It's happened time after time."

It's important to overlook past differences and concentrate on the present goal of the coalition, agrees Dr. Paul A. Kerschner, associate director for legislation, research, and programs at the National Retired Teachers Association/American Association of Retired Persons, Washington. "Two organizations can be in deep dissent on some issues," he says. "On those issues, we know we disagree. But on the issues where we do agree, it's much more powerful to speak in a unified voice."

Of course, sometimes your association's allies are obvious. Such was the case when the Distributive Services Committee was formed 17 years ago. Eighteen Ohio associations whose members were involved in distributing formed the coalition to reduce property tax on retail inventory. At the time, the tax was 70 percent of the value of the inventory. The coalition has successfully obtained several reductions since its formation, and the coalition's goal of a 35 percent inventory tax will go into effect in two years.

In this case, both the allies and the enemy were obvious. The allies: trade associations with retail merchant members. The enemy: the state legislature.

SO MANY SUCCESS STORIES

Case after case of association coalitions that have been successful in their pursuits can be cited. William T. Robinson, CAE, senior vice president of the American Hospital Association, Chicago, relates one coalition success story.

Several years ago, he says, the annual rate of increase in the level of expenditures for health care was out of control. Predictions were that if health care costs continued at the same rate it would be necessary to spend the entire gross national product on health care alone by the year 2010. In fact, the government's outlay for health care—Medicare and Medicaid—was beginning to compete with the defense budget.

Government officials, concerned, issued a challenge to the health care field to voluntarily control the rate of increase. A coalition called Voluntary Effort was created. It represented the interests of trade associations, commercial insurance companies, and others. Now, three years after the start of the coalition, "the rate of increase has been sufficiently retarded," Mr. Robinson says.

Edie Fraser, president of Fraser/Associates, Washington, has been involved in enough similar success stories to become a firm believer in their power. "Coalitions are the new trend in business relations on policy issues," she says. "I believe they are the most effective means of achieving results."

WHAT'S THEIR PURPOSE?

She explains that the basic purpose of a coalition is "to join forces together behind a mutual interest—generally a policy issue—and work together for common effectiveness and results."

"More and more associations are recognizing the power of coalitions," Ms. Fraser continues, "because they can achieve far more by integrating their resources and dividing the effort behind a common cause."

Paul Korody, director of public affairs for the National Meat Association, Washington, says coalitions are growing in numbers in response to a changing Congress. "Within the past 10 years, we have seen a decentralization of power on Capitol Hill. Today, every congressmen is almost as important as another. They all have to be talked to."

That means, he says, that only the really large associations with members in every congressional district can tackle an issue alone. "The rest of us have to pool our memberships to be effective in Congress. Whereas we have a lot of meatpackers in the Northwest and Southwest, there are many congressional districts where we have no members at all. We would be less effective in those states [without a coalition]. By combining resources with a number of associations with different memberships but the same goals, you can cover the country."

He adds that, in most cases, congressional staffs appreciate a coalition's efforts. Why? Because it makes their jobs that much easier. They can get one document or have one conversation with a coalition leader and know who and how many are for or against an issue. That's in lieu of speaking with 50,000—a number that five association executives involved in a coalition can easily represent.

CHOOSING A LEADER

In order for any coalition to be successful, it has to have a leader or coordinator with a commitment to the cause and time to devote to it, says Sheldon Steinbach, American Council on Education. "The effectiveness of the ICR repeal was solely due to the continuous scrutiny and daily monitoring of one person.

"A coalition functions only when one person is given responsibility to make that issue move. Someone must call the shots. A leader must have ample time to spend on the issue, almost to the point of making it his or her primary preoccupation."

Because of the considerable time requirement, choosing a coalition coordinator is often simply a process of elimination. Who has the time to spend on it? Who has the expertise on the issue?

When these questions are answered, only a few eligibles are likely to remain. Usually it's the executive of the association which the outcome of the issue most affects.

Or as Ms. Fraser puts it, "The leader usually represents the one association that has the most to gain . . . or lose."

GUIDELINES FOR EFFECTIVENESS

Obviously, the selection of the leader can either make or break a coalition. But other factors also enter into the outcome of your association's coalition.

Here are just a few elements common to successful coalition efforts:

- A commitment by members to work, not in their own self-interest, but in the interest of the group.
- Expertise on the part of all members on the subject matter and its ramifications.
- Knowledge of how the legislature—either state or federal—works.
- Ability to plan a strategy and allow enough lead time to develop it detail by detail so nothing slips through the cracks and is left undone.
- Communication with members of the coalition—whether it's through meetings, newsletters, memos, or telephone calls.
- Keeping on the offensive, rather than the defensive. "Use facts, data, and public opinion to build on your important points," Ms. Fraser says. "It's not necessary to attack your opposition." She ticks off campaign after campaign that was lost because one side began to react defensively to the opposition.
- Member involvement. "If the issue is important to your members— and it should be or your shouldn't be part of the coalition—get them involved," Ms. Fraser urges. "The grassroots campaign is important. The work should really come from members; your association should serve as the catalyst."
- Latitude from you and your board of directors. "Our board sets broad policy," says John C. Mahaney, Jr., president of the Ohio Council of Retail Merchants in Columbus. "After that, my board leaves me alone. It doesn't tie the staff's hands."

A COMMITMENT TO GO

The last point, the latitude you give to your chief paid executive, can be a crucial item to your association's contribution to the coalition. "The board gives us a broad delegation of authority," Sheldon Steinbach says. "We are paid to exercise good judgment and proceed. If you are hamstrung, it will slow you down, if not completely cripple your coalition."

He explains that if he had to go back to his board of directors every time a decision was made in a coalition, he would lose valuable time—not to mention the confidence of other coalition members.

SURVEY OF MEMBERSHIP

To make sure his board of directors will agree with his decisions, Mr. Steinbach surveys his membership on major issues that concern the association. "If they think it is important, they tell us to go," he says. "But they don't tell us how to go."

Dr. Kerschner explains that the only time he goes back to his board for a coalition decision is when the issue is controversial and the association's stance involves a change in previous policy.

"What do you do with dissent among coalition members?" asks Dr. Kerschner. "How do you handle it? Do you avoid the issue? Do you go with the majority?"

He explains that chief paid officers must answer these questions, and answer them adequately, for a coalition to work. He has found one possible answer for the coalitions he has been involved with: If there is a disagreement on one particular point of an issue, the dissenting party removes his or her name and endorsement from that specific letter but continues to endorse the remainder of the issue.

"Trade-offs are important because one small issue can divide the coalition," he says. "Before you say 'I will not sign that,' look at all sides. You might have to make a compromise. Internal negotiations are necessary to present a united front to those you are dealing with."

GOODWILL A KEY INGREDIENT

William Robinson advises associations to go into a coalition with the idea that there might have to be a trade-off. "Your pet ideas are going to be examined by others," he says. "You might have to accept the fact that the publicity will be given to the coalition and not to your association. A coalition takes goodwill by the participants. Sometimes the goodwill is there in the beginning; sometimes it takes time for it to grow."

Speaking realistically, Edie Fraser says it almost never happens that members of a coalition agree on every item, every detail of a coalition. "That's where the art of negotiation is important. The common end of the allies is more important than the priority of any one association."

SHARING IN THE GLORY

You may wonder why your association's past efforts in coalitions have not been more heavily publicized. . . . why your association didn't take more credit for the outcome.

"A coalition, to be effective, is without limelight or glory for the association involved," says Paul Korody. "The purpose is to get a particular job done. We're there to serve our members, and coalitions are the most effective means of doing that. Any glory is in the fact that we satisfactorily served our members."

Sheldon Steinbach admits that sharing the spotlight is a problem for some associations. Sometimes, they are so greedy for the recognition that they won't participate in a coalition—and risk losing the fight. Other times, they might participate in a coalition, but afterwards they will attempt to garner all of the credit for their association alone.

When William Robinson was working on Voluntary Effort, he says that the businesses and associations involved had no qualms about giving complete credit to the coalition, not to themselves. "It would have been counterproductive to publish under any one member's name," Mr. Robinson says. "We wanted the coalition to become a familiar name . . . to have its own identity."

POTENTIAL PROBLEMS

Powerful though they may be, coalitions are not perfect. Problems arise, and they have to be alleviated before the cause can be won. Here are some snags that can occur. With negotiation, respect, and planning, all can be overcome.

1. One Member Dominates. Sometimes, when a coalition is composed of one or two large, domineering associations and a variety of small ones, representatives from the smaller associations are not given the chance to express their opinions. Or, if they are given the opportunity, they are not given priority. All members must listen to one another.

2. Jealousy between Members. This usually occurs at the outset, Ms. Fraser points out, until coalition members realize that "they can achieve far more by integrating their resources and dividing the effort behind a common cause."

3. Conflicting Goals. "You've got to go for the greatest good for the greatest number," Mr. Steinbach says.

4. Conflicting Strategy. This occurs most often when two or more coalition members have considerable legislative experience. Because of their backgrounds, each thinks his own plan of attack is best.

5. Minor disagreements. Even though the association executives agree on the major issue, they sometimes bicker about a minor part of it. "You can't let a specific point divide and conquer the group," Dr. Kerschner says.

6. Too Formal. Dr. Kerschner differentiates between organization, which you can never have enough of, and formalization, which you can. He says it's important to remember that each member of the coalition has an association to which he is responsible and that the coalition should not become a substitute for it.

7. Too Many Meetings. Some coalitions are permanent. Others are temporary—disbanded as soon as their cause is settled. Dr. Kerschner warns

---

TWENTY TIPS FOR MAKING A COALITION WORK

If you aren't convinced of the value of coalitions, talk to Edie Fraser, president of Fraser/Associates, Washington, D.C. She's a firm believer in their effectiveness and presents a persuasive argument on their behalf.

She asserts that coalitions are the wave of the future. "On most policy issues, a coalition is the only way to go—if you have a common interest," she says.

In her opinion, more and more association executives are recognizing the potential—and power—of coalitions, but they aren't sure how to proceed. "Carrying out the program is where they often fall down."

Here are her 20 rules for participating in an effective coalition:

1. Clearly define issues and strategy.
2. Determine a timetable and needs.
3. Identify both allies and opposition.
4. Build constituency and recruit allies.
5. Select leadership from within allies.
6. Devise a clear plan of action.
7. Determine resources, budget, and meet those needs.
8. Divide up tasks within the coalition.
9. Establish a working task force or executive committee.
10. Keep coalition members informed and involved.
11. Establish a communication program plan; clearly distribute tasks.
12. Build supportive case materials.
13. Develop an internal communication program with each association involving its members.
14. Enlist experts to support the coalition's case.
15. Explain the issue in economic impact terms when possible; use appropriate public opinion.
16. Utilize all pertinent media for greatest impact.
17. Remember to keep all coalition constituents informed and involved.
18. If it's a legislative issue, review the congressional strategy on a regular basis.
19. Determine if the coalition leadership is serving as a catalyst for communication.
20. Prove the results and communicate them to the member constituencies.

---

that members of permanent coalitions have to be careful not to call a meeting just to be calling a meeting. Unless a crisis has occurred or a new development has come up, he recommends meeting about once a month. Between meetings, he uses the phone for exchanges of information.

8. Lack of Follow-Through. Sometimes a coalition member will slip up, and the work assigned to him or her will not get done. If that happens, and it is not caught in time, all of the coalition efforts will be wasted.

EVERYONE'S DOING IT

Coalitions are not limited to associations. Business groups, consumer groups—just about any group you can think of is involved in some type of coalition. "On any side of any issue, you can find a coalition that has formed, is being formed, or will be formed," Mr. Korody says.

Whatever type of coalition your association may now be involved in, your chances for victory are better through unity. Mr. Mahaney firmly believes Ohio merchants would not have received inventory tax relief without the Distributive Service Committee. "We could not have done it alone," he states. "It took everyone in the coalition to do it."

"Sometimes a coalition is the only way to do something," he continues. "Especially now, as the problem becomes more complex. It seems like they are too big for any one—or even two—associations to handle."

Paul Korody couldn't agree more. "A smart association executive seeks his peers and works through a coalition. The days of trying to do it all yourself are long gone."

Personality

Are some people "born negotiators?" Many observers of negotiation have argued that some negotiators, by virtue of their personality, are simply much more capable of winning a negotiation or getting the best outcome. They argue that if we can understand which dimensions of personality contribute to negotiation effectiveness, we would be able to select potentially good negotiators with greater accuracy, or better understand how to train certain people to adapt their behavior to accommodate to situations that their personality style does not normally provide.

In spite of these assertions and a great deal of research that has been devoted to identifying the characteristics and personality styles of more effective and less effective negotiators, the exact role of a negotiator's personality and its impact on outcomes is not well known. Many of these studies have yielded inconclusive results, and others have often yielded contradictory findings. Nonetheless, some facts are known. The articles represented in this section cover three different areas of personality style and type with implications for understanding effectiveness in negotiation.

The first article, "The Machiavellis among Us" by Richard Christie, describes a type of individual personality style known as Machiavellianism. Christie began his study of Machiavellianism because of his interest in the effectiveness of certain individuals who were good manipulators. His research lead him to propose that the perfect manipulator was characterized by four attributes. First, the perfect manipulator was not basically concerned with conventional morality. Second, he/she was basically cool and detached with other people. Third, he/she was more concerned with the means than with the ends; that is, how he conned people was more important than what he conned out of them. Lastly, rather than being a psychologically disturbed individual, he/she was very rational—in fact, overrational in dealing with people.

Based on this characterization, Christie then set out to investigate the ways that Machiavellian people manipulate others, and the conditions under which they are most likely to be successful at it. The research findings lead to an important conclusion about the role of personality factors in negotiation, one that we will see repeated again and again: Machiavellians, like other types of personalities who may be more effective in negotiation, are only most effective under certain kinds of conditions. Thus, no personality type is likely to be effective in all situations; rather, different personalities can be more or less effective depending on certain situational factors. These situational factors may include the kind of relationship one can develop with the other person, the nature of the conflict, or the strategic and tactical opportunities available to the negotiator himself.

Gwilym Brown, in the second article, "Winning One for the Ripper," also explores the nature of personality and its impact on effectiveness. The focus here is not the world of negotiation, but the world of professional sports. We know that professional football and basketball players, and other athletes are rigorously screened for their physical capabilities and agilities. Less known, however, is the psychological screening that is also conducted to determine which types of individuals are likely to perform best given the demands of certain sports. Thus, the temperament and individual style necessary to be a successful race car driver may not be the same necessary to be a successful linebacker or distance runner. By developing and studying the psychological profiles of individuals and matching them against the profiles of successful sports figures in a variety of sports and competitive positions, investigators are able to determine the likelihood that a person with the physical capability will also be psychologically fit for the sport and position that he or she will play. William J. Beausay's conclusions are similar to the ones we drew about Machiavellianism earlier, no one temperament type would be psychologically suited for all sports, and that profiling the athlete to fit the sport is likely to lead to the most successful outcomes. Hence, the answer to our opening question is—no one is born equipped to handle all types of negotiations or negotiating situations.

The third article, "Trust and Gullibility" by Julian Rotter, focuses on another dimension of personality: interpersonal trust. An easy assumption is that trusting people are more easily duped, mislead, or taken advantage of. Is this true? Rotter's research shows that individuals differ widely in what he calls their "generalized expectancy for trust"—that is, the degree to which they trust others, or the speed with which they develop this trust. Research demonstrates that individuals do vary in this capability to trust, and that this capability is closely tied to the individual's ability to develop successful relationships with others. High trusters are more trustworthy in their nature, and they are seen as more likable by other people. They are not necessarily more gullible or naive, or more moralistic or prone to be "do-gooders" than less trusting people. We would also expect that high trusters would be able to establish better relationships with other people, and be able to arrive at cooperative negotiating agreements which would be more long lasting and more problem-free in their implementation.

RICHARD CHRISTIE

Reading 11–1
The Machiavellis among Us

*Because this is to be asserted in general of men, that they are ungrateful,
fickle, false, cowardly, covetous, and as long as you succeed they are yours
entirely; they will offer you their blood, property, life and children when the
need is far distant; but when it approaches they turn against you . . . and
men have less scruple in offending one who is beloved than one who is feared,
for love is preserved by the link of obligation which, owing to the baseness of
men, is broken at every opportunity for their advantage; but fear preserves you
by the dread of punishment which never fails.*

The Prince (XVII)
Niccolò di Bernardo Machiavelli

The use of guile and deceit to influence and control others is a popular theme
in myth and folklore throughout history. Political theorists in all ages and
countries have been fascinated by the topic, even in cultures as remote as
those of ancient China and India. For example, the Arthaśāstra of Kautilya
gives rulers very detailed advice on espionage: who should be kept under
surveillance, what roles spies should take, how they should be paid, how to
verify the accuracy of their reports, how to keep from being stabbed while
one is busy in the harem, and so on. He even discussed the use of classmates
as spies—more than two millennia before the FBI.

Kautilya's advice to rulers suggests that India in 300 B.C. would have
made Machiavelli's Florence in the 1500s look like a kindergarten. Yet it is
Machiavelli we remember for his cynical view of man and the way in which
man should be manipulated. This may be unfair, and in fact eminent
historians are in violent disagreement about Machiavelli's writings. Mat-
tingly Garrett, an American, has argued convincingly that *The Prince* was
written as political satire. G. P. Gooch, an Englishman, felt that Machiavelli

was unfair to mankind because he saw a limited portion of the vast field of experience. And the German Friedrich Meinecke thought that Machiavelli rose to the highest ethics in advocating that a prince behave unlawfully, cruelly and shamefully for the sake of the state.

THINKERS

My interest in Machiavellianism began some 15 years ago when I was puzzling over the nature of individuals who are effective in manipulating others. At the time I was at the Center for Advanced Study in the Behavioral Sciences (Stanford) for a year with nothing to do but think great thoughts. To relieve anxiety over this ominous responsibility, my fellow thinkers and I formed work groups on various topics. Some six of us met to discuss the psychology of leaders—manipulators—having discovered that most of the literature was on followers—the manipulated.

Our early conversations led to four hunches about the perfect manipulator:

1. He is not basically concerned with morality in the conventional sense.
2. He is basically cool and detached with other people. Once a person becomes emotionally involved with another person it is difficult to treat him as an object.
3. He is more concerned with means than ends, thus more interested in conning others than in what he is conning them for. Good manipulators, therefore, come in all ideological colors.
4. He is not pathologically disturbed nor would he have clinical symptoms of neurosis or psychosis. The manipulator must be able to function successfully in the real world, and thus must have an undistorted view of reality. If anything, he would be overrational in dealing with others.

SCALE

To get some ideas for a test that could identify this ideal type, we examined the writings of power theorists throughout history. Viewed in this broad perspective, Machiavelli is not unique. He differs from other power theorists in being explicit in the assumptions he made about human nature. Most political theorists or philosophers base their prescriptions on implicit assumptions; namely, that man is basically weak and gullible, and a rational man takes advantage of the foibles of others. Machiavelli's essays in *The Prince* and the *Discourses* each illustrated a particular point.

This explicitness enabled us to construct a scale. Some of the items we chose for it came directly from his essays, with slight updating, such as: *Most men forget more easily the death of their father than the loss of their property.* Some comments we reversed to avoid wholesale agreement or disagreement; for example, his reflection on man's cowardice became *Most men are brave*. Finally, we invented some new statements that we felt Machiavelli would have approved, such as *Barnum was right when he said there's a sucker born every minute*.

CAMOUFLAGE

After pretesting, revising, and eliminating some of our original 71 statements, we ended up with 20 items: 10 worded in a pro-Machiavelli direction and 10 in an anti-Machiavelli direction. This balanced scale, our fourth variation on the theme, was dubbed Mach IV.

However, many persons are reluctant to agree unequivocally with Machiavellian statements, even if they believe in them, because in our culture agreement with Machiavellianism has low social desirability. Thus we constructed another form of the scale (Mach V) to minimize this effect, using the same 20 items.

This done, we began studies that attempted to relate the Mach scales to other pencil-and-paper tests, and to identify the kinds of persons most likely to agree with Machiavelli's precepts. We found:

1. Males are generally more Machiavellian than females.

2. High Machs do *not* do better than Low Machs on measures of intelligence or ability.

3. High Machs, though they are detached from others, are not pathologically so, at least as measured by the Minnesota Multiphasic Personality Inventory psychopath scale or Lykken's sociopath scale.

4. Machiavellianism is not related to authoritarianism, although superficially it seems that it should be. We decided that there is a basic philosophical difference between these two orientations: the moralistic authoritarian says, "People are no damn good *but they should be*"; the Machiavellian says, "People are no damn good, *so why not take advantage of them?*"

5. High Machs are more likely to be in professions that primarily control and manipulate people. Lawyers, psychiatrists and behavioral scientists, for example (including social psychologists), are more Machiavellian than accountants, surgeons and natural scientists.

6. Machiavellianism is not related to a respondent's occupational status or education, marital status, birth order, his father's socioeconomic position, or most other demographic characteristics. We base these conclusions on results from a representative national sample of adults, another study of thousands of college students, and findings from a variety of nonstudent samples by other investigators.

7. On a societal level, industrialization and urbanization apparently contribute to the emergence of Machiavellianism. Survey studies have shown that High Machs are likely to come from urban rather than rural

backgrounds. In addition, young adults have higher Mach scores than older adults, perhaps because they grew up in a period of transition toward a cosmopolitan society.

GLOBAL

In fact, studies in the United States and in other cultures indicate that increased cosmopolitanism is creating a generation of Machiavellis—worldwide. Armando de Miguel gave a Spanish version of Mach V to 15 groups of Spanish students from nine provinces and found that scores were highly related to the degree of industrialization of the provinces these students were from. Lois Oksenberg translated Mach IV into Mandarin Chinese and gave it to high school students in Hong Kong. She found that those attending a westernized school, where the language of instruction was English and where the curriculum followed the British system, scored higher on Machiavellianism than students attending a traditional (Confucian) Chinese high school.

A Machiavellianism score, of course, represents only the degree to which a person believes that people in general are manipulable. He does not necessarily claim that *he* would, or does, manipulate. However, we inferred that agreement with such cynical views of human nature might go along with the emotional detachment and amoral attitude necessary for successful deception.

CHEATERS

Ralph Exline and his colleagues constructed a devious experiment that piqued our curiosity. Exline used a confederate—who posed as another subject—to induce individual subjects to cheat on a test. The experimenter then returned for a posttest interview, during which the eye movements of the subjects were recorded. The experimenter first expressed surprise at the subjects' unusually good performances on the test, then became suspicious, and finally accused the subjects of cheating. In this stressful confrontation, subjects who had scored high on Mach IV resisted confessing. They also looked the experimenter in the eye significantly longer while denying that they had cheated than low-scoring subjects did.

MONEY

This defensive maneuver appeared to be consistent with what we might expect from a good manipulator and it suggested that there were behavioral correlates of Machiavellian attitudes. Would High Machs behave just as predictably when they had the opportunity for aggressive rather than defensive manipulation?

To find out, Florence Geis and I did an experiment we came to call the

A Test: Are You Machiavellian?

	Disagree			Agree	
	A Lot	A Little	Neutral	A Little	A Lot
1. The best way to handle people is to tell them what they want to hear.	1	2	3	4	5
2. When you ask someone to do something for you, it is best to give the real reasons for wanting it rather than giving reasons which might carry more weight.	1	2	3	4	5
3. Anyone who completely trusts anyone else is asking for trouble.	1	2	3	4	5
4. It is hard to get ahead without cutting corners here and there.	1	2	3	4	5
5. It is safest to assume that all people have a vicious streak and it will come out when they are given a chance.	1	2	3	4	5
6. One should take action only when sure it is morally right.	1	2	3	4	5
7. Most people are basically good and kind.	1	2	3	4	5
8. There is no excuse for lying to someone else.	1	2	3	4	5
9. Most men forget more easily the death of their father than the loss of their property.	1	2	3	4	5
10. Generally speaking, men won't work hard unless they're forced to do so.	1	2	3	4	5

Check the point on the scale that most closely represents your attitude. To find your Mach score, add the numbers you have checked on questions 1, 3, 4, 5, 9 and 10. For the other four questions, reverse the numbers you checked—5 becomes 1, 4 is 2, 2 is 4, 1 is 5, Total your 10 numbers. This is your score. The National Opinion Research Center, which used this short form of the scale in a random sample of American adults, found that the national average was 25.

$10 game. Three subjects—with high, middle, and low scores on the Mach scales—took seats around a table. We placed 10 $1 bills on the table with the following simple instructions: any *two* of the players could divide the money between themselves in any fashion—five and five, six and four, eight and two, etc. The game would end when two of the subjects came to a final decision, with the crucial stipulation that no agreement could be made to cut the third person in after the session. Theoretically this is an endless game: the excluded person can always break any tentative agreements by offering one of the other two a better deal. And on and on the game goes.

When we started we had no notion how long the subjects would sit, dividing and redividing the dollars. It turned out that the game, far from being endless, varied in duration from 15 seconds to 15 minutes. The High Mach was in the winning combination in every group. Overall, High Machs won significantly more money than would be expected by chance. In this case, their winning was due to their persistence and the reluctance of the Low Machs to hassle over money.

MISS RHEINGOLD

High Machs impressed us as being much more curious about the nature of our experiments than Low Machs did. They asked more questions about the ground rules and in general seemed to case the experimental situation with an eye to taking maximum advantage of it. We began to wonder: were they more attuned to subtle cues in the environment?

Virginia Boehm and I attempted to answer this question in our Miss Rheingold experiment. Perhaps you remember the Miss Rheingold contest. For over 20 years the Liebmann Breweries annually selected six young ladies to vie for the honor of being used in promotional advertising the following year. Before the contest was ended, some 20 million votes per year were being cast.

We decided to use these pictures in our experiment partly on the basis of a grocery clerk's remark that he could always pick the winner. This seemed highly unlikely; the brewery selected fresh-faced, wholesome types who might have been the proverbial girl next door, and it was hard to tell one from another. For this reason, the pictures appeared to be a good way of testing whether High Machs were more perceptive of subtle cues. If so, they should learn more quickly than Low Machs to identify winners.

So we obtained color photographs of the contestants for the preceding 20 years, and made slides of the six girls for each year. We presented the slides in chronological order, and after each exposure, respondents guessed the winner and runner-up. We gave them feedback about the identities of the winners after they made their choices.

To our surprise there was no difference between High Machs and Low Machs in learning to identify the winners. All respondents chose the winner with greater-than-chance accuracy on the first block of 10 trials, and made a much greater number of correct choices on the second block of 10.

PARAMETERS

Why did degree of Machiavellianism make a difference in the $10 game but not in the Miss Rheingold contest? Florence Geis and I have since analyzed some 50 laboratory studies and have found three parameters that determine whether Machiavellianism is salient. High Machs make out better when three crucial conditions are met:

1. When the laboratory interaction is face-to-face with another person.
2. When there is latitude for improvisation; that is, the subject has a chance to respond freely and is not restricted to pushing buttons or taking tests.
3. When the situation permits the arousal of emotions; that is, where the experiment has serious consequences. Playing for money rather than, say, points, is an example.

Of the 50 Machiavelli experiments that we tabulated, High Machs were more likely to "win"—that is, get more money or points, con someone else, or otherwise perform successfully—when all three of these conditions are met. They did not win when the conditions were absent.

	Number of Parameters Present			
	0	*1*	*2*	*3*
High Machs win	0	5	7	13
High Machs don't win	11	8	5	1
Total: 50 studies				

It became clear why High Machs won consistently in the $10 game but not the Miss Rheingold contest. In the latter case, there was no face-to-face interaction since all subjects responded to pictures. There was no latitude for improvisation since the choice was limited to one of six pictures per year. There was no competition with other subjects and no reward, except perhaps self-satisfaction for improving one's guesses. And the stimuli were unlikely to arouse much emotional involvement, since the young ladies were characterized by a bland, homogenized wholesomeness. The money game, however, met all three conditions.

COOL

Other experimental studies have shown that the High Machiavellian is extremely resistant to social influence, although he can be persuaded by rational arguments; he appraises a situation logically and cognitively rather than emotionally; and he tends to initiate and control the structure of the situation when possible. The cool syndrome is his trademark.

The Low Machiavellian, by contrast, is the perfect soft touch. He is susceptible to social influence, he empathizes with others, and he tends to accept the existing definitions of the situation. Far from being cool, he is warm and gets caught up in ongoing human interaction.

Geis and I have the impression that the High Machiavellian is an effective manipulator *not* because he reads the other person and takes advantage of his weakness, but because his insensitivity to the other person permits him to bull his way through in pursuit of coolly rational goals. The Low Mach's empathic ability prevents him from being detached enough to take advantage of the other.

Geis and I concluded that Machiavellianism shows up as an interaction between some enduring interpersonal orientation and specified kinds of situations. We then began to wonder about the genesis of such a manipulative style—how soon it appears in children and how it is acquired.

Susan Nachamie ingeniously constructed a Kiddie-Mach scale—modified Mach IV items—for use with elementary-school children, and gave it to a ghetto-school's sixth-graders (mostly of Chinese, black and Puerto Rican parentage). The children played a dice game that provided immediate payoffs in M&M candies. The game matrix was asymmetric, so that successful bluffing and challenging were rewarded disproportionately. Children with High Mach scores won significantly more M&Ms than those with low scores.

CRACKERS

Dorothea Braginsky administered a modified version of the scale to fifth-grade children in two small Northeastern cities. Those scoring high and low on the test were chosen as subjects, and the middle scorers were used as targets. Braginsky was introduced as a home economist working for a large bakery that was testing a new health cracker—actually a cracker soaked in quinine. After each child had fully savored the bitterness he rated the cracker's flavor on a graphic rating scale and was then given water and chocolate to help kill the taste. (A few children who said they liked the cracker were not used in the rest of the study.)

Braginsky told the children that although they did not like the cracker, it had been found that sometimes if people ate enough crackers they developed a fondness for them. She offered the children a chance to help her by asking each to persuade another student (the Middle-Mach target) to eat as many crackers as possible. For this help, she said, she would give the child one nickel for every cracker he could persuade the target to eat.

Needless to say, the High-Mach children talked the targets into eating over twice as many crackers as the Low Machs did. Interestingly there were no sex differences in scores or persuasive ability.

PARENTS

Machiavellianism apparently does exist in nascent form in preadolescence. Do the children acquire this orientation by modeling themselves after their manipulative parents?

Braginsky obtained Mach-IV and -V scores on the parents of some two thirds of the children. To her surprise, she found that consistently Low-Mach parents had children who were significantly higher on her version of the Kiddie-Mach scale. The children who were more successful in pushing noxious crackers came from Low-Mach parents. This finding seemed to contradict much current research in developmental psychology—and theory that emphasizes the importance of identification with adults (usually parents). How do we account for this?

An infant sends out many signals, from coos to cries, to bring his needs to the attention of a responsible adult, most often the mother. Some of these behaviors are successful, others are not; and those that are rewarded with the mother's attention are more quickly learned. Mothers, of course, vary in their degree of Machiavellianism; some are more manipulable than others. We would therefore predict that the small children of Low-Mach mothers are able to get away with a greater variety of manipulative actions than children of High-Mach mothers.

A preliminary check on these speculations has been started by Dora Dien in Japan. She related Machiavellianism scores of a group of mothers to the amount of cheating done by their nursery-school children. Children of Low-Mach mothers did cheat considerably more when they were alone in the laboratory situation. This study is currently being replicated in the United States.

WRANGLE

It is remarkable to me that the Mach tests seem simple enough and the meaning universal enough to be readily translated into other languages. In 16th-century Italian, modern English, Mandarin Chinese, or Spanish, Machiavelli's concept of human nature still serves to locate individuals along a continuum of agreement to disagreement with his precepts. Whether his advice to rulers was valid or not, I am not qualified to say. I am content to let historians and politicians wrangle about their interpretation of Machiavelli, secure in my appraisal that he was a most astute observer of man.

GWILYM S. BROWN

Reading 11–2

Winning One for the Ripper

The last thing in the world that psychologist William J. Beausay wants to be accused of is generalizing. None of this casual, flat-statement lumping together in categories, such as "All race drivers are aggressive" or "Everybody knows that linebackers are mean rascals." The art of psychology as applied to sport is much more exacting; men must be examined one at a time and their profiles carefully charted. And what has Dr. Beausay found after years of exhaustive study? Among other things, he has found that all race drivers are aggressive—and linebackers are nothing if not mean. And more.

By individual profile, a race driver is nervous, depressed, withdrawn, insensitive, self-absorbed, dominating, hostile, uncontrolled. And if that isn't enough, he also is slow of eye, at least slower than the average person. On Dr. Beausay's charts, a driver who makes the lineup for the Indianapolis 500 tests so high on hostility that some psychiatrists might declare that improvement was urgent. He checks out as being so tense and highstrung that it seems a wonder he can buckle his crash helmet, let alone get his car out of the pits.

The data is right there, as Exhibit 1 shows. No escaping the data: Beausay is the executive director of a small research institute he calls the Academy for the Psychology of Sports International, and the Toledo psychologist has run off personality profile tests on hundreds of practicing athletes, including 50 Indy drivers. After three years of examinations conducted at the Speedway during the race month of May, Dr. Beausay's data point to the conclusion that the most successful hard chargers who race there appear to be average in only one of nine vital personality characteristics. Further, the eyesight of the drivers is no better than the man's in the stands.

The following article is reprinted courtesy of *Sports Illustrated* from the November 26, 1973 issue. © 1973 Time Inc. "Winning One for the Ripper," by Gwilym S. Brown.

EXHIBIT 1
Nice Guys Finish off the Chart

Called the Taylor-Johnson Temperament Analysis Profile, the graphs tell all: linebackers (solid line) score high in nerves, dominance, hostility. Indy race starters (dotted line) are withdrawn and almost as hostile. But distance runners (bars) are a different breed—composed, submissive and self-disciplined.

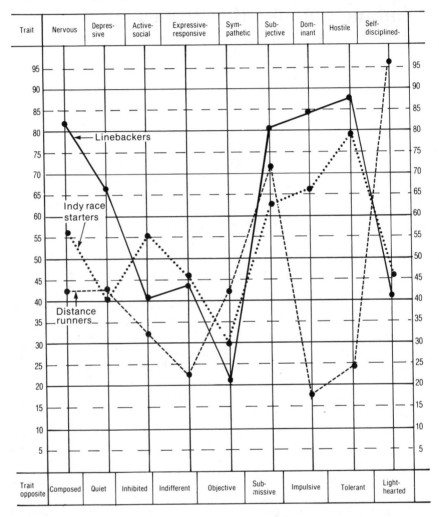

Tests by Beausay have shown that while the Indy driver has no trouble picking out the gibberish posted on an eye doctor's wall, he scores significantly lower than other athletes his age in examinations designed to show how quickly and efficiently his eyes can focus and refocus.

Beausay has more dandies. If racing drivers don't sound exactly stable, consider football linebackers and defensive linemen. Beausay's profiles reveal that these men possess personality patterns that deviate even more. They are more nervous and depressed. Their profiles show that football's primary defenders are also more hostile, socially averse, insensitive and impulsive than the drivers.

This sort of situation is fine on the fields of sport, but what of the social side? Say, a young woman was shopping for a mate; what should she do? Answer: Go for the quarterback every time. Despite a certain suspicion that they are all long-haired, arrogant playboys, the quarterbacks, say Beausay, are not all bad. "While they test almost as high in hostility as drivers and linebackers," he says, "it is for different reasons. It is because the quarterbacks are extreme perfectionists. Otherwise, they are a pretty cool bunch. They tend to be more lighthearted, free of themselves, compassionate and self-disciplined."

The alltime safest choice for reliable stability turns out to be distance runners. According to Beausay's profiles, they tend to be passive, compliant, tolerant and even more self-disciplined than the quarterbacks.

But what of Beausay himself, this snoop who prowls the sports scene with his meddlesome 180-part quizzes, computer printout codes and charts and graphs? Is he intent upon proving that all the hotshot athletes are hopeless neurotics? Is nobody safe with Beausay?

With a couple of notable exceptions, everybody is safe with the good doctor. Beausay is a large and affable 42-year-old assistant professor currently working at the psychology department of Bluffton College in Ohio. He has a pretty wife, Milane, three athletically active sons and two daughters. Beausay takes to the pulpit only on rare occasions, but he is an ordained minister in the United Church of Christ. He also has a certificate in dental technology and a B.A. in psychology from Ohio State, an M.A. in counseling and a Ph.D. in administration from Bowling Green. Drilling, quizzing or searching souls—those are the credentials for a man who likes to probe personalities.

The profile charts are part of a larger plan. Beausay is seeking an improvement of the breed. "The psychological aspect of what produces a super athlete is an overlooked and yet highly valuable subject for study," says Beausay, a high school star whose own athletic development stopped in college well short of super. "I have no doubt that this knowledge also can help an average athlete to change himself into a superior one."

There are enough believers around the country to have hired Beausay to profile the personalities of more than 300 National Football League players, 100 motor racers, a wide assortment of pro and college basketball, football and hockey players, sky divers and even a women's semipro tackle-football team. "The girls tested out the same as their male counterparts," he says.

Beausay was first turned on to a study of the athletic psyche back in the early 1960s by Bill Glass, who played defensive end in the NFL, first with the Detroit Lions and later with the Cleveland Browns, where he was once rated All-Pro. The two met through a mutual friend and immediately started picking each other's brains. All his football life Glass had listened to coaches ascribe victory and defeat to whether or not a team was "up" for a particular game. "But never did I hear a coach define what 'up' meant or just how to attain that state," says Glass. "I decided to find out for myself. It was a difficult search because the only advice available on the subject was in books on salesmanship."

Enter Beausay. At dinner one night the psychologist and the defensive end were discussing the game that Glass would soon be playing against the New York Giants and their outstanding quarterback, Y. A. Tittle. Glass sought a method by which he could get prodigiously "up" for a busy afternoon of playing sack the quarterback. Beausay introduced the concept of autosuggestion.

"What is the chief obstacle you must overcome to get at Tittle?" Beausay recalls asking.

"The offensive tackle."

"How do you want to handle the offensive tackle?'

"I take a quick step across the line, throw him off and then shoot for Tittle."

Beausay distilled this description into an explosive three-word command—"Charge! Throw! Shoot!"—which Glass was to repeat to himself frequently during the preceding week and then during the game. The psychologist calls this Super Psyching. Neither Glass nor Beausay can now recall how often, if at all, Glass was able to shoot Tittle down when next they met across the line of scrimmage. But what did happen was that Glass soon became a master of this psychological pep pill, popping it in many forms.

"I would lie on my bed before a game and imagine that I had pulled down a motion picture screen and was watching a film of myself in action, constantly getting past the offensive tackle," says Glass. "This was putting positive pictures into my subconscious—in the same way that performing well in a real game would have done—and it built up my confidence."

When the tape cassette came into popular use Glass would record a series of commands on tape and play them back continuously during game weeks. A typical Glass-to-Glass taped Super Psyching might go something like this: "When the ball is snapped you are going to CHARGE. You are going to charge across the line of scrimmage and PURSUE, PURSUE, PURSUE. You are going to pursue for 40, 50, and 60 yards until you make the tackle or until the whistle blows." Always the trigger word would be "charge." The belief was that when repeated on the field it would activate the taped instructions buried in the Glass subconscious.

Glass' most successful tape job was done prior to the Browns-Washington Redskins game on the opening weekend of the 1966 season. The game was in Washington and the temperature was an enervating 105°. To offset the heat, the message that Glass fed into his tape cassette was that heat was beautiful and that it kept the muscles loose. But best of all, the heat would help Glass because he was now psychologically programmed to use it, while his opponents, in their ignorance, would dissolve into sweat-soaked exhaustion. During the game, while all around him seemed to blur in slow motion, Glass charged through and shot for the quarterback, Sonny Jurgensen, like a man possessed (which, of course, he was). The Browns won 38–14 and it is generally agreed around Cleveland that this was just about the finest game of Glass' outstanding career.

Bill Beausay was often an enthralled spectator at these violent testimonials to the effectiveness of Super Psyching. "It was incredible," he recalls. "Bill Glass, a completely warm, outgoing and friendly guy, ceased to be a human being. He played like a carefully programmed machine. It really got me interested in the psychology of athletes, expecially so because I soon discovered that little testing had been done on them."

Beausay started out in Gasoline Alley at Indianapolis during time trials for the 500 in 1968, talking with the drivers and even wandering through the stands, trying to figure out why spectators turned out in such huge droves just for the time trials. He decided to make Indy his first major testing ground. With tips provided by Astronaut Neil Armstrong, a boyhood friend, on the personality tests used by NASA, plus some insights offered by Dr. Robert Taylor, co-author of the Taylor-Johnson Temperament Analysis Profile, Beausay returned to Indy during the 1969 time trials. This time he was armed with the 180-question Taylor-Johnson test and the blessing of Indy's medical director, Dr. Thomas A. Hanna.

That first year Beausay ran tests on 35 drivers—17 went on to qualify for the starting grid and 18 did not. All the starters showed in their personality profiles an unusually high level of hostility and impulsiveness, traits that would seem a bit dicey to ride with through the crowded, high-speed furor of the Indy race. Beausay also found it significant that in every one of nine listed characteristics, the 17 who qualified for the race were, as a group, from 5 to 10 degrees further removed from what could be described as average disposition than the 18 men who didn't make the lineup. The conclusion seemed inescapable that it was the extra hostility and aggressiveness that got the starters into the race.

Beausay was back again in 1970 for further testing, and the results served to confirm his earlier findings. Then, in 1971, he was on hand with a lineup of complex eye-testing equipment, at which time he discovered that many of the drivers had questionable peripheral vision. In the vital matter of how quickly the eyes could focus and refocus on different objects, they scored lower than athletes from other sports. The driver average on the number of focal points on which the eyes could focus during a period of one second was 2.3. The mark for the 50 major league baseball players Beausay has tested is 2.9 and the champ eye-baller of all is Chuck Ealey, the former University of Toledo quarterback now starring in Canada (*Sports Illustrated,* December 11, 1972), who scored a phenomenal 4.6.

The idea, for Beausay, is to transform all this data into something pragmatic. This is where he claims to differ sharply from the more widely known team of Bruce Ogilvie and Thomas Tutko, who also have conducted hundreds of personality tests on athletes (*Sports Illustrated,* January 18, 1971). "My purpose is to help the individual athlete improve performance through knowledge of his own psychology and how to get the most of it," claims Beausay. "Ogilvie and Tutko have made what I think is the mistaken choice of aligning themselves too closely with coaches and owners, which puts the emphasis more on manipulation."

Ogilvie and Tutko, in fact, are the authors of a book entitled *Problem Athletes and How to Handle Them* and their surveys done for numerous NFL clubs have so irritated the players that their Players Association has called for a ban on all psychological testing. Several players also have suggested that there is a far greater need for a book entitled *Problem Coaches and How to Handle Them.*

The methods used by Beausay to improve the breed are wondrously various and some even contain an element of risk—for Beausay. He once punched a Toronto Argonaut center squarely in the mouth in a dramatic attempt to suddenly raise his low hostility quotient so that the center would fire out at the opposing middle linebacker. The center might easily have preferred to fire out at Beausay. The psychologist also claims to have discovered the key to success for a punter on the New Orleans Saints—who scored low on hostility—when he found out that the man went partially berserk when pinched. An assistant coach was instructed to give the kicker's biceps a sharp, painful squeeze just as he was being sent into the game. The autosuggestion method via tape recorder, à la Bill Glass, is still a Beausay favorite to help an athlete overcome inconvenient Mr. Nice Guy tendencies. Another is a form chart he uses with athletes who score low in persistence, as determined in a test Beausay has devised himself. "It teaches a guy to set goals for himself," he says. "That's important because a guy without goals is usually too complacent to succeed."

Overly complacent subjects are asked to fill out four boxes on the chart. In the first box they record what goals they would like to reach during the coming season or year. In the second box they list the various methods they plan to use to achieve those goals. In the third box they sketch out a proposed timetable. The fourth is the evaluation box. When the season is over and the chips have fallen, they must look back and decide whether they made good on preseason predictions or just fell flat on their faces.

"If a person sticks to that process," claims Beausay, "there is almost nothing he can't do. The issue becomes not 'can I,' but 'will I.' I use it myself."

Beausay now is working on some ingenious training devices to improve visual efficiency, principally for quarterbacks. He is putting together a slide show that depicts what a quarterback might see as he peers downfield for a receiver. On each slide a receiver and a defender are pictured in a different one-on-one situation. As the slides flash briefly on the screen the quarterback must call out whether he would throw or not throw in each situation.

Sometimes distracting lights flash off and on to one side, or taped crowd noises roar in his ears. This is a device thought capable of demonstrating whether or not a quarterback is a risk taker or too cautious, as well as training his eye and his mind to act quickly in unison under game conditions.

Not long ago, after studying his research, Beausay forwarded to the brass at Indy a plan he thinks would do much to improve the track's accident record. "Right now the cars are too jammed up at the start and so those drivers who squeeze ahead to improve their starting positions cause accidents that can wreck the race," he says. "What this means is that drivers are being penalized for demonstrating the very quality—impulsiveness—that makes them successful.

"My suggestion is to imprint a highly visible grid pattern over the start-finish straight, pair the cars in rows of two instead of three, and station plenty of marshals along the track at the start who could, with the aid of the grid, easily determine who is trying to sneak up. A one-lap penalty would be assessed for each infraction. I think all drivers should also be given an eye test that simulates dynamic race conditions, not just some lettered chart, and that each driver should go through visual efficiency training. After all, things are happening out there at 200 miles per hour now. It's vital to have something better than just normal perception." So far the Indy brass has taken Beausay's suggestion calmly.

Beausay even sees potential rejuvenation for those passive Milquetoasts of sport, the runners. "It's surprising how low a person like Dave Wottle, the Olympic 800-meter champion, as well as other distance runners, score on such things as hostility and self-confidence," says Beausay. "Most runners seem to be passive, submissive followers. But once you know the profile you can work with them to develop more aggressiveness and stronger self-confidence. The research is still continuing and someday we are going to have runners with the race driver's psychic attitude. When that happens I predict that the world mile record will come down a full 10 seconds."

JULIAN B. ROTTER

Reading 11-3
Trust and Gullibility

"People are more hypocritical than ever."

"In dealing with strangers, one is better off being cautious until they provide evidence of trustworthiness."

"The judiciary is a place where we can all get unbiased treatment."

"By and large, people who repair appliances like washing machines and television sets are honest."

"Given the opportunity, most people would steal if there were no way of being caught."

Responses to propositions like these tell us something about how trusting people are, and a great deal more. Ultimately, combined with information about how trusting and nontrusting people are likely to act, they suggest answers to two fundamental questions: What are the costs of trusting too much, and what are the costs of trusting too little?

About 14 years ago, at the University of Connecticut, my students and I began a program of research dealing with interpersonal trust. We developed an Interpersonal Trust Scale consisting of 25 statements (like those above) with which people can express their opinions on a five-point scale ranging from "strongly agree" to "strongly disagree." The scale measures both trust in peers and people we come in contact with every day, and trust in powerful, distant figures and institutions, such as the press and the judiciary. In the studies to be described, those who score in the top 50 percent we call high trusters, while those whose scores fall in the lower half we call low trusters. (Scores can range from 25 to 125 points.)

Some psychologists, like Erik Erikson, see trust as a basic belief in the goodness of others and in the benign nature of the world. They believe that

---

the capacity for trust is largely determined early in life by the mother's care of the infant in the first few weeks of life. I think that the inclination to trust or distrust is probably learned over a longer period of time, and that it results from a person's cumulative experiences.

In our research we have defined trust as a "generalized expectancy" that the word, the promise, the verbal or written statement of another individual or group can be relied upon. From a social-learning point of view, people's expectancy for a particular kind of reward (or punishment) in a given situation will be determined not only by their past experience in a given situation but also, to varying degrees, by experiences that they generalize from other situations that they perceive as similar. As a result of such generalizations, they develop a relatively stable personality characteristic of trusting others (or not trusting them). But that does not mean that they will trust or distrust others equally. For example, a man may have a generalized distrust of women based on a series of bad experiences during adolescence. He may still trust his own mother, however, believing that she is an exception to the rule.

The Interpersonal Trust Scale (ITS) is designed to measure generalized expectancy for trust. Considerable evidence has now accumulated showing the scale to be successful in predicting a wide range of attitudes and behavior. The various experiments that have made use of the scale suggest that high trusters are no less intelligent or more gullible than others; however, they are happier, more likable—and more trustworthy.

HIGH TRUSTERS ARE MORE TRUSTWORTHY

One of the clearest advantages of trusting others, we have found, is that people who do so are themselves likely to be regarded as dependable. This conclusion was suggested by one of our earliest studies, in which we asked members of two sororities and two fraternities at the University of Connecticut—83 women and 73 men—to choose the one person among their peers who had the most trust in others and the one who had the least. We also asked the students to rate themselves on the trust scale.

We found that people who scored high on the ITS were perceived by others as being both trusting and trustworthy. By the same token, students who scored low in trust were chosen most often by their peers as lowest in trust of others and less trustworthy.

In a number of subsequent studies we have replicated the strong relationship between trust and trustworthiness. Indeed, these experiments demonstrate that low trusters are not only perceived as less trustworthy than others but also are actually more likely to lie and cheat.

Herbert Hamsher, a former student of mine, has used a stock market game in which students bet money on various imaginary stocks. The experimenter gives the students tips on which stocks are about to rise—both correct and false tips. They are allowed to pass on the tips to the other players, if they wish, by writing them notes. According to the rules, the student who makes the most money is the winner.

Hamsher's results indicate that high trusters are somewhat more likely than low trusters to believe the notes passed on to them, whether correct or false, but the difference is not statistically significant. However, high trusters are significantly less likely to pass on false notes and less likely to lie about whether they have received a correct tip from the experimenter. Apparently, high trusters found it difficult to lie even when the rules of the game explicitly permitted them to do so.

In the course of investigating sex guilt, Daniel Boroto, a psychologist at Florida State University, discovered in one experiment that low trusters are more likely than others to behave in an untrustworthy manner in certain situations—when they believe they will not be caught. After gathering a group of volunteer subjects in an office, Boroto left the room, supposedly to answer a telephone call. On his way out, he "accidentally" dropped on the floor a folder that the students could see contained pornographic pictures. He left a second folder, which the students had been led to believe contained personal information about them, on a desk. Then, through a peephole, Boroto observed which students looked at either of the folders and which did not.

Boroto had previously given the trust questionnaire to all the students; he found a substantial difference in trust between those who had invaded the experimenter's privacy by looking at the folders while he was gone and those who had not. Students who looked at neither of the folders had an average trust score of 80, while those who looked at either one or both of the folders had an average of 66.

In another University of Connecticut study, psychologist Thomas Wright and Afshan Kirmani, a research scientist, established an association between low trust and actual thefts. Wright and Kirmani asked 214 high school students to fill out an anonymous questionnaire that asked them how often they had shoplifted from local stores, along with the Interpersonal Trust Scale and other inventories measuring social attitudes. Overall, the girls in the study admitted to shoplifting less often than the boys did. But female low trusters reported significantly more shoplifting than did female high trusters. Low trusters of both sexes were also more likely to believe that people in their communities distrusted students.

The relationship between low trust and untrustworthy behavior seems readily explainable. If low trusters truly feel that other people cannot be trusted, then there is less moral pressure on them to tell the truth. They may also feel that lying, cheating, and similar behaviors are necessary under some circumstances for defensive reasons—"because everybody else is doing it."

Before some low-trusting readers get upset, I should emphasize that we are talking only about statistical averages. There are, in our data, many instances of low trusters behaving in an honest and moral fashion. In addition, most of our work has been done with college students; whether these findings can be generalized to other populations is not known. I also recognize that in exploring trust, we may fall into good-guy/bad-guy stereotypes. But that may be due to built-in value judgments our culture makes about "trusting" and "distrusting."

HIGH TRUSTERS ARE MORE LIKABLE

The evidence suggests that people who are high in trust are both better adjusted psychologically and more likable than others. We have measured adjustment with a semiprojective test called the Incomplete Sentences Blank. On this test, people complete sentences such as "I like _____" or "I worry about _____." Trained raters then analyze the completed sentences, looking for evidence of personality conflict and adjustment. For example, a response such as "I like to have a good time" would be considered adjusted, while "I like to be alone" would be labeled conflicted.

In six studies we have done with college students, we have found high trusters to be better adjusted and less conflicted than low trusters.

Dorothy Hochreich, a psychologist at the University of Connecticut, found that people generally like high trusters more than they like low trusters. Hochreich asked 365 students to read a sample of an ITS questionnaire that they were told had been filled out by a real person. Only the sex of the respondent was indicated on the forms (which had been filled out by the experimenter to portray a person who was either high or low in trust). The 365 student volunteers included both men and women, high and low trusters. After reading the questionnaire, they were asked to rate the anonymous respondent on various personality characteristics—including likability.

The results were somewhat surprising. While some psychologists have demonstrated that people tend to like others who are most like themselves in attitudes, opinions, and personality, Hochreich found that, in general, everyone likes a high truster—even low trusters. More specifically, the student volunteers were inclined to rate the high-trust respondent as being happier, more ethical, more attractive to the opposite sex, and more desirable as a close friend than the low-trust respondent.

HIGH TRUSTERS ARE NOT MORE GULLIBLE

Some people, obviously low trusters, would say that high trusters are just plain dumb. Although we have not had access to the IQ scores of students who have taken part in our studies, we have correlated their trust scores with their performances on the Scholastic Aptitude Test (SAT). In each of several studies, we found no relationship between the two sets of scores. That is, people who are high in trust do no better or worse on the SATs, on the average, than low trusters do. Thus, assuming that scholastic aptitude is one measure of intelligence, high trusters are no less intelligent than anyone else.

A gullible person might be described as one who is naive and easily fooled. To translate such a description into experimental criteria is not always easy. In a series of studies, we defined gullibility as a willingness to believe another person's statement even when there is some clear-cut evidence that the person should not be believed. To trust a stranger who has not lied to you before would not be gullible; to believe a politician who has lied to you many times before is.

In none of our studies did we find any evidence that high trusters behaved in a manner that we, somewhat arbitrarily perhaps, described as more gullible than that of low trusters. For example, we asked our fraternity and sorority volunteers to pick out the person among their peers whom they considered most gullible and the one they felt was least gullible. Members of both groups tended to cite the same people as highest or lowest in gullibility. But these choices were not related in a statistically significant way to those they selected as most and least trusting. Moreover, the Trust Scale scores of those selected as most gullible showed no common pattern.

Another former student, Jesse Geller, a psychologist who is now at Yale, tested the gullibility of 114 male students by displaying to them, one at a time, a piece of electrical apparatus that seemed to give him a powerful and sudden shock. After jumping up and down with pain, Geller would proceed to "fix" the machine and explain to the student that it was now functioning properly.

Prior to this scene, a confederate of Geller's had told one group of subjects that Geller had deceived *him* in an earlier phase of the research. Under the circumstances, the behavior of both high- and low-trusting students showed signs that they were suspicious of both Geller and the apparatus. In a postexperiment interview, high trusters who had seemed suspicious *admitted* that they were, in fact, suspicious of both Geller and the apparatus; low trusters, in contrast, denied feeling suspicious. In other words, the high trusters, having evidence of previous deception by the experimenter, were no more inclined than low trusters to accept Geller's statement that the faulty apparatus had been repaired. Indeed, they were more likely to be candid about their suspicions.

Finally, in another experiment, Ronald Lajoy of the Clackamas County Mental Health Center in Oregon studied whether people who are high in trust are less discriminating than those who are low in trust when weighing the advice of physicians and auto mechanics. Lajoy showed his subjects eight videotapes. In the first, a professional actor portrayed a physician giving a diagnosis to a patient and answering his questions in an arrogant manner. In the second, the same actor gave the same diagnosis and advice, but in a nonarrogant manner. And in the third and fourth tapes, the same actor, still described as a physician, gave advice on a zoning referendum—a topic presumably outside his area of expertise—in an arrogant and then a nonarrogant manner.

Different groups of student volunteers were shown the four tapes, as well as four similar ones with an auto mechanic in the role of expert advice-giver.

All the students had been tested earlier on the Trust Scale. In addition to rating the trustworthiness of the central character on the tapes, they were asked to assess his competence, his altruism, and whether or not they themselves would have taken the advice given by him on the tape.

In this study, high and low trusters did *not* differ overall in their ratings of the trustworthiness of physicians compared with that of auto mechanics. High trusters, however, gave significantly lower ratings on trustworthiness to the arrogant character than to the nonarrogant one. These results do not have direct bearing on the gullibility of high trusters, but they do suggest that high trusters are differentiating whom to trust from whom not to trust on the basis of specific cues. We have no evidence that they are better or worse at making such distinctions than low trusters, but the results indicate the two groups may use *different* cues in making decisions.

It might be added parenthetically that arrogance lowered the trustworthiness ratings of both physicians and auto mechanics, especially in the case of the physician not speaking in his area of expertise. Not surprisingly, most students indicated that they would be less likely to follow the advice of both physicians and auto mechanics who seem arrogant.

To summarize our findings on gullibility, I would say, most conservatively, that we have failed to establish that high trusters are any more likely than low trusters to be fooled or taken in by others. I am, of course, aware of the problems of trying to prove the null hypothesis; that is, a hypothesis that no significant difference exists. However, we have studied enough different situations, using a variety of measures of gullibility that have proven valid and reliable, to convince me that our conclusion is plausible.

HIGH TRUSTERS ARE DO-GOODERS

While high trusters may not be less intelligent or more gullible than low trusters, they may be more conventional and moralistic. To many people, these are hardly positive qualities.

In interviews with very high trusters, we have found that their code of ethics is often based more on conventional morality than on a personal set of moral principles. High trusters are frequently involved in traditional good works; they may be Eagle Scouts or belong to the college equivalent of a 4-H Club. On the other hand, the person with the lowest ITS score we've ever seen was the son of a Madison Avenue advertising executive.

In a study using the "prisoner's dilemma" game, Thomas Wright, a psychologist now at Catholic University, has found that high trusters are likely to be more punitive in certain situations than low trusters. The game is called prisoner's dilemma because it resembles plea bargaining by two prisoners charged with the same crime, who can adopt either a selfish or a joint bargaining strategy. What the players actually do is choose to cooperate or compete with each other about how much money they can win in the game. By cooperating, each player may win a modest amount; by competing—and taking higher risks—one player may either win a lot of money at the expense of the other, or both may lose a lot. The players are not allowed to talk in Wright's study; as in the stock market game, they pass notes back and forth through the experimenter—choosing amounts of money that indicate either a cooperative or a competitive strategy. The notes may be truthful or deceptive (and the experimenter may decide to change them to test a player's response, as Wright did).

When one partner deceived a high truster in the exchange of notes in Wright's experiment, the high truster would "punish" the partner by becoming uncooperative. Only when the high truster received an apology from the partner would he or she be more likely than the low truster to play cooperatively. Of course, some might interpret the high truster's willingness to cooperate after an apology as gullibility. But I prefer to regard it as a moral belief that people should be given a second chance.

Before attempting to draw some conclusions from these studies, I should emphasize that none deal with deprived populations or with those who are exposed to extreme prejudice. We simply do not know whether or not our findings would hold up in such populations. Also, we have not systematically considered the influence of different degrees of risk on people's trust in others. Several of the studies reported here involve only minor losses or discomforts, such as the prisoner's dilemma game, the stock market game, and the apparatus that may or may not deliver a strong shock.

Other experiments do involve moderate risk—for example, the investigations of cheating and shoplifting. However, the data are insufficient to generalize our results easily to activities that involve very high risk, such as making large investments in a speculative venture, participating in a bank robbery, or promoting international cooperation.

Judging from the situations we have studied, however, it seems safe to conclude that high trusters can read cues as well as or as poorly as low trusters. They differ, however, in their willingness to trust a stranger when there is no clear-cut data. The high truster says, "I will trust him until I have clear evidence that he can't be trusted." The low truster says, "I will not trust him until there is clear evidence that he can be trusted."

We can make a strong statement about the consequences to society of people's being more trusting. People who trust more are less likely to lie and possibly less likely to cheat or steal. They are more likely to give others a second chance and to respect the rights of others. The personal consequences for high trusters also seem beneficial. High trusters are less likely to be unhappy, conflicted, or maladjusted, are liked more and sought out more often as friends, by both low-trusting and high-trusting people.

High trusters are no less capable of determining who should be trusted and who should not be trusted, although in novel situations the high truster may be more likely to trust others than the low truster. It may be true that high trusters are fooled more often by crooks, but low trusters are probably fooled just as often by distrusting honest people; they thereby forfeit the benefits that trusting others might bring. As Samuel Johnson wrote: "It's happier to be sometimes cheated than not to trust."

Finally, what does this mean for us? While we cannot control all the forces at work in society, within our own smaller circles of influence, we can model and encourage more trust. The consequences can be beneficial; the risks do not seem too great; and a younger generation may be a little more ready for a better world—just in case there is one coming.

Conflict Resolution

In the earlier sections of this book, we focused on the fundamentals of the negotiation process: planning and setting objectives, understanding the fundamental strategic approaches to negotiation, and procedures for developing tactics. We also explored the underlying components and processes of negotiation that lead to particular outcomes—that is, persuasion processes, the use of power, the personality of the negotiator, and so on. These all help in assessing what type of negotiation situation we face, what resources we have to draw upon, how to set objectives and establish a strategy—all things we do to prepare for negotiation.

At the center of any negotiation is conflict. The parties do not agree—and the negotiation that occurs is an effort to resolve that conflict. Even in integrative bargaining, while conflict may be transformed into a more malleable and muted form, it is still there. Both parties want to actively contribute to the joint outcome—and some may want to contribute "more than their 'fair' share." Both parties want to benefit—but can they benefit equally? Tensions become heightened, positions become polarized, parties become deeply committed to their own point of view and no longer trust their opponent. If the parties do not recognize these dynamics as they are occurring, conflicts can grow and threaten to destroy the negotiated agreement they are seeking.

In this section, we examine conflict and the tensions and dynamics that it engenders. The articles here examine various techniques either for resolving disputes more amicably, or for allowing third parties to become involved in the resolution of the dispute.

The first article, "A Businesslike Way to Resolve Legal Disputes" by Stephen Solomon, examines the recent tendancy for executives to solve their disputes by negotiation rather than by lawsuits. Many business disputes have traditionally been handled by turning the conflict over to the corporate legal department or law firm, and allowing the attorneys from both firms to either take the dispute to court, or to eventually arrange a settlement. This procedure has resulted in frequent and lengthy delays in resolving the problems, and skyrocketing legal fees for both sides. In the past, these costs were endured because it was assumed that the litigation route was likely to lead to the best settlement (or, perhaps, even to victory over the other). Hard experience, however, had led businesspeople to recognize that victories are few and far between, that the legal costs (time and money) are enormous, and that the gain may not be worth the cost. As a result, businesspeople are turning more and more to expert negotiators to resolve disputes more promptly out of court.

The second article, "For the People: Prosecutor Rudgers Speeds Justice along in Akron Courts," by Philip Revzin, gives a brief but interesting portrait of the work of a small county prosecutor, James Rudgers, in Akron, Ohio. As the earlier article shows businesspeople turning away from the civil court system to resolve disputes quickly and efficiently, Revzin points to another recent trend in the criminal justice system: the role of plea bargaining in resolving criminal cases before they go to trial. The job of James Rudgers (and many other prosecuting attorneys) is to arrive at an agreement between prosecution and defense attorneys on the defendant's plea. Agreement on this plea, and the defendant's willingness to plead guilty to it, saves the courts and the defendant considerable time and money. Understanding the criminal justice system, and being able to persuade defendants and their attorneys to accept reasonable pleas, is an integral part of Mr. Rudgers' effectiveness as a negotiator and dispute resolver.

The last two articles in this section focus on the specific role of third parties in resolving disputes. The first article, "Results of Final Offer Arbitration of Bargaining Disputes" by Paul Staudohar, examines the process of final offer arbitration. An arbitrator is a neutral third party who resolves a dispute by recommending or imposing a specific settlement on the conflicting parties. Arguments and evidence are presented to the arbitrator, and once this evidence is considered and evaluated, the arbitrator proposes or imposes a specific settlement.

Arbitration has been an extremely popular form of dispute resolution, particularly in labor disputes and in ruling on labor grievances. In the past, conflicting parties, knowing that an arbitrator would be involved, often made outrageous demands and charges to the arbitrator in the hopes of persuading him to rule more in their favor. Over time, the demands and counterdemands of conflicting parties have become more and more extreme; as a result, the arbitrator has been forced to forge a compromise solution which may favor neither side, or may actually punish the party who was making less extreme demands. Final offer arbitration has been proposed as a way to curtail this destructive trend.

Final offer arbitration differs from conventional arbitration in that each side must present to the arbitrator its last best offer or position. Rather than developing a compromise solution from the parties' two positions, the arbitrator *picks* one side's solution to be the binding agreement between the two sides. This procedure thus encourages the negotiators to be more reasoned and considered in their development of a final offer, since they know that their own reasonableness, rather than extremeness, may lead to victory for their own side. Staudohar evaluates the final offer arbitration process and its impact on a variety of labor settlements.

In the next article, "The Role of the Mediator," Thomas Colosi describes the strategy and tactics that mediators use to help bring the parties to agreement. (This selection was originally a continuation of the "core model" article presented in the "Social Context of Negotiation," Section Nine of this volume.) Colosi suggests that mediators must follow several key steps in order to bring negotiating parties together. First, mediators must win the negotiators' trust through neutrality, listening, and supportiveness. Second, mediators must then transfer that trust from themselves to the negotiating process, such that the parties believe that productive negotiations can solve the problem. Finally, the mediator must transfer the trust a second time, from the negotiation process to helping the parties learn to trust one another. Colosi gives several examples of the ways that effective mediators work to execute this process.

Colosi also briefly discusses how negotiation and mediation can be an effective solution to problems that traditionally were worked out in the courts. In the past, the involvement of lawyers and the courts frequently lead to solutions that neither side found acceptable, as well as heavy legal fees that drained what little financial resources were available. Divorce cases, environmental disputes, and even minor civil and criminal cases are areas in which this trend is prevalent, and which have been significantly helped by substituting the negotiation-mediation process. While the parties in these situations are not experienced negotiators, and while their hostility levels are usually very high, research has shown that mediation can be a significantly cheaper, quicker, and more satisfactory resolution process for all concerned.

STEPHEN SOLOMON

Reading 12–1
A Businesslike Way
to Resolve Legal Disputes

In his most famous soliloquy, delivered at the royal castle of Elsinore, Hamlet complained of ''the law's delay.'' Many American businessmen have more reason for complaint than the Prince of Denmark had—it's doubtful, after all, that he ever had to sit for two days giving a sworn deposition. Litigation, with its huge and evergrowing lawyer bills and the toll it takes on executive time, has become a serious management problem for American business. Often the most effective way to avoid or lighten these burdens, some executives are finding out, is to use their own negotiating abilities to resolve the substantive issues in lawsuits. This approach can sometimes yield sensible agreements based on practical business considerations rather than legal technicalities.

Business executives and lawyers tend to have different ways of looking at and dealing with disputes. Executives, being problem solvers, are inclined to weigh the practical realities of the situation with an eye to working out a resolution. But lawyers are gladiators rather than conciliators, and their adversary stance is fundamentally at odds with the idea of settling lawsuits by commercial give-and-take. Lawyers, indeed, can become an obstacle to settlement, especially during the pretrial discovery phase of the suit, when they often skirmish over what documents and depositions are relevant as potential evidence. Moreover, the by-the-clock fee system, $100 per hour or more for a partner's time, rewards the protracted jousting that characterizes large-scale litigation.

Lawyers do settle most suits before they get to trial, but usually not until both sides have wearied of the escalating costs and the disruptive effects on operations. More cases could probably be settled at an earlier stage if lawyers brought their business clients to a conference to hear a presentation of the arguments in the case. Having assessed the strengths and weaknesses that both sides would bring to a trial, executives would have a basis for pursuing negotiation and settlement. Especially in disputes that involve corporate policy and operations, it is better for businessmen to reach a settlement they can live with than to play roulette with a judge and jury.

EVERY MONTH ANOTHER BLANK CHECK

The American Bar Association plans to test the businessman-to-businessman avenue of settlement this spring, in an experiment involving perhaps a score of federal and state courts. If successful, this mode of arriving at settlements would cut away much of the cost, delay, and disruption that accompany corporate litigation. Nearly a quarter of the cases pending trial in federal district courts have been on the docket for two years or more, and the backlog in state courts is often worse. And every month of litigation represents another blank check for legal assistance; perhaps in no other area of business is so much money spent with so few controls or so little attention to cost-effectiveness. The cost of a deposition can reach $5,000 a day, and pretrial discovery in litigation of moderate scale can run to $500,000 or more.

All this is forcing some legal disputes into alternative channels, such as arbitration. The number of commerical cases handled by the American Arbitration Association has doubled since 1970, despite arbitration's reputation among many lawyers as a compromise forum that cuts the baby in two when parentage is in dispute. But some businessmen, attracted by the advantage of personally helping to mold a settlement to their company's interests, have turned away from judges and arbitrators to negotiate the issues themselves.

The most innovative approach has been the use in a major patent- infringement case of what lawyers involved in the matter called a "mini- trial." It consisted of a two-day presentation of arguments by both sides in a nonbinding forum outside the legal system. The case shared the characteristics of much large-scale commercial litigation: costliness, complexity, and issues whose resolution seemed likely to have a substantial impact on how the companies operated in the future.

The lawsuit began early in 1974, when Telecredit, Inc., a Los Angeles-based company providing computerized check and credit-card authorization services, claimed that TRW had infringed several of its patents. Telecredit asked for an injunction against future infringement and for treble damages, which the company later put at $6 million. TRW denied the infringement charges and counterclaimed that the patents were invalid and unenforceable.

When lawyers for the two sides got going on their pretrial discovery work, more than 100,000 documents changed hands. Understandably, companies are not always cheerful about handing over records. Eric D. Green, who was one of the lawyers for TRW, recalls what happened when that company requested documents from IBM, hoping to uncover evidence backing its claim that Telecredit's patents were invalid. "They told us the files were in palletized boxes, bound with metal bands, and unmarked. And they said the warehouse was infested with black-widow spiders."

After the passage of three years, many heated battles between lawyers, and the expenditure of about half a million dollars in legal fees by each side, there was still no settlement in sight. Finally, Ronald A. Katz, Telecredit's patent-licensing administrator and a co-founder of the company, suggested a form of binding arbitration as an alternative way to settle the lawsuit. When TRW refused, the parties discussed a nonbinding forum. That clicked with Ronald L. Olson, the principal outside counsel for TRW. Olson, a member of the Los Angeles firm of Munger, Tolles & Rickershauser, had been serving as chairman of the American Bar Association's committee on litigation management and economics, which was searching for more efficient ways of resolving lawsuits. This case seemed a good place to begin.

In subsequent meetings, the parties worked out the concept of a mini-trial: six weeks of expedited discovery, the exchange of briefs, and then a two-day session during which top management would hear each side present its case on the issues. The proceedings would be moderated by a neutral party, who turned out to be James F. Davis, a leading patent attorney and formerly a trial judge on the U.S. Court of Claims. If the executives were unable to reach a settlement after the mini-trial, Davis was to issue a nonbinding opinion. Then the executives would meet again.

A MILLION LESS FOR THE LAWYERS

The mini-trial took place in a Los Angeles hotel in July, 1977. Among the more than two dozen people present were two men who had authority to settle the lawsuit: Lee A. Ault III, Telecredit's president and chief executive, and Richard A. Campbell, A TRW vice president (since promoted to executive vice president). In the agreed-upon format, one side presented its case, followed by a rebuttal, then a reply, and finally questions from the executives. Then the other side put on its case.

When the mini-trial was over, Katz and Campbell met privately. Within half an hour, they had the rough beginnings of a settlement that Ault and Campbell negotiated during the following 11 weeks. Ault agreed to resubmit the patents for review by the U.S. Patent Office. If the Patent Office reissued them, TRW would take licenses at a reduced fee. Both executives were satisfied with the results—and relieved that between them they had saved at least a million dollars in legal fees. Says Campbell: "We had been told the case could have gone on for another few years and ended in a three-week trial, and I was sitting there putting a dollar figure on that. When we both saw the total case, the nature of a settlement became obvious."

The mini-trial approach can be structured to fit other types of controversies, and it can be used much earlier in the course of a dispute. It requires only that counsel frame the issues after a limited amount of discovery. On the other hand, this approach is not meant for cases that present novel questions of law, requiring a judge to establish a new precedent; nor would it be likely to work in some of the largest cases where even trial-court opinions are merely preliminary to the real battleground, the appeals courts.

THE DRINKS WERE ON THE JUDGE

Face-to-face negotiations between executives have recently led to settlements in several of the multimillion-dollar Westinghouse Electric Corp. uranium cases. Top managers of Westinghouse, including the chairman and chief executive, Robert E. Kirby, have been meeting with executives of various utility companies to settle what may be the largest private civil litigation in U.S. history—Westinghouse's potential liability amounts to more than $2 billion. It was primarily to give Kirby more time to participate in settlement discussions that the Westinghouse directors created the new position of vice chairman and chief operating officer last June.

The dispute began in September 1975, when Westinghouse informed 27 utility customers that it would not deliver about 70 million pounds of uranium it had contracted to provide at an average price of $11 a pound. The price of a pound of uranium had jumped to $25 (it has since reached $43), and Westinghouse claimed it was excused from performance under the commercial-impracticability clause of the Uniform Commerical Code. The utilities sued.

Since the cases involved the same set of facts, 10 of them were consolidated, at the request of Westinghouse, under U.S. District Court Judge Robert R. Merhige Jr., in Richmond, Virginia. Judge Merhige did some imaginative things to spur out-of-court settlements. On three consecutive evenings in September 1976, he hosted cocktail parties on the veranda of his handsome Georgian house in Richmond, providing the lawyers and executives a chance to talk informally over mint juleps. Then he appointed a special master to oversee the settlement process.

Executives were better suited than the court to resolve the disputes. If the court forced Westinghouse to pay cash damages, the financial drain would not only cripple Westinghouse but also jeopardize completion of the nuclear-power plants it was building for the utilities. The goal of the management negotiators was to devise a *business* solution to the lawsuits—one that the court, limited to traditional contract remedies, was not able to produce.

Four of the cases were resolved by the end of 1978. In formulas that varied with each agreement, Westinghouse settled the claims by providing cash, equipment and services for the nuclear plants, interest in uranium-mining operations, mining technology, and so forth. The inclusion of non-cash payments reduced the burden on Westinghouse, since the cost of providing the goods and services was less than their market value.

Typical of these settlements was the one between Westinghouse and

Texas Utilities Services, Inc. (TUSI), a service company for three Texas utilities. The two companies had been deadlocked on the contents of a shopping list of Westinghouse equipment and services that might be included in an agreement. TUSI's president, Perry Brittain, who was directing the utility's negotiations, had recently put his company into the uranium-mining business, and Westinghouse offered uranium property rights in Wyoming as part of the settlement. But Brittain was unsure about their value. With the talks in the eleventh hour, Brittain dispatched a geologist to check drill records and ore estimates and to call with an appraisal that same night. The report was bullish. After Westinghouse added cash and uranium-mining technology to the deal, Brittain agreed.

AN INGENIOUS CORNERSTONE

The other settlements—with Alabama Power Co., Houston Lighting & Power Co. and three utilities headed by Dusquesne Light Co.—were also tailored to fit each plaintiff's particular needs. In the *Alabama Power* case, for example, a major disagreement arose from the fact that after the Westinghouse default, the utility bought uranium on the market for delivery before it was actually needed. The talks deadlocked when Westinghouse refused to pay Alabama Power's costs of carrying this uranium in inventory. But Westinghouse finally agreed to purchase the uranium and then sell back the same amount of fuel, at the same price, a few years later, when the utility needed it. Alabama Power would be rid of idle and expensive inventory, and Westinghouse would receive uranium it needed anyway to fulfill other contracts. That ingenious solution became the cornerstone of the settlement.

Judge Merhige has held Westinghouse liable for breach of the uranium contracts, but he has also urged other utilities involved in the Richmond cases to reach out-of-court agreements. Most of them may eventually come to share the view expressed by George W. Oprea Jr., executive vice president of Houston Lighting & Power Co. and the principal negotiator of the utility's settlement with Westinghouse. Says Oprea: "I'm not a believer in letting lawyers solve business problems."

PHILIP REVZIN

Reading 12–2
For the People: Prosecutor Rudgers Speeds Justice along in Busy Akron Courts

AKRON, Ohio—James Rudgers stands at the prosecutor's table in the nearly deserted courtroom, rapidly leafing through papers atop a pile of manila folders. His voice has a distant, automatic quality: "Your honor, the state understands that the defendant" (still riffling through papers) "wishes to waive his constitutional and statutory rights to a trial and to plead guilty to the charge of breaking and entering. . . ." It is almost as if by rote.

Judge Daniel B. Quillen turns to the defendant, one Kevin Finch, and asks him if this is his plea and if he is indeed guilty of breaking into the grocery store. Mr. Finch admits his guilt, and the judge gives him 2 to 10 years in prison.

For Mr. Finch and the defendants like him who daily crowd the calendars of the nation's courts, this appearance in the musty, echoing courtroom has been a deeply haunting experience. But for Mr. Rudgers, an assistant prosecutor for Summit County (which includes metropolitan Akron), this case is just one out of 12 he will be handling during this typical Wednesday morning in county court.

For the next two hours he will be working his way through that pile of folders, calling cases for sentencing, meeting with defense attorneys in the judge's chambers to negotiate pleas, and making recommendations for sentencing of the guilty. A parade of often well-paid lawyers will file in and out of the courtroom with their clients. But Mr. Rudgers, burdened with work and modestly paid, will handle each case for the state.

The scene is repeated daily in hundreds of metropolitan courtrooms across the country as local prosecutors (or district attorneys) face the almost overwhelming task of representing the state's side in the endless stream of criminal cases. How well these prosecutors do their jobs affects the lives of all who come into contact with the law and sets the standard for the quality of justice in much of America today.

"The prosecutor is the one smack in the middle of the system," says Patrick Healy, executive director of the National District Attorneys Association in Chicago. "He's the most central pivot point in the criminal justice system because he sets the tone of law enforcement for a community. How he handles his cases affects the public defender system, the prisons, everything."

In a perfectly functioning system, a prosecutor's duties would mesh smoothly with those of the police, the judge, the defense counsel and the jury in determining guilt or innocence. The prosecutor's role is to assess the evidence, to decide who should be prosecuted for a crime and then to compile and forcefully present the evidence at a trial. But in practice, because of heavy case loads and limited budgets, the system rarely works that way.

"ASSEMBLY LINE" JUSTICE

"The prosecutor has complete control over the criminal justice system because he has the ability to dispose of cases as he sees fit," says Lewis R. Katz, professor of law at Case Western Reserve University in Cleveland. But, he adds, "at the same time he has the greatest burden because the sheer number of cases makes his ability to prepare each one very limited."

In fact, because of an ever-rising crime rate, prosecutors' offices in most urban areas, like Akron, have become little more than processing centers where cases are shuffled along with one eye on justice and the other on court-docket backlogs and overcrowded prisons. Such is not the case in most rural areas, where, for the most part, the prosecutor still has time to prepare carefully the infrequent felony cases that come his way, to advise local government agencies on legal matters and often to maintain a sizable private law practice on the side.

"Urban justice just bumps along. It's an assembly line," says Mr. Healy of the district attorneys association. "Much of the time the prosecutor's main concern is how he can get through the day without drowning in his cases. In a small town the press of business is so much less that people don't feel abandoned. They think they have a better chance of the prosecutor listening to their problems and helping them."

Jim Rudgers's daily routine is representative of that of other urban prosecutors. Summit County embraces Akron and its suburban communities and is an altogether typical U.S. urban area. Its 550,000 residents are predominantly working-class people, mostly employed in the rubber and supporting industries. More than 12 percent are black.

SHUNTING CASES ASIDE

Last year, the Summit County prosecutor's office handled about 1,600 new felony cases. Each of seven assistant prosecutors in the criminal division was responsible for about 230 felony cases, from arrest to final disposition. Each assistant also handles appeals or requests for adjustments of sentence. In addition, two senior prosecutors assist on more complex cases. (In Summit County, as in other urban counties, the city or suburban town, rather than the county, handles misdemeanors, such as traffic offenses, within its borders. The county prosecutor's office has a separate staff for civil matters.)

This heavy case load keeps Mr. Rudgers and his colleagues constantly on the go and leaves little time for work on each individual case. "You try to give each case the time it requires, but you always find yourself devoting more time to cases that seem more important, and you have to shunt some of the seemingly minor cases aside," he says.

A typical workweek spent with Mr. Rudgers is centered on Wednesday morning, his "call day," when a batch of pending cases is called into his assigned courtroom. The cases all involve sentencing or pretrial hearings, the latter usually being a matter of negotiating pleas. If a guilty plea can't be negotiated between the prosecution and the defense, a trial date is set.

Just about all of the felony cases in Summit County, as in other county courts across the United States, don't go to trial but are resolved with guilty pleas or dismissals. Last year only 84 cases out of 1,600, or about 5 percent of the total, came to trial (which is close to the national average). Of these 84 trials, 71 resulted in convictions, seven in acquittals and six in mistrials.

One reason there aren't more trials is the unhappy fact that the great majority of crimes go unsolved. Suspects who are arrested often have the weight of evidence against them. Defense lawyers, rather than risk a stiff sentence at a trial, often prefer to negotiate a guilty plea on a reduced charge with the guarantee of a lesser sentence.

In this, both prosecutors and judges are willing partners because of their desire to cut down on time-consuming and expensive trials. Prosecutors also take the view that if they are convinced of a defendant's guilt, but their case isn't 100 percent airtight, it is better to offer the deal of a guilty plea on a reduced charge rather than see the accused acquitted at a trial.

On this particular Wednesday morning, Mr. Rudgers arrives at his sparsely furnished office on the seventh floor of the City-County Building at 8 A.M. Over coffee he refreshes his memory of the cases he will be presenting in court at 9.

In the first case, Charles Smith is accused of robbing a man after his wife had solicited him and lured him to her home (Mrs. Smith is on probation after pleading guilty to the offense). Mr. Smith has already admitted his guilt to the police. But before his lawyer, Charles Grisi, will agree to recording the guilty plea, a sentence has to be negotiated. Mr. Rudgers and Mr. Grisi meet in Judge Quillen's chambers to discuss the sentence.

Mr. Rudgers scans a report prepared by the probation department and tells Mr. Grisi, "I'll bet they pulled this thing several times at least before they got caught. If they had been any good at it, they could have gotten away with it for a long while."

Mr. Grisi agrees. But, he says, "they were just amateurs." Amateurs or not, Mr. Rudgers says, he will have to recommend the state penitentiary for Mr. Smith. But since the crime was not violent, he has no objection to a minimum sentence of six months.

Mr. Grisi goes into the courtroom to consult with his handcuffed client. There is no objection, so Mr. Rudgers, Mr. Grisi and Judge Quillen return to the courtroom to put the guilty plea and the sentence on the official court record. Mr. Smith is led away by sheriff's deputies.

PARADE OF CRIME

Throughout the morning the parade of crime passes through the court. Ronald Lewis Jr. pleads guilty to receiving a stolen stereo system, breaking church windows, and resisting arrest. Franklin Deem pleads guilty to armed robbery of a delicatessen and is sentenced to serve 4 to 25 years in prison. William Cain, charged with stealing merchandise from a warehouse where he had been employed as a security guard, won't accept Mr. Rudger's offer of a plea bargain: a guilty plea in return for probable probation. So a trial date is set.

To Mr. Rudgers and most other prosecutors, this plea bargaining is crucial to keeping the wheels of justice turning. "If more money was allotted by counties for more prosecutors and investigators, then maybe we could prosecute more cases all the way," he says.

The only "evil" that Mr. Rudgers sees in plea bargaining is that "it tends to give a prosecutor too much power." But, he says, "if he keeps asking himself, am I doing this in the best interest of the people I'm supposed to be serving, and if he can answer yes, then he won't be abusing his power."

Because of plea bargaining, Mr. Rudgers was involved in only 17 trials last year (he expects no more than that number this year). But the trial procedure can result in great frustration for a prosecutor. Often he will go to great lengths to prepare the state's case, only to have the defendant suddenly agree to plead guilty to a lesser charge. "One of my colleagues calls the feeling, the post-plead-'em blues," says Mr. Rudgers.

JUST WORDS ON PAPER

If it all seems a bit cut and dried and impersonal, that's because it is. Big-city prosecutors and defense attorneys (often court-appointed) rarely have any personal knowledge of defendants. Mr. Rudgers says he tries to fight the habit of looking at defendants and their crimes as only words on paper. But with so many cases to handle, that is often unavoidable. "I try to base sentencing and plea recommendations on whether the guy has a job he could return to, and whether he is a violent, confirmed criminal who has chosen crime as a way of life, he says. "I'm much more sympathetic to people who have simply committed a crime but haven't made crime their occupation."

For his efforts, the 30-year-old Mr. Rudgers, who has been an assistant prosecutor since graduating from the University of Akron law school two years ago, is paid $18,000 a year. This is far below the income of most private lawyers, and Mr. Rudgers concedes that he stays on "only because I love the job." His boss, Summit County prosecutor Stephan Gabalac, says that "Jim could easily make double what he gets here if he worked at a private firm."

Because of the low salaries, the high turnover of lawyers is a perennial problem in prosecutors' offices. "Assistants may stay two or three years on the average, certainly less than five years in most cases," says Michael Foley, executive director of the Ohio Prosecuting Attorneys Association.

There was a time, says Mr. Foley, when the political power and prestige of working in the prosecutor's office outweighed the burden of low pay. Now, he says, the job has become too complicated and strenuous to attract any but the most dedicated. "It might still give you a leg up to a judgeship. But that's about it," he says.

EXCITEMENT IS RARE

Nor can it be said that there is a great deal of excitement in the assistant prosecutor's job. Most of the cases he handles are striking only in their sameness. Headline-catching murders or armed robberies are usually handled by the chief prosecutor, an elected official who must keep publicity value in mind for the next election. Other highly publicized crimes, such as bank robbery and kidnapping, fall under the jurisdiction of federal courts and are handled by federal prosecutors.

Mr. Rudger's routine duties can be grueling. On alternate Wednesday afternoons he presents a fresh batch of cases (from police departments and the county sheriff) to the sitting county grand jury. If the jurors return an indictment, the case goes into Mr. Rudgers's case load.

Mondays (that aren't occupied with trials) and Tuesdays are spent reviewing and investigating cases for Wednesdays. Thursdays and Fridays are spent on paperwork and preparations for trials and the following week's "call day." He is also frequently summoned late at night to help police at the scene of a crime. Recently he dashed to a murder scene at 10:30 at night to interview possible witnesses and to direct the police photographer and the gathering of evidence. He didn't get home until 5:30 A.M. Luckily, he says, "my wife Lois is very understanding about my schedule."

Despite the constant pressures of the system, Mr. Rudgers remains fairly optimistic about the quality of justice he sees around him. He says he had qualms about joining the prosecutor's office because he had worked for the Urban League in Akron, setting up a job-finding program, before going to law school. "I didn't think prosecutors or law enforcement officials in general were sensitive to the problems of poor people and minorities," he says. "I learned differently once I got into it."

The system of justice, he says, boils down to this: "If a guy is innocent, you can dismiss the case a million different ways. If he is guilty, he deserves to be punished."

PAUL D. STAUDOHAR

Reading 12–3
Results of Final-Offer Arbitration
of Bargaining Disputes

The past few years have seen an increase in the use of innovative procedures for resolving collective bargaining disputes. Experiments have sprung up in both the private and public sectors that seek to provide an alternative to pressure tactics. A procedure that appears to have particular merit is final-offer arbitration of negotiation impasses. Under this arrangement labor and management make a final offer on issues in dispute, and an arbitrator is empowered to select one of the offers as binding on the parties. The purpose of this article is to examine the final-offer arbitration model and experience with its use.

Before proceeding, it is useful to distinguish between two types of labor disputes, those over interests and rights. Interest disputes arise over determination of future terms and conditions of employment, referring to situations in which the parties are seeking to negotiate either an initial or renewed collective bargaining agreement. Rights disputes are those stemming from interpretation or application of an already existing contract, and these are commonly handled through a grievance procedure spelled out in the contract. Arbitration, a mechanism for submitting disputes to an outside third party for final binding decision, can be used for either type of dispute. Where the arbitration is required by law for resolution of interests disputes, it is known as compulsory arbitration.

FINAL-OFFER MODEL

The final-offer method of arbitration may be used in interests disputes as an alternative to the traditional way of arbitrating, whether voluntary or compulsory. There is a tendency in traditional arbitration for the parties to put forth exaggerated claims to the arbitrator because of a suspicion—not without justification—that the arbitrator will split the difference. Unless the participants take extreme positions, the compromise fashioned by the arbitrator is likely to disfavor the more candid or realistic side. Negotiations prior to intended arbitration therefore may be only a device to set the stage for arbitration, without either party seriously interested in compromise or agreement at this juncture. What distinguishes the "either-or" arrangement is that if one side gets too far out of line the arbitrator is apt to choose the other's offer. By trying to come up with a figure likely to be chosen by the arbitrator the parties often move closer together in their positions, the result of which may be total compromise and agreement. The availability of final-offer arbitration is thus thought to provide a catalyst for settlement.

Two ways to apply the final-offer approach are (1) ruling on an entire package proposal, known as the "selector method," and (2) choosing either party's offer on each issue in dispute. Ruling issue by issue avoids the potential problem, raised by the selector method, of mixing undesirable demands into a package that overall is appropriate to select. However, deciding on individual issues may encourage submission of extraneous matters to the arbitrator on the theory of "nothing ventured, nothing gained."[1]

Efficacy of final-offer arbitration is inversely related to the number of issues in dispute and, of course, it is not a perfect substitute for a negotiated settlement. A balance among possible outcomes on individual issues and an integrated whole results from a negotiated agreement. The parties best know their interests and problems and negotiation is the best way to compromise them with a reasonable degree of acceptability to both sides. While arbitrators can fashion balance by trading off items among the offers on individual issues, the interissue balance and total outcome have a greater chance of being inappropriate the larger the number of issues involved. At the same time, however, this risk of impropriety is a factor inducing voluntary agreement. And, when the parties simply cannot come to agreement, even a less-than-perfect substitute is often preferable to the onus of a strike.

SOME APPLICATIONS AND EXPERIENCE

Final-offer arbitration was proposed for inclusion in national economic policy in 1970 when the Nixon administration introduced a bill to modify the emergency strike provisions of the Taft-Hartley Act as applied to transportation industries (including railroads, airlines, maritime, longshore, and trucking).[2] Three options were set forth for dealing with strikes that imperil the

---

[1] J. R. Grodin, "Either-Or Arbitration for Public Employee Disputes," *Industrial Relations*, May 1972, p. 264.

[2] B. Aaron, "National Emergency Disputes: Some Current Proposals." Proceedings of the 1971 Annual Spring Meeting, Industrial Relations Research Association, in *Labor Law Journal*, August 1971, pp. 465–474.

public health or safety, one of which was to require each party to submit two final offers on all issues in a proposed collective bargaining agreement. One of the four offers would then be chosen by a neutral group. The bill, opposed by organized labor, was dropped prior to the 1972 election, but has since been restudied in committee and may be reintroduced.

The final-offer method as a substitute for the strike appears on its way to extensive development in the public sector. This gives emphasis to Aaron's observation that:

> Whether it is possible to devise a collective bargaining system that denies the right of employees to strike but provides acceptable alternatives is almost certainly going to be decided in the government employment sector, not the private sector. What this means is that, contrary to the common assumption, public employment may provide the model for private employment, rather than the reverse.[3]

In 1971, Eugene, Oregon was the first known U.S. city to try final-offer arbitration for resolution of negotiation impasses. More recently, Minnesota (1973) and Iowa (1974) have adopted it for public employees, and Wisconsin (1972), Michigan (1972), and Massachusetts (1973) for police and firefighters as a strike alternative. These laws all spell out criteria—involving such issues as comparability, cost of living, and ability to pay—to guide the arbitrator's decision. Although experience under these laws is limited, results are generally favorable.

Under the Wisconsin law disputes are subject to mediation before arbitration can take place, and the Wisconsin Employment Relations Commission will order arbitration only if it finds that a bona fide impasse exists. This process tends to screen cases in which the parties are not sincerely attempting to resolve their differences through negotiation. Early results with making awards on a total package basis indicate that there has not been a narcotic effect on negotiations. In 1973 arbitration awards were issued in only 9 percent of the 173 negotiations.[4] This is in accord with experience in Eugene, where in the first six sets of negotiations the parties' incentive to negotiate their own agreements was found to be preserved.[5]

The Michigan final-offer statute provides for adopting the final offer as to each economic issue in dispute. Limited results indicate that the final-offer feature had not moved the parties any closer together in bargaining than was the case with traditional arbitration procedures.[6]

An interesting case occurred in Indianapolis in 1972 when, in the absence

---

[3] B. Aaron, "How Other Nations Deal with Emergency Disputes," *Monthly Labor Review,* May 1972, p. 41.

[4] J. L. Stern, "Final Offer Arbitration—Initial Experience in Wisconsin," *Monthly Labor Review,* September 1974, p. 40.

[5] G. Long and P. Feuille, "Final Offer Arbitration: 'Sudden Death' in Eugene," *Industrial and Labor Relations Review,* January 1974, pp. 186–203.

[6] C. M. Rehmus, "Is a 'Final Offer' Ever Final?" *Monthly Labor Review,* September 1974, p. 43.

of a law, the city and union agreed to arbitrate disputed issues. The arbitrators were instructed to choose the "most reasonable" package offer. They found the union's proposal on the wage issue more reasonable, but chose instead the city's overall package because the union's request for family insurance and extra sick leave made its package offer unreasonable.[7] The case illustrates how requiring choice of an entire package can cause problems through undesirable results being mixed in with an overall outcome that is relatively more favorable.

BASEBALL RESULTS

One of the most innovative experiments with final-offer arbitration is its use by major league baseball for resolving salary disputes between individual players and their ball clubs. Established in the 1973 collective bargaining agreement between the Major League Baseball Players Association and the club owners, salary arbitration began with the 1974 season. The system is novel to the sport in that it allows an outside third party to become a part of the salary-determination process, which heretofore rested solely with the parties and resulted in either mutual agreement through negotiation or the player's ineligibility to participate.

(Salary is the only significant item that the major league baseball player negotiates separately and individually. Other issues are handled through a multiemployer bargaining unit consisting of 24 clubs in the major leagues. The players are represented by the Major League Baseball Players Association, which is an exclusive bargaining agency for all employees in the unit. Under baseball's reserve clause the player is committed to a particular club for his entire professional career unless released, traded, or sold to another team. The player is, in effect, owned by the club, and part of the ownership right is that the player cannot perform for another professional team if he goes unsigned. This has had the result of reducing his bargaining power within the league, but probably lends stability to the game through restricting player mobility and promoting fan loyalty.)

The salary-determination process is initiated when proposed contracts for the coming season are sent to the players by the clubs by December 20. If agreement is not reached, either a player or his club may submit the dispute to 1 of 14 arbitrators mutually selected by the parties. The club must comply with the player's request for arbitration, but the player does not have to arbitrate if the request is made by the club. Each party gives the arbitrator a salary figure for the coming season, from which he chooses one or the other. Submissions to arbitration are to be made between February 1 and 10, with hearings scheduled from February 11 to 20. Decisions are due within 72 hours of the hearing. The arbitrators do not write opinions giving reasons for their decisions; they only choose the salary.

---

[7] F. Witney, "Final-Offer Arbitration: The Indianapolis Experience," *Monthly Labor Review*, May 1973, p. 22.

Criteria used by the arbitrators in decision making are set forth in the agreement, and include "quality of the Player's contribution to his Club during the past season, . . . the length and consistency of his career contribution, the record of the Player's past compensation, comparative baseball salaries, . . . the existence of any physical or mental defects on the part of the Player, and the recent performance record of the Club. . . ." The arbitrator is instructed not to consider evidence on the financial position of the parties, costs to them, previous offers in negotiations, press comments and testimonials on performance, and salaries in other sports or occupations. Lists of players' salaries were provided to the arbitrators by the owners, the first time such figures were made available in negotiations. Costs of the hearings are shared by the parties.

In 1974, 54 players of the 500 or so eligible submitted their disputes to arbitration, although 25 of these subsequently decided to settle their cases prior to actual arbitration. Of the 29 arbitrations, the player's offer was chosen in 13 instances and the club's offer in 16. (The players' previous salaries, player and club offers, and arbitrators' selections are shown in Exhibit 1.) The overall advantage going to the clubs in the arbitrations may be misleading in that it was reported that in only one instance did a club submit a salary figure lower than what it offered in negotiations prior to arbitration.[8] What commonly occurred is illustrated by Gene Tenace of the Oakland A's. He had to accept the club's offer of $45,000, which was chosen by the arbitrator, but that figure was about $5,000 more than the club's top offer in negotiations. In these cases less was more.

The primary advantage of the final-offer procedure in baseball appears to be that it gives rise to less extreme positions on the part of the contestants and stimulates compromise through negotiation. This is illustrated by the 25 players who opted for arbitration but resolved their differences prior to the hearing, as well as the fact that only about 6 percent of the league's eligible players had their salaries arbitrated.

An interesting result of the arbitrations was the increase in salaries of Oakland A's players. Nine of the A's participated in arbitration, five more than from any other club. This was a result of the argument that salaries were relatively low, as evidenced by the A's being the seventh-best-paid team in baseball in 1973 but winners of the championship among all 24 teams for the second consecutive season. Indeed, part of the disagreement was over World Series money. The club argued that Series money earned by players should be considered by the arbitrator, while the players contended that this was prize money unrelated to salary. In arbitration the A's players won five and lost four. However, the players who won cost an additional $87,000 more than was offered, while $28,650 was recouped from the players who lost their cases.

Apart from the special situation of the Oakland A's, nearly all of the

---

[8] R. F. Boyle, "This Miller Admits He's a Grind," *Sports Illustrated,* March 11, 1974, p. 22.

EXHIBIT 1
Baseball Salaries Arbitrated in 1974

Player, Team	1973 Salary	1974 Offer	1974 Request	1974 Salary
R. Jackson, A's	$ 75,000	$100,000	$135,000	$135,000
Sal Bando, A's	60,000	75,000	100,000	100,000
Ken Holtzman, A's	66,500	80,000	93,000	93,000
Rollie Fingers, A's	48,000	55,000	65,000	65,000
Darold Knowles, A's	50,000	55,000	59,000	59,000
Joe Rudi, A's	50,000	55,000	67,500	55,000
Gene Tenace, A's	33,000	45,000	52,500	54,000
Ted Kubiak, A's	30,000	37,000	42,500	37,000
Jack Heidemann, A's	15,750	12,600	15,750	12,600
B. Sudakis, Yankees	20,000	25,000	30,000	30,000
W. Granger, Yankees	47,500	42,000	46,000	46,000
G. Michael, Yankees	55,000	55,000	65,500	55,000
Duke Sims, Yankees	50,000	50,000	56,000	50,000
D. Evans, Braves	27,500	47,500	52,500	52,500
N. Miller, Braves	35,000	30,000	35,000	35,000
M. Perez, Braves	20,000	27,500	39,500	27,500
F. Tepedino, Braves	15,500	20,000	23,000	20,000
S. Braun, Twins	18,000	25,000	31,000	31,000
D. Woodson, Twins	18,500	23,000	30,000	30,000
L. Hisle, Twins	18,000	23,000	29,000	29,000
D. McNally, Orioles	105,000	105,000	115,000	115,000
P. Blair, Orioles	50,000	60,000	70,000	60,000
B. Grich, Orioles	38,000	46,000	49,000	46,000
C. May, White Sox	70,000	70,000	85,000	70,000
S. Bahnsen, White Sox	65,000	70,000	82,500	70,000
T. Foli, Expos	30,000	40,000	55,000	40,000
Cookie Rojas, Royals	45,000	67,500	80,000	67,500
C. Gaston, Padres	38,000	42,000	50,000	42,000
K. Brett, Pirates	22,000	35,000	40,000	35,000

Source: *New York Times,* March 3, 1974, Sec. 5, p. 1.

players who elected to go to arbitration were of average ability. It has been determined that the better the player, the closer his wage will come to the value of his services to the club.[9] Superstars have a high degree of uniqueness which, if they recognize and exploit it in negotiations, results in their getting not only an absolutely but a proportionately better deal than players with average ability for whom there are many substitutes. Arbitration may therefore have the effect of narrowing the range between salaries of exceptional and average players.

It is unclear whether, on the basis of yearly salary data, overall salaries went up more under the arbitration system than they would have without it. It

---

[9] H. G. Demmert, *The Economics of Professional Team Sports* (Lexington, Mass.: Lexington Books, 1973), pp. 33–34.

EXHIBIT 2
Major League Baseball Salaries, 1969–1974

Year	Average Salary	Median Salary	Annual Percent Increase in Average Salary
1969	$24,909	$19,750	—
1970	29,303	21,750	17.6
1971	31,543	24,750	7.6
1972	34,892	27,000	10.6
1973	37,606	28,000	7.8
1974*	42,871	31,360	14.0

* Author's estimate.
Source: Marvin Miller, Executive Director, Major League Baseball Players Association.

has been estimated that salaries would increase in 1974 by about 14 percent,[10] compared with 7.8 percent in 1973 and an average of about 10 percent in each of the past five years (see Exhibit 2). While the 1974 estimate is higher than the average of past years, the high rate of inflation in 1973-74 makes the real wage increase less than would otherwise be the case.

It is interesting to note that the number of cases arbitrated in 1975 was down to 16 from the 29 cases in 1974. In 10 of the decisions the owner's lower offer was chosen, while the players were awarded their selections on six occasions. This further indicates the parties' desire to negotiate rather than arbitrate.[11]

CONCLUSIONS

Final-offer arbitration appears to have much potential. Primary areas of application are to situations in which strikes cannot be tolerated by the public, involving such problems as inordinate economic loss and danger to public health and safety, and fields such as sports, in which the performer is contractually tied to an organization and has no practical voluntary employment alternative. The baseball scheme was designed by the parties to accommodate to the unique salary structure of the industry, and it is different from other applications of the procedure. Yet, as can be seen from the varied circumstances in which the final-offer arrangement has been suggested or utilized, its qualities of providing stimulus to negotiation, equitable results, and final adjudication of the dispute make it worth considering as a conflict-resolution device.

---

[10] *New York Times,* March 3, 1974, Sec. 5, p. 2; and Boyle, "This Miller Admits He's a Grind," p. 22.

[11] *San Francisco Sunday Examiner & Chronicle,* April 20, 1975, Sec. C, p. 4.

THOMAS COLOSI

Reading 12–4
The Role of the Mediator

Because the essence of negotiations is to provide an opportunity for parties or disputants to exchange promises and thus resolve their differences, some measure of trust between the parties is critical. While some students of negotiation contend that trust is irrelevant to negotiations, it is hard to see how a serious exchange of promises can occur without trust. Each side must have some confidence that the other will keep its word once a promise is given (whether the promises involve benefits or threats). Trust need not be blind, of course. It may be supported by information that is uncovered and processed in the course of negotiation; it may rest on relationships that have strengthened in the course of negotiation; ultimately it may emerge even from the shared experience of coming to understand the negotiation process.

Parties can reach an impasse in negotiations, where no further discussion is possible because either their trust has run out or there was too little trust in the first place. Indeed, in the absence of trust, negotiations might never even begin. Parties with no trust between them can be said to be in a trust vacuum. This underlies their fears of each other. Moreover, it interferes with the very communication that might dispel such fears. Without open lines of productive communication, very little education can take place.

The necessary trust between the parties may be developed in three steps. First, a mediator must work to win the trust of the parties. Next, the mediator educates the parties about the negotiation process (not the mediation process) and works to encourage them to transfer their trust from him to it. Finally, the mediator persuades the parties to begin trusting each other, again using the negotiation process as a vehicle to demonstrate that trust.

Adapted from Thomas Colosi, "Negotiation in the Public and Private Sectors," *American Behavioral Scientist,* vol. 27, no. 2 (November/December 1983), pp. 237–47. Copyright © 1983 by Sage Publications, Inc. Reprinted by permission of Sage Publications.

THE EVOLUTION OF TRUST

Trust in the Outside Third-Party Mediator

The mediator wins the trust of the parties principally by demonstrating that he or she is truly neutral. The capacity of a mediator to win trust may be at its highest if intervention occurs when the situation is particularly polarized and trust between the parties is at its lowest.

Others contend that a mediator should intervene before the parties are frozen into positions, but the particular mediator (and mediation in general) may very well be rejected early in the dispute. At best, the mediator may be underutilized or "bargained with" by parties, both of which make it difficult for him to determine their true objectives.

Just as nature abhors a vacuum, the negotiation process abhors the absence of trust. When parties are polarized, they also have a better idea of what they want the mediator to do. The issues and alternatives are better defined and, as a result, the disputants will be more likely to understand that it is they (and not the mediator) who must assume responsibility for the outcome of negotiations. This is, after all, a fundamental objective of the mediator. In addition, the more time the mediator is involved in the dispute, the less he or she will appear neutral to everyone involved. This perception, of course, can sabotage the mediator's effectiveness.

Mediators may use a number of techniques to demonstrate their neutrality and win the parties' trust. Mediators must learn, for example, how to listen and not say much; likewise, they cannot reveal their emotions and attitudes. Taking care to express only positive or neutral opinions of the groups involved in the dispute is one important approach. Mediators should listen to people's ideas with an open mind, not only to obtain a comprehensive view of the problem but to set an example by showing that there is little risk in entertaining other points of view. Mediators should emphasize that they are only there to help the parties, and have absolutely no decision-making authority regarding the substance or the issues. Mediators must also assure the parties that all conversations will be held in strict confidence. Additionally, a hard-won reputation for helping people in other cases obviously provides a solid foundation for winning the parties' trust.

A mediator may also be able to use other processes for gaining trust. For example, parties who shy away from mediation nevertheless may be willing to engage in fact-finding. Viewed narrowly, fact-finding is a process of gathering information, understanding and organizing the issues in a dispute, and giving advice about a possible settlement; the parties are not bound by the fact-finder's recommendations. Sophisticated mediators, however, see broader potential in fact-finding: It can serve as a first step in negotiations, the mechanism by which the mediator gets to meet with all the parties and begins to win their trust.

The process of enhancing trust in the mediator is not without risk.

Inexperienced mediators frequently feel empowered by the confidence and acceptance that the disputants may quickly show toward them. Mediators must keep in mind, however, that their perception of power comes from the parties' need to fill the trust vacuum. Furthermore, their perceived power is only an early stage in a developmental process that ideally should lead to the empowering of the negotiators themselves through the help of the mediator.

Trust in the Process

Having obtained the parties' trust, the mediator must next work to transfer it from himself to the negotiation process. The parties must be shown that the negotiation process is the way through their problem. They must become comfortable with the negotiation process, experiment with it, and use it to achieve success. In the early stages of a dispute, the best kind of intervenor often will avoid substantive issues and concentrate instead on procedural matters in order to educate the parties about negotiation and mediation. The parties should know that mediation is available if they want it, but they should not move into mediation until they really need it.

Because negotiating skills are not taught in our society to any great extent, there is very poor understanding about how the negotiation process works. People tend to concentrate on whether or not another *party* should be trusted, rather than on trusting the process itself. Learning to trust negotiations is a useful interim step between no trust and trust in another party. Disputants who do not take the interim step usually end up using alternative dispute resolution processes. In some cases, the alternative may be litigation; in others, a strike or a riot. The role of the mediator is to call attention to the need for establishing an understanding of, and confidence in, the negotiation process before trust in the other parties is sought.

Trust among the Parties

Once the interim steps have been taken and trust in both the mediator and in the negotiation process is established, the professional mediator must work hard to transfer that trust to the parties themselves. This can occur in two ways. First, the mediator acts as a role model: demonstrating good listening skills; showing respect for other people's opinions and constraints; and creating an atmosphere of trust by encouraging the negotiators to develop a statement of common goals. Second, trust is established among the parties through practice. The preliminary stages of negotiation involve some cooperation among the parties in relatively simple process decisions. These may involve minor procedural matters—''housekeeping issues'' if you will—yet over time they provide a shared experience that allows the parties slowly to develop a more trusting relationship, one that is essential when more fundamental, high stakes issues are tackled.

The case that follows illustrates how these trust-building steps are implemented in practice.

Building Trust: An Example in Community
Multilateral Negotiations

In 1973 a riot in a Rochester, New York, high school sent 16 students and teachers (8 blacks and 8 whites) to the hospital. I was one of two intervenors from the American Arbitration Association's National Center for Dispute Resolution in Washington, D.C., who entered the dispute as fact finders. In truth, we borrowed from the public sector labor-management model to characterize our roles, using the Newman model of "mediators wearing fact finders' hats." The particular intervenors were teamed because one is white and the other black.

About 18 different organizations, representing students, specific racial and ethnic groups, teachers, parents, and local citizens, were identified by the school board and one another as interested parties. They were invited by the American Arbitration Association to meet each other and the fact finders. The purpose of the meeting was to determine what had caused the riot and to try to set up a process for avoiding future disruption. Once this group was assembled, one of the first questions that had to be answered was whether still other parties and organizations should be involved. Some groups already present voiced objections about inviting certain others, contending that they would ruin the process. Nevertheless, as mediator/fact-finders, we encouraged those who were involved to invite the threatening groups to participate on the ground that any outsiders who had enough power to stymie the process would likely be important to implementing any agreement. Ultimately, the original participants did decide who would be at the table and added several parties. In effect, the negotiators defined themselves.

Once the group's composition was established, the parties had to determine how decisions would be made. Two competing models of decision making were offered: majority vote and full consensus. Some conservative groups supported the majority vote, while the minority organizations felt better protected by full consensus; indeed, they threatened to leave the table over this issue. The intervenors kept the parties together by observing that an effective solution to the high school problem would be possible only if all the groups present were involved in the negotiations. The intervenors pointed out that a settlement unanimously endorsed by a group as broadly based as those convened would carry a great deal of clout with the school board and the public. The parties remained at the table because they had begun to believe that some common goals and solutions were possible, even though these had yet to take concrete form.

Each group's attitudes on the decision-making issue was affected, in part, by its own internal structure and experience. Some groups that were accustomed to operating under an authoritarian model assumed that the mediator/fact-finders would make the decisions. Others thought that committees would be formed to discuss the issues and be given delegated powers.

Majority rule, with and without minority opinion reports, were other suggestions. Before long, participants came to see how differently they all made decisions, and began to educate one another about the relative merits of each process.

The intervenors had to conduct sidebar meetings (caucuses with groups in isolation from other groups) because of one minority group's flat refusal to participate under any process except full consensus. The mediator/fact finders created doubts in the conservative camp as to the viability of the majority rule process by asking its members if they realized how much power was available to them through the full consensus process. The intervenors pointed out that a simple veto could be exercised by any group to prevent proposals and directions that were perceived to be inappropriate or undesirable from being adopted. After many internal discussions with the conservative group, full consensus decision making was accepted.

Continuing the process discussions, we next suggested to the group that they begin their negotiations by agreeing upon a common goal. The initial proposals were sweeping and often contradictory. Some said that the goal should be to stop busing. Others said that desegregation should be eliminated. One proposal was to abolish the school board. Even amendments to the U.S. Constitution were put forth. It was clear that the parties were still a long way from reaching a mutually acceptable goal.

We worked patiently in a variety of process configurations and settings to try to close the many gaps. Talks took place chiefly in informal meetings. Internal discussions took place within some of the parties; there was also direct talk between the parties, both with and without the mediators. In the course of these discussions, the mediators came to realize that despite the parties's obvious differences, they shared a common attitude: fear. They feared each other, but beyond that they feared what might happen in the schools and in the community if accommodation could not be achieved. Still, they were not ready to trust each other to be reasonable or to deliver on promises.

The parties met over a six-month period with the mediators and a local coordinator. A church basement was used as the formal meeting area. There was near-perfect attendance at all the weekly and biweekly meetings; no group pulled out of the process. Ultimately, the groups agreed on a common goal: to have *safe schools*. In retrospect, the goal may seem obvious, yet the fact that it eluded the parties for so long shows that polarization and lack of trust can keep disputants from recognizing their shared interests that, under other circumstances, might be easily perceived. Once the common goal was articulated, the parties tried to formulate an overall strategy for achieving it. Their initial strategy was to continue negotiations. Trust in the negotiation process and in each other was beginning to be established, and as the parties assumed greater responsibility for tasks, the mediators of course did less.

The outside neutrals entered this polarized situation as fact finders, worked to establish trust—first in themselves and then in the negotiation process—by showing the parties how mediation could help them. By encouraging the parties to work together on small, seemingly procedural issues, the intervenors demonstrated how people with different priorities and outlooks could work cooperatively.

Once trust is established in the negotiation process and in each other, the negotiators will find that they no longer need a mediator. When this happens, the mediator should begin to leave the dispute, as his job may essentially be over. The mediator may make himself available for other process-management tasks, of course, or to resume mediation if the trust relationship breaks down for any reason.

THE MEDIATOR'S CAPACITY TO RAISE AND MAINTAIN DOUBTS

Effective mediators create and maintain doubts by raising questions about alternatives and implications that the negotiator may not have considered or fully appreciated. Like any good negotiator, the mediator avoids flat statements. If, for instance, a mediator wants a negotiator to think about the reaction of the negotiator's superiors to a certain proposal, the mediator is better off asking, "What would your boss say?" rather than declaring, "Your boss may not support you on that." The same axiom would apply in a situation in which a mediator and a negotiator are discussing a negotiator's decision to leave the bargaining table. Assuming that the negotiators are using full consensus in their decision-making process, the mediator might privately say to the reluctant negotiator, "The other parties might come to some decision in your absence. Have you considered the implications of your not being present to veto decisions that would hurt your side?" The use of questions rather than statements gives negotiators more room to respond and more freedom to consider what the mediator is saying. It also allows the mediator to play a more neutral, laissez-faire role as declarations tend to be more leading and value-loaded than questions. The negotiators are thus subtly encouraged to take maximum responsibility in the negotiation process.

As noted earlier, most important negotiating takes place in the internal team caucuses. As a consequence, this usually is where the mediator is most active as well. Private meetings are normally the best forum for the mediator to raise doubts.

During horizontal (across-the-table) negotiations, each team tries to educate the other about its position. The negotiators try to raise new doubts in the minds of their counterparts. As a result, a new set of assumptions and proposals may become plausible, and new issues and problems may arise as well. In this phase of negotiation, the stabilizers and nonstabilizers tend to open up to each other in the caucuses when these new concerns are discussed. If the quasi-mediator is unable to create doubts in the nonstabilizer's mind, an outside, neutral mediator may be enlisted before the team resorts to autocratic decision making, or internal disciplinary measures to bring the dissenter along. Committed to stability, the mediator concentrates on internal team bargaining and similarly tries to raise doubts about the viability of nonsettlement in the mind of the nonstabilizer. Sometimes the emphasis is less on outcomes and more on process. If the nonstabilizer does not trust the negotiation process because of preconceived notions, the mediator must raise doubts about the competing process alternatives. By contrast, of course, effective mediators would not work to create doubt in the minds of the stabilizers, since this group wants settlement.

Parties Who Will Not Settle

The mediator's function is thus to create and maintain doubts in the minds of individual negotiators who oppose settlement. What can a mediator do if an entire team is composed of nonstabilizers?

Some negotiators enter the process quite committed to talking but not to settling. For them negotiation may only be a device to stall for time. They may be waiting for the other side to exhaust its strike fund or other resources. They may have calculated that in time public opinion will shift in their favor. Time may be needed to prepare a lawsuit, launch a media campaign, or use some other external pressure on the other side. It may simply be that these "negotiators" prefer the status quo to any foreseeable alternative.

When one team is negotiating just to buy time, the situation between the contending parties is similar in many respects to the internal process that occurs within a team between stabilizers and nonstabilizers. The non-stabilizers are the ones who must be convinced by the quasi-mediator (and the stabilizers) to remain at the table, to listen to the other teams, to consider their arguments, and, ideally, to revise their positions to enable their negotiating team to offer deliverable proposals. The quasi-mediator first tries to raise doubts in the mind of the uncooperative teammates about the consequences of nonsettlement. (What losses would have to be incurred: a strike, litigation, violence; can the group afford such losses?)

A team dedicated to nonsettlement occupies the same position in horizontal negotiations as does the nonstabilizer within his team. It, too, is uninterested in settlement. In this instance, however, it is the mediator rather than the quasi-mediator who steps in. Although the person is different, the role is much the same. The mediator relies on the same basic technique of raising doubts about the team's decision to stall, probing to see if all the implications of nonsettlement have been evaluated.

In any case when it becomes obvious that a party has carefully considered its position and has determined that settlement is not in its interest, then, after appropriate probing, the mediator ultimately must accept the party's own judgment. When a party believes that it is better to stall than to settle, the mediator might reasonably continue with the process if the other party accedes.

NEGOTIATION AND LITIGATION

Deadlines are important monitors of the parties' success at reaching an agreement. Timing is a critical factor in a mediator's assessment of a party's willingness to settle. When there is no court-imposed or other "natural" deadline (for example, the expiration of a labor contract), the mediator can help the parties set the clock. He can warn the parties that if settlement is not reached by a certain time, then the parties may have to proceed without him. Mediators have to take care in using this tactic. The deadline should not be artificial; disputes are not poker games for bluffing. Instead, the mediator should use his general experience, combined with his knowledge of the specific dispute, to determine at what future point a failure to agree would show that his time was spent inefficiently.

The difficulty a mediator may have in getting negotiators to settle within a time limit gives much support to arguments that favor the deadlines imposed by the litigation process. In litigation, deadlines are perceived to be firmer and more believable. Disputes therefore can be settled within a set period of time. Although some proponents of negotiation extoll it as an alternative to the courts, nothing settles a dispute better than the combined force of the strong arm of the court (or an arbitrator) and active negotiation.

Negotiation is often called an "alternative" dispute resolution process, a characterization that implicitly regards the judicial system as dominant. This view also seems predicated on a belief that negotiation and litigation represented entirely divergent paths, yet practice often reveals that the two can be inextricably bound.

This point is illustrated by a heated land use dispute in New York State in which negotiation and litigation occurred in tandem. A group of Mohawk Indians occupied some open land, and town officials moved to have them evicted. Before the state police were deployed, however, help was sought from the National Center for Dispute Settlement. The center (a division of the American Arbitration Association) was contacted to serve as "Rumor Control Experts." (This term was carefully chosen to help the intervenors win the trust of all the parties, as rumors were potentially harmful to everyone.) Under that authority, representatives of the center began the delicate process of building trust. In time, the process came to be directed explicitly at negotiation. Prosecutorial actions were held in abeyance. Nevertheless, the specter of a court-imposed resolution kept the process on track. The mediators assured the parties that no action would be taken by the court so long as the negotiation process was reported as being fruitful. Neither side was confident what the judge would order if negotiation broke down.

In disputes that erupt spontaneously (such as the one just described), parties often find themselves simultaneously involved in lawsuits and negotiations. Usually their lawyers are likewise involved in both processes. But is a lawyer the best representative for a party in a negotiation process? Cer-

tainly, lawyers are assumed to be good negotiators. Yet the parties themselves may be just as good if they are educated properly about the process.
Moreover, many lawyers are biased in favor of the judicial process and act
with little enthusiasm for negotiation. Sophisticated clients could become
knowledgeable about the negotiation process (using the mediator as a men-
tor, if necessary) and employ lawyers for advice on how the negotiations
could influence the simultaneous litigation. In such a case, the lawyers
should not take over the negotiation process, though their advice could be
useful. The mediator, in turn, could help the negotiator and the lawyers
coordinate their respective responsibilities. In a sense, this is just another
example of building team cohesion: It is similar to the work a mediator does
to produce greater harmony among the stabilizers and nonstabilizers.

SECTION THIRTEEN

Bargaining and Personal Values

In this last section of the book, we focus on the role that personal values and ethics plays in negotiation. This area of negotiation has received very little attention as a topic of research or even more general writing. Nevertheless, ethics and morality are a subject of common discussion in everyday life, and particularly in the news media's analysis of current events. As an example, the world of professional sports is governed by an extensive series of rules and regulations, determining what the players, owners, and managers can, or cannot, do on the field and in the conduct of their business. In contrast, the world of politics is not so well regulated; as a result, events like Watergate, motivated by a desire to win at any cost, occur more frequently. Similarly, cheating on examinations, falsifying research studies, or falsifying personal backgrounds and credentials are just some of the tricks that people use to gain temporary tactical advantage—all of which are receiving considerable attention in the press. It thus seems appropriate to pay attention to the important ethical questions raised when considering what is right or appropriate to do in negotiation.

In the first article, "Sales Tricks of a Con Artist," Clark McCauley and Mitchell Handelsman document a number of tricks and tactics used by salesmen in promoting their products. Many of these tactics, most would argue, are highly unethical. One difficulty is that we are only likely to recognize these tactics after they have been worked on us, and to our disadvantage. This article effectively points out how these tactics work, and how we may more intelligently recognize them as manipulative efforts.

The remainder of the articles in this section take the approach of social commentary rather than descriptive statement. Each one highlights a question of personal values or ethical conduct and challenges the reader to consider the key questions in depth. Harry Stein's articles deal with two questions: vengeance and greed. In the first article, "Ah, Sweet Vengeance!" he comments on the natural tendency to seek revenge—and the equally natural tendency to ignore the costs or consequences for such motivation. While parties who have been "wronged" by their opponent frequently feel a strong urge to gain revenge, retribution for its own sake is hardly a rational or cost-effective approach to successful negotiation. Moreover, there are a number of moral and ethical dilemmas in vengeance that are seldom experienced until after the "deed is done." In the second article, "Easy Money, Easy Virtue," Stein focuses on greed—the commonplace trend in American society to value and pursue economic riches at the expense of other standards of worth. Stein comments on the passion with which many pursue wealth for its own sake, and the manner in which the "revolution of rising expectations" has caught many others in a whirlwind of pursuit for big bucks. Again, Stein points out how his all-consuming passion in some undermines other social values, and questions the society that condones and encourages such behavior.

Two other articles in this section also raise an important value concern—playing and winning within the rules. Pete Axthelm in "Psst, Somebody May Be Cheating," comments on rules—and the great desire to stretch them until they break. Rules govern sports and competitions of all varieties—baseball, hockey, yachting, and negotiating. Without rules, there would be little left of any orderly procedure; without procedure, any competitive event would immediately resort to a test of power and strength for one side to have its own way. Thus, while every competitive interaction needs rules to govern it—and both fans and players know it—there is nevertheless a constant temptation to "stretch and test" the rules to find out how much deviation can be tolerated. Whether it be the amount of pine tar on a baseball bat used by George Brett, or the substance inside the boxing gloves, Axthelm argues fans like it even better when the rules are violated and controversy surrounds the rules themselves. If in fact breaking the rules is more exciting than playing within the rules, then the very fabric of competitive interaction is challenged. The reputation for corruption and dishonesty has threatened to kill certain professional sports (e.g., wrestling and boxing), and the problem may spread to all other sports which are overtaken by the same reputation. Finally, Joseph Sorrentino, in the last article, "The Cult of Winning," comments on the very nature of the predisposition in American culture toward competition and winning. He sees a pressure to win at any cost, and the tendency to use questionable tactics and methods in order to achieve this victory. As Sorrentino states, the way the game is played is just as important as who wins. A society which does not value adherence to some set of moral rules is likely to find its victories hollow and meaningless.

CLARK R. MCCAULEY, JR.
and MITCHELL HANDELSMAN

Reading 13–1
Sales Tricks of a Con Artist

A jam joint is a place where fast-talking salesmen peddle merchandise at inflated prices. Jam joints exist in resort areas like Las Vegas, Atlantic City, and Miami. Jams are also done at fairs and carnivals. Wherever large numbers of people can be found with money in their pockets and time on their hands, jam joints are likely to prosper. Lured off the street or board-walk, Mr. and Mrs. America are persuaded to spend between $3 and $300 for overpriced items that they don't need and didn't want—until they met the jammer. The jammer employs means of persuasion that are not quite illegal. The details of his pitch vary widely, but the basic procedure is the same.

The doors are rolled aside, opening the entire front of the joint, and two young men bring out a portable counter and position it facing the street. On it are a pineapple, oranges, grapefruit, lemons, tomatoes, potatoes, glasses, orange juicers, spiral potato slicers, and usually some knives or olive forks. The floor help stands out front to provide the nucleus of an audience, and the bally is under way.

"Watch! Watch!! WA-A-A-ATCH!!!" the tipman begins as he steps a few feet out onto the street and taps a glass with a paring knife. (The crowd is called the tip, and the man who works the tip is called the tipman.) His voice is magnified by the cheap sound system activated from a microphone he wears around his neck.

"Watch it!! We're going to do it on the pineapple! In three seconds, all that marvelous juice will come cascading down into the glass. If you don't have a pineapple, take a fresh grapefruit. . . ."

As he's talking he takes a grapefruit, orange, tomato, and the pineapple, and sticks a spiral slicer into the top of each. "If you've never seen this demonstration, you're in for a treat." A little later, he will take the slicers out of the fruits, having done nothing with them. The pineapple is never used again.

"N'watch, n'look. This is the most incredible thing I've ever seen," he says as he winds the slicer down a potato. "Apples for slicing, carrots for creaming, beets for pickling, potatoes for frying—isn't that remarkable. I get so excited every time I do this! Look, every slice, cut to perfection. Let me show you what to do with this. . . ."

Now the tipman introduces the story. "The reason why I'm here telling you these things is that the Wilkinson Company, who made these, has instructed me to give everybody out here one of these *free,* so you can try them, tell your friends and neighbors about them, and they can go out and buy one for 98 cents. That's called *advertising.* They gave us 10,000 of these, *free, free!*" The moment people hear that word, they are hypnotized. People who had started to saunter away return now. The magic has begun. The tipman is turning ordinary people into K mooches (good customers).

"TEN FREE SAMPLES!"

He pulls a knife out from under the counter and continues his barrage. "This is the world's sharpest knife. Guaranteed never to get dull. It's going on sale in every Sears store in the country on Labor Day for $3.95. These are made by Wilkinson . . . Watch this, unbelievable. . . ." He then demonstrates the knife by cutting up some fruit. "Look how thin these slices are. One tomato can last you a summer. This knife is so sharp, you can cut a cow in half, and that's no bull!" Corny jokes like this are very effective in holding the tip's attention and taking their minds off what's happening.

The bally continues. "These knives are going to be sold in boxes for $3.95, but I want somebody here to take a desperate chance and, for the one I work with, give me a quarter. Who else would give me a quarter?" He sells a few knives, then says, "Now wait a minute. For everyone who bought a knife, I have 10 free gifts to give you. Everybody's going to get these 10 free samples!" The tip is given something to expect, something to wait for.

Then comes the juicer demonstration. The tipman pulls a small boy out of the crowd and squeezes the juice from a grapefruit and an orange into his mouth. "Governor Reubin Askew, of the great state of Florida, calls this the most amazing thing he's ever seen. Look at that, unbelievable! You're all going to get one of these free.

"I promised you all 10 free gifts; I'm going to give them out right now. I'm going to give you the juicer, the extractor, the corer, the cutter, the slicer, the rosette cutter, all this stuff, *free, free.*" Each set of three words is describing only one object. "Here's what I want you to do. Take a nickel out of your pocket, and *don't give it to me.* Just hold it up in the air. Hold a nickel up. I can do this for 40 people." He proceeds to collect the nickels, counting more nickels than he actually collects. This is called coining the tip. Then he asks the floor help to pass out as many bags as he counted nickels, saying that he will fill the bags with free gifts.

Everybody gets a bag, whether he gave a nickel or not. The counter is moved away, and the tipman throws a few juicers into the crowd as he moves farther and farther into the joint. Most of the tip follow the tipman. Once inside, they are encouraged to take seats. The bally has served its purpose; people who had been strolling down the street are now sitting in their seats, expecting something for nothing.

THE JAM

The jam itself begins with the takeover. As the tipman hands out some more plunder (small giveaways), the J-man (jammer) enters unobtrusively, picks up some plunder, and gives it to a mooch. "Oh, Bill! There you are," the tipman says, as if surprised. "I want you to do me a favor. I promised all my friends here all these gifts. This is my friend, Bill; let's give him a big round of applause." As the tip claps, the J-man takes the microphone and says, "Isn't he wonderful! Do you know why he's so happy? 'Cause today's his birthday! Give him a hand." As the tip is clapping again, they hardly realize that the man who made the promises is gone, and a new man is standing before them. All they know is that they're going to get something for nothing.

As the tipman is walking out, he points to a few people and says, "Bill, favor these people. And *favor them*. Give out all that crap!"

The J-man starts giving out plunder left and right, telling a joke or story about each item. "Do you need some money?" he asks a mooch.

"Sure!"

"Well, here is a pencil; write home for some. Here's a pencil for you, another over here. . . . Here's a comb I'd like to give out. These combs are guaranteed never to break; absolutely unbreakable," he says as he snaps one in half and throws it on the floor.

The plunder time keeps people expecting better things. "Each article I give away is going to be more expensive than the last. Who likes that stereo? We're going to get rid of a couple of those today." The J-man also uses the plunder time to get to know the tip, to banter with them until they feel comfortable and become responsive. "Who here is from New York? How about Philadelphia? You are? Do you know where the Ellis Theater used to be? . . ."

As he is plundering the tip, he reintroduces the advertising story. "Who's seen Monty Hall on TV, giving away furniture and appliances like mad? Does he pay for that stuff he dishes out? Of course not! His sponsors do. Well, we get this merchandise to distribute to you from our sponsors, so you'll take them home, use them and advertise them.

"We could just put a big box of merchandise outside with a big sign that said *free,* but you know what would happen. One guy would get five or six articles, and some old lady would get five or six bumps on the head trying to get them. That wouldn't be advertising, that would be paralyzing. So we do it this way.

"I know how to tell which ones are the snatchers and grabbers, and which ones are my responsible advertisers, who'll really make good use of these articles, like the stereo, and show them to their nosy neighbors."

THREE BLACK BOXES

At this point, he holds up three lighters. "I have three lighters here to give away free; who wants one? Everybody. Who'd give me $1 for one of these lighters? Ah, not as many hands up this time. Okay, you, you and you. You three people, I want you to dig down into your pocket, your purse, or the tip of your shoe, and hold up $1. Don't *send* it up, *hold* it up." He asks each person if he's satisfied to spend $1 for the lighter. Each says yes. He then throws the lighters out to the three people. "I wasn't really going to sell those lighters for $1, because—if you remember—I said I was going to give them away free. I just wanted to see who are my good advertisers. If those three people were sincere enough to spend $1 of their hard-earned money, that shows me that they're the type of people who will take these products home, use them, and advertise for us."

The plundering is over. Now the J-man takes out three black boxes from behind a counter. "I have this box here. As I said, each article gets more valuable, so naturally the price has to go up. This box is $2. But this box comes with two guarantees. First, this box is worth a lot more than any one of you will ever actually pay me for it; and, you're going to get a lot more than that box and what's in it. That's my guarantee. Now, for the box and its contents—and the two guarantees that go with it—who'd pay $2?"

He collects $2 from three people, qualifies it (i.e., asks them if they're satisfied to spend the money), shows the piece of cheap jewelry that was inside the box, and explains the guarantee. "This is worth more than any one of you will pay for it, because you're actually going to pay *nothin'!* And you're going to get more because I'm giving you the $2 back." As with the lighters, he impresses upon the people that he has backed up his guarantees, and that he is finding out who his responsible citizens are.

Now the J-man points to a series of articles (called the cops) lined up on a counter. "Who likes this Snoopy dog? The special advertising price of this is a penny. Who likes this electric toothbrush, with its own waterproof carrying case? We have to sell certain articles; this is a nickel. This salad set is going for a dime. How about this knife set that you see the Galloping Gourmet use every day on TV? I'm going to sell that for a quarter."

The J-man has introduced the cops, but now turns away from them to bring out a number of white boxes. "I'm going to form me a little advertising committee. I need about 25 good, honest, responsible citizens, who are not too proud to get a little something for nothing, not too proud to say 'thank you,' and not too proud to show these things to 10 or 12 of your nosy neighbors and do a little advertising, that's the main thing. From now on, anyone who gets any advertising merchandise at special prices—like a knife set for a quarter—is going to be somebody with a white box. The lucky person who takes home a stereo or a sewing machine is going to be somebody with one of these white boxes.

"Lady, do you want to be on my committee? OK, I'm going to call you advertiser number one. Remember your number. If I take this watch and say, 'This belongs to advertiser number one,' and you forget your number, you may as well forget the article. Everybody who wants a number raise up your hand."

Everybody raises his hand, and he gives them each a number. To prove that they're sincere, he asks everybody to hold up $3; don't send it up. "I see some people who raised their hand before, but aren't holding up their three, so I'm going to have to separate this crowd one more time. If you said three, if you meant three, but most important, IF YOUR WORD IS WORTH $3, send up your three."

SNATCHERS AND GRABBERS

The people who send up the $3—and the number of people could range from about five to more than 20—are nailed. These people are the K mooches, the marks, the prospects. Those $3 will never be returned to them. The white boxes are held on the counter with the money for most of the pitch, so the people still think that when they get the boxes, they'll get the money, too. "At this point, I must ask those people who did not have enough interest to send up $3 to please leave; I have nothing else for you. You just can't see what I'm trying to do up here." Those who did not pay leave, and the doors are closed but not locked; people are free to go at any time.

"There, we've gotten rid of all the snatchers and grabbers. Now I know that those who are left are responsible advertisers. You're the people I will treat and favor."

The J-man returns to the cops. Money collected for the cops is always returned. "Who'd give me a penny for the Snoopy dog? Everyone. Who'd give me $1? You would? Send up your dollar." He puts the dollar with the dog and gives them both back to the mooch. "I didn't want your dollar, because I said I was going to sell it for a penny, and I have to back up my word."

The second cop is the electric toothbrush. It is handled like the first except that $5 are collected and returned. The third cop is a little different. The jammer takes out an empty paper bag and "sells" it to "a sport, a speculator" for $10. As the price goes up, the qualifications get stronger. "You sent up $10 for this bag. It's my $10, it's your bag, right? Satisfied? You're not going to come back later and say that was the baby's whiskey money, are you? If I give you the bag and nothing else, you can't complain, because that's all we bargained for, right? See that sign on the wall? It says *all sales final*. A bargain is a bargain. Satisfied? OK.''

He takes the $10 and says, ''I'm going to give you some time to think about this, so I'll hold your bag and my money up here.'' He then shows the stereo and sewing machine again, likening them to the big deal of the day on ''Let's Make a Deal.'' Once more, he is making the tip expect something. He gives the man back his bag, into which he has put the $10, the salad set, and various other cheap articles. He plays another such game with the knife set, for which he collects and returns $30.

The jammer is now ready to begin selling, although virtually nobody realizes it. From this point on, no money is given back.

''OK, I can only advertise one more article, favor one more person.'' He does his story on five articles, usually including watches, a razor, a hair styler, and a whiskey-decanter set. ''For choice of any one of these five articles, I want someone—first hand up gets it, 'cause I can only advertise one—who'd say . . . $30!''

At this point, the procedure becomes variable; different J-men handle this part of the pitch differently. The most deceptive procedure goes as follows: ''OK, sir, you picked the razor, send up your $30.'' After getting the money, he qualifies the sale. ''Some articles we give away, some we sell. The price of this razor is $30. Are you satisfied to spend $30? OK?''

As the J-man hands the razor to the mooch, he says, ''Wait a minute! Give me back that razor! I'm sorry, sir. Would you trust me with your razor up here for a second? Good, then I'll trust you with my $30.'' He hands back the money, and suddenly appears to get angry. ''I just heard a remark in here, and I'm not going to stand for it. Somebody just whispered that this man works for me. Mr. Man, do you work for me?''

''No,'' the bewildered mooch answers. Everybody is looking around to see who made the remark, a remark that wasn't made at all. The jammer doesn't give the tip a chance to breathe as he continues.

''I'll show you that nobody here works for me. Whoever wants one of these five articles, raise up your hands.'' For effect, one of the floor help says, ''But Bill, you said only one arti—.'' ''Shut up! I know what I'm doing; you don't! You just mark it down on the sheet and I'll sign for it.''

TEN TO TAKE A GAMBLE

As each person chooses an article, the assistant puts that article up on the counter. About every third person who chooses is asked, ''If I asked you to send up $30, would you?'' When they are all through, the jammer says, ''Now just to show that you're sincere—and to show that pokey-nose, that busybody—that nobody here is working for me, I want everyone who chose an article to hold up $30. We're going to collect your $30 and give you this card as a receipt.'' The floor help collects the money quickly. The mooches are completely confused; all this has happened lightning-fast.

"Now, some of you are a little short of cash today, so I'm going to give everybody a chance to get in on this one.'' The switch from anger back to jamming is almost instantaneous. "Who's ever gambled and lost? I want 10 people to take a gamble with me. I'm thinking of something. It could be a stereo, or it could be nothing. I want 10 people who have faith to say—not $30, $20, or even $15—I want 10 people who have faith to raise up their hands and say $10!'' He collects the money from those who have their hands up, and qualifies each one carefully.

We now have the white boxes, the $30 articles, and the money all sitting on the counter. Some people still expect to get their money back, others are just beginning to realize that they've *bought* something, and the others don't know what's going on. The J-man has the money *and* the goods; he remains in control.

"Now, let's leave that aside for a while, and get to the real reason I'm here. This is what I get paid for.'' He then does a long and beautiful advertisement for the sewing machine and the stereo, talking about the lifetime guarantee, how the speakers on the stereo are solid fruitwood, and all kinds of truths and half-truths. Then he pulls out a Manila envelope. "For the two lucky people who take away one of these two articles, I have a special bonus that's worth at least as much as the stereo or the sewing machine itself. So, for either the sewing machine or the stereo, plus the extra added bonus that Monty Hall gives away every day—forget $400 for the stereo, forget $309.95 for the sewing machine, forget $300 or $250 or even $200. If I were to say $175, it would be the best deal you ever made in your life, you know why? Because the *dealers* can't even get it for that! I want two people with the sense that God gave to a six-year-old to raise up their hands and say $150, and leave the rest to me! If you don't have cash, we'll take credit cards, Spanish pesetas, Russian rubles, or Italian lire. We'll even take Chinese money, if you have a yen for it. If you're ever going to buy a sewing machine or a stereo, now's the time to do it!''

The game is over. What's going on now is extremely high-pressure salesmanship. If he has no takers at first, he goes around the room to each person individually and tries again and again to talk someone into buying. He then asks if anyone can leave a deposit. Sometimes he will take personal checks.

After selling the stereo and sewing machine, the J-man reveals the contents of the envelope. It is a trip to Las Vegas or Florida for four days and three nights. He does not show the actual certificate, on which it says that transportation and meals are not included.

The J-man returns to his folksy manner. "Now it's time to give you what you paid for, and *spend* some money back with you.'' He then gives out all the merchandise on the counter, so the people get all the articles at the same time. In the mailers (the white boxes) are found pen-and-pencil sets or perfume. The J-man reveals that the people who had sent up $10 will get "a genuine Royalite Gem man-made diamond necklace, which sells for $110 at all the fine jewelry stores. Never mind how we got them; the store we got'em from doesn't even know they're missing yet. . . ."A little more plunder tops off the deluge of merchandise, to help make the tip forget about the money they spent.

"Who thinks I've worked hard up here?" Everyone raises a hand. "Who thinks I deserve a tip?" Everyone. "Who would give me a dollar so my helpers and I can go out for a drink tonight?" Virtually everybody gives a dollar, and the pitch ends.

SUSCEPTIBLE WOMEN

One of the assistants stands at the door as people file out, giving each person a little good-luck charm and getting him out as fast as possible. The other assistant starts to sweep the floor to make it look as if they're finished for the day. The doors are closed and, after 10 minutes to clean up the joint, the doors are opened, the tipman appears, and the jam starts again. A two-hour jam can make anywhere from about $200 to well over $1,000. For items that cost a mooch $10, the jam joint pays an average of $1; for a $30 article, the joint pays about $9; and for the $150 articles, the joint pays about $55.

It should be made clear that not everybody gets jammed. Only a fraction of the people on the street are lured inside, and many of those leave before the J-man forms his advertising committee. But neither does it appear that there are types of people who will not enter the joint, and other types who are easy marks. Many people who buy white boxes just watch the rest of the show, and don't buy anything else. Many who go in very skeptical wind up buying merchandise.

It does appear that women are more susceptible to the jammers than men are. Raymond A. Bauer, author of "The Obstinate Audience," has reported research indicating that women, in general, are more easily persuaded than men. The J-men seem to know this, and they aim their pitch primarily toward the women, even though the men usually have the money. "Treat your wife to the sewing machine," they tell him, hoping the wife will agree. Many men will turn to their wives with a look that says, "Should I do it?" Her decision is usually final.

The entire process of the jam can be broken down into three major objectives: to get the people into the joint, to keep them there, and to make them buy. Naturally, the first two are secondary to the third, but they must be fulfilled in order for the selling part of the pitch to work. This is why the pitch builds for more than an hour before any selling takes place.

The first objective, getting people into the joint, is accomplished by appealing to greed, one of the most stable and effective ways of influencing people. Darrell Lucas and Charles Benson, in their book *Psychology for*

Advertisers, identify ownership as a fundmental urge. "The desire to possess worldly goods goes to the limit of reason with most people but fortunately for the advertiser is seldom so well satisfied that it cannot be used further." Greed will lead people to do things like sitting in a store, if they can get something for nothing.

SOMETHING FOR NOTHING

The tipman gives out bags, promises to fill them, then throws out a few juicers. The bags and the promise to fill them develop the expectation of free merchandise. The first few gifts actually thrown out serve to strengthen the expectation and make it more immediate: "I'm going to give you 10 free gifts RIGHT NOW." The effectiveness of the bally in producing greed and expectation is seen after some pitches, when people who have just spent over $200 will come up to the jammer and ask, "Can we have one of those potato slicers the man promised us? That's all we came in for."

Once people are in the joint, the objective is to keep them there. This is done by developing longer range expectations. While handing out little plastic combs for free, the jammer is talking about the stereo and sewing machine. The effect is the creation of a mental set. Ernest Dichter, a psychologist known to the advertising world as "Mr. Motivational Research," notes that "In the field of communication the mistake is often made that either no time is provided or effort is made to establish a mental set." The jammer does not make this mistake. In fact, the mental set of "something for nothing" must be produced if the jam is going to work at all.

There is another force, no less powerful than greed, that keeps people in a jam. This force arises from the personality of the jammer and from his relationship with his audience. The jammer works hard to make himself rewarding and attractive in ways that go far beyond his giveaway image.

The jammer is first of all an entertainer. His vaudeville performance is a reinforcement for staying in the joint. The performance, with its continual bantering and joking, also creates for the jammer a "nice-guy" image. In his book, *Attitude Change and Social Influence,* Arthur Cohen points out that "An attractive, decent, warm person can generally get us to do what he wants us to do; if we do something unpleasant because he asks us to, . . . his admirable traits are compelling reasons for doing it."

This power is not well understood theoretically; psychologists argue as to whether it depends on liking or identification or some other process. But the experimental data are consistent with the common wisdom of salesmen that when it comes to persuasion, nice guys finish first.

The jammer also works to make the tip see him as expert and trustworthy. Expertness and trustworthiness together determine the credibility of a communicator, and dozens of experiments have confirmed that more credible communicators are more persuasive.

One way the jammer appears expert is by name-dropping. Names such as Wilkinson, Westinghouse, Governor Askew and Monty Hall, bring the J-man closer as a trusted authority. If the mooch agrees with the jammer that Westinghouse is a reputable firm, he gets the impression that the jammer knows what he's talking about. Being told that the J-man is just like Monty Hall also leads the mooch to see the J-man as an expert.

PHONY ACCUSATION

The jammer develops trust in several ways. The most explicit way is telling and showing the tip that he can be trusted: "You knew I wasn't going to take your dollar, because I said I was only going to sell it for a penny, and I always keep my word." The jammer's display of anger at the (phony) accusation of dishonesty adds to the effect.

The jammer also builds trust by occasionally showing that his products are not perfect. He starts out small, by breaking a comb while jokingly saying that it's guaranteed never to break. Sometimes the jammer mentions that an article comes from a new company and is no better than the well-known brand, but that "we just want to help them out by advertising for them."

What we have at the end of the cops is a highly persuasive communicator—powerful, entertaining, likable, expert, and trustworthy—talking to selected and committed people who are expecting good things and are having a good time. Greed brought people in; more greed and the developing relationship with the J-man keeps them there. Only one thing remains to be done: push the expensive articles.

THE REWARDS GET LARGER

Even though the obvious objectives of the bally and plunder are to get the people in and waiting for the bigger free stuff, the pitchmen have been working on the third objective, buying, from the very start of the pitch. The jam has conditioned buying responses through a successive approximations technique very much like that used in animal learning experiments. The responses the mooch is asked to make start out very small and grow progressively larger from just standing and watching, to holding up a nickel, to giving a nickel, to sitting down, to holding up a dollar, to sending up a dollar, to holding up $2, etc. Each response is reinforced. Standing is rewarded with a bag, sitting is rewarded with something free, and each time money is sent up, it is given back. (The nailer money is not given back, but the tip expects that it soon will be.) As the responses get larger, the rewards also get larger, because more money is being given back.

In addition to operant shaping of buying behavior, the jammer uses something like a classical conditioning technique to encourage positive verbal responses. Saying "yes" to the jammer's questions is developed through the use of a staggering number of positive questions. "Who's here for the first time? . . . Would you like to take home a nice gift? . . .

Who's seen Monty Hall on TV? . . . Who could make good use of one of these articles? . . . Who's ever gambled and lost?'' These positive questions elicit yes responses, over and over again, until any question from the jammer tends to elicit a yes. The jammer moves the mooch through repeated yeses to buy a $30 or $150 article that he would never have bought an hour ago.

Another way of understanding things like coining the tip, or collecting money for the lighters and black boxes and giving it back, or the fact that the tipman sells knives for a quarter (a sale so early that it violates the logic of successive approximations) is the foot-in-the-door principle. Social psychologists Jonathan Freedman and Scott Fraser found that a person who had already agreed to take some small action was more likely to take larger action upon request: "Once he has agreed to a request, his attitude may change. He may become, in his own eyes, the kind of person who does this sort of thing, who agrees to requests made by strangers. . . .''

THE LABELING EFFECT

Whether the mooches label themselves as yeasayers, the jammer undoubtedly labels the mooches. He begins early in the pitch with explicit labeling: "She sent up $1, so I know she is a good advertiser . . . You people who are left . . . are my advertising committee, you really want this merchandise." The dollars-and-cents power of this kind of labeling has been established by Robert Kraut, in a study of door-to-door solicitations. Givers labeled charitable gave more to a second charitable appeal than did givers who were not labeled, and nongivers labeled uncharitable gave less than those not labeled. Kraut concluded that ". . . labeling a person, i.e., giving him a feedback based on his behavior, causes him to behave consistently with the label and with his past behavior."

In the jam, the labeling effect is immensely strengthened by group pressure. When the mooch sends up that $3 for the nailer, his commitment is public. From that point on, in all future behaviors, the mooch is under real pressure from the group—whose members are now all committed—to act as a "responsible citizen who'll do a little advertising." Buying quickly becomes the group norm with the tip. If one member of the group doesn't conform, the jammer can turn the rest of the people against him, calling him a "stingy devil," which means that he's not a good advertiser. The group support for the role of good advertiser lasts until there is no way to get any money back.

It is interesting to note that when the buying norm is broken by one person who jumps up and starts complaining during a pitch, other members of the group find it easier to jump up and complain. As in Solomon Asch's studies of conformity, one deviate encourages nonconformity in others. Chain reactions of this type occasionally result in an entire tip coming up and asking for their money back before the pitch is over. From such incidents it appears that group pressure is essential to the success of the jam. Even if it were practical to apply the jam procedure to each person individually, the jam probably would not succeed outside the group situation.

Finally, the jam uses specific instructions to control behavior. From his studies of campaigns to sell U.S. War Bonds, Dorwin Cartwright argued that, "To induce a given action, an appropriate cognitive and motivational system must gain control of the person's behavior at a particular point in time. . . . The more specifically defined the path of action to a goal (in an accepted motivational structure), the more likely it is that the structure will gain control of behavior."

The jam fulfills these requirements by giving the mooch a motivational structure (something for nothing) and a cognitive structure (the advertising story, social labels) that culminate in the instructions to take a specific action (send up money) at a specific time (now!).

The techniques of persuasion used in the jam—conditioning, labeling, norm formation, and specific instruction—are aimed directly at controlling behavior. It is this concentration on behavior, together with the manipulation of group norms, that sets the jam apart from more familiar selling techniques. Other salesmen lie a little and misrepresent a lot. Many salesmen, notably those on Madison Avenue, know the techniques by which the jammer establishes himself as a persuasive communicator. But most salesmen do not work face-to-face with a group, and most salesmen do not aim their persuasion directly at buying behavior. The jammer is different in that he sells the act of buying rather than a particular product.

There are many different reactions to the jam. Most people do not complain. Some of them go out satisfied, while others are not satisfied at all, but just sit in their seats for a little while, or leave as if defeated. Nearly all those who complain do so after the pitch, almost apologetically. The quiet and apologetic people never get their money back. But a very small minority are more forceful in demanding a refund. By sheer persistence, screaming and yelling, or bringing in the police, these people do get their money back.

THE PRESSURE OF EMBARRASSMENT

The most likely answer to the question of why there are not more complaints is that complaints would contradict the behaviors induced by the jam. The nailers, together with any subsequent purchase, represent a clear and public commitment to the jam and the jammer. In this situation, Leon Festinger's cognitive-dissonance theory clearly predicts the adoption of attitudes consistent with the commitment, namely, positive attitudes toward the jam. The prediction can be made with great confidence: the tendency of attitudes to follow behavior has been demonstrated in a great number of dissonance studies. Indeed, the empirical result is now more certain than its explanation, as attribution theory and self-concept theory now vie with dissonance theory to explain why people don't like to admit they were had.

Even if a person walks away angry there is pressure of embarrassment. As one local newspaper reported, "Outside, the buyers dispersed quickly, some obviously embarrassed. A young woman from Pittsburgh was arguing with her husband as he lugged off a lamp and other appliances.

"'Well, at least we got the $30 back,' he said.

"'We didn't get it back the second time,' she shouted.

"'What?' he said, 'Shut up and get going.'"

HARRY STEIN

Reading 13–2

Ah, Sweet Vengeance!

Martha had a plan. In circumstances like these, Martha always had a plan. Her friend Jake, a minor executive at the New York office of a film studio, had been maneuvered out of a promotion by an ambition-consumed rival, and Martha damn well wasn't about to take it sitting down.

"Here's what we do," she said, leaning forward conspiratorially although the restaurant was empty except for the five of us at the table. "We're gonna make a total fool out of the guy. We're gonna make him the laughingstock of the industry."

Jake grinned. "I could go for that," he said.

"How?" I asked.

Martha drummed her fingers on the table. "It's complicated," she said. "We're going to need some help out on the Coast, but I think I know where to get it." And then she presented the plan, a caper rivaling that of *The Sting* in its scope. A few days hence, the rival would receive a call from an actor friend of Martha's posing as an important executive at Twentieth Century-Fox in California. The friend would hint at a job offer and urge him to drop everything in New York and come to California the next day. This important executive would add, casually, that the rival should fly out first class, register at the Beverly Hills Hotel, and drop the receipts off with the executive's secretary when he arrived for the meeting. Then—this was the beauty part—another pal of Martha's, who worked as a secretary at the studio, would make sure there was a pass in the rival's name waiting at the gate. He would actually make his way up to the executive's office—to face the humiliation of learning that no one there had the slightest idea who he was.

From Harry Stein, "Ah, Sweet Vengeance," *Esquire*, May 1981, pp. 14–16. Reprinted by permission.

"Who knows?" concluded Martha triumphantly. "With luck, his current boss will find out about it. He might even get fired!"

There followed such an eruption of good cheer around the table that a waitress was drawn over to inquire whether we might be interested in a bottle of champagne. Only one of us—Jake's wife, Susan—remained aloof from the bonhomie.

"I'd just like to ask one thing," she ventured finally. "What is all of this going to accomplish?"

The rest of us looked at her in bald astonishment. "What will it accomplish?" repeated Martha. "It will accomplish *revenge.*"

In the end, thanks to Susan's considerable powers of dissuasion, Jake refused to give the plan his go-ahead, and Martha was left more than a little disappointed. But I don't mean to convey the wrong impression about Martha. She is, in general, a very decent woman—thoughtful, courteous, and as loyal as anyone I have ever known. Indeed, that is why she lashes out with such energy at those who cross her or hers, why she will arrange to screw those who are needlessly vicious in their professional dealings.

That impulse is understandable because it is so terribly human. Most of us have felt surges of hostility so violent, so compelling, that we have literally fantasized murder. There was a period five or six years ago—it lasted a month—when I used to lie awake at night wondering how I might do away (inconspicuously yet very, very painfully) with a particularly loathsome agent who had double-crossed me. I still have to swallow hard when I think about the creep.

Indeed, imagining any act of violence seems far more comprehensible than maintaining utter calm in the face of terrible provocation. That "don't get mad, get even" mentality has been embraced not only by the efficiency experts who direct organized crime but by legions of political leaders and chamber of commerce types as well. It is a major reason that the machinations of *Dallas's* J. R. ring true to so many millions of us, and it has something to do with the unhappy state of our society.

However, as Jake's wife pointed out, retribution for its own sake is hardly a reasonable alternative. Almost all of Martha's acts of revenge appear to have been justly motivated, and some of them have even worked, but not one has succeeded in righting the initial wrong. Nor, for that matter, has one served to make Martha or her friends feel better for more than a few minutes. For, of course, none has ever touched the source of the pain.

With depressing frequency, the traveler along the low road actually ends up feeling a lot worse. For starters, we *look* so irredeemably small when we're caught being vindictive. I shudder to imagine how Jake would have reacted if the California scheme had gone through and his rival or—Jesus!— his boss had chanced upon its origin.

But detection is almost beside the point. The fact is, vindictive behavior and meanness of spirit finally make us as small as those we despise. Even when we do manage to hurt others as we have been hurt, we succeed, in a real sense, only in further victimizing ourselves. Obviously, that is not an easy thing for one fixated on vengeance to recognize. The vengeful impulse tends to obscure our better instincts and to stymie logic as well.

Vindictive behavior is not only self-destructive; it can also wound people who had nothing to do with the initial dispute. A friend of mine told of arriving at her office one morning to find her boss, a prominent magazine editor, in tears. "She'd recently been dumped by her husband," said my friend, "and she was absolutely shattered. But suddenly she stopped crying. 'I'm going to get even,' she announced. 'I'm going to tell our daughter how her father screwed around when I was pregnant.' And I swear to God, she meant it!"

Relatively few people would be quite that candid about their vindictive intentions, but it is a pretty good bet that the editor would not be the first on her block to have adopted such a tactic.

"I tried to get her to calm down," continued my friend. "I explained to her how sorry she'd be later.

"'Okay, she replied, 'then what do you suggest I do to him?'

"'Nothing. Just go along as best you can, and eventually you'll get past this. The best way to get back at him is to show him how well you can do without him.'"

My friend, as you might surmise, is a soul of staggering sweetness, and she continued to express dismay at her boss's reaction. The editor ordered her from the room forthwith. Like most of us, my friend's boss was so used to operating the other way—to getting even—that she was incapable of recognizing the elementary truth of that famous maxim: Living well *is* the best revenge.

At this juncture another, more recent, adage springs to mind: What goes around comes around. It is, all in all, a terrific sentiment, and I know a lot of people who would turn handsprings if only they could be assured it was true.

Well, I'm here to do some assuring. The fact is, the editor's husband (if he is as vicious a bastard as she maintains) will almost certainly get his, and so will Jake's rival and all of Martha's many wrongdoers. They might be successful professionally—might even, conceivably, seem to lead placid domestic lives—but it is almost a sure thing that all of those people are in knots inside. People at peace with themselves simply don't act cruelly toward others. When the rest of us finally accept that law of human behavior, we'll be a hell of a lot better off ourselves.

I am all too well aware that such wisdom about the way of the world is easier to set down on paper than to apply to one's own experience. Just a couple of weeks ago, I laid aside the beginnings of this piece to thumb through a local magazine of some repute, and there, to my astonishment, I found a vicious attack on the character of a very close friend of mine, whose much-acclaimed first novel had recently been published. Now, I care immensely about this fellow and am familiar with the fragility of his ego, and I found myself irate on his behalf. Not only had the attack—by a supposedly reputable journalist—been needlessly vituperative, it was also, I knew, completely without foundation. When I called my friend, I discovered that he had moved from deep depression to rage and was now ready to sling a little mud himself. "What do you think," he asked, "of my getting a friend in the press to blast the son of a bitch? Or would it be better just to call his editor myself? *I want the bastard to pay."*

So, as it happened, did I, but for the moment we decided to do nothing more dramatic than discuss it over dinner. As I was leaving for this rendezvous I got a call from another old friend, a guy just back from a long business trip, and I suggested that he join us.

This other fellow made it to the restaurant just as the novelist and I were warming to the unpleasant subject at hand. When he'd gotten an earful, he broke into a broad grin.

"What's so funny?" I demanded. "Did you read what that guy wrote?"

"Yeah, I read it."

"So what's so funny?" I asked.

He laughed. "That you two are taking it so seriously." He turned to our friend. "Don't you know about that guy?" he asked. "For years he's been trying to get someone to pay attention to his own fiction. He's the most bitter guy in town."

This last, I understood, was hyperbole—the town in question was, after all, New York—but the revelation was more than enough to restore our friend's good mood. After eliciting a few more details about his adversary's ugly disposition, he settled back to enjoy his meal.

And enjoy it he did. By dessert he was in better spirits than I'd seen him in for months.

"No more plotting?" I inquired.

He laughed. "His private demons seem to be handling him just fine."

Reading 13-3

Easy Money, Easy Virtue

The other afternoon, co-op hunting in the newspaper, I ran across an ad for an apartment on the Upper West Side of Manhattan available to rent for $1,850 a month. Now the Upper West Side, though markedly more chic today than in years past, remains an essentially middle-income district, and I was thus curious to discover just what this place (which was not located at a particularly chic address) might look like.

The snappy young real estate lady who met me in the lobby, though she would be collecting 15 percent of a year's rent for her services, had not yet seen the apartment herself. But that didn't stop her from pushing it. "What a fabulous lobby," she exclaimed as we rose in the elevator. "Did you notice the ceiling?" Then, a few floors higher: "I'm so excited! I adore these big, old apartments!"

And the apartment was indeed awfully nice, with rooms all over the place and a pretty view of Upper West Side rooftops. But my companion behaved as though we'd been afforded an inside track to paradise. "I can't believe this! How gorgeous! Look at this, you could have *four* bedrooms here. I have to tell you the truth. Frankly, I didn't expect it to be much, but this is gorgeous!" A beat. "The lady who owns it has another offer, but she doesn't like the people. Let's hurry down to the office and sign a contract."

When, despite a fair amount of cajoling and a little bullying, I convinced her at last that, no, I didn't think I was going to take the place, she was not at all disappointed. I stood beside her on the street while she dialed her office and barked into the phone: "Tell her not to rent it. Tell her I'll get her $2,400 for it."

Even in the best of times, of course, those who deal in the roofs over our heads—agents, realtors, landlords—are in many quarters regarded with

---

From Harry Stein, "Easy Money, Easy Virture," *Esquire*, September 1981, pp. 15–16. Reprinted by permission.

suspicion. So it is perhaps courting incredulity to begin building a general case upon such an incident. However, my visit with the real estate agent occurred toward the end of a day marked by half a dozen not dissimilar episodes. One acquaintance of mine, a staunch liberal, had informed me by phone, and without the merest hint of irony, that he could kick himself for having failed to buy defense stocks prior to Reagan's election. Another guy, a fine writer, had told me over lunch that on the basis of the big numbers dropped by an independent producer, he has opted to work on a film project that will, at best, be inane, and might turn out to be morally reprehensible. I had heard from another acquaintance, who was thrilled to death because his old Ford had been broadsided by a very wealthy hosiery manufacturer with expired plates. The unfortunate hosiery manufacturer was reportedly ready to pay through the nose.

This frenzied hustling after the big score has become, quite literally, inescapable. Suddenly it seems that everyone is looking to make a great deal of money in return for the least possible effort, and scruples be damned. Indeed, the truth is, the excessive greed of the lady in the big apartment had not even struck me as anomalous. Friends of mine hoping to sell their own apartments for 5 or 6 or 10 times what they paid for them are hardly more admirable; nor are all those otherwise respectable citizens who a year ago attached themselves so readily to pyramid schemes; nor those anxious souls who today study the silver or commodities markets the way, in calmer times, they used to study box scores; nor those many thousands who have guaranteed the fortunes of authors of books with titles like *The Lazy Man's Way to Riches*.

Of course, easy money and lots of it is not exactly a new addition to the catalog of human fantasies. And in this society, where from the very beginning people have been measured, and tended to measure themselves, by the bottom line, the fantasy of unearned wealth has been as persistent as hope itself. It was the impetus behind the great gold and land rushes of the last century, behind all those many thousands of quirky devices listed with the U.S. patent office, and behind all the idol makers of show business and more than a few of the idols themselves. It is no accident that the big-money quiz shows and supermarketlike gambling casinos were born in this country.

But in the past, I think, we kept the fantasy in perspective. While as Americans it was the birthright of each of us to play Walter Mitty, we always regarded those who turned themselves inside out in pursuit of the mirage— those who actually *bought* the Brooklyn Bridge—as fools, and rather pathetic ones at that. In the end our values were very nearly consistent with those of our forebears. From the time of Miles Standish to the era of Frank Capra films, the lessons had been handed down—nothing truly worthwhile comes easily; one makes something of oneself by setting goals and working toward them; character is ultimately what counts—and for most people these values were as sound as the dollar.

In a sense they still are—which is one excellent explanation for why they have fallen so widely out of favor. "People are scared," notes a friend of mine, in self-defense, "and principles don't do terribly well in times of fear. With prices and interest rates where they are, salaries don't leave people feeling very secure. A lot of us are ready to do whatever we have to to produce income, short of illegality—and some of us haven't excluded that."

Different today, too, is that those subscribing to the "anything for a buck" mentality have grown shamelessly brazen. What is an 11-year-old to make of a television ad campaign for a product called Goldigger jeans that features two of his contemporaries picking up each other in a disco?

What, for that matter, is a 40-year-old to make of his government, under pressure from the infant-formula lobby, standing alone among the industrialized nations of the world in opposing a measure designed to save the lives of a million newborns annually?

And, of course, there is also the matter of rising expectations. With the incessant reports of entertainers, ballplayers, businessmen, realtors, actors, and even writers who have become, often with stunning swiftness, indecently wealthy, we have become an entire nation with its nose pressed up against the candy store window. As my friend puts it, "people feel like fools for not getting their share." He smiles, "I'm a fool and don't I know it, but even fools can have their charms. . ."

But the other side—how they feel, or should feel, after a few years of assiduously playing the angles—cannot be so lightly shrugged off. The fact is that the real estate agent seemed so intent on financial gain that she might have summoned up the Ghost of Christmas Past right there on the fourteenth floor. Those part-time fortune makers, similarly fixated on the quick score and equally ready to put aside qualms about right and wrong to achieve it, are little better.

At the time that John Lennon was killed last year, I was visiting a tiny upstate New York community. I will not soon forget the shock of seeing, within 36 hours of the murder, a young woman turn up in a diner wearing a Lennon memorial T-shirt.

That the awful event was being squeezed for dollars should not, in retrospect, have come as a surprise, not after the exploitation of so many other tragedies in recent years. Indeed, in the months since the murder, we have witnessed many, many others—from button manufacturers, to organizers of "Beatles conventions," to publishers and record company executives—cash in, in their turn. But, finally, the question must be asked: What does all of this say about us as a people? At long last, to paraphrase Joseph Welch's lament at the Army-McCarthy hearings, have we left no sense of decency?

I did not know John Lennon, but I did know Jean Seberg, and reasonably well. She was a remarkably fine human being, fragile as crystal but animated by spunk and vivid humor—in contrast to the way she has lately been portrayed, and to the way she will probably be depicted in most of the forthcoming books and movies.

When I came to know her in Paris, several years before her apparent suicide, Jean was quite obviously troubled, and not just by the profound personal woes that have made grist for so many mills over the last couple of years. She was, lest we forget, an actress of some standing; but the public, particularly on this side of the water, had lost interest and the film offers had all but stopped coming. And so, in her late 30's and by no means wealthy, she found herself examining other career options. She enjoyed writing, so life behind an Olivetti seemed the way to go; indeed, at one point she broached the idea of a monthly column from Paris for this magazine. But it was rejected, as were most of her other brave attempts to sell herself in this new guise.

The easy sell, she knew, was an autobiography. Seberg was, after all, a beauty who had had influential friends and lovers on both sides of the Atlantic; who had helped shape contemporary cinema; who had moved between the worlds of show business and politics, from glitzy stardom to bold experimentation, from state dinners to clandestine activity on behalf of revolutionaries, in a manner unique in her generation.

But it was a notion she approached with great trepidation. "My problem," she told me one evening, "is my parents. It would cause them such enormous embarrassment. I don't know, I think I'll wait. . ."

Forget for a moment about all of those so suddenly interested in Jean Seberg. Would you, if the money were waiting on the table, let yourself be stopped by such a consideration?

PETE AXTHELM

Reading 13–4
Psst, Somebody May Be Cheating

In his sleeves, which were long,
He had twenty-four packs—
Which was coming it strong,
Yet I state but the facts;
And we found on his nails, where were taper,
What is frequent in tapers—that's wax.

Bret Harte,
"The Heathen Chinee," 1870

No, those weren't extra packs of marked cards up New York Yankee manager Billy Martin's pinstriped sleeve last week. And it wasn't a dealer's paraffin that adorned the bat of Kansas City Royals' smoothie George Brett; it was dark and sticky pine tar. But the high-noon shoot-out of gamesmanship that made a Brett home run disappear and then suddenly reappear belonged to a saga that is centuries old, reenacted from the riverboats of Mississippi to the roulette wheels of Monte Carlo: the eternal search for the edge.

PINE TAR

The affair can be quickly summarized. Brett, one of baseball's best hitters, uses pine tar to improve his grip. But since he doesn't want too much on the handle, he slathers it up the bat where he can palm it when he needs more. This method is clean, comfortable and gives Brett an edge. Martin and some Yankee players noticed that Brett placed the tar so far up the bat that it violated a rule. And when George hit a ninth-inning homer against Yankee reliever Goose Gossage, the Yankees presented the bat to the umpires—who cited the rule and nullified the home run. This gave the Yankees a very big edge, and the ball game.

The Yankees had scarcely stopped gloating before American League president Lee MacPhail reversed the decision. Tempering justice with mercy in Solomonic proportions, MacPhail differentiated the anti-tar rule from other rules regarding illegal bats: use of wax or cork to increase a hitter's distance was clearly illegal, but the pine-tar regulation was largely hygienic. Tar doesn't add clout; it is messy and a nuisance, but it does not threaten the integrity of the national pastime. Sticky bats should be spotted and tossed out of the game, but they should not be ground for depriving players of home runs. "Although manager Martin and his staff should be commended for their alertness," MacPhail said, "it is the strong conviction of the league that games should be won and lost on the playing field."

This sensible decision did little to still the furor on the saloon-and-water cooler frontiers of the tar wars. The reason goes far beyond the effect of the ruling on the pennant chances of the Yankees and Royals. Ever since the first serpent stole a base in the Garden of Eden, sports fans have been fascinated by rules and the heady possibility that someone will figure out a new way to break them.

Bret Harte's "Chinee" cardsharp has descendants in almost every modern sport. It was fitting that one of the Royals who tried to abscond with Brett's viscous bat was the venerable master of the illegal spitball, Gaylord Perry. But connoisseurs of foreign substances were also quick to recall the glory days of football's old Oakland Raiders. Once the Raiders were accused of greasing the jerseys of defensive linemen so blockers couldn't hold them—a clear case of one rulebreaker seizing an edge from another. Raider fans will always treasure the memory of a Ken Stabler pass hitting receiver Fred Biletnikoff in the back of the helmet and staying there for a completion, because of the stickum that Freddie applied to every target on his slim body.

Ice hockey fans always hope that their favorites will curve the blades of their sticks just enough to be more effective in their shooting. If that fails, they hope the opponents will curve their sticks beyond the allowable limits— and have a crucial goal nullified. In college basketball, sly coaches make sure that the heat is turned up in the visitors' locker room, to enervate the foes before they take their first shot. And if a visiting team likes to play the fast break, it doesn't hurt a bit to wet down the twine on the basket. The tightened net makes the ball go through slower, and gives the defense more time to set up.

Many tricks of the trade have been outlawed, but two events that were overshadowed by the Brett affair last week indicate that the spirit of chicanery is alive and well. In New York, Alexis Arguello and Aaron Pryor signed for a rematch of their brutal junior welterweight fight last fall. Much of the appeal of the bout is that when Pryor savaged Arguello, it was widely believed that he had help: his horsehair gloves may have been kneaded between rounds to expose his knuckles to Arguello's face, and he drank lustily from a mysterious black bottle that might have contained stimulants. His cornerman, Panama Lewis, his since been suspended for alleged dirty tricks. The mere chance that Pryor won illegally makes the rematch hugely attractive in the nether world of boxing.

In more aristocratic circles off Newport, R.I., a crewman for the Canadian yacht was apprehended in his wet suit, taking underwater pictures of the America's Cup boat from Australia. Charges were dropped, but the suspicion remained that yacht racing had finally found a way into the public consciousness: somebody may be cheating.

The Newport incident also raises one dark specter. In the wake of Ronald Reagan's Debategate, the *New York Post* called the Brett controversy De-Bat-Gate. It seems that "gate" has become the most tired suffix in the language since Madison Avenue types popularized "wise." Cheatingwise, we may finally have come full circle. If a guy in a wet suit steals another boat's secrets in the water, are we faced with another Watergate?

GAMBLE

George Brett pondered no such problems as he recovered his multishaded beige bat and resumed his pursuit of the pennant last week. The Royals and the Yankees will probably put their little edges out of their minds, at least until one of the teams finishes within a game of the division lead—and they have to resume the suspended game that "ended" when Brett's homer was incorrectly declared a final out. In the meantime, the baseball races will proceed on schedule, and the fans will continue to be delighted. The great edge-seeking hustler Wilson Mizner once admitted that he would rather gamble honestly than not at all. The enduring sports fan feels the same way. The next best thing to the home team getting the edge is a game that is on the level.

Reading 13–5

The Cult of Winning

Winning is a gloriously gratifying ecstasy for the ego. In every sports arena, adoring crowds flock and flurry to touch the charismatic magic of the victor. The two-gunned Texan tank general George Patton once observed: ''America loves a winner.'' So true is this view that after winning seven Olympic gold medals, amateur athlete Mark Spitz was enshrined as a national hero and conferred with gifts and commerical offers that ensured him a multi-million dollar future.

To recent years, however, America's win-orientedness has been whipped into a near win-obsessiveness, threatening to undermine other traditions and values which have made this nation great. In the current atmosphere, from age five in the toddler division of Little League and beyond, our children are being instilled with a hyper go-go drive to push for the prize. The slogan ''We're Number One'' is gaining on ''In God We Trust'' as the national motto. ''We try harder'' has become the rallying cry for every red-blooded, Wheaties-eating, Dad-loving, patriotic American boy—and more and more girls. The possibility exists of American life becoming one big existential superbowl.

In political campaigns U.S.A. style, the candidates typically start out in a candid fashion, charging straightforward on the issues. Eventually though, they begin to hedge and fudge, obscure and evade, squiggle and slither, until they are assured of victory by standing up for nothing.

Collegiate sports have been scandalously quaked with headlines arising out of what 12-time All-American Bob Cousy calls a ''grotesque over-emphasis on winning.'' At the University of Montana, administrative officials were charged with fraudulently diverting $200,000 of federal

Joseph N. Sorrentino, ''The Cult of Winning,'' *Flightime* magazine, September 1974. Reprinted by permission.

scholarship money to bolster their sagging football team. At the same time in a California sailing race, the captain of the winning craft was disqualified shortly after receiving the gold cup when it was discovered that during the race he had ducked his sailboat into a cove and turned on its power motor. The most shockingly ominous case of the "win-by-any-means" mentality was seen in the 1973 American Soap Box Derby in which one third of the 12-year-old entrants were expelled for cheating.

"Winning," champion football coach Vince Lombardi once exclaimed, "is not important. It is everything." Yet to be obsessed with winning in every endeavor is an infantile attitude—an insistence of one's primacy, an urge to blow out all the candles. Winning should be pursued with excellence, not excess, and losing should be taken disappointedly, not neurotically, and on both sides there should be a more valuable lesson to be gained.

Winners are sometimes inclined to snobbishly take themselves too seriously. Ability is a prerequisite for achievement but there are many equally gifted losers who have made way for the winners. How many races have been won by a fractional margin that could have gone to another with the tiniest tilt in conditions? Thomas Hardy, in *Far From The Madding Crowd*, suggests that there is no justice in the universe or rational pattern to events. What happens to everyone, regardless of who he is, happens as a matter of time and chance.

The story behind the casting of *The Graduate* illustrates the dramatic weight of fate. Director Mike Nichols had been searching for a male lead for six months when Dustin Hoffman, who for years had been an unsuccessful though highly talented actor, showed up. By this time both Nichols and the producers were extremely weary and eager to get the film underway. As everyone knows, Hoffman was chosen for the role and he went on to become a superstar. The question he must ask himself is what would have happened if he had shown up on the first day, not the last, of auditioning?

Winning has its rewards but the price can be extreme sacrifice. The Japanese Women's Volleyball Team won a Gold Medal at the 1964 Olympics, but it was well publicized that as a part of training the girls had given up all social life for two years. Divorce proceedings abound with stories of successful businessmen who reached the top over the wreckage of their family life because of the time and energy consumed by ambition. Far more tragic are the political figures who ascended the ladder by surrendering their souls. Win-obsessiveness even infects our colleges and universities in the fierce clash for recognition through the annual "Academy Awards" for academic achievement, and the price paid is seen in the statistics on ulcers, heart attacks and suicides among college students and professors.

At the highly competitive Harvard Law School I became well acquainted with the "win at all cost" philosophy. One student in my dormitory, as a tactic to fret his competition, kept his lights on during sleeping hours to give the appearance of an all-night vigil. During law school exams, marshals patrolled the corridors and rest rooms to guard against cheating, and they strictly enforced time limits by yanking out typewriter cords the moment exams were over. Caught up in the mania myself, to prepare for exams I carried a tape recorder wherever I went, playing back lectures at the dinner table, on my way to class, in the shower. Even while sleeping, I had the tape recorder going in the minispeaker in my ear.

Competitive men have an especially attractive allure to competitive women. Aware of reports that Harvard Law graduates average $50,000 a year, hordes of girls, sometimes outnumbering the men 10 to 1, descend on the law school at the monthly social mixers, which in derisive parlance are known as "cattle shows." It is no wonder, then, that Harvard Law students were committing suicide on the eve of exams. In a system which puts such an emphasis on winning or success at all costs, failure is intolerable. William Carlos Williams, in his poem "The Yachts," accurately portrays of failure in our society:

> Bodies thrown recklessly in the way are cut aside.
> It is a sea of faces about them in agony, in despair
> until the horror of the race dawns staggering the mind,
> the whole sea becomes an entanglement of watery bodies
> lost to the world . . . Broken.
> Beaten, desolate, reaching from the dead to be taken up
> they cry out, failing, failing.

Perhaps among the more competitive men and women in the nation are insurance agents, who by selling a million dollars of insurance each year are nominated to the celebrated Million Dollar Round Table. Immersed as these agents are in pushing, driving and hustling to sell insurance, they take a week out each year to attend a convention that features a flood of information and knowledge from a host of different fields.

Attending their convention in Florida this year, I was impressed by the range of perspectives represented by their 52 guest speakers. While these agents were eager to add to their insurance sales, they also sought an expansion of vision and understanding in their general knowledge. Not only does it emancipate an individual from the rut of the success race, it helps him to perform better when he returns.

Winning is a beautiful creation of culture to enhance life. Without goals of merit to chase, and heights of excellence to climb, human experience stagnates in biological functions of nature. What is there to do on this planet after survival but to try to stimulate ourselves by inventing ego games and rewards?

In criticizing the extremes of some players, I do not deny the intrinsic worth of competition. Ardent discipline toward a goal is an expression of the purest idealism. Competition is healthy, but what needs to be reaffirmed in America today is that equally as important as winning are the rules of playing. The profound tragedy of Watergate is that the "guilty" participants were willing to go to any immoral lengths to ensure victory.

No matter how many impressive titles or luxurious symbols one accrues, a human being's ultimate worth, cynical rationalizations notwithstanding, is based on how he played the game. One humble but good man is worth a hundred successful but unscrupulous men.

EXERCISES

The Disarmament Exercise

INTRODUCTION

The purpose of this exercise is to engage you in working together in a small group, making decisions about the nature of your relationship with another group. Your group will be paired with another group. Each group will have the opportunity to make a decision on a series of "moves." The outcome of those moves (in terms of the amount of money that your team wins or loses) will be determined by the choice that your group makes, *and* the choice that the other group makes. Your group cannot independently determine its outcomes in this situation. The nature of your group's choices, and how well it performs in this exercise, will be determined by: (1) your group's behavior toward the other group, (2) the other group's behavior toward your group, and (3) the communication between groups when this is permitted.

ADVANCE PREPARATION

None.

PROCEDURE

Step 1: 5 Minutes

Divide the class into three to six persons per group (your group leader will tell you how to do this). Pair off the groups so that all groups are paired. If there is more than one pair, the group leader will assign a referee to monitor each pair of teams. He may also designate specific rooms for each team.

Step 2: 15 Minutes

Read the following instructions—"Rules for the Disarmament Exercise"— carefully. When you have finished reading the instructions, the group leader

---

Adapted by Roy J. Lewicki from an exercise developed by Norman Berkowitz and Harvey Hornstein. Reprinted from *Experiences in Management and Organizational Behavior*, by Douglas T. Hall, Donald Bowen, Roy J. Lewicki, and Francine Hall (Chicago: St. Clair Press, 1975).

will answer any questions that you have. You will then be given time to discuss the rules with your teammates, and plan the strategy you will use.

RULES FOR THE DISARMAMENT EXERCISE

The Objective

You and your team are going to engage in a disarmament exercise in which you can win or lose money. In this exercise, your objective as a team is to win as much money as you can. The team opposing yours has the identical objective.

The Task

1. Each team is given 20 cards. These are your *weapons*. Each card has a marked side X and an unmarked side. The marked side of the card indicates that the weapon is armed; conversely, the blank side shows the weapon to be unarmed. Each team also has an A (Attack) card; this will be explained later.

2. At the beginning of the exercise, each team places 10 of its 20 weapons in their armed positions with the marked side up, and the remaining 10 in their unarmed positions was the marked side down. These weapons will remain in your possession, but they must be placed so that the referee (group leader) can see them, and out of the sight of the other team.

3. During this exercise, there are rounds and moves. Each round consists of seven moves (perhaps fewer; see below) by each team. There will be two or more rounds in this exercise. The number of rounds will depend on the time remaining. Payoffs are calculated after each round.

   a. A move consists of a team turning two, one, or none of its weapons from armed (X) to unarmed (blank) status, *or* vice versa.

   b. Each team has 2½ minutes to decide on its move and to make that move. There are 30-second periods between moves. At the end of 2½ minutes, a team must have turned two, one, or none of its weapons from armed to unarmed status, or from unarmed to armed status. Failing to decide on a move in the allotted time means that no change can then be made in weapon status until the next move.

   c. The length of the three-minute period (move and after-move time) is fixed and unalterable.

4. Each new round of the experiment begins with all weapons returned to their original positions, 10 armed and 10 unarmed.

The Finances

If your referee chooses to use *real* money in this exercise, money will be distributed as described. If you use *imaginary* money, assume that each team member has made an imaginary contribution of $2.00, and that the money is also distributed as described.

1. Each member will contribute to the treasury. The money you have contributed will be allocated in the following manner:

    a. 60 percent will be returned to your group to be used in the task. Your group may diminish or supplement this money during the course of your work. At the end of the exercise your group's treasury will be divided among the members.

    b. 40 percent will be donated to the World Bank, which is to be managed by the referee. This money will *not* be returned at the end of the exercise, and should be considered as no longer yours.

    c. The opposing team's money will be allocated in the same way.

The Payoffs

1. If there is an *attack:*

    a. Each team may announce an attack on the other team (by notifying the referee) during the 30 seconds following any 2½-minute period used to decide upon a move (including the seventh, or final, decision period in any round). To attack, you must display your A (attack) card to the referee. You may not attack without a card. The choice of each team during the decision period just ended counts as a move. An attack may not be made during negotiations (see below).

    b. If there is an attack (by one or both teams), the round ends.

    c. The team with the greater number of armed weapons wins 5 cents per member for each armed weapon it has *over and above* the number of armed weapons of the other team. These funds are paid directly from the treasury of the losing team to the treasury of the winning team. If both teams have the same number of armed weapons, the round is declared a draw.

2. If there is *no attack:*

    a. At the end of each round (seven moves), each team's treasury *receives* from the World Bank 2 cents per member for each of its weapons that is at that point unarmed, *and* each team's treasury *pays* to the World Bank 2 cents per member for each of its weapons remaining armed.

    b. When both teams win funds, they are awarded by the World Bank. When both teams lose funds, they are paid to the World Bank.

    c. When one team wins while the other loses, the winning team receives funds from the World Bank, while the losing team forfeits funds to the World Bank. Thus, in effect, the losing team pays part or all of its losses to the other team.

The Negotiations

1. Between moves, each team has the opportunity to communicate with the other team through negotiators chosen by the team members for this purpose.
2. Either team may call for negotiations (by notifying the referee) during any of the 30-second periods between decisions. A team is free to accept or reject any invitation from the other team.
3. Negotiators from both teams are *required* to meet after the third and sixth moves.
4. Negotiators can last no longer than five minutes. When the two negotiators return to their teams, the 2½-minute decison period for the next move begins.
5. Negotiators are bound only by: (*a*) the five-minute time limit for negotiations, and (*b*) required appearance after third and sixth moves. They are otherwise free to say whatever they choose, and to make an agreement which is necessary to benefit themselves or their teams. They are not required to tell the truth. Each team is similarly not bound by any agreements made by their negotiators, even when those agreements were made in good faith by the negotiators.

Reminders

1. Each move can consist of turning over two, one, or zero or your weapons to the unarmed side—*or* back again to the armed side.
2. You have 2½ minutes to decide which of the above you will choose.
3. If there is *no* attack, at the end of the round (seven moves) your team receives 2 cents per member for each unarmed weapon and loses 2 cents per member for each armed weapon.
4. If there *is* an attack, the team with the greater number of armed weapons wins 5 cents per minute for each armed weapon it has *over* the number the other team has.
5. A team may call for negotiations after any move. Mandatory meetings of negotiators occur after moves three and six.

Step 3: 15 Minutes

1. Once you have clarified and understood the rules, each team has 15 minutes to organize itself and to plan team strategy.
    a. You must select people to fill the following roles (the persons can be changed at any time by a decision of the team): (1) A

negotiator—activities as stated under "The Negotiations." (2) A team spokesperson to communicate decisions to the referee about team moves, attacks, initiations or acceptances of negotiations, etc. The referee will only listen to the team spokesperson, and the spokesperson cannot also be the negotiator. (3) A team recorder to record moves of the team, and to keep running accounts of the team's treasury.

b. You should discuss with your team members the way that you want to play, what the other team might do and how that affects your strategy, the first move that you will make for the first round, whether or not you desire negotiations, and what you might say to the other team if you or they initiate them.

Step 4: 10–20 Minutes

Round 1:

1. The referee will signal that the first round begins.
2. Your team has 2½ minutes to decide on its first move, and then to actually move 1, 2, or no cards.
3. When the referee returns, show him your move. You may also attack at this point, and/or you may call for negotiations.
4. If neither team attacks or calls for negotiations, the referee will proceed to the second move.
5. Remember that there will be mandatory negotiations after moves three and six. Also remember that the game will proceed for seven moves, unless there is an attack.
6. When the game ends, the referee will determine the winnings and losses for each team. These will be announced, and money (if used) will be transferred from one team's treasury to the other, or to/from the World Bank.
7. After accounts are settled, return the cards to their "opening" position (10 *X*-side up and 10 *X*-side down).

Step 5: 5 Minutes (at the Referee's Discretion)

Answer the questions for round 1 on the Disarmament Exercise Questionnaire below.

Disarmament Exercise Questionnaire

For round 1, circle the appropriate number on each scale which best represents your feelings. (For subsequent rounds, uses boxes or triangles or colored pencils to indicate appropriate number.)

1. To what extent are you satisfied with your team's current strategy?

highly satisfied   1   2   3   4   5   6   7   highly dissatisfied

2. To what extent do you believe the other team is now trustworthy?

| highly trustworthy | 1 | 2 | 3 | 4 | 5 | 6 | 7 | highly untrustworthy |

3. To what extent are you now satisfied with the performance of your negotiator?

| highly dissatisfied | 7 | 6 | 5 | 4 | 3 | 2 | 1 | highly satisfied |

4. To what extent is there now a consensus in your team regarding its moves?

| great deal | 7 | 6 | 5 | 4 | 3 | 2 | 1 | very little consensus |

5. To what extent are you now willing to trust the other people on your team?

| more than before | 7 | 6 | 5 | 4 | 3 | 2 | 1 | less than before |

6. Select one word to describe how you feel about your team:

7. Select one word to describe how you feel about the *other* team:

Negotiators Only: Please respond to the following question.

How did you see the other team's negotiator?

| phoney and insincere | 1 | 2 | 3 | 4 | 5 | 6 | 7 | authentic and sincere |

Step 6: 5 Minutes

Evaluate your team's strategy and outcomes in round 1. Use your reactions to the Disarmament Exercise Questionnaire as a guide, then discuss the strategy you wish to pursue in round 2.

Step 7: 5–20 Minutes

Round 2. Proceed as in round 1 (Step 3).

Step 8: 5 Minutes (at the Referee's Discretion)

Complete the questions for round 2 on the questionnaire.

Step 9: 5–20 Minutes

Additional rounds may be played at the discretion of the referee.

Disarmament Exercise Team Record Sheet

	Round 1		Round 2		Round 3		Round 4	
	Armed	Unarmed	Armed	Unarmed	Armed	Unarmed	Armed	Unarmed
Start:	10	10	10	10	10	10	10	10
Move 1								
Move 2								
Move 3								
Negotiation								
Move 4								
Move 5								
Move 6								
Negotiation								
Move 7								
Financial status prior to first move:								
Funds in team treasury								
Funds of other team								
Funds in World Bank								
At end of each round:								
Funds in team treasury								
Funds of other team								
Funds in World Bank (include penalties)								

DISCUSSION QUESTIONS

1. How effectively did your team work together?
   a. How did your team make decisions? (Did one or two persons make the decision for the whole team? A minority make decisions for the whole team? Always a democratic vote? Majority kept overriding the minority?)
   b. Did your team make maximum use of information available? Did the team members really listen to each other? Why not? Were the opinions of the less vocal members sought? Why not? Did the team really try to obtain every piece of information from the negotiators, which was the team's only direct source of information about the other team?
2. Did your team have a viable strategy?
   a. Did your team have a *consistent* plan or was it "pushed around" by other teams?
   b. Was your team's plan *naive?* If so, why?
   c. To what extent was your team trying to "win a lot," but not risking anything to do that?
3. How did your team react to cooperation and competition?
   a. Why is cooperation so difficult to achieve?
   b. What are the barriers that stand in the way of developing trust?
   c. What assumptions did your team have about the other team which may have prevented trust and cooperation?
   d. What happened to your team's morale and decision-making structure when it won? When it lost?
4. How did the negotiator get chosen? Delegated? Volunteered? Discussion of "qualifications"?
   a. How committed were you to your negotiator? Where you willing to stand by him through thick and think, or did you abandon trust in your negotiator at some point?
   b. Did some of the negotiators lie? If they are not basically dishonest people, why did they? If they lied, how did they feel about this afterward?

Precision Plastics

INTRODUCTION

This exercise creates a situation in which you and the other person(s) will be making separate decisions on how to manage your firm. In this situation, the outcomes (costs and profits) are determined not only by what you do, but also by a number of other factors, such as the goals and the motives that you and the other party have and the communication that takes place between you and the other party.

ADVANCE PREPARATION

None.

PROCEDURE

Step 1: 5 Minutes

The class will be broken into six-person groups; three will play the role of Manufacturing Committee for Xercon Corporation, three will play the role of Manufacturing Committee for Yenton Corporation.

The two committees should sit close enough to talk but also able to caucus among themselves.

Step 2: 10 Minutes

Read the "Background Information" for Precision Plastics below. If you have any questions, clarify them with the instructor at this time.

In this exercise, you will represent your company in negotiations with another company about the use of a production facility that you both share. You and the other company manager will be making decisions simultaneously, and your firm's profits will be directly affected by these decisions. How well you perform will depend in part on your goals, the other manager's goals, and the communication between you.

BACKGROUND INFORMATION

Zercon and Yenton are both small, rapidly growing manufacturers of electrical hand tools. To break even, each must hold its factory costs to $50 per item. Both use 10,000 pieces a month of a precision molded plastic part in their products. Both have been successful in holding factory cost, exclusive of the plastic part, to $40. Each has production equipment to make the plastic part, which is old and inefficient, resulting in an average cost of $12 a part. Newer equipment can produce the same quality parts for much less. However, because of the high capital investment needed for this equipment and the relatively small quantities of plastic parts used, both companies use outside subcontractors to make their plastic parts.

The most desirable supplier in terms of quality, delivery, and price is Precision Plastics, which will deliver the part at a cost of $2. Precision Plastics has most of its capacity committed to long-term contracts but does have one day a month available during which it can produce 10,000 pieces of the part needed by both Xercon or Yenton. The setup time and costs are such that Precision Plastics will accept orders no smaller than for one day's production.

The management of Precision Plastics has become tired of the hassle of deciding between Xercon or Yenton in allocating this one day's capacity. They have told the vice presidents of both companies that they must settle this among themselves and that, if Precision Plastics does not receive an order by the first of each month, they will simply use that one day's production capacity to build inventory of their other contract items.

Precision Plastics management has gone further and set these conditions:

1. It will take an order for 10,000 parts at $2 a part from either Xercon or Yenton. The parts will be shipped to the company sending in the order.

2. It will take an order from each company for 5,000 parts at $2 a part and ship that amount to both Xercon and Yenton.

3. If Precision Plastics receives a 20,000 order from both Xercon and Yenton, it will ship 5,000 parts to each at a cost of $4 each.

The managers of Xercon and Yenton have agreed to meet the last Friday of every month to work out which order for parts Precision Plastics will receive for the next month's day of available production. They understand the terms Precision Plastics has established and recognize that, if no order is sent in by the deadline, neither will get any materials from Precision Plastics the next month. They also recognize the possibility of receiving part of their monthly needs for the plastic part from Precision Plastics and making the remainder on their own equipment. Hence, there are four possible outcomes in regard to their production costs:

1. Receive all plastic parts from Precision Plastics at a cost of $2 a

piece, resulting in a factory cost of $42 and a profit of $8 for each hand tool.
2. Receive half of the needed plastic parts from Precision Plastics for $2 a piece and make the other half on their own equipment for $12 a piece for an average cost for the plastic part of $7 or a total factory cost of $47 and a profit of $3 per tool.
3. If both Xercon and Yenton send in 20,000 orders, each will receive 5,000 pieces at a cost of $4. They will also have to make the remaining 5,000 parts needed at a cost of $12 for an average cost per part of $8, resulting in a factory cost of $48 and a profit of $2 per tool.
4. Receive no parts from Precision Plastics and make them all on their own equipment, resulting in a factory cost of $52 and a $2 loss on each tool.

You are a member of the Manufacturing Committee (for either Xercon or Yenton), which will meet with your counterpart from the other company to negotiate an order for Precision Plastics that will make the largest profit for your company.

Step 3: 10 Minutes

Review the details of the situation and understand how you can make or lose money. Familiarize yourself with the Production Planning Report below. Members of each Manufacturing Committee should plan their strategy for their negotiations. There is to be no communication between the negotiating teams at this time.

There will be seven one-minute negotiating sessions during which the committees or their representatives negotiate each month's production. A three-minute planning session separates each negotiating session. There is no communication between the negotiating teams during the planning sessions. At the end of each negotiating period, the representative sends his/her order to the referee. The referee will then announce each side's profit.

Step 4: 30 Minutes

The instructor will indicate when round one negotiating begins and ends. He or she will then indicate the end of each subsequent three-minute planning session and each one-minute negotiating session. Each team will record the outcome of each negotiating session on the Production Planning Report.

Step 5: 30 Minutes

The instructor will record the total profit for each team in each negotiating group. Difference in performance will be noted and possible reasons explored. Participants should describe what happened, particularly in regard to their perceptions of and reactions to the other party. Some suggested questions and issues for discussion are given below.

Production Planning Report

Round	Decision	Xercon Profit	Yenton Profit
1			
2			
3			
4			
5			
6			
7			

Total profit

DISCUSSION QUESTIONS

1. What were your basic objectives and strategy when you started the simulation? Did they change? What outcomes did you achieve as a result of these plans?
2. What did you talk about after the first round of negotiation?
3. Did the content of your negotiating discussion change? Why?
4. What were the most important things that lead to the outcome you had?

The Used Car

INTRODUCTION

The scenario for this role-play involves a single issue: the price of a used car that is for sale. While there is a great deal of other information that may be used to construct supporting arguments or to build in demands and requests in addition to the price, the sale price will ultimately be the indicator used to determine how well you do in comparison to other role-play groups.

ADVANCE PREPARATION

1. The instructor is likely to assign preparation for this exercise in advance. If so, read and review the "Background Information" section on the used car, and the buyer or seller position information that you have been assigned. Read *only* your own position.
2. If you are working with others as a team, meet with the team and prepare a negotiation strategy. If you are working alone, plan your individual strategy for your position.
3. Whether working in a small group or alone, make sure that you complete the section at the bottom of your confidential information sheet.

PROCEDURE

Step 1: 5 Minutes

The instructor will determine whether this exercise is to be conducted individually or in small groups. If it is individual, pairs of individuals may be assigned buyer and seller roles. Alternatively, groups of two or three persons will be assigned buyer and seller roles.

Role-play was developed by Professor Leonard Greenhalgh, Dartmouth College. Used with permission.

Step 2: 30 Minutes

Read and prepare your negotiating position, if this assignment was not done as part of the advanced preparation.

Step 3: 40 Minutes or as Recommended by Instructor

Meet with the opposite side to negotiate a price for the used car. During this time, you may observe the following procedures:

1. Use any plan or strategy that will help you achieve your objectives.
2. Call a caucus at any time to evaluate your strategy or the opponent's strategy.
3. Reach an agreement by the end of the specified time period, or conclude that you are not able to agree and that buyer and seller will explore other alternatives.
4. Complete the Statement of Agreement form and submit it to the instructor. Be sure to write down any additional terms or conditions that were agreed to.

Step 4: 30 Minutes

Be prepared to discuss your settlement with your opponents, and with other groups in the role-play.

BACKGROUND INFORMATION

You are about to negotiate the purchase/sale of an automobile. The ~~buyer~~ *seller* advertised the car in the local newspaper. (Note: Both role-players should interpret "local" as the town in which the role-play is occurring.) Before advertising it, the ~~buyer~~ *seller* took the car to the local Volkswagen dealer, who has provided the following information:

1982 VW Rabbit diesel, standard shift.

White with red upholstery, tinted glass.

AM/FM radio.

30,450 miles; steel-belted radial tires expected to last 65,000.

45 miles per gallon on diesel fuel at current prices (usually about 10 percent less than regular gasoline).

No rust; dent on passenger door barely noticeable.

Mechanically perfect except exhaust system, which may or may not last another 10,000 miles (costs $300 to replace).

"Blue book" retail value, $5,000; wholesale, $4,400 (local 1984 prices).

Car has spent its entire life in the local area; it is the only used diesel Rabbit within a 60-mile radius.

Statement of Agreement for Purchase of the Automobile

Price: _____

Manner of Payment: _____

Special Terms and Conditions: _____

_____

_____

_____

_____

_____   _____
Seller   Buyer

_____

DISCUSSION QUESTIONS

1. Did you reach an agreement in this negotiation? If so, how satisfied are you with the price? If not, are you satisfied that you did not agree? Why?
2. If you reached a settlement, how does the settlement price compare to your target price, to the buyer's opening offer, and to the lowest (highest) price that you were willing to accept? Who "won" in this simulation?

Buyer/Seller Negotiation

INTRODUCTION

Negotiations can be described as a process that combines economic transactions with verbal persuasion. A great deal of what transpires in negotiation is the verbal persuasion—people arguing for and supporting their own preferred position, and resisting similar arguments from the opponent. Underlying this layer of persuasive messages is a set of economic transactions—bids and counterbids—that are the economic core of the negotiation process.

The purpose of this exercise is to give you some experience with the process of economic transactions, independent of much of the persuasive rhetoric that typically goes with it. As a result, you will be able to see how the simple trading of bids and counterbids allows negotiators to influence one another even without a great deal of verbal interaction.

ADVANCE PREPARATION

None. Bring a calculator to class.

PROCEDURE

Step 1: 15 Minutes

Your instructor will assign you to the role of buyer or seller for this activity. If you are a buyer, please turn to the instructions on page 585; if you are a seller, turn to the instructions on page 609. Your instructor will also assign you a partner for this exercise.

Step 2: 20 Minutes

Once you have read the instructions, turn to the first blank record sheet. There will be *two* practice trials, and then 20 bids. Keep track of the bids and your profit on the chart. At the end of 20 bids, add up your profit on each bid to determine your total profit.

Adapted from S. Siegel and L. Fouraker, *Bargaining Behavior*. Used with permission.

Step 3: 20 Minutes

Your instructor will give the signal to proceed. Using the table that your instructor has provided, engage in *two* practice trials and 20 new sequenced bids. Then compute your total profit for this second round of bidding.

Step 4: 20 Minutes

Your instructor will ask you for information regarding the two bidding rounds. Your results will be compared with other pairs in the class, and the bidding process will be discussed.

DISCUSSION QUESTIONS

1. What were the results of round 1? (What was the price and quantity on the last trial, and how much did each party earn?)
2. How satisfied did you feel with this outcome at the time? Why?
3. What kind of strategy and tactics did you use to exert influence in round 1? How effective were your strategy and tactics?
4. What were the results of round 2? What was the price and quantity on the last trial, and how much did each party earn?
5. How satisfied did you feel with this outcome? Why?
6. Did your satisfaction with your outcomes on round 1 change after you saw the tables for round 2? What does this say about the impact of information on your satisfaction level?
7. What strategy and tactics did you use in round 2 in order to exert influence on your partner? How effective were your strategy and tactics?

Buyer/Seller Bidding Exercise: Bid Record Sheet

Check One: Buyer_____ Seller_____ *Check one:* Round 1_____ Round 2_____

Bid No.	Price	Quantity	Profit to You
Practice A	_____	_____	_____
Practice B	_____	_____	_____
1.	_____	_____	_____
2.	_____	_____	_____
3.	_____	_____	_____
4.	_____	_____	_____
5.	_____	_____	_____
6.	_____	_____	_____
7.	_____	_____	_____
8.	_____	_____	_____
9.	_____	_____	_____
10.	_____	_____	_____
11.	_____	_____	_____
12.	_____	_____	_____
13.	_____	_____	_____
14.	_____	_____	_____
15.	_____	_____	_____
16.	_____	_____	_____
17.	_____	_____	_____
18.	_____	_____	_____
19.	_____	_____	_____
20.	_____	_____	_____

TOTAL _____

How satisfied are you with your total profit in this round? (Circle one number below)

1	2	3	4	5	6	7
Extremely dissatisfied			Neither satisfied nor dissatisfied			Extremely satisfied

2nd round

Exercise Section

Buyer/Seller Bidding Exercise: Bid Record Sheet

Check One: Buyer_____ Seller ✓   *Check one:* Round 1_____ Round 2_____

Bid No.	Price	Quantity	Profit to You
Practice A			
Practice B			
1.	4	15	2470
2.	16	12	5260
3.	5	1	530
4.	16	1	750
5.	14	1	710
6.	16	1	750
7.	4	15	2470
8.	16	4	2220
9.	3	18	2020
10.	16	2	1260
11.	4	15	2470
12.			
13.			
14.			
15.			
16.			
17.			
18.			
19.			
20.			

TOTAL _____ 43140

How satisfied are you with your total profit in this round? (Circle one number below)

1	2	3	4	5	6	7
Extremely dissatisfied			Neither satisfied nor dissatisfied			Extremely satisfied

49,400

Alta Electronics

INTRODUCTION

This simulation is intended to demonstrate how the structure of the situation influences the type of negotiation that exists, and how it sets the basic condition for choosing a negotiating strategy.

ADVANCE PREPARATION

Read the Alta Electronics Company "Background Information" section and the role you have been given by your instructor. Prepare to play that role in an upcoming in-class meeting. Familiarize yourself with the facts. At the meeting, act as you think you would if you were the person in that situation.

PROCEDURE

Step 1: 5 Minutes

You and five other people will be designated as a group, and your individual roles within the group will be identified.

Step 2: 20–30 Minutes

The member of your group who plays the role of Fran Meltzer will be in charge of the group and call you to a meeting. Fran will explain the purpose of the meeting.

Step 3: 20–40 Minutes

The instructor will notify you when the time for the meeting is over. At that time, the instructor will gather certain information from each group that has taken part in the role-play.

You will then be asked to examine the outcomes in the different groups and find explanations for why those outcomes are similar or different.

BACKGROUND INFORMATION

Assume that you are an electronics engineer working for the Alta Electronics Company, a medium-sized firm manufacturing a variety of electronics products. You design new products. You and the other engineers work individually on projects aided by technicians and, when needed, draftsmen. All engineers in your group are proud of the products they have designed, both for the technical developments they incorporate and their reliable performance in use.

For the last several years the company has been experiencing financial difficulties. While these have not resulted in layoffs, there has been a severe restriction on wage increases and an absolute freeze on building alterations, travel to professional meetings, magazine subscriptions, and similar expenditures. While most of these have been of a minor nature, some (like not attending professional meetings) have made it difficult for you and other engineers to keep abreast of technical developments and to maintain your professional contacts. Recently you have heard that the company has begun to see a modest economic upturn.

Here is the roster of people who work for Fran Meltzer, section head of your group.

Lee Clark   Senior design engineer—21 years with the company, has two technicians

Chris Manos   Senior design engineer—16 years with the company, has one technician

B. J. Pelter Senior design engineer—15 years with the company, has two technicians

Pat Rosen   Design engineer—8 years with the company, has one technician

Sandy Solas   Design engineer—3 years with the company, has one technician

Company policy dictates that engineers are responsible for a project not only through the design phase but also to see it through production startup to the point where acceptable products are regularly being produced. On many projects the amount of time spent on handling problems in production is minor. On others, especially those with particularly difficult standards, the time spent in handling production problems can be considerable.

You will be one of the persons mentioned in the case. In addition to the information above, you will be given additional information for your role. In taking your role accept the facts as given and add to them as you see appropriate. Act the way you feel you would in such a position.

DISCUSSION QUESTIONS

1. What made this meeting difficult? What made it easy?
2. Were all members of your group equally pleased or displeased with the

outcome of the meeting? Specifically, what things happened when group members shared the same opinion on the outcome? What things happened when they held different opinions on the outcome?

3. Why did different groups have different outcomes? Specifically, what did Fran, Lee, Chris, B. J., Pat, and Sandy do to make things come out the way they did?

4. How would you recognize this type of situation again?

5. If you were in such a situation again what would you do to help reach an outcome all group members could support?

Twin Lakes Mining Company

INTRODUCTION

In this role-play, you will have the opportunity to negotiate a real problem—
a conflict between a mining company and the government of a small town
regarding an environmental cleanup. While the issues in this scenario have
been simplified somewhat for the purpose of this role-play, such conflicts
between industry and governmental groups are typical throughout the country. Try to introduce as much realism into this situation as you can, based on
your own personal experiences.

ADVANCE PREPARATION

The nature of advanced preparation will be determined by your instructor.
You may be required to read these materials and/or to meet with your other
team members in advance of the class session in which this problem will be
actually negotiated.

PROCEDURE

1. You will be assigned to a small group to represent either the
Twin Lakes Mining Company or the Tamarack Town Council in this
negotiation.

2. Before meeting with your group, you should read the common
"Background Information" statement, and your own individual briefing sheet for either the company or the council.

3. When you meet with your group, review the issues and determine a strategy that you intend to pursue. Also divide your group up
into realistic individual roles that might actually be represented if this
were a real-life negotiation. These roles are described in your individual briefing sheets.

4. Negotiate for as long as you need to arrive at a solution, or follow
the time limits set by your instructor.

5. When you arrive at an agreement, make sure that you write down

exactly what was agreed to. Have a representative of each side sign this document and either submit it to your instructor or bring it to class as instructed.

BACKGROUND INFORMATION

The Twin Lakes Mining Company is located in Tamarack, Minnesota, in the northen part of the state. It was established there in 1941. The town of Tamarack has a population of approximately 12,000. Although there is a growing revenue that accrues to the town as a result of heavy summer tourism (summer homes, fishing, etc.) and several "cottage industries," Tamarack is basically a one-industry town. Two thousand five hundred people, 60 percent of whom live within town limits, work for the Twin Lakes Mining Company; 33 percent of the town's real estate tax base consists of Twin Lakes property and operations. Both in terms of direct tax revenue and indirect contribution to the economic stability of the local population, Tamarack is strongly dependent on the continued success of the Twin Lakes Company.

The Twin Lakes Mining Company is an open-pit, iron ore mine. Open-pit mining consists of stripping the top soil from the ore deposit with the use of power shovels. Train rails are then laid, and most of the ore is loaded into railroad cars for transportation to a central collecting point for rail or water shipment. As mining operations progress, rails are relaid or roads constructed to haul ore by truck. The ore is transported to a "benefication plant" located on the outskirts of Tamarack. Benefication of ore involves crushing, washing, concentrating, blending, and agglomerating the ore. In the early days of ore production, such treatment was unnecessary; however, benefication is necessary today for several reasons. First, transportation costs of rejected material (gangue) are minimized. The crude ore may lose as much as one third its weight in grading, and, in addition, impurities are removed at a much lower cost than if removed during smelting. Second, ores of various physical and chemical properties can be purified and blended during this process. Finally, fine ore materials, which previously may have been rejected as a result of smelting problems, can now be briquetted and pelletized to increase its value. After the ore proceeds through this process of cleaning and agglomerating into larger lumps or pellets, it is shipped by railroad car to steel mills throughout the Midwest. Rejected materials are returned to "consumed" parts of the mine, and the land restored.

Twin Lakes' benefication plant is located approximately five miles outside of Tamarack. As a result of both the expansion of the residential areas of the town, summer home development and various Twin Lakes operations, the plant has become a major problem for local citizens. For years, the Tamarack Town Council has been pressing the company to clean up the most problematic operations.

While most of these discussions have been amicable, Twin Lakes has done little or nothing to remedy the major concerns. Now, as a result of more stringent environmental laws and regulations, Twin Lakes has come under pressure from both the state of Minnesota and the federal government for environmental cleanup. Both the state and the Federal Environmental Protection Agency have informed Twin Lakes that they are in the major violation of water and air pollution quality standards, and that immediate action must be taken. Twin Lakes' estimates indicates that total compliance with the cleanup regulations will cost the company over $9 million. Because Twin Lakes is now mining reasonably low-grade ore and because foreign competition in the steel market has significantly eroded the demand for ore, environmental compliance will put the company out of business. Many local citizens, as individuals and through the local chapter of the United Mineworkers Union, are putting significant pressure on the Town Council to help the Twin Lakes Company in its environmental cleanup operations.

The imposition of the environmental controls on Twin Lakes, and the resulting pressure from all segments of the community, has lead to renewed discussions between company officials and the Town Council. As a result of these discussions, the following environmental issues have emerged:

1. Water Quality. The Twin Lakes plant requires large amounts of water to wash the crushed ore. In addition, much of the highest quality ore is reduced to an almost powderlike texture after washing, and was being lost in the washing operation. As a result, the company has built a series of settlement recovery ponds alongside Beaver Brook near the plant. Water that has been used for washing ore is allowed to stand in these ponds; they are then periodically drained and the ore recovered. Nevertheless, granules of iron ore and other impurities continue to wash downstream from the plant.

The environmental agents have insisted that the effluent from the plant and the ponds be cleaned up. Estimates for the cost of a filtration plant are $5 million. Twin Lakes claims that it cannot afford to build the plant with its own revenue. Since Tamarack has periodically talked about Beaver Brook as a secondary water source for the town (and residential development makes this a more pressing concern in two–three years) the Twin Lakes officials hope that they might interest Tamarack in a joint venture.

2. Air Quality. The entire process of mining, transporting, and crushing ore generates large amounts of dust. This has significantly increased the levels of particulates in the air. In addition, during the dry summer months, the operation of many large trucks along dirt roads intensifies the problem considerably.

Twin Lakes believes that it can control a great deal of the dust generated immediately around the plant at a cost of approximately $2 million. The most significant debate with the town has been over a series of roads around the outskirts of town. Approximately half of the roads are town-owned; the rest have been specially constructed for the transportation of ore and material. Estimates for paving all the roads are $1.2 million with a yearly maintenance cost of $150,000; periodic oil spraying of the roads, to keep down the dust, would run approximately $200,000 annually, but an agreement to do this as a short-term measure may not satisfy the environmental agencies.

3. Taxation of Company Land.   The land for the mine itself is outside of town limits. However, the plant lies within township boundaries, and current taxes on the town land are $200,000 annually. The company has always felt that this taxation rate is excessive.

In addition, several of the railroad spurts used to move ore into the plant, and out to the major railway line, cross town land. The town has continued to charge a flat rate of $100,000 annually for right-of-way use. (It has occasionally offered it for sale to the company at rates varying from $550,000–$600,000.) Again, the company has felt that this rate is excessive.

Both the company and the town believe that if some resolution could be obtained on these three major issues, the remaining problems could be easily resolved, and Twin Lakes would agree to keep the mine open.

DISCUSSION QUESTIONS

1. How did you go about preparing for this role-play? What type of strategy did you decide to employ?
2. Did you set goals or targets that you wanted to achieve on each issue or the total package, and did you set "bottom lines" or resistance points? How did having these (or not having these) affect your own negotiation effectiveness?
3. What roles did group members decide to play? How did this affect your own team and the way that it worked with the other group?
4. How satisfied are you with the final agreement (if you reached one)? What factors in your negotiation make you feel satisfied or dissatisfied with this outcome?
5. What did you personally learn from this situation that you feel you will want to continue (or try to change) in future negotiation situations?

Universal Computer Company

INTRODUCTION

In this exercise you will play the role of a plant manager who has to negotiate some arrangements with another plant manager. You will be in a potentially competitive situation where cooperation is clearly desirable. Your task is to find some way to cooperate, when to do so might seem to put you at a disadvantage.

ADVANCE PREPARATION

Prior to class, read the Universal Computer Corporation "Background Information" section and the role that the instructor has assigned you. Do not discuss your role with other class members. Plan how you will handle the forthcoming meeting with the other plant manager. Record your initial proposal on the Initial Settlement Proposal form. Do not show this to the other party you are negotiating with until after the negotiations are completed.

PROCEDURE

Step 1: 5 Minutes

The class will be broken into teams of two, one person in the dyad representing the Crawley plant manager and the other representing the Phillips plant manager.

Step 2: 20–45 Minutes

Each dyad of plant managers conducts their meeting, trying to reach a solution to their problems. When an agreement is reached, both parties record the outcome on the Final Settlement Agreement form.

Step 3: 10–20 Minutes

With your partner in the dyad, review the Initial Settlement Proposals you each prepared. What bargaining range did you have? What actions by either party lead to the particular outcome you reached and recorded on the Final Settlement Agreement form?

Step 4: 15–20 Minutes

The instructor will poll each dyad on the Initial Settlement Proposals of the parties and the final agreement reached. The instructor will also ask any groups who have not been able to reach an agreement where they are at the time negotiations are halted, and what may be standing in the way of their reaching an agreement.

BACKGROUND INFORMATION

Universal Computer Company is one of the major producers of computers. Plants in the company tend to specialize in producing a single line of products or, at the most, a limited range of products. The company has considerable vertical integration. Parts made at one plant are assembled into components at another which in turn are assembled into final products at still another plant. Each plant operates on a profit center basis.

The Crawley plant produces modules, cable harnesses, and terminal boards which in turn are shipped to other company plants. It makes more than 40 different modules for the Phillips plant. The two plants are about five miles apart.

The Quality Problem

Production at the Phillips plant has been plagued by poor quality. Upon examination it has been found that a considerable portion of this problem can be traced to the quality of the modules received from the Crawley plant.

The Crawley plant maintains a final inspection operation. There has been considerable dispute between the two plants as to whether the Crawley plant was to maintain a 95 percent acceptance level for all modules shipped to the Phillips plant, or to maintain that standard for each of the 42 modules shipped. The Phillips plant manager has insisted that the standard had to be maintained for each of the 42 individual modules produced. The Crawley plant manager maintains that the requirements mean that the 95 percent level has to be maintained for the sum of modules produced. Experience at the Phillips plant shows that while some module types were consistently well above the 95 percent acceptance level, 12 types of modules had erratic quality and would often fall far below the 95 percent level. As a result, while individual types of modules might fall below standard, the quality level for all modules was at or above the 95 percent level.

This raised serious problems at the Phillips plant since the quality of its products is controlled by the quality of the poorest module.

The Interplant Dispute

The management of the Phillips plant felt that the quality problem of the modules received from the Crawley plant was causing them great difficulty.

It caused problems with the customers, who complained of the improper operation of the products that contained the Crawley modules. As a result, the Phillips plant operation had earlier added secondary final inspection of its completed products. More recently it had added an incoming inspection of 12 poor quality modules received from the Crawley plant. There were times when the number of modules rejected was large enough to slow or even temporarily stop production. At those times, to maintain production schedules, the Phillips plant had to work overtime. In addition, the Phillips plant had the expense of correcting all the faulty units received from the Crawley plant.

Ideally the management of the Phillips plant would like to receive all modules free of defects. While this was recognized as impossible, they felt that the Crawley plant should at least accept the expense of repairs, extra inspections and overtime required by the poor quality of the parts.

Since installing incoming inspection procedures on the 12 modules, the Phillips plant had been rejecting about $8,000 of modules a week. For the most part these had been put into storage pending settlement of the dispute as to which plant should handle repairing them. Occasionally, when the supply of good modules had been depleted, repairs were made on some of the rejected units to keep production going. The Phillips plant had continued to make repairs on the remaining 30 types of modules as the need for repairs was discovered in assembly or final inspection.

From its perspective the Crawley plant management felt that it was living up to its obligation by maintaining a 95 percent or better quality level on all its modules shipped to the Phillips plant. Further, they pointed out that using sampling methods on inspection meant that some below-standard units were bound to get through, and that the expense of dealing with these was a normal business expense which the Phillips plant would have to accept as would any other plant. They pointed out that when buying parts from outside suppliers it was common practice in the company to absorb the expenses from handling the normal level of faulty parts.

The Phillips plant management argued that the Crawley plant management was ignoring its responsibility to the company by forcing the cost of repairs on to their plant where only repairs could be made—rather than to have the costs borne by the Crawley plant where corrections of faulty processes could be made.

DISCUSSION QUESTIONS

1. What differences in strategy and tactics were followed in groups that completed negotiations versus those that did not? Were relationships competitive or cooperative, conflictful, or problem solving?
2. What factors did the various dyads find that contributed most to the outcome they reached?

Initial Settlement Proposals

_____ Plant

How do you propose that the following expenses and repairs should be handled?

Expense of repairing all faulty modules _____

_____

Expense of repairing faulty modules other than the 12 types that fall below 95 percent

level _____

_____

Expense of repairing the faulty modules of the 12 types that fall below the 95 percent

level _____

_____

How to handle the repair of the faulty modules of the 12 types that fall below the 95

percent level _____

_____

How to handle the repair of the modules other than the 12 types that fall below the 95

percent level _____

_____

3. Did the members of dyads change their feelings about the settlement after they learned how well they did relate to their initial goals for the negotiation? Why? What does this say about how we evaluate "good" and "bad" actions in negotiation?

Final Settlement Agreement

How, exactly, did you agree that the following expenses and repairs would be handled?

Expense of repairing all faulty modules _____

_____

Expense of repairing faulty modules other than the 12 types that fall below 95 percent level _____

_____

Expense of repairing the faulty modules of the 12 types that fall below the 95 percent level _____

_____

How to handle the repair of the faulty modles of the 12 types that fall below the 95 percent level _____

_____

How to handle the repair of the modules other than the 12 types that fall below the 95 percent level _____

_____

_____   _____
Representative, Phillips Plant   Representative, Crawley Plant

Salary Negotiations

INTRODUCTION

In this simulation, you will play the role of either a manager or subordinate in a negotiation over salary. Both in securing employment as well as promotions, we frequently are in a position to negotiate with our superiors over salary; and, once we achieve managerial rank, we do the same with subordinates. This is one of the most common and, at the same time, most personal forms of negotiation; for many people, it is also the most difficult. Since salary can be a means of satisfying many needs—economic, recognition, status, or competitive success measure—it leads to complex negotiations.

PROCEDURE

Step 1: 5 Minutes

The class will be divided into groups of three; two will be assigned the roles of manager and subordinate, the other as an observer. Role-players will be assigned either an "A" or a "B" role in one of the Salary Simulations below. Assemble with your trio in the place specified by the instructor.

Step 2: 5 Minutes

Read your assigned role and prepare a strategy. If you are an observer, review the Observer Reporting Sheet and make sure you understand what to look for.

Step 3: 10 Minutes

Carry out your discussion with your counterpart. If you finish before the allotted time is up, review the sequence of events with the other party and tell the other what he or she did that was productive or unproductive to the negotiations.

If you are an observer, make brief notes during the role-play on your Observer Reporting Sheet. When the role-play is over, review the sheet and add further details where necessary.

Developed from examples used by John Tarrant, *How to Negotiate A Raise*, Van Nostrand Reinhold, 1976.

Step 4: 10 Minutes

In your trio, discuss the outcome of the negotiation. The observer should report what he or she saw each party doing. Review what steps or positions seemed most and least useful.

At the end of the time for step 4, the observer should hand his Observer Reporting Sheet to the instructor.

Step 5: 5 Minutes

In your trio, change role assignments so that the person filling an A role now fills a B role, the person filling the B role now becomes observer, and the previous observer now fills an A role.

Step 6: 5 Minutes

Repeat step 2.

Step 7: 10 Minutes

Repeat step 3.

Step 8: 10 Minutes

Repeat step 4.

Steps 9, 10, 11, 12: 30 Minutes

Repeat steps 5, 6, 7, 8.

Observer Reporting Sheet

Round _____ .

How did A open the meeting? _____

_____

_____

How did B respond to the way A opened the meeting? _____

_____

_____

Was an agreement reached? Yes _____, no _____.

What was the salary agreed to, if there was an agreement? _____

Were there any other added features in the settlement achieved? _____

_____

Will future relations between A and B be better (+), worse (−), or the same (=) as a result of this meeting? List the opinions of A, B, and the observer.

A _____, B _____, Observer _____.

Step 13: 30 Minutes

The instructor will post the results from the three sets of role-plays. Examine the different outcomes and explore reasons why they occurred and their consequences.

DISCUSSION QUESTIONS

1. Were there any differences in the way negotiations were handled when:
   a. Both parties in a role-play were satisfied?
   b. One was satisfied?
   c. Both were dissatisfied?
2. Were some people playing the same role dissatisfied with an outcome that others in the same role found satisfying? Why? How do you account for this?
3. Poll quickly those who were satisfied with the outcome. Ask why they were satisfied.
4. Poll quickly those who were dissatisfied with the outcome. Ask why they were dissatisfied.
5. What was the effect of observing another's negotiation on how you negotiated? Did what you see as an observer affect how satisfied you felt with your own outcome?

One-on-One Negotiation

INTRODUCTION

The purpose of this negotiation is to test your skill as a negotiator of several uncontroversial issues. The strategy that you use to approach this problem will ultimately determine your success in the exercise.

ADVANCE PREPARATION

None.

PROCEDURE

Step 1: 5 Minutes

Your instructor will divide the group into pairs. You will be assigned a role as Negotiator Able or Baker.

Step 2: 10 Minutes

Read your briefing sheet for *your side*. *Hide* your instructions and payoff table from your opponent—do *not* permit your opponent to see your point values in this exercise.

Step 3: 15 Minutes

Achieve the best possible point value that you can for your side. Use the blank record sheet to record offers and counteroffers, and your ultimate settlement.

Step 4: 15 Minutes

Be ready to reveal your settlement letters and the point value for you and your opponent to the instructor when the information is shared in general session.

Adapted from an exercise developed by N. Berkowitz and Bert Brown. Used with permission.

INSTRUCTIONS—NEGOTIATORS ABLE AND BAKER

Hide this sheet from your opponent. Do not permit your opponent to see any of the point values on your payoff table.

The purpose of this exercise is to test your skill as a negotiator of purely quantitative issues. On your payoff table, there are three columns of numbers, labeled "Issue I," "Issue 2," and "Issue 3." These are the three issues on which you will negotiate. For each issue, there is a range of possible settlement points, labeled A through T. Each point has assigned to it a certain number of satisfaction units. During negotiations, you will trade "offers" (suggested settlement points) back and forth on each issue until you arrive at a settlement point (A–T) for that issue. You may eventually agree on a single settlement point for all three issues, or different settlement points for each of the three issues. In this exercise, your objective is to maximize the total number of satisfaction units that *you individually* receive. Your opponent may or may not have the same units attached to each settlement point as you do.

Before the negotiations begin, you will have a few minutes to review these directions with the instructor and to determine a strategy. When the negotiations begin, one of you will make an "offer" on any issue. You will state to the other party the number of the issue you want to negotiate (I, II, or III), and the letter corresponding to the settlement point that you would like to propose. (Example. "I'd like to discuss issue I, and to propose settlement point T.") The other party can then agree, respond with a different letter, or propose to discuss a different issue. Offers and information are then traded back and forth until the parties agree. Agreement occurs when each party accepts the *same* letter as a settlement point for an issue, and when a settlement is arrived at for all three issues. Each negotiator then obtains the number of points for that issue and settlement point on his own payoff chart. Agreement on any issue is tentative until all three issues are settled.

Your instructor will give you a time limit for these negotiations. Results will be compared to other negotiating pairs in order to assess your effectiveness. Remember to hide your point value sheet from your opponent, and aim to maximize your own individual point total from the sum of the three issues.

DISCUSSION QUESTIONS

1. What was your strategy in this game? What factors (e.g., your opponent, the instructions, the setting, etc.) led you to adopt that particular strategy?
2. Did that strategy change during the game? How? Why? What did you do or did your opponent do that might have contributed to this change?
3. How satisfied are you with your settlement now that you have seen what other groups achieved? Why did you achieve the particular settlement that you did?

Record Sheet

Bid No.	Issue	(Offer)	(Counteroffer)
1	_____	_____	_____
2	_____	_____	_____
3	_____	_____	_____
4	_____	_____	_____
5	_____	_____	_____
6	_____	_____	_____
7	_____	_____	_____
8	_____	_____	_____
9	_____	_____	_____
10	_____	_____	_____
11	_____	_____	_____
12	_____	_____	_____
13	_____	_____	_____
14	_____	_____	_____
15	_____	_____	_____
16	_____	_____	_____
17	_____	_____	_____
18	_____	_____	_____
19	_____	_____	_____
20	_____	_____	_____

Final Package Report

Issue	Settlement Letter	Settlement Value To Me
I	_____	_____
II	_____	_____
III	_____	_____

Total Points _____

Name: _____

Opponent: _____

My bargaining group is: _____

Newtown School Dispute

INTRODUCTION

In this simulation, you will play a member of either a school board or teachers' association bargaining team. You and the other members of your team, and the members of the other team, are negotiators representing constituencies. You will deal with a complex mix of bargaining issues which have differing preference functions for each side, and you will be subject to a variety of pressures during the negotiations.

ADVANCE PREPARATION

Prior to class, read the "Background Material" on the Newtown School Dispute. You have been assigned to either the Board of Education or the Teachers' Association. Read the appropriate position paper the instructor has given you.

Prior to class, meet with the members of your bargaining team, determine your objectives and strategy, and prepare your initial offer. Record this offer on the Initial Offer Form.

PROCEDURE

Step 1: 5 Minutes

The instructor will announce the team assignments and time schedules and designate locations for negotiations and caucuses.

Step 2: 60–90 Minutes

Teams negotiate. Teams may negotiate as a whole or through spokespersons. Who makes the first offer, how time is used for caucus, and so on, are all controlled by the negotiators themselves. At the end, record your settlement on the Final Settlement form and hand it to the instructor. If there has not been a complete settlement, note which items have been agreed upon.

Developed by Bert R. Brown and Frank W. Masters. Used with permission.

Step 3: 30–60 Minutes

The instructor will post the initial offers and the final settlements.

BACKGROUND INFORMATION

It is now September 10, the opening day of the school year in Newtown. The contract between Newtown School District and the Newtown Teachers' Association expired on 30 June. Since then the Board of Education and representatives of the Teachers' Association have met on several occasions in an attempt to finalize a contract, but these attempts have not be successful.

Prior to June 30 and during the summer months, there was increasing talk among the membership of the Teachers' Association of the desirability of calling a strike if the contract was not finalized by opening day. However, the leadership of the Teachers' Association agreed, for the benefit of the community, to resume normal operations throughout the system (without a contract) on opening day *on a day-to-day basis.* This is in response to parent pressures to resume normal operations. Parents have been placing pressure on both teachers and the board to keep the schools operating, but have twice defeated referendums for increased taxes to cover budgetary increases over and above those of the previous year. Due to decreases in enrollments, income from local taxes and state and federal aid, as well as increased costs, maintenance of the school budget at par with the previous year would produce a 4.98 percent budgetary shortfall, which the board feels would begin to exhaust budgetary categories beginning in April of the present school year. Therefore, the board feels that programs and personnel must be cut while, at the same time, productivity (work load) of teachers must be increased if the system is to function effectively within its budgetary constraints to the end of the current fiscal year (June 30). In this regard, the district must provide 190 instructional days, as mandated by state law.

The Board of Education is caught between the Teachers' Association and community pressure groups. The board believes that it must satisfy these pressure groups, while at the same time keeping the teachers on the job with a contract that is acceptable to the bargaining unit's membership. The board is concerned that if it fails to respond appropriately to community pressures for cost reductions, it may be removed. The board's primary objective, therefore, is to cut costs while retaining as many programs as possible. It hopes to do so through cutbacks in teaching personnel and increases in teacher productivity (work load). The board also wishes to eliminate certain existing agreements in order to increase productivity. In this connection, the board wants to negotiate a three-year contract that will "stabilize" the situation by creating orderly and predictable budgetary needs that will be less apt to be seen as excessive by various community groups. In contrast, the Teachers' Association wants to obtain a one-year contract to maintain flexibility.

The Teachers' Association also feels caught between community pressure groups, who want to avert a strike, and the board's apparent unwillingness to fight for increased budget allocations to run the system. The teachers feel the board has not faced up to the community's unwillingness to accept increased taxation to pay for education, and that the board is simply responding to community unwillingness by passing the burden along to teachers.

Newtown is a relatively settled and stable upper middle-income community, with a strong interest in quality education, but is disinclined to increase its already burdensome tax rate. The Newtown School District consists of 12 schools: 9 elementary schools (K–8) and 3 senior high schools. The student population is 12,000, with 8,000 elementary and 4,000 high school stu-

Newtown School District Teachers' Salary Schedule

Step	Amount	Last Year's Number of Teachers	Cost	Current Year's Number of Teachers	Cost
Entry	$12,500	20	$250,000	0	0
1	13,000	20	260,000	20	$260,000
2	14,000	28	392,000	20	280,000
3	15,000	31	465,000	26	390,000
4	16,000	30	480,000	28	448,000
5	17,500	23	402,500	26	455,000
6	18,500	24	444,000	23	425,500
7	19,500	15	292,500	22	429,000
8	21,000	16	336,000	15	315,000
9	22,000	13	286,000	16	352,000
10	23,000	180	4,140,000	179	4,117,000
TOTALS		400	$7,748,000	375	$7,471,500

CURRENT SCHOOL YEAR
July 1–June 30
Projected Budget

1. INCOME

    1.1 Local tax (same rate as last year will continue, $4.86 per $1,000. No significant increase in values expected.)

        $12,151,000

    1.2 State (formula yield per pupil will remain the same. Legislature may meet and possibly raise formula for next year.)

        4,916,880

    1.3 Federal   750,000

        Total $17,817,880

Note: This is a decrease of $380,517 (−2.09%) for the previous year's income.

2. EXPENDITURES

2.1 Administration

2.1.1	Professional salaries	$1,137,500[b]
2.1.2	Clerical/secretaries	281,250
2.1.3	Other	250,000
	Total	1,668,750

2.2 Instruction

2.2.1	Teachers	
	Salaries	$7,471,500[a]
	Fringes	1,420,000
2.2.2	Aides	1,187,600
2.2.3	Materials/supplies	943,750[b]
	Total	11,022,850

2.3 Plant operation/maintenance

2.3.1	Salaries	$1,266,250
2.3.2	Utilities	975,000[c]
2.3.3	Other	258,750[d]
	Total	2,500,000

2.4 Fixed charges

2.4.1	Retirement	$1,176,450[e]
2.4.2	Other	428,700[f]
	Total	1,605,150

2.5 Debt service — $ 1,026,000[g]

2.6 Transportation

2.6.1	Salaries	400,000
2.6.2	Other	395,000[h]
	Total	$ 795,000

Grand Total — $18,617,750

Notes:
Total number of pupils = 12,000
Total number of teachers = 375
Per pupil expenditures = $1,551

	Percent of Last Year's Total Expenditures
a. Twenty-five teachers did not return to the system either due to retirement or other reasons.	−1.52%
b. Costs of materials and supplies will be up 12 percent over last year's cost based upon currently known price increases.	+.96%
c. Cost of utilities is expected to increase by more than 20 percent for the current year.	+.89%
d. Cost projections indicate a 15 percent increase in this category.	+.18%
e. Teacher retirement is up 5 percent due to increases mandated by legislature to pay for new benefits. This was partially offset by attrition.	+.31%
f. Other fixed charges are up 32 percent for this current year.	+.87%
g. Debt service is up 14 percent due to increased difficulty in floating bonds.	+.69%
h. Transportation 31 percent due to increases in operating and maintenance costs.	+.51%
Total cost adjustments	+2.89%
Summary: Change in costs including income decrease	+4.98%

LAST SCHOOL YEAR
July 1–June 30
Actual Audit

1. INCOME
   1.1 Local tax ($4.86 per $1,000 worth assessed real property. Assessment is at full value.) ... $12,204,444
   1.2 State (based on an equilization formula, improved during the last legislative session. Yielded $409.74 per pupil in administration last year.) ... 5,244,709
   1.3 Federal ... 749,244

   Total ... 18,198,397

2. EXPENDITURES
   2.1 Administration

2.1.1 Professional salaries	$1,137,248	
2.1.2 Clerical/secretarial	281,067	
2.1.3 Other	261,129	
Total		1,679,444

   2.2 Instruction

2.2.1 Teachers		
Salaries	$7,748,000	
Fringes	1,394,643	
2.2.2 Aides	1,183,275	
2.2.3 Materials/supplies	842,633	
Total		11,168,551

   2.3 Plant operation/maintenance

2.3.1 Salaries	$1,266,250	
2.3.2 Utilities	812,268	
2.3.3 Other	225,198	
Total		2,303,716

   2.4 Fixed changes

2.4.1 Retirement	$1,120,428	
2.4.2 Other	324,773	
Total		1,445,201

   2.5 Debt service ... $900,260

   2.6 Transportation

2.6.1 Salaries	$399,698	
2.6.2 Other	301,527	
Total		$701,225

   Grand Total ... 18,198,397

Notes
   Total number of pupils = 12,800
   Total number of teachers = 400
   Per pupil expenditures = $1,421

Initial Offer Form

Board of Education _____ Teachers' Association _____

Item	"Bottom Line" Position	Desired Settlement	Opening Offer
Salary			
Reduction in staff			
Work load			
Evaluation of teachers			
Binding arbitration			
Benefits			

Final Settlement

Board of Education _____ Teachers' Association _____

Item	Settlement
Salary	
Reduction in staff	
Work load	
Evaluation of teachers	
Binding arbitration	
Benefits	

dents. The bargaining unit, representing 95 percent of all teachers, consists of 250 elementary teachers in all categories and 125 high school teachers in all categories.

Both sides wish to conclude an agreement to avert a strike. However, the Teacher's Union bargaining team is adamantly committed to improving the lot of its membership and the board is just as committed to keeping its costs as low as possible. Nevertheless, each side feels it has some room to move on certain issues.

DISCUSSION QUESTIONS

1. The different sides in the negotiations should describe their initial strategies and positions, how well they worked together, and how their positions and strategies changed during negotiation.
2. The different sides should identify changes they made in their objectives during negotiations, what they saw to be the strengths and weaknesses of their own position, and of the opposing team's position.
3. Was there any discussion at the beginning of negotiation about how the discussions were to be handled? If so, did they have any effect? If not, would some have had an effect? How?
4. What was the bargaining range that existed at the beginning of negotiation?
5. Who made the opening offer? What effect did it have on the conduct of negotiations?
6. Were there attempts to use constituencies and/or bystanders? To what effect?
7. Who made the final offer? How was it structured?

The Power Game

INTRODUCTION

The concept of "power" is a complete, elusive, and almost paradoxical one. It is complex because there is a wide variety of definitions of what constitutes power, and how it is effectively accumulated and used. It is elusive because there seems to be very little consensus about the definitions, or the best way to describe power and talk about it in action. Finally, power is paradoxical because it doesn't always work the way it is "expected" to; sometimes those who seem to have the most power really have the least, while those who may appear to have the least power are most in control.

This simulation offers an opportunity to experience power in a wide variety of forms and styles. During the activity, you will become aware of your own power, and the power of others. Your objective will be to determine who has power, how power is being used, and how other's power may be effectively counteracted with your own power in order for you to achieve your goals. This type of analysis is essential to effective negotiations in power-laden situations.

ADVANCE PREPARATION

Your instructor will probably ask you to make a monetary contribution for this activity. Otherwise, no advance preparation is necessary.

PROCEDURE

Step 1

Your instructor will ask you for your monetary contribution. This money is to be given to the instructor. He will then announce what he will do with it.

Adapted from an exercise developed by Lee Bolman and Terrence Deal, Harvard Graduate School of Education, and published in *Exchange: The Organizational Behavior Teaching Journal.* Used with permission.

Step 2

Your instructor will assign you to a group. You will become acquainted with the group that you are assigned to, and that others are assigned to. You will be given a place to meet.

Step 3

Your instructor will give you descriptions of the duties and responsibilities of the group that you are assigned to. Please read this information closely.

Step 4

You will have exactly one hour to conduct the exercise, unless your instructor gives you different instructions.

DISCUSSION QUESTIONS

1. What did you learn about power from this experience?
2. Did this experience remind you of events you have experienced in other organizations? If so, what were the similarities?
3. What did you learn about yourself personally, and the way that you react to power or use?
4. What events occurred in your own subgroup? Did you feel satisfied with the amount of power you had? With the way you used it? Why?
5. What did you or your group do to exercise power, or to gain more power? How did it work out?

Coalition Bargaining

INTRODUCTION

A coalition may be loosely defined as a group of individuals, or subgroups, that assemble together to exert influence on one another. In an environment where there are many individuals, there are often many different points of view. Each individual views things differently, and each individual would like to have the "system" represent his views. In a dictatorship, the system usually represents the views of the dictator, but in a democratic environment, the views that are represented are usually those of a subgroup who have agreed to "work together" and collectively support one another's views in exchange for having a stronger impact on the system than each individual could have by himself.

Many of us are familiar with the work of coalitions. The patterns of influence in national politics and government provide us with some excellent examples. Whether it be the "coalitions" that are formed along traditional party lines—Democrats or Republicans—or along the concerns of special interest groups—Common Cause, The Sierra Club, AFL-CIO, National Rifle Association, National Spore Conference, or hundreds of others—each group is attempting to influence the direction of the larger system by effectively pooling its resources, working together as a team, and persuading those who have control of the current system.

This activity will help you understand, in the process of participation, how coalitions can form and how they can exert influence. You will probably be also able to see what they feel they deserve in return if the coalition is successful.

ADVANCE PREPARATION

None

Adapted by Roy J. Lewicki from an exercise originated by Robert M. Norman and adapted by John J. Sherwood. Reprinted from *Experiences in Management and Organizational Behavior* by Douglas T. Hall, Donald Bowen, Roy J. Lewicki, and Francine Hall, St. Clair Press, 1975. Used with permission of John Wiley & Sons.

PROCEDURE

Step 1: 5 Minutes

Form three teams of four to eight members each, with approximately an equal number of members on each team. Your group leader may assign you to teams, or this may be done randomly. Designate teams A, B, and C.

Step 2: 5 Minutes

Each member should contribute $1 to the "stake" or "prize" for the game. (You may want to use "points" rather than real money. Discuss this with your group leader.)

Step 3: 10 Minutes

Read the following rules:

Rules of the Game

Objective

To form a coalition with another team, in order to divide the stake. The coalition must also decide on a way of dividing the stake so as to satisfy both parties.

The Stake

Each team has *unequal* resources. In spite of the fact that you each contributed $1, you will receive a different stake, depending on the coalition you form. The following table should be filled in with information provided by the group leader (the individual payoffs are determined by the number of participants in the activity):

AB coalition will receive a stake of $_____ .

AC coalition will receive a stake of $_____ .

BC coalition will receive a stake of $_____ .

The Strategy

Each team will meet separately to develop a strategy before the negotiations. You should also select a negotiator.

Rules for Negotiation

1. All members on a team may be present for negotiations; however, *only* the negotiator may speak.
2. Notes may be passed to negotiators if desired.

3. A team may change its negotiator between conversations.
4. At the termination of the experiment, the stake will be allocated only if a coalition has been formed.
5. Only one formal coalition is permitted.
6. If no coalition is reached, no funds are allocated.
7. Negotiations will be conducted in the following *fixed* order, and for the following *fixed* periods of time:

Order of Negotiation	Time for First Round of Negotiation	Time for Second and Third Rounds of Negotiation
Team A and B	5 min.	3 min.
Team A and C	5 min.	3 min.
Team B and C	5 min.	3 min.

8. The team *not* in negotiations—that is, while the other two teams are negotiating—must leave the negotiation room.

Valid Coalitions

1. A coalition will be recognized by the group leader only if (*a*) no two teams are permitted to receive the same amount of money, *and* (*b*) neither team in the coalition is allowed to receive zero.
2. After negotiations, all three teams are given the opportunity to submit a written statement in the following form: "Team X has a coalition with Team Y, whereby Team X gets $9 and Y gets $3." When written statements meeting the above requirements from any two teams *agree,* a valid coalition has been formed.

Step 4: 15 Minutes

Meet in a separate area with your team to plan your strategy. During the strategy session, you will want to decide which team you might want to coalesce with, how you might want to divide resources, what kind of offers the other team might make, etc. You must also select a negotiator.

Step 5: 15 Minutes

Each team will report to the "negotiating area" for *five* minutes to conduct its discussions. Only the negotiators will speak, but other team members can be present and pass notes. At the end of each five-minute block, the group leader will stop the negotiations and move to the next pair. The team *not* in negotiations on a particular round *must leave the negotiating room.*

Step 6: 20 Minutes

Each team reports to the negotiating area for three-minute discussions for the *second* and *third* rounds (in the same sequence as above).

Step 7: 10 Minutes

The group leader will report to each team's separate room and ask them if they have formed a coalition. If so, each team in the coalition has five minutes to prepare a written statement of their coalition, acceptable within the conditions given above.

Step 8: 5 Minutes

Each team brings its written statement to the negotiating room. The instructor determines if a coalition has been formed. If it has been formed, the funds are allocated according to the written statements. If a coalition has *not* been formed, or where the coalition does not exhaust the initial stake, a problem will arise as to what to do with the funds.

DISCUSSION QUESTIONS

1. What was the initial strategy that each team decided on?
2. How were these strategies influenced by the resources (funds) that each team could contribute to a coalition?
3. How was your strategy modified as you began talking to the other teams?
4. How did the sequence of conversations between teams influence strategy?
5. How did individuals feel about being advantaged or disadvantaged in terms of unequal resources, and how did these feelings influence their behavior during this session?
6. How were strategic decisions made within your team?
7. How free did the negotiator feel to act for the team?
8. How did the negotiator establish credibility with the other teams?
9. What did the negotiators do that encouraged or impaired the development of trust with the other teams?
10. How did the negotiator's "prior reputation" (in terms of his specific behavior or your knowledge of him before this activity) influence people's assumptions about how he would behave?
11. Were negotiators ever changed? If so, for what reasons?

Elmwood Hospital Dispute

INTRODUCTION

In this exercise, you will be dealing with a very complex negotiation situation. Often, some individuals' and groups' agendas for negotiation are hidden. In this situation, people's desires are forcibly obvious. Also in this exercise, the role of the mediator is introduced as an aid to reaching an agreement.

ADVANCE PREPARATION

Read the "Background Information" section for the Elmwood Hospital Dispute in this exercise; then read the role the instructor has assigned to you. Prepare to play this role. Familiarize yourself with the facts and be prepared to act as you think you would act if you were a person in the situation described in this case.

PROCEDURE

Step 1: 30 Minutes

Participants assigned to the same role, that is, board members and administrators, members of the Community Coalition, and the mediators will meet separately to plan how they will handle the forthcoming meeting. If there are several sets of roles, that is, the class is so large that there are several Elmwood City hospitals, the role teams for each hospital will meet separately to plan strategy.

Step 2: 60 Minutes

The mediator(s) will call the parties together for the meeting. Discussion begins on the purpose of the meeting.

Adapted from an activity developed for the Institute of Mediation and Conflict Resolution, 1972.

BACKGROUND INFORMATION

The situation described below is a composite, with some data drawn from a number of similar disputes, and other information constructed specifically for this training exercise. The scenario is not to be interpreted as an account of any actual dispute. This simulation is one of several developed and tested by the Institute for Mediation and Conflict Resolution in New York, and adapted with permission by the Community Conflict Resolution Program.

* * * * *

Elmwood is a medium-sized, 450-bed private hospital in a southwestern city of approximately 600,000. It is well equipped for inpatient care, and has an open-heart surgery team which is a matter of special pride to the board of trustees and the hospital's director. None of the trustees lives in the hospital's immediate neighborhood, though some of their parents once did. Most of them are professionals or businesspeople and one of their main functions as trustees is to help in fund-raising for the hospital.

Until five to seven years ago, Elmwood was in the middle of a white, middle-class community. Now, however, it is on the eastern edge of an expanding low-income neighborhood, which has moved across the nearby expressway and is continuing to grow eastward. A good part of the low-income community is served by West Point Hospital, back on the western side of the expressway. People on the east, however, are turning to Elmwood. There are very few private physicians left in the Elmwood area, and the hospital, through its outpatient clinic, is the main source of medical care for the newer residents.

These newer residents, who now make up approximately 65 percent of the service area, are a mix of relatively recent newcomers to the city, some from other parts of the United States and others from various foreign countries. Most are in low-paying service jobs. Many are on public assistance. Infant mortality is three times as high as the rest of the city. Malnutrition is a problem, as are tuberculosis, lead poisoning, and other diseases associated with a slum environment. Most of these new residents cannot afford to be admitted to the hospital when sick, and rely instead on outpatient treatment in what is now an overburdened facility at Elmwood.

Like most hospitals, Elmwood is in a financial squeeze. In addition, it has become increasingly difficult to attract new interns and residents and harder to retain present professionals. Although the hospital director is somewhat sympathetic to the medical care problems of the community, he sees his first priority as building the hospital's institutional strength by such measures as increasing intern- and resident-oriented research opportunities and adding facilities which would induce the staff to stay on rather than go elsewhere. He has apparently given some thought to sponsoring a neighborhood health center, but it has been put off by location problems. He has also heard about some heated conflicts over control of services at other hospitals in the state that took state and federal health grants. Right now, the director apparently intends to put these matters on the "back burner" until he gets the other things going.

Residents of the low-income community have organized a Concerned Community Coalition (CCC). The community has been asking the hospital to increase its almost nonexistent efforts in preventative medical care, improve and expand outpatient facilities, establish a satellite health center with day-care facilities, and train a roving paraprofessional health team to administer diagnostic tests throughout the community. Elmwood is their neighborhood hospital and, to them, this is what a neighborhood hospital should be doing for the residents.

Two weeks ago, the CCC sent a letter to the director asking that the hospital initiate these efforts and requesting that he meet with them to discuss how the community and the hospital could work together. Although the community is deeply concerned about its medical problems and resents the fact that a city institution has not acted before this of its own volition, the letter was not unfriendly.

To date, the letter has not been answered.

Three days ago, the director and the chairman of the board announced the acquisition of a site about 15 blocks from the hospital on which it said it would build a heart research facility, a six-story nurses residence, and a staff parking lot, with shuttle bus service to the hospital grounds.

On learning of the plans, the leaders and members of the CCC were incensed. They decided to sit in at the director's office until the hospital met their needs.

The day before yesterday, about 50 CCC adherents took over the director's office vowing not to leave until the hospital agreed to meet the following demands:

1. Replacement of the board of trustees with a community-controlled board.
2. A 100 percent increase in outpatient facilities.
3. Establishment of a neighborhood health center and a day-care facility on the newly acquired site.
4. Establishment of a preventative diagnostic mobile health team, consisting of neighborhood residents chosen by CCC.
5. Replacement of the director by one chosen by the community.

While the hospital director indicated that he would be glad to meet with the group's leader to discuss the matters raised in its letter, he also stated quite forcefully that he considered the new demands arrogant and destructive and that, in any event, he would not meet under duress (i.e., as long as the sit-in continued).

The CCC said it would not leave until a meeting took place and the demands were accepted.

The sit-in began to days ago. This morning the hospital's lawyers moved to get an injunction against the sit-in. The CCC, aided by a Legal Services attorney, resisted.

The judge reserved decision, stating that to grant an injunction might only make the situation worse. He noted that both the hospital and the CCC would have to learn to live together for their own joint best interest. He therefore instructed the parties to meet to try to work out the problems between them, and has appointed a mediator to assist them. The mediator is a staff member of the city's Human Rights Commission, a unit of the municipal government.

At the judge's suggestion, the sides have agreed to meet with the mediator in the hospital library. The meeting has been scheduled for later today.

Step 3: 15–30 Minutes

At the end of the meeting, meet with your team members and answer the following questions.

  a. Review your original plans. Did you follow them? Meet your objectives? Why? Why not?

  b. For those playing a board member or CCC member: Did having a mediator help or hinder you? How? For those filling the role of mediator: What strategy did you try to employ? What things did the other parties do that helped or hindered you in your work as mediator?

  c. If you were in this position again, what would you do differently?

  d. What things did you notice or think about that would have helped people in the other roles be more effective in dealing with you in your role?

  e. For members of CCC: What power tactics did you employ? How effective were they?
  For board members and mediators, what power tactics did the CCC employ? How did you react to these tactics?

  f. What characteristics did this bargaining situation have that were different from those of other bargaining situations you have been in?

Step 4: 30–60 Minutes

Next, join the rest of the class and report what you have concluded for (*a*) through (*f*).

Central Industries, Inc.— Operation Expansion

INTRODUCTION

In this simulation, you will be a member of the management group of a wholly owned but autonomous division of Central Industries, Inc. Your management group will be dealing with the management groups of other divisions of Central Industries. Your objective is to exchange resources that each possess so that your division can carry out its business strategy. Top management of Central Industries has left the decisions regarding the reallocation of resources in the hands of the division managements.

PROCEDURE

Step 1: 5 Minutes

The class will be divided into four groups, each comprising the top management of a subsidiary company of Central Industries, Inc. The subsidiary companies are: Delta Co., Excel Co., Key Co., and Valco Co.

Step 2: 15 Minutes

Read the Central Industries, Inc., "Background information" section given below. Then read the instructions for the company whose management you represent. Soon, you will meet with the managements of the other subsidiary companies in order to obtain land for your division's expansion. Plan how you want to handle those meetings.

BACKGROUND INFORMATION

Central Industries, Inc., is a holding company in the commercial goods industry. It holds four major subsidiary companies, each of which is well

---

This exercise is based on "Operation Suburbia" as described in *Human Elements of Administration*, H. R. Knudson, Jr., Holt, Rinehart & Winston, 1963.

regarded in the business community. For various economic and legal reasons, each subsidiary is established as a separate company; the president of each sits on the board of directors of Central Industries, Inc.

Each subsidiary has experienced continuous growth over the years. This growth has already overtaxed the present facilities of each subsidiary company, and anticipated future growth has made urgent the need for immediate building of new facilities.

Some years ago, Central Industries located a large tract of land which was judged to be ideal for subsidiary expansion when their growth required new facilities. The tract was not available for purchase in total, so plots of land within it were acquired over time as they became available. The actual purchase of these plots was made by the subsidiary company which was in the most favorable cash position when the plot became available for sale.

Last year the final plot was purchased; so, at this time, the entire tract is owned by the various subsidiaries. Acquiring the land in this fashion has resulted in plot ownership being somewhat random insofar as each subsidiary is concerned. Exhibit 1 presents land holdings of each company and describes the tract in terms of current plot ownership by subsidiary company; that is, Delta Co., Excel Co., Key Co., and Valco Co.

Subsidiary expansion plans, which have been approved by Central, will require a different plot configuration than present ownership. Each subsidiary has carefully surveyed the site and has developed specific plans for the plots needed to accommodate their unique expansion requirements.

Following the decentralization policy which has been characteristic of Central Industries, the task of proper plot rearrangement has been delegated by Central to the subsidiaries for solution. Consequently, the president of each subsidiary has appointed a key staff group and has chartered them with the responsibility of working out required land transactions. Central has made it clear, however, that they expect the most effective possible utilization of the land.

It was decided that the top-management groups of the four subsidiary companies would convene in a general meeting and complete the required land transactions. This meeting is now at hand.

Your group will assume the role of the top management of one of the subsidiary companies. You will be given the particular plot configuration you require. Your task will be to conduct the required transactions with the other three companies.

Certain rules for the transactions have been established. These are:

1. Plots of land may be purchased, sold, or traded (evenly or with cash incentive).
2. Any transfer of land requires a properly executed deed (Exhibit 2).
3. Options (Exhibit 3) to transfer plots may be extended to you, to others, and vice versa. Options may be given free or sold for

Exhibit 1
Present Land Holdings of Each Company

A	B	C	D
EXCEL	EXCEL	VALCO	DELTA
E	F	G	H
VALCO	DELTA	KEY	DELTA
I	J	K	L
KEY	KEY	VALCO	EXCEL
M	N	O	P
EXCEL	KEY	DELTA	VALCO

N ↑

cash. Once an option is extended, it is valid for a period of 10 minutes only. During its valid period, the option requires the plot owner to transfer to the option holder the designated plot if the option holder requests it.

4. All lots are nominally priced at $10,000 each. However, this is purely a nominal figure and in no way should restrict the principle of supply and demand. Therefore, each plot owner is free to set whatever value on his plots he desires.

5. At the instant of transfer of property by a duly executed deed, both seller and buyer must notify the instructor so that such trans-

fer can be recorded on the Central Land Chart. Failure to do so will render the transfer invalid.

6. A time period for planning and another for transacting will be specified by the instructor.

Step 3: 45–60 Minutes

Meet and negotiate with the other subsidiary companies to acquire the land needed for your expansion. Make sure you follow the rules set out at the end of the "Background Information" section.

INSTRUCTIONS TO LANDHOLDERS

The chart given to you shows your present landholdings. Your site expansion team has identified your required lots as indicated. You have been supplied with two alternatives. Your preferred configuration is shown by solid lines; this configuration would be optimum for your company. The alternative shown by dotted lines would be acceptable, but would create some difficulties. It should be obtained *only* if it becomes *impossible* to obtain your preferred configuration.

It is anticipated that one or more of the plots you now own may be desired by one or more of the other subsidiaries. This could result in those plots being of considerably more value than the nominal price.

If, for any reason, you are unable to obtain either your preferred or alternate configurations, your company will be required to locate in another area than this total land. This would mean additional expense. In the event of this possibility, your president has directed you to sell all your plots at the maximum price you can obtain in order to help offset the added cost of other location.

You are authorized to spend up to $25,000 of company funds for the procurement of needed land, if you must do so. You cannot operate in a deficit cash position. You may, of course, obtain cash by selling plots you own.

You must maintain continuous accounting of your financial standing.

You are encouraged to involve all members of your group in some way during the transactions.

Step 4: 15 Minutes

Complete all your financial calculations and assemble all documents resulting from your negotiations.

Individually complete the "Analysis Guide" (see Exhibit 4) below. Then, in your group, compare your answers and summarize those points on which you agree or disagree.

Step 5: 20 Minutes

Individual teams report their summaries on the Analysis Guide and discuss.

Exhibit 2
Deed

Lot _____ Originally owned by_____
                                                         (Company)

Transferred to_____ By _____
                    (Company)   (Company)

              Authorized signature: _____

Transferred to_____ By _____
                    (Company)   (Company)

              Authorized signature: _____

Transferred to_____ By _____
                    (Company)   (Company)

              Authorized signature: _____

Exhibit 3
Option

Option to obtain lot_____ At $_____
                                                                            (Cost of lot)

Option expires _____ (10 minutes from original issue)
                      (Time)

Initial issue to_____ for $_____
                      (Company)   (Cost of option)

            Signature of lot owner:_____

First transfer of option to_____ for $_____
                              (Company)   (Cost of option)

            Signature of transferring agent:_____

Second transfer of option to_____ for $_____
                                (Company)   (Cost of option)

            Signature of transferring agent:_____

Note: Lot owner must sell to option holder on demand at stated cost of lot.

Exhibit 4
Analysis Guide

Instructions: First, complete this questionnaire individually according to your personal reactions and experiences. Second, discuss together your responses, focusing particularly on the Why answers.

On each scale below, record two answers. Mark a W to record your impression of the process occurring *W*ithin your own subsidiary company, and a B for the process occurring *B*etween subsidiaries.

1. Amount of trust.

Low   High

Why: _____

_____

_____

2. Character of interactions.

Competitive   Cooperative

Why: _____

_____

_____

3. Basis of decision making.

Power, threats,   Problem solving,
bluff, strategies   mutual and open,
                                                                           exploration

Why: _____

_____

_____

Exhibit 4 *(concluded)*

4. Problem-solving stance.

Fixed, rigid	Adaptable, flexible

Why: _____

_____

_____

5. Which of the other three subsidiaries were the most:

Cooperative _____ Competitive _____

Why: _____

_____

_____

6. What personal behaviors and actions would need to be different, and what would they need to be in order for the Central Industry goal to be fully met?

_____

_____

_____

_____

_____

_____

DISCUSSION QUESTIONS

1. Did all groups see the other groups the same way; that is, trusting, flexible, competitive, etc.? If there were differences, what explains the differences?
2. Did most groups accomplish their objectives? What things lead to some groups being successful or unsuccessful?
3. Were Central Industries' goals achieved? Why?

Jordan Electronics Company

INTRODUCTION

In this simulation, you will play the role of a committee member on the New Products Committee of Jordan Electronics Company. The committee oversees the development of all new products. In particular, it approves the research and design of all new products and authorizes their release from R&D to begin the manufacturing process. At the moment, the committee is faced with a decision: whether or not to authorize the manufacture of a new model of the Jordan Auto Correlator Model 36, known as the JAC 36.

As a member of the committee working on this problem, you will face some of the complex and tense deliberations that often confront senior management. You will have several levels of concern on the committee: your own job and the problems you may have in getting it done, representing the members of your unit whom you supervise, and worrying about the welfare of Jordan Electronics as a whole.

ADVANCE PREPARATION

Prior to class, read the "Background Information" section of the Jordan Electronics Company. Also read the information sheet on the role you have been assigned by your instructor. Plan what you are going to do in the forthcoming meeting.

BACKGROUND INFORMATION

Jordan Electronics is a manufacturing company that produces two major lines of scientific measuring instruments: instruments for use in scientific laboratories (Laboratory Products) and industrial instruments for use in manufacturing processes (Industrial Products). The management of Jordan Electronics is currently confronted with a problem in authorizing the manufacture of a redesigned model of the Jordan Auto Correlator Model 36 (JAC 36).

The original measuring instrument was designed over 20 years ago by Norman Bass (now president of the company but at that time, a professor at the State University). Bass had teamed up with two others to found Jordan Electronics: Kenneth Lawson (now director of research and development but at the time also a State University professor) and John Snyder (now senior engineer but then an independent electronics engineer specializing in computers).

The original mission of the company was to manufacture the auto correlator and other scientific instruments. (An auto correlator is a device used to monitor flow processes by measuring data at different points in the process. It might measure the rate of flow of chemicals through a pipeline as well as changes in temperature of the chemical at two different points along a pipeline and then correlate that information.) At the time, the instrument revolutionized the market. The JAC 36 (so called because it was launched on Bass' 36th birthday) permitted a researcher to make correlations simultaneously on 64, 128, or 256 channels (monitoring levels). The device was initially picked up by physicists doing research in defraction and gradually was adopted by scientists from other fields and by manufacturing firms using complex chemical processes. The JAC 36 became the market leader in its field and maintained that position for over 15 years.

However, the past few years have brought changes. First, revolutionary developments in electronics technology now permit the manufacture of the entire JAC circuitry in solid state microcircuits, or "chips." Using these components reduces the size and weight of the completed machine, permits a smaller-size box, and allows the design of a portable unit. Changeover to this manufacturing process is costly, but once the "bugs" are worked out, manufacturing cost per unit could be cut significantly.

Second, although the JAC 36 holds a strong share of the market, Jordan's competitors have been nibbling away at that share by adding a variety of new features to their own instruments. One addition has been to provide automatic scanning over all the data in the channel (rather than to do this manually). A second feature is to provide a built-in oscilloscope to display data from several channels simultaneously. Competing products with these features sell for $1,000–$1,500 more than the present JAC 36. Finally, as mentioned above, some competitors are rumored to be working on a design that also uses microcircuitry, which could make their machines lighter and therefore portable. While the JAC 36 typically is used as a laboratory instrument, scientists now seem to want the flexibility of a lighter machine for field experiments and mobile laboratories. Lightness and ease of movement is even more attractive in industrial applications. Though the use of chips requires some change in the basic circuit design, it requires extensive change in the physical design of the instrument and in the manufacturing methods.

Six months ago, Sales Vice President Joe Little made a very strong pitch to management to encourage production of a JAC 36 that incorporated the reduced size, automatic scanning, and multiple scanning features. He pointed out that Jordan's sales representatives were becoming increasingly embarrassed by customer complaints about the outdated nature of the JAC 36 and their requests for a newer version similar to the competition. Little also said he would like to see two versions of the JAC 36 in the future, a portable machine and a stationary one, but that the portable machine was clearly second priority because strong demand was not anticipated for several years.

In response to this request, President Norm Bass requested an intensive study of the market for an updated JAC 36 and an estimate of manufacturing costs. The market study, conducted by an independent marketing research firm, reported that there was still a very strong market for the current JAC 36. In fact, many of the consumers who had purchased auto correlators from competitors—machines that included the advanced scanning features—reported that they rarely used those features. In other words, many of the newer machines on the market were "overdesigned" for their customers' actual use. Market research on the portable versus nonportable machines was inconclusive: Some purchasers clearly wanted it, but the overall demand for portability was not strong.

Cost estimates for an updated JAC 36 were developed by John Snyder, Peter O'Malley (vice president of manufacturing), and Ted Slocum (director of engineering). They calculated that there would be a very high cost in changeover to the microcircuit technology. Adding automatic scanning capability, while continuing to use the present digital readers, was the most simple and least costly change. Adding an oscilloscope for graphic displays of data in several channels simultaneously would involve considerable redesign of the cabinet and manufacturing methods and would cost considerably more than adding the automatic scanning but considerably less than switching to microchip circuits. Moreover, there were a few nagging technical problems in the electronic design of a suitable portable instrument; the longer it took to work these problems out, the higher the R&D costs would go and the longer it would take to get the portable JAC 36 on the market.

Bass reviewed all of this information. He decided that in spite of these reports, Jordan needed to come out with a new JAC 36 model, if only to satisfy the need to appear to be competitive with other machines. Since the old standard JAC 36 machines were holding their market share and since development of the portable microchip model was plagued with problems, Bass decided to proceed with a redesign of the old JAC 36 machine that would include both the automatic scanning features and the ocilloscope. At the meeting announcing the decision, Bass stated that he wanted the new model to maintain Jordan's reputation for providing flexible, high-quality equipment. Joe Little commented that the new JAC 36 should be offered at about the same price as the present model. Since the revised model was not designed to be portable, weight was not a problem for the new machine. Snyder and Slocum, after reviewing the design specifications, said they could probably have the development work done in three to four months.

Synder and Slocum finished the development work in early January. Production was sent the information it needed to set production methods and to estimate costs. After talking it over with his factory superintendent, Peter O'Malley described the production methods and costs in detail in a memorandum to Norman Bass. O'Malley's estimates were considerably higher than anticipated. The current JAC 36 sold for $16,000, but O'Malley estimated that it would be impossible to sell the new model for less than $20,000. Bass and Little were very upset by this memorandum. They asked O'Malley to thoroughly review all figures and distribute them to all members of the New Products Committee, who would then make the decision whether to start manufacturing the revised JAC 36.

It is now early March, and the meeting of the New Products Committee is about to occur. O'Malley's revised figures were not substantially different from his original estimates. The basic costs are presented in Exhibit 1.

The committee has a real problem on its hands. In addition, Bass, who normally chairs the meeting, will not be present because he is scheduled to undergo minor surgery; he has asked Vince D'Moro, vice president for finance, to chair the meeting in his place. The purpose of the meeting is to determine if the JAC 36 should be put into production and, if so, at what price it should be marketed. In attendance will be:

Vince D'Moro, vice president, finance (chairman)

Ken Lawson, director of R&D

Joe Little, vice president, sales

Pete O'Malley, vice president, manufacturing

John Snyder, senior electrical engineer

EXHIBIT 1
Jordan Electronics Company Cost Structures

	Present Cost Structure JAC 36	Estimated Cost Structure Revised JAC 36
Factory price	$16,000	$20,000
Costs:		
Direct labor	1,650	2,300
Raw materials	6,700	8,500
Factory overhead	3,700	5,200
Margin	3,950	4,000

	Variance Report Last Year JAC 36
Labor:	
Metal shop	−2%
Electronic components	+8%
Other components	—
Assembly	+5%
Test	+10%
Materials:	
Metal	−3%
Electronics	+10%
Overhead	−11%

PROCEDURE

Step 1: 5 Minutes

If this has not already been done, you will be assigned a role on a pricing committee.

Step 2: 45 Minutes

The New Products Committee will meet and work toward settling the major issues.

Step 3: 15 Minutes

If you have not reached an agreement, stop the discussion at this point. Each member of the group should state the goals they were trying to achieve, the least-preferred solution that they would still accept for a settlement, and any other issues that must be included in a minimally acceptable deal. Then each member should state what factors in the group's discussion blocked achieving a settlement within the time limits.

If a settlement was reached, each member of the group should report what their minimally acceptable terms were and what factors helped the group reach a solution.

Step 4: 30 Minutes

The instructor will gather information from each New Products Committee on their outcome and the information assembled by each group in step 3. The exercise will then be reviewed and evaluated.

DISCUSSION QUESTIONS

1. What were the most frequently cited obstacles to reaching agreement?
2. What was or could be done to overcome these obstacles?
3. Were there any common features to the groups that did successfully achieve agreement? That did not achieve agreement?
4. Should this type of issue be handled by a committee in organizations? What are the pros and cons of this approach?

Personal Bargaining Inventory

INTRODUCTION

One way for negotiators to learn more about themselves, and about others in a negotiating context, is to clarify their own personal beliefs and values about the negotiation process, and their style as negotiators. The questionnaire in this section can help you clarify perceptions of yourself on several dimensions related to negotiation—winning and losing, cooperation and competition, power and deception—and your beliefs about how a person "ought" to negotiate. Your instructor is likely to ask you to share your responses with others after you complete the questionnaire.

ADVANCE PREPARATION

Complete the Personal Bargaining Inventory questionnaire in this exercise. Bring the inventory to class.

PROCEDURE

Option 1: 60–90 Minutes

a. Pick six–eight statements from Part I (rating yourself) and six–eight statements from Part II (rating people's behavior in general) that you feel most strongly about.

b. In groups of four to five (as organized by the instructor), discuss those statements in Part I that you feel most strongly about. Working around the group, each individual should reveal (1) the statements he/she selected, and (2) whether the statements are characteristic or uncharacteristic of him/her. Other group members may then ask questions of clarification. The group as a whole then should help the individual arrive at a two or three sentence summary description of that individual's *self-image as a negotiator.*

Note. The role of the group is *not* to challenge, confront, or attempt

---

Adapted from an exercise developed by Bert Brown and Norman Berkowitz.

to change an individual's view of himself. Group members are encouraged to be supportive of an individual's self-view, and try to understand how that individual sees himself/herself.

c. Using the same groups, members should now proceed to Part II (people's behavior in general) of the questionnaire. The same format and approach should be followed. Individuals should identify the six–eight statements that they most strongly agree or disagree with. Each individual should state these to the group, and the group should then help each individual to identify that individual's *philosophy of negotiation effectiveness.* Again, the purpose of the groups is not to talk an individual out of his/her beliefs, but to try to understand how people approach this process with very different beliefs and values. Individuals should work to understand how their own view is *similar* or *different* to other individuals in the group and class.

d. One person from the group should be selected as spokesperson to prepare a report to the class. The reporter should *not* identify individuals, but try to summarize the different "types" of individuals that were identified in the group.

Option 2: 60–90 Minutes

a. The instructor will give you six–eight 3 × 5 file cards. Select *six* statements from the first group of 23 that you feel most strongly about (statements which are either characteristic or strongly uncharacteristic of you). Write each statement on a separate 3 × 5 card—statement number, full text of the statement, and whether it is characteristic or uncharacteristic of you.

c. Your instructor will give you further information on how to proceed.

Personal Bargaining Inventory Questionnaire

The questions in this inventory are designed to measure your responses to your perceptions of human behavior in situations of bargaining and negotiation. The first group of statements ask you about *your own behavior* in bargaining; the second group asks you to judge *people's behavior in general.*

Part I: Rating Your Own Behavior

For each statement, please indicate how much the statement is *characteristic of you* on the following scale:

1 Strongly uncharacteristic
2 Moderately uncharacteristic
3 Mildly uncharacteristic
4 Neutral; no opinion
5 Mildly characteristic
6 Moderately characteristic
7 Strongly characteristic

Rate each statement on the seven-point scale by writing in one number closest to your personal judgment of yourself:

Rating   *Statement*

_____   1. I am sincere and trustworthy at all times. I will not lie, for whatever ends.

_____   2. I would refuse to bug the room of my opponent.

_____   3. I don't particularly care what people think of me. Getting what I want is more important than making friends.

_____   4. I am uncomfortable in situations where the rules are ambiguous and there are few precedents.

_____   5. I prefer to deal with others on a one-to-one basis rather than as a group.

_____   6. I can lie effectively. I can maintain a poker face when I am not telling the truth.

_____   7. I pride myself on being highly principled. I am willing to stand by those principles no matter what the cost.

_____   8. I am a patient person. As long as an agreement is finally reached I do not mind slow-moving arguments.

_____   9. I am a good judge of character. When I am being deceived I can spot it quickly.

_____   10. My sense of humor is one of my biggest assets.

_____   11. I have above-average empathy for the views and feelings of others.

_____   12. I can look at emotional issues in a dispassionate way. I can argue strenuously for my point of view, but put the dispute aside when the argument is over.

_____   13. I tend to hold grudges.

_____   14. Criticism doesn't usually bother me. Any time you take a stand people are bound to disagree, and it's ok for them to let you know they don't like your stand.

_____   15. I like power. I want it for myself, to do with what I want. In situations where I must share power I strive to increase my power base, and lessen that of my co-power holder.

_____   16. I like to share power. It is better for two or more to have power than it is for power to be in just one person's hands. The balance of shared power is important to effective functioning of any organization because it forces participation in decision making.

_____   17. I enjoy trying to persuade others to my point of view.

_____   18. I am not effective at persuading others to my point of view when my heart isn't really in what I am trying to represent.

_____   19. I love a good old, knockdown, drag-out verbal fight. Conflict is healthy, and open conflict where everybody's opinion is aired is the best way to resolve differences of opinion.

_____   20. I hate conflict and will do anything to avoid it—including giving up power over a situation.

_____   21. In any competitive situation I like to win. Not just win, but win by the biggest margin possible.

_____ 22. In any competitive situation I like to win. I don't want to clobber my opponent, just come out a little ahead.

_____ 23. The only way I could engage conscionably in bargaining would be by dealing honestly and openly with my opponents.

Part II: Rating People's Behavior in General

For each statement, please indicate how much you agree with the statement on the following scale:

1 Strongly disagree
2 Moderately disagree
3 Mildly disagree
4 Neutral; no opinion
5 Mildly agree
6 Moderately agree
7 Strongly agree

Rate each statement on the seven-point scale by writing in one number closest to your personal judgment of people's behavior in general:

Rating	Statement

_____ 24. If you are too honest and trustworthy, most people will take advantage of you.

_____ 25. Fear is a stronger persuader than trust.

_____ 26. When one is easily predictable, one is easily manipulated.

_____ 27. The appearance of openness in your opponent should be suspect.

_____ 28. Make an early minor concession; the other side may reciprocate on something you want later on.

_____ 29. Personality and the ability to judge people and persuade them to your point of view (or to an acceptable compromise) are more important than knowledge and information about the issues at hand.

_____ 30. Silence is golden—it's the best reply to a totally unacceptable offer.

_____ 31. Be the aggressor. You must take the initiative if you are going to accomplish your objectives.

_____ 32. One should avoid frequent use of a third party.

_____ 33. Honesty and openness are necessary to reach equitable agreement.

_____ 34. It is important to understand one's values prior to bargaining.

_____ 35. Be calm. Maintaining your cool at *all* times gives you an unquestionable advantage. Never lose your temper.

_____ 36. Keep a poker face: never act pleased as terms are agreed upon.

_____ 37. A good negotiator must be able to see the issues from the opponent's point of view.

_____ 38. An unanswered threat will be read by your opponent as weakness.

_____ 39. In bargaining, winning is the most important consideration.

_____ 40. The best outcome in bargaining is one which is fair to all parties.

_____ 41. Most results in bargaining can be achieved through cooperation.

_____ 42. Principles are all well and good, but sometimes have to be compromised to achieve your goals.

_____ 43. You should never try to exploit your adversary's personal weakness.

_____ 44. A member of a bargaining team is morally responsible for the strategies and tactics employed by that team.

_____ 45. Good ends justify the means. If you know you're right and your goal is worthy, you needn't be concerned too much about *how* your goal is achieved.

_____ 46. Honesty means openness, candor, telling all and not withholding pertinent information, not exaggerating emotion. One should always be honest during bargaining.

_____ 47. Imposing personal discomfort on an opponent is not too high a price to pay for success in negotiation.

_____ 48. Regardless of personal considerations one should accept any role assigned to him by the bargaining team.

_____ 49. There is no need to deal completely openly with your adversaries. In bargaining as in life, what they don't know, won't hurt them.

_____ 50. There is nothing wrong with lying to an opponent in a bargaining situation as long as you don't get caught.

DISCUSSION QUESTIONS

Option 1

1. Which six–eight statements did you identify for Part I? What summary statement did you arrive at to characterize your self-image as a negotiator?
2. Which six–eight statements did you identify for Part II? What summary statement did you arrive at to characterize your philosophy of negotiation effectiveness?
3. How similar or different were you to other people in your group? In your class? Did this surprise you? Why?
4. What do you believe are the good and bad aspects of your self-image as a negotiator? Are there aspects that you would like to change? Which ones?

Option 2

1. Which six statements did you begin with? Which six statements did your group end with? How much do your statements still represent your own self-image?
2. How much influence do you think you had in the group meetings? If you had a lot of influence, how were you influential? If you had very little influence, how were others influential?
3. Are you comfortable with the group's statements? Do you wish you had behaved any differently in group discussions?
4. How do the groups' statements differ from one another? What does this say about personal views of negotiation?

Questionnaire on Machiavellianism

INTRODUCTION

The questionnaire in this section explores your orientation to a personality dimension known as Machiavellianism. Please complete the questionnaire, and then your instructor will explain how to score the instrument and how to interpret these scores.

ADVANCE PREPARATION

As provided by your instructor.

PROCEDURE

Complete the M–V Personality Profile.

Your instructor will hand out a scoring key. Follow the key in order to score your questionnaire.

The M–V Personality Profile

Below are 20 sets of statements. In each set, there are three statements lettered A, B, and C.

For *each set,* you are to mark the statement that is *most descriptive* of you with an M, and to mark the statement that is *least* descriptive of you with an L. Leave the third statement blank. At the end of the test, therefore, you will have 20 statements (one in each set) marked M, 20 marked L, and 20 left blank. Even if the choices are difficult, select a "most" and "least" descriptive statement from each set.

1. _____ A. It takes more imagination to be a successful criminal than a successful businessman.

   _____ B. The phrase, "the road to hell is paved with good intentions" contains a lot of truth.

   _____ C. Most men forget more easily the death of their father than the loss of their property.

2. _____ A. Men are more concerned with the car they drive than with the clothes their wives wear.

_____ B. It is very important that imagination and creativity in children be cultivated.

_____ C. People suffering from incurable diseases should have the choice of being put painlessly to death.

3. _____ A. Never tell anyone the real reason you did something unless it is useful to do so.

_____ B. The well-being of the individual is the goal that should be worked for before anything else.

_____ C. Since most people don't know what they want, it is only reasonable for ambitious people to talk them into doing things.

4. _____ A. People are getting so lazy and self-indulgent that it is bad for our country.

_____ B. The best way to handle people is to tell them what they want to hear.

_____ C. It would be a good thing if people were kinder to others less fortunate than themselves.

5. _____ A. Most people are basically good and kind.

_____ B. The best criteria for a wife or husband is compatability—other characteristics are nice but not essential.

_____ C. Only after a man has gotten what he wants from life should he concern himself with the injustices in the world.

6. _____ A. Most people who get ahead in the world lead clean, moral lives.

_____ B. Any man worth his salt shouldn't be blamed for putting his career above his family.

_____ C. People would be better off if they were concerned less with how to do things and more with what to do.

7. _____ A. A good teacher is one who points out unanswered questions rather than give explicit answers.

_____ B. When you ask someone to do something, it is best to give the real reasons for wanting it rather than giving reasons which might carry more weight.

_____ C. A person's job is the best single guide as to the sort of person he is.

8. _____ A. The construction of such monumental works as the Egyptian pyramids was worth the enslavement of the workers who built them.

_____ B. Once a way of handling problems has been worked out it is best to stick to it.

_____ C. One should take action only when sure it is morally right.

9. _____ A. The world would be a much better place to live in if people would let the future take care of itself and concern themselves only with enjoying the present.

_____ B. It is wise to flatter important people.

_____ C. Once a decision has been made, it is best to keep changing it as new circumstances arise.

10. _____ A. It is a good policy to act as if you are doing the things you do because you have no other choice.

_____ B. The biggest difference between most criminals and other people is that criminals are stupid enough to get caught.

_____ C. Even the most hardened and vicious criminal has a spark of decency somewhere within him.

11. _____ A. All in all, it is better to be humble and honest than to be important and dishonest.

_____ B. A man who is able and willing to work hard has a good chance of succeeding in whatever he wants to do.

_____ C. If a thing does not help us in our daily lives, it isn't very important.

12. _____ A. A person shouldn't be punished for breaking a law that he thinks is unreasonable.

_____ B. Too many criminals are not punished for their crimes.

_____ C. There is no excuse for lying to someone else.

13. _____ A. Generally speaking, men won't work hard unless they are forced to do so.

_____ B. Every person is entitled to a second chance, even after he commits a serious mistake.

_____ C. People who can't make up their minds are not worth bothering about.

14. _____ A. A man's first responsibility is to his wife, not his mother.

_____ B. Most men are brave.

_____ C. It's best to pick friends that are intellectually stimulating rather than ones it is comfortable to be around.

15. _____ A. There are very few people in the world worth concerning oneself about.

_____ B. It is hard to get ahead without cutting concerns here and there.

_____ C. A capable person motivated for his own gain is more useful to society than a well-meaning but ineffective one.

16. _____ A. It is best to give others the impression that you can change your mind easily.

_____ B. It is a good working policy to keep on good terms with everyone.

_____ C. Honesty is the best policy in all cases.

17. _____ A. It is possible to be good in all respects.

_____ B. To help oneself is good; to help others even better.

_____ C. War and threats of war are unchangeable facts of human life.

18. _____ A. Barnum was probably right when he said that there's at least one sucker born every minute.

_____ B. Life is pretty dull unless one deliberately stirs up some excitement.

_____ C. Most people would be better off if they control their emotions.

19. _____ A. Sensitivity to the feelings of others is worth more than poise in social situations.

_____ B. The ideal society is one where everybody knows his place and accepts it.

_____ C. It is safest to assume that all people have a vicious streak and it will come out when they are given a chance.

20. _____ A. People who talk about abstract problems usually don't know what they are talking about.

_____ B. Anyone who completely trusts anyone else is asking for trouble.

_____ C. It is essential for the functioning of a democracy that everyone vote.

Developed by Richard Christie and Florence Geis.

Read, if your instructor does not cover the concepts in class, the article entitled "The Machiavellis among Us," by Richard Christie in the "Readings" section of this volume.

DISCUSSION QUESTIONS

1. What was your score?
2. How does this score compare to other students in the class? How does it compare to the national norms reported by Christie and Geis?
3. Do you think that this score is an accurate reflection of your tendencies toward Machiavellianism as described by Christie and Geis? Why or why not?
4. How might individuals who are high in Machiavellianism behave in negotiating situations? Have you seen examples of this behavior in class activities? Describe.

Career Style Inventory: An Assessment Exercise

PURPOSE

1. To engage in an assessment of the personal style that one currently expresses, or intends to express, in organizational life.
2. To explore the dynamics of that style with others of similar disposition, and understand how individuals of different styles perceive one another in organizational environments.

ADVANCE PREPARATION

The questionnaire may be completed as a homework assignment, if specified by the instructor.

INTRODUCTION

There have been a number of efforts by behavioral scientists to describe, categorize, and classify different personal styles in organizations. Many of these efforts have concentrated on describing different styles of leaders (e.g., Blake and Mouton, 1964; Tannenbaum & Schmidt, 1958; Hersey & Blanchard, 1977), while other works have focused on the basic characteristics of those who work for organizations (e.g., Jay, 1968, 1971; Whyte, 1956).

The following questionnaire was developed to measure individual dispositions toward another set of personal styles in organizations, proposed by Michael Maccoby (1976). After completing the questionnaire below, you will have the opportunity to read about these styles, and to evaluate your own responses to the questionnaire.

Developed by Roy J. Lewicki. Reprinted from *Experiences in Management and Organization Behavior* by Douglas T. Hall, Donald Bowen, Roy J. Lewicki and Francine Hall. New York: John Wiley & Sons, Rev. Ed., 1981.

EXHIBIT 1
Career Style Inventory

Below are a number of descriptive paragraphs. They describe a set of beliefs or perceptions that may be held by different individuals that work for large organizations. The paragraphs are divided into four sections: Life Goals, Motivation, Self-Image, and Relations with Others. For each section, there are four paragraphs. Please evaluate these paragraphs as follows:

1. Read the paragraph. Treating the paragraph as an entity—that is, using *all* of the information in the paragraph, not just one or two sentences—*rate* the paragraph as it describes you. Indicate in a scale from "not at all characteristic of me" (1) to "highly characteristic of me" (7). Rate each paragraph in the section on this scale.
2. Rate each paragraph in terms of the way you would *like* to be. Regardless of how you are now, rate each description as it represents an "ideal" managerial style. Rate each on a scale from "not like to be like this at all" (1) to "very much like to be like this" (7).

Please be as honest, realistic and candid in your self-evaluations as possible. Try to accurately describe yourself, not represent what you think others might want you to say or believe.

Scales:

1	2	3	4	5	6	7
Not at all characteristic of me	Somewhat characteristic of me		Generally characteristic of me		Highly characteristic of me	

1	2	3	4	5	6	7
I would not like to be like this at all		I would somewhat like to be like this		I would generally like to be like this		I would very strongly like to be like this

A. Life Goals

1. I equate my personal success in life with the long-term development and success of the organization that I work for. I enjoy a sense of belonging, responsibility, and loyalty to an organization. I believe that I will benefit most if my organization prospers. I would be satisfied with my career if I progressed no higher than a middle management level.

   How characteristic is this of you (1–7) _____?
   How much would you like to be like this (1–7) _____?

2. I have two major goals in life: to do my job well, and to be committed to my family. I believe strongly in the work ethic, and want to succeed by skillfully and creatively accomplishing goals and tasks. I also want to be a good parent and provider for my family. Work and family are equally important.

EXHIBIT 1 *(continued)*

How characteristic is this of you (1–7) _____?
How much would you like to be like this (1–7) _____?

3. My goal in life is to acquire power; success for me means being involved in a number of successful, diverse enterprises. I generally experience life and work as a jungle; like it or not, it's a dog-eat-dog world, and there will always be winners and losers. I want to be one of the winners.

   How characteristic is this of you (1–7) _____?
   How much would you like to be like this (1–7) _____?

4. I tend to view life and work as a game. I see my work, my relations with others, and my career in terms of options and possibilities as if they were part of a strategic game that I was playing. My main goal in life is to be a winner at this game.

   How characteristic is this of you (1–7) _____?
   How much would you like to be like this (1–7) _____?

B. Motivation

1. My interest in work is in the process of building something. I am motivated by problems that need to be solved; the challenge of work itself or the creation of a quality product gets me excited. I would prefer to miss a deadline rather than do something halfway—quality is more important to me than quantity.

   How characteristic is that of you (1–7) _____?
   How much would you like to be like this (1–7) _____?

2. I like to take risks, and am fascinated by new methods, techniques, and approaches. I want to motivate myself and others by pushing everyone to their limits, beyond their normal pace. My interest is in challenge, or competitive activity, where I can prove myself to be a winner. The greatest sense of exhiliration for me comes from managing a team of people and gaining victories. When work is no longer challenging, I feel bored and slightly depressed.

   How characteristic is this of you (1–7) _____?
   How much would you like to be like this (1–7) _____?

3. I like to control other people and to acquire power. I want to succeed by climbing the corporate ladder, acquiring greater positions of power and responsibility. I want to use this power to gain prestige, visibility, financial success, and to be able to make decisions that affect many other people. Being good at "politics" is essential to this success.

   How characteristic is this of you (1–7) _____ ?
   How much would you like to be like this (1–7) _____?

4. My interest in work is to derive a sense of security from organizational membership, and to have good relations with others. I am concerned with the feelings of people who I work with, and am committed to maintaining the integrity of my organization. As long as the organization rewards my efforts, I am willing to let my commitment to my organization take precedence over my own self-interest.

EXHIBIT 1 *(continued)*

How characteristic is this of you (1–7) _____?
How much would you like to be like this (1–7) _____?

C. Self-Image

1. I am competitive and innovative. My speech and my thinking are dynamic, and come in quick flashes. I like to emphasize my strengths, and I like to be in control. I have a lot of trouble realizing and living within my limitations. I pride myself on being fair with others; I have very few prejudices. I like to have limitless options to succeed; my biggest fears are being trapped, or being labeled as a loser.

   How characteristic is this of you (1–7) _____?
   How much would you like to be like this (1–7) _____?

2. My identity depends upon being part of a prestigious, protective organization. I see myself as trustworthy, responsible, a "nice guy" who can get along with almost everyone. I'm concerned with making a good impression on others, and representing the company well. I'm not sure that I have as much confidence, toughness, aggressiveness, and risk-taking as I would like. I am aware of these weaknesses, but I also think I should receive credit for the contributions I have made to my organization.

   How characteristic is this of you (1–7) _____?
   How much would you like to be like this (1–7) _____?

3. My sense of self-worth is based on my assessment of my skills, abilities, self-discipline, and self-reliance. I tend to be quiet, sincere, modest, and practical. I like to stay with a project from conception to completion.

   How characteristic is this of you (1–7) _____?
   How much would you like to be like this (1–7) _____?

4. I tend to be brighter, more courageous, and stronger than most of the people I work with. I see myself as bold, innovative, and an entrepreneur. I can be exceptionally creative at times, particularly in seeing entrepreneurial possibilities and opportunities. I am willing to take major risks in order to succeed, and willing to be secretive or manipulative with others if it will further my own goals.

   How characteristic is this of you (1–7) _____?
   How much would you like to be like this (1–7) _____?

D. Relations with Others

1. I tend to dominate other people because my ideas are better, and/or I am willing to take risks and withstand a lot of criticism. I generally don't like to work closely and cooperate with others. I would rather have other people working for me, following my directions. I don't think anyone has ever really freely helped me; either I controlled and directed them, or they were expecting me to do something for them in return.

   How characteristic is this of you (1–7) _____?
   How much would you like to be like this (1–7) _____?

EXHIBIT 1 *(concluded)*

---

2. My relations with others are generally good. I value highly other people who are trustworthy, committed to this organization, and act with integrity in the things that they do. In my work group, I attempt to sustain an atmosphere of cooperation, mild excitement, and mutuality. I get "turned off" by others in the organization who are out for themselves, who show no respect for others, or who get so involved with their own little problems that they lose sight of the "big picture."

    How characteristic is this of you (1–7) _____ ?
    How much would you like to be like this (1–7) _____ ?

3. I like to be in control; I am tough and dominating, but I don't think I am destructive. I tend to classify other people as winners and losers. I evaluate almost everyone in terms of what they can do for the team. I coax other people to share their knowledge with others, trying to get a work atmosphere that is both exciting and productive. I am impatient with others who are slower and more cautious, and don't like to see weakness in others.

    How characteristic is this of you (1–7) _____ ?
    How much would you like to be like this (1–7) _____ ?

4. My relations with others are generally determined by the work that we do. I feel more comfortable working in a small group, or on a project with a defined and understandable structure. I tend to evaluate others (my co-workers and superiors) in terms of whether they can help or hinder me in doing a craftsmanlike job. I do not compete against other people as much as I do against my own standards of quality. On the other hand, I often find myself on the defensive, trying to preserve my integrity from the exploitative demands of the more aggressive managerial types around me.

    How characteristic is this of you (1–7) _____ ?
    How much would you like to be like this (1–7) _____ ?

THE CORPORATE CLIMBER HAS TO FIND HIS HEART[1]

A new type of man is taking over the leadership of the most technically advanced large companies in America. In contrast to the jungle-fighter industrialists commonly associated with the turn of the century, the new leader is driven not to build or preside over empires, but to organize winning teams. Unlike the security-seeking organization man who became the stereotype of the 50s, he is excited by the chance to cut deals and to gamble.

The new industrial leader is not as hardhearted as the autocratic empire builder, nor is he as dependent on the company as the organization man. But he is more detached and emotionally inaccessible than either. And he is

---

[1] Excerpt from article by Michael Maccoby in *Fortune* (December 1976). Reprinted by permission of Dr. Maccoby.

EXHIBIT 2
Career Style Inventory Scoring Key

For *each* orientation, refer back to the respective sections and paragraphs in Exhibit 1. *Add* the rating scale values for the "characteristic of me" scales, and for the "would like to be" scales, in each grouping.

	Characteristic of Me	Would Like to Be Like This
Craftsman Orientation		
Life goals—Paragraph 2		
Motivation—Paragraph 1		
Self-image—Paragraph 3		
Relations with others—Paragraph 4		
TOTAL score for Craftsman		
Company Orientation		
Life goals—Paragraph 1		
Motivation—Paragraph 4		
Self-image—Paragraph 2		
Relations with others—Paragraph 2		
TOTAL score for Company Man		
Jungle Fighter Orientation		
Life goals—Paragraph 3		
Motivation—Paragraph 3		
Self-image—Paragraph 4		
Relations with others—Paragraph 3		
TOTAL score for Jungle Fighter		
Gamesman Orientation		
Life goals—Paragraph 4		
Motivation—Paragraph 2		
Self-image—Paragraph 1		
Relations with others—Paragraph 1		
TOTAL score for Gamesman		

troubled by that fact: he recognizes that his work develops his head but not his heart.

As a practicing psychoanalyst, I reached these conclusions on the basis of interviews with 250 managers, ranging from chief executives down to lower-level professional employees in 12 well-known corporations. The study was sponsored by the Harvard Seminar on Science, Technology, and Public Policy and supported by the Andrew W. Mellon Foundation. With the help of Douglass Carmichael, Rolando Weissmann, Dennis M. Greene, Cynthia Elliott, and Katherine A. Terzi, I conducted the interviews over six years.

In some cases we returned to particular managers several times to talk about how their work was influencing the development of their characters.

All together, we spent at least 3 hours with most, as long as 20 hours with some. In a few cases we also interviewed their wives and children, and 75 executives took Rorschach tests.

In contrast to psychoanalysts who study the emotionally disturbed, we concentrated on healthy people in healthy companies. Most of the companies have sales exceeding $1 billion a year and all are highly technological, creators of some of the most advanced products of our age. They practice, and some invented, managerial techniques and business strategies that others admire and copy. Their top managers tend to speak out on major public issues, and a few have held high government positions. No one has accused these companies of trying to overthrow governments, bribe officials, or beg Washington to bail them out of their mistakes.

Creatures in a Corporate Culture

I wanted to find out what motivates the managers of these corporations—what mix of ambition, greed, scientific interest, security seeking, or idealism. How are managers molded by their work? What is the quality of their lives? What type of person reaches the top (and which falls by the wayside)? Once we had studied the interviews and Rorschach tests, it became clear that the corporation is populated by four basically different character types. These are "ideal" types in the sense that few people fit any one of them exactly. Most executives are mixtures of two or more, but in practically every case, we were able to agree on which type best described a person. And the individual and his colleagues almost always agreed with our assessment.

The types are as follows:

The craftsman, as the name implies, holds traditional values, including the work ethic, respect for people, concern for quality, and thrift. When he talks about his work, he shows an interest in the *process* of making something; he enjoys building. He sees others, co-workers as well as superiors, in terms of whether they help or hinder him in doing a craftsmanlike job.

Many of the managers in the great corporate laboratories, such as Du Pont and Bell Labs, are craftsmen by character. Their virtues are admired by almost everyone. Yet they are so absorbed in perfecting their own creations—even to the exclusion of broader corporate goals—that they are unable to lead complex and changing organizations.

The jungle fighter lusts for power. He experiences life and work as a jungle where it is eat or be eaten, and the winners destroy the losers. A major part of his psychic resources are budgeted for his internal department of defense. Jungle fighters tend to see their peers as either accomplices or enemies, and their subordinates as objects to be used.

There are two types of jungle fighters, lions and foxes. The lions are the conquerors who, when successful, may build an empire. In large industry, the day of the lions—the Carnegies and Fords—seems virtually ended. The foxes make their nests in the corporate hierarchy and move ahead by stealth and politicking. The most gifted foxes we encountered rose rapidly, by making use of their entrepreneurial skills. But in each case they were eventually destroyed by those they had used or betrayed.

The company man bases his sense of identity on being part of the protective organization. At his weakest, he is fearful and submissive, seeking security even more than success. At his strongest, he is concerned with the human side of the company, interested in the feelings of the people around him, and committed to maintaining corporate integrity. The most creative company men sustain an atmosphere of cooperation and stimulation, but they tend to lack the daring to lead highly competitive and innovative organizations.

The gamesman sees business life in general, and his career in particular, in terms of options and possibilities, as if he were playing a game. He likes to take calculated risks and is fascinated by techniques and new methods. The contest hypes him up and he communicates his enthusiasm, energizing his peers and subordinates like the quarterback on a football team. Unlike the jungle fighter, the gamesman competes not to build an empire or to pile up riches, but to gain fame, glory, the exhilaration of victory. His main goal is to be known as a winner, his deepest fear to be labeled a loser.

Molded by the Psychostructure

The higher our interviews took us in the corporation, the more frequently we encountered the gamesman—he is the new corporate leader. Again, it must be emphasized that the top-level executive is not a pure type, but rather a mixture. He most often combines many of the traits of the gamesman with some attributes of the company man. He is a team player who identifies closely with the corporation.

The gamesman reaches the top in a process of social (in contrast to natural) selection. The companies that excel tend to be run by people who are well adapted to fulfill the requirements of the market and the technology, and who create an atmosphere that encourages productive work. These executives in turn stimulate traits in their subordinates that are useful to the work, while discouraging those that are unnecessary or impede it. As an executive moves to the top, therefore, his character is refined.

Any organization of work—industrial, service, blue or white collar—can be described as a "psychostructure" that selects and molds character. One difference between the psychostructure of the modern corporate hierarchy and that of the factory is the fineness of fit required between work and character. Managers must have characters closely attuned to the "brain work" they perform. Only a minimal fit is required to perform simplified, repetitive tasks in a factory.

The gamesman's character, which might seem a collection of near paradoxes, can best be understood in terms of its adaptation to the requirements of the organization. The gamesman is cooperative but competitive, detached and playful but compulsively driven to succeed, a team player but a would-be superstar, a team leader but often a rebel against bureaucratic hierarchy, fair and unprejudiced but contemptuous of weakness, tough and dominating but not destructive. Competition and innovation in modern business require these gamelike attitudes, and of all the character types, only the gamesman is emotionally attuned to the environment.

DISCUSSION QUESTIONS

Discuss the different career styles in terms of the following questions:

1. In this program or class, what would be your guess as to the style that most people use to describe themselves? What is the least frequently used style? Why?
2. In this program or class, what would be your guess as to the style that most people would like to be? What is the style that they would least like to be? Why?
3. Survey the members of the class. How many are there of each type? How many are there of each "desired" (would like to be) type? Do you think these numbers would be characteristic of other student groups completing this questionnaire?
4. How many people wanted to be styles different from the ones that they are now? What were their reasons for wanting to be different?
5. Do you think there are any significant differences in how males and females would rate their present styles or their ideal styles? Why?
6. What would be the best type of job, managerial role, or organization for each style? Why?
7. What would be the advantages, or assets, for individuals possessing each style, in an organizational setting? What would be the disadvantages, or weaknesses, of each style?
8. What can people in each style learn to do, in order to function more effectively in a variety of organizational roles and responsibilities?

READINGS AND REFERENCES

Blake, R. R., and Mouton, J. S., *The Managerial Grid* (Houston, Tx.: Gulf Publishing Co., 1964).

Hersey, P., and Blanchard, K., *Management of Organizational Behavior: Utilizing Human Resources* (Englewood Cliffs, N.J.: Prentice Hall, 1977).

Jay, A., *Management and Machiavelli* (New York: Holt, Rinehart and Winston, 1968).

Jay, A., *Corporation Man* (New York: Random House, 1971).

Maccoby, M., *The Gamesman* (New York: Simon and Schuster, 1976).

Maccoby, M., "The Corporate Climber Has to Find His Heart," *Fortune*, December (1976), 98–108.

Tannenbaum, R., and Schmidt, W., "How to Choose a Leadership Pattern," *Harvard Business Review*, March–April (1958), 95–102.

Whyte, W. F., *The Organization Man* (New York: Simon and Schuster, 1956).

EXERCISE 19

Social Power Inventory

INTRODUCTION

The questionnaire in this exercise is designed to measure your predisposition to be responsive to certain forms of social power. In responding to these questions, you will learn something about the types of power that you are most responsive to, or least responsive to, depending on who is exercising it.

ADVANCE PREPARATION

At the discretion of the instructor.

PROCEDURE

Step 1: 45 Minutes

Identify three *different* people who have influence over you. One must be a teacher, a second may be a roommate or spouse, a third may be a boss. Others might include friends, business associates, parents, or people that you negotiate with regularly. Specify the three people you have identified:

Person 1: *Boss*
Person 2: *Teacher*
Person 3: *Good Friend*

Step 2: 20 Minutes

For *each* of the three people work completely through the questionnaire with that person in mind. For each of the 30 questions, pick A or B depending on which one of the two best describes the way that they affect you more. Make sure to *pick one* even if neither are very good answers.

Step 3: 30 Minutes

Your instructor will hand out a scoring key. Follow the key in order to score your questionnaire.

Questionnaire developed by David W. Jamieson and Kenneth W. Thomas. Used with permission.

Boss Teacher Friend

Person 1	Person 2	Person 3	
A	A	A	1. A. I sometimes do what the other person says in order to get something I want. B. I sometimes have to go along to avoid trouble.
B	A	B	2. A. The person always convinces me with his reasoning. B. I sometimes do things for that person because I admire him.
A	B	A	3. A. The person might do good things for me in return. B. I don't know as much about it as the other person does.
B	A	A	4. A. That person's suggestions always make sense. B. I could receive things I want from that person.
B	B	A	5. A. I want that person to like me. B. I often feel that it is legitimate for that person to influence my behavior.
B	A	B	6. A. I take his word for things. B. I sometimes try to avoid trouble by doing what is asked.
A	B	B	7. A. The other person has the right to tell me what to do. B. That person is able to harm me in some way.
B	A	B	8. A. The other person knows better. B. I will receive something I want.
B	B	A	9. A. That person's friendship is important to me. B. The other person seems fairly intelligent.
B	B	A	10. A. The reasoning of the request usually agrees with my way of thinking. B. The other person is in a position to legitimately ask things of me.
A	B	B	11. A. I will receive something I want. B. I sometimes go along with the other person to make him happy.
B	A	B	12. A. The other person's knowledge usually makes him right. B. I feel that the other person has the right to ask things of me.

Boss teacher Friend

Person 1	Person 2	Person 3	
B	B	A	**13.** A. I want that person to like me. B. I sometimes have to go along to avoid trouble.
B	B	A	**14.** A. I would sometimes like to get things from that person. B. Sometimes I feel that the person might do something which is unpleasant to those who do not do what is suggested.
B	B	A	**15.** A. That person's suggestions always make sense. B. I do what is asked to keep the other person from taking actions which could be unpleasant for me.
A	A	B	**16.** A. That person should be listened to. B. That person's friendship is important to me.
A	A	B	**17.** A. That person can do things which I would not like. B. The other person always knows what he's doing.
B	A	B	**18.** A. I sometimes have to go along in order to get things I need. B. I often feel that it is legitimate for that person to influence my behavior.
B	A	B	**19.** A. The request is sometimes appropriate, considering the other person's position. B. At times, that person's suggestions make sense.
B	B	A	**20.** A. I sometimes do so because I feel that the person is my friend. B. The other person's expertise makes him more likely to be right.
A	B	B	**21.** A. The other person has the right to tell me what to do. B. The other person could do something unpleasant to me.
A	B	A	**22.** A. The person is able to do things which benefit me. B. The person always convinces me with his reasoning.
A	A	B	**23.** A. The other person's position permits him to require things of me. B. The other person's knowledge usually makes him right.
A	A	A	**24.** A. I trust the other person's judgment. B. I agree with what the other person says.

Boss teacher Friend

Person 1	Person 2	Person 3	
A	A	B	25. A. Sometimes I feel that the person might do something which is unpleasant to those who do not do what is suggested.
			B. I always do what is asked because that person's ideas are compelling.
B	A	A	26. A. The other person might help me get what I want.
			B. It would not be proper sometimes for me to do otherwise.
A	A	B	27. A. The other person can make things uncomfortable for me if I don't comply.
			B. I do what is asked to make the other person happy.
B	B	A	28. A. I would like to be his friend.
			B. The other person can help me.
A	A	A	29. A. That person always gives me good reasons for doing it.
			B. I sometimes do what is asked to gain that person's friendship.
B	B	A	30. A. What the other person says seems to be appropriate.
			B. That person has had a lot of experience and usually knows best.

DISCUSSION QUESTIONS

1. What was your score for each of the different forms of power?

Scoring Key

	Expert	Legitimate	Coercive	Reward	Referent	Informational
Person 1						
Person 2						
Person 3						

2. Find others in the class who rated the same *type* of person (e.g., teacher, parent, roommate, and so on). How do your scores compare to theirs in terms of the types that are most and least influential? Why do you suppose that this is so?
3. How do the *situations* that these people are in—for example, their objectives and your objectives, the differences in your ages, the kind of resources they control and you want, etc.—affect the kind of power they

are likely to use, and the kind of power that has impact on you? Explain.

4. If you were the "powerful" party in these situations, would you try to use different forms of power from those now being used? Explain.

5. As a power-user yourself, which forms of power are you most comfortable in using? Least comfortable? In which situations?

Questionnaire on Ethics

INTRODUCTION

The purpose of the Questionnaire on Ethics is to inquire about your general disposition toward questions of ethics, particularly those ethical issues related to negotiations. Please complete the two questionnaires in this activity. The instructor will explain how to score the questionnaires and interpret their results.

ADVANCE PREPARATION

None, unless specified by the instructor.

PROCEDURE

1. Complete the Ethics Position Questionnaire.
2. Complete the Incidents in Negotiation Questionnaire.
3. Your instructor will hand out a scoring key for the Ethics Position Questionnaire. Follow the key in order to score your questionnaire. A description of the questionnaire and what it measures can be found following the questionnaire.
4. Be prepared to share your answers to the Incidents in Negotiation Questionnaire with others in a small group or class discussion.

The Ethics Position Questionnaire

You will find a serious of general statements listed below. Each represents a commonly held opinion, and there are no right or wrong answers. You will probably agree with some items and disagree with others. We are interested in the extent to which you agree or disagree with such matters of opinion.

Please read each statement carefully. Then indicate the extent to which you agree or disagree by placing in *front* of the statement the number corresponding to your feelings, where:

1 = Completely disagree	4 = Slightly disagree	7 = Moderately agree
2 = Largely disagree	5 = Neither agree or disagree	8 = Largely agree
3 = Moderately disagree	6 = Slightly agree	9 = Completely agree

Rating

_____ 1. A person should make certain that their actions never intentionally harm another, even to a small degree.

_____ 2. Risks to another should never be tolerated, irrespective of how small the risks might be.

_____ 3. The existence of potential harm to others is always wrong, irrespective of the benefits to be gained.

_____ 4. One should never psychologically or physically harm another person.

_____ 5. One should not perform an action which might in any way threaten the dignity and welfare of another individual.

_____ 6. If an action could harm an innocent other, then it should not be done.

_____ 7. Deciding whether or not to perform an act by balancing the positive consequences of the act against the negative consequences is immoral.

_____ 8. The dignity and welfare of people should be the most important concern in any society.

_____ 9. It is never necessary to sacrifice the welfare of others.

_____ 10. Moral actions are those which closely match ideals of the most "perfect" action.

_____ 11. There are no ethical principles that are so important that they should be a part of any code of ethics.

_____ 12. What is ethical varies from situation in society to another.

_____ 13. Moral standards should be seen as being individualistic; what one person considers to be moral may be judged to be immoral by another person.

_____ 14. Different types of moralities cannot be compared to one another as to "rightness."

_____ 15. Questions of what is ethical for everyone can never be resolved, since what is moral or immoral is up to the individual.

_____ 16. Moral standards are simply *personal* rules, which indicate how a person should behave, and are not to be applied in making judgments of others.

_____ 17. Ethical considerations in interpersonal relations are so complex that individuals should be allowed to formulate their own codes.

_____ 18. Rigidly codifying an ethical position that prevents certain types of actions could stand in the way of better human relations and adjustment.

_____ 19. No rule concerning lying can be formulated; whether a lie is permissible or not permissible totally depends on the situation.

_____ 20. Whether a lie is judged to be moral or immoral depends upon circumstances surrounding the action.

Ab. (1–10) _____   Rel. (11–20) _____

Source: Donelson R. Forsyth, "A Taxonomy of Ethical Ideologies," *Journal of Personality and Social Psychology* 39 (1980), pp. 175–84. Copyright 1980 by the American Psychological Association. Reprinted by permission of the author.

Incidents in Negotiation Questionnaire

Listed below you will find a number of negotiating tactics. People frequently disagree about these tactics and whether they are ethically acceptable or unacceptable in negotiation. Please think about each tactic, and then rate each one on the scale below, based on your judgment of the ethical or unethical nature of the tactic:

1	2	3	4	5	6	7
Not at all ethical			Somewhat ethical			Very ethical

Rating

_____ 1. Threaten to harm your opponent if he/she doesn't give you what you want, even if you know you will never follow through to carry out that threat.

_____ 2. Promise that good things will happen to your opponent if he/she gives you what you want, even if you know that you can't (or won't) deliver those good things when the other's cooperation is obtained.

_____ 3. Lead the other negotiator to believe that they can only get what they want by negotiating with you, when in fact they could go elsewhere and get what they want cheaper or faster.

_____ 4. Hide your real bottom line from your opponent.

_____ 5. Make an opening demand that is far greater than what one really hopes to settle for.

_____ 6. Gain information about an opponent's negotiating position and strategy by "asking around" in a network of your own friends, associates, and contacts.

_____ 7. Gain information about an opponent's negotiating position by paying friends, associates, and contacts to get this information for you.

_____ 8. Gain information about an opponent's negotiating position by trying to recruit or hire one of your opponent's key subordinates (on the condition that the key subordinate bring confidential information with him/her).

_____ 9. Gain information about an opponent's negotiating position by cultivating his/her friendship through expensive gifts, entertaining, or "personal favors."

_____10. Make an opening offer or demand so high (or low) that it seriously undermine's your opponent's confidence in his/her own ability to negotiate a satisfactory settlement.

_____11. Talk directly to the people who your opponent reports to, or is accountable to, and tell them things that will undermine their confidence in your opponent as negotiator.

_____12. Talk directly to the people who your opponent reports to, or is accountable to, and try to encourage them to defect to your side.

_____13. Convey a false impression that you are in absolutely no hurry to come to a negotiation agreement, thereby trying to put more time pressure on your opponent to concede quickly.

_____14. Threaten to make your opponent look weak or foolish in front of a boss or others to whom he/she is accountable.

_____15. Intentionally misrepresent factual information to your opponent in order to support your negotiating arguments or position.

_____16. Intentionally misrepresent the nature of negotiations to the press or your constituency in order to protect delicate discussions that have occurred.

_____17. Intentionally misrepresent the progress of negotiations to the press or your constituency in order to make your own position or point of view look better.

_____18. Intentionally misrepresent factual information to your opponent when you know that he/she has already done this to you.

WHEN YOU HAVE FINISHED, REVIEW ALL 18 STATEMENTS AND PICK THE FIVE WHICH ARE MOST ETHICAL, AND THE FIVE WHICH ARE MOST UNETHICAL. WRITE THE NUMBERS BELOW, AND BE PREPARED TO STATE HOW YOU MADE YOUR CHOICES.

Most Ethical	*Least Ethical*
1. _____	1. _____
2. _____	2. _____
3. _____	3. _____
4. _____	4. _____
5. _____	5. _____

DISCUSSION

The Ethics Position Questionnaire was developed by Donelson Forsyth, and designed to measure individual variations in approaches to making moral judgments along two major dimensions. The first dimension is the degree to which an individual makes moral judgments based on universal moral rules versus relativistic criteria. When considering moral and ethical issues, some individuals tend to rely upon "moral absolutes" (e.g., "Thou shalt not lie"), while others rely upon the circumstances of the situation to determine what to do (e.g., it's OK to lie in some situations). The second major dimension is the amount of idealism in an individual's moral judgments. Some individuals are high in idealism, and believe that if one always does the "right" thing, good consequences will occur (e.g., if I always tell the truth, everything will work out OK). Others, lower in idealism, believe that doing the "right" thing will not always lead to the desirable consequences (e.g., if I always tell the truth, sometimes the truth will get me in more trouble than a lie would.)

Based on responses to the items in the questionnaire, Forsyth proposed that an individual's general ethical ideology could be described by one of four different types, depending upon whether the respondent scored high or low on the idealism and relativism scales (see Exhibit 1). In Forsyth's research, an individual's ethical ideology has been demonstrated to be related

EXHIBIT 1
Taxonomy of Ethical Ideologies

Relativism

	High	*Low*
Idealism High	*Situationalists* Rejects moral rules; advocates an individual analysis of each act in each situation to determine what is right; relativistic.	*Absolutists* Assumes that the best possible outcome can always be achieved by following universal moral rules.
Low	*Subjectivists* Appraises the situation based on own personal values and perspectives rather than universal moral principles; relativistic.	*Exceptionists* Moral absolutes guide personal judgments but pragmatically open to exceptions to these standards; utilitarian.

to attitudes on contemporary moral issues and on ways to deal with people who violate moral and ethical codes. Absolutists—particularly males—are much more moralistic than the other types, and wish to deal significantly more harshly with those who violate the rules. Subjectivists, on the other hand, were much more pragmatic and much more likely to judge events and actions based on the specific facts, circumstances, and outcomes that resulted, rather than on moralistic grounds.

The Incidents in Negotiation Questionnaire was prepared by the authors based on a number of incidents that have occurred in negotiation, and which usually are very controversial because of the moral and ethical judgments that surround these actions. As you can probably conclude, there are no "right" or "wrong" answers to these statements. However, people in your class or seminar will probably strongly disagree about which events are more or less acceptable in negotiation, and which ones are the most or least serious. Group discussion can focus around the questions below.

DISCUSSION QUESTIONS

1. What were your scores on the Relativism and Idealism scales? Based on information provided by your instructor, what is your predominant ethical ideology? Is this score consistent with the way you think you make judgments about moral or ethical issues?
2. How do your scores compare to others in your class or group? Are there

differences based on age or sex? What might be some other ways to explain differences among the group?

3. How did you respond to the Incidents in Negotiation Questionnaire? Are some of these tactics ethically acceptable? Which ones? Are some ethically wrong? Which ones? Are there some that are OK depending upon the circumstances? What might those circumstances be?

4. Do you agree with the following quotation? (Think about it and then discuss with your classmates):

There is no such thing as an "honest bluff" as distinguished from the empty promise or the treacherous falsehood. If an "honest bluff" fails, the bluffer may be forgiven for trying a legitimate strategem, but if he has lied he may be cold shouldered out of the game.[1]

5. Do you agree with the following quotation? (Think about it and then discuss with your classmates):

Falsehood ceases to be a falsehood when it is understood on all sides that the truth is not expected to be spoken. [attributed to Sir Henry Taylor, British statesman].[1]

---

[1] Quotations from Albert Carr, "Is Business Bluffing Ethical?" *Harvard Business Review,* January–February 1968.

CASES

CASE STUDY

Capital Mortgage Insurance Corporation (A)

Frank Randall hung up the telephone, leaned across his desk, and fixed a cold stare at Jim Dolan.

> OK, Jim. They've agreed to a meeting. We've got three days to resolve this thing. The question is, what approach should we take? How do we get them to accept our offer?

Randall, president of Capital Mortgage Insurance Corporation (CMI), had called Dolan, his senior vice president and treasurer, into his office to help him plan their strategy for completing the acquisition of Corporate Transfer Services (CTS). The two men had begun informal discussions with the principal stockholders of the small employee relocation services company some four months earlier. Now, in late May 1979, they were developing the terms of a formal purchase offer and plotting their strategy for the final negotiations.

The acquisition, if consummated, would be the first in CMI's history. Furthermore, it represented a significant departure from the company's present business. Randall and Dolan knew that the acquisition could have major implications, both for themselves and for the company they had revitalized over the past several years.

Jim Dolan ignored Frank Randall's intense look and gazed out the eighth-floor window overlooking Philadelphia's Independence Square.

> That's not an easy question, Frank. We know they're still looking for a lot more money than we're thinking about. But beyond that, the four partners have their own differences, and we need to think through just what they're expecting. So I guess we'd better talk this one through pretty carefully.

Capital Mortgage Insurance Company (A)–(F) 9-480-057-062.

Copyright © 1980 by the President and Fellows of Harvard College.

This case was prepared by James P. Ware as a basis for class discussion rather than to illustrate either effective or ineffective handling of an administrative situation. Reprinted by permission of the Harvard Business School.

COMPANY AND INDUSTRY BACKGROUND

CMI was a wholly owned subsidiary of Northwest Equipment Corporation, a major freight transporter and lessor of railcars, commercial aircraft, and other industrial equipment. Northwest had acquired CMI in 1978, two years after CMI's original parent company, an investment management corporation, had gone into Chapter 11 bankruptcy proceedings.

CMI had been created to sell mortgage guaranty insurance policies to residential mortgage lenders throughout the United States. Mortgage insurance provided banks, savings and loans, mortgage bankers, and other mortgage lenders with protection against financial losses when homeowners defaulted on their mortgage loans.

Lending institutions normally protected their property loan investments by offering loans of only 70 percent to 80 percent of the appraised value of the property; the remaining 20 percent to 30 percent constituted the homeowner's down payment. However, mortgage loan insurance made it possible for lenders to offer so-called high ratio loans of up to 95 percent of a home's appraised value. High ratio loans were permitted only when the lender insured the loan; although the policy protected the lender, the premiums were paid by the borrower, as an addition to monthly principal and interest charges.

The principal attraction of mortgage insurance was that it made purchasing a home possible for many more individuals. It was much easier to produce a 5 percent down payment than to save up the 20 percent to 30 percent that had traditionally been required.

CMI had had a mixed record of success within the private mortgage insurance industry. Frank Randall, the company's first and only president, had gotten the organization off to an aggressive beginning, attaining a 14.8 percent market share by 1972. By 1979, however, that share had fallen to just over 10 percent even though revenues had grown from $18 million in 1972 to over $30 million in 1979. Randall attributed the loss of market share primarily to the difficulties created by the bankruptcy of CMI's original parent. Thus, he had been quite relieved when Northwest Equipment had acquired CMI in January 1978. Northwest provided CMI with a level of management and financial support it had never before enjoyed. Furthermore, Northwest's corporate management had made it clear to Frank Randall that he was expected to build CMI into a much larger, diversified financial services company.

Northwest's growth expectations were highly consistent with Frank Randall's own ambitions. The stability created by the acquisition, in combination with the increasing solidity of CMI's reputation with mortgage lenders, made it possible for Randall to turn his attention more and more toward external acquisitions of his own. During 1978 Randall, with Jim Dolan's help, had investigated several acquisition opportunities in related insurance industries, with the hope of broadening CMI's financial base. After several unsuccessful investigations the two men had come to believe that their knowledge and competence was focused less on insurance per se than it was on residential real estate and related financial transactions. These experiences had led to a recognition that, in Frank Randall's words, "we are a residential real estate financial services company."

THE RESIDENTIAL REAL ESTATE INDUSTRY

Frank Randall and Jim Dolan knew from personal experience that real estate brokers, who played an obvious and important role in property transactions, usually had close ties with local banks and savings and loans. When mortgage funds were plentiful, brokers often "steered" prospective home buyers to particular lending institutions. When funds were scarce, the lenders would then favor prospective borrowers referred by their "favorite" brokers. Randal believed that these informal relationships meant that realtors could have a significant impact on the mortgage loan decision and, thus, on a mortgage insurance decision as well.

For this reason, CMI had for many years directed a small portion of its marketing effort toward real estate brokers. CMI's activities had consisted of offering educational programs for realtors, property developers, and potential home buyers. The company derived no direct revenues from these programs, but offered them in the interest of stimulating home sales and, more particularly, of informing both realtors and home buyers of how mortgage insurance made it possible to purchase a home with a relatively low down payment.

Because he felt that real estate brokers could be powerful allies in encouraging lenders to use mortgage insurance, Randall had been tracking developments in the real estate industry for many years. Historically a highly fragmented collection of local, independent entrepreneurs, the industry in 1979 appeared to be on the verge of a major restructuring and consolidation. For the past several years many of the smaller brokers had been joining national franchise organizations in an effort to gain a "brand image" and to acquire improved management and sales skills.

More significantly, in 1979, several large national corporations were beginning to acquire prominent real estate agencies in major urban areas. The most aggressive of these appeared to be Merrill Lynch and Company, the well-known Wall Street securities trading firm. Merrill Lynch's interest in real estate brokers stemmed from several sources; perhaps most important were the rapidly rising prices on property and homes. Realtors' commissions averaged slightly over 6 percent of the sales price; *Fortune* magazine estimated that real estate brokers had been involved in home sales totaling approximately $190 billion in 1978, netting commissions in excess of $11 billion (in comparison, stockbrokers' commissions on all securities transactions in 1978 were estimated at $3.7 billion).[1] With property values growing

---

[1] "Why Merrill Lynch Wants to Sell You a House," *Fortune,* January 29, 1979.

10–20 percent per year, commissions would only get larger; where 6 percent of a $30,000 home netted only $1,800, 6 percent of a $90,000 sale resulted in a commission well in excess of $5,000—for basically the same work.

There were also clear signs that the volume of real estate transactions would continue to increase. Although voluntary intercity moves appeared to be declining slightly, corporate transfers of employees were still rising. One of Merrill Lynch's earliest moves toward the real estate market had been to acquire an employee relocation company several years earlier. Working on a contract basis with corporate clients, Merrill Lynch Relocation Management (MLRM) collaborated with independent real estate brokers to arrange home sales and purchases for transferred employees. Like other relocation companies, MLRM would purchase the home at a fair market value and then handle all the legal and financial details of reselling the home on the open market. MLRM also provided relocation counseling and home search assistance for transferred employees; its income was derived primarily from service fees paid by corporate clients (and augmented somewhat by referral fees from real estate brokers, who paid MLRM a portion of the commissions they earned on home sales generated by the transferred employees).

Later, in September 1978, Merrill Lynch had formally announced its intention to acquire at least 40 real estate brokerage firms within three to four years. Merrill Lynch's interest in the industry stemmed not only from the profit opportunities it saw, but also from a corporate desire to become a "financial services supermarket," providing individual customers with a wide range of investment and brokerage services. In 1978 Merrill Lynch had acquired United First Mortgage Corporation (UFM), a mortgage banker. And in early 1979 Merrill Lynch was in the midst of acquiring AMIC Corporation, a small mortgage insurance company in direct competition with CMI. As *Fortune* reported:

> In combination, these diverse activities hold some striking possibilities. Merrill Lynch already packages and markets mortgages through its registered representatives. . . . If all goes according to plan, the company could later this year be vertically integrated in a unique way. Assuming the AMIC acquisition goes through, Merrill Lynch will be able to guarantee mortgages. It could then originate mortgages through its realty brokerages, process and service them through UFM, insure them with AMIC, package them as pass-through or unit trusts, and market them through its army of registered representatives. (January 29, 1979, p. 89.)

It was this vision of an integrated financial services organization that also excited Frank Randall. As he and Jim Dolan reviewed their position in early 1979, they were confident that they were in a unique position to build CMI into a much bigger and more diversified company. The mortgage insurance business gave them a solid financial base with regional offices throughout the country. Northwest Equipment stood ready to provide the capital they would need for significant growth. They already had relationships with important lending institutions across the United States, and their marketing efforts had given them a solid reputation with important real estate brokers as well.

Thus, Randall, in particular, felt that at least he had most of the ingredients to begin building that diversified "residential real estate financial services company" he had been dreaming about for so long. Furthermore, Randall's reading of the banking, thrift, and real estate industries suggested that the time was ripe. In his view, the uncertainties in the financial and housing industries created rich opportunities for taking aggressive action, and the vision of Merrill Lynch "bulling" its way into the business was scaring realtors just enough for CMI to present a comforting and familiar alternative.

THE METROPOLITAN REALTY NETWORK

Frank Randall spent most of the fall of 1978 actively searching for acquisition opportunities. As part of his effort, he contacted David Osgood, who was the executive director of The Metropolitan Realty Network, a national association of independent real estate brokers. The association, commonly known as "MetroNet," had been formed primarily as a communication vehicle so its members could refer home buyers moving from one city to another to a qualified broker in the new location.

Randall discovered that Osgood was somewhat concerned about MetroNet's long-term health and viability. Though MetroNet included over 13,000 real estate agencies, it was losing some members to national franchise chains, and Osgood was feeling increasing pressures to strengthen the association by providing more services to member firms. Yet the entrepreneurial independence of MetroNet's members made Osgood's task particularly difficult. He had found it almost impossible to get them to agree on what they wanted him to do.

One service that the MetroNet brokers *were* agreed on developing was the employee relocation business. Corporate contracts to handle transferred employees were especially attractive to the brokers, because the contracts virtually guaranteed repeat business in the local area, and they also led to intercity referrals that almost always resulted in a home sale.

MetroNet brokers were also resentful of how Merrill Lynch Relocation Management and other relocation services companies were getting a larger and larger share of "their" referral fees. Osgood told Randall that he had already set up a committee of MetroNet brokers to look into how the association could develop a corporate relocation and third-party equity[2] capability of its own. Osgood mentioned that their only effort to date was an independent firm in Chicago named Corporate Transfer Services, Inc. (CTS), that had been started by Elliott Burr, a prominent Chicago broker and

---

[2] The term *third-party equity capability* derived from the fact that a relocation services company actually purchased an employee's home, freeing up the owner's equity and making it available for investment in a new home. Within the industry the terms *third-party equity company* and *employee relocation services company* were generally used interchangeably.

a MetroNet director. CTS had been formed with the intention of working with MetroNet brokers, but so far it had remained relatively small and had not met MetroNet's expectations.

As Randall explained to Osgood the kinds of activities that CMI engaged in to help lenders and increase the volume of home sales, Osgood suddenly exclaimed, "That's exactly what *we're* trying to do!" The two men ended their initial meeting convinced that some kind of working relationship between CMI and MetroNet could have major benefits for both organizations. Osgood invited Randall to attend the next meeting of MetroNet's Third-Party Equity Committee, scheduled for March 1. "Let's explore what we can do for each other," said Osgood. "You're on," concluded Randall.

THE THIRD-PARTY EQUITY BUSINESS

Randall's discussion with David Osgood had opened his eyes to the third-party equity business, and he and Jim Dolan spent most of their time in preparation for the March 1 committee meeting steeped in industry studies and pro forma income statements.

They quickly discovered that the employee relocation services industry was highly competitive, though its future looked bright. Corporate transfers of key employees appeared to be an ingrained practice that showed no signs of letting up in the foreseeable future. Merrill Lynch Relocation Management was one of the two largest firms in the industry; most of the prominent relocation companies were well-funded subsidiaries of large, well-known corporations. Exhibit 1 contains Jim Dolan's tabulation of the seven major relocation firms, along with his estimates of each company's 1978 volume of home purchases.

Dolan also developed a pro forma income and expense statement for a hypothetical firm handling 2,000 home purchases annually (see Exhibit 2). His calculations showed a potential 13.1 percent return on equity. Dolan then discovered that some companies achieved a much higher ROE by using a Home Purchase Trust, a legal arrangement that made it possible to obtain enough bank financing to leverage a company's equity base by as much as 10 to 1.

Randall and Dolan were increasingly certain that they wanted to get CMI into the employee relocation services business. They saw it as a natural tie-in with CMI's mortgage insurance operations—one that could exploit the same set of relationships that CMI already had with banks, realtors, savings and loans, and other companies involved in the development, construction, sale, and financing of residential real estate. The two men felt that real estate brokers had a critically important role in the process. Brokers were not only involved in the actual property transactions, but in addition they almost always had local contacts with corporations that could lead to the signing of employee relocation contracts. Equally important, from Randall's and Dolan's perspective, was their belief that a close relationship between CMI

EXHIBIT 1
Major Employee Relocation Services Companies

Relocation Company	Parent Organization	Estimated 1978 Home Purchases	Estimated Value of Homes Purchased*	Estimated Gross Fee Income†
Merrill Lynch Relocation	Merrill Lynch	13,000	$975,000,000	$26,800,000
Homequity	Peterson, Howell, & Heather	12,000	900,000,000	24,750,000
Equitable Relocation	Equitable Life Insurance	5,000	375,000,000	10,300,000
Employee Transfer	Chicago Title and Trust	5,000	375,000,000	10,300,000
Relocation Realty Corporation	Control Data Corporation	3,000	225,000,000	6,200,000
Executrans	Sears/Coldwell Banker	3,000	225,000,000	6,200,000
Transamerica Relocation	Transamerica, Inc.	3,000	225,000,000	6,200,000

* Assumes average home values of $75,000.
† Assumes fee averaging 2.75 percent of value of homes purchased.

EXHIBIT 2

HYPOTHETICAL EMPLOYEE RELOCATION COMPANY
PRO FORMA INCOME STATEMENT

Key assumptions:
1. Annual purchase volume of 2,000 homes.
2. Assume average holding period of 120 days. Inventory turns over three times annually, for an average of 667 units in inventory at any point in time.
3. Average home value of $75,000.
4. Existing mortgages on homes average 50 percent of property value. Additional required capital will be 40 percent equity, 60 percent long-term debt.
5. Fee income from corporate clients will average 2.75 percent of value of properties purchased (based on historical industry data).
6. Operating expenses (marketing, sales, office administration) will average 1 percent of value of properties purchased (all costs associated with purchases, including debt service, are billed back to corporate clients).

Calculations	
Total value of purchases	
(2,000 units at $75,000)	$150,000,000
Average inventory value	50,000,000
Capital required:	
Existing mortgages	25,000,000
New long-term debt	15,000,000
Equity	10,000,000
Fee income at 2.75%	4,125,000
Operating expenses at 1%	1,500,000
Net income	$ 2,625,000
Tax at 50%	(1,312,500)
Profit after tax	$ 1,312,500
Return on equity	13.1%

and the MetroNet brokers would also lead to significant sales of CMI's mortgage insurance policies.

The March 1 meeting with MetroNet's Third-Party Equity Committee turned into an exploration of how CMI and MetroNet might help each other by stimulating both home sales and high ratio mortgage loans. After several hours of discussion, Frank Randall proposed specifically that CMI build an operating company to handle the corporate relocation business jointly with the MetroNet brokers. As a quid pro quo, Randall suggested that the brokers could market CMI mortgage insurance to both potential home buyers and lending institutions.

The committee's response to this idea was initially skeptical. Finally, however, they agreed to consider a more formal proposal at a later date. MetroNet's board of directors was scheduled to meet on April 10; the Third-Party Equity Committee could review the proposal on April 9 and, if they approved, present it to the full board on the 10th.

As the committee meeting broke up Randall and Dolan began talking with

Elliott Burr and Thomas Winder, two of the four owners of Corporate Transfer Services, Inc. (CTS). Though Burr had been the principal founder of CTS, his primary business was a large real estate brokerage firm in north suburban Chicago that he operated in partnership with William Lehman, who was also a CTS stockholder.

The four men sat back down at the meeting table, and Randall mentioned that his primary interest was to learn more about how an employee relocation business operated. Burr offered to send him copies of contracts with corporate clients, sample financial statements, and so on. At one point during their discussion Burr mentioned the possibility of an acquisition. Randall asked, somewhat rhetorically, "How do you put a value on a company like this?" Burr responded almost immediately, "Funny you should ask. We've talked to an attorney and have put together this proposal." Burr reached into his briefcase and pulled out a two-page document. He then proceeded to describe a complex set of terms involving the sale of an 80 percent interest in CTS, subject to guarantees concerning capitalization, lines of credit, data processing support, future distribution of profits and dividends, and more.

Randall backed off immediately, explaining that he needed to learn more about the nature of the business before he would seriously consider an acquisition. As Jim Dolan later recalled:

> I think they were expecting an offer right then and there. But it was very hard to understand what they really wanted; it was nothing we could actually work from. Besides that, the numbers they were thinking about were ridiculously high—over $5 million. We put the letter away and told them we didn't want to get specific until after the April 10 meeting. And that's the way we left it.

Preparation for the April 10 Meeting

During the next six weeks Randall and Dolan continued their investigations of the employee relocation industry and studied CTS much more closely.

One of their major questions was how much additional mortgage insurance the MetroNet brokers might be able to generate. Frank Randall had CMI's marketing staff conduct a telephone survey of about 25 key MetroNet brokers. The survey suggested that most brokers were aware of mortgage insurance, although few of them were actively pushing it. All of those questioned expressed an interest in using CMI's marketing programs, and were eager to learn more about CMI insurance.

By early May a fairly clear picture of CTS was emerging. The company had been founded in 1975; it had barely achieved a break-even profit level. Annual home purchases and sales had reached a level of almost 500 properties, and CTS has worked with about 65 MetroNet brokers and 35 corporate clients. Tom Winder was the general manager; he supervised a staff of about 25 customer representatives and clerical support staff. Conversations with David Osgood and several MetroNet brokers who had worked with CTS suggested that the company had made promises to MetroNet about developing a nationwide, well-financed, fully competitive organization. To date, however, those promises were largely unfulfilled. Osgood believed that CTS' shortage of equity and, therefore, borrowing capacity, had severely limited its growth potential.

Jim Dolan obtained a copy of CTS' December 1978 balance sheet that, in his mind, confirmed Osgood's feelings (see Exhibit 3). The company had a net worth of only $420,000. Three of the four stockholders (Elliott Burr, William Lehman, and Michael Kupchak) had invested an additional $2 million in the company—$1.3 million in short-term notes and $700,000 in bank loans that they had personally guaranteed. While CTS owned homes valued at $13.4 million, it also had additional bank loans and assumed mortgages totaling $9.8 million. Furthermore, the company had a highly uncertain earnings stream; Frank Randall believed the current business could tail off to almost nothing within six months.

During late March both Randall and Dolan had a number of telephone conversations with Burr and Winder. Their discussions were wide-ranging and quite open; the CTS partners struck Randall as being unusually candid. They seemed more than willing to share everything they knew about the business and their own company. On one occasion, Burr asked how much of CTS Randall wanted to buy, and how Randall would feel about the present

EXHIBIT 3

CORPORATE TRANSFER SERVICES, INC.
Unaudited Balance Sheet
December 1978

Assets:	($000)
Cash	$ 190
Homes owned	13,366
Accounts and acquisition fees receivable	665
Other (mainly escrow deposits)	143
	$14,364
Liabilities:	
Client prepayments	$ 1,602
Notes payable to banks	4,161
Assumed mortgages payable	5,670
Loan from stockholders	700
Advance from MetroNet	300
Other liabilities	211
	$12,644
Capital:	
Subordinated debenture due stockholder (April 1981)	1,300
Common stock	450
Deficit	(30)
	$14,364

owners retaining a minority interest. Burr's question led Randall and Dolan to conclude that in fact they wanted full ownership. They planned to build up the company's equity base considerably, and wanted to gain all the benefits of a larger, more profitable operation for CMI.

In early April, Randall developed the formal proposal that he intended to present to MetroNet's board of directors (see Exhibit 4). The proposal committed CMI to enter negotiations to acquire CTS and to use CTS as a base for building a third-party equity company with a capitalization sufficient to support an annual home purchase capability of at least 2,000 units. In return, the proposal asked MetroNet to begin a program of actively supporting the use of CMI's insurance on high ratio loans.

Randall and Dolan met again with the Third-Party Equity Committee in New York on April 9 to preview the CMI proposal. The committee reacted favorably, and the next day MetroNet's board of directors unanimously accepted the proposal after discussing it for less than 15 minutes.

FORMAL NEGOTIATIONS WITH CORPORATE TRANSFER SERVICES

On the afternoon of April 10, following the MetroNet board meeting, Randall and Dolan met again with Elliott Burr and Tom Winder. Now that CMI was formally committed to acquisition negotiations, Burr and Winder were eager to get specific and talk numbers. However, Randall and Dolan remained very cautious. When Burr expressed an interest in discussing a price, Randall replied, "We don't know what you're worth. But we'll entertain any reasonable argument you want to make for why we should pay more than your net worth." The meeting ended with a general agreement to firm things up by April 25.

Later, reflecting on this session, Jim Dolan commented:

> Our letter of agreement committed us to having an operating company by July 12, so the clock was running on us. However, we knew that after the April 10 board meeting they would be hard pressed not to be bought, and besides they were obviously pretty eager. But at that point in time we had not even met the other two stockholders; we suspected the high numbers were coming from them.

Further Assessment of CTS

Even though the April 10 meeting had ended with an agreement to move ahead by April 25, it quickly became evident that a complete assessment of CTS and preparation of a formal offer would take more than two weeks. Other operating responsibilities prevented both Randall and Dolan from devoting as much time as they had intended to the acquisition, and the analysis process itself required more time than they had expected.

During the first week of May, Jim Dolan made a "reconaissance" trip to Chicago. His stated purpose was to examine CTS' books and talk with the

EXHIBIT 4

Board of Directors
The Metropolitan Realty Network
New York, NY

April 9, 1979

Gentlemen:

It is our intention to enter negotiations with the principals of Corporate Transfer Services, Inc., for the acquisition of the equity ownership of this Company by Capital Mortgage Insurance Corporation.

In the event Capital Mortgage Insurance Corporation is successful in the acquisition of Corporate Transfer Services, Inc., it is our intention to capitalize this Company to the extent required for the development of a complete bank line of credit. The initial capital and bank line of credit would provide the MetroNet association members an annual equity procurement 1,500–2,000 units. In addition, we would be prepared to expand beyond this initial capacity if the MetroNet Association volume and profitability of business dictates.

We are prepared to develop an organizational structure and support system that can provide a competitive and professional marketing and administrative approach to the corporate transfer market.

Our intentions to enter negotiations with Corporate Transfer Services, Inc., are subject to the following:

1. The endorsement of this action by you, the board of directors of MetroNet, for Capital Mortgage Insurance Corporation to acquire this organization.
2. The assurance of the MetroNet Association for the continuation of their support and use of CTS. Upon the completion of the acquisition, the MetroNet Association would agree to sign a Letter of Agreement with the new owners of Corporate Transfer Services.
3. The assurance of the MetroNet Association to cooperate in the development of a close working relationship with CMI for the influence and control they may provide when seeking high-ratio conventional mortgage loans using mortgage insurance.

Capital Mortgage Insurance will need the support of expanded business by the MetroNet Association, due to the heavy capital commitment we will be required to make to CTS to make this acquisition feasible. In this regard, CMI is prepared to offer the MetroNet nationwide members a range of marketing programs and mortgage financing packages that will help earn and deserve the mortgage insurance business and expand the listings, sales and profitability of the MetroNet members.

Upon receiving the endorsement and support outlined in this letter from the board of directors of MetroNet, we will proceed immediately with the negotiations with Corporate Transfer Services, Inc. It would be our intention to have the acquisition completed and the company fully operational by the time of the MetroNet national convention in San Francisco in July 1979.

Sincerely,

Franklin T. Randall
President and Chief Executive
Officer

company's local bankers. He also scrutinized the office facilities, met and talked with several office employees, observed Tom Winder interacting with customers and subordinates, and generally assessed the company's operations. Dolan spent most of his time with Winder, but he also had an opportunity to have dinner with William Lehman, another of CTS' stockholders. Dolan returned to Philadelphia with a generally favorable set of impressions about the company's operations, and a much more concrete understanding of its financial situation. He reported to Randall, "They're running a responsible organization in a basically sensible manner." At the same time, however, Dolan also reported that CTS was under increasing pressure from its bankers to improve its financial performance.

Dolan's trip also provided him with a much richer understanding of the four men who owned CTS: Elliott Burr, William Lehman (Burr's real estate partner), Michael Kupchak (a private investor), and Tom Winder. Of these four, only Winder was actively involved in the day-to-day management of the company, although Elliott Burr stayed in very close touch with Winder and was significantly more involved than either Lehman or Kupchak. From their meetings and telephone conversations, Randall and Dolan pieced together the following pictures of the four men:

Elliott Burr, in his middle 50s, had been the driving force behind Corporate Transfer Services. He was a "classic" real estate salesman—a warm, straightforward, friendly man who enthusiastically believed in what he was doing. An eternal optimist, he had been an early advocate of MetroNet's getting into the employee relocation business. Burr knew the relocation business extremely well; he personally called on many of the large Chicago corporations to sell CTS' services.

Burr appeared to be very well off financially. Burr and Lehman Real Estate was one of the largest realty firms on Chicago's North Shore, and Burr was held in high regard by local bankers. One banker had told Dolan, "Burr's word is his bond."

William Lehman, Burr's real estate partner, was in his mid 60s. He appeared to be much more of a financial adviser and investor than an operating manager. Lenman personally owned the shopping center where Burr and Lehman Real Estate was located, as well as the office building where CTS was leasing space.

Dolan characterized Lehman as an "elder statesman—a true gentleman." Dolan recalled that when he had dinner with Lehman during his visit to Chicago, Lehman had kept the conversation on a personal level, repeatedly expressing concern about Dolan's plane reservations, hotel accommodations, and so on. He had hardly mentioned CTS during the entire dinner.

Michael Kupchak was the third principal stockholder. Kupchak, who was about 50, had been a mortgage banker in Chicago for a number of years. Recently, however, he had left the bank to manage his own investments on a full-time basis.

Dolan met Kupchak briefly during his Chicago visit, and characterized him as a "bulldog"—an aggressive, ambitious man much more interested in financial transactions than in the nature of the business. He had apparently thought Dolan was coming to Chicago to make a firm offer, and had been irritated that one had not been forthcoming.

Frank Randall had not yet met Kupchak face to face, although they had talked once by telephone.

Thomas Winder, 44, had spent most of his career in real estate-related businesses. At one time he had worked for a construction company, and then he had joined the mortgage bank where Michael Kupchak worked.

Kupchak had actually brought Winder into CTS as its general manager, and the three original partners had offered him 25 percent ownership in the company as part of his compensation package.

Winder was not only CTS' general manager, but its lead salesperson as well. He called on prospective corporate clients all over the country, and he worked closely with MetroNet as well. That activity primarily involved appearing at association-sponsored seminars to inform member brokers about CTS and its services.

It was obvious to Jim Dolan that CTS had become an important source of real estate sales commissions for the Burr and Lehman partnership. Most of CTS' clients were in the Chicago area, and a large portion of the real estate transactions generated by CTS were being handled by Burr and Lehman Real Estate.

Dolan also inferred that the three senior partners—Burr, Lehman, and Kupchak—were close friends socially as well as professionally. The men clearly respected each other and valued each other's opinions. On one occasion Burr had told Dolan, "It's because of Bill Lehman that I have what I do today. I can always trust his word." Tom Winder was also woven into the relationship, but he was apparently not as closely involved as the other three. Randall and Dolan both sensed that Elliott Burr was the unofficial spokesman of the group: "I have the impression he can speak for all of them," commented Dolan.

In late April, Randall obtained a copy of a consultant's report on the employee relocation industry that had been commissioned by MetroNet's Third-Party Equity Committee. The report estimated that there were more than 500,000 homeowner/employees transferred annually, generating over 1 million home purchases and sales. However, fewer than 55,000 of these transfers were currently being handled by relocation services companies. Dolan's own analysis had projected a 10 percent–15 percent annual growth rate in the use of relocation companies, leading to industry volume estimates of 60,000 in 1979, 67,000 in 1980, and 75,000 by 1981.

The consultant's report stressed that success in the relocation business depended upon a company's ability to provide services to its corporate clients at lower cost than the clients could do it themselves. In addition, profitability depended on a company's ability to turn over its inventory of homes quickly and at reasonable prices.

Dolan's own financial projections showed a potential return on equity of over 30 percent by 1983, assuming only an 8 percent share of the market. And that return did not include any incremental profits resulting from new sales of CMI mortgage insurance policies generated by MetroNet brokers. Randall in particular was confident that the close ties between CMI and MetroNet would result in at least 5,000 new mortgage insurance policies annually—a volume that could add over $400,000 in after-tax profits to CMI's basic business.

On May 10, Randall and Dolan attended a Northwest Equipment Corporation financial review meeting in Minneapolis. Prior to their trip west Randall had prepared a detailed analysis of the CTS acquisition and the employee relocation industry. The analysis, in the form of a proposal, served as documentation for a formal request to Northwest for a capital expenditure of $9 million. Randall had decided that he was willing to pay up to $600,000 more than the $420,000 book value of CTS' net worth; the remaining $8 million would constitute the initial equity base required to build CTS into a viable company.

The financial review meeting evolved into a lengthy critique of the acquisition proposal. Northwest's corporate staff was initially quite skeptical of the financial projections, but Randall and Dolan argued that the risks were relatively low (the homes could always be sold) and the potential payoffs, both economic and strategic, were enormous. Finally, after an extended debate, the request was approved.

FORMAL NEGOTIATIONS WITH CTS

When Randall and Dolan returned from Minneapolis, they felt it was finally time to proceed in earnest with the acquisition negotiations. Randall sensed that at present CTS was limping along to no one's satisfaction—including Elliott Burr's. The company was sucking up much more of Burr's time and energy than he wanted to give it, and its inability to fulfill MetroNet's expectations was beginning to be an embarrassment for Burr personally.

In spite of these problems, Randall remained interested in completing the acquisition. Buying CTS would get CMI into the relocation business quickly, would provide them with immediate licensing and other legal documentation in 38 states, and would get them an experienced operations manager in Tom Winder. More importantly, Randall knew that Elliott Burr was an important and respected MetroNet broker, and buying CTS would provide an effective, influential entry into the MetroNet "old boy" network. Though he couldn't put a number on the value of that network, Randall believed it was almost more important then the acquisition of CTS itself. Randall was convinced that the connection with the MetroNet brokers would enable him to run CTS at far lower cost than the established relocation companies, and he also expected to realize a significant increase in CMI's mortgage insurance business.

May 21, 1979

Now, as Randall and Dolan sat in Randall's office on May 21, they discussed the draft of a formal purchase offer that Dolan had prepared that morning (see Exhibit 5 for relevant excerpts). The two men had decided to make an initial offer of $400,000 more than the $420,000 book value of CTS' net worth,

---

EXHIBIT 5
Excerpts from Draft of Purchase Letter

The Board of Directors and Stockholders
Corporate Transfer Services, Inc.
Chicago, IL

May 24, 1979

Gentlemen:

Capital Mortgage Insurance Corporation (the "Purchaser") hereby agrees to purchase from you (the "Stockholders") and you, the Stockholders, hereby jointly and severally agree to see to us, the Purchaser, 100 percent of the issued and outstanding shares of capital stock of Corporate Transfer Services (the "Company") on the following terms and conditions.

Purchase Price.   Subject to any adjustment under the following paragraph, the Purchase Price of the Stock shall be the sum of $400,000.00 (four hundred thousand dollars even) and an amount equal to the Company's net worth as reflected in its audited financial statements on the closing date (the "Closing Date Net Worth").

Adjustment of Purchase Price.   The Purchase Price shall be reduced or increased, as the case may be, dollar-for-dollar by the amount, if any, by which the net amount realized on the sale of homes owned as of the Closing Date is exceeded by, or exceeds, the net value attributed to such homes in the Closing Date Net Worth.

Continuation of Employment.   Immediately upon consummation of the transaction, the Purchaser will enter into discussion with Mr. Thomas Winder with the intent that he continue employment in a management capacity at a mutually agreeable rate of pay. Mr. Winder will relocate to Philadelphia, Pennsylvania, and will be responsible for the sale of all homes owned by the Company at the Closing Date.

Covenant-Not-to-Compete.   At the closing, each Stockholder will execute and deliver a covenant-not-to-compete agreeing that he will not engage in any capacity in the business conducted by the Company for a period of two years.

If the foregoing correctly states our agreement as to this transaction, please sign below.

Very truly yours,

CAPITAL MORTGAGE INSURANCE
CORPORATION

By_____
President

The foregoing is agreed to and accepted.

---

subject to a formal audit and adjustments depending on the final sales prices of all homes owned by CTS as of the formal purchase date. This opening bid was $200,000 below Randall's ceiling price of $600,000 for the firm's goodwill. The offer also included a statement of intent to retain Tom Winder as CTS' general manager and to move the company to CMI's home office in Philadelphia.

As Randall and Dolan reviewed their plans, it was clear that they were more concerned about how to conduct the face-to-face negotiations than with the formal terms themselves. In the telephone call he had just completed, Randall had told Elliott Burr only that they wanted to meet the other stockholders and review their current thinking. At one point during the conversation Jim Dolan commented:

> I really wonder how they'll react to this offer. We've been putting them off for so long now that I'm not sure how they feel about us anymore. And our offer is so much less than they're looking for . . .

Randall replied:

> I know that—but I have my ceiling. It seems to me the real question now is what kind of bargaining stance we should take, and how to carry it out. What do you think *they* are expecting?

DISCUSSION QUESTIONS

1. Prepare, and be ready to discuss, a negotiating strategy for Randall and Dolan.
2. What should CMI be expecting from CTS?

Pacific Oil Company (A)

For the session on Pacific Oil Company, please prepare the following:

1. As background information, *read:* "Petrochemical Supply Contracts: A Technical Note."
2. After reading Pacific Oil Company (A), prepare the following questions for class discussion:

   A. Describe the "problem" that faced Pacific Oil Company as it reopened negotiations with Reliant Chemical Company in early 1975.
   B. Evaluate the styles and effectiveness of Messrs. Fontaine, Gaudin, Hauptmann, and Zinnser as negotiators in this case.
   C. What should Frank Kelsey recommend to Jean Fontaine at the end of the case? Why?

THE PACIFIC OIL COMPANY

"Look, you asked for my advice, and I gave it to you," Frank Kelsey said. "If I were you, I wouldn't make any more concessions! I really don't think you ought to agree to their last demand! But you're the only one who has to live with the contract, not me!"

Static on the transatlantic telephone connection obscured Jean Fontaine's reply. Kelsey asked him to repeat what he had said.

"OK, OK, calm down, Jean. I can see your point of view. I appreciate the pressures you're under. But I sure don't like the looks of it from this end. Keep in touch—I'll talk to you early next week. In the meantime, I will see what others at the office think about this turn of events."

Frank Kelsey hung up the phone. He sat pensively, staring out at the rain pounding on the window. "Poor Fontaine," he muttered to himself. "He's so anxious to please the customer, he'd feel compelled to give them the whole pie without getting his fair share of the dessert!"

Kelsey cleaned and lit his pipe as he mentally reviewed the history of the

---

This case was prepared by Roy J. Lewicki for use in executive seminars.

negotiations. "My word," he thought to himself, "we are getting eaten in little bites in this Reliant deal! And I can't make Fontaine see it!"

BACKGROUND

Pacific Oil Company was founded in 1902 as the Sweetwater Oil Company of Oklahoma City, Oklahoma. The founder of Sweetwater Oil, E. M. Hutchinson, pioneered a major oil strike in north central Oklahoma that touched off the Oklahoma "black gold" rush of the early 1900s. Through growth and acquisition in the 1920s and 30s, Hutchinson expanded the company rapidly, and renamed it Pacific Oil in 1932. After a period of consolidation in the 1940s and 50s, Pacific expanded again. It developed extensive oil holdings in North Africa and the Middle East, as well as significant coal beds in the western United States. Much of Pacific's oil production is sold under its own name as gasoline through service stations in the United States and Europe, but also it is distributed through several chains of "independent" gasoline stations. In addition, Pacific is also one of the largest and best known worldwide producers of industial petrochemicals.

One of Pacific's major industrial chemical lines is the production of vinyl chloride monomer (VCM). The basic components of VCM are ethylene and chlorine. Ethylene is a colorless, flammable, gaseous hydrocarbon with a disagreeable odor; it is generally obtained from natural or coal gas, or by "cracking" petroleum into smaller molecular components. As a further step in the petroleum "cracking" process, ethylene is combined with chlorine to produce vinyl chloride monomer, also a colorless gas.

VCM is the primary component of a family of plastics known as the vinyl chlorides. VCM is subjected to the process of polymerization, in which smaller molecules of vinyl chloride are chemically bonded together to form larger molecular chains and networks. As the bonding occurs, polyvinyl chloride (PVC) is produced; coloring pigments may be added, as well as "plasticizer" compounds that determine the relative flexibility or hardness of the finished material. Through various forms of calendering (pressing between heavy rollers), extruding and injection molding, the plasticized polyvinyl chloride is converted to an enormous array of consumer and industrial applications: flooring, wire insulation, electrical transformers, home furnishings, piping, toys, bottles and containers, rainwear, light roofing and a variety of protective coatings. (See Exhibit 1 for a breakdown of common PVC-based products.)

In 1969, Pacific Oil established the first major contract with The Reliant Corporation for the purchase of vinyl chloride monomer. The Reliant Corporation was a major industrial manufacturer of wood and petrochemical products for the construction industry. Reliant was expanding its manufacturing operations in the production of plastic pipe and pipe fittings, particularly in Europe. The use of plastic as a substitute for iron or copper pipe was gaining rapid acceptance in the construction trades, and the European

EXHIBIT 1
Polyvinyl Chloride Major Markets, 1972 (units represented in MM pounds)

Market	MM Pounds	Percent of Market Share
Apparel		
Baby pants	22	0.6
Footwear	128	3.2
Misc.	60	1.5
	210	5.3
Building and Construction		
Extruded foam moldings	46	1.2
Flooring	428	10.8
Lighting	10	0.3
Panels and siding	64	1.6
Pipe and conduit	720	18.5
Pipe fittings	78	2.0
Rainwater systems	28	0.7
Swimming pool liners	40	1.0
Weather stripping	36	0.9
Misc.	50	1.2
	1,500	38.2
Electrical		
Wire and cable	390	9.9
Home Furnishings		
Appliances	32	0.8
Misc.	286	9.8
Wall coverings	418	10.6
Housewares	94	2.4
Packaging		
Blow molded bottles	64	1.6
Closure liners and gaskets	16	0.4
Coatings	16	0.4
Film	124	3.2
Misc.	80	2.0
	300	7.6
Recreation		
Records	136	3.4
Sporting goods	46	1.2
Misc.	68	1.7
	250	6.3
Transportation		
Auto mats	36	0.9
Auto tops	32	0.8
Misc.	164	4.2
	232	5.9

EXHIBIT 1 *(concluded)*

Market	MM Pounds	Percent of Market Share
Miscellaneous		
Agriculture (including pipe)	106	2.6
Credit cards	24	0.4
Garden hose	40	1.0
Laminates	44	1.1
Medical tubing	42	1.1
Novelties	12	0.3
Stationery supplies	32	0.8
Misc.	12	0.3
	312	7.6
Export	146	3.7
Misc.	98	2.5
Total	3,960	100.0

Source: Modern Plastics.

markets were significantly more progressive in adopting the plastic pipe. Reliant already had developed a small polyvinyl chloride production facility at Abbeville, France, and Pacific constructed a pipeline from its petrochemical plant at Antwerp to Abbeville.

The 1969 contract between Pacific Oil and Reliant was a fairly standard one for the industry, and due to expire in December of 1972. The contract was negotiated by Reliant's purchasing managers in Europe, headquartered in Brussels, and the senior marketing managers of Pacific Oil's European offices, located in Paris. Each of these individuals reported to the vice presidents in charge of their company's European offices, who in turn reported back to their respective corporate headquarters in the States. (See Exhibits 2 and 3 for partial organization charts.)

THE 1972 CONTRACT RENEWAL

In February 1972, negotiations began to extend the four-year contract beyond the December 31, 1972 expiration date. Jean Fontaine, Pacific Oil's marketing vice president for Europe, discussed the Reliant account with his VCM marketing manager, Paul Gaudin. Fontaine had been promoted to the European vice presidency aproximately 16 months earlier after having served as Pacific's ethylene marketing manager. Fontaine had been with the Pacific Oil for 11 years, and had a reputation as a strong "up and comer" in Pacific's European operations. Gaudin had been appointed as VCM marketing manager eight months earlier; this was his first job with Pacific Oil, although he had five years of previous experience in European computer sales with a

EXHIBIT 2
Partial Organization Chart—Pacific Oil Company

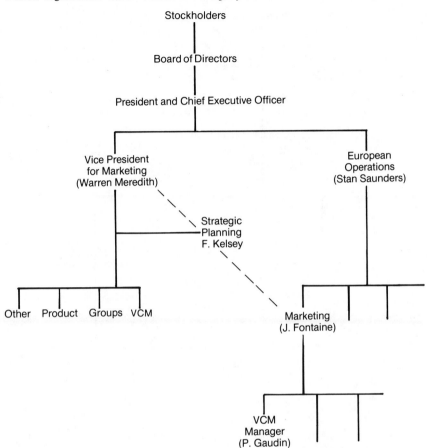

large American computer manufacturing company. Fontaine and Gaudin had worked well in their short time together, establishing a strong professional and personal relationship. Fontaine and Gaudin agreed that the Reliant account had been an extremely profitable and beneficial one for Pacific, and believed that Reliant had, overall, been satisfied with the quality and service under the agreement as well. They clearly wanted to work hard to obtain a favorable renegotiation of the existing agreement. Fontaine and Gaudin also reviewed the latest projections of worldwide VCM supply which they had just received from corporate headquarters. (See Exhibit 4.) The data confirmed what they already knew—that there was a worldwide shortage of VCM and that demand was continuing to rise. Pacific envisioned that the current demand-supply situation would remain this way for a number of

EXHIBIT 3
Partial Organization Chart—Reliant Chemical Company

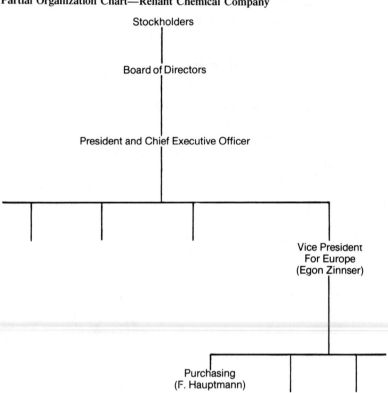

years. As a result, Pacific believed that it could justify a high favorable formula price for VCM.

Fontaine and Gaudin decided that they would approach Reliant with an offer to renegotiate the current agreement. Their basic strategy would be to ask Reliant for their five-year demand projections on VCM and polyvinyl chloride products. Once these projections were received, Fontaine and Gaudin would frame the basic formula price that they would offer. (It would be expected that there would be no significant changes or variations in other elements of the contract, such as delivery and contract language.) In their negotiations, their strategy would be as follows:

a. To dwell on the successful long-term relationship that had already been built between Reliant and Pacific Oil, and to emphasize the value of that relationship for the success of both companies.
b. To emphasize all of the projections that predicted the worldwide shortage of VCM, and the desirability for Reliant to ensure that they would have a guaranteed supplier.

EXHIBIT 4

Memorandum

TO: All VCM Marketing Managers
FROM: F. Kelsey, Strategic Planning Division
RE: Worldwide VCM Supply/Demand Projections
DATE: January 17, 1972

CONFIDENTIAL—FOR YOUR EYES ONLY

Here are the data from 1970 and 1971, and the five-year projections that I promised you at our last meeting. As you can see, the market is tight, and is projected to get tighter. I hope you will find this useful in your marketing efforts—let me know if I can supply more detailed information.

Year	Demand Total Projected Demand (in MM Pounds)	Supply Plant Capacities	Operating Rates to Meet Demand (percent)
1970	4,040	5,390	75%
1971	4,336	5,390	80
1972	5,100	6,600	77
1973	5,350	6,600	81
1974	5,550	6,600	83
1975	5,650	7,300	75
1976	5,750	7,300	78

c. To point out all of the ways that Pacific had "gone out of its way" in the past to ensure delivery and service.
d. To use both the past and future quality of the relationship to justify what might appear to be a high formula price.
e. To point out the ways that Pacific's competitors could not offer the same kind of service.

Over the next six months, Gaudin and Fontaine, independently and together, made a number of trips to Brussels to visit Reliant executives. In addition, several members of Pacific's senior management visited Brussels and paid courtesy calls on Reliant management. The net result was a very favorable contract for Pacific Oil, signed by both parties on October 24, 1972. The basic contract, to extend from January 1973 to December 1977, is represented as Exhibit 5 on pages 526 through 530.

A CHANGED PERSPECTIVE

In December of 1974, Fontaine and Gaudin sat down to their traditional end-of-year review of all existing chemical contracts. As a matter of course, the Reliant VCM contract came under review. Although everything had been

EXHIBIT 5
Agreement of Sale

This Agreement, entered into this ___24th___ day of ___October___ , ___1972___ , between ___Pacific Oil Company___ , hereinafter called Seller, and ___Reliant Chemical Company of Europe___ , hereinafter called Buyer.

WITNESSETH:

Seller agrees to sell and deliver and Buyer agrees to purchase and receive commodity (hereinafter called "product") under the terms and conditions set forth below.

1. Product: Vinyl Chloride Monomer

2. Quality: ASTM requirements for polymer-grade product

3. Quantity: 1973:   150 million pounds
   1974:   160 million pounds
   1975:   170 million pounds
   1976:   185 million pounds
   1977:   200 million pounds

4. Period: Contract shall extend from January 1, 1973 and extent until December 31, 1977, and evergreen thereafter, unless terminated within 180 days prior notification at the end of each calendar year, but not before December 31, 1977.

5. Price: See Contract formula price.

6. Payment Terms:
   a. Net   ___30 days___ .
   b. All payments shall be made in United States dollars without discount or deduction, unless otherwise noted, by wire transfer at Seller's option, to a bank account designated by Seller. Invoices not paid on due date will be subject to a delinquency finance charge of 1 percent per month.
   c. If at any time the financial responsibility of Buyer shall become impaired or unsatisfactory to Seller, cash payment on delivery or satisfactory security may be required. A failure to pay any amount may, at the option of the Seller, terminate this contract as to further deliveries. No forebearance, course of dealing, or prior payment shall affect this right of Seller.

7. Price Change:

   The price specified in this Agreement may be changed by Seller on the first day of any calendar half-year by written notice sent to the Buyer not less than thirty (30) days prior to the effective date of change. Buyer gives Seller written notice of objection to such change at least ten (10) days prior to the effective date of change. Buyer's failure to serve Seller with written notice of objection thereto prior to the effective date thereof shall be considered acceptance of such change. If Buyer gives such notice of objection and Buyer and Seller fail to agree on such change prior to the effective date thereof, this Agreement and the obligations of Seller and Buyer hereunder shall terminate with respect to the unshipped portion of the Product governed by it. Seller has the option immediately to cancel this contract upon written

EXHIBIT 5 *(continued)*

notice to Buyer, to continue to sell hereunder at the same price and terms which were in effect at the time Seller gave notice of change, or to suspend performance under this contract while pricing is being resolved. If Seller desires to revise the price, freight allowance or terms of payment pursuant to this agreement, but is restricted to any extent against doing so by reason of any law, governmental decree, order or regulation, or if the price, freight allowance or terms of payment then in effect under this contract are nullified or reduced by reason of any law, governmental decree, order or regulation, Seller shall have the right to cancel this contract upon fifteen (15) days written notice to purchaser.

8. Competitive Offers:

If Buyer receives a bona fide offer to purchase product of the same specification as contained in this agreement and of no greater quantity, at a price, including terms and conditions, lower than applicable under this Agreement, and if Buyer furnishes written evidence specifying the details of such an offer to the seller, Seller will, within 15 days, either meet such prices on the same quantity offered or allow Buyer to purchase the product so offered. Buyer shall give Seller prompt notice of any quantity of Product purchased or to be purchased in accordance with the provisions of this paragraph. Such quantity shall be deducted from the quantity specified in this Agreement for the year in which it is so purchased. In addition, Seller at its option may also deduct such quantity for each year thereafter remaining under this Agreement. Election of such option by seller shall be given to Buyer by written notice within 90 days after Seller receives Buyer's notice of purchase.

9. Measurements:

Seller's determinations, unless proven to be erroneous, shall be accepted as conclusive evidence of the quantity of Product delivered hereunder. Credit will not be allowed for shortages of ½ of 1 percent or less of the quantity and overages of ½ of 1 percent or less of the quantity will be waived. The total amount of shortages or overages will be credited or billed when quantities are greater and such differences are substantiated. Measurements of weight and volume shall be according to procedures and criteria standard for such determinations.

10. Shipments and Delivery:

Buyer shall give Seller annual or quarterly forecasts of its expected requirements as Seller may from time to time request. Buyer shall give Seller reasonably advanced notice for each shipment which shall include date of delivery and shipping instructions. Buyer shall agree to take deliveries in approximately equal monthly quantities, except as may be otherwise provided herein. In the event that Buyer fails to take the quantity specified or the pro rata quantity in any month, Seller may, at its option, in addition to other rights and remedies, cancel such shipments or parts thereof.

11. Purchase Requirements:

a. If during any consecutive three-month period, Buyer for any reason (but not for reasons of force majeure as set forth in Section 13) takes less than 90 percent of the average monthly quantity specified, or the prorated minimum monthly quantity

EXHIBIT 5 *(continued)*

---

then applicable to such period under Section 13, Seller may elect to charge Buyer a penalty charge for failure to take the average monthly quantity or prorated minimum monthly quantity.

b. If, during any consecutive three-month period, Buyer, for any reason (but not, however, for reasons of force majeure as set forth in Section 13) takes Product in quantities less than that equal to at least one half of the average monthly quantity specified or the prorated minimum monthly quantity originally applicable to such period under Section 13, Seller may elect to terminate this agreement.

c. It is the Seller's intent not to unreasonably exercise its right under (*a*) or (*b*) in the event of adverse economic and business conditions in general.

d. Notice of election by Seller under (*a*) or (*b*) shall be given within 30 days after the end of the applicable three-month period, and the effective date of termination shall be 30 days after the date of said notice.

12. Detention Policy:

Seller may, from time to time, specify free unloading time allowances for its transportation equipment. Buyer shall be liable to the Transportation Company for all demurrage charges made by the Transportation Company, for railcars, trucks, tanks, or barges held by Buyer beyond the free unloading time.

13. Force Majeure:

Neither party shall be liable to the other for failure or delay in performance hereunder to the extent that such failure or delay is due to war, fire, flood, strike, lockout, or other labor trouble, accident, breakdown of equipment or machinery, riot, act, request, or suggestion of governmental authority, act of God, or other contingencies beyond the control of the affected party which interfere with the production or transportation of the material covered by this Agreement or with the supply of any raw material (whether or not the source of supply was in existence or contemplated at the time of this Agreement) or energy source used in connection therewith, or interfere with Buyer's consumption of such material, provided that in no event shall Buyer be relieved of the obligation to pay in full for material delivered hereunder. Without limitation on the foregoing, neither party shall be required to remove any cause listed above or replace the affected source of supply or facility if it shall involve additional expense or departure from its normal practices. If any of the events specified in this paragraph shall have occurred, Seller shall have the right to allocate in a fair and reasonable manner among its customers and Seller's own requirements any supplies of material Seller has available for delivery at the time or for the duration of the event.

14. Materials and Energy Supply:

If, for reasons beyond reasonable commercial control, Seller's supply of product to be delivered hereunder shall be limited due to continued availability of necessary raw materials and energy supplies, Seller shall have the right (without liability) to allocate to the Buyer a portion of such product on such basis as Seller deems equitable. Such allocation shall normally be that percent of Seller's total internal and

EXHIBIT 5 *(continued)*

external commitments which are committed to Buyer as related to the total quantity available from Seller's manufacturing facilities.

15. Disclaimer:

Seller makes no warranty, express or implied, concerning the product furnished hereunder other than it shall be of the quality and specifications stated herein. Any implied warranty of FITNESS is expressly excluded and to the extent that it is contrary to the foregoing sentence; any implied warranty of MERCHANTABILITY is expressly excluded. Any recommendations made by Seller makes no warranty of results to be obtained. Buyer assumes all responsibility and liability for loss or damage resulting from the handling or use of said product. In no event shall Seller be liable for any special, indirect or consequential damages, irrespective of whether caused or allegedly caused by negligence.

16. Taxes:

Any tax, excise fee, or other charge or increase thereof upon the production, storage, withdrawal, sale, or transportation of the product sold hereunder, or entering into the cost of such product, imposed by any proper authority becoming effective after the date hereof, shall be added to the price herein provised and shall be paid by the Buyer.

17. Assignment and Resale:

This contract is not transferable or assignable by Buyer without the written consent of Seller. The product described hereunder, in the form and manner provided by the Seller, may not be assigned or resold without prior written consent of the Seller.

18. Acceptance:

Acceptance hereof must be without qualification and Seller will not be bound by any different terms and conditions contained in any other communication.

19. Waiver of Breach:

No waiver by Seller or Buyer of any breach of any of the terms and conditions contained in this Agreement shall be construed as a waiver or any subsequent breach of the same or any other term or condition.

20. Termination:

If any provision of this agreement is or becomes violate of any law, or any rule, order or regulation issued thereunder, Seller shall have the right upon notice to Buyer, to terminate the Agreement in its entirety.

21. Governing Law:

The construction of this Agreement and the rights and obligations of the parties hereunder shall be governed by the laws of the State of New York.

EXHIBIT 5 *(concluded)*

22. Special Provisions:

BUYER: SELLER:

_____   PACIFIC OIL CORPORATION
            (firm)

By: _____   By: _____

Title: Senior Purchasing Manager   Title: Marketing Vice President

Date: _____   Date: _____

---

proceeding very smoothly, the prospects for the near and long-term future were obviously less clear, for the following reasons:

1. Both men reviewed the data that they had been receiving from corporate headquarters, as well as published projections of the supply situation for various chemicals over the next 10 years. It was clear that the basic supply-demand situation on VCM was changing. (Exhibit 6.) While the market was currently "tight"—the favorable supply situation that had existed for Pacific when the Reliant contract was first negotiated—the supply of VCM was expected to expand rapidly over the next few years. Several of Pacific's competitors had announced plans for the construction of VCM manufacturing facilities that were expected to come on line in 20–30 months.

2. Fontaine and Gaudin knew that Reliant was probably aware of this situation as well. As a result, they would probably anticipate the change in the supply-demand situation as an opportunity to pursue a more favorable price, with the possible threat that they would be willing to change suppliers if the terms were not favorable enough. (Although rebuilding a pipeline is no simple matter, it clearly could be done, and had been, when the terms were sufficiently favorable to justify it.)

3. Fontaine was aware that in a situation where the market turned from one of high demand to excess supply, it was necessary to make extra efforts to maintain and "re-sign" all major current customers. A few large customers (100 million pounds a year and over) dominated the marketplace, and a single customer defection in an oversupplied market could cause major headaches for marketing and sales. It would simply be impossible to find

EXHIBIT 6

MEMORANDUM

TO: All VCM Marketing Managers
FROM: F. Kelsey, Strategic Planning Division
RE: Worldwide VCM/Supply/Demand Projections
DATE: December 9, 1974

CONFIDENTIAL—FOR YOUR EYES ONLY

This will confirm and summarize data that we discussed at the national marketing meeting last month in Atlanta. At that time, I indicated to you that the market projections we made several years ago have changed drastically. In early 1973, a number of our competitors announced their intentions to enter the VCM business over the next five years. Several facilities are now under construction, and are expected to come on line in late 1976 and early 1977. As a result, we expect a fairly significant shift in the supply/demand relationship over the next few years.

I hope you will give this appropriate consideration in your long range planning effort. Please contact me if I can be helpful.

Year	Demand Total Projected Demand (in MM pounds)	Supply Plant Capacities	Operating Rates to Meet Demand (percent)
1972	5,127 (actual)	6,600	78%
1973	5,321 (actual)	6,600	81
1974	5,572 (rev. 11/74)	6,600	84
1975	5,700	7,300	78
1976	5,900	8,450	70
1977	6,200	9,250	64
1978	6,500	9,650	67
1979	7,000	11,000	63

---

another customer with demands of that magnitude; a number of smaller customers would have to be found, while Pacific would also have to compete with spot market prices that would cut profits to the bone.

4.   In a national product development meeting back in the States several weeks prior, Fontaine had learned of plans by Pacific to expand and diversify its own product line into VCM derivatives. There was serious talk of Pacific manufacturing its own PVC for distribution under the Pacific name, as well as the manufacture and distribution of various PVC products. Should Pacific decide to enter these businesses, not only would they require a significant amount of the VCM now being sold on the external market, but Pacific would probably decide that as a matter of principle, it would not want to be in the position of supplying a product competitor with the raw materials to

manufacture his product line, unless the formula price were extremely favorable.

As they reviewed these factors, Gaudin and Fontaine realized that they needed to take action. They pondered the alternatives.

A NEW CONTRACT IS PROPOSED

As a result of their evaluation of the situation in December of 1974, Fontaine and Gaudin decided to proceed on two fronts. First, they would approach Reliant with the intent of reopening negotiation on the current VCM contract. They would propose to renegotiate the current agreement, with an interest toward extending the contract five years from the point of agreement on contract terms. Second, they would contact these people at corporate headquarters in New York who were evaluating Pacific's alternatives for new product development, and inform them of the nature of the situation. The sooner a determination could be made on the product development strategies, the sooner that the Pacific office would know how to proceed on the Reliant contract.

Gaudin contacted Frederich Hauptmann, the senior purchasing manager for Reliant Chemicals in Europe. Hauptmann had assumed the position as purchasing manager approximately four weeks earlier, after having served in a purchasing capacity for a large German steel company. Gaudin arranged a meeting for early January in Hauptmann's office. After getting acquainted over lunch, Gaudin briefed Hauptmann on the history of Reliant's contractual relationships with Pacific Oil. Gaudin made clear that Pacific had been very pleased with the relationship that had been maintained. He said that Pacific was concerned about the future, and about maintaining the relationship with Reliant for a long time to come. Hauptmann stated that he understood that the relationship had been a very productive one, too, and also hoped that the two companies could continue to work together in the future. Bouyed by Hauptmann's apparent enthusiasm and relative pleasure with the current agreement, Gaudin said that he and Jean Fontaine, his boss, had recently been reviewing all contracts. Even though the existing Pacific-Reliant VCM agreement had three years to run, Pacific felt that it was never too soon to begin thinking about the long-term future. In order to ensure that Reliant would be assured of a continued supply of VCM, under the favorable terms and working relationship that was already well established, Pacific hoped that Reliant might be willing to begin talks now for contract extension past December 31, 1977. Hauptmann said that he would be willing to consider it, but needed to consult other people in the Brussels office, as well as senior executives at Corporate headquarters in Chicago. Hauptmann promised to contact Gaudin when he had the answer.

By mid-February, Hauptmann cabled Gaudin that Reliant was indeed willing to begin renegotiation of the current agreement, with interest in extending it for the future. He suggested that Gaudin and Fontaine come to Brussels for a preliminary meeting in early March. Hauptmann also planned to invite Egon Zinnser, the regional vice president of Reliant's European operations and Hauptmann's immediate superior.

MARCH 10

Light snow drifted onto the runway of the Brussels airport as the plane landed. Fontaine and Gaudin had talked about the Reliant contract, and the upcoming negotiations, for most of the trip. They had decided that while they did not expect the negotiations to be a complete "pushover," they expected no significant problems or stumbling points in the deliberations. They thought Reliant negotiators would routinely question some of the coefficients that were used to compute the formula price as well as to renegotiate some of the minimum quantity commitments. They felt that the other elements of the contract would be routinely discussed, but that no dramatic changes should be expected.

After a pleasant lunch with Hauptmann and Zinnser, the four men sat down to review the current VCM contract. They reviewed and restated much of what Gaudin and Hauptmann had done at their January meeting. Fontaine stated that Pacific Oil was looking toward the future, and hoping that it could maintain Reliant as a customer. Zinnser responded that Reliant had indeed been pleased by the contract as well, but that it was also concerned about the future. They felt that Pacific's basic formula price on VCM, while fair, might not remain competitive in the long-run future. Zinnser said that he had already had discussions with two other major chemical firms who were planning new VCM manufacturing facilities, and that one or both of these firms were due to come on line in the next 24–30 months. Zinnser wanted to make sure that Pacific could remain competitive with other firms in the marketplace. Fontaine responded that it was Pacific's full intention to remain completely competitive, whether it be in market price or in the formula price.

Zinnser said he was pleased by this reply, and took this as an indication that Pacific would be willing to evaluate and perhaps adjust some of the factors that were now being used to determine the VCM formula price. He then presented a rather elaborate proposal for adjusting the respective coefficients of these factors. The net result of these adjustments would be to reduce the effective price of VCM by approximately 2 cents per pound. It did not take long for Fontaine and Gaudin to calculate that this would be a net reduction of approximately $4 million per year. Fontaine stated that they would have to take the proposal back to Paris for intensive study and analysis. The men shook hands, and Fontaine and Gaudin headed back to the airport.

Throughout the spring, Gaudin and Hauptmann exchanged several letters and telephone calls. They met once at the Paris airport when Hauptmann stopped over on a trip to the States, and once in Zurich when both men discovered that they were going to be there on business the same day. By May 15, they had agreed on a revision of the formula price that would adjust the price downward by approximately 85 cents per pound. Gaudin, relieved that the price had finally been established, reported back to Fontaine that significant progress was being made. Gaudin expected that the remaining issues could be closed up in a few weeks, and a new contract signed.

MAY 27

Hauptmann contacted Gaudin to tell him that Reliant was now willing to talk about the remaining issues in the contract. The two men met in early June. Gaudin opened the discussion by saying that now that the formula price had been agreed upon, he hoped that Reliant would be willing to agree to extend the contract five years from the point of signing. Hauptmann replied that Reliant had serious reservations about committing the company to a five-year contract extension. He cited the rapid fluctuations in the demand, pricing structure, and competition of Reliant's various product lines, particularly in the construction industry, as well as what appeared to be a changing perspective in the overall supply of VCM. Quite frankly, Hauptmann said, Reliant didn't want to be caught in a long-term commitment to Pacific if the market price of VCM was likely to drop in the foreseeable future. As a result, Reliant only wanted to make a commitment for a two-year contract renewal.

Gaudin tried to give Hauptmann a number of assurances about the continued integrity of the market. He also said that if changing market prices were a concern for Reliant, Pacific Oil would be happy to attempt to make adjustments in other parts of the contract to ensure protection against dramatic changes in either the market price or the demand for Reliant's product lines. But Hauptmann was adamant. Gaudin said he would have to talk to Fontaine and others in Paris before he could agree to only a two-year contract.

The two men talked several times on the telephone over the next two months, and met once in Paris to discuss contract length. On August 17, in a quick 45-minute meeting in Orly Airport, Gaudin and Hauptmann agreed to a three-year contract renewal. They also agreed to meet in early September to discuss remaining contract issues.

SEPTEMBER 10

Hauptmann met Gaudin and Fontaine in Pacific's Paris office. Hauptmann stressed that he and Zinnser were very pleased by the formula price and three-year contract duration that had been agreed to thus far. Fontaine echoed a similar satisfaction on behalf of Pacific, and stated that they expected a long and productive relationship with Reliant. Fontaine stressed, however, that Pacific felt it was most important to them to complete the contract negotiations as quickly as possible, in order to adequately plan for product and market development in the future. Hauptmann agreed, saying that this was in Reliant's best interest as well. He felt that there were only a few minor issues that remained to be discussed before the contract could be signed.

Fontaine inquired as to what those issues were. Hauptmann said that the most important one to Reliant was the minimum quantity requirements, stipulating the minimum amount that Reliant had to purchase each year. Gaudin said that based on the projections for the growth of the PVC and fabricated PVC products over the next few years, and patterns established by past contracts, it was Pacific's assumption that Reliant would want to increase their quantity commitments by a minimum of 10 percent each year. Based on current minimums stipulated in the current contract, Gaudin expected that Reliant would want to purchase at least 220 million pounds in year 1, 240 million pounds in year 2, and 265 million pounds in year 3.

Hauptmann responded that Reliant's projections were very different. The same kind of uncertainty that had led to Reliant's concern about the term of the contract also contributed to a caution about significantly overextending themselves on a minimum quantity commitment. In fact, Reliant's own predictions were that they were likely to take less than the minimum in the current year ("underlifting," in the parlance of the industry), and that if they did so, they would incur almost a $1 million debt to Pacific. Conservative projections for the following year (1977) projected a similar deficit, but Reliant hoped that business would pick up and that the minimum quantities would be lifted. As a result, Hauptmann and Zinnser felt that it would be in Reliant's best interest to freeze minimum quantity requirements for the next two years—at 200 million pounds—and increase the minimum to 210 million pounds for the third year. Of course, Reliant *expected* that, and most likely, they would be continuing to purchase much more than the specified minimums. But given the uncertainty of the future, Reliant did not want to get caught if the economy and the market truly turned sour.

Fontaine and Gaudin were astonished at the conservative projections Hauptmann was making. They tried, in numerous ways, to convince Hauptmann that his minimums were ridiculously low, and that the PVC products were bound to prosper far more than Hauptmann seemed willing to admit. But Hauptmann was adamant, and left Paris saying he needed to consult Zinnser and others in Brussels and the States before he could revise his minimum quantity estimates upward. Due to the pressure of other activities, vacation schedules, and so on, Gaudin and Hauptmann did not talk again until late October. Finally, on November 19, the two men agreed to a minimum quantity purchase schedule of 205 million pounds in the first year of the contract, 210 million pounds in the second year, and 220 million pounds in the third year. Moreover, Pacific agreed to waive any previous underlifting charges that may be incurred under the current contract when the new contract was signed.

OCTOBER 24

Jean Fontaine returned to Paris from meetings in New York and a major market development meeting held by senior Pacific executives at Hilton

Head. After a number of delays due to conflicting market research, changes in senior management, as well as the general uncertainty in the petroleum and chemical markets, Pacific had decided not to develop its own product lines for either PVC or fabricated products. The decision was largely based on the conclusion—more "gut feel" than hard fact—that entry into these new markets was unwise at a time when much greater problems faced Pacific and the petrochemicals industry in general. Fontaine had argued strenuously that the VCM market was rapidly going soft, and that failure to create its own product lines would leave Pacific Oil in an extremely poor position to market one of its basic products. Fontaine was told that his position was appreciated, but that he and other chemical marketing people would simply have to develop new markets and customers for the product. Privately, Fontaine churned on the fact that it had taken senior executives almost a year to make the decision, while valuable time was being lost in developing the markets; but he wisely decided to bite his tongue and vent his frustration on 36 holes of golf. On the return flight to Paris, he read about Pacific's decision in the October 23rd issue of *The Wall Street Journal,* and ordered a double martini to soothe his nerves.

DECEMBER 14

Fontaine and Gaudin went to Brussels to meet with Hauptmann and Zinnser. The Pacific executives stressed that it was of the utmost importance for Pacific Oil to try to wrap up the contract as quickly as possible—almost a year had passed in deliberations, and although Pacific was not trying to place the "blame" on anyone, it was most concerned that the negotiations be settled as soon as possible.

Zinnser emphasized that he, too, was concerned about completing the negotiations quickly. Both he and Hauptmann were extremely pleased by the agreements that had been reached so far, and felt that there was no question that a final contract signing was imminent. The major issues of price, minimum quantities and contract duration had been solved. In their minds, what remained were only a few minor technical items in contract language. Some minor discussion of each of these should wrap things up in a few weeks.

Fontaine asked what the issues were. Zinnser began by stating that Reliant had become concerned by the way that the delivery pipeline was being metered. As currently set up, the pipeline fed from Pacific's production facility in Antwerp, Belgium, to Reliant's refinery. Pacific had built the line, and was in charge of maintaining it. Meters had been installed at the exit flange of the pipeline, and Reliant was paying the metered amount to Pacific. Zinnser said that some spot-checking by Reliant at the manufacturing facility seemed to indicate that they may not be receiving all they were being billed for. They were not questioning the integrity of the meters or the meter readers, but felt that since the pipe was a number of years old, it may have developed leaks. Zinnser felt that it was inappropriate for Reliant to absorb the cost of VCM that was not reaching its facility. They, therefore, proposed that Pacific install meters directly outside of the entry flange of Reliant's manufacturing facility, and that Reliant only be required to pay the meter directly outside the plant.

Fontaine was astonished. In the first place, he said, this was the first time he had heard any complaint about the pipeline or the need to recalibrate the meters. Second, if the pipeline was leaking, Pacific would want to repair it, but that it would be impossible to do so until spring. Finally, while the meters themselves were not prohibitively expensive, moving them would mean some interruption of service and definitely be costly to Pacific. Fontaine said he wanted to check with the maintenance personnel at Antwerp to find out whether they could corroborate such leaks.

Fontaine was unable to contact the operating manager at Antwerp, or anyone else who could confirm that leaks may have been detected. Routine inspection of the pipeline had been subcontracted to a firm which had sophisticated equipment for monitoring such things, and executives of the firm could not be reached for several days. Fontaine tried to raise other contract issues with Zinnser, but Zinnser said that this was his most important concern, and this issue needed to be resolved before the others could be finalized. Fontaine agreed to find out more about the situation, and bring the information to the next meeting. With the Christmas and New Year holidays approaching, the four men could not schedule another meeting until January 9.

JANUARY MEETINGS

The January 9 meeting was postponed until January 20, due to the death of Mr. Hauptmann's mother. The meeting was rescheduled for a time when Hauptmann needed to be in Geneva, and Gaudin agreed to meet him there.

Gaudin stated that the investigation of the pipeline had discovered no evidence of significant discharge. There were traces of *minor* leaks in the line, but they did not appear to be serious, and it was currently impossible to determine what percentage of the product may be escaping. The most generous estimate given to Gaudin had been 0.1 percent of the daily consumption. Hauptmann stated that their own spot monitoring showed it was considerably more, and that Reliant would feel infinitely more comfortable if the new metering system could be installed.

Gaudin had obtained estimates for the cost of remetering before he left Paris. It was estimated that the new meters could be installed for approximately $20,000. Tracing and fixing the leaks (if they existed) could not be done until April or May, and may run as much as $50,000 if leaks turned out to be located at some extremely difficult access points. After four hours of debating with Hauptmann in a small conference room off the lobby of the Geneva Hilton, Gaudin agreed that Pacific would remeter the pipeline.

Hauptmann said that as far as he was concerned, all of his issues had been settled, however, he thought Zinnser might have one or two other issues to raise. Hauptmann said that he would report back to Zinnser, and contact Gaudin as soon as possible if another meeting was necessary. Gaudin, believing that Pacific was finally beginning to see the light at the end of the tunnel, left for Paris.

JANUARY 23

Hauptmann called Gaudin and said that he and Zinnser had thoroughly reviewed the contract, and that there were a few small issues of contract language which Zinnser wanted to clarify. He said that he would prefer not to discuss them over the telephone, and suggested that since he was going to be in Paris on February 3, they meet at the Pacific offices. Gaudin agreed.

Fontaine and Gaudin met Hauptmann on February 3. Hauptmann informed them that he felt Reliant had been an outstanding customer for Pacific in the past, and that it probably was one of Pacific's biggest customers for VCM. Fontaine and Gaudin agreed, affirming the important role that Reliant was playing in Pacific's VCM market. Hauptmann said that he and Zinnser had been reviewing the contract, and were concerned that the changing nature of the VCM market might significantly affect Reliant's overall position in the marketplace as a purchaser. More specifically, Reliant was concerned that the decline in market and price for VCM in the future might endanger its own position in the market, since Pacific might sign contracts with other purchasers for lower formula prices than were currently being awarded to Reliant. Since Reliant was such an outstanding customer of Pacific—and Fontaine and Gaudin had agreed to that—it seemed to Reliant that Pacific Oil had an "obligation" to write two additional clauses into the contract that would protect Reliant in the event of further slippage in the VCM market. The first was a "favored nation's" clause, stipulating that if Pacific negotiated with another purchaser a more favorable price for VCM than Reliant was receiving now, Pacific would guarantee that Reliant would receive that price as well. The second was a "meet competition" clause, guaranteeing that Pacific would willingly meet any lower price on VCM offered by a competitor, in order to maintain the Reliant relationship. Hauptmann argued that the "favored nation's" clause was protection for Reliant, since it stipulated that Pacific valued the relationship enough to offer the best possible terms to Reliant. The "meet competition" clause, he argued, was clearly advantageous for Pacific since it ensured that Reliant would have no incentive to shift suppliers as the market changed.

Fontaine and Gaudin debated the terms at length with Hauptmann, stressing the potential costliness of these agreements for Pacific. Hauptmann responded by referring to the costliness that the absence of the terms could have for Reliant, and suggesting that perhaps the Pacific people were truly *not* as interested in a successful long-term relationship as they had been advocating. Fontaine said that he needed to get clearance from senior management in New York before he could agree to these terms, and said that he would get back to Hauptmann within a few days when the information was available.

FRANK KELSEY'S VIEW

Frank Kelsey was strategic planning manager, a staff role in the New York offices of the Pacific Oil Corporation. Kelsey had performed a number of roles for the company in his 12 years of work experience. Using the chemistry background he had achieved in college, Kelsey worked for six years in the research and development department of Pacific's Chemical Division, before deciding to enter the management ranks. He transferred to the marketing area, spent three years in chemical marketing, and then assumed responsibilities in marketing planning and development. He moved to the strategic planning department four years ago.

In late 1975, Kelsey was working in a staff capacity as an adviser to the executive product vice president of the Pacific Oil Company. Pacific had developed a matrix organization. Reporting relationships were determined by business areas and by regional operating divisions within Pacific Oil. Warren Meredith, the executive vice president, had responsibility for monitoring the worldwide sale and distribution of VCM. Jean Fontaine reported to Meredith on all issues regarding the overall sale and marketing of VCM, and reported to the president of Pacific Oil in Europe, Stan Saunders, on major issues regarding the management of the regional chemicals business in Europe. In general, Fontaine's primary working relationship was with Meredith; Saunders only became involved in day-to-day decisions as an arbiter of disputes or interpreter of major policy decisions.

As the negotiations with Reliant evolved, Meredith became distressed by the apparent turn that they were taking. He called in Frank Kelsey to review the situation. Kelsey knew that the VCM marketing effort for Pacific was going to face significant problems following the company's decision to stay out of the PVC/fabrication business. Moreover, his dominant experience with Pacific in recent years had been in the purchasing and marketing operations, and knew how difficult it would be for the company to maintain a strong negotiation position in VCM contracts.

Meredith asked Kelsey to meet with Fontaine and Gaudin in Paris, and review the current status of negotiations on the Reliant contract. While Kelsey could only act in an advisory capacity—Fontaine and Gaudin were free to accept or reject any advice that was offered, since they were the ones that had to "live with" the contract—Meredith told Kelsey to offer whatever services the men would accept.

Kelsey flew to Paris shortly after New Year's Day 1976. He met with Fontaine and Gaudin, and they reviewed in detail what had happened in the Reliant contract negotiations over the past year. Kelsey listened, asked a lot of questions, and didn't say much. He felt that offering "advice" to the men was premature, and perhaps even unwise; Fontaine and Gaudin seemed very anxious about the negotiations, and felt that the new contract would be sealed within a month. Moreover, they seemed to resent Kelsey's visit, and clearly didn't want to share more than the minimum amount of information. Kelsey returned to New York, and briefed Meredith on the state of affairs.

When Fontaine called Meredith for "clearance" to give Reliant both "favored nation's" and "meet competition" clauses in the new contract, Meredith immediately called Kelsey. The two of them went back through the history of events in the negotiation, and realized the major advantages that Reliant had gained by its negotiation tactics.

Meredith called Fontaine back and advised against granting the clauses in the contract. Fontaine said that Hauptmann was adamant, and that he was afraid the entire negotiation was going to collapse over a minor point in contract language. Meredith said he still thought it was a bad idea to make the concession. Fontaine said he thought he needed to consult Saunders, the European president of Pacific Oil, just to make sure.

Two days later, Saunders called Meredith and said that he had complete faith in Fontaine, and Fontaine's ability to determine what was necessary to make a contract work. If Fontaine felt that "favored nation's" and "meet competition" clauses were necessary, he trusted Fontaine's judgment that the clauses could not cause significant adverse harm to Pacific Oil over the next few years. As a result, he had given Fontaine the go-ahead to agree to these clauses in the new contract.

MARCH 11

It was a dark and stormy night, March 11, 1976. Frank Kelsey was about to go to bed when the telephone rang. It was Jean Fontaine. Kelsey had not heard from Fontaine since their meeting in Paris. Meredith had told Kelsey about the discussion with Saunders, and he had assumed that Fontaine had gone ahead and conceded on the two contract clauses that had been discussed. He thought the contract was about to be wrapped up, but he hadn't heard for sure.

The violent rainstorm outside disrupted the telephone transmission, and Kelsey had trouble hearing Fontaine. Fontaine said that he had appreciated Kelsey's visit in January. Fontaine was calling to ask Kelsey's advice. They had just come from a meeting with Hauptmann. Hauptmann and Zinnser had reported that recent news from Reliant's corporate headquarters in Chicago projected significant downturns in the sale of a number of Reliant's PVC products in the European market. While Reliant thought it could ride out the downturn, they were very concerned about their future obligations under the Pacific contract. Since Reliant and Pacific had already settled on minimum quantity amounts, Reliant wanted the contractual right to resell the product if it could not use the minimum amount.

Kelsey tried to control his emotions as he thought about this negative turn of events in the Reliant negotiations. He strongly advised against agreeing to the clause, saying that it could put Pacific in an extremely poor position. Fontaine debated the point, saying he really thought Reliant might default on the whole contract if they didn't get resale rights. "I can't see where agreeing to the right to resale is a big thing, Frank, particularly given the size of this contract and its value to me and Pacific."

> **Kelsey:** "Look, you asked for my advice, and I gave it to you. If I were you, I wouldn't make any more concessions. Agreeing to a resale clause could create a whole lot of unforeseen problems. At this point I think it's also the principle of the thing!"
>
> **Fontaine:** "Who cares about principles at a time like this! It's my neck that's on the line if this Reliant contract goes under! I'll have over 200 million pounds of VCM a year to eat in an oversupplied market! It's my neck that on the line, not yours! How in the world can you talk to me about "principle" at this point?"
>
> **Kelsey:** "Calm down, Jean! I can see your point of view! I appreciate the pressures on you, but I really don't like the looks of it from this end. Keep in touch—let me ask others down at the office what they think, and I'll call you next week."

Kelsey hung up the telephone, and stared out of the window at the rain. He could certainly empathize with Fontaine's position—the man's neck was on the block. As he mentally reviewed the two-year history of the Reliant negotiations, Kelsey wondered how they had gotten to this point, and whether anyone could have done things differently. He also wondered what to do about the resale clause, which appeared to be the final sticking point in the deliberations. Would acquiescing to a resale clause for Reliant be a problem to Pacific Oil? Kelsey knew he had to take action soon.

Petrochemical Supply Contracts: A Technical Note

Supply contracts between chemical manufacturing/refining companies and purchasing companies are fairly standard in the industry trade. They are negotiated between supplier and purchaser in order to protect both parties against major fluctuations in supply and demand. Any purchaser wishing to obtain a limited amount of a particular product could always approach any one of a number of chemical manufacturing firms and obtain the product at "market price." The market price is controlled by the competitive supply and demand for the particular product on any given day. But purchasers want to be assured of a long-term supply and do not want to be subject to the vagaries of price fluctuation; similarly, manufacturers want to be assured of product outlets in order to adequately plan manufacturing schedules. Long-term contracts protect both parties against these fluctuations.

A supply contract is usually a relatively standard document, often condensed to one page. The major "negotiable" elements of the contract, on the "front side" of the document, include the price, quantity, product quality, contract duration, delivery point, and credit terms (see Exhibit 1 for a sample blank contract). The remainder ("back side") of the contract is filled with traditionally fixed legal terminology that govern the conditions under which the contract will be maintained. While the items are seldom changed, they may be altered or waived as part of the negotiated agreement.

The primary component of a long-term contract is the price. In the early years of the petrochemical industry, the raw product was metered by the supplier (either in liquid or gaseous form) and sold to the purchaser. As the industry became more competitive, as prices rose rapidly, and as the products developed from petrochemical supplies (called "feedstocks") became more sophisticated, pricing became a significantly more complex process. Most contemporary contract prices are determined by an elaborate calculation called a "formula price," composed of several elements:

This note was prepared by Professor Roy J. Lewicki for use in executive seminars.

1. Feedstock Characteristics. Petrochemical feedstock supplies differ in the chemical composition and molecular structure of the crude oil. Differences in feedstocks will significantly affect the refining procedures and operating efficiency of the refinery that manufactures a product, as well as their relative usefulness to particular purchasers. While some chemical products may be drawn from a single feedstock, large-volume orders may necessitate the blending of several feedstocks with different structural characteristics.

2. Fuel Costs. Fuel costs include the price and amount of energy that the manufacturing company must assume in cracking, refining, and producing a particular chemical stream.

3. Labor costs. Labor costs include the salaries of employees to operate the manufacturing facility for the purpose of producing a fixed unit amount of a particular product.

4. Commodity costs. Commodity costs include the value of the basic petrochemical base on the open marketplace. As the supply and demand for the basic commodity fluctuate on the open market, this factor is entered into the formula price.

A formula price may therefore be represented as a function of the following elements:

$$\text{Formula price} = \text{Feedstock cost} + \text{Energy cost} + \text{Labor cost} + \text{Commodity cost (per unit)}$$

If only one feedstock were used, the chemical composition of the feedstock would determine its basic cost, and the energy, labor, and commodity costs of producing it. If several feedstocks were used, the formula price would be a composite of separate calculations for each particular feedstock, or a weighted average of the feedstock components, multiplied by the cost of production of each one.

Each of the elements in the formula price is also multiplied by a weighting factor (coefficient) that specifies how much each cost will contribute to the determination of the overall formula price. The supplier generally sets a "ceiling price," guaranteeing that the formula price will not exceed this amount. Below the ceiling price, however, the supplier endeavors to maximize profits while clearly specifying the costs of production to the purchaser, while the purchaser attempts to obtain the most favorable formula price for himself. Since basic cost data and cost fluctuations are well known, negotiations typically focus on the magnitude of the coefficients that are applied to each element in the formula. Hence, the actual formula computation may be represented as:

$$\text{Formula price} = (\text{Weighting coefficient} \times \text{Feedstock cost}) + (\text{Weighting coefficient} \times \text{Energy cost}) + (\text{Weighting coefficient} \times \text{Labor cost}) + (\text{Weighting coefficient} \times \text{Commodity cost})$$

EXHIBIT 1
Agreement of Sale

This Agreement, entered into this __day of _, _____, between Pacific Oil Company, hereinafter called Seller, and _____, hereinafter called Buyer.

WITNESSETH:

Seller agrees to sell and deliver and Buyer agrees to purchase and receive commodity (hereinafter called "product") under the terms and conditions set forth below.

1. PRODUCT:

2. QUALITY:

3. QUANTITY:

4. PERIOD:

5. PRICE:

6. PAYMENT TERMS:

(a) Net _____ .

(b) All payments shall be made in United States dollars without discount or deduction, unless otherwise noted, by wire transfer at Seller's option, to a bank account designated by Seller. Invoices not paid on due date will be subject to a delinquency finance charge of 1% per month.

(c) If at any time the financial responsibility of Buyer shall become impaired or unsatisfactory to Seller, cash payment on delivery or satisfactory security may be required. A failure to pay any amount may, at the option of the Seller, terminate this contract as to further deliveries. No forebearance, course of dealing, or prior payment shall affect this right of Seller.

7. PRICE CHANGE:

The price specified in this Agreement may be changed by Seller on the first day of any calendar _____ by written notice sent to the Buyer not less than thirty (30) days prior to the effective date of change. Buyer gives Seller written notice of objection to such change at least ten (10) days prior to the effective date of change. Buyer's failure to serve Seller with written notice of objection thereto prior to the effective date thereof shall be considered acceptance of such change. If Buyer gives such notice of objection and Buyer and Seller fail to agree on such change prior to the effective date thereof, this Agreement and the obligations of Seller and Buyer hereunder shall terminate with respect to the unshipped portion of the Product

EXHIBIT 1 *(continued)*

governed by it. Seller has the option immediately to cancel this contract upon written notice to Buyer, to continue to sell hereunder at the same price and terms which were in effect at the time Seller gave notice of change, or to suspend performance under this contract while pricing is being resolved. If Seller desires to revise the price, freight allowance or terms of payment pursuant to this agreement, but is restricted to any extent against doing so by reason of any law, governmental decree, order or regulation, or if the price, freight allowance or terms of payment then in effect under this contract are nullified or reduced by reason of any law, governmental decree, order or regulation, Seller shall have the right to cancel this contract upon fifteen (15) days written notice to purchaser.

8. COMPETITIVE OFFERS:

If Buyer receives a bona fide offer to purchase product of the same specification as contained in this agreement and of no greater quantity, at a price, including terms and conditions, lower than applicable under this Agreement, and if Buyer furnishes written evidence specifying the details of such an offer to the seller, Seller will, within 15 days, either meet such price on the same quantity offered or allow Buyer to purchase the product so offered. Buyer shall give Seller prompt notice of any quantity of Product purchased or to be purchased in accordance with the provisions of this paragraph. Such quantity shall be deducted from the quantity specified in this Agreement for the year in which it is so purchased. In addition, Seller at its option may also deduct such quantity for each year thereafter remaining under this Agreement. Election of such option by seller shall be given to Buyer by written notice within 90 days after Seller receives Buyer's notice of purchase.

9. MEASUREMENTS:

Seller's determinations, unless proven to be erroneous, shall be accepted as conclusive evidence of the quantity of Product delivered hereunder. Credit will not be allowed for shortages of ½ of 1% or less of the quantity and overages of ½ of 1% or less of the quantity will be waived. The total amount of shortages or overages will be credited or billed when quantities are greater and such differences are substantiated. Measurements of weight and volume shall be according to procedures and criteria standard for such determinations.

10. SHIPMENTS AND DELIVERY:

Buyer shall give Seller annual or quarterly forecasts of its expected requirements as Seller may from time to time request. Buyer shall give Seller reasonably advanced notice for each shipment which shall include date of delivery and shipping instructions. Buyer shall agree to take deliveries in approximately equal monthly quantities, except as may be otherwise provided herein. In the event that Buyer fails to take the quantity specified or the pro rata quantity in any month, Seller may, at its option, in addition to other rights and remedies, cancel such shipments or parts thereof.

11. PURCHASE REQUIREMENTS:

(a) If during any consecutive three month period, Buyer for any reason (but not for reasons of force majeure as set forth in Section 13) takes less than 90 percent of

EXHIBIT 1 *(continued)*

the average monthly quantity specified, or the prorated minimum monthly quantity then applicable to such period under Section 13, Seller may elect to charge Buyer a penalty charge for failure to take the average monthly quantity or prorated minimum monthly quantity.

(b) If, during any consecutive three month period, Buyer, for any reason (but not, however, for reasons of force majeure as set forth in Section 13) takes Product in quantities less than that equal to at least one half of the average monthly quantity specified or the prorated minimum monthly quantity originally applicable to such period under Section 13, Seller may elect to terminate this agreement.

(c) It is the Seller's intent not to unreasonably exercise its rights under (a) or (b) in the event of adverse economic and business conditions in general.

(d) Notice of election by Seller under (a) or (b) shall be given within 30 days after the end of the applicable three month period, and the effective date of termination shall be 30 days after the date of said notice.

12. DETENTION POLICY:

Seller may, from time to time, specify free unloading time allowances for its transportation equipment. Buyer shall be liable to the Transportation Company for all demurrage charges made by the Transportation Company, for railcars, trucks, tanks or barges held by Buyer beyond the free unloading time.

13. FORCE MAJEURE:

Neither party shall be liable to the other for failure or delay in performance hereunder to the extent that such failure or delay is due to war, fire, flood, strike, lockout, or other labor trouble, accident, breakdown of equipment or machinery, riot, act, request, or suggestion of governmental authority, act of God, or other contingencies beyond the control of the affected party which interfere with the production or transportation of the material covered by this Agreement or with the supply of any raw material (whether or not the source of supply was in existence or contemplated at the time of this Agreement) or energy source used in connection therewith, or interfere with Buyer's consumption of such material, provided that in no event shall Buyer be relieved of the obligation to pay in full for material delivered hereunder. Without limitation on the foregoing, neither party shall be required to remove any cause listed above or replace the affected source of supply or facility if it shall involve additional expense or departure from its normal practices. If any of the events specified in this paragraph shall have occurred, Seller shall have the right to allocate in a fair and reasonable manner among its customers and Seller's own requirements any supplies of material Seller has available for delivery at the time or for the duration of the event.

14. MATERIALS AND ENERGY SUPPLY:

If, for reasons beyond reasonable commercial control, Seller's supply of product to be delivered hereunder shall be limited due to continued availability of necessary

EXHIBIT 1 *(continued)*

---

allocate to the Buyer a portion of such product on such basis as Seller deems equitable. Such allocation shall normally be that percent of Seller's total internal and external commitments which are committed to Buyer as related to the total quantity available from Seller's manufacturing facilities.

15. DISCLAIMER:

Seller makes no warranty, express or implied, concerning the product furnished hereunder other than it shall be of the quality and specification stated herein. Any implied warranty of FITNESS is expressly excluded and to the extent that it is contrary to the foregoing sentence; any implied warranty of MERCHANTABILITY is expressly excluded. Any recommendations made by Seller makes no warranty of results to be obtained. Buyer assumes all responsibility and liability for loss or damage resulting from the handling or use of said product. In no event shall Seller be liable for any special, indirect or consequential damages, irrespective of whether caused or allegedly caused by negligence.

16. TAXES:

Any tax, excise fee or other charge or increase thereof upon the production, storage, withdrawal, sale or transportation of the product sold hereunder, or entering into the cost of such product, imposed by any proper authority becoming effective after the date hereof, shall be added to the price herein provided and shall be paid by the Buyer.

17. ASSIGNMENT AND RESALE:

This contract is not transferable or assignable by Buyer without the written consent of Seller. The product described hereunder, in the form and manner provided by the Seller, may not be assigned or resold without prior written consent of the Seller.

18. ACCEPTANCE:

Acceptance hereof must be without qualification and Seller will not be bound by any different terms and conditions contained in any other communication.

19. WAIVER OF BREACH:

No waiver by Seller or Buyer of any breach of any of the terms and conditions contained in this Agreement shall be construed as a waiver or any subsequent breach of the same or any other term or condition.

20. TERMINATION:

If any provision of this agreement is or becomes violate of any law, or any rule, order or regulation issued thereunder, Seller shall have the right upon notice to Buyer, to terminate the Agreement in its entirety.

EXHIBIT 1 *(concluded)*

21. GOVERNING LAW:

The construction of this Agreement and the rights and obligations of the parties hereunder shall be governed by the laws of the State of New York.

22. SPECIAL PROVISIONS:

BUYER: SELLER:

_____   PACIFIC OIL CORPORATION
            (firm)

By: _____   By: _____

Title: _____   Title: _____

Date: _____   Date: _____

A fairly typical ratio of the weighting coefficients in this formula would be 70 percent (0.7) for feedstock cost, 20 percent (0.2) for energy costs, 5 percent (.05) for labor costs and 5 percent (0.05) for commodity costs. Multiple feedstocks supplied in a particular contract would be composed of a different set of costs and weighting elements for each feedstock in the supply.

The computation of a formula price, as opposed to the determination of a market price, has a number of advantages and disadvantages. Clearly, it enables the supplier to pass costs along to the purchaser, which minimizes the risk for both parties in the event of rapid changes in cost during the duration of the contract. The purchaser can project directly how cost changes will affect his supply costs; the supplier is protected by being able to pass cost increases along to the purchaser. However, when the market demand for the product is very high, the formula price constrains the seller in the ceiling price he can charge, hence curtailing potential profit for the product compared to its value on the open marketplace. Conversely, when market demand is very low, the contract may guarantee a large market to the supplier, but at a price for the product that could be unprofitable compared to production costs.

QUANTITY

Formula prices are typically computed with major attention given to quantity. Costs will fluctuate considerably based on the efficiency with which the production plant is operated, number of labor shifts required, and so on. Hence, in order to adequately forecast demand, attain particular "economics of scale" in the manufacturing process, and plan production schedules, suppliers must be able to determine the quantities that a particular customer will want to acquire. (Because of the volumes involved, no significant inventory is produced.) Quantities will be specified in common units of weight (pounds, tons, and so forth) or volume (gallons, and so on).

Quantity specifications are typically treated as minimum purchase amounts. If a purchaser desires significantly more than the minimum amount ("overlifting") in a given time period (e.g., a year), the amount would be sold contingent on availability, and delivered at the formula price. Conceivably, "discount" prices or adjustments in the formula price could be negotiated for significant purchases over minimum quantity. Conversely, underpurchase of the minimum amount ("underlifting") by a significant degree typically results in penalty costs to the purchaser. These are typically referred to as "liquidated damages" in the industry, and may be negotiated at rates anywhere from a token fine of several thousand dollars to as much as 30 percent of the formula price for each unit underlifted. Faced with the possibility of underlifting (due to market or product demand changes that require less raw material in a given time period), purchasers typically handle underlifting in one of several ways:

a. Pay the underlifting charges ("liquidated damages") to the supplier, either as stated or according to some renegotiated rate.

b. *Not* pay the liquidated damages, under the assumption that the supplier will not want to press legal charges against the purchaser at the expense of endangering the entire supply contract.

c. Resell the commodity to another purchaser who may be in need of supply, perhaps at a discounted price. Such action by the purchaser could cause major instability in the market price and in supply contracts held at the original manufacturer or other manufacturers. For this reason, sellers typically preclude the right of the purchaser to resell the product as part of the "standard contract language."

QUALITY

The quality of the product is related to the particular feedstock from which it is drawn, as well as the type and degree of refining that is employed by the supplier. Standard descriptions for gradations of quality are common parlance for each major chemical product.

DELIVERY

Most contracts specify the method of delivery, point of delivery, and way that the quantity amounts will be measured as the product is delivered. Gases are typically metered and delivered by direct pipeline from the manufacturer to the purchaser; liquids and liquified gases may be sold by pipeline, or shipped via tank truck, railroad tank car, tank barges, and tank ships.

CONTRACT DURATION

Most typical supply contracts extend for a period from one to five years; significantly longer or shorter ones would probably only be negotiated under extreme circumstances. Negotiations for contract renewal are typically begun several months prior to contract expiration.

PAYMENT TERMS

Payment terms are determined by the credit ratings and cash flow demands of both parties. Typical contracts specify payment within 30 days of delivery, although this time period may be shortened to payment on delivery, or lengthened to a period of 3 months between delivery and payment.

CONTRACT LANGUAGE

As can be determined from Exhibit 1, there are a number of elements in the contract that delineate the conditions under which the parties agree to bind themselves to the contract, or to deviate from it. Terminology and agreements were typically standard, unless altered by negotiation prior to contract signing. These elements include:

1. Measurements.   A mechanism for specifying how quantity amounts will be determined, and how disputes over differences in delivered quantity will be resolved.

2. Meet Competition.   The seller agrees to meet competitive market prices for the product if they become substantially lower than the current negotiated formula price.

3. Favored Nations.   The supplier agrees that if he offers a better price on the product to any of the purchaser's competitors, he will offer the same price to this buyer.

4. Purchase Requirements.   These govern the conditions and terms under which liquidated damages may be invoked.

5. Force Majeure.   This clause exempts the parties from contract default in the event of major natural disasters, strikes, fires, explosions, or other events that could preclude the seller's ability to deliver the product or the buyer's ability to purchase.

6. *Disclaimers*. These protect both buyer and seller against unreasonable claims about the product or its quality.

7. *Assignability*. This clause limits the right of either party to assign the contract to another purchaser or supplier if they so desire.

8. *Notifications*. This is the lead time specified during which one or both parties must notify the other party of any change in the contract or its renewal.

9. *Other Clauses*. These include conditions under which the product may be assured delivery, application of taxes, provisions for resale, definitions of contract breach and termination, the legal framework used to enforce the contract (in the event of cross-state or cross-national agreements), and methods of notification of one party to the other.

CONTRACT MANAGEMENT AND MAINTENANCE

While a supply contract is a legally binding document that attempts to articulate the way two companies will work together, it more commonly stands as the cornerstone of a complex long-term social relationship between buyer and seller. This relationship requires constant monitoring, evaluation, and discussion by representatives of both organizations. Thus, while similar supply contracts may exist between a particular manufacturer and three different buyers, there may be major differences in the day-to-day interactions and quality of relationships between the manufacturer and each buyer. Experienced sales representatives have defined a "good" seller-buyer relationship as meeting the following criteria:

The purchaser can be counted on to live up to the terms and conditions of the contract as negotiated. The purchaser accepts a fair formula price in price negotiations, and does not attempt to push the supplier into an artificially low price. The purchaser lifts as much of the product per time period as he agreed to lift under the contract. The purchaser is trustworthy, and follows a course of action based on sound business ethics.

The purchaser does not attempt to take advantage of fluctuations or abberations in the spot market price to gain advantage. He accepts the fact that a formula price has been negotiated, and that both parties agree to live up to this price for the duration of the contract. He does not seek contract price changes as the market price may drop for some time period.

When there is a mutual problem between seller and purchaser, it can be openly discussed and resolved between the two parties. Problems resulting from the continued inability of the supplier to provide the product, and or the continued inability of the buyer to consume the product, can be openly addressed and resolved. Problems in the quality of the product, labor difficulties resulting in problems in manufacturing, loading, shipping, unloading, cleanliness of the shipping equipment, and so on, can be promptly explored and resolved to mutual satisfaction. Finally, changes in the business projections of one or both parties can be shared, so that difficulties anticipated by the supplier in providing all of the product, or difficulties anticipated by the purchaser in consuming all of the product, can lead to amicable and satisfactory resolutions for both parties. Ability to resolve these problems requires mutual trust, honesty, open lines of communication, and an approach to problem solving that seeks the best solution for both sides.

A Contract with the Kremlin

By William Oscar Johnson

They want us to be like three scorpions fighting in a bottle. When it's over, two will be dead and the winner will be exhausted.

Thus spoke Roone Arledge, president of ABC Sports, of the way it was when the three major American televison networks joined in bitter battle with the government of the Soviet Union over the U.S. rights to televise the 1980 Summer Olympic Games. It was a Cold War confrontation with an absolutely classic—if also a somewhat comic—cast of adversaries. On one side stood the network executives, representing all that is richest, sleekest, most glamorous about the free-enterprise system. They came from stately Manhattan skyscrapers, quick-witted, supersophisticated salesmen given to Gucci shoes and manicured hands. If they were not the cream of U.S. business, the network men were certainly from the tip of the vast capitalist iceberg.

On the other side stood a battery of grim Russian bureaucrats—burly, pallid fellows, some former peasants with hands still hard from years of labor in the fields of Mother Russia. They were canny technocrats and politicians from the cold corridors of the Kremlin; some were in their 70s, and their longevity alone made it clear that they were among the wiliest of men in this land of purges. It also is worth noting that the network representatives were not entirely without this instinct for survival, being no less vulnerable than Soviet politicians to swift turns of fortune that could send them to the Siberias of American business.

So they joined the conflict well matched—the minions of Red Square, Moscow versus the moguls of Sixth Avenue, New York. It would be nice to report that the result was a hard, clean, clear-cut battle between two ideological juggernauts, that two gleaming machines performed in a way that displayed the best of both systems. This did not happen.

The big Olympic TV deal became bogged down in misunderstanding, misjudgment and mistakes.

Reprinted from *Sports Illustrated,* February 21, 1977.

In fact, during the critical closing phase of negotiations that concluded three weeks ago with an astonished National Broadcasting Company being presented with the Olympic rights for $85 million, the only real link between the two adversaries was a garrulous little German named Lothar Bock. He is a small-time "impresario" (the term he uses to describe himself) who had more experience as a booking agent for Georgian saber dancers and Mongolian tumblers than as the indispensable middle-man between a bunch of cold-eyed Soviets and high-rolling TV executives. It is true that one network man described Bock as being "a bit of a klutz," but it was Bock—and Bock alone—who plodded between Moscow and Manhattan to forge the final bond that gave the Olympics to NBC. In the bargain, he earned himself a million bucks and made his name a household word from the bar at P. J. Clarke's to the boardroom at the A. C. Nielsen Company.

This bizarre situation officially began in Vienna in October 1974, when the International Olympic Committee awarded the Soviet Union the 1980 Summer Olympics. All three networks were there just to shake hands with their new adversaries. No one was selling, no one was buying. Only one network—ABC—was absolutely certain that it would bid for the Moscow Games. Under the masterful guidance of Arledge, ABC had won the rights to six of the last eight Olympics, and it covered each with increasing excellence. But except for sport, the network had been No. 3 in the ratings for many years. That changed in the 1976–77 TV season when ABC burst to the fore, partially because of its hugely successful telecasting of the Montreal Games.

CBS had televised the Rome Olympics of 1960. That was in TV's dark ages, when rights could be purchased for $550,000. Since then, CBS had never bid successfully—or even seriously—for an Olympics. The network had been rated No. 1 for so long that it seemed to be living on its own Mount Olympus, showing a godlike disdain for the Games of mere mortals. However, in mid-1974, Robert F. Wussler became CBS's vice president in charge of sports, and he was very interested in the Moscow Games.

As for NBC, it had televised the 1972 Winter Olympics from Sapporo—an esthetic disaster and a financial disappointment. Top management was at best neutral toward the Moscow Olympics. Carl Lindemann Jr., NBC's vice president for sports, made a couple of trips to the Soviet capital in the early going but says, "I was essentially there to wave the flag. Higher network management was ambivalent. I wanted the Games in the worst way. We had lost the Munich Olympics because of a lousy $1 million." (ABC paid $13.5 million for the rights.)

During 1974 and 1975 the American network executives—Arledge, Wussler, Lindemann, and an ever-growing cast of presidents, board chairmen, lawyers, diplomats, politicians and public relations men—launched into a lumbering courtship that was intended to win the hearts and minds of the Soviet Olympic hierarchy. In the end, none of it seems to have made any difference in the selection of NBC. Yet the courtship was fervent, relentless—and sometimes quite public.

For example, in the fall of 1975, ABC's faltering morning show, "A.M. America," woke up the nation to a week of reports on life in the Soviet Union that were so uncritical an embarrassed ABC man said, "We made Moscow look like Cypress Gardens without the water skiers." In 1976 CBS aired a prime-time bomb that featured a shivering Mary Tyler Moore standing on a wintry Moscow street corner, hosting a show about the Bolshoi Ballet. When Wussler was asked if this was part of his Olympic campaign, he replied, "No question about it."

As the time approached for the Montreal Games, there was a constant shuttling of network people to Moscow to wine and dine with Soviet Olympic officials. East and West became palsy-walsy, even kidding each other about whether it was the KGB or the CIA that was bugging their conversations. Mostly it was social, but in Montreal the plot at last thickened.

The USSR's Olympic Organizing Committee glittered with Kremlin stars. The leader was a hulking, dark-haired Ignati Novikov, 70. He had started his career as a laborer in the Ukraine, rising through the ranks until he became one of the top half dozen men in the USSR, the deputy premier in charge of all power construction projects. Second in command was Sergei Lapin, 64, a stern and polished diplomat who had been ambassador to Austria and China and general director of Tass. Now, as Minister of the State Committee for Television and Radio, Lapin became the Soviet Union's head propagandist. They were invariably accompanied by a battery of deputy chairmen, vice commissars, translators, and stenographers. The Americans quickly noted a difference between two factions: Novikov, an old Kremlin hand, came on in the intransigent shoe-rapping manner of Nikita Khrushchev, while Lapin and others on the TV-radio committee seemed more subtle.

On a Saturday afternoon in Montreal, the Soviets gave a lavish party on the good ship *Alexander Pushkin,* which was moored in the St. Lawrence. The decks were awash with gallons of Stolichnaya vodka and Armenian cognac. The tables groaned beneath platters of cracked lobster, sliced sturgeon, caviar. The event was purely social, even jolly. But Novikov & Co. were in town to do some serious shoe-rapping. They contacted the networks one by one and made their demand: they wanted $210 million. In cash. The networks laughed. An NBC man said to a Russian, "210 million dollars? We were thinking of 210 million *pennies.*" The Soviet representative stalked off in anger, but one of his comrades confided to a CBS representative that no one in Moscow expected more than $65 million.

In fact, none of the numbers meant much of anything. NBC's Lindemann says, "We all knew the price would be between $70 and $100 million. I think all three of us would have gone to $100 million." Perhaps so. But the real numbers would come later. The most troubling aspect of the Russian demands in Montreal had to do with the sensitive issue of just how much selling of the Soviet Union a U.S. network would have to do to buy into the Olympics. The fine line between propaganda and news seemed particularly fuzzy to Novikov. Wussler recalls, "He made it clear to us he expected some kind of favorable political coverage. We said we could *not* compromise CBS News. We might do something like the Mary Tyler Moore show, ice shows, circuses, sports."

Arledge says, "I wanted a clause in the contract that said ABC would have total control over our telecast of the Olympics. Novikov had said to me earlier in the year, 'If you show things we don't like, we will pull the plug.' I doubt they would do that, but the problem of even *seeming* like a propaganda arm for the Russians is delicate. For example, if you show the subways of Moscow—and they are superb—some people in the United States are going to see it as a selling job for the Soviets just because it isn't something negative."

The Soviets did not demand specific schedules of pro-USSR programming, but the prospect of having to do such shows hung heavy over the networks throughout the negotiations.

As the Montreal Games ended, the Soviets said they would like to see some preliminary money bids in Moscow that fall. They would be secret, of course. NBC was particularly careful about security. It wrote a two-sentence bid on a page of company stationery, sealed it in a film can, sent it by courier to New York's Kennedy Airport where it was given to an airline pilot, who carried it in the cockpit to Moscow. There he gave it to the driver for NBC News, who took it straight to the committee. An hour later in New York Wussler knew NBC's bid.

The early bids received by the Soviets were: NBC $70 million, CBS $71 million and ABC a surprising $33.3 million for nonexclusive rights, meaning that it was already thinking of the possibility of pool coverage in which all three networks would participate. Arledge later bid $73 million for exclusive rights.

The autumn of 1976 arrived in New York, but in Moscow it suddenly seemed to be the season of CBS. Almost two years earlier Wussler had gotten enthusiastic encouragement in his Olympic quest from William Paley, the venerable CBS board chairman. Paley said, "I'm delighted you boys want to go after this, just delighted!" Thus blessed, Wussler and Arthur Taylor, then president of the network's parent company (CBS Inc.), had begun a series of trips between Manhattan and Moscow where they established warm friendships with important committee members. However, nothing they did was as important as the signing of Bock to be CBS's representative in Moscow.

Wussler had first met Bock, 38, in the spring of 1975 as the result of a phone call from film producer Bud Greenspan. "Bob, if CBS is really serious about the Olympics, the man to get them for you is sitting here in my office," Greenspan said. Wussler met Bock and invited him to dinner. Later Taylor met Bock in Moscow, and a consulting contract was arranged for him.

Who is Bock? And how did this energetic little fellow with a real-estate salesman's smile ingratiate himself with a pathologically suspicious crowd of Kremlin politicians? The answers are not clear. Was it because Bock arranged a few years ago to have a memorial plaque placed on the house in Munich where Lenin did some of his most important writing? This impressed the Soviets. Beyond that, Wussler says, "The Russians trust him at least partly because in 1968 Lothar imported a troupe of Russian singers for a tour of West Germany. They were there at the same time the Russians invaded Czechoslovakia to crush the uprising. That week the West Germans wouldn't touch anything Russian with a 10-foot pole. Lothar had to eat about a $75,000 loss. And he did. The Russians never forgot that. They thought Lothar showed class. They trusted him."

There are stories around Munich that contradict this theory. Some people say they cannot understand why the Soviets even let Bock into the USSR because he allegedly once left a troupe of Georgian saber dancers flat broke in Hamburg until the Soviet government sent money to pay their bills. On another occasion, Bock reportedly marooned 60 Mongolian tumblers in a Bavarian country inn, forcing Moscow to come to the rescue again.

Whatever else he may be, Bock is a loquacious chap who is seemingly quite open about himself. Sitting in his office, which is located in the basement of a green bungalow on an unpaved street in a Munich suburb, he explained last week how his prosperous Soviet connection came to be: "In 1965 I happened to see the Osipov Balalaika Orchestra, and I thought I would bring it to Germany. I wrote to Moscow and got a letter back in Russian. I hardly even speak the language now, and I certainly didn't understand it then. But instead of having it translated, I took the next flight to Moscow. They translated it for me there. It said: 'Dear Mr. Bock. We are not interested in your offer.' But I was insistent, I continued talking to them. After a while, they saw my point, and I have been dealing with them ever since. We are fair and square with each other."

Pressed further for his formula for gaining friends in the most remote recesses of the Kremlin, Bock said, "I always tell them I am a capitalist, making no attempt to hide that I am working for profit. They accept it. They love it."

That seems all too simple. But whatever the reasons, the Soviets trust Bock. As one Russian told Wussler, "All U.S. networks are bad, but you are less bad, because you know Lothar Bock." By October 1976, with Bock running interference, Wussler and Taylor felt they were on the brink of closing a deal. "We had contracts all drawn up between CBS and the organizing committee," says Wussler. They came triumphantly back to New York to tell the network the Olympics were wrapped up, and arranged a big party for the Russians at the IOC meetings that were scheduled in Barcelona a day later. Wussler was packing to go to Spain when he got the stunning news: Taylor had been fired by Paley.

If there is one thing the Soviets understand with razor-sharp clarity, it is the sudden purge of high-level personnel. And it makes them nervous. "They were shook, I mean *shook!*" Wussler, who six months before had moved up from head of CBS sports to the presidency of the network. "I tried to assure them it had nothing to do with the Olympics, but it was hard for them to believe." Even the sprightly Bock was numb—for a while. Then he phoned Wussler and said, "I think if Mr. Paley would come to Moscow himself, we could put the deal together again." Wussler doubted whether Paley would agree, but when he asked him to go, Paley's only question was "How soon do we leave?" Early in November, the patriarch of American television and a leading patrician of world capitalism was welcomed with almost adoration by the old Ukrainian laborer, Novikov. They toasted each other warmly during a lavish dinner of chicken Kiev fit for a czar. Then, after two long days of meetings, the two old lions had a tête à tête in a small room. They toasted each other. They shook hands. Wussler recalls, "Mr. Paley and I left Moscow with the definite feeling that the deal was firm."

Oddly, nothing further was heard from Moscow until December 8. Then the networks received a communication outlining the framework under which the final bidding for the rights would take place. It was an amazing document. Only ABC's men had heard anything like it mentioned in Montreal, and nothing resembling it had come up in CBS's private talks. No one was quite sure what it meant.

Nevertheless, all three networks went to Moscow to find out. NBC was planning to seriously enter the fray now. Robert Howard, president of the network, went to Moscow along with Lindemann and nine other executives and technicians. "Most of our guys had never been to Moscow," says Lindemann. "I had been there only four times. I was surprised when Wussler said he had been there 11 or 12 times."

When the Americans arrived for the showdown on December 15, two of the networks—CBS and ABC—were dead certain they had been chosen. Only NBC figured it was an underdog, and it was correct. NBC was about as far under as a dog could be. Novikov could never remember the network's call letters; even during the final signing, he twice referred to it as ABC.

Nevertheless, the Soviets treated the three networks exactly the same— like dirt. One by one, they were informed of the new conditions for bidding—which were outrageous. For one thing, the USSR demanded $50 million for equipment and facilities, to be paid in staggering increments of $20 million in 1977 and $30 million in 1978.

All along one of the Russians' most irrational demands had been for huge sums of cash to be paid two or three years before the Games. Recent Olympics have taken place in such a politically charged atmosphere that it was not unreasonable to fear that an international incident might cancel the Moscow Games, leaving the Soviets with the loot and TV with no programs. But the network executives were less afraid of losing money because of political disruption—after all, in a tightly controlled country like the USSR, the chances of disruption are slim—than because of an old-fashioned business reason.

Though the networks would have no problem raising the money, an enormous amount of interest would be lost if millions of dollars were tied up over such a long period. Arledge figured that if the $50 million for facilities was paid on the timetable the Soviets demanded, $17.5 million in interest would be forfeited.

Along with the ruinous pay schedule for the equipment, the Soviets had decided to hold an auction to sell the actual rights to the Games. In effect, the $50 million was merely an admission ticket to the final round of bidding. Arledge recalls, "Their plans involved an unending series of bids that went on as long as two guys were able to stand. There was a new sealed bid every 24 hours. The winner would be announced, then the losers could up the ante by a minimum of 5 percent. That's when I made the remark about scorpions in a bottle."

Wussler was most shocked by the USSR proposal. He had a letter with him from Paley reminding Novikov of their deal, and he asked for an audience with the chairman. They talked for 45 minutes. Novikov was stony. He told Wussler, "We are here to get the most money possible. That is our sole purpose. We need it for the Games." Wussler asked him about the agreement with Paley. Novikov replied, "It is a pity."

Wussler was appalled. He hurried to his hotel room. It was 4 P.M. Moscow time, 7 A.M. in the eastern United States. He phoned Jack Schneider, president of CBS Broadcasting, at home in Greenwich, Conn., and told him that CBS's deal had collapsed. He suggested that Schneider contact the other networks and arrange a pool. Within two hours, CBS, NBC, and ABC had agreed to file a brief with the Justice Department, asking it to waive the antitrust laws so the three networks could negotiate as a unified front.

Now it was 7 P.M. in Moscow, and the Soviets had decided to throw one last lavish supper before they put the three scorpions into the bottle. It was held in an elegant banquet room of the Hotel Sovietskaya. The party was a mistake. It was the first time that the three networks had been brought together in the same room in Moscow, and they were seething. At this point, no one but Wussler knew that a pool was in the works. The others were shouting angrily about the crude and insulting tactics of the Soviets. Almost immediately there was talk of walking out en masse. The hosts stood against the wall, aghast at the uproar among the Americans. Linemann says, "They had figured there was no limit to the manic competitive zeal of the networks. That was insulting, of course. But what bothered me even more was the fact that this wasn't just another ball game, this wasn't a spat with Bowie Kuhn or Pete Rozelle. This was the United States against the Soviet Union—and we just couldn't let this happen.''

The next day, taking a page from the Soviet book on diplomacy, the Americans walked out. At a meeting attended by Arledge, Wussler, and Howard, Novikov was impassive. He told them, ''If any of you leave Soviet soil on this day, you will never, *never* be allowed to return.'' The three said they had no choice. After leaving Novikov's office, they promised to leave the USSR and they showed each other their airline tickets as a display of good faith.

Arledge had earlier made an appointment for a private session with Novikov. He decided to keep the date. ''I was bound not to negotiate,'' says Arledge, ''but I didn't think Novikov understood. He said he would make a deal with me right there on the spot. He said the Olympics were mine. I told him I couldn't take the Olympics at that point if he gave them to me for five million.''

A few days after the networks left, the Soviets announced that the rights now belonged to a mysterious fourth party, an American trading and manufacturing company called SATRA, which does a lot of business with the USSR. This move was—and still is—seen by most network men as both a threat and a face-saving move by the Soviets. But SATRA apparently took it seriously and has filed a $275 million suit against NBC for interfering with its agreement with the Soviets.

Back in Manhattan, each network pledged to have no contact of any kind with the Soviets while the Justice Department considered the pool waiver request. However, Bock was still loose in Moscow. When the networks departed, he was shaken. Technically he was not a network employee, but he still had his contract with CBS. Soon Bock got word to Wussler that Novikov was sorry, that the Soviets wanted CBS to please come back. Then Novikov wired Paley, saying, in effect, that the USSR-CBS deal was still on. Meanwhile, Bock continued to negotiate.

Was this a breach of the agreement between the networks? Wussler claims Bock was working on his own. ''I told him specifically and in person when we left Moscow that he was not to continue any talks with the Russians on our behalf,'' Wussler says.

Arledge got disturbing news from Moscow in late December. ''I heard that Lothar was negotiating for CBS,'' he says. ''I kept hearing it. Then in mid-January I got word of the terms of a new contract. And I said, 'This has gone too far.' ''

Arledge contacted Wussler and told him, ''The Russians believe Bock is speaking in your behalf.'' Wussler said no, he is not. Arledge said that CBS could verify that by sending the Moscow Olympic Committee a wire stating that Bock had no authorization to bargain for CBS. Later, ABC indicated it would be satisfied if CBS sent a letter to Bock telling him he could not act in its behalf or sent a letter to ABC saying the same thing. CBS pondered this move for several days, then out of the blue it announced it was not only dropping out of the pool but also, because of various "imponderables," would have nothing further to do with the 1980 Olympics.

The shocking decision had been made after a series of CBS senior staff meetings, the last a 24-hour marathon. Bock had indeed brought a letter from Moscow that gave the Olympics to CBS for $81 million; he also brought assurances that a reasonable payment schedule could be worked out. It was a very good deal. Why did CBS quit with the battle at last won? Wussler says, "We saw nothing but trouble ahead. We couldn't see living with their deviousness. Their refusal to stick to the deal they made with Mr. Paley was the most telling point. I figured if they'd go back on a deal with him, how could I ever trust them with anything?"

Some people thought this explanation less than complete—especially after CBS had undertaken such an intense, well-organized two-year campaign to land the Games. It was suggested that perhaps a more compelling reason was that Bock's unauthorized work in Moscow on CBS's behalf would be embarrassing if it got out. As one network man says, "They got caught with their hand in the cookie jar."

Bock was stricken. He pleaded his case with Wussler, then took a Lear jet to the Bahamas to plead with Paley. The answer was no, although the network arranged for Bock to be paid a little extra cash for his trouble. Bock asked to be released from his CBS contract so he could contact NBC. It was done.

With the CBS pullout, the attempts to form a pool had disintegrated, and both NBC and ABC were free to operate unilaterally. Bock and Lindemann met for breakfast at the Edwardian Room of Manhattan's Plaza Hotel. Lindemann recalls, "The conversation was remarkably low key, considering its substance. Lothar started telling me his deal. We ordered something to eat. He kept talking. We drank our orange juice, then it dawned on me what he was saying. He was delivering the Olympics to us. We left without eating." Within hours, NBC signed a contract with Bock to pay him $1 million, to buy 15 programs he would produce, to retain him as a special consultant for four years. It was a dazzling package. Bock then delivered his part. A series of phone calls to Moscow clinched the deal that night. A day later Lindemann, Howard and an NBC lawyer were on their way to Moscow for the final negotiating and the formal signing.

NBC had hoped to complete the entire contract in Moscow before ABC learned it was there. It could not be done, even though the Soviets sent a wire telling Arledge not to come to Moscow. ABC was not dissuaded. Arledge says, "I knew the Russians were panicky. Novikov made a terrible mistake in December. Even his peers were accusing him of having bungled the deal with CBS. He was faced with the prospect of no American network at all. And by that time, he figured all Americans were crazy anyway, so when Bock said he had NBC, Novikov jumped at it. NBC was never in the Russian plans until CBS quit.

"And Novikov never understood what we were doing about the pool and why I had never contacted him after we walked out. When I finally saw him, he said, 'You never phoned, you never wrote. I waited and waited, and you never called.' I suppose if I had it to do over, maybe I'd do things differently. But I really felt relieved when it was over. I hated to lose the Games, but I had been wondering way back last summer whether I really wanted to have them."

ABC's presence at the last minute in Moscow did boost the price some. Lord Killanin, president of the previously somnolent IOC (which shares the rights fees with the host country), had heard ABC would go higher, and he had wired the Soviets to be certain they were getting top dollar. The deal wound up at $85 million—but there was no demand this time for the kind of pro-Soviet propaganda old Ignati Novikov had once seemed so determined to have.

Now the question is: Who won this confrontation between the USSR and the networks? No one knows. This was just the first skirmish in the conflict. Only late in the summer of 1980, when the Games are over and the NBC cameras and crews have gone home, will we know exactly who sold what, who bought what and who got the better of whom.

Appendix

Role for Fran Meltzer

SECTION HEAD DESIGN ENGINEERING GROUP

You are the section head of the design engineering group and have reporting to you a competent group of engineers who individually handle design projects. Because of financial difficulties the compay has not allocated funds to send engineers to professional meetings for the last several years. You have just heard from your superior that enough money has been appropriated to send one engineer from each group to the national meetings of your professional society next month. He also stated that the vice president of engineering thought it would be best if the limited travel funds were allocated to engineers rather than to managerial personnel which includes section heads like yourself.

You are quite sure that all of your engineers will want to go and know that there is the possibility of hurt feelings and resentment developing over this matter unless it is handled properly. Therefore, you have decided that rather than make the decision yourself you will call a meeting of your group and turn the matter over to them and let them make the decision. You will tell them of the funds available for travel and that you want them to make the decision as to who will go in the way they feel most fair. Your superior has also reminded you that these funds can only be used to send someone to the professional meetings. Do not take a position yourself as to who should be selected to go to the meetings.

Confidential Information for Buyer of the Used Car

Your car was stolen and wrecked two weeks ago. You do a lot of traveling in your job, so you need a car that is economical and easy to drive. The diesel Rabbit that was advertised looks like a good deal, and you would like to buy it right away if possible.

The insurance company gave you $4,000 for your old car. You have only $700 in savings that you had intended to spend on a trip with an *extremely* attractive companion—a chance you really don't want to pass up.

Your credit has been stretched for some time, so that if you borrow money, it will have to be at an 18 percent interest rate. Furthermore, you need to buy a replacement car quickly, because you have been renting a car (a 1983 Ford Fairmont) for business purposes, and it is costing you a great deal. The diesel Rabbit is the best deal you've seen, and the car is fun to drive. As an alternative, you can immediately buy a used 1981 Ford Pinto for $3,800 (the wholesale value), which gets 28 miles per gallon and will depreciate much faster than the Rabbit.

The seller of the Rabbit is a complete stranger to you.

Before beginning this negotiation, set the following targets for yourself:

1. The price you would like to pay for the car ⎯⎯⎯⎯⎯

2. The price you will initially offer the seller ⎯⎯⎯⎯⎯

3. The highest price you will pay for the car ⎯⎯⎯⎯⎯

Negotiator Able

	Issues		
Settlement Point	*Issue I*	*Issue II*	*Issue III*
A	7	12	5
B	7	14	6
C	7	15	7
D	8	16	7
E	10	17	8
F	11	18	9
G	11	20	9
H	11	22	10
I	12	22	13
J	13	24	15
K	13	26	17
L	14	28	18
M	16	30	18
N	20	40	19
O	25	45	19
P	30	50	20
Q	35	55	25
R	40	60	30
S	45	65	35
T	50	70	40

Note: Your maximum settlement = 50 + 70 + 40 = 160
Your minimum settlement = 7 + 12 + 5 = 24 (assuming all issues settled)

Role for B. J. Pelter

The line of work you are now on is taking you in exciting new directions not only for yourself and the company but for your professional area. You feel a real need to talk to other engineers doing similar work both to confirm what you have been doing and also to get ideas on some problems you have been facing. You know that several will be giving papers on topics right in the new area at the professional meetings next month. Fortunately you recently finished debugging the production problems on the last product you designed and now have more time to travel.

Employee Position 3B

You are the director of mail order sales for the Rapid Leathergoods Company, and have been in that job for the past two years. On the whole, you believe that you have done a satisfactory job. When you took the job of director, you had several talks with your boss (the marketing vice president), learned about the job requirements that were seen as important. You were able to work out an informal set of job objectives, and have been able to produce a good record against each of these criteria—with one exception. The exception is a major one, and it looms as the biggest stumbling block to your raise.

One of your objectives was to come up with a way of selling Rapid's Top Flite line, the company's most expensive line of leather wallets, purses, and so on, by mail. It had never been done successfully in the past. You have worked hard on methods of improving the Top Flite line. You had experimented with different mailing lists, tried premiums, money-back guarantees, and still the results were relatively insignificant. But in the past months you have been working hard on Top Flite. One particular appeal applied to a new list has had better results than most. It's too early to come to a definite conclusion. Further testing will be required, but the signs are good enough to be optimistic.

You know your boss is a hard negotiator at raise time. You also know that failure to achieve a breakthrough on Top Flite will make it easy for him to deny you anything but the most nominal raise. But you have not told your boss of the most recent results with the new list. You plan to save them to counter any argument he raises about your lack of performance in that area.

You plan on asking for a large $6,000 raise (normally, your raises have been 5–10 percent). Your current compensation has a base salary of $30,000. The projects that you have been working on have been MaxFli, Fireball, and Thunderhead. These projects have been excellent successes and have exceeded the projected growth. The Top Flite program was the only blemish in an otherwise excellent record.

Take a few minutes to review these facts and then devise a strategy to approach your boss for this raise.

Confidential Information for Seller of the Used Car

You have bought a diesel Mercedes (used) from a dealer. The down payment is $4,700 on the car, with steep monthly payments. You are stretched on credit, so if you can't make the down payment, you will have to borrow at 18 percent. You're going to pick up the Mercedes in two hours, so you want to sell your old car, the Rabbit diesel, before you go.

You advertised the car (which is in particularly good condition) in the newspaper and have had several calls. Your only really good prospect right now is the person with whom you are about to bargain—a stranger. You don't *have* to sell it to this person, but if you don't sell the car right away, you will have to pay high interest charges until you do sell it.

The Mercedes dealer will only give you $4,400 for the Rabbit, since he will have to resell it to a Volkswagen dealer. The local VW dealer is not anxious to buy the car from you since he just received a shipment of new cars; in any case, he probably would not give you more than $4,400 either.

Before beginning this negotiation, set the following targets for yourself:

1. The price you would like to receive for the car _____

2. The price you will initially request from the buyer _____

3. The lowest price you will accept for the car _____

Employer Position 1A

You are the vice president for finance at the Ace Company. During a time of crisis three years ago, you had jumped up a young person to the credit manager position, discounting his young age and inexperience because the previous credit manager had quit and you were desperate. In time the word "Acting" had been removed from (his) title, and the subject of a raise had come up. You had said, "Let's see how this works out. After all, you're pretty young and inexperienced for this job. I don't have any doubts about your handling the job, but I'd like to wait. If you're able to handle it, we'll take care of you."

You have had consistent negotiations with this man about making up the differential between himself and other managers. He is the lowest paid manager at that level, and the others earn between $5,000–$7,000 more. Every time salary negotiations have come up, you have used your skill to play on the awe that this manager still holds for his good turn of fate as the argument to justify giving him a lower raise. It's almost been a game with you. He starts out determined to make up the financial spread, but he never really forces you to give it to him. The last time you negotiated you again were able to whittle him down. He is an excellent worker and you have no intention of firing him; as a matter of fact, in higher levels of management he has been declared a comer. You feel that if he really stuck to his initial demands you would give him the large raise he deserves. You just want him to drag it out of you.

You previously met with this individual a few days ago, and after hard negotiating, you got (him) to agree to a raise of $1,800 to his base salary of $22,000. In your eyes, you "won" this negotiation by your persistent skills and the special circumstances of this particular manager.

Today is the day of the office party, the day when clerical and office staff receive their "bonus checks" of up to $100. (Managers used to receive checks too, but there was a policy change this year and it was decided that managers would be compensated for their efforts through their salary increases.) Here comes the credit manager now. He doesn't look very happy—you wonder what's on his mind.

Take a few minutes to review these facts and devise a strategy for managing the discussion with your manager about a pay raise.

Role for Lee Clark

If funds become available for sending people to professional meetings and there are not enough to send everyone you feel that you should be the person to go because you have the most seniority. You feel strongly that in professional work seniority should count. In addition, you have a wide array of contacts developed over the years through which you can pick up much information useful to the company.

Capital Mortgage Insurance Corporation (E)

Randall and Dolan stopped only briefly at the hotel before going out for dinner; Randall was certain Elliott Burr would be trying to reach them before too long. Sure enough, when they returned to the hotel at 11:00 P.M., there were several phone messages. They ignored the messages and went to bed, since they had to get up at 6:00 A.M. to catch their flight back to Philadelphia.

Promptly at 6:00 A.M., Jim Dolan's telephone rang. As he groggily picked up the phone, a familiar voice said, "Good morning, Jim. This is your wake-up call. It's Elliott Burr. I tried to reach Frank and couldn't; but I would like to talk some more before you leave." Now fully awake, Dolan responded, "All right, I'll listen. But let's be clear that this is *not* a negotiating session."

Dolan met Burr in the hotel coffee shop at 6:30 A.M. after a quick shower and shave. Burr had CMI's offer letter with him. He had crossed out the offer to pay $400,000 over net worth and replaced it with $1 million. Jim was deliberately noncommittal in responding to Burr. All he said was that he and Randall were flying back to Philadelphia immediately and, "Frank will let you know."

Teachers' Association Position

You and your teammates are the bargaining team of the Newtown Teachers' Association. You are to select one or more of your members to serve as chief negotiator(s) representing your side in contract negotiations with the Newtown School District. Members of your team not designated as chief negotiator(s) may function in any capacity that the team decides upon.

As indicated in your "Background Information" sheet, the previous contract with the school district has expired. It is now the opening day of the school year and, as a result of various community pressures, the Teachers' Association has agreed to return to work on a day-to-day basis, with the provision that it is free to call a strike at any time so long as the contract is not finalized. In this regard, the bargaining team has considered several options ranging from a systemwide strike to a variety of more limited actions.

You represent 95 percent of the teachers in the Newtown system. Information available to you indicates that a majority of the membership prefers to conclude an agreement but is willing, if necessary, to engage in a strike action. The remainder of the membership is split, in that one subgroup wants to avoid any strike, while a second group is pressing to call one immediately. You, along with the other members of your team, prefer to conclude a contract rather than strike, but you are ready to do the latter if necessary. You are aware of increasing community pressure on your associaton and on the school board to conclude an agreement in order to avert a closing of the schools.

The Teachers' Association membership is aware of the budget cuts being imposed on the district. However, it has certain demands which it feels are justified and reasonable in light of the increased cost of living and recent gains received by Teachers' Associations in neighboring communities.

In general, the bargaining team wants to avoid a situation where the Teachers' Association loses benefits that have been gained over the past several years. In this connection it is felt that the Board of Education is essentially trying to reduce staff and, at the same time, obtain a considerable increase in teachers' work load in order to meet externally imposed budgetary reductions. You feel that the board is attempting to pass the burden of the budget cuts along to teachers rather than apportioning them in an equitable manner. Many members of the association also want salary increases that, at the very least, are sufficient to offset the rise in cost of living. Many teachers are willing to share some responsibility in the cutting of the budget and are willing to make a reasonable contribution to this end. A sizable portion of the membership is willing to accept an increase in work load, provided that the increases are reasonable *and* that they have some choice as to how this would be accomplished. However, it is felt that the board is asking teachers to incur most of the costs, make most of the sacrifices and seeking to retain its prerogative to make all decisions in these matters.

The issues that remain to be settled fall into six general categories:

1. Salary
2. Evaluation of teachers
3. Reduction in staff
4. Work load
5. Benefits
6. Binding arbitration of grievances

These general categories are ranked (above) in order of importance to the teachers. The bargaining team's position on specific issues within these categories is spelled out below. State law requires that all issues in dispute are negotiable.

1. *Salary*. The Teachers' Association wants the following:

   1.1 Retroactivity: All salary increases retroactive to July 1, the anniversary date of the contract. However, information available to the bargaining team suggests that the membership may be willing to accept a partial retroactivity formula in exchange for concessions on other issues. Possibilities include a reasonable percentage of full retroactivity, differential retroactivity linked to criteria such as years of service and present salary level, or other formulas devised by the bargaining team that any formula agreed upon yields satisfactory concessions on other priority issues.
   1.2 Cost-of-living increase: The membership prefers a cost-of-living increase commensurate with the regional increase in cost of living during the previous year, as determined by official government sources. However, information available to the bargaining team suggests that the membership might be willing to accept either a differential formula or one providing a reasonable percentage of the full increase in cost of living in exchange for concessions on other issues.
   1.3 Across-the-board increases in salary schedule: In order to equalize salaries with those in surrounding districts, the

membership is in favor of a $750 across-the-board increase. Information available to the bargaining team suggests that this figure is somewhat flexible so long as pronounced inequities at the lower steps of the salary schedule are brought into line with those of surrounding districts.

2. *Evaluation of Teachers.* The bargaining team has information indicating that the School Board is about to hire a consultant to develop a systematic evaluation procedure to be used by the board in determining individual teacher's salary increases and assignments to specific schools and duties. The board also wants to use these evaluations in making decisions pertaining to the granting of tenure and teacher layoffs. The membership is wary of this approach. Instead, teachers want the following:

2.1 Representation in the design and execution of teacher evaluations with particular reference to the specification of performance criteria and rules concerning the conditions under which such evaluations will be made.

2.2 Access by individual teachers to any and all evaluation data obtained and on file.

2.3 The opportunity to challenge, through a specified procedure, any data or entries felt by individual teachers to be inappropriate, inaccurate or otherwise damaging to them, and to have such entries expunged.

In general, the teachers want an explicit agreement, incorporating their input, spelling out the content of teacher evaluations, the procedures to be followed in obtaining such data and their use by the board in the areas of teacher salary, school assignments, tenure, and staffing.

3. *Reduction in Staff.* The Teachers' Association wants the following:

3.1 Minimal and selective reductions in staff, offset wherever possible by activating early retirements, using teachers to fill administrative positions that are presently vacant and using laid-off teachers to fill vacancies created by teachers on both long- and short-term leave.

3.2 Layoffs to be jointly determined on a case-by-case basis by representatives of the Teachers' Association and the Board of Education.

3.3 Layoffs to become effective on the last day of the present school term (January 28).

3.4 Written notification of layoff to affected teachers at least 60 days prior to layoff date.

3.5 Right to dispute layoff of individual teachers by meeting and conferring with the board in order to resolve such differences. Where disputes cannot be resolved in this manner, case to be submitted to an arbitrator whose decision would be binding on both sides. In the event of a reversal of layoff resulting from either procedure, the reinstated teacher would receive full salary for any period on layoff status.

3.6 Laid-off teachers to be placed on a recall list in the order of their layoff dates. Teachers to be carried on this list for a period not to exceed three years. In the case of ties between teachers on recall list, recall to be determined by length of service prior to layoff date. Tied teachers not recalled through this procedure to be placed at the top of the remaining recall list for next consideration.

3.7 Recall notification shall be in writing and teachers shall have 10 days following receipt of notification to inform board of their intention to accept or decline recall.

In general, the teachers want to minimize layoffs through placement of teachers in existing administrative vacancies, activation of early retirements and the use of laid-off teachers as substitutes for those on leave. Also, representation in layoff decisions, maximization of forewarning to affected teachers, specified recall procedures and a procedure permitting challenges of board layoff decisions are wanted. Within these overall membership preferences, however, the bargaining team recognizes a need to remain flexible in order to make trade-offs wherever necessary.

4. *Work Load.* The bargaining team has information indicating that the membership, though somewhat divided, wants the following:

4.1 Pupil/teacher ratio (average class size): The present system-wide ratio is approximately 32:1. However, this figure is an average, encompassing some smaller and some larger classes. The membership wants to hold the ratio at its present level, but might be willing to accept an increase in certain types of classes in exchange for concessions on other priority issues.

4.2 Workday: The present workday, as established in previous contracts, is seven hours and five minutes. Although there is strong feelings in the membership against any formal increase, the bargaining team feels that it might agree to certain limited increases, particularly where individual teachers voluntarily agree to assume additional responsibilities on an ad hoc basis. The bargaining team wishes to use this option as a lever to gain concessions on other priority issues.

4.3 "Prep" time: Teachers currently have a 50-minute "prep" time period each workday. Much of the membership feels rather strongly about retaining this period "as is" but the bargaining team feels that it might be able to offer a nominal reduction on a rotational or otherwise "shared" basis. The bargaining team feels that any concession on this issue should yield approriate concessions in return.

4.4 Duty-free time: In the previous contract, the teachers made a concession to the board which called for a reduction in their 1-hour lunch period, to a 50-minute period. Furthermore, the teachers also agreed to divide this 50-minute period into two parts: 25 minutes for lunch, per se, and 25 minutes of "duty-free" time. The teachers are adamantly opposed to any demands made by the board for additional service during the 25-minute "duty-free" period.

4.5 Emergency assignments and general obligations: The teachers are opposed to giving the board discretionary power to assign teachers to various duties during their daily "prep" time or "duty-free" time periods. Such assignments would include emergency substitute fill-in, bus duty, hall duty, disciplinary duty, committee service, and duties involving the monitoring and/or chaperoning of after-school athletic and social events. The bargaining team feels that it can design schemes filling some of these needs, provided that:

a. Decisions pertaining to such assignments are made jointly by representatives of the Teachers' Association and the board.

b. Such assignments are rotated in order to both minimize and equalize such service.

c. Individual teachers have choice in the duties to which they are assigned.

The bargaining team is willing to make such proposals in exchange for concessions on other priority issues. In general, the teachers are willing to make certain concessions on work load, provided that assignments are not made arbitrarily by the board and that any increases are kept to a minimum and are distributed equitably.

5. *Benefits.* The Teachers' Association wants the following:

5.1 Accumulated sick leave upon severance: In light of the fact that teachers in most surrounding communities receive payment for unused sick leave upon severance, the Newtown membership feels it too is entitled to such benefits. However, the bargaining team believes that various formulas can be devised that might be acceptable to the membership if concessions on other priority issues were forthcoming from the board. These might include a percentage of accumulated sick leave, payments keyed to years of service, reasons for severance, and so on. The bargaining team also sees possibilities of phasing such benefits in over several years.

5.2 Bereavement leave: According to a poll taken by the bargaining team, the membership is seeking up to five days of paid leave in the event of death of an immediate member of a teacher's family, including spouse, children, and parent. Also sought are the two days' bereavement leaves in the death of a spouse's parent. However, the results of the poll indicate that these preferences are somewhat flexible.

5.3 Civic duty leave: The membership has indicated that it wants full pay from the school district while serving on jury duty, without deductions for any pay received as a result of such duty. However, the bargaining team's information suggests that the membership could be induced to accept a formula in which any pay received for performing civic duty would be deducted from regular pay, so long as teachers incur no less of pay as a result of such service to the community. The bargaining team feels that such an agreement would only be appropriate if the board is willing to meet salary demands satisfactorily.

5.4 Childbirth leave: The membership wants 15 days for child-birth leave, for both female and male (spouse) employees. A number of teachers also want childbirth leave benefits to be independent of sick leave taken for other reasons. However, the bargaining team feels that trade-offs might be made on this issue in exchange for salary and/or reduction in staff concessions. The bargaining team feels it can develop proposals tying childbirth leave to specific work load issues so as to reduce the overall costs of such leaves to the system.

6. *Binding Arbitration of Grievances.*

6.1 The teachers are seeking binding arbitration of grievances, but are willing to temporarily accept advisory arbitration provided that teacher's interests are represented to their satisfaction. The bargaining team wants to use this as a lever for gaining concessions from the board on issues related to work and reduction in staff.

Mediator Position

As you can see from the "Background Information" regarding the development of this conflict, you have been appointed by the judge in an attempt to resolve the current impasse between the Hospital Board and Administration and the CCC. As a group, you will have to decide what actions you wish to take in order to carry out the judge's orders, and to facilitate some sort of resolution between the two sides.

The parties have asked for one final opportunity to meet together in an attempt to resolve their differences. If, however, they are unable to make substantial progress by the announced deadline, you have stated that you will enter the conflict and attempt to initiate actions that may help to facilitate a resolution of the remaining issues.

In developing your strategy and tactics as mediators, you ought to consider a number of factors related to the effective functioning of third parties:

1. You probably will want to remain *disinterested* with respect to preference for particular solutions, but *interested* with respect to moving the parties toward *some* solution. That is, your major goal is to get the parties to a settlement *they* can live with, not necessarily some solution *you* prefer.

2. You will probably want to control the *process* of conflict and negotiation more than the *substance*. In general, you ought to try to "regulate" the conflict in order to prevent eruptions of unproductive arguments, name calling, demonstrations, or other incidents that are likely to perpetuate the current polarization. Some techniques for controlling the conflict might include:

   a. Separating the parties into different rooms, including perhaps at some point separating chief negotiators from their teams.
   b. Meeting with each side separately to try and clarify their true demands, and to identify (if possible) their true "resistance points," strength of commitment to various issues, areas where concession making is possible, etc.
   c. Carrying offers, communications or other messages between separated teams.

d. Developing impressions among the mediation team as to (1) areas where teams could make easy concessions or trade concessions, (2) ways to "fractionate" issues that currently seem difficult to resolve, (3) identifying "settlement points" on issues where there currently seems to be no overlap in the bargaining range, and so forth. In most mediation, these impressions are not mandated on the parties, but are "suggested" or "introduced" to one or both sides as ways to help the parties make concessions they would not normally want to make.

e. Arranging public negotiations between the teams to discuss or review specific proposals, issues, and so on.

f. "Moderating" negotiations between the groups to control communication and keep it from escalating into unproductive argument, and so forth.

3. You will probably want to work up some brief description of your qualifications to be mediators, so as to communicate prestige, authority, and impartiality to both sides.

4. You may want to think about ways to help negotiators on one or both sides "unhook themselves" from commitments or positions they have already taken publicly, and feel they cannot back down from without losing face.

5. You may want to think about how much you want to use:

a. "Persuasion" of one or both sides to change their positions.

b. "Coercion" (e.g., public pressure) to move people.

c. "Transmission" of information about one team to the other team in order to identify resistance points or settlement areas.

d. "Reconstitution" of the original bargaining relationship in public view.

In summary, the science (and art) of mediation involves systematic efforts at defusing unproductive hostility, separating or combining the parties to maximally facilitate productive exchange of offers and communications, and helping the parties envision settlement ranges and settlements that they can agree to without looking weak or losing face. All of this should be accomplished in such a way that the parties feel comfortable in working with you, believe you have their best interests at heart, and come to feel more generally satisfied that they have arrived at an agreement.

Role for Sandy Solas

You feel like the low man on the totem pole in this group. A lot of your equipment is old and frequently breaks down. You do not think Fran has been particularly concerned about the inconvenience this has caused you. Further ever since you have graduated from college you have not been able to attend a professional meeting because of the freeze the company has had on travel of this sort. You feel that this has kept you from making the contacts you need to professionally develop. You hope that the recent upturn in the company's business will finally make some money available to go to professional meetings.

EXERCISE 8
Salary Negotiations

Employee Position 1B

You are fairly young for the responsibility that the Ace Company has given you as credit manager. You were elevated up from the ranks at a moment of crisis to take over this vital management function when the previous credit manager moved on, and you have handled the situation well. After a few months, the word "Acting" has been deleted from your title, and you had been confirmed in your new role.

When you were first promoted, you had asked for a raise, but your boss had countered: "Let's see how this works out. After all you're pretty young and inexperienced for this job. I don't have any doubts about your handling the job, but I'd like to wait. If you're able to handle it, we'll take care of you."

It had now been three years since that crisis. You've been confirmed as credit manager, and have gotten raises every year. But they were raises in the same order as when you were a toiler in the ranks. You still have not received the one big jump that would put you in the same financial class as the older, more experienced personnel, those who are holding down jobs no more responsible than yours.

In the past you had made a few tries to obtain the big jump, but you were still somewhat in awe of the position you held given your tender age. Your boss is a skilled negotiator, and each time you've gone in for a raise asking for big money, he has maneuvered the conversation around so that you're very thankful for the small raise and equally thankful he hasn't held this against you.

This was the status on the day of the annual office party. Traditionally, this was also the day the company distributed small bonus checks to every one on the payroll. These checks were never large—$100 was tops. But as they were passing out the checks, you realized there was none for you. After talking with another manager about this mistake, he said there was no mistake. There was a new policy this year, and only the "rank and file," not "management," would receive bonuses.

This has moved you to action. You currently make $22,000. A few days ago you had a "tentative" (in your eyes) salary discussion with your boss, and you agreed to a raise of $1,800. But now that there are no bonuses, you have decided to go in and renegotiate for the "big money." It's about time you got financially even with the rest of the managers at your level.

You're on your way to see your boss. You plan on withdrawing your request for $1,800 and ask for $6,000. This will be that big jump you have been after for three years, and will put you even with other managers who earn $5,000–$7,000 a year more than you. You are going to be tough this time, and not let him wear you down.

Take a few minutes to review these facts and then devise a strategy to approach your boss for this raise.

EXERCISE 4
Buyer/Seller Negotiation

Instructions to Buyer

You are about to engage in a bidding game. In this game, you will be playing with imaginary money. Your objective in this game is to win as much money for yourself as you can. At the end of the game, your winnings will be compared to all of the other buyers in the room.

You have been paired with another person, playing the role of seller. In this game, you and your partner will engage in a series of transactions by means of bids. Imagine that you and s(he) are exchanging some commodity. You have been selected (at random) to act as the buyer of this commodity; your opponent will act as the seller. You must deal *only* with the opponent to whom you are assigned, s(he) must deal only with you.

You will be furnished with a table showing the various levels of profit you can attain. Prices are listed on the left-hand side of the table, and quantities of purchase are listed across the top. The figures in the body of the table represent the profit you will receive, depending on the price and quantity selected. For example, at a price of 7 and a quantity of 4, your profit is $0.51 or 51 cents.

The seller will start the process by offering a price. S(he) may select any one of the prices on the left-hand side of the table. S(he) will then announce the price to you verbally. You will then consult your table and respond with a quantity—any one of the quantities listed across the top of the table. In other words, the seller chooses the price line, and the buyer chooses the quantity column. The box where these two intersect represents *your* profit for this transaction. You know how much you made from that transaction; however, you do not know whether your opponent's payoff table is the same, and whether s(he) made more or less. Similarly, the opponent knows his/hers own profit, but not yours. You should record the price, quantity, and your payoff on the blank record sheet.

The process is repeated for 20 trials. The seller may select the same price each time, or may vary; similarly, you may select the same quantity each time, or may vary. You will proceed until you have each recorded 20 transactions. Remember, your overall objective is to maximize the amount of imaginary money that you earn over the 20 trials.

Profit Table for Buyer

Price	0	1	2	3	4	5	6	7	8	9	10	11	12	13	14	15	16	17	18
																			Quantity
1	0.00	0.28	0.45	0.60	0.75	0.88	1.01	1.12	1.23	1.32	1.41	1.48	1.55	1.60	1.65	1.68	1.71	1.72	1.73
2	0.00	0.28	0.43	0.58	0.71	0.84	0.95	1.06	1.15	1.24	1.31	1.38	1.43	1.48	1.51	1.54	1.55	1.56	1.55
3	0.00	0.26	0.41	0.54	0.67	0.78	0.89	0.98	1.07	1.14	1.21	1.26	1.31	1.34	1.37	1.38	1.39	1.38	1.37
4	0.00	0.26	0.39	0.52	0.63	0.74	0.83	0.92	0.99	1.06	1.11	1.16	1.19	1.22	1.23	1.24	1.23	1.22	1.19
5	0.00	0.24	0.37	0.48	0.59	0.68	0.77	0.84	0.91	0.96	1.01	1.04	1.07	1.08	1.09	1.08	1.07	1.04	1.01
6	0.00	0.24	0.35	0.46	0.55	0.64	0.71	0.78	0.83	0.88	0.91	0.94	0.95	0.96	0.95	0.94	0.91	0.88	0.83
7	0.00	0.22	0.33	0.42	0.51	0.58	0.65	0.70	0.75	0.78	0.81	0.82	0.83	0.82	0.81	0.78	0.75	0.70	0.65
8	0.00	0.22	0.31	0.40	0.47	0.54	0.59	0.64	0.67	0.70	0.71	0.72	0.71	0.70	0.67	0.64	0.59	0.54	0.47
9	0.00	0.20	0.29	0.36	0.43	0.48	0.53	0.56	0.59	0.60	0.61	0.60	0.59	0.56	0.53	0.48	0.43	0.36	0.29
10	0.00	0.20	0.27	0.34	0.39	0.44	0.47	0.50	0.51	0.52	0.51	0.50	0.47	0.44	0.39	0.34	0.27	0.20	0.11
11	0.00	0.18	0.25	0.30	0.35	0.38	0.41	0.42	0.43	0.42	0.41	0.38	0.35	0.30	0.25	0.18	0.11	0.02	-0.07
12	0.00	0.18	0.23	0.28	0.31	0.34	0.35	0.36	0.35	0.34	0.31	0.28	0.23	0.18	0.11	0.04	-0.05	-0.14	-0.25
13	0.00	0.16	0.21	0.24	0.27	0.28	0.29	0.28	0.27	0.24	0.21	0.16	0.11	0.04	-0.03	-0.12	-0.21	-0.32	-0.43
14	0.00	0.16	0.19	0.22	0.23	0.24	0.23	0.22	0.19	0.16	0.11	0.06	-0.01	-0.08	-0.17	-0.26	-0.37	-0.48	-0.61
15	0.00	0.14	0.17	0.18	0.19	0.18	0.17	0.14	0.11	0.06	0.01	-0.06	-0.13	-0.22	-0.31	-0.42	-0.53	-0.66	-0.79
16	0.00	0.14	0.15	0.16	0.15	0.14	0.11	0.08	0.03	-0.02	-0.09	-0.16	-0.25	-0.34	-0.45	-0.56	-0.69	-0.82	-0.97

This procedure is to be conducted as quietly as possible. There should be *no verbal exchanges between you other than the quoting of prices and quantities.* You will have a chance to discuss the process after it is completed.

Review these rules again to make sure you understand what you are to do. When everyone has read the rules, there will be an opportunity to ask questions. There will be two practice trials before the bidding begins.

Capital Mortgage Insurance Corporation (B)

By late afternoon on May 21, 1979, Frank Randall and Jim Dolan had finished putting together Capital Mortgage Insurance Corporation's formal offer to purchase all the outstanding stock of Corporate Transfer Services, Inc. The offer they settled on was virtually identical to the draft that Jim Dolan had already prepared, with one significant addition: an offer to retain Elliott Burr as a consultant to help build a strong relationship between the relocation company and MetroNet.

Randall considered the offer to keep Burr actively involved as a key ingredient in the total package. As he told Jim Dolan: "Burr fathered this company, and now he's putting it up for adoption. I want to give him every assurance that we'll be an adequate foster parent. Besides, he can be a key link to MetroNet for us." The consulting arrangement would also be a way to provide Burr with some extra income beyond what he stood to make by selling his stock.

In addition to the purchase offer letter, Randall also prepared a letter formally stating CMI's interest in acquiring CTS. The letter (see Exhibit 1) opened by expressing Randall's gratitude to the four stockholders for their help and cooperation during the past several months. Randall planned to distribute this letter to the four men before discussing the formal purchase offer.

Once the purchase offer details were settled, Randall telephoned Elliott Burr again to arrange the details of their meeting. At Randall's suggestion it was agreed that he and Dolan would fly to Chicago on the morning of May 24 and meet with the CTS stockholders at the Burr and Lehman Real Estate office. Again, however, Randall was intentionally vague about his agenda for the meeting.

THE MAY 24 MEETING

When Randall and Dolan arrived in Chicago, they found only Elliott Burr, William Lehman, and Tom Winder in attendance. Burr explained that

Exhibit 1

Board of Directors and Stockholders
Corporate Transfer Services
Chicago, IL

May 24, 1979

Gentlemen:

The purpose of this letter is to express our sincere appreciation for the help and cooperation you and your staff have provided over the past several months to enable us to understand the employee relocation service business. You have been most liberal with your time and candid in the sharing of your knowledge of the industry.

As you know, we have conducted an extensive study of the employee relocation service industry and we realize there is still much for us to learn. During our analysis, we have gained a high regard for CTS and the manner in which you have conducted your business.

Capital Mortgage Insurance Corporation would like to acquire the ownership of Corporate Transfer Services. We will make every effort to do so on a mutually fair and equitable basis. We enter these negotiations with you fully aware of your personal feelings as individuals who have created and nurtured CTS for several years.

Upon acquiring CTS, I want to assure you that we are committed to building and expanding the operations on a nationwide basis that will continue the high business standards you have established.

Sincerely,

Franklin T. Randall
President

Michael Kupchak, the fourth stockholder, was tied up in a meeting in Gary, Indiana, and would not be able to get back in time.

The five men sat down at a conference table in a private room in the back of the Burr and Lehman Real Estate office. Burr sat on one side of the table, flanked by Winder and Lehman. Randall and Dolan settled into the seats directly opposite. Randall opened the meeting with a brief but warm statement of thanks for all the help the CTS group had provided. He then distributed his formal letter of intent and expressed his continuing interest in developing a formal relationship with Corporate Transfer Services. Randall concluded:

We appreciate the fact that you have created this company out of nothing, and that you care a great deal about its future. We understand those feelings, and we respect them. We are definitely interested in acquiring you, but we want to do so only on terms that will satisfy your concerns about the future of Corporate Transfer Services.

Elliott Burr then replied, "What is your offer?" Randall responded:

We find it exceedingly difficult to put a price on your company. Most acquisitions are completed on the basis of a projected earnings stream; you don't have one. Most acquisitions involve a careful analysis of a company's management team; you have only one man. You have only very small exposure to the MetroNet brokers, and your business is basically self-liquidating with no residual value. But we do want to buy you on the basis of your goodwill and reputation.

Burr: What is your offer?
Randall: We will pay you $400,000 above your audited net worth.
Burr: We are very disappointed in that offer price.
Randall: What did you have in mind?
Burr: We wanted $5 million.

Negotiator Baker

	Issues		
Settlement Point	Issue I	Issue II	Issue III
A	80	30	50
B	70	28	47
C	60	26	43
D	50	26	37
E	40	20	33
F	30	18	27
G	25	10	25
H	20	10	23
I	19	9	20
J	19	7	18
K	18	7	17
L	17	5	17
M	17	5	16
N	16	3	15
O	15	3	15
P	14	2	14
Q	14	1	13
R	13	0	13
S	13	0	12
T	12	0	12

Note: Your maximum settlement = 80 + 30 + 50 = 160
Your minimum settlement = 12 + 0 + 12 = 24 (assuming all issues settled).

Role for Peter O'Malley
Vice President, Manufacturing

Bass talked to you before he left to enter the hospital. As usual, he did not want to get himself involved in working out this problem, yet he did want results—and he wanted them quickly. "I want the new JAC 36 soon, Pete, and the more up-to-date it is, the better. Above all, I want it to sell." You agreed to do everything you could to get the JAC 36 costs into line and begin production as soon as possible.

You have been vice president of manufacturing for a little over a year, having previously been superintendent of the major Jordan manufacturing plant. You are annoyed with Bass's decision to go ahead with a redesign of the JAC 36. Adding the new scanning features is turning out to be trickier than it had first seemed, and adding the oscilloscope is going to require considerable reworking of several production positions, adding some extra tests and retraining several workers. Production costs are always hard to estimate when a lot of new features have to be handled.

About a month ago, you had your first performance review with Bass since becoming VP of manufacturing. One big negative factor in your review was cost overruns in manufacturing new products. With the cost of labor and materials skyrocketing these days, you might as well use a dart board to make estimates. In estimating costs on the JAC 36, you've decided it is better to be safe than sorry; hence you have padded your estimates by 5–10 percent to give yourself some margin for error. This way, if you keep costs down you will really look good; on the other hand, if the likely (but unforeseeable) problems occur, you will be covered. At least Bass had decided to not go for the portable unit using the microchips; that would have made costs really difficult to estimate.

John Snyder, senior engineer, is probably going to be the biggest problem in the upcoming meeting. He has a frustrating way of thinking that he knows more about your business than you do and will continually push you to defend your costs. Your last cost estimate would set the selling price at

$20,000. If really pressured, you probably could reduce the cost estimate but at the expense of reducing your own cushion in the budget. You would be willing to do this only as a last resort. The higher the selling price you get the group to agree to, the more security you have against unanticipated cost overruns.

Board of Education's Position

You, along with the other members of your team, constitute the whole of the Newtown Board of Education. You are to select one or more of your members to serve as chief negotiator(s) representing your side in contract negotiations with the Newtown Teachers' Association. Members of your team not designated as chief negotiator(s) may function in any capacity that the team decides upon.

As indicated in your "Background Information" sheet, the previous contract with the Teachers' Association has expired. It is now the beginning of the school year and, as a result of various pressures, the teachers have agreed to return to work on a day-to-day basis, with the reservation that they may call a strike at any time so long as the contract is not finalized. Your responsibility as far as the board is to conclude an agreement with the Teachers' Association to avert a strike. However, the teachers are not fully informed of just how important it is to you to conclude an agreement. In order to conclude an agreement (in light of the budget situation described in the Background Information sheet), you feel that you have to minimize concessions, reduce staff, obtain an increase in teachers' work load, and retain your prerogatives to make final decisions wherever possible. The board has been informed privately that if it cannot succeed in preventing a strike and finalizing a contract at minimal cost, the community may withdraw its support of the board and ask for your resignation. All members of the board, however, wish to retain their positions on it. Also, the board has discretionary power to transfer funds among budgetary categories if the need arises.

The issues that remain unsettled fall into six general categories:

1. Reduction in staff.
2. Work load.
3. Evaluation of teachers.
4. Salary.
5. Binding arbitration of grievances.
6. Benefits.

These general categories are ranked in order of importance to the board. The board's position on specific issues within these categories is spelled out below. State law requires that all issues in dispute are negotiable.

1. *Reduction in Staff.* The board wants the following:

   1.1 Systemwide reduction in staff as deemed necessary by the board. The board wishes to retain as much control as possible over layoffs, but may provide opportunities for the Teacher's Association to make informal recommendations of various kinds.

   1.2 Final decisions about layoffs of individual teachers, as well as quotas within schools and/or grade levels, should remain with the board. The board wishes to retain as much control as possible, but may offer mechanisms enabling the Teacher's Association to voice its views.

   1.3 Layoffs to become effective 20 working days after contract is finalized. The board wishes to expedite layoffs as quickly as possible, but has some room to negotiate on this issue.

   1.4 Notification of layoff to affected teachers not more than 10 working days prior to layoff date. The board wishes to minimize notification period. However, the board feels that there is some room to negotiate on this issue.

   1.5 Members of the board are generally resistant to hearing grievances from individual teachers who have been laid off. However, the board is willing to accept an informal review procedure so long as it minimizes time investment and permits retention of final discretionary power by the board.

   1.6 Recall: The board is willing to accept a recall list but wishes to limit formal eligibility to one year from the date of layoff. The board also wishes to retain full discretion in recalling individual teachers, particularly those whose one-year recall period has expired, if it wishes to do so.

   1.7 Notification and acceptance of recall: The board wants written response within 72 hours of notification of recall in order to expedite recall. Again, the board wants to minimize its efforts and obtain clear indication of recall acceptances as quickly as possible. However, there is some room to negotiate within the context of this principle.

   In general, the board wishes to reduce teaching staff in order to absorb part of the overall budget decrease. It also hopes to partially cover increased costs that would result from finalization of the contract presently being negotiated through such layoffs.

2. *Work Load.* The board wants the following:

2.1 Pupil/teacher ratio: The board wants an increase in the systemwide ratio from its current level of 32, to approximately 35. Although there is some flexibility on this issue, the board feels it important for budgetary reasons to come as close to 35 as possible.

2.2 Workday: The board wants an increase in the length of the present workday from seven hours, five minutes, to a full eight hours. The shorter workday was agreed to in better times when the budget was able to tolerate it. Now, the board feels that it wants the time "returned."

2.3 "Prep" time: The board wants elimination of the 50-minute prep time period given to each teacher, each workday. (One period per day.) Same reasons as in 2.2.

2.4 "Duty-free" time: The board wants elimination of duty-free time given to each teacher, each workday. This amounts to 25 minutes per day, in addition to a 25-minute lunch period. Same reasons as in 2.2.

2.5 Emergency assignments and general obligations: The board wants discretionary power to assign teachers to activities during the 75 minutes gained from 2.3 and 2.4 above. These activities include: emergency substitute fill-in; bus duty; hall duty; disciplinary duty and committee service. Also, the board wants to assign teachers to monitor and chaperone after-school athletic and social activities.

In general, the board wishes to increase teachers' work load so as to regain coverage lost by layoffs and budget cuts while at the same time minimizing costs.

3. *Evaluation of Teachers.* The board wants to hire its own consultant to develop a systematic evaluation procedure. It wishes to use these evaluations as aids in each of the following areas:

    a. Determination of pay increases.
    b. Assignment of teachers to schools and classes.
    c. Granting of tenure.
    d. Removal of teachers.

3.1 The board feels that evaluation is a legitimate management activity and that the Teachers' Association should provide only advisory assistance when asked in the design and execution of the evaluations.

3.2 The board does not want these evaluations to be freely available to teachers due to the confidential nature of the material included and the notes likely to be made by supervisors. Instead, the board is willing to provide limited access through a procedure in which a teacher's supervisor, principal, or assistant principal, outlines the contents to individual teachers. Here, the board wishes to retain discretion as to information revealed to individual teachers.

3.3 The board is seeking "unannounced visitations" into classrooms for purposes of conducting observations as a part of the evaluation procedure. The board wishes to be unrestricted in its freedom to conduct these observations, but is prepared to accept scheduled visitations.

4. *Salary*. The board wants the following:

4.1 Retroactivity: No retroactivity of salary increases prior to date of contract finalization. However, if necessary, the board feels it can provide a nominal percentage of full retroactivity but it would prefer not to do so.

4.2 Cost-of-living increase: The board feels that it can only provide a percentage of the previous years' increase in cost of living, as determined by official government figures. However this limit may be approached in many ways, and the board is willing to entertain suggestions.

4.3 Across-the-board increases in salary schedule: The board feels that it cannot provide such increases unless budgetary resources can be obtained through sacrifices made by the Teacher's Association on other issues in the present negotiation.

5. *Binding Arbitration of Grievances.*

5.1 The board is hesitant to consent to a binding arbitration procedure as a result of certain groups in the community who are adamantly opposed to erosion of management prerogatives. The board is willing to agree to some form of advisory arbitration.

6. *Benefits*. During this time of severe budgetary curtailment the board wants to minimize expenditures for benefits. This includes their direct costs, as well as costs for administering such programs that would be incurred by the school system.

6.1 Accumulated sick leave upon severance: The board wishes to minimize such expenditures.

6.2 Bereavement leave: The board is willing to go up to two days' bereavement leave in the case of the death of a member of the teacher's immediate family (spouse or children).

6.3 Civic duty leave: The board is willing to grant salary for jury duty only. The board also wishes to deduct the amount received for jury duty from a teacher's regular daily rate of pay.

6.4 Childbirth leave: The board is seeking the following limits on childbirth leave: up to 10 days' leave for female employees; not more than 5 days' leave for male employees (spouse). In addition, the board prefers that childbirth leave be included in teachers' total sick-leave benefits.

Role for Bower, Plant Manager of the Phillips Plant

The quality problem on the modules coming from the Crawley plant has been the most frustrating problem you have had for some time. Not only has the expense of rework and repairs, overtime, and additional inspections increased the cost of operation of your plant but complaints from customers and occasionally failing to meet production schedules have gotten you a lot of unfavorable attention from higher management. What is particularly frustrating is the fact that difficulty comes from a single area and also that there is so little you can do directly about the matter.

You would like the additional expenses resulting from these problems to be transferred to the Crawley plant. J. Leavitt, manager at the Crawley plant has been very stubborn about this matter and has refused to accept any of the costs. Leavitt has been working on the problem and quality has improved somewhat, but you have doubts that it will ever be of a desired level for all modules you receive from his plant. Leavitt has made the argument to you that expenses incurred because of faulty modules should be borne as a regular business expense the way they are for all products purchased outside. While it is true that the company has repaired poor quality items from vendors this is usually done to avoid interrupting production by sending them back to the supplier. You do not know why the company does not charge the supplier for these costs, but assume that it is because it is difficult to write into a purchasing agreement. In any event when the materials received from an outside supplier do occasionally get bad enough a shipment will be rejected and sent back.

In addition you do not think it is to the company's benefit to accept these costs on items made in its own plants. If the supplying plant had to absorb the costs pressure would be created within that plant to reduce, if not eliminate, these expenses.

Because the company does not have this practice, however, you are not sure you can get the other plant to accept all repair expenses for all poor quality modules. You are determined, however, that they will have to absorb the expenses on the cost of repairing faulty items of the 12 types of modules where quality has been found to be below the 95 percent level. You feel strongly that the plant manager of the Crawley plant is taking an inaccurate and unfair interpretation of the way 95 percent level of quality is to be applied.

You are also troubled by the delays in production (often requiring overtime) when large numbers of rejects occur on the 12 types of modules often found with poor quality. You are not too optimistic about getting the Crawley plant manager to accept overtime costs for production, but you are going to insist that either they accept the faulty parts back to replace or repair them quickly or that they pay you to put repairmen to work on them, even if overtime is necessary.

Unfortunately, while this dispute has gone on modules have been rejected in incoming inspection at a rate of about $8,000 a week. You have refused to work on these arguing that they should be handled by the Crawley plant. They have refused to accept any responsibility for them. Before long this will come to the attention of the vice president of manufacturing and you feel quite sure that both you and the Crawley plant manager will be called on the carpet for not having solved this problem.

You have set up a meeting with the Crawley plant manager at his plant for one last effort to try to settle this matter.

Employer Position 2A

You are the financial manager of the Western Division of the Modern Finance Agency. This company is made up of several regional divisions, each structured in a similar way. Your division has a separate financial analysis staff group. One of your analysts has been with the Western Division since his graduation three years ago. This particular analyst has in the past year done some exceptional work. The projects have been well thought out, and have been implemented without any major problems. This employee has had normal raises in the past years, and the one last year was from $17,500 to $18,500, a raise determined by last year's salary negotiation between yourself and the employee. You believe that this raise reflects the increased worth of the employee toward the Western Division.

The work of this employee has been so good that on one occasion you showed his project to Joe Short, the financial manager of the Central Division. Short was quite impressed with the work, and has used the plan in his own division. He has kidded you recently about stealing this analyst away from Western for his own staff. You wonder if there is anything serious behind this talk. You would hate to lose this employee, as your efforts in this employee's development have created an outstanding asset which is now paying off in a substantially larger return than expected.

You are a fairly hard negotiator and have given salary increases of about $1,200 to other analysts in the division. You plan on giving more to this outstanding analyst, but still not the world. Yet you don't want to lose the analyst to the Central Division and let Short get all the future benefits. A large raise to keep your star would be in order, but only as a last resort.

Take a few minutes to review these facts and devise a strategy for managing the discussion with your analyst about a pay raise.

Role for Kenneth Lawson
Director of Research and Development

Bass talked to you before he entered the hospital. As usual, he did not want to get involved with the problem, yet he did want results—and quickly. "I want the JAC 36 as soon as possible, Ken. The more up-to-date it is, the better. Above all, I want it to sell." You have agreed to do everything you could to get the new model into production and at a reasonable price.

You and Norm, along with John Snyder, started this company about 25 years ago to manufacture the first model of the JAC 36. You pride yourself on running a tight R&D operation, one that continues to work at the frontier of scientific knowledge and one that makes continual contributions to Jordan's products. You are annoyed with Bass's decision to go ahead with a simple redesign of the old JAC 36. You believe the real future of the industry is with the microcircuitry. Redesigning the old machine is a waste of your department's time and energy. Moreover, Joe Little continues to be a pain. He is the one who pushed Bass to develop the simple redesign and said that the portable model was of secondary importance. *Now* he says that the portable JAC 36 is what he needs to make a really big splash in sales. You can understand that the sales picture changes, but you do wish Little would make up his mind on what he really needs.

Fortunately, your department's reputation for quality and innovation is still on a solid base. On the way into your office today you stopped in to see Ted Slocum, your electronic designer, and he told you that his team has solved two of the major technical snags that have stymied development of the portable JAC 36. There is a good chance that all the bugs will be worked out in four or five weeks. With some cooperation from John Snyder, a portable design should be feasible in the very near future.

Consequently, you are very reluctant to devote any more of your department's time to redesigning the old JAC 36 by adding a few scanning features. It has taken too many man-hours already, and most of your people are anxious to get on with developing the new microcircuitry technology. As a result, you have decided to do the following things at the meeting:

1. Tell Joe Little and the others that you are close to a breakthrough in the design of the portable JAC 36.
2. Persuade stubborn John Snyder that the portable model is the best alternative and that he should begin working on his part of the project.
3. Dissuade the others from continuing with the simple addition of scanning features to the JAC 36 so that your department's time and energy can be focused on the development of a really new product. You have no real information on the price of either design, but that does not matter since all your costs are covered by the general R&D budget.

Role for Chris Manos

You have been feeling a strong need to get to some professional meetings. Through no fault of your own you missed attending meetings for several years before the freeze on travel was imposed. For two years there were crash projects that kept you tied to the plant. The year before that you had to testify at a patent suit the company was pressing. The year before that your daughter had gotten married. An unplanned chain of events, but one that has kept you from building new professional contacts or even maintaining old ones. As a result you feel you are in serious danger of slipping professionally and getting stale.

Confidential Memorandum—
Tamarack Town Council

You represent members of the Town Council of Tamarack, Minnesota. Among you, there is the mayor of Tamarack, the chairman of the Town Council, and several councilmen. Two councilmen who work for Twin Lakes have excused themselves from the discussions because of conflict of interest; the rest of you are local businesspeople. Please assign roles to individuals in your group before you begin the role-play.

The problems of air and water pollution that were described in the "Background Information" have existed for a long time. The Town Council has met periodically with the officials of the Twin Lakes Mining Company to discuss these problems. While the discussions have been friendly, and some small cleanup measures have been taken, the meetings have usually ended with the major issues unresolved. The Twin Lakes representatives have always maintained that they did not have the economic resources to spend that much money on cleanup activities. Now the federal and state agencies have mandated a cleanup. While you are pleased that the company people are under some pressure to make some changes, you certainly do not want to see the company close its operations. To do so would be economic disaster for the town of Tamarack. Within the Town Council, you have taken the following positions on the three major issues:

1. Water Quality. Growth of the other small industries in town and the summer home development will require a new water supply in several years. Beaver Brook is the most logical choice for a variety of reasons, but construction of a water filtration plant is essential to using this water source.

You have been in touch with the civil engineering department of the nearby university. They have told you about the most recent technology in filtration plants, and assured you that a plant could remove all impurities and make the water potable. In addition, they have been experimenting with several techniques for recovering the fine iron particles that now go over the spillway from the recovery ponds. Additional revenue from the sale of this recovered iron (and other minerals) could amount to $8,500 annually.

The town has a very small tax base and cannot possibly afford to build the filtration plant on its own. It has been suggested, however, that the town might float a 25-year bond issue to cover the cost of improvements, with payment of interest and repayment of principal to be made by the company. The proposal would need approval by the state legislature, which the town is not sure of getting. If the legislature did approve, the state would require the company to guarantee repayment of the bond issue. The Twin Lakes Company has requested that the town share in 50 percent of the interest payments on the bonds. Given current interest rates, total payments will be $500,000 annually (not including repayment of principal).

2. *Road Paving.* You have been working with the state, and with several paving companies, on the cost of paving on the town roads. Paving of the town-owned roads will cost $600,000 with yearly maintenance of $75,000; you have no concern for how the company takes care of the roads that are not town-owned. As you have discussed this among yourselves, you have determined that if you can get the company to pay for all or a large part of the capital cost of paving, you will assume complete responsibility for routine maintenance in the future.

3. *Taxation of Company Land.* You have agreed to listen to several proposals that may be brought forth by the company for tax relief or tax abatement of land owned by the company, or right-of-ways used for moving ore. Naturally, you wish to maintain the tax package as it is, but you are willing to trade this off for major concessions on the first two issues. However, you have decided that any *major* program of tax relief (short term or long term) will require approval by public ballot of the town's citizens. You are afraid of any decision that will result in losing significant tax revenue without public support of the position.

Review these positions and develop a plan of action for your team.

EXERCISE 4
Buyer/Seller Negotiation

Instructions to Seller

You are about to engage in a bidding game. In this game, you will be playing with imaginary money. Your objective in this game is to win as much money for yourself as you can. At the end of the game, your winnings will be compared to all of the other sellers in the room.

You have been paired with another person, playing the role of buyer. In this game, you and your partner will engage in a series of transactions by means of bids. Imagine that you and s(he) are exchanging some commodity. You have been selected (at random) to act as the seller of this commodity; your opponent will act as the buyer. You must deal *only* with the opponent to whom you are assigned, s(he) must deal only with you.

You will be furnished with a table showing the various levels of profit you can attain. Prices are listed on the left-hand side of the table, and quantities of purchase are listed across the top. The figures in the body of the table represent the profit you will receive, depending on the price and quantity selected. For example, at a price of 7 and a quantity of 4, your profit is $0.75 or 75 cents.

The seller (you) will start the process by offering a price. You may select any one of the prices on the left-hand side of the table. You will then announce the price to the buyer verbally. The buyer will then consult his/her table and respond with a quantity—any one of the quantities listed across the top of the table. In other words, the seller chooses the price line, and the buyer chooses the quantity column. The box where these two intersect represents *your* profit for this transaction. You know how much you made from that transaction; however, you do not know whether your opponent's payoff table is the same, and whether s(he) made more or less. Similarly, the opponent knows his/her own profit, but not yours. You should record the price, quantity, and your payoff on the blank record sheet.

The process is repeated for 20 trials. The seller may select the same price each time, or may vary; similarly, the buyer may select the same quantity each time, or may vary. You will proceed until you have each recorded 20 transactions. Remember, your overall objective is to maximize the amount of imaginary money that you earn over the 20 trials.

Profit Table for Seller

Price		Quantity																	
	0	1	2	3	4	5	6	7	8	9	10	11	12	13	14	15	16	17	18
1	0.00	0.22	0.33	0.42	0.51	0.58	0.65	0.70	0.75	0.78	0.81	0.82	0.83	0.82	0.81	0.78	0.75	0.70	0.65
2	0.00	0.24	0.35	0.46	0.55	0.64	0.71	0.78	0.83	0.88	0.91	0.94	0.95	0.96	0.95	0.94	0.91	0.88	0.83
3	0.00	0.24	0.37	0.48	0.59	0.68	0.77	0.84	0.91	0.96	1.01	1.04	1.07	1.08	1.09	1.08	1.07	1.04	1.01
4	0.00	0.26	0.39	0.52	0.63	0.74	0.83	0.92	0.99	1.06	1.11	1.16	1.19	1.22	1.23	1.24	1.23	1.22	1.19
5	0.00	0.26	0.41	0.54	0.67	0.78	0.89	0.98	1.07	1.14	1.21	1.26	1.31	1.34	1.37	1.38	1.39	1.38	1.37
6	0.00	0.28	0.43	0.58	0.71	0.84	0.95	1.06	1.15	1.24	1.31	1.38	1.43	1.48	1.51	1.54	1.55	1.56	1.55
7	0.00	0.28	0.45	0.60	0.75	0.88	1.01	1.12	1.23	1.32	1.41	1.48	1.55	1.60	1.65	1.68	1.71	1.72	1.73
8	0.00	0.30	0.47	0.64	0.79	0.94	1.07	1.20	1.31	1.42	1.51	1.60	1.67	1.74	1.79	1.84	1.87	1.90	1.91
9	0.00	0.30	0.49	0.66	0.83	0.98	1.13	1.26	1.39	1.50	1.61	1.70	1.79	1.86	1.93	1.98	2.03	2.06	2.09
10	0.00	0.32	0.51	0.70	0.87	1.04	1.19	1.34	1.47	1.60	1.71	1.82	1.91	2.00	2.07	2.14	2.19	2.24	2.27
11	0.00	0.32	0.53	0.72	0.91	1.08	1.25	1.40	1.55	1.68	1.81	1.92	2.03	2.12	2.21	2.28	2.35	2.40	2.45
12	0.00	0.34	0.55	0.76	0.95	1.14	1.31	1.48	1.63	1.78	1.91	2.04	2.15	2.26	2.35	2.44	2.51	2.58	2.63
13	0.00	0.34	0.57	0.78	0.99	1.18	1.37	1.54	1.71	1.86	2.01	2.14	2.27	2.38	2.49	2.58	2.67	2.74	2.81
14	0.00	0.36	0.59	0.82	1.03	1.24	1.43	1.62	1.79	1.96	2.11	2.26	2.39	2.52	2.63	2.74	2.83	2.92	2.99
15	0.00	0.36	0.61	0.84	1.07	1.28	1.49	1.68	1.87	2.04	2.21	2.36	2.51	2.64	2.77	2.88	2.99	3.08	3.17
16	0.00	0.38	0.63	0.88	1.11	1.34	1.55	1.76	1.95	2.14	2.31	2.48	2.63	2.78	2.91	3.04	3.15	3.26	3.35

This procedure is to be conducted as quietly as possible. There should be *no verbal exchanges between you other than the quoting of prices and quantities.* You will have a chance to discuss the process after it is complete.

Review these rules again to make sure you understand what you are to do. When everyone has read the rules, there will be an opportunity to ask questions. There will also be two practice trials before the bidding begins.

Capital Mortgage Insurance Corporation (D)

Frank Randall paused only briefly before saying, "That's still way too high."

Burr: But we control MetroNet.

Randall: No you don't; you have no control there—no ability to guarantee their performance.

Burr: You don't understand . . .

Randall: No, *you* don't understand. You can't deliver MetroNet. In fact, I'll have to live down your poor performance with MetroNet.

Dolan: Just how much time have you spent working with MetroNet?

Winder: Well, I spoke at half a dozen regional seminars in 1976. I made up a bunch of slides, passed out brochures, and answered a lot of questions. That was a lot of work.

Dolan: How much of that effort is still valid? Has it generated much business?

Winder: Well, I really don't know . . . I guess we probably haven't grown as fast as we should have to satisfy MetroNet . . .

Burr interrupted, cutting Winder off:

We're still awfully far apart. Can we work out a deal giving us some now and something more in the future?

Dolan: If you want to take on some future risks, we'll pay you net worth now and a fixed dollar payout in the future, based on the ROE we can get. The fact is, the future performance of this company will depend a lot more on the capital we're going to put in than it will on what it's worth today.

Burr: That's not acceptable. But I'm still certain we can work something out. You have a John F. Kennedy stadium in Philadelphia, don't you? I remember he used to say that people of goodwill can always get things done.

Randall: You've got my geography misplaced. I'm originally from Missouri; you've got to show me. Besides, I preferred Harry Truman to J.F.K. I especially like one of his sayings: "If you can't stand the heat, get out of the kitchen."

Look, why don't you all get together and discuss our offer in more detail. Maybe you can quantify your performance with MetroNet, and sign a written warranty or pledge to produce the business.

Meanwhile, let's keep the lines of communication open. Come on, Jim, let's get back to the hotel. I want to get some dinner.

Hospital Board and Administration Role Description

The director, his aides, and some members of the board of trustees are now meeting in a hospital lecture room to decide what to do next. From what the judge said, or, at least, the way you interpret it, he expects you to settle the dispute soon, in joint discussion with the CCC.

From the show of community support outside the hospital, it looks like the CCC could stay here forever. And while you can't make a showing that the occupation is injurious to patient life, it has become hard to run the hospital while they're in there. Besides, such a spectacle is eroding your authority. You have got to settle things fast if you're going to have any authority and respect left.

You believe you simply cannot turn that site over to the uses the community wants. Your own uses are just too important. Besides, you've got specific grants and fund-raising drives lined up.

You have to figure out how to get the CCC out of there and buy some time. One possible strategy, if you can't pressure them out, might be to offer them two or three seats on the board (demand number one), and talk them into dealing with all other issues at the board level. With bimonthly meetings, difficulties in getting quorums, and so on, you could keep them talking for months—and settle the controversy in a rational, responsible way.

On the other demands, you just don't know where the money is going to come from. You could increase the efficiency of outpatient services if you could get community patients to keep their appointments, but you're not even sure how to do that.

As part of the strategy you develop for the negotiations, you should consider carefully the roles of the persons on your negotiating team and how they will be portrayed. Some suggested administration representative include:

Hospital administrator

Representative(s) of the board of trustees

Representative(s) of the hospital's Medical Executive Committee
Someone from outpatient services
Hospital attorney
Community relations person

Some of the factors you should consider during your strategizing include:

1. The position of the administration on each of the issues.
2. An assessment of the sanctions available to the administration.
3. Possible restrictions on those sanctions.
4. An assessment of the CCC's power.
5. The possible impacts of internal relationships on the administration (i.e., doctors, nurses, trustees, and so on).
6. Some estimate of the maximum concessions the hospital might be willing to make.

At the outset, please designate one of your team to take notes of your deliberations, conclusions and assumptions for discussion and comparison purposes after the exercise is completed.

These instructions and information are given only to the hospital board and administration.

Role for John Snyder
Senior Engineer

Bass talked to you before he left for the hospital. As usual, he did not want to get involved in the present problem. Yet he wanted results, and he wanted them quickly. "I want the new model of the JAC 36, John, and I want it soon. Above all, I want it to sell." You agreed to do everything you could to get the new model of the JAC 36 into production at a reasonable price.

You and Norm started this company almost 25 years ago. In the years you've worked together, Norm has always shown confidence in your problem-solving ability. It does anger you that some people who joined the company after you did now have better jobs. When the company was small, you (along with everyone else) did a fair amount of selling, and for a long time, you were effectively in charge of production.

You finally worked out all the bugs in the redesign of the JAC 36. It took a while to add features and yet not add to the size or cost of the unit. Of course, they are really going to have to be on their toes in purchasing and in the factory if the costs are going to come in on target. Thank God they decided to not go ahead with the portable unit! Some people seem to think that the only problem with a portable unit is using a microprocessor; but there is a great deal involved with mounting meters and counters to make them shockproof, making the unit dust and moisture tight, and other refinements not obvious to the nonprofessional engineer. Actually you would feel better if you had more training in the design and manufacture of the microprocessors. Sooner or later, Bass is going to want a portable unit. Now that you will have a little breather from the JAC redesign, perhaps you can get the company to send you to an engineering seminar this summer to learn more about microprocessors.

You know that the new design has really added very little to the cost of the JAC 36. Working with Pete over the last several months, you also know that he runs a pretty sloppy manufacturing operation. You are pretty sure that if there are going to be cost problems, they will be in his area. If you dug into them, you probably could cut $500 off those costs in a day or so. Moreover, if you had the time (probably two or three months), you bet you could further redesign the gadget and knock an additional $300–$400 off the cost of the product by eliminating some frills and by selecting lower-cost materials.

Most of all, you are loyal to Norm and want to defend his interests as much as possible for the good of the company.

Employee Position 2B

You are an analyst in the Western Division of the Modern Finance Company. This company is made up of several regional divisions, all of which have a staff of analysts working in positions similar to yours. You have a diligent boss whom you have worked for since you came to Modern three years ago. You have been doing a good job, and have been complimented by your boss on a number of occasions for outstanding work. As far as salary raises, however, you have had what you consider adequate raises, but nothing truly substantial. You feel that your consistently strong efforts, and the exceptionally good project work you have done, merits a larger than normal raise.

To strengthen your hand, you have been doing a little "seed planting" with Joe Short, the financial manager over in the Central Division. While you don't have a firm commitment from him, Short has given you signals that he would like you to come to work for him in Central. He has seen several of your projects, and was very impressed with the quality of your analysis as well as your ability to put the plan into action.

Your boss knows that Short has seen some of your work. He has shown some of it to Short, and has told Short what a valuable member of the Western Division staff you are.

Since your boss feels that you are valuable (and your work has proved it), isn't it time to get the company to show it with dollars? Your last raise moved you from $17,250 to $18,500, which was about a year ago. Why not try for the big jump—a $3,000 raise. You have the leverage on your boss, as you have an implied offer from Short. While you really enjoy working for the Western Division, you don't want to limit your options, especially when it involves money.

Take a few minutes to review these facts and then devise a strategy to approach your boss for this raise.

Capital Mortgage Insurance Corporation (C)

On hearing Elliott Burr's demand for $5 million for CTS, Frank Randall replied:

"If you're serious, we might as well leave right now. But why don't you listen to our complete offer?

Jim Dolan then read through CMI's formal offer letter, which spelled out all the details of the proposed agreement. Dolan took the CTS group slowly through the letter, explaining the meaning of each item in great detail.

Elliott Burr then suggested that they skip the price issue momentarily. He reviewed the offer step by step, asking questions to clarify the implications of each part of the proposal. Winder and Lehman remained silent during this exchange.

The tremendous difference in the asking and offering prices continued to be the major source of contention, however. After several minutes of open debate, Randall finally asked in exasperation, "How did you ever come up with that figure?" Tom Winder mentioned hearing that 60 percent of another employee relocation company had been sold recently for something in excess of $3 million.

Dolan: How does that relate to us?
Winder: Well, I guess it really isn't the same thing. I suppose we made a mistake using that as a base.

There was a long silence following Winder's comment. Finally, after several minutes, Elliott Burr said:

Let me tell you about Mike, who isn't here. I have his proxy, and he'll sell right now for $3.5 million.

Randall replied, "That's ridiculous."

The meeting then degenerated for several minutes, as Burr, Lehman, and Winder whispered among themselves. They finally announced their willingness to sell for $2 million.

Role for Leavitt, Plant Manager
of the Crawley Plant

You have been quite concerned about the quality problem on some of the modules your plant sends to the Phillips plant. Over the last several months considerable progress has been made and you intend to keep pushing on the matter and expect some further improvement, although it will probably not be as great as that realized before. Some poor quality items are bound to occur with a product as complicated as a module. Given the volume with which these are produced, 100 percent inspection is impossible and sampling, especially at the 95 percent level of acceptance is an accepted practice even though it means that some faulty items will get through.

You feel that the position taken by the Phillips plant manager that your plant accept the costs of repairing all faulty parts is ridiculous. You have to bear the expense of repairing items from outside vendors that are not returned and you do not see why the same practice should not apply to within-company vendors. Of course, if shipments were refused because of poor quality they could be shipped back to your plant—just as faulty shipments are returned to outside suppliers occasionally. You would like to avoid having the faulty shipments returned to you since you would have to pick up transportation expenses. If you had to repair a rejected lot of modules it might be cheaper to send a repairman to the Phillips plant.

You are particularly puzzled and troubled that 12 types of modules are found to be below the desired quality level when they arrive at the Phillips plant even though they were apparently at the desired level when they left your plant. It is a company policy that plants are responsible to see that products shipped meet stated quality levels, regardless of whether they go to an outside or a within-company user. Overall, all modules shipped to the Phillips plant are above the 95 percent level so you think that you are complying with company policy but you are nonetheless concerned about the 12 modules that at times do not measure up to the standard. First, because you want to get the plant output to a high standard and second, because you fear that if this matter gets to higher management they may revise the interpretation of how the 95 percent level of quality is to be applied making it applicable to each individual type of product line rather than to the overall output of a plant.

If you had to accept any of these expenses you would like to charge part of them to the department in the plant that makes the faulty modules and part to the final inspection department to give them feedback on their performance and to put pressure on both of them to improve.

In addition, the Phillips plant manager has been urging that you absorb this overtime costs that come from delayed production caused by shortages of modules when a great number of them have to be rejected. You think he is way out of line on this matter and would never accept any arrangement like that.

Unfortunately while this dispute has gone on, modules have been rejected at incoming inspection at the Phillips plant at a rate of about $8,000 a week. The plant manager at the Phillips plant is just letting them sit there while he tries to get you to accept responsibility for them. Before long this will come to the attention of the vice president of manufacturing and when it does you feel that both you and the Phillips plant manager will be called on the carpet for not having solved this problem.

The Phillips plant manager has an appointment with you this afternoon on what he has said is one last try to settle the matter.

Pacific Oil Company (B)

Kelsey called Meredith the next day. They both agreed that a resale clause would be a dangerous commitment and an even more dangerous precedent for Pacific Oil. They made an appointment for a conference call to Saunders for the following morning. When they talked to him, they learned that Saunders had approved the concession, and that Fontaine had already talked to Hauptmann and told him it was OK to include it in the revised agreement.

Capital Mortgage Insurance Corporation (F)

As the big jet banked over the city and began its final approach toward the Philadelphia Airport, Frank Randall closed his briefcase and looked at Jim Dolan.

> Well, I don't know about you, Jim, but I think we're in good shape. We brought their price down into our range, and we established our feelings about CTS' intrinsic value—or lack of value.
>
> And I know my ceiling price; I won't go a dollar over it. If they won't accept it, we'll just forget them. But one way or another, we're going into the business.

FURTHER NEGOTIATIONS WITH CORPORATE TRANSFER SERVICES

Once again, Randall and Dolan let their relationship with Elliott Burr and his partners cool off a bit. There were several phone conversations over the next two weeks, but Randall often "forgot" to return calls, and he remained deliberately neutral in his discussions with Burr. The conversations that did occur tended to focus on technical matters such as alternate payout arrangements; the price issue was hardly mentioned.

Randall kept David Osgood of MetroNet up to date on the negotiations. During one of their conversations Randall told Osgood about Burr's claim that he "controlled" the MetroNet brokers and could "deliver" them. Osgood was incensed; he told Randall he was going to write a letter to Burr calling attention to CTS' failure to meet commitments the company had made to MetroNet.

During this time Randall also hired the consultant who had prepared the relocation industry report for MetroNet earlier in the spring. The consultant spent several days in Philadelphia helping Randall and Dolan think about how to structure and operate a relocation business, and suggesting the names of experienced managers they might want to recruit. The consultant also put Randall in touch with the parent organization of one of the well-established relocation companies. The consultant hinted that the parent was not satisfied with its subsidiary and might be willing to sell it, even though it was one of the largest in the industry. Randall made an appointment for early June to "discuss matters of mutual interest" with the Executive Vice President responsible for the subsidiary.

Jim Dolan was beginning to question whether they really wanted to acquire CTS. The discussions with the consultant had given him new insights into the business, and now he not only had someone to compare Elliott Burr and Tom Winder with, but there was the possibility, however remote, of buying a much bigger and clearly more successful operation.

Finally, on June 5, Burr called again. He told Randall, "We've thought about your offer and talked it over. How about $750,000 over book value?" Randall replied, "We're not even sure we want to go through with it. I'll get back to you in a day or two."

Randall and Dolan spent most of June 6 rethinking their whole assessment of Corporate Transfer Services. As Dolan later recalled:

> At that point we had a chance to do some real soul-searching. It was fully in our hands; we knew we could get the company, and get it at a price we considered reasonable. The negotiations were in a sense over; the next move was our real commitment. We talked ourselves into and out of doing it several times, and we thought about our other options as well.

Finally, late in the day, Randall called Elliott Burr and offered $600,000 over net worth. Burr, without any hesitation, agreed.

EXERCISE 15
Jordan Electronics Company

Role for Vincent D'Moro
Vice President, Finance

Bass talked with you shortly before he left for his surgery. As usual, he did not want to get involved in working out this problem, yet he did want results—and quickly. "I want the new model of the JAC 36, Vince, and I want it soon. The more up-to-date it is, the better. Above all, I want it to sell." Other than that, he left you with no instructions on what he wanted or how you were to proceed. He did ask you to chair the meeting and to get the group to come to a consensus on these decisions: (1) Should the new model of the JAC 36 be manufactured? (2) If it is to be manufactured, at what price should it be sold? (3) If 'he new model is not to be manufactured, what should be done next?

In thinking about the meeting, you are not sure how to proceed. You believe the best thing would be for each person at the meeting to briefly report on his area's position on the new model and the group's proposals for items (1) and (2). Item (3) should only be considered if there is a negative conclusion to (1). After hearing the report, you should try to see if there is an obvious and easy solution. Otherwise you will help the group search for compromises and trade-offs. Given Bass's instructions to you, you feel personally responsible for having the committee reach a consensus before the meeting breaks up. The worst thing that could happen is for Bass to return and find the issue still unsettled; *you* would probably be held responsible for that.

Employer Position 3A

You are the marketing vice president of the Rapid Leathergoods Company, and have been in this position for the past four years. One of the people you have working for you is the director of mail order sales. This person has been in the position for the past two years. In your discussions with (him), you have informally set up the requirements and the objectives of the mail order sales position. The director has over the past two years done an excellent job. (He) has improved the response in the campaigns of the MaxFli, the Fireball and the Thunderhead lines. The thinking that has gone into these programs has been developed in an excellent manner and the execution has been quite effective. You are quite pleased with the efforts on these lines.

There has been one problem area. One of the objectives for this past year was to get more action in the Top Flite line (Rapid's most expensive line of wallets, purses, key cases, and so on). The returns on this year's Top Flite sales have been quite poor. This is not a change from Top Flite's past history, as it has never really been successful. The director seems not to have been able to change the results of the Top Flite via any of his recent efforts. While you haven't learned of anything on Top Flite in the past month, you have no indication that anything in this program has changed.

It is currently salary review time. And while the director has had excellent results in the other lower priced line, the failure to get Top Flite moving is the reason you expect to only give a nominal raise for this year. If he can demonstrate new achievements on Top Flite, you could see your way clear to a larger raise. The director's current salary is $30,000 base pay. You feel that a raise of $2,000 (6⅔ percent) is a fair raise for this year's efforts (normal raises are usually in the 5–10 percent range). You are not constrained in granting a raise of more than that figure, but you want some justifiable evidence why the director should get more. You consider yourself a firm but fair negotiator, and are willing to give a raise above $2,000 if the director can show he is worth the money.

Take a few minutes to review these facts and devise a strategy for managing the discussion with your director about a pay raise.

Role for Pat Rosen

Lately you have been swamped with making numerous lengthy tests on some new equipment you have designed. The work has completely swamped your technician and you have had to work along with him to keep the job moving. Even with your effort however it looks like you may be on this a long time. You would like very much to get to the professional meetings next month to see the new testing equipment that wil! be on display on the hope that some manufacturer may have come out with an item that would ease your testing problem. You are thinking seriously of making a strong pitch for this to Fran even though you know there has been no money for such trips for the last several years. Additional technician help would be an alternative but you doubt there is any possibility of hiring a new technician.

Concerned Community
Coalition Role Description

You almost wish that judge had issued his injunction because you're having trouble sustaining this thing. With people's jobs in jeopardy and no negotiations taking place, you're going to start losing people soon and you may be worse off than before. You've got to get some kind of visible victory—some change in behavior. You know you can't get everything at once, but you have to show the community that health care is going to be different—*now*. Maybe these facilities they announced are needed, maybe not—but not at the expense of your people's needs.

You also have to make sure that these needs are always heard and understood.

As a part of the strategy which you develop for the negotiations, you should consider carefully the roles of the people on your team and how they will portray them. The CCC team for the meeting might include:

The Coalition chairman.

The legal representative.

Representative of a community corporation.

Member of hospital paraprofessional or housekeeping staff.

Representatives of other typical community interest groups.

Some of the factors which should be considered during your strategizing for the meeting include:

1. The goals and demands of the CCC.
2. The priority ordering the demands.
3. The relative power and sanctions presently possessed by the CCC, and the hospital's apparent perception of that power.
4. Possible allies and additional leverage which the CCC might tap.
5. Limitations on the coordination and use of available and potential resources.